D1104376

# The Best of New York

Written by
**HENRI GAULT & CHRISTIAN MILLAU**

Translated by
**ROBERT GRAY**

Contributing Editors
**YVES BRIDAULT, ROBERT EGAN,
ROBERT LOW, VERONIQUE PREVOST,
ALEXANDER & JOAN SHIHWARG,
CHRISTOPHER VAUGHN**

Designed by
**BORDNICK & ASSOCIATES**

Crown Publishers & The Knapp Press

Published in the United States of America in 1982
Crown Publishers/The Knapp Press
Copyright©1982 by Knapp Communications Corporation
5900 Wilshire Boulevard, Los Angeles, California 90036

All rights reserved. No part of this book may be reproduced, stored, or transmitted
in any form or by any means, electronic or mechanical, including photocopying,
recording, or by any information storage and retrieval system, without permission
in writing from the copyright owner.

Published by Crown Publishers, Inc.,
One Park Avenue, New York, New York 10016
(simultaneously in Canada by General Publishing Company Limited).

Printed in the United States of America

Library of Congress Cataloging in Publication data

Includes index.
Main entry under title: The Best of New York
1. New York (N.Y.)—Description—1981 — Guide-books.
I. Millau, Christian.   II. Title.
F128.18.G3313      1982B      917.47'10443      82-13058

ISBN:  0-517-547708
0-517-547716 (paperback)

10  9  8  7  6  5  4  3  2  1

First Edition

# CONTENTS

# NEW YORK

## THE MOST ELECTRIC
## CITY IN THE WORLD

Ugly and beautiful, tender and violent, greedy and generous, bewitching and horrifying, lyrical and melodramatic —New York is unquestionably the world's most exciting city. The mornings are bracing—it's a time when you can feel the city shaking itself to alertness, like a young jungle beast—but we have come to love the evenings most, that extended moment when the dusk is glowing rosily on the skyscraper windows, and the city is awakening to its febrile, nocturnal life. Each time we leave New York, something within us is not quite as it was before.

New York, which until quite recently was the subject of regular obituaries, is constantly reinventing itself; it is a fluid city, a place of perpetual motion. Which was our problem, by the way. In Europe, cities and people tend to grow old together. There are changes, but they occur slowly. Not so New York, where things change in a twinkling, and one is always needing to reorient oneself to changing modes; to readjust one's psychic watch, so to speak. A guide such as ours cannot claim to be exhaustive. This is the city as we found it. If things have changed here and there, or if we have overlooked some new bloom, forgive us—there's always the next time.

Although we have now been preparing guidebooks for some twenty years, we still regard ourselves as amateurs—maybe a bit nosier than others, admittedly. Also, we are passionate, perhaps unfair sometimes, certainly far from perfect; but we have freely expressed our likes, dislikes, enthusiasms, prejudices—our pleasures and our pains. Like lovers we are sometimes satisfied, sometimes frustrated, but always enthralled, and just as a novelist might, we want you to share in our passions. If you disagree with one of our judgments, or if you have something to add, please let us know. We received a letter the other day that ran: "I almost never agree with you. But I've been reading you since you began, and I hope to continue reading you for a long time to come." That letter, believe it or not, made us very happy indeed.

*Henri Gault and Christian Millau*
Gault Millau America—5900 Wilshire Boulevard—
Los Angeles, California—90036

# THE RESTAURANTS

# Eating in America

## ═══════════TASTE LEVELS═══════════

T o quote an excellent journalist who is also a true connoisseur of things culinary, John Hess, for many years the Paris correspondent for *The New York Times:* "Most Americans are completely out of touch with natural flavors, and are so conditioned by the dictates of industry and marketing that, more often than not, they reject anything that comes close to its natural form."

A brand of ice-cream made only with fresh fruit and pure sugar was poorly received by the public at large. A manufacturer who had put on the market a tomato sauce that contained nothing but tomatoes met with bitter failure, and scarcely had time to enrich it with the chemical additives necessary for consumers to enjoy the "real" tomato taste of which they had been deprived.

Without going so far as to accuse chemicals of killing people, it's certainly true that they can kill flavor. More or less everything is pasteurized, from Camembert to caviar. Even palates have become pasteurized, and anything that might disturb their neutrality arouses the greatest mistrust.

Trapped in a dietary regime totally dominated by manufacturers, prisoners of its freezers, baby food, mixes and margarine, a good part of America is totally estranged from original flavors and the changing seasons.

A re we exaggerating? Are we being dreadfully chauvinistic? We sincerely think not, especially as we are waging the same battle on the European front. This isn't an American phenomenon, but a problem facing all of modern civilization—it's just more obvious in the United States, where everything goes further and faster than anywhere else. Then how is it that, despite everything, we remain optimistic? For a very simple reason, one that has always been proven right: the greater the limitations placed upon a society, the greater the need for the society to liberate itself.

This has been true as well in the United States, where over the past decade there has been a trememdous surge of interest in cooking and gastronomy. It used to be that only the well-to-do and certain professionals could afford the luxury of indulging in the snobbery or the sincere pleasure of posing as a gourmet. It was a way of standing out from the crowd. Nowadays, however, social status and wealth are not exclusively determinant. People from all walks of life and from extremely varied milieus experience the same need to escape the mass dictates of taste.

In some, this need is expressed by a total belief in natural health foods; among others, by an increasing concern with and search for quality, whether it be in cooking at home or in restaurants.

In no other country in the world (including France) is cooking the subject of so many books, magazine and newspaper articles, and television programs as in the United States.

Now obviously this incredible infatuation is going to have its negative side in a country where marketing skills are so perfected, and where hyperbole is accepted at face value. Housewives are assured, for example, that good cooking requires absolutely no effort, and it's hard not to be carried away in many restaurants by the elegant and voluptuous descriptions of the dishes— until you're confronted with the sad reality on your plate.

Cooking can be staged like a Hollywood spectacular, and it's easy to understand why this sumptuous and intricate cuisine of ceremony, which lends itself readily to pageantry, was so popular. You devoured a dish with your eyes while maitres d'hôtel poured brandy over the plates, then lit them, making the dining room look like a war zone.

French chefs from before and immediately after the war, abetted by Swiss and German colleagues trained in the sinister schools of international luxury hotels, were often far too quick to accept this nouveau riche style of cooking. These flame-thrower specialists and masters of trompe l'oeil still ravage the country, but are fortunately losing ground.

If you need more evidence, just compare some New York restaurant menus from the '60's and even the '70's with those of today. The steaks Diane, tournedos Rossini, and other specialties—as boring as they are pretentious—of so-called haute cuisine used to hold unchallenged sway over practically all the fancy restaurants, with a few notable exceptions. Today, menus have been almost systematically liberated of their knock-out dishes, from their abusive flambées and heavy sauces. New ideas and healthier methods of cooking have been introduced, and restaurant fare is infinitely more seductive and diverting than it was twenty years ago.

Never before has it been possible to dine so well in New York. In this regard, nouvelle cuisine has been a great inspiration—though it's true that results vary considerably. As is the case in Europe, it has served as a screen for the ridiculous fantasies of amateurs with little talent, failed professionals, and twisted aesthetes who believe themselves artists because they are willing to mix anything with almost anything else. All that is new is not necessarily praise-worthy. But it would be unfair to condemn a movement (whether in painting, literature, or cooking) simply because its banners attract incompetents and impostors. There were mediocre Impressionists and Cubists, but that didn't stop these schools from attaining their triumphs.

It is undeniable that the phenomenon of modern cuisine, whose effects are discernible around the world, has given new life to a slumbering profession and has redirected cooking, including classical cooking, towards simplicity, naturalness, and true refinement. If nouvelle cuisine should, in turn, get bogged down in routine, clichés, and commercialism, there will obviously be a counter-reaction. But we must be indebted to it for the tremendous renaissance currently sweeping American gastronomy.

Of particular importance is the appearance of a generation of American cooks (both men and women) absolutely intent upon joining ranks with the best. As we point out in the restaurant section of this guide, a few have already earned their place in this category.

This decolonization of the kitchens is a source of great joy for us. It's obviously not a question of banning European and Asian cooks—there's room enough for everyone in this big country—but it would be abnormal if America were to leave foreigners in complete control of its stoves. America has its great architects, painters, writers, and musicians: why should it be any different with regard to cooks? And the more American chefs there are, the higher the level of cuisine in the country will tend to rise. It's a matter of creating a style of cooking which truly reflects the tastes of the nation. The young chefs you meet along both the East and the West Coast share the neophyte's zeal (and sometimes his awkwardness), but they represent the future of American cooking, and it's our aim to help encourage and promote them.

In a modest café-restaurant near Lausanne a few years back, we made the acquaintance, quite by chance, of a young unknown chef, whose cuisine was entirely different from that (in our eyes terribly conventional) served in other Swiss restaurants at that time. His name is Freddy Girardet, and he seemed to us to have a sort of genius. Not only did the Swiss themselves eventually discover him, but, very quickly, as if by contagion, other highly talented chefs appeared, and a country which had seemed unflinchingly devoted to fondue Zürichoise and overcooked veal scallops became a haven of fine eating.

**A**nother element which has transformed the American gastronomic landscape is the discovery—the rediscovery really—of good domestic produce. A century ago America produced, under the same conditions as those prevailing in Europe, good dairy products, poultry, fruit and vegetables. Industry subsequently wrought its well-known devastations, and, out of laziness or convenience, restaurateurs and the public put up with what was offered. The most demanding chefs prided themselves on having first-rate produce, impossible to find locally, imported from elsewhere, notably from France. Now, however, these same cooks happily admit that they can find almost everything where they are. The greatest professionals, like André Soltner (Lutèce), Michel Fitoussi (The Palace), Barry Wine (The Quilted Giraffe), and Lawrence Forgione (The River Café) are in complete agreement. Of course, it requires a good deal of effort to unearth quality products in a swamp of mediocrity, but the important thing is that they are available.

"The change over the last five years has been spectacular," says André Soltner. "I find almost everything I need." Maine lobsters are exquisite if one is careful to cook them lightly. The small scallops fished on the East Coast in the autumn are even better than those from Brittany. Atlantic fish are of superb variety and quality when they're fresh. The red-footed crayfish from Louisiana, superior to the white-footed ones from California, are excellent, and wild mushrooms (morilles, chanterelles, cèpes, etc.) are finally being gathered in the forests and offered to restaurants—at terrifying prices. Montana and New Jersey lamb are extraordinarily delicate, and, although the quality of prime beef has been for a long time more even than in France, that wasn't the case for veal, which André Soltner still refused to buy five years ago. The veal he serves today is always first-rate, as are the fresh sweetbreads and kidneys. The extremely fat Long Island ducks are delicious so long as they haven't been frozen, and, though good chickens are rare, they can still be found, grain-fed by Italian families living in New Jersey and Pennsylvania. There are even squabs, raised with incredible results by a Frenchman living near Albany.

Flour, severely criticized in the past, seems to be much improved. The same for butter: while it's still impossible to find the equivalent of French butter from Normandy and Charente, the quality of the sweet butter served in some restaurants has for a while now been pleasantly surprising. This observation holds true for fresh cream, which, though a little thinner than French cream, is made much better than before, and gives very satisfactory results when reduced.

**W**e could multiply these examples. One thing is certain: a small market for quality produce—generally very expensive —is developing. It's not a question of attaching greater importance to this fact than it deserves. For the moment, it only meets the needs of a small elite—but, if there's a prospect of doing good business in the field of quality produce, have no doubt: this industry will grow. American caviar production, which at the turn of the century was greater than that of Russia, is picking up again under pressure of recent events in Iran. It is quite inexpensive and, although admittedly not yet first-rate, one of these days producers will learn to select the roe properly, to add precise quantities of salt, and to make high-quality sturgeon caviar. Californians are beginning to raise snails, frogs, and even truffles, all symbols par excellence of French cuisine. Why not foie gras soon as well?

For a long time, the thought that Americans could produce anything good to eat or drink would have produced sniggers on the Champs Elysée. But, Californians have done exactly that with their wine.

In 1973, after we dared, in our magazine *Le Nouveau Guide,* to praise California wines, more or less unknown in France at the time, we were bitterly attacked. Certain Bordeaux wine producers and some journalists went so far as to accuse us of stabbing the French wine patrimony in the back. But this idiotic and chauvinistic extremism didn't last long, and today French wine growers not only loyally recognize the quality of American wines, some have even bought vineyards in the Napa and Sonoma Valley.

This tremendous and quite recent infatuation on the part of the American public for wine is not due to mere whim. It is in keeping with a general movement towards a more refined and higher quality gastronomy. Good meals require good wines to accompany them: this is common knowledge in Europe but, in the United States, the idea is relatively new. Fifteen years ago we were struck by how few tables, even in the best American restaurants, had bottles of wine on them. Diners anaesthetized their palates with a few preliminary dry martinis, then washed down their canard à l'orange with chlorinated water. Now you only have to look around you in New York and Boston, or Los Angeles and San Francisco, to see that the cult of Bacchus is thriving as never before.

And we are convinced that America today is only at the beginning of what will be its rise as a wine-producing power. Wines are constantly improving, and pleasant surprises may be in store from along the Oregon coast and from Washington, both of which are beginning to produce truly fine wines.

This is all very positive, but it presents a danger too, for cuisine and for wines. After suffering from an inferiority complex in the realm of taste vis-à-vis Europe, it would be disastrous for the United States to commit the opposite error. There are already signs of an unchecked overreaction which threatens to become dangerous. Some people now claim that California produces "the best wines in the world" and that "You eat infinitely better in New York than in Paris." It's only vanity, you may be tempted to say, hardly a menace. But we're not so sure: humans are only human, and if you compliment them too much, they tend to believe you. It simply isn't true that California wines are the best in the world. They are pleasant, flattering, slightly heavy (because they are bursting with sunshine), somewhat coarse, and, to be perfectly honest, their ability to age cannot be compared to that of great Bordeaux and Burgundies with their substantially more complex aromas. Nonetheless, the excessive praise enjoyed by these wines has directly caused their prices to increase unjustifiably. It's a dangerous game, and a few of the better sommeliers, like Kevin Zraly of Windows on the World, have expressed a sense of shock, and have immediately reduced their purchases in favor of foreign wines, especially the French ones.

In the same way, it would be wrong to attribute talent to an American chef when he obviously doesn't have any, just because he's American. It is frustrating that critics who, in other domains (such as politics, the economy, and the arts) exercise an exemplary and sometimes fearful rigor are so uncritical when it comes to cooking. The inflationary spiral of superlatives doesn't serve the cause of gastronomy and taste in any way. In order to help truly gifted people, you musn't be lax on those who aren't.

# Symbol Systems

Restaurants are marked on a scale of 0 to 20, and are judged only on their cooking. Decor, welcome, atmosphere, and service do not influence the rating, but are otherwise commented upon quite explicitly within the reviews. Restaurants that score 13 and above are distinguished with toques (chef's hats), according to the following table:

| | | |
|---|---|---|
| Exceptional | 🎩🎩🎩🎩 | 4 toques, for 19/20 |
| Excellent | 🎩🎩🎩 | 3 toques, for 17/20 or 18/20 |
| Very good | 🎩🎩 | 2 toques, for 15/20 or 16/20 |
| Good | 🎩 | 1 toque, for 13/20 or 14/20 |

We should point out that these marks are *relative*. One toque for 13/20, when awarded to a highly reputed restaurant, is not a very good mark, whereas it is for a small restaurant without much culinary pretention.

Except when otherwise indicated, the restaurant prices listed are for an average meal comprising an appetizer, a main course, a dessert, and a half-bottle of wine. The prices are obviously only approximate and unfortunately, many will have changed by the time you read these lines.

Many chefs have the bad habit of changing restaurants, and thus a good restaurant can turn mediocre or even bad in just a few days. Restaurants whose chef is also the owner are, in theory, more stable, but even they are liable to deteriorate: success can turn an owner's head, and he may be tempted to accept too many diners, and quality generally suffers for it. Should this have occurred, please be indulgent with us. Our profession is not an easy one—we can't be held responsible! And one last word: menus can change often. The dishes we have described were available pre-publication. We apologize if what we reviewed is no longer available: it's out of our control!

# Lower Manhattan • Tribeca

13

## Acute Cafe
**110 West Broadway**
**349-5566**
*Mon. to Sat. nightly until 12:30 A.M.; late supper until 3:00 A.M.*
*AE, MC, V.*
French (nouvelle)

Bruno Oliver—grandson of Raymond Oliver, owner of the Grand Vefour in Paris, and France's answer to Julia Child—has brought his not inconsiderable talents to the kitchen of this stunning Tribeca restaurant and late night spot. Its sharp art deco lines are set off by a handsome mahogany and glass entrance, white tile floors, beige-cushioned wicker chairs—and, in the center, the main dining area dropped a few steps down like a giant conversation pit.

Young Oliver is no stranger to America—he did a stint at Les Castelets in St. Bart's, where he served plenty of American tourists, and he is married to a lady from Idaho (although you won't find trout or potato on the menu). Despite this exposure to things American (or perhaps because of it), he believes the way to show his affection for his customers at Acute Cafe is to embrace them with feuilletage. You will be encouraged to nibble on puffed pastry cheese sticks with your drinks, le feuille au bouquet de légumes or le feuille aux belons as appetizers, and then a soupe de moules en croute—a cap of feuilletage placed atop the marmite.

If you are still hungry after this farinaceous beginning, you will enjoy entrees reflecting the chef's conversion to nouvelle cuisine: émincé de veau aux courgettes, éventail de boeuf et de poulet, poisson au vin rouge et gingembre. By the time you have finished your desert (a delicious mocha cake in a bath of an exquisite crème anglaise or the house's fresh fruit sherbets) you'll be happy you didn't leave after the soup and appetizers. About $40 with a modest Pinot Grigio or 1970 Marques de Caceres Riojo, a good value.

## 14 ♧
# The American Harvest Restaurant
**Vista International Hotel (World Trade Center complex)**
**938-9100, x-7231**
*Lunch and dinner Mon. to Fri. until 9:45 P.M., Sat. dinner; closed Sun.*
*All major credit cards*
American

The Hilton organization, which manages the Vista International Hotel, offers some intriguing alternatives to the array of restaurants in the adjacent World Trade Center towers: The American Harvest Restaurant and (less ambitious) The Greenhouse, both one flight above the street level. Obviously the Vista could not compete with the view from the 107th floor, so in The American Harvest Restaurant, Hilton created an opulent setting with a feeling of space that is matched by few restaurants in the entire city. Attractive drapes hang from the twenty foot ceiling and are left open to permit a view across the Hudson. Tables are widely separated, and tables for two are set against deep-cushioned, plush banquettes.

To compete with the French-accented cuisine at the Cellar in the Sky, Hilton came up with something of a gimmick: a menu based on *American* ingredients and dishes that changes every month. But to carry this off, Hilton imported an Austrian chef, who has talent and imagination. The menu generally includes fresh oysters and clams, Maryland crab bisque, Southern fried chicken with corn fritters, roast beef, Yankee pot roast, and apple pie with cheddar cheese or ice cream. These traditional dishes are all quite well prepared. But those dishes in which the chef takes American ingredients or dishes and gives them his own interpretation will give the most interest and pleasure to the adventurous diner. The chef coats native mushroom caps (instead of snails) with a delicious Burgundian garlic dressing; he combines squash and apple in a (November) soup; he provides orange slices and ginger as a garnish to poached red snapper; he prepares a zesty pear sauce to accompany roast duck, and he bakes a whole battery of interesting desserts, such as pumpkin cheesecake, walnut chiffon cake (better than carrot cake), and an apple and cranberry pie. The whipped cream served with these delights is as good as you would expect from a Austrian master pastry chef, and you have one here. One word about the vegetables. Whether puréed or whole, they are perfectly prepared, an unusual phenomenon in New York. It's just a pity the service plods so.

The wine list stresses American wines, from the better known smaller California vineyards, at prices in the $15 to $25 range. The Dry Creek Chardonnay at $20 is well rounded and a good value, as is the Simi Cabernet Sauvignon at $17.50. Good value is not limited to the wine card. Complete dinners—appetizer, soup, main course, salad, dessert, and coffee—will cost you between $21.50 and $26.50, depending on main course selected. If you have already seen the view from the 107th floor, this may well be your best bet downtown.

**10/20**

# La Bourse
**53 Beaver St. (between William and Broad Sts.)
425-0665**
*Mon. to Fri. lunch only*
French (provincial)

There aren't many acceptable lunch places in the Wall Street area, perhaps because there is no dinner business to speak of and ambitious restaurateurs usually think of dinner as their raison d'être. La Bourse is a possibility at lunchtime—if you are on an expense account. Prices are high for what you can expect in front of you: $25 to $30 for a three-course meal with a glass of the house wine. The appetizers (pâté, snails, quiche, coquille St. Jacques) are in the $4 to $5 range; the entrees (striped bass, beef bourguignon, veal piccata) in the $12 to $15 range. The dishes are less genuine than many French counterparts uptown, and the chef has a somewhat heavy hand with his sauces. But if you don't expect too much, you can have a pleasant enough lunch. There is a sister establishment called La Tour, at the top of 14 Wall Street, managed by the sister of the patron here.

**11/20**

# The Bread Shop Cafe
**157 Duane St. (between W. Broadway and Hudson St.)
964-0524**
*Dinner nightly until midnight
All major credit cards*
American

There is a plain brick wall along one side of a deep, narrow space; plantation fans and frosted globe lights hang from the high tin ceiling. Behind a counter along the opposite side, the chef and his helpers are in full view, working at the range, the grill, the oven—and the sink. The show behind the counter is not very exciting, and some of the dishes they produce lack the finish of a professional kitchen. Perhaps this is because the management is constantly encouraging the chef to do something new. "Food should be in constant transition," says Tom Roberts, the owner and an architect by trade. So you find any number of unusual combinations on the blackboard menu: a tasty and fresh arugola salad with ham and mushrooms as an appetizer or an acceptable spinach ravioli with asparagus and smoked trout in a cream sauce as a main course.

Desserts include the high-quality ices and ice creams of The New York Ice Company, and a good dacquoise baked on the premises. There is an astute selection of boutique California wines (as well as some standard French names) and the Pedroncelli Zinfandel at the steal price of $7 could encourage you to overlook one or two of the chef's shortcomings.

## 11/20
# Capsouto Frères
**451 Washington St.
(south of Canal St.)
966-4900**
*Lunch and dinner daily until 2:00 A.M., closed Mon., bar open until 4:00 A.M.*
French (provincial)

Capsouto Frères occupies an 1891 warehouse (now designated a landmark) south of Canal Street, an area that is seeing the conversion of dozens of loft buildings into apartments. The brothers Capsouto have been in New York for some time, but they were born in Egypt and lived for a time in Lyon. With help from their mother, they have converted the huge ground-level space into a stunning bistro. Along Washington Street, they have created a narrow gallery with an ornate iron rail and marble-topped tables for twosomes. Inside the immense ceilings, cast-iron supporting columns, brick walls, and red satin drapes framing the high corner windows give the feeling of Gilded Age chic. Tables are well spaced. Waiters and waitresses in black pantaloons and vests are alert and attentive. The Capsouto brothers do not attempt to serve meals as breathtaking as the setting. This is a New York bistro. The all-day menu includes omelets and some interesting salads, such as cucumber with smoked whitefish and entrees such as calf's liver with a tarragon and mustard sauce, as wall as the usual simple chicken and steak dishes. There is a more sophisticated second menu that changes daily. This might include gravlax as a starter or poached salmon with a sauce verte as a main course. The list of moderately priced French and California wines include a Côtes du Ventoux at $9 and a Saint Véran at $11.75. If you want to sample that placid ambience of the 1890s, where you can actually hear what your dinner companion is saying, this is your chance.

## 9/20
# The Commissary
**99 Hudson Street
(between Franklin and Harrison Sts.)
431-1017**
*Dinner nightly until 12:30 A.M.; weekend late supper until 3:00 A.M.; Sat. and Sun. brunch*
*All major credit cards*
American

The Commissary, with its twenty-foot ceiling, mezzanine-like gallery across the back of the premises, and theater floodlights along one side, gives the appearance of an off-Broadway theater. Out front a snappily attired doorman guides patrons to the door after they have alighted from their taxis and limousines. This is definitely showbiz, and from time to time the staff appears in costume to prove it.

Over the years William Mehlman, the chef, has worked in Brooklyn and earned a certain reputation for his "nouvelle" dishes and the generally high level of his kitchen. His performance in Manhattan casts doubt on the reputation accorded him by diners across the river. Or it's possible that Mr. Mehlman simply lost his touch when he moved to Manhattan. In any event, at The Commissary you will be paying $30 to $35 per person, and you will probably not get your money's worth. Appetizers are disappointing. The oil dressing with the squid lacks seasoning; the liver and spinach terrine is heavy and the combination does not come off well; and the fish soup is a weak sister to the lusty Mediterranean version which it seeks to imitate. There are, however, a couple of acceptable entrees, including veal chops in a Calvados-scented sauce with apples and a cornish game hen in a tarragon sauce. There is an excellent mocha cake, but the fruit tart should be avoided.

The wine list features several solid California Cabernet Sauvignons, such as Beringer at $13 and Chappellet at $24. The cavernous setting is curious enough, but is the food good enough to merit the trip to Tribeca? When you add the cost of your taxi or limousine to your bill, you may decide to dine Midtown.

## 11/20
## Delphi
**109 West Broadway (corner of Reade St.)**
**227-6322**
*Lunch and dinner daily until midnight; no reservations*
*No credit cards*
Greek

Right in the heart of Tribeca, a district of artists' lofts west of Chinatown, this small, rather seedy-looking Greek restaurant offers authentic Greek dishes at heavenly prices. They admittedly don't leave the beaten paths (moussaka, vine leaves, shish-kebab) but are executed with unusual care.

## 10/20
## Fraunces Tavern
**54 Pearl St.**
**(corner of Broad St.)**
**269-0144**
*Mon. to Fri. until 9:00 P.M.*
*Lunch and dinner*
*All major credit cards*
American

You step from the canyons of Wall Street skyscrapers into a Revolutionary War tavern. Upstairs in the Longroom, now a museum, General Washington (on December 4, 1783) toasted his officers with wine, shook each of them by the hand, and departed by barge across the Hudson on the first leg of his return trip to Mount Vernon at the end of the Revolutionary War. The main dining room downstairs, which gives out onto Broad Street, has been restored to its early colonial simplicity, while the tap room offers a bar, though it's somewhat lacking the feeling of what Fraunces must have been like in another time.

About the only connection the menu claims with food served two hundred years ago is the specialty of the house, baked chicken à la Washington, described as an original tavern recipe: cubed chicken and mushrooms in a cream sauce cooked in a casserole and then passed under a broiler. Pretty tricky dish for 1783 cooking facilities, but then Sam Fraunces was reputed to be a competent innkeeper (when General Washington became President Washington, he made Sam his steward). Otherwise, the menu reflects the cuisines of the world: Italian pastas, Spanish paellas, French crêpes, curried Indian shrimp, Yankee pot roast, salads, sandwiches, steaks, burgers, roast beef, and lamb chops. There are also some sophisticated dishes like a striped bass with lobster sauce. There are not many colonial buildings left in Manhattan. This one with its small museum should be visited. If you want to sample the cuisines of the world, you probably can do better elsewhere.

## 11/20
## Odeon
**145 West Broadway**
**233-0507**
*Lunch and dinner daily until*
*2:30 A.M. (full menu until*

A godsend for the night's hungry. Until recently it was impossible to dine properly south of SoHo after the theater; an engaging oasis has appeared in the desert that looms after dusk between Canal Street and the World Trade Center. News of the apparition was quick to spread.

*midnight ); closed Sat. at lunch*
*AE, V, MC*
French (nouvelle)

Now the capriciously garbed beautiful young set from all over town, including uptown, regularly turn up for dinner—even for lunch—at the brand new Odeon, a large, spare dining room lit by opalescent globes, with an enormous 1930s bar. Don't be misled by the word "cafeteria," whose red letters illuminate the restaurant's facade (it's a vestige of the former management) or by the hideous green and pink clock that dominates the bar: this place has boasted some of the more inventive and refined cooking downtown: from poached oysters with julienne of vegetables, smoked breast of chicken salad, ragoût of duck, lamb roasted with garlic and herbs, spinach salad with mushrooms and bacon, to steamed fish. But times have changed and we have become increasingly disappointed with a good idea that has not come to fruition. Everything is served with great friendliness, but also at times with immense incompetence, by waiters from all nations—France included.

**11/20**
### Sammy's Roumanian Jewish Restaurant
**157 Chrystie St.**
**(near Delancey St.)**
**673-0330**
*Daily until 2:00 A.M.*
Kosher

The Lower East Side luxury restaurant, very fashionable and rather expensive. Sausages, icra (whitefish caviar), and various Romanian peasant dishes. On each table (in addition to the usual pickles) are milk, chocolate, and soda water, to accompany the traditional egg cream.

**10/20**
### Sloppy Louie's
**92 South Street**
**(Fulton Market)**
**952-9657**
*Lunch and dinner Mon. to Fri.*
*until 8:00 P.M.;*
*closed Sat. and Sun.*
*No reservations*
*No credit cards*
Seafood

The only "harbor bistro" in New York, with three-masters anchored at the nearby docks. So much for the romantic setting. Outside, the smell of stale fish from Fulton Market; inside, an antediluvian, slightly grimy setting, with two rows of long wooden tables and small notices on the walls announcing the catch of the day—fresh, but often overcooked and served by waiters who look as if they came over with Peter Stuyvesant. The shellfish, limited in variety, are of good quality, and you won't be disappointed if you stick to simply prepared dishes—such as the fried oysters, sauteed bay scallops, or seafood combination broiled—but avoid any of the dishes with sauces—the cook goes overboard. No alcoholic beverages, thus no white wine: bring a bottle with you. And at exactly 8:00 P.M., they throw you ashore.

**11/20**
### Sweets
**2 Fulton St.**
**(Fulton Market)**
**825-9786**

The subject of much debate in New York. What this forerunner of the seafood restaurants meant to us last time was a slightly vulgar bistro for snobbish fishmongers and in-the-know stockbrokers. The clatter of the heavy crockery, which Mediterranean busboys

*Lunch and dinner daily until
10:30 P.M. closed weekends
No reservations
No credit cards*
Seafood

launched with incredible violence into a trashbin at the end of the long room, still resounded in our ears. But things are quieter now: the red-jacketed Italo-Greek waiters no longer imagine themselves to be discus throwers, and the ceiling has been soundproofed with its windows (decorated with half-moon shaped hinges) looking out on the fish market. Now Sweets is a pleasant enough spot for lunch. The fried oysters are good, and the small sauteed scallops are as sweet as they are fresh. On the other hand, we've eaten here (not more than a mouthful of) the world's most overcooked sole, for which the recipe seems to be: boil the fillets for twelve hours, freeze, defrost, broil for three hours, refreeze, pass under the broiler and serve warm. The coffee, prepared with similar attention, is also remarkable. Count on spending about $25.

**12/20**
# Tenbrooks
**62 Reade St.
(between Broadway
and Church St.)
349-5900**
*Lunch and dinner daily
until 11:00 P.M.;
closed Sat. lunch and Sun.
All major credit cards*
American

Peter Klein, thirty-two, specialized in Oriental studies and obtained a degree in comparative literature, then did graduate work in the theater. Somehow, he wound up running Tenbrooks, a small restaurant frequented at lunch by politicians from City Hall, a block away, where the fresh and cheery decor—a light bar, cane chairs— give an idea of what the food is all about.

There's a galantine of veal, with spinach and pistachio stuffing, either as an appetizer or as a main entree, and a scallop pâté, scented with fresh dill in vinaigrette. A standard entree is lamb Louisiana, good-quality médaillons marinated in fennel, garlic, and Chinese bean paste, and then grilled steak-style, a crust on the outside and pink inside. The whole-wheat Italian bread is fresh and crunchy. Desserts include a variety of fruit ices and ice cream from the New York Ice Company. Try the espresso/marsala ice cream.

The short wine list has some notable California names at reasonable prices, including Zinfandels at $12.50. Two can have an interesting meal for $40 to $50, wine and tip included. Peter Klein has talent and imagination. As he completes the metamorphosis from academician to professional chef, he should win a toque.

**11/20**
# Vincent Petrosino
**100 Greenwich St.
(near Rector St.)
227-5398**
*Lunch and dinner weekdays until
7:30 P.M.; closed weekends
V, AE, MC*
Seafood

A young Manhattan lawyer, well versed in good, little-known eating places, introduced us some fifteen years ago to this small wholesale and retail fish store, where the four tables are always busy. Sitting in a non-decor of violent neon light, we were offered all that the Atlantic had given forth that morning, prepared in the simplest possible manner. It was 11:30 A.M., and for $5 we enjoyed one of the best brunches of our life. Prices have obviously changed since then, but if hunger ever sets in while you're near the stock exchange, pay a visit to Petrosino's to eat oysters, fresh crab, haddock, bass, or gray sole—avoiding the dishes au gratin or with sauces, as well as the vegetables and desserts, which are nothing to get excited about. Here, it's fish that talks, in its natural (or almost natural) state.

# WORLD TRADE CENTER

F ive years ago, its future looked bleak. The vertical city, rising over a quarter of a mile into the sky, was accumulating a weight of vexation and frustration, and some critics even went so far as to demand that the two 110-story towers, which remained half-empty, be torn down.

Today, people who wouldn't touch a square foot when it cost $7 now scramble for it at $40. A whole new district is being constructed along the Hudson on an immense platform built from the millions of square yards of earth dug up during excavation of the World Trade Center, and experts predict that in three years the Trade Center will be one of the most elegant and lively districts in Manhattan. Surprising as it may seem, food has undoubtedly played a large part in the success of this difficult project.

Windows on the World and the twenty-seven restaurants, snack bars, and cafeterias variously located in its two towers, which together serve close to 33,000 meals a day, have acted as a powerful magnet— for which credit is due to Toni Aigner, the thirty-eight-year-old Bavarian president of Inhilco (a subsidiary of Hilton International) who runs this giant, surely unique in the world of restaurants.

No matter what the cuisine, whether haute or fast-food, the quality is exceptional, with standards carefully controlled, and the usual traps of assembly-line feeding or pretentious "international gastronomy" have been avoided.

The restaurants that feed the fifty thousand people who work in the towers and the thousands of visitors who flock there every day form a vast complex that deserves a brief introduction. Around Market Square on the ground floor of One World Trade Center there are the fast-food restaurants: the Big Kitchen, with counters where American cuisine is served, and the Market Dining Room and Bar, where the food is considerably more elaborate.

W indows on the World is the collective name of a group of restaurants (Cellar in the Sky, The Restaurant, and L'Hors d'Oeuvrerie), bars (City Lights Bar), and reception lounges (The Ball Room and The Hudson River Suites), perched on the 106th and 107th floors of One World Trade Center. Here, along with Warren Platner's spectacular decor, one of the most imaginative ever created for a restaurant, you'll discover what is surely among the most fantastic panoramas in the New World: the parade of Manhattan skyscrapers, scraping no skies as they jut up toward you. Drink in the Hudson and East Rivers like silver ribbons, the merry-go-round of shipping and, no larger than a matchbox floating on the water, the Statue of Liberty. A magnificent spectacle especially at dusk, when beneath a mauve sky the towers light up and thousands of tiny lightbulbs thread the Brooklyn Bridge like so much incandescent dew.

Windows on the World has been open for seven years under the direction of Alan Lewis, an accomplished professional in the restaurant business, and it is still a curiosity, visited by people from all over the world. For heads of state and celebrities who don't care to venture into town, it's also one of the safest places in New York: the World Trade Center enjoys the protection of a totally autonomous corps of two hundred policemen, who also act as fire brigade and emergency first-aid crew, as well as a squad of secret agents and a private elevator, discreetly isolated, for V.I.P.s.

Windows on the World is reserved for members of the World Trade Center Club from lunchtime until 3:00 P.M. Restaurant facilities, a large buffet, eighteen private rooms and conference rooms, are put at their disposal, as well as a Finnish sauna, a Japanese "soak," an electronic stock quoter, newspapers from all over the world, and free parking. Dues at the club vary from $50 to $420 per year. Nonmembers of the Club may make reservations for lunch (938-1111). There is a $7.50 surcharge per person.

## 17
## Cellar in the Sky

*Dinner Mon. to Sat. at 7:30 P.M.;*
*formal; reservation necessary*
*All major credit cards*
French
(classical/nouvelle)

Thirty-six privileged diners punch in at 7:30 P.M. sharp and take their places at one of the pine tables in what must be the world's highest cellar. One of the regulars has already made a reservation for New Year's Eve 2000! In fact, most of the guests in this luxurious (and somewhat too dark) enclave come back regularly to partake of the fixed meal that is changed every two weeks. Their fidelity is entirely understandable, as the meal, which costs $55 including wine, is not only one of New York's most sophisticated but, for the quality it offers, one of the least expensive as well. The young sommelier Kevin Zraly, famous in the United States and even in Europe where he has many friends, and his remarkable assistant, Ray Wellington, have chosen a formula unique in New York: they serve with each course a glass of outstanding wine, French or Californian, changing from week to week according to their inspiration. Thus, after a dish of two sorts of Californian caviar, one dark (far better and less salty than is usually found in New York) and the other red salmon caviar, we were served an exceptional Fino Sherry 1908 for the duck consommé with Chinese mushrooms and watercress. Accompanying an admirable lobster and crayfish blanquette with chanterelles and asparagus was a

Les Clos Chablis 1978. Next, the Mondavi Pinot Noir 1978 harmonized marvelously with the tarragon and orange sauce served with some incredibly tender and juicy Wisconsin lamb, and then carried over for a tasty radicchio salad before ceding its place to a glass of Brane-Cantenac 1976, which valiantly held its own against some French Roquefort. Finally, a Schwarzhofberger Riesling Auslese 1976 finished off the meal with a flourish, served with a cantaloupe sherbet with fresh blueberries and raspberry sauce, followed by a delicious Colombian coffee.

A special team is responsible for the cuisine of the Cellar in the Sky, and the formula of a single menu served at a set time to a very limited number of people obviously allows it to do wonders.

## 14 ♧
## The Restaurant

*Dinner Mon. to Sat. 10:00 P.M.; formal; reservation necessary; grand buffet lunch on Sat. noon to 3:00 P.M. and Sun. noon to 7:30 P.M. All major credit cards*
French
(classical/nouvelle)

The real decor of this, the largest of the Windows on the World restaurants, lies outside beyond the large bay windows, next to which you should do your best to obtain a table. A full-course meal is served for $23.95, including, for example, a salmon pâté with dill mustard sauce, a boneless breast of chicken with broccoli cream and American caviar, salad, dessert, and a cup of Colombian coffee. The a la carte menu offers some thirty appetizers and main courses, of classical inspiration but with a modern touch: excellent oysters baked with a julienne of leeks; a very good Gulf shrimp cocktail that, for once, didn't have the consistency of papier mâché, sauteed shrimps wrapped in leeks served with an entirely successful broccoli flan; then an old favorite with a new look, the roast boneless Cornish hen with prune stuffing and armagnac sauce; a selection of charcoal-broiled meat and fish; and a good choice of desserts, including a superb chocolate pecan soufflé and a delicious hazelnut dacquoise. The list of wines is exceptional too, as much for its variety as for its reasonable prices, and our last find was a Robert Keenan Chardonnay 1977, memorably fresh and fruity.

## 13 ♧
## L'Hors D'Oeuvrerie
**938-1111**

*Mon. to Sat. lunch and dinner until 1 A.M.; Sun. brunch; afternoon tea daily 3 to 6 P.M.; no reservations accepted, except for the brunch*
International

A warm and intimate dining room, where specialized cooks prepare delicious dishes and appetizers from the Middle East, China, Japan, Indonesia, Brazil, Morocco, and Sweden right before your eyes. They're all tasty, admirably presented, and absolutely authentic. This is definitely the most unusual of all the restaurants in the complex, and the most relaxed (although men are required to wear jackets).

## 13 ♧
## The Market Dining Room
**938-1155**

This unfortunately rather drab dining room, with its discreetly distant white linen-covered tables, attracts the cream of neighboring Wall Street's businessmen at lunch. The food is admirably fresh: excellent seafood, fresh daily

*Mon. to Fri. 11:30 A.M. to
2:30 P.M.; Mon. to Sat. 5:30 to
10:00 P.M.; reservations
recommended.*
Steaks/Seafood

(we have a tender memory of some sublime scallops), comes from the finest provisioners in New York, their names listed on the menu. There are also very fine meats, as well as several more elaborate dishes in which the flavor of the main ingredient is never masked. A generous wine list and speedy, friendly service. How lucky are those lower Manhattan business people who, for less than $20, can enjoy such marvelously healthy meals!

# Chinatown • Little Italy

## 11/20
### Benito's I and Benito's II
**174 Mulberry St.**
**226-9007**
**163 Mulberry St.**
**226-9012**
*Dinner nightly until 11:00 P.M.;
closed Sun. Benito I, Fri. and
Sat. only
No credit cards*
Italian

Located right across from each other, these two very friendly Sicilian restaurants offer good quality family-style cooking at extremely reasonable prices. Excellent fried zucchini, good mussels in tomato sauce, several types of fish (overcooked) in well-seasoned sauces, and, to end the meal, zabaglione prepared as it should be.

## 11/20
### Il Cortile
**125 Mulberry Street**
**(between Canal and Hester Sts.)**
**226-6060**
*Lunch and dinner daily until
midnight; jacket and tie preferred
All major credit cards*
Italian

A pretty place, done with bricks and wood paneling, draws well-to-do customers who don't come for pizza and spaghetti. This is "new style" Little Italy—slightly stiff, but indisputably elegant. The chef is from the south, but his cooking ranges over the entire peninsula and at times even skips across the border. Sometimes overly ambitious (is this really the place to serve chicken au Champagne?) he is certainly not lacking in talent, as you'll agree after having tasted his Sardinian-style eel, his bouillabaisse "marinero," or his chicken "du cordonnier," sautéed in garlic sauce with Italian sausage and mushrooms. The service is excellent, the choice of Italian cheeses particularly wide (something rare in New York), and the prices quite high. $30–35.

## 12/20
### Dragon Garden
**47 Division St.**
**(between Bowery and Market Sts.)**

The family comes from Ningpo, and the style of cuisine is therefore Shanghainese, though hot and spicy Szechuan dishes are also featured. Starters include a delicious creamy salad of fresh tofu, dressed with soy and sesame oil and topped with finely chopped, crunchy Szechuan pickle. Vegetarians may enjoy the mock duck rolled in

*Lunch and dinner daily until
10:00 P.M.; weekends until
10:30 P.M. V, MC*
Chinese

bean curd skin, but we found it a bit chewy and more mock than duck. "Drunken" chicken and crisp scallion pancakes were excellent; but the star turn was undoubtedly steamed ting buns, a speciality of Shanghai. Served in a bamboo steamer, these small, round, fluted dumplings were so full of juice that they had to be eaten gingerly with a spoon. Accompanied by a spicy soy dip, they were among the best dim sum we encountered in New York. Green fish fritters were cooked in a light and crispy batter with chopped seaweed for color. Delicately flavored but a bit on the bland side, they were cheered up by a side order of sweet-and-sour sauce.

Hot and spicy dishes are indicated by a red star, and include such favorites as carp in hot sauce, chicken with orange flavor, and double sauteed sliced pork. The cooking is competent with a genuine homey touch. This small family restaurant is a rare find and certainly worth the journey. $10; bring your own rice wine.

## 7/20
## Grotta Azzurra
**387 Broom St.
(at Mulberry St.)
226-9283**
*Lunch and dinner daily until
11:30 P.M.; closed Mon.;
no reservations
No credit cards*
Italian

We spent some rather gloomy moments in this "blue grotto" in Little Italy, which has an inexplicably high reputation. If you're subject to vertigo, we don't recommend you descend the tumbling steep staircase into this infernal cavern. And if you like good Sicilian cooking, look elsewhere for it. The pasta, served lukewarm, sticks to your fork, the veal scallops are drowned in an alleged bolognese sauce that tastes as though it's poured straight out of the ketchup bottle, the grated parmesan tastes like Gruyère, and the desserts are sad enough to make you weep.

## 12/20
## Home Village
**20 Mott St.
964-0381**
*Daily lunch and dinner until
1:30 A.M.
No credit cards*
Chinese

Molded plastic panels proclaim an "instant" Chinese restaurant. Neat and obliging waiters will explain the sinister-sounding entries under the "exotic Hakka" section. Whatever your persuasion, try a dish or two and you will understand why miles of tripe are sold here each month. Large but light egg rolls made entirely from tofu skin with different fillings arrive on the table accompanied by a sweet-and-sour dip. Moist and subtly flavoured salt-baked chicken, pink at the bone, was served with ginger and star anise-flavored soy, or a dip of salt, pepper, and cinnamon.

Home Village is renowned for its seafood, with over fifty dishes to choose from. Pass over the clams in black bean sauce, bland and rubbery, and go instead for the mussels in the pot cooked with coriander, scallions, and greens. Baked crabs with curry proved an agreeable surprise and if there are five or more of you, try the steamed sea bass in a soy-and-scallion or sweet-and-sour sauce. Also recommended are prawns baked with chili and spiced salt.

Chinese pork chops could have been a disaster. In fact they were delicious, crunchingly crisp yet tender and served in a reddish-brown honeyed sauce, just enough to glaze the meat without drowning it. A certain tendency to flirt with American ingredients results in such bizarre combinations as lobster topped with processed cheese and chicken à la king in a nasty whitish sauce. Fried rice "special" bore the marks of ordeal by tomato ketchup. All three to be avoided.

But the prize dish was undoubtedly deep-fried fresh pig's intestines. Forget that you are eating pig's entrails: these red crispy sausages with their meltingly soft innards couched on a bed of cabbage are sensational, and merit the Golden Offal Award of the year. There are set feasts for parties but with a menu as large and varied as this it must pay to be adventurous. $15 for a feast and bring your own wine.

## 12/20
## Hwa Yuan
**40 East Broadway**
**966-5534**
*Daily lunch and dinner until 10:00 P.M.; weekends until 11:00 P.M.*
*All major credit cards*
Chinese

It's certainly not the depressing (ugly beige) decor, or the brusque (but smiling and quick) service, or the concessions that Szechuan cooking is forced to make for American palates, or the choice of alcoholic beverages (limited to Chinese beer) that draws New Yorkers here. Rather, it's the very reasonable prices, the incredibly generous portions (one dish is enough for three people), and above all the quality of some of the dishes, in particular the soups (such as the hot and sour, and the noodles with shredded pork), the unusual bean curd, the remarkably tender chicken, cut into thin strips and served with snow peas, and the very spicy double sauté of pork, as well as a few other bizarre preparations we didn't taste. The shrimp, by contrast, tough and tasting sadly of the freezer, are not as good as in France—or in China.

## 12/20
## Little Szechuan
**31 Oliver St.**
**349-2630**
*Lunch and dinner daily until 10:00 P.M.; closed Mon.; no reservations*
*No credit cards*
Chinese

Only initiates frequent this tiny, out-of-the-way restaurant tucked away between the Manhattan and Brooklyn Bridges not far from the Civic Center, where they dine on marvelously spiced dishes at absolutely ridiculous prices. One of the most authentic Chinese restaurants in New York.

## 12/20
## Peking Duck House
**22 Mott St.**
**227-1810**
*Daily lunch and dinner until 10:30 P.M.; weekends until 11:30 P.M.; dim-sum weekends from 11:30 A.M. to 3:00 P.M.*
*AE*
Chinese

Of the many restaurants in Chinatown, this is one of the most active and most frequented, by a clientele both Chinese (lots of families from the neighborhood) and Occidental (to which a photo of Dr. Kissinger bears witness). You won't scale any peaks of glory, but you're assured of enjoying hearty, solid cooking here, not overly subtle but superbly copious, low-priced, and essentially honest. The great turnover assures more or less constant freshness. As for the decor, it's as naked as the large popular restaurants in Singapore and Hong Kong. In fact, you could almost fancy yourself really there.

## 13 ♧
# Say Eng Look
**1 East Broadway**
**732-0796**
*Lunch and dinner daily until
10:30 P.M.; weekends until
11:30 P.M.
V, MC*
Chinese

One of the oldest and most reputable restaurants in
Chinatown, Say Eng Look has recently had a facelift. The
name means "4–5–6," a winning hand in mahjongg, and
the ancient waiters in their crumpled jackets shuffle
around like croupiers in a Hong Kong casino. Nothing has
really changed and already the new look is, mercifully,
beginning to fade. Red-check oilcloth covers the tables
and there is a small bar, red and black like a Chinese
shrine, that dispenses nothing stronger than beer. So bring
your own booze.

The food is Shanghai style as both owners and chefs
come from Ningpo. The waiters are scrutable, but there is
no hard sell: they will advise you if you smile nicely.
Connoisseurs like Say Eng Look because it has always
stuck to its style and standards. Ingredients are fresh and
of high quality: above all, the cooking is consistent.

Special dishes are cryptically worded. "Fried roll fish
with bean curd sheet" turned out to be a seafood spring
roll wrapped in light and crisp fried tofu skin. Tai chi
chicken released such flavors and aromas that we ended
up eating the sauce with a spoon. Undoubtedly Say Eng
Look scores with its sauces, as anyone who has tasted the
whole fish in brown sauce will confirm. Lions Head
proved to be jumbo-sized meatballs in a star anise pepper
sauce with greens; a remote and exalted cousin of the
American burgers. For real Chinatown aficionados there is
a choice of casseroles and the chicken with cellophane
noodles was much praised at a neighboring table. It's a
meal in itself.

The menu is large and helpings enormous. It is futile to
ask for half portions, as the chefs all wield the same
standard ladles. Clear your palate with a refreshing
spumoni or tortoni, Marco Polo's way of saying "thank
you" for his discovery of China. $10 with Tsingtao beer.

True to its name, no sooner had the clicking of
chopsticks died down than we heard the rattling of
mahjongg tiles at the staff table.

## 12/20
# Silver Palace
**50 Bowery**
**(near Canal St.)**
**964-1204**
*Daily lunch and dinner until
10:00 P.M.; no reservations;
Chinese brunch on Sun.
All major credit cards
(accepted for dinner only)*
Chinese

On the Bowery, where winos sleep off the effects of cheap
liquor, there are rows of Chinese restaurants, all different.
Of these the immense Silver Palace is the most surprising
and the best; the dim sum served Sunday mornings is a
must. The dining room looks like the engine room of
some South Seas tub whose engines have been replaced
by chopsticks. An infernal din, with tables of Chinese
families from howling infants to silent grannies. The
waitresses charge to the front in waves, brandishing trays
that threaten to buckle under the piles of small Cantonese
bite-sized treats, each more delicate than the last, allow
you to enjoy the best Chinese brunch in town for no
more than a few dollars. And that's no secret either:
Sunday morning, between 10:00 A.M. and 2:00 P.M., the
Silver Palace serves close to three thousand meals in this

room, where a sign on the wall serenely proclaims, "Occupancy by more than 137 is dangerous and unlawful."

# SoHo

## 11/20
## Ballato's
**55 East Houston St. (between Mulberry and Mott Sts.)**
**226-9683**
*Lunch and dinner daily until 8:45 P.M.; closed Sun. No credit cards*
Italian

For twenty-three years until his death in June 1980, short, dapper John Ballato presided over this tiny Italian restaurant on East Houston Street. Neither the vagrants on the sidewalk nor the trailer trucks rumbling down the street deterred the rich and the famous. Photos, cartoons, and posters attest to their affection for Ballato, and his for them. Today, his widow carries on with something like the same aplomb, and many of the same customers keep coming.

What is the attraction? There is intimacy here; you feel you are in an inner circle, one of the fortunate few who have discovered a New York restaurant. In fact, the essentially northern Italian cooking (the chef is from Yugoslavia) is steady, but certainly not outstanding. The prices are extremely modest. Antipasti—mussels reganate, baked clams, roast peppers with anchovies—are in the $3 to $4 range. The zuppe di pesce, assorted seafood and shellfish in a garlicky broth, is surely good value at $8.75. Or try the halibut steak, fresh and nicely grilled, or the bass livornese, in a light tomato dressing. By contrast, the rolatini of veal Margherita, rolled veal with prosciutto and cheese, was overcooked and not as tender as it should be. There is one dessert worth ordering: a frothy zabaglione well flavored with a good marsala.

An exceptional chianti, the Reserva Ducale of Ruffino, costs $12.75; and there are standard Valpolicellas and Soaves for under $10. If the taxi meter hits $5. each way, you'll still be ahead. The chances are that you'll enjoy your meal.

## 9/20
## Central Falls
**478 West Broadway (between W. Houston and Prince Sts.)**
**533-9481**
*Lunch and dinner daily until 1:00 A.M. All major credit cards*
American

Once Central Falls was a box factory. Today, it is a SoHo restaurant, bar, and meeting place. The huge mahogany bar dominates the scene. And what other establishment in town can boast bar stools upholstered in red velour? This is a place to relax and have fun. Down the center, Ionic columns support the eighteen-foot ceiling and separate the bar crowd from a somewhat more sedate atmosphere across the room, where diners sit in wicker chairs along a gallery of prints and photographs.

The food doesn't quite live up to expectation, but it's passable. At lunch, there are omelets and pastas (spinach ravioli with dill-scented cream sauce, or fettucine with leeks, prosciutto, and mushrooms.) At dinner there are a handful of additional entrees, including a fish of the day with lemon butter sauce, lamb chops, or steak. The wine list is short. The Phelps Pinot Noir at $12 and the Chappellet Chenin Blanc at $14 are good choices.

Central Falls is a good bet to sample the spirit of SoHo. Don't expect too much from the kitchen, and you will no doubt join in the good times around you.

## 13 ♀
## La Chanterelle
**89 Grand St.**
**(at Greene St.)**
**966-6960**
*Lunch and dinner daily until*
*10:00 A.M.; closed Sun. and Mon.*
*AE, MC, V*
French
(provincial/nouvelle)

A wholesale store built around the turn of the century has been converted into a restaurant whose only attempts at decoration are the pink walls and the molding on the ceiling from which hang two large Dutch copper chandeliers. Twelve tables served by young student types, small, scrawled menus, a trendy clientele—all this smacks of amateurism, but doubts are dispelled when the food arrives. Chef David Waltuck's repertoire may be limited, but he masters it perfectly, confining himself to a simple cuisine as refreshing as the atmosphere that reigns in the restaurant. His pigeon mousse is a mite too fat, but good all the same; the fresh, tiny scallops served with lime melt in your mouth; the chicken poached in a cabbage leaf is a true joy, and his lamb chops, served with baked garlic cloves and a very light potatoes au gratin (one of Guérard's dishes) are succulent. It's only a pity that the praline and coffee cake, one of the two desserts on the menu, should taste so little of coffee. Nonetheless, the bill is the only real trouble spot: it's high enough to suggest that La Chanterelle is one of the truly great restaurants, which it quite obviously is not.

## 10/20
## Elephant and Castle
**183 Prince St.**
**260-3600**
*Breakfast, lunch and dinner daily*
*until 1:00 A.M.;*
*2:00 A.M. weekends*
*No reservations*
*All major credit cards*
International

*The* hang-out for artists, hustlers, and all SoHo aficionados. A choice of nineteen different omelets is offered by the charming waitresses in addition to an excellent sesame chicken. Very attractive wood-paneled dining room. Another branch in Greenwich Village, at 68 Greenwich Avenue (near 7th Avenue).

## 13 ♀
## Greene Street Restaurant
**101 Greene Sts.**
**(between Prince and**
**Spring Sts.)**
**925-2415**

There is a submarine quality to the light in this immense, two-tiered hangar inhabited by giant green plants, models, and the (richer) intelligentsia. At first, it looks far too trendy to be honest, and you expect the worst. But you're wrong, because the two young Frenchmen, Jean-Pierre Laporte and Jean-Pierre Lauret, who created this

*Lunch Mon. to Fri. until 3:00 P.M.;
dinner Sat. and Sun. until
midnight; Sun. brunch
Reservation recommended
AE, MC, V*
French (nouvelle)

restaurant are firm believers in the virtues of good cooking. And to our great surprise, after a critical false start (a lukewarm salad of insipid, insignificant bay scallops and a slightly dry feuilleté of snails), we were served three delicious dishes: lobster à l'orange, sweetbreads poached with basil, and sautéed médaillons of veal accompanied by an exquisite mushroom mousse. The ingredients were first-rate, the cooking perfect, and the lightly creamed sauces showed finesse—the one hesitation being that all the sauces had exactly the same base. The entire menu is both modern and imaginative, and there's not a single dish we didn't want to taste, from the sautéed magret of Long Island duck in raspberry vinegar sauce and liver mousse to the feuilleté of veal kidneys in Pommery mustard sauce—not to mention the roast baby pheasant with poached figs and chestnut mousseline or the millefeuille of salmon with ginger. Also a dozen desserts, including a good bittersweet chocolate cake and delicious hot apple tart with almonds. Make sure, however, that you're not seated too near the pianist, who sits on a platform in the center of the room—he plays well, but you'll hardly be able to hear yourself talk.

## 5/20
## Oh-Ho-So
**395 West Broadway
(Spring St.)
966-6110**
*Lunch and dinner daily
until 1:00 A.M.
AE*
Chinese

The most spectacular restaurant in all of SoHo, and also one of the worst. This huge joint, launched about a dozen years ago by the art dealer Leo Castelli, Andy Warhol, and the French painter Arman (one of the co-owners), continues to delight lovers of the unusual with its neo-Renaissance sculptures and ornate balcony grills (as corrected by the decadents), stained glass, and green plants. Unfortunately, the cooking—theoretically Chinese—is absolutely dreadful. Drop in long enough for a quick drink.

## 12/20
## Raoul's
**180 Prince St.
(Sullivan St.)
966-3518**
*Dinner daily until midnight
AE, V, MC*
French (provincial)

The sign outside proclaims, "Le bistro de SoHo"; and indeed, this is New York's most authentic French bistro. Nothing is missing: a somber dining room with a long counter along one side where you can drink kir and order Champagne by the glass, posters and photos from the Old Country (including one of General de Gaulle), a large slate listing the daily specials (representing the entire repertoire of traditional French bistro fare): leeks vinaigrette, pâté maison, snails, fish panaché, fillet of sole, brains with beurre noir, sauteed calf's liver, kidneys à la moutarde, boeuf bourguignon, partridge paysanne, leg of lamb, and all that. You'd think yourself transported across the Atlantic, especially as the dishes are prepared honestly, although without genius, and according to the rules of good French provincial cooking. You'll understand how this little miracle was made possible when Serge Raoul, the owner, sits down at your table after you've eaten and tells the story of his life over a glass of the house Burgundy. He arrived in America in 1962 as a specialist in telecommunications, and soon became a French radio correspondent. Eight years later he took over an old Italian restaurant in SoHo, Gallicized it, and called his brother Guy (at the time second chef at the Palace). And so it came to pass that in 1976 a society of journalists, painters, fashion types, and artists from all over set up camp in this exact replica of an old-fashioned French bistro.

As one might expect, prices have started to rise, and the clientele is now a mixed breed, including numerous sightseers. But the quality has remained as straightforward and the atmosphere as relaxed as when the restaurant opened. At last, a real French bistro that will not make a Frenchman feel ashamed.

---

**11/20**
## SoHo
## Charcuterie
**195 Spring St.
(Sullivan St.)
226-3545**
*Lunch and dinner daily
until 11:00 P.M.; Sat until
midnight; closed Mon. dinner;
Sun. brunch
All major credit cards*
Continental

Actually, this is nothing more than a deli, but it must be admitted that the format devised by the young owners, Francine and Madeline, is clever as anything. Whereas the decor in most delicatessens keeps them in a bygone era, this is a chic charcuterie where everything, from lamps to fans, is immaculately white. In front you can buy sausages, head cheese, salads—everything you need for a park-bench picnic in Washington Square—and in the room at the back you can choose from omelets, quiches, cold cuts, and excellent pies, on which you can lunch comfortably for about $20, including a California wine. But the two ladies pride themselves on their culinary talents, and in the evening prepare dishes that are not so much unappealing as borderline, and much too expensive. Pine nuts adorn the fillet of sole, cucumbers are served in a Champagne sauce, and Mornay sauce is poured over the stuffed chicken—all of which reeks of total amateurism. Asexual fare perfect for a transvestite tea party. It's a pity, because the products used are really rather good, and the atmosphere of this charcuterie is authentic New York. Go on Sunday morning for their popular brunch: with croissants, brioches, preserves and scrambled eggs, and you will run no risks.

---

**12/20**
## Wings
**76 Wooster St.
(between Spring and
Broome Sts.)
966-1300**
*Nightly dinner until midnight;
weekends until 1:30 A.M.;
Sun. brunch; reservations required
AE*
American

New Yorkers looking for something different seem especially to enjoy dining in converted warehouses, lofts, factories, carriage houses, or whatever—particularly if the location is SoHo. The ambience, not the food, is the attraction. At Wings, the food is decent and the decor is striking. You enter at street level, pass beyond a bright, stylish bar, and find yourself on a balcony overlooking the dining area below. (A waiter asserts it was once a box factory.) Everything is one hue or another of pink— ceiling, walls, carpeting, upholstery, napery—except a single tube of white flourescent light that circles around the square ceiling some twenty feet above the tables. In one corner at the foot of the stairway descending from bar to dining area, a four-foot imitation pink calla lily sprouts from a giant flower pot; in another corner a piano indicates that this is a place to have fun (even if the acoustics are terrible). The chef is twenty-seven-year-old Jonathan Bennet, once the sous-chef at Joanna—not an extravagant recommendation. But Jonathan apprenticed at Lyon, where he learned about good bourgeois cooking and about nouvelle, as well. The results at Wings demonstrate that he didn't waste his time in Lyon. Furthermore, he has resisted concocting the absurd combinations that some SoHo establishments offer proudly as their own versions of nouvelle. The menu is short. Standard dishes are prepared with a flair, and innovations with restraint. Among the former are appetizers of mussels in white wine cream sauce and sweetbreads in puff pastry. Among the latter is a plate of lightly sautéed vegetables with ginger. In the same vein is a smoked salmon salad in a hazelnut dressing. Standard chicken and veal entrees are exceptionally flavorful, such as chicken with a rosemary and garlic sauce and veal with a basil sauce.

We have had some exciting meals here, but our last experience left us wondering why things can change so quickly with a chef who certainly has potential. It is a shame that something that started with such excitement appears to be settling into a less than inspired pattern. We urge Mr. Bennet to reclaim his creativity and talent. About $80 for two in this very pink place.

13
## Wise Maria
**210 Spring St.
(at 6th Ave.)
925-9257**
*Lunch and dinner daily
until midnight; Sat. dinner only;
closed Sun.*
*AE*
Italian

Wise Maria, according to Susan and Philip Idone, proprietors of this year-old establishment, was a medieval Tuscan alchemist who knew something about mixing brews in a steaming cauldron, and is credited as the first to use a double boiler; in Italian the bagna Maria, in French the bain Marie. Whatever, Susan, after an erratic few months of getting herself and her kitchen organized, now produces delicious twentieth-century results. The menu is small and the emphasis is on northern Italian. Susan has a light touch, and you'll be surprised and pleased by her approach to traditional items that appear on Italian menus around town.

For example, among the appetizers, a crisp pizza emphasizes the freshness of the tomatoes and omits the cheese; spinach tortelloni is dressed in clarified butter instead of the usual cream. For an intriguing starter not so often found on New York menus, try the sautéed fennel in a light olive oil dressing. Among entrees, the baby roast quail with polenta is pink and moist, the brook trout is nicely poached and accompanied by superbly flavored rice, mushrooms, and almonds. However, the bordetto, or the fish stew, does not quite capture the zest intended. A la carte salads of arugula or radicchio are outstanding.

# Greenwich Village • Lower East Side

## 10/20
### Bernstein-On-Essex Street
**135 Essex St.**
**(Orchard and Rivington Sts.)**
**473-3900**
*Breakfast, lunch, and dinner daily until 1:00 A.M.; closed Fri. nights and Sat. day.*
Chinese

Incredible! A Sino-Kosher restaurant. Chinese recipes are prepared with "lawful" meats (chicken and veal instead of pork and shellfish), the results being entirely acceptable. The proof: numerous imitations of the format. Sino-Kosher cooking is booming in New York, much to everyone's surprise. The majority of waiters are Jewish, dressed in Chinese garb—others really are Chinese, and speak broken American with a Yiddish accent.

## 12/20
### Black Sheep
**342 W. 11th St.**
**242-1010**
*Dinner daily until 11:00 P.M.; midnight weekends; Sun. brunch All major credit cards*
French (provincial)

The quintessential modish Greenwich Village bistro, tucked away on a nicely quiet street, with bare brick walls, very ugly still-lifes depicting flowers and tablescapes, luxuriant plants, tables crammed together, murky lighting (de rigeur in such locales) and the beautiful Bohemians who, going by prices, aren't exactly destitute. The cooking aims at being absolutely French—rural French at that—and largely succeeds. The menu opens commandingly with an honest plate of crudités à l'aïoli, continues with a very good cream of watercress soup, and is followed by a respectable pâté de campagne served with slices of brioche. Next, you may choose from nine main dishes, including fish—grilled or à la provençale—meats in wine sauce, steak forestière, and lamb chops or pork chops. Honest only, but generously served. And, to finish, salad and pastry (including a good almond tart). Despite several California wines offered on the wine list, everyone here drinks French wine, beginning with a kir or glass of Pineau des Charentes to whet the appetite—not forgetting the ubiquitous Perrier water. No gastronomic spasms of delight, but a friendly and relaxed atmosphere that is just right for the neighborhood.

## 11/20
### Cafe Espanol
**172 Bleecker St.**
**(between Sullivan**

Cafe Espanol is as close as you'll get in New York to the tasca of Spain—the small, intimate, crowded, and noisy restaurant noted for its good cheer, good fellowship, and

**and MacDougal Sts.)**
**475-9230**
*Lunch and dinner daily*
*until 1:00 A.M.*
*All major credit cards*
Spanish/Mexican

its ample food and wine. Here, as often in Spain, the bar is in the back, and you have to push your way through the packed tables to get there. On weekends, the crowds wait on the sidewalk outside to get in.

There is good reason for the popularity of this little place. The Spanish and Mexican dishes are tasty, the portions are huge, and the prices are right. At dinner you can gorge yourself on a steaming paella with lobster, or a mariscada (fish stew) of scallops, shrimps, mussels and lobster for $9.95. With a carafe of lusty Spanish wine ($7.50), and a cup of coffee (you won't have room for dessert), two can feast for $35, tip included. If that is too steep for your pocketbook, you can turn to the Mexican side of the menu and select one of the combination platters of tacos, enchiladas, and tamales for as little as $6.50. Or plan your visit at lunch (not so crowded) and enjoy a complete lunch of soup, any dinner entree item (the lobster meat left out), wine or beer, and coffee for $6.50. Is there better value anywhere in New York?

**11/20**
## Café Loup
**18 E. 13th St.**
**255-4746**
*Lunch and dinner daily*
*until 11:00 P.M.; closed Sat. lunch*
*and Sun.*
*All major credit cards*
French (provincial)

If you're curious to see how New Yorkers prepare simple French fare, walk right into this small, elegant, and tranquil wood-paneled bar. Young blue-jeaned waiters, attentive and well groomed, will recommend the onion soup, spinach salad with mushrooms from Paris, an amusing seafood sausage accompanied by fresh pasta, a hot sausage "comme à Lyon" (unfortunately, the potatoes served with it are undercooked, and crack when you bite), crème caramel, and a surprising charlotte with very creamy chocolate. The spot is friendly and cheerful, the final attraction being the unpretentious bill: $12 for lunch with beer, $20-25 for supper.

**11/20**
## Café New Amsterdam
**284 W. 12th St.**
**242-7929**
*Dinner nightly until 11:00 P.M.;*
*Sun. brunch; closed Tues.*
*AE, MC, V*
Continental

A ravishing, madly fashionable bistro where chic people unflinchingly swallow the latest American culinary discoveries such as fried Brie (you read that right), which some have described as a triumph of nouvelle cuisine. . . . Still the cook is not without talent; his sauces are delicate, and his fish dishes quite successful.

**10/20**
## Caffé da'Alfredo
**17 Perry St.**
**(and Seventh Ave.)**
**989-7028**
*Dinner nightly until 11:00 P.M.;*
*Sat and Sun. lunch*
*No credit cards*
Italian

BYOBOW ("bring your own bottle of wine") to this minuscule Italian bistro where people fight for the right to sit at one of the twelve tables. Young crowd, lots of atmosphere, good pasta alla carbonara, mediocre meats, and a few interesting dishes such as stuffed mushrooms and zucchini with garlic. None of this is particularly light—except the prices—but the place is charming. And the prices are right ($10–$15).

## 13
# The Coach House

**110 Waverly Place (west of Washington Square)**
**777-0303**

*Dinner nightly until 10:30 P.M.;*
*closed Mon.; formal;*
*reservation necessary*
*All major credit cards*
American/Continental

It has long been accepted that this famous and elegant restaurant in the old Washington Square district serves the best "American" cooking in New York. However, a glance at the menu (which sluggishly remains more or less unchanged all year long) is enough to convince that this reputation is founded on myth, and is perpetuated for reasons that remain unclear. The Coach House's American specialties are in fact more or less limited to a black bean soup (lightly flavored with lemon, and delicious); thin slices of smoked turkey served with an excellent horseradish sauce; buttered ears of corn; and a chicken pie that, with its dry crust and overseasoned sauce, leaves much to be desired. Neither the owner, Léon Leonides, nor the chef seems ever to have had enough curiosity to push their investigations of native recipes any further, falling back instead on Gruyère cheese quiche, escargots de Bourgogne, mushrooms à la Grècque, and shish kebab, none of which—so far as we know—is a New World specialty. It's a pity, since most of the dishes are perfectly made from first-rate ingredients. The striped bass poached in court-bouillon, flavored with anise and surrounded by small vegetables, is as delightful to look at as to eat; the fresh crab in a deliciously spiced butter sauce is highly successful; the rice is exquisite, and no meats are juicier or better cooked than the rack of lamb and western steer sirloin. And if the chocolate cake is too compact and flavorless, the pecan pie takes its rightful place in a glorious tradition. Léon Leonides, present in the dining room every night, doesn't trouble to greet each table; and despite the presence of a charming old maitre d'hôtel, the service is not polished: our waiter, for example, forgot to uncork a bottle of wine after having shown us its label. But that's not serious, and you can spend a pleasant evening in this somewhat colonial-style decor, with sixteen-branched candelabra, dark brickwork, and charming paintings of equestrian and hunting scenes. $30–$35, excluding wine.

## 13
# Da Silvano

**260 Avenue of the Americas (Bleecker St.)**
**982-0090**

*Lunch and dinner daily*
*until 11:30 P.M. Sat. and Sun.*
*dinner only*
*No credit cards*
Italian

When the weather is nice you can sit at one of a handful of tables outside, European-style, and enjoy the sights, sounds, and smells of New York's Greenwich Village. You may even see a nearby manhole pop open and a pair of overalled genii emerge from the subway world below. There are a few more tables inside and a tiny bar with a huge espresso machine. This is a gregarious, intimate, and fashionable Village establishment. The short menu lists some old standbys (grilled shrimps or tortellini alla panna), but there are also departures from the usual. As starters try the calamari and mussel salad dressed in a well-seasoned olive oil, or the crostini, chopped chicken liver with capers, onions, and anchovies on Italian bread. Fresh pasta is imported daily from Little Italy a few blocks across town, and it is carefully cooked to order with several interesting accompaniments. Spaghetti puttanesca, for example, with its black olives, capers, and anchovies, is a change of pace from the more usual tomato, meat, or cheese sauce. Among the meats is a veal chop with chicken liver, tomatoes, and peas that holds its own against more expensive veal chop preparations uptown.

Acceptable Italian wines are available at $12. But there are bottles listed at outlandish prices that seem out of place here. You can order a bottle of Brunello di Montalcino, Biondi Santi (1971) for $110—almost double the price two would pay for two three-course dinners with a bottle of Villa Antinori or an Orvieto. Skip the Montalcino. You'll have the $110 to return a second and third time to sample some of the dishes you missed on your first visit.

## 12/20
### Fish Place
**570 Hudson St.
(11th St.)**
243-4212
*Dinner nightly until
11:30 P.M.; brunch on Sun.
AE, V, MC*
Seafood

Only faithful Village regulars frequent this charming, very modestly decorated bistro, where you can eat your fill without emptying your wallet, and gorge on all sorts of seafood, including superb fresh scampi cooked in court-bouillion, and served simply with melted butter. Good unpretentious American wines. Relaxed, very friendly atmosphere.

## 10/20
### Garvin's
**19 Waverly Place**
473-5261
*Lunch and dinner daily
until midnight, Fri. and Sat.
until 1:00 A.M.
All major credit cards*
International

Some ten yards from the hurly-burly of Washington Square is this large, mauve dining room, slightly "retro" with its 1900s lamps and long wooden bar where you can listen to the pianist plinking out old tunes as you drink. A young, relaxed very "Village" crowd comes to nibble on clams and Long Island oysters, unfussy hamburgers, a sirloin steak that remains tender despite the abuse it suffers in the kitchen, good pecan pie, and an apple strudel whose white pastry they must have forgotten to bake. Good wine list with affordable prices (a rarity): Spanish sparkling wine for the price of a Côte du Roussillon, and a fantastic Cabernet Sauvignon served by the glass.

## 14
### La Gauloise
**502 6th Ave.
(12th-13th Sts.)**
691-1363
*Lunch and dinner daily
until 11:00 P.M.;
Sat. and Sun. brunch;
jacket preferred
All major credit cards*
French (provincial)

On the edge of the Village, a lone window stands out, an elegant presence among the sad Sixth Avenue boutiques. Inside, a long, quite large restaurant boasts mahogany-framed mirrors, 1925 lighting, and an eclectic clientele. The French co-owners take turns on duty, and the menu is terse and rather ordinary: artichokes, pâtés, fish soup, leeks vinaigrette, oysters, sautéed chicken, a mousse of pike, calf's liver with shallots, sole meunière, breast of duck with green peppercorns, veal "zingane," and hearty salads. Banal, but well done, well prepared and cooked with good ingredients, as with the daily specials, chosen from the classics: cassoulet on Sunday, bouillabaise on

Friday, choucroute on Wednesday, confit of duck on Thursday. Weekend brunches consist mainly of egg dishes. The service is provided by animated young men in long aprons. We've eaten the best local Belon oysters in New York here, a superb pudding of onions and apples, and a very serious salad consisting of fresh (but pasteurized) crab, celery, cucumber, hearts of palms, and more. With good little wines served by the glass and excellent coffee, this adds up to a very healthy lunch for about $30 (a little more in the evening).

## 10/20
## Horn of Plenty
**91 Charles St.
(corner of
Bleecker St.)
242-0636**
*Dinner nightly until 2:00 A.M.
All major credit cards*
American

Without question one of the most fun places in the Village, with its deep South bar in dark wood, long bladed fans, and a lively, good-natured, preponderantly Black clientele. Vast dining rooms have been converted into a sort of big, flowered barn, with a glass ceiling and an immense baroque fountain where lively conversation and streams of water flow. Good unpretentious California wines drunk by the glass (the red wine is particularly fruity) wash down clams, good herring with sour cream, and some examples of soul food such as an enormous platter of slightly greasy short ribs of beef with black beans. The spareribs though, are much better at Joe Allen's in Paris. Attractive, granny-style desserts, very friendly service, very New York prices: about $35.

## 11/20
## John Clancy's Restaurant
**181 W. 10th St.
242-7350**
*Dinner nightly until 11:30 P.M.;
Sun. brunch
All major credit cards*
Seafood

John Clancy, a tall, affable New Yorker, ran a cooking school in the city for a number of years. Along with his students, he saw there was a dearth of good seafood establishments. His response was logical enough: he opened his own.

An enormous, pretentious electric sign announces that this is Clancy's Restaurant. But once down a couple of steps into the premises, the atmosphere is pleasant: white walls, white chairs, and pretty table settings of imported English china. The menu is exclusively seafood. Stick to the simple preparations both among the appetizers and the entrees. The clams and oysters are fresh and the pickled mussels of some interest. The mushrooms stuffed with crabmeat and the broiled clams are routine. The swordfish, described as "mesquite grilled," is your best bet among entrees. The fishermen's stew is acceptable, but you can have a zestier version a few blocks away in Little Italy for less money. The fillet of sole is apt to be overcooked, and the sauce undistinguished.

The wine list is tilted to whites (this is a fish restaurant) and there are a number of good California bottles. Try the Chappelet Chenin Blanc ($12) or the Joseph Phelps Sauvignon Blanc ($12.50). A dinner for two can easily run to $80, including wine and tip. In a world where students are as apt to grade teachers as the other way around, students might give Professor Clancy a passing grade—but not much more. The professor's command of the basics is adequate enough, but he is not yet ready for the advanced curriculum.

## 11/20
## Marylou's
**21 W. 9th St.**
**533-0012**
*Lunch and dinner daily until*
*1:00 A.M.; Sun. until 10:00 P.M.*
*All major credit cards*
International (Seafood)

Marylou Baratta learned about bringing fresh fish to the public at her own retail fish store little more than a block away on University Place. For more than a year she has been running Marylou's, the restaurant, with her brother Thomas as partner. Logically enough, the restaurant features fish, and it is invariably fresh. Marylou also likes crisp, fresh vegetables, nouvelle style. A Thai chef combines both in a number of commendable dishes.

One delicious appetizer is shrimp Bangkok, sautéed shrimp with a julienne of zucchini, red and green peppers, and tomato. A commendable entree is bass or red snapper in a zesty Thai dressing. There are a number of pastas and Italian dishes on the menu that don't come off as well. A rice pudding, inexplicably called Angel Cloud, with white raisins steeped in rum and a raspberry sauce, is a good dessert. The espresso is exceptional.

The narrow dining rooms with their banquettes are somewhat formal in contrast to the lack of pretension in the dishes served. But there is some imagination here, and two can experience a rather novel cuisine blending East and West, with wine and tip, for $50–$60.

## 12/20
## La Métairie
**189 W. 10th St.**
**989-0343**
*Nightly dinner seatings at*
*7:00 P.M. and 9:30 P.M.;*
*closed Sun.*
*No credit cards*
French (provincial)

This minuscule, well-polished farmhouse looks as if it might have been decorated by Laura Ashley but in fact was done up by the young woman who owns the restaurant, a be-skirted American chef who bustles about in her closet-sized kitchen. A hostess with glowing cheeks hands you a slate on which are chalked the specials of the day, and places a basket of hot, fresh, wonderfully crusty bread next to the candlestick on your table. The repertoire is quite limited, and the cooking smells faintly of accomplished amateurism, reminiscent of the better Franglais bistros in London's Chelsea. A salad of marinated mushrooms, celery, and lettuce sprinkled with a well-mixed vinaigrette; whiting with capers, garnished with small crisp vegetables; a bass with grapes in wine sauce, veal with olives and garlic in tomato sauce, a pie with caramelized apples, flambéed in Calvados—agreeable eating, if nothing higher, for those who enjoy the chic peasant look.

## 11/20
## One Fifth Avenue
**1 Fifth Avenue**
**260-3434**
*Lunch and dinner daily until*
*1:30 A.M.; no reservations,*
*casual dress*
*All major credit cards*
International

Out of the wreckage of the "S.S. Caronia," a British liner cut in three by a South Seas typhoon in 1974, one of New York's liveliest and most informal restaurants has been created. A large, noisy bar popular with singles is at the entrance, and this extends into the vast white-tiled dining room whose pink walls are pierced with portholes offering "ocean views." In the diffuse, underwater lighting, attractive waiters in black pants and ties gallop about between tables beneath the fishy eye (a fish in aspic, to be more exact) of the master of ceremonies, too British for words, in tails and gray trousers. And all the while, the constant din of the air-conditioning gives you the impression that the ship is about to get underway.

The cooking has the advantage of not standing on ceremony, so we cannot be overly critical. For once, the salad (green pepper, lettuce, watercress, and cherry tomatoes) didn't taste of water, the level of starch in the clam chowder is acceptable, the oysters are excellent (provided you don't touch the purée of shallots accompanying them: seemingly put through the blender, give off a very unpleasant odor), the red snapper and sole meunière are passable, the vegetables are fresh though undercooked, the cheesecake is remarkable, and the Mondavi white Sauvignon nice and fruity. About $20 with wine.

## 12/20
## Patrissy's
**98 Kenmare St.**
**(corner of Mulberry**
**and Lafayette Sts.)**
**226-8509**
*Lunch and dinner daily until*
*midnight*
*All major credit cards*
Italian

One of the Italian colony's favorite haunts. In a modern and relatively discreet setting, casual and reasonably efficient waiters serve the mostly Neapolitan and very satisfying dishes: good homemade lasagna and ravioli, Patrissy steak alla pizzaiola, Italian sausage with green peppers, chicken cacciatore, excellent ricotta cheesecake, and several Italian wines—although these, as it happens, are by no means exceptional. $50–$60 for two to have a full meal with wine.

## 12/20
## Le Petit
## Robert
**314 W. 11th St.**
**691-5311**
*Dinner daily until midnight;*
*closed Mon.*
*AE*
French
(provincial/nouvelle)

The owner is French, the cook American, and the menu asserts: "cuisine bourgeoise." If the grayish-white decor veers frantically between that of a renovated shed and a dentist's waiting room, the dishes are rather promising. A pleasant artichoke salad with pecans, a light cheese soufflé, and a good terrine of rabbit as appetizers. While the seafood ragoût of oysters, mussels, and scallops is well cooked in butter with curry, the civet of doe errs on the side of being too well done. Some effort is made where the accompanying vegetables are concerned: potatoes au gratin, zucchini in butter, steamed turnips and beans. Good desserts: a rich bitter chocolate cake, small pots de crème with ginger. But the splended surprise is a wine list full of moderately priced treasures, including a stunning Ponnelle Vougeot 1977 with sumptuous bouquet, practically a gift at $13. Pleasant service, and a bracing check: about $30–$40.

## 10/20
## Pink Tea Cup
**310 Bleecker St.**
**243-8117**
*Daily 24 hours*
*No credit cards*
Soul Food

Where else can you enjoy Village atmosphere as much as in this bistro for broke students, amicable gays (Christopher Street is a minute away), and those older, but still spry people who come to revel in soul food for practically nothing? If the fatty smell, the sight of a floor that looks like it's never been subjected to the ordeal of a scrubbing, and the greasy ceiling don't put you off, you can dine for about $5–$8 on coleslaw, salad, tomato soup, spareribs (slightly resembling cardboard), good barbecued chicken with black beans and potato salad, and a curious cinnamon pudding—under the portraits of Martin Luther King and John Fitzgerald Kennedy, served with a smile by a young woman—and contemplate all the important intellectuals who've parked their fannies on the red stools near the bar.

13 ♧
## Sabor
**20 Cornelia St.
(near Bleecker St.)
243-9579**
*Dinner nightly until 11:00 P.M.;
weekends until midnight*
*AE, MC*
Cuban

Cubans eating at the Sabor are often surprised by the excellence and originality of the food here, different and more appetizing than in its country of origin. The answer, surprisingly enough, is that the two girls who cook here on alternate nights are in fact American—a Cuban ex-husband being the only Latin link. Keeping the best of the ethnic dishes, but refining them a little, they have produced a very seductive menu.

The outstanding starters here are the various escabeches (raw fish marinated in lime juice with a crisp garnish of onion, celery, carrots, olives and capers). If you are lucky enough to catch the scallop escabeche, it's the best of the lot—absolute perfection. Avoid the frituras de malangas, deep-fried fritters made from a singularly tasteless variety of hairy sweet potato. Of the main dishes the lightest and freshest is the whole red snapper, poached in a green sauce of parsley, wine, garlic, and lime juice. Chicken with prunes and a hint of curry was dark, sweet, and good, but beef dishes tend to be a bit fibrous— especially one with the unappetizing name of ropa vieja, or "old clothes." All dishes should be eaten with that perfect complementary trio, white rice, black beans, and sweet-fried plantains.

By all means leave room for a superb warm tart of freshly grated coconut, sherry, and cinnamon, topped with whipped cream, called coco quemado. It's a glutton's dream. The coffee is faultless, and the tiny bar at the back makes fantastic daiquiris—fresh strawberries or peaches whipped up with dark rum and lime juice. About $20 with a glass of wine or a cocktail.

13 ♧
## Texarkana
**64 W. 10th St.
254-5800**
*Daily dinner until midnight, late
supper until 4:00 A.M.*
*AE*
American

The menu claims that crawfish, catfish, shrimp, frogs legs, and other ingredients (including mesquite charcoal from Laredo, Texas) are flown in from the Gulf states. Whatever, this is one of New York's most interesting new eating establishments. Essentially, the dishes are prepared as they would be along the Gulf Coast, which means generally hot and spicy. But Texarkana recognizes that some palates hanker for milder food, and most condiments are served at the side so the diner can take as much of the hot stuff as he or she likes. For example, the charred raw beef, consisting of barely grilled thin slices of exquisite tenderloin, is served with tiny side dishes of green chili sauce and anchovy mayonnaise. It is a superb appetizer. Also recommended are the pickled shrimp, quickly boiled and then marinated in olive oil, vinegar and lemon, and the crawfish cocktail, served with a hot cayenne sauce and a less hot cocktail sauce, on the side.

Flavorful main courses include Southern fried chicken, here served with a honey butter and Cajun mustard; breaded, pan-fried catfish with a tangy tartare sauce on the side, or Gulf shrimp (better texture than most around town), with lemon, garlic, and scallion greens. Desserts (black-bottom pie, mousse, fruit tarts) don't add up to much except calories. But then if you nibble the wondrous corn bread (placed on the table when you sit down) through the meal, you won't feel like dessert anyway. The wine list focuses on California reds and whites and a handful of French. A good bottle is the Clos du Val 1978 Cabernet Sauvignon.

This is not a copycat restaurant. There is an effort to do something other than to recreate the dishes of the Southwest, and this effort extends to the setting. Abe and Alene de la Houssaye, owners of the Louisiana restaurant, have taken the premises of the old Peter's Backyard establishment and created a setting that perfectly complements the food. Mahogany-colored louvers cover the windows (to keep out the heat of the Gulf sun) while the pale peach walls give a cool backdrop for the hot food. Wooden balconies run along each side (as in a small country church) and a ten-foot copper hood hangs over the grill and fireplace (where you might expect to see the preacher).

Are there regional American cuisines? If this is a sample, New York could use a few dozen more establishments like Texarkana to give diners some alternatives to the copycat French, Italian, or what-have-you that sprout up every day. To experience the cuisine of the Southwest in New York, it will cost you and a friend close to $80. But that is still a lot cheaper than two tickets to Laredo.

## 10/20
### Trattoria da' Alfredo
**90 Bank St.
(Hudson St.)
929-4400**
*Lunch and dinner daily until
10:00 P.M.; Sun. until 9:30 P.M.;
closed Tues.*
*No credit cards*
Italian

A small restaurant with a big reputation, which means you'll have great difficulty getting in. "The best Italian food in New York" (or even the U.S.A., according to *Playboy*); but Signor Alfredo, a shrewd, bearded character with piercing blue eyes, very sensibly pooh-poohs all this. "The best? There's no such thing. On a night when the chef has a hangover it could just as easily be the worst." Nevertheless, the word has got around, and now he's turning away sixty covers a night—it's like trying to get into Studio 54 or Elaine's. To be perfectly frank there's nothing dramatically different about Alfredo's food. The pastas are good, the meat dishes nothing special, but the mere fact that it's difficult to get a table will probably be enough to ensure its popularity for the foreseeable future.

The place itself is very unassuming, with bare wooden tables, classical bric-a-brac, a blue ceiling with floor to match, and masses of plants. The cuisine is from northern Italy, with heavy emphasis on cream and butter, but various interesting regional dishes turn up on the menu— pastas with fresh sardines (a Sicilian speciality), or with sauces of aubergine; spicy Italian sausage and cacciocavallo cheese. Alternatively you can start with mushrooms Sora Rosa stuffed with herbs, prosciutto and parmesan; or artichokes eaten Roman style with fresh lemon, olive oil, garlic, and parsley.

Entrees tend to be uninspired, and you might well risk ordering the meal that Italian restaurateurs hate most— antipasti and pasti, with a zabaglione and an espresso to round things off. If you've enjoyed Signor Alfredo's specialties and want to reproduce them at home, there's a nicely illustrated book, *Alfredo Viazzi's Italian Cookery*. About $20–$25, with an Italian wine.

## 16 ⬤
## La Tulipe
**104 W. 13th St.**
**691-8860**
*Dinner nightly until 10:00 P.M.;*
*closed Mon. jacket and tie*
*recommended*
*All major credit cards*
French (nouvelle)

We couldn't believe our eyes. Usually, as soon as you enter a New York restaurant, even one of some elegance, you're herded into line, watched over, and admonished like boy scouts: "Stay here, wait your turn, don't move." In this small private house you may think for a moment that you've made a mistake and gone into the neighbor's: a friendly man, getting on in years, shows you to your table, and seats you with considerate diffidence. Highly unusual—but then it's true that La Tulipe isn't just another restaurant. Sally Darr, wife of John (the charming man mentioned above, who has the modest mien of a prince consort) was long employed trying out recipes for *Gourmet*, until she thought of putting the experience to work for her own benefit. On the ground floor of their house (which, in France, would be considered a small mansion) she opened a tiny bar and a small dining room, whose sophistication paradoxically derives from their extreme simplicity. The walls, upholstery, and even the trim on the white plates are all in the same shades of burgundy. A few mirrors, some lamps with floral motifs, and large, white tablecloths are enough to create a subtle atmosphere. While the husband shows other guests to their table, the head waiter, a young, entirely likable Frenchman who hasn't yet taken on the blasé and disdainful air that years of overseas service confer on most of our countrymen, intelligently explains the dishes on the menu (itself, sad to say, disastrously laid out). Here you are able to enjoy a delightful cuisine characterized by honest flavors—a cooking style typical of feminine good taste. A limited choice of dishes, which are, however, changed daily, rigorously fresh ingredients, careful attention to cooking time, very light sauces: in short, the antithesis of high-flown, reheated haute cuisine. The small Nantucket scallops, tastier than our own larger ones from Brittany, are served in a perfect butter sauce; the lightly fried zucchini are divine; the bass—ever so slightly overcooked, but still exquisite—has its flavor highlighted by a mixture of expertly seasoned vegetables slowly cooked with the fish en papiotte. The tender lamb chops, pink and juicy, are almost as good as those at the Quilted Giraffe, and the veal sweetbread with cream and noodles is sumptuously fresh. To round things off, the warm apple tart and hot apricot soufflé will make you want to leap up and kiss the cook on both cheeks. A good choice of relatively inexpensive wines: the Saint Véran, an excellent white Châteauneuf-du-Pape, and the extremely rare Château Latour 1955, a steal at $150 (the 1959, less exceptional, costs $600 at La Grenouille). About $29–$36 for the fixed price menu, depending on dishes selected.

9/20
## The Ukrainian Restaurant
**140 Second Ave. (8th-9th Sts.)**
**533-6765**
*Dinner nightly until 11:00 P.M.; closed Sun. and Mon.*
*No credit cards*
Russian

The facade and foyer of New York's Ukrainian Restaurant has all the appeal of a Y.M.C.A. in Outer Siberia—but once through the grisly entrance hall, the actual restaurant has quite a cheerful and welcoming air. There are checked tablecloths, Tiffany lamps, pictures of dancing Cossacks, and girls in peasant blouses. Although once part of the Ukrainian Community Center it has now gone public, and although the menu is longer so, the atmosphere is still very innocent and unsophisticated. Off the restaurant lies an austere and cavernous hall with an upright piano and a couple of rather incongruous-looking chandeliers, optimistically labeled "Party Room." In fact our evening was enlivened by a very jolly and noisy group of Ukrainian youngsters celebrating their graduation.

After two bowls of delicious soup—honeycomb tripe and beetroot borscht, both ample enough for a full meal—we were faced with the daunting Combination Platter No. 1. Its centerpiece was a huge oblong galubsi (stuffed cabbage, rather overcooked), flanked by sauerkraut, tasteless lumps of kielbasa sausage, and the famous pirogis. These heavy, crescent-shaped dumplings came with four stuffings—meat or potato, both nice, cabbage, very nasty indeed, and sweet cottage cheese, which would have seemed more at home in the dessert section. This last we attacked purely in the line of duty, having heard of a legendary old babushka whose jelly doughnuts—dark, greasy, and heavy as cannonballs— were formerly a great draw. Alas, she has ceased to operate, so we ordered homemade apple cake, and lived to regret it.

This is food for a Russian winter, honest, heavy, and extraordinarily cheap—you can be sure that neither your wallet nor you will depart any the lighter. Our meal, with a hot toddy and a Ukrainian cocktail, cost us $12 a head.

9/20
## Village Green
**551 Hudson St.**
**255-1650**

How pleasant to have a drink in this delightful old Greenwich Village house, as one sits facing the piano under the well-waxed beams, in the shadow of a few green plants that, in the evening, give the place the air of a

*Daily until midnight; Sun. brunch
but no dinner
AE, MC, V*
French (provincial)

comfortable winter garden. But things take a decided turn for the worse when you are led to your dining table. Why? The service is as friendly as one could wish, the place settings neat and clean, and the candles stand straight in their holders. But neither the absolutely tasteless giant frogs legs à la provençale (in fact, a very bland ratatouille), nor the chicken breast poached in a totally incongruous mussel sauce, nor the duck stupidly flambéed in Grand Marnier, nor the doughy chocolate soufflé, managed to rouse any enthusiasm. Is this supposed to be a campy parody of what French cooking used to be like? Yet the cook (an American) was fairly successful with the fricassee of snails (a mite bland, nonetheless) in a good sorrel cream. And the management can't totally despise good ingredients, as we were brought some marvelous raspberries for dessert. They score another point for their wine list, with a stunning Rioja du Marquès de Riscal 1973 reasonably priced at $6 the half bottle. The check, by contrast, was less agreeable: $45 without any effort.

**11/20**
## Ye Waverly Inn
**16 Bank St.**
**929-4377**
*Lunch and dinner daily until
11:00 P.M.; no lunch Sat. or Sun.;
no liquor
All major credit cards*
American

The simple, friendly atmosphere of a New England tavern (without the ale), where charming waitresses serve simple but tasty dishes (roast lamb, meatloaf, pot roast) and, above all, fine desserts. A pleasant lunch for under $10; dinner is somewhat more expensive, but this is always a good spot to come when payday seems far away.

# East 14th to 42nd Streets

13
## Ararat
**4 E. 36th St.**
**686-4622**
*Lunch and dinner daily until
10:00 P.M.; closed for lunch Sun.
All major credit cards*
Armenian

"Everything is good here," a friendly old waiter told us disarmingly, recalling in a sometimes trembly voice his trip from Constantinople to Paris in 1919. And the elderly gentleman was right. This purebred Armenian restaurant serves authentic Middle Eastern cuisine in a comfortable fake-Byzantine-palace setting (just avoid the harshly lit back room). The light and delicate dishes are made from good, robust ingredients. Order the Ararat Special, a selection of homemade hors d'oeuvres; and try the vine leaves, mussels with rice, the delicious hummos (puree of chickpeas) and perfectly done shoulder of lamb with tomatoes, the moussaka served with surprisingly delicate rice. Finish with a baklava in real honey, which is sweet, but not overly so. Other grounds for rejoicing: with excellent American wines served by the glass, it will cost you less than $25 per person, tax and gratuities included. That makes this restaurant one of New York's most agreeable surprises.

**12/20**

## Balkan-Armenian

**29 E. 27th St.
(between Lexington and Park)
689-7925**

*Lunch and dinner daily until 9:00 P.M. (10:30 P.M. Sat.); closed Sat. and Sun. afternoons*
*AE, DC, CB, MC*
Armenian

The old Armenian neighborhood, located between 22nd and 40th Streets east of Lexington Avenue and dominated by the gilded cupola of St. Vartan's Cathedral, is slowly being colonized by Indians! Word has it that this little spot, in business since 1912 and run by the Berberian family, is the best of its genre. This is true. The hot yogurt soup is delicious, the Armenian shish-kebab served with well-prepared rice is excellent, as are the mantar kebab (lamb with mushrooms, green peppers, onions) and yaprak sarma (vine leaves stuffed with meat and rice). And, to wind things up, a few sturdy desserts to send your blood-sugar level soaring, and a very reasonable check. Very pleasant, clean decor, and an extremely friendly welcome.

**11/20**

## Caliban

**360 Third Ave.
(26th-27th Sts.)
689-5155**

*Dinner nightly until 11:30 P.M.; closed Mon.*
*All major credit cards*
American (nouvelle)

A paradox: a remarkable wine list alongside an unremarkable cuisine. The great houses of Bordeaux, the most important areas of Burgundy, and many outstanding California vineyards are represented. Wine prices are not exorbitant given the quality of the offerings. There are adequate choices in the $9–$14 range, and superior choices from $18 to $25, from such West Coast vineyards as Phelps, Mayacamas, Heitz, Freemark Abbey, and Clos du Val. The Clos du Val 1972 at $24 is particularly satisfying, and will add lustre to your meal. If you discover a hundred-dollar bill in your wallet, you can add yet more lustre with two bottles of a Margaux in the $50–$60 range or a bottle of the Lynch-Bages 1966, at $108.

Unlike the lengthy wine list, the menu is short. Appetizers are perhaps more exciting than entrees. Oysters are fresh and invariably excellent. Try the poached oysters, served in their shells with a tasty beurre blanc, or the raw oysters with a mignonette dressing. Double lamb chops, steak, or duck with a port sauce are good bets as entrees. The swordfish, by contrast, is sometimes overcooked and tasteless. The Cornish game hen, apparently precooked, remains pale and not as hot as it should be. Decor is simple enough: up front are a huge saloon bar and a handful of tables; in the back is a dining room seating thirty with bare brick walls, high ceiling, and cathedral windows giving out on a courtyard.

The young kitchen staff, influenced by New York nouvelle, seems dedicated to matching the excellence of the cellar. For about $35 per person, you can find out what progress they have made.

## 12/20
## La Colombe
## d'Or
**134 E. 26th St.**
**689-0666**
*Dinner nightly until 10:30 P.M.;*
*lunch Mon. to Fri.*
*All major credit cards*
French (provincial)

Items on menus at most informal French restaurants around town have become so standard that the diner doesn't need a menu at all. He can confidently order a chef's pâté, onion soup, coq au vin, beef Wellington, or chocolate mousse, and he'll be served without question. So it's a welcome change to find an unpretentious French restaurant with a menu that goes considerably beyond the old standbys. Emphasis at La Colombe d'Or is on the cuisine of Provence, where fragrant herbs, garlic, and tomatoes are dominant. Among the hors d'oeuvres are the traditional pissaladière, a Provençal pizza with onions, black olives, and anchovies, as well as sautéed scallops in a light tomato dressing and crêpes with eggplant, spinach, and ricotta cheese in a more lusty tomato sauce. The bouillabaisse of Marseilles ($19.50 or $22.50 with lobster) is featured, and it is better than most offered in comparable restaurants this side of the Atlantic. There are several varieties of fish (properly poached) and shellfish in a rich, Pernod-scented broth. The traditional toasted garlic bread and rouille (garlic mayonnaise) is served on the side. How to manage all of this is quite a trick, since the seafood is served on an eight-inch, black cast-iron frying pan. Another hefty dish is the cassoulet of white beans, sausage, pork, and confit of duck. It is a passable version of the real thing from Toulouse or Carcassonne.

La Colombe d'Or is named for the stylish small inn and restaurant with sunny terrace outside the walls of Saint Paul de Vence, in the hills just inland from the Mediterranean between Nice and Cannes. The interior of the New York restaurant hardly captures the ambience of its namesake, but still the surroundings provide a pleasant setting for an enjoyable meal. Walls are red brick and white stucco, flowers in miniature casks grace the plain, wood-topped tables, and a billowing canvas overhead adds to the feeling of freshness. With a bit more consistency in the kitchen (the pastry in the pizza, bass en croute, and fruit tarts could be more delicate), this could be one of the best of the New York's smaller French restaurants. As it is, you'll have a better-than-average meal for $30 to $35. And you'll be offered tapenade, the Provençal purée of black olives, anchovies, garlic, and olive oil, instead of butter, to spread on crusty French bread, at no extra charge.

## 6/20
## La Coupole
**2 Park Ave.**
**(entrance on**
**32nd St.)**
**696-0100**
*Lunch and dinner daily until*
*2:00 A.M.*
*All major credit cards*
French (provincial)

Jean Denoyer—the French fashion designer who is the successful proprietor of the trendy uptown bistro, La Goulue—understands how to fill up an eating establishment with diners more interested in who is at the next table than what is served at their own. In this second venture (now with Jean Manuel Rozan as his partner), Mr. Denoyer has recreated in New York a replica of the huge Left Bank brasserie of the same name. The place has been packed since it opened in January 1982. As you enter from 32nd Street, you can take in the expanse of the enormous premises (partitions are waist-high) and see, some sixty-five feet away at the other end of the room, the "Bar Américain." Waiters, in dark vests and jackets and white aprons, scurry about taking care not to slip on the floor of brightly colored, broken mosaic tile.

The menu offers the standard French bistro fare of New York. But serving 210 people at a sitting (and most days several hundred more) is not very easy, and you can expect to wait. Do you care? You can wave to friends fifty feet or more away, and take in the show around you. The potage St. Germain is apt to arrive cold anyway, and it may not be much improved after a trip back to the kitchen, almost half a city block away. The pot au feu, which should be served in its broth in a soup dish like a New England boiled dinner, arrives instead on a flat plate without the broth. When specially requested, it can be served as a side dish, but the broth has no flavor or character at all. The baby whole salmon has been too long out of the water. The cassoulet contains tasty white beans, but the duck (scarcely a bite) is stringy and the sausage is totally undistinguished. The coq au vin, by contrast, appears in a lusty red wine sauce and is to be recommended.

The bombe praliné and a chocolate mousse tart are excellent, and the wine list is among the best in town. Two of the best values are a Château Simard (St. Emilion '74) at $15 and a dry and fruity Macon-Lugny at $11.

Is it impossible to serve good food to so many people? Ten blocks north of La Coupole it is being done five days a week at the Oyster Bar in Grand Central Terminal.

## 9/20
# Francesca's
**129 E. 28th St.**
**685-0256**
*Lunch and dinner daily until 11:00 P.M.; closed Sun. AE, V, MC*
Italian

A seasoned restaurant critic will always rely on his intuition. And when we visited Francesca's for the first time our infallible sixth sense immediately started humming: "This place is good!" Consider the odors wafting in from the kitchen, as you pass through to reach one of the six tables crowded together in a small room decorated with homey simplicity, and the alluring menu with its promise of fresh herbs and country flavors, not to mention the hot, crusty bread, that melts in your mouth. Our taste buds quivered in expectation of the dishes, each individually cooked to order, as we had heard it through the grapevine that Francesca's is the most personal and best intentioned of all the new Italian restaurants. The moment of truth was rather disappointing, everything being merely half good or three-quarters bad. The stuffed zucchini would have been perfect had the sauce been added, but without it they were dreadfully dry; the contents of the steamed fresh vegetable platter were undercooked, bland, and hard as marbles; the "veal rollatine," with mozzarella, sautéed onions, and mushrooms, was about as tender as a wooden leg; and the lemon chicken stuffed with a wad of herbed brown rice as impenetrable as a bullet-proof vest. "Where's

Francesca?" we asked the waiter. "At home," he replied, uncoaxed. Francesca no longer fusses with the cooking, we were told, leaving this task to a small team of young people who fend as best they can with her recipes. Alas! Francesca has turned cook by proxy.

## 10/20
## Hubert's
**102 E. 22nd St.**
**673-3711**
*Lunch and dinner*
*until 11:30 P.M.; closed Sun.*
American (nouvelle)

While in Brooklyn, Karen Hubert and Lenny Allison succeeded in converting the better part of New York to their brand of new American cooking. In September 1981 they moved to a lovely old-fashioned bistro-style setting in Manhattan, and this dedicated young couple have won unanimous praise for their light, inventive dishes, using the best made-in-America ingredients in their painstaking recreations of Grandma's recipes. Our previous meals of hot delicate oysters and shrimp in a cream sauce with coriander; sautéed duck's liver en croustade; a perfect Muscovy duck; a magret served very rare and accompanied by a beet mousse, spätzele, and brandied sickle pears; a miraculous sautéed lobster served on a bed of green and white pasta with basil; and the white chocolate mousse with dark chocolate sauce were sensational.

However, Karen no longer cooks, but now manages the front of the house, and the quality of food at Hubert's has changed drastically. Our last meal was a disappointment in every case except for the seasonal fiddlehead ferns that were superb. We are saddened that this charming place has lost its original chef, and we can only hope that her talent and direction will upgrade the quality of the food to the two-toque level we had once awarded it.

## 10/20
## Joanna
**18 E. 18th St.**
**(between Fifth Ave.**
**and Broadway)**
**675-7900**
*Daily until 2:00 A.M.*
*AE.*
Continental

It's a pity you don't get to see more of the delectable young Texan whose name adorns this brasserie, which was opened by her dashing husband, Sheldon Haseltine (former owner of the Hoexter), on the ground floor of an abandoned warehouse. A bearded, Edwardian sort of man who, if he's not quite British can certainly pass, he greets you with great friendliness at the entrance to the large green-walled dining room, which, we were told, was an attempt to recreate the atmosphere of La Coupole in Paris. A doubtful kinship, somewhat redolent of pastiche. Rather than the imitation leather seat-covers, the round lamps or the slick poisonous-looking flowers, you will probably admire the authenticity of the toilets that are flushed by pulling a chain—a supreme luxury in New York.

Customers can drink the white house wine from jam-jar styled glassware. The somewhat fussy bistro fare is grandly topped by caviar-stuffed potatoes, but the everyday fare of gravlax isn't bad. Also, there are mediocre hamburgers, sauerkraut that would be good if the meats garnishing it didn't taste of dust, and a delicious chocolate cake. The menu includes some interesting information: the half-chicken with lime is served (we translate): "at the temperature of the room."

**11/20**
## Louisiana
**132 Lexington Ave.**
**686-3959**
*Dinner nightly until midnight;*
*closed Sun.*
*No credit cards*
American

Hidden away in the Indian district, this small restaurant defends the honor of Southern cooking (basically Louisiana-style here), which on the whole is badly represented in New York. The defense is skillful: we enjoyed a very pleasant meal here for about $25 per person, consisting of Louisiana blood sausage, chicken Jolie Blande garnished with sauteéd vegetables, fillet of pork with onions, and (the weak spot of the establishment) a mediocre dessert. Unless your teeth are made of steel, avoid the steak de coquillages—various giant shellfish that seem to have come off a Goodyear assembly-line.

**7/20**
## Mary Elisabeth
**6 E. 37th St.**
**683-3018**
*Lunch daily until 3:00 P.M.;*
*dinner Thurs. only until 8:00 P.M.;*
*closed Sun.*
*AE, DC, MC*
International

This is a big, old-fashioned tea room in the heart of Manhattan, a minute from the Empire State Building. With its brownish walls and grey formica tables, it would appear gloomy but for the elderly women chattering gaily in eccentric hats, the pretty models nibbling on salads, the businessmen buried in the *Wall Street Journal* and earnestly swallowing fish croquettes, a mixture that gives Mary Elisabeth its inimitable atmosphere. Pure New York. Mary herself, a debonaire granny, is on hand to welcome you, and attentive waiters take your orders with a good humor that will surprise anyone used to being stranded in long lunchtime waiting lines.
There's just one drawback. The food. Ingesting an avocado salad with fresh fruit, drowned in an indescribable honey dressing, overcooked (that's a euphemism) calf's liver served with a sugary potato and boiled green beans, and a tasteless nut cake, wasn't our idea of fun. But there are still the "old-fashioned" sandwiches and doughnuts, which the delightful Mary lets you take out. A cafeteria adjoining the restaurant looks after these orders. About $13–$18 with a cold Budweiser.

**12/20**
## Mr. Lee's
**337 Third Ave.**
**(25th St.)**
**689-6373**
*Lunch and dinner daily*
*until 11:00 P.M.; dinner only Sat.;*
*closed Sun.*
*All major credit cards*
International

If you are tired of keeping to the rules—French, Italian, Chinese, Japanese, or whatever—and want to try something different, Mr. Lee's may be your answer. But before you call for a reservation, make sure that you have the $125 that it will cost the two of you to find out whether Mr. Lee's blend of East and West is for you.
Gim Lee, born in China, educated in France (where he became a friend of Paul Bocuse) lists himself on his business card as proprietaire; his wife, the chef, is a

native of Hawaii. They have transla (
fiendish skill) their cultures and e
food and decor of their tiny resta
cuisines of East and West is not/
appetizers, which are French and .
garlic butter, terrine, spinach crêpe, or a ͜
with mussels. More exotic is a Polynesian bro͜.
pungent flavors of the Orient. Some of the entrees a.
also generally associated with the West: chicken Kiev,
lobster cardinal, and even a bouillabaise. But the
blending of cultures is more apparent in various other
entrees: lemon chicken, poached striped bass with
banana, roast squab with a teriyaki-scented sauce, or the
boneless breast of duck, skin crisp, with a slightly sweet-
and-sour kumquat sauce. If you with to exercise your
taste buds further, try "veal Venetian," sliver of veal in a
cheese-flavored dressing. Desserts are more Western than
Eastern, and not outstanding.

A further word about prices. Everything is a la carte:
appetizer, soup, salad, entree, vegetable, dessert, and
coffee. And an 18 percent gratuity is added to the bill. At
these prices you have a right to expect extremely
attentive service. Mr. Lee, in his ruffled formal shirt and
colorful Mondrian print bow tie, is regularly on hand to
see that you get it.

How does this perplexing meeting of East and West
come off? If not brilliantly, at least satisfactorily. In fact
you will probably enjoy yourself—until you are
presented with the bill.

## 13
## Mon Paris
**111 E. 29th St.**
**683-4255**
*Lunch and dinner Mon. to Fri.*
*until 10:00 P.M.; Sat. dinner only;*
*closed Sun.*
*AE, V, MC*
French (provincial)

This is a long-time favorite of New Yorkers who cherish
French cooking with no frills. Here there are no
concessions to nouvelle, no pretensions. Robert Stephan,
the proprietor, watches over the dining room from
behind the small bar at the door, as he has for nineteen
years. Perhaps his attention to detail is what makes the
difference, because standards in service and food are a
cut above the usual found in all but the most expensive
Midtown establishments. Try the veal kidneys in a
mustard sauce, the calf's brains with capers, or the
roast squab.

The pastries are delivered daily from Délices la Côte
Basque, and they are first-rate. There is a better than
adequate wine list. With the house-recommended petit
Bordeaux ($9), two can manage a satisfying meal for $50
to $60. You will eat as well as you would at an auberge in
the French countryside, and you will have saved yourself
the Apex fare.

## 10/20
## Once Upon
## a Stove
**325 Third Ave.**
**(24th-25th Sts.)**

Into the wee hours people from all walks of life—angst-
ridden intellectuals, upright middle-class citizens,
families on a binge—visit this labyrinth of tiny, old-
fashioned rooms where a second-hand furniture dealer

**44**
*nd dinner daily until
.M.; Sat. and Sun. brunch
ajor credit cards*
ontinental

used to store his treasures. The food is perfectly banal, but copious and cheap, and the atmosphere intimate and good-natured.

The suppertime shows in Valentine Room every Friday and Saturday night (8:45 to 11:45 P.M.) shouldn't be missed. The young actors and singers who also serve as waiters put on extraordinarily funny and irreverent acts between courses, and are reminiscent of French "café–théatre" at its best. One of the most entertaining evenings New York has to offer, at very reasonable prices.

**7/20**
## Tom's Shangri-la
**237 Madison Ave. (37th St.)**
**683-0996**
*Lunch and dinner daily until midnight*
*AE, DC, CB*
Chinese

The entrance to the Shangri-la, one of New York's oldest Chinese restaurants, is through a Western-style bar plunged in stygian gloom—a kind of Sino-American speakeasy with Chinese muzak—where the businessmen hunched over their martinis seem happier than the wilting, sun-starved array of exotic plants. The brightest spotlight is that directed onto the cash register.

Beyond the bar lies a cavernous earth-colored dining-room, lit by tulip-shaped lamps hardly bright enough to read your fortune cookie by. The tables, set Western-style with cruets, potato crisps, and packets of Sweet'n'Low (for your jasmine tea?) give ample warning that real Chinese cuisine is not the name of the game. So does the menu, where every other entree is simply described as "with brown sauce." We toyed with some dried-up appetizers, heavily battered and breaded, but served on a rather cute tray with an illuminated Spanish onion in the center. This was followed by an equally dehydrated and deep-fried sea bass, and both were accompanied by what looked—and tasted—like warm, pink, melted Jell-O. The twice-cooked chicken with coarsely cut lumps of green pepper and some ammonia-tasting prawns completed a meal that made one long for an honest hamburger.

Between $10 and $15, including rice and tea. Less if you choose the American menu, which includes bread and butter, vegetable, and coffee.

**12/20**
## Z
**117 E. 15th St.**
**254-0960**
*Lunch and dinner daily until 11:00 P.M.; closed Mon.*
*AE*
Greek

Three rooms in a row, an indoor garden, and sober folk decorations are the setting for a large Greek taverna two minutes away from Union Square, which would differ little from any number of other Greek restaurants if the cuisine weren't so authentic. You'll greatly enjoy the mezadakia (liver, sweetbread, and meatballs) served hot, the tarama, the special eggplant dish, Greek cheese, and the lamb "Yuvetsi" with pasta. Although the shish-kebab is slightly dry, and the flogliera (an orange pastry) without much taste, the baklava is honest and, above all, the wine list has a wide and interesting range of Greek wines. We discovered a light, fruity wine from the Peloponnese, Achaia, which is light on your wallet as well. On the whole, prices at Z (homage to Costa

Gavras' famous film) remain splendidly moderate: $16 per person. Which makes up for the overly relaxed service.

# East 42nd to 59th Streets

**9/20**
## Akbar
**475 Park Ave.
(57th-58th Sts.)
838-1717**
*Lunch and dinner daily until
10:30 P.M; closed Sun. afternoon
All major credit cards*
Indian

Just read the menu, and you imagine yourself miraculously transported to a large restaurant in Bombay or Delhi. It's all listed: the samosas and pakoras, tandoori-cooked meat and fish, vegetarian dishes, various sorts of chicken (kashmiri, patiala) and lamb (a total of five) plus all sorts of bread and pancakes (with vegetables, meat, or fruit, both hot and cold, crunchy and soft). Everything's there. The only thing missing is a bit of sparkle. This pretty little restaurant with its discreetly Mongol decor has indeed fallen prey to the most ruinous international flavors. All the subtlety of the original spices is gone! Every morsel of vegetable or meat is drowned in a tide of creamy sauce: neither taste nor nuance remains. Even the hottest dishes (there are a few) are strangely heavy and bland. On its journey across the Atlantic, the normally light Indian cuisine lost all its character and sense of harmony. Or it may simply be that the opulence of Park Avenue is ill-suited to Third World cooking.

**12/20**
## Ambassador Grill
**United Nations
Plaza Hotel: 44th St.
and First Ave.
355-3400**
*Lunch and dinner daily until
10:00 P.M.; Sun. brunch; jacket
and tie required.
All major credit cards*
International

A floor of white and green marble, dark walls, large linen-draped tables at which sit beautiful women and the powers that be in diplomacy and politics, all reflected to infinity in mirrors—no wonder that lunch at the Ambassador Grill is one of the obligatory stopovers in New York's fashionable life. If there are no ineffable gastronomic pleasures to be had here, it offers at least (provided you avoid the woolly shrimp cocktail) civilized foods (poached salmon with sauce verte, smoked chicken in vinaigrette, lamb chops) which allow one to leave the table clear-headed, ready to face the problems of the world.

**8/20**
## Beijing Duckhouse
**144 E. 52nd St.**

The Beijing—Chinese newspeak for Peking—is the uptown version of James Wu's Chinatown Peking Duckhouse. It has minimal decor, with the usual

**759-8260**
*Lunch and dinner daily until 11:00 P.M.; weekends until midnight*
*V, MC, AE*
Chinese

mandatory scrolls of flowers and mountain peaks, waiters in dinner jackets, and a largely Western clientele who come mainly for the famous lacquered duck.

In China of course, the Peking Duck ritual starts with the Duck Blower, a gentleman not too popular on dates, whose main occupation in life is to blow up the duck's orifice, thus loosening the skin and making it more crispy. It can also be done more hygenically with a bicycle pump, but we preferred not to ask which method was in use at the Beijing. Afterwards the bird is scalded and hung up for twenty-four hours, before being anointed with honey and roasted in a hot oven. In most restaurants you'd have to order this a day in advance, but here you can have it in a mere twenty minutes.

Our friend, who speaks excellent Chinese, rather rashly asked the waiter a few questions—how was the duck prepared, was it good, and so on. "If you like it it's good. If you don't it's bad," came the rather Confucian answer. By this time other people's ducks were flying out of the kitchen on silver platters, neck, beak, and all, some reclining languidly, head on breast, like Victorian ladies in a swoon, others peering anxiously over the rim. A bit unnerving this, especially as their webbed feet, garnished with celery, had already preceded them as a cold appetizer.

Our bird arrived, and the waiter with a sharp cleaver proceeded to hack it into huge slices, skin and all—no nonsense about wafer-thin slivers or the skin served separately, as in most good Peking restaurants. The scallions and cucumber too were crudely cut into large chunks instead of being julienned, so although the pancakes in their bamboo container were nicely thin and hot, the final package was unwieldy—quite impossible to eat with decorum. Even worse, the first bite unleashed a faintly unpleasant aroma of hot oil. Our stony-faced waiter, under some pressure from the China expert, finally admitted that the duck was not roasted but deep-fried— which probably explains the conveyor-belt speed of the whole operation.

As regards the other dishes, one was excellent, an appetizer of transparent noodles tossed in a mustardy dressing with shrimp, pork, and cucumber. Apart from that, the deep-fried sea bass with sweet–sour sauce— presumably dumped in the same vat as the duck—was overcooked and oversauced, and one was hard put to judge the quality of the fish under all that dark batter and hot fruit salad. The eggplant with garlic suffered from an overdose of cornstarch and, although pleasantly spicy, looked like a dog's dinner. Everything we tried, in fact, suffered from lack of finesse and bad presentation—a coarse cuisine without any delicacy.

Most indelicate of all was the manner of our eviction. At a mere 10:30 P.M. the fortune cookies and the bill arrived on our table simultaneously, with a most uncompromising thud. No desserts were offered, no tea or coffee suggested. Looking nervously around we discovered ourselves in a totally deserted restaurant—apart, that is, from the staff happily tucking into large bowls of noodles.

The whole duck—enough for six—will cost you $25. Otherwise an average meal would be about $26 a head with wine.

## 11/20
# Benihana
**120 E. 55th St.**
**593-1627**
*Daily until 11:00 P.M.;*
*weekends until midnight and*
*Sun. until 10:00 P.M.*
*All major credit cards*
Japanese

Benihana was something of a pioneer when he opened what he called a Japanese steak house in New York fourteen years ago. His formula was sound: quick, good food at decent prices plus a little entertainment thrown in. It works just as well today. The chef still expertly slices, seasons, and sautées the shrimp, chicken, or steak on the grill before you. Can you beat the hibachi steak lunch for $6.95? You are served Western-style iceberg lettuce salad (not inspiring), a shrimp appetizer, neatly sliced good-quality beef (more than you'll want if you're going back to the office), with mushrooms, onions, squash, and a bowl of rice, plus a serving of bean sprouts before ice cream or lemon sherbet that are better than you'd expect.

At dinner ("to suit the heartier appetite"), a complete meal with a double portion of steak is $16; the steak and lobster tail is $17.50. Tea is served with the meals. There are wines and Japanese beer and sake.

The Benihana formula works in forty establishments around the world. Watch out, McDonalds! For fun, food, and frolic Benihana beats you hands down.

## 12/20
# Le Bistro
**827 Third Ave.**
**(near 50th St.)**
**759-8439**
*Lunch and dinner; Mon. to Fri.*
*until 10:00 P.M.; Sat. dinner only;*
*closed Sun.*
*All major credit cards*
French (provincial)

Unlike most of the restaurants around the country that go by the same name, Le Bistro is an honest French bistro with turn-of-the-century decor and down-to-earth food. You enter through a tiny vestibule, turning immediately to avoid the side of a zinc-topped bar. A tubular brass rail rims the red-backed banquettes across from the bar and in the dining room to the rear. Glass partitions, etched with hanging bunches of grapes, separate the rooms. A single long-stemmed rose graces each table. Appetizer and entree items that you would expect to find on a bistro menu here are carefully prepared and ingredients are of good quality. The country terrine is tasty, the leeks in a spicy vinaigrette a nice change from the usual celery remoulade. But the garlic sausage, with potatoes in oil, lacks zest, and is one of a handful of disappointments. Calf's brains are tender (no crust of flour to spoil the texture); the accompanying vegetable and potato retain their natural flavors. Scallops are well seasoned in herbs, and the omelets are cooked so they are soft inside, French-style, unless you order them firm.

In the evening there are several items from southwestern France that are not standard in New York: a lusty cassoulet, a confit d'oie (goose aged in its own fat in a crock), and an interesting braised duck. The wine list is sound, and sensibly priced for the most part. The house wine at $10.50 is good quality and good value. If you are eager for a more substantial bottle at a reasonable price, try the Chateau Lynch Bages (1976) at $30, or an excellent Puligny Montrachet at $35.

This is a professional establishment. The owner, Georges, is on top of every detail in the dining room, and he copes with the noonday crowds in a manner that leaves one feeling good, even should you have to wait for your reserved table. In any event, he seems to be able to greet almost everyone by name. A three-course lunch with wine will run $20 to $25, and at dinner $5 to $10 more.

Le Bistro has been around since 1938, under one management or another. It was one of these managements that refused to sell the little building housing the restaurant to Third Avenue developers. Today, New Yorkers can be thankful for this Gallic haven in a landscape of glass and metal.

**11/20**
## Box Tree
**242 E. 50th St.**
**758-8320**
*Lunch and dinner daily until*
*9:30 P.M.; closed Sun.*
*Jacket and tie required*
*No credit cards*
French (classical)

One of the Kennedy clan's favorite hangouts, apparently. Not surprising. This doll's house goes in for luxury in the English style, meaning well-polished and sizable tables, Edwardian stained glass and Wedgwood porcelain. Actually, this is a French restaurant owned by a Bulgarian, featuring American and Hungarian chefs, and has a very likable maitre d' hôtel, a direct import from France. This eclecticism is reflected in the cooking—which leaves one perplexed. Depending on the dishes ordered, you might justifiably conclude that the cooking is rather good, or then again, that it's frankly bad. On the one hand a very pleasant salmon bisque with saffron, and a perfectly cooked calf's liver; and on the other, a puréed duck pâté, a haddock mousse into which the cook must have accidentally dropped his salt-cellar, a veal with morilles as dry as a bone, and a Madeira sauce reduced to nothingness. The desserts, fortunately, do not partake of this cruel ambivalence: the crème brulée and the vacherin, the house specialties, are both excellent. The coffee is particularly vile; but a rose accompanies the check, which will come to thirty-odd dollars for lunch, including a minor domestic wine. In the evening the prices are quite a lot higher, which was of no concern to us since we didn't go.

**11/20**
## La Brasserie
**100 E. 53rd St.**
**751-4840**
*Daily 24 hours; no reservations*
*All major credit cards*
French (provincial)

Since 1959, this big, noisy brasserie has worked 24 hours a day, seven days a week, to feed the crowds honest cooking: a good Alsatian choucroute garnie, admirable quiches, omelets with none of the telltale signs of reheating, excellent steak tartare and grilled steaks, a comforting onion soup. A likable spot for meals on the run.

## 12/20
## Café 58
**232 E. 58th St.**
**758-5665**
*Lunch and dinner daily*
*until midnight*
*All major credit cards*
French (provincial)

The decor is somewhat affected; not so the cooking. Marguerite Bruno, born and raised in France, has a passion for variety in meats, and cooks them perfectly. It would be hard to find elsewhere in New York pig's feet, kidneys, tripe, or calf's head done so well. She also serves an honest choucroute garnie, bouillabaisse (on weekends) that is well spoken of, and a delicious crème au chocolat. Several good French wines, in particular the Burgundies, and a bill that comes to about $20—an excellent price-to-quality ratio.

## 10/20
## La Camelia
**225 E. 58th St.**
**751-5488**
*Lunch and dinner Mon. to Fri.*
*until 1:00 A.M.; Sat. dinner only;*
*closed Sun.*
*All major credit cards*
Italian

Handsome glass chandeliers and a skylight with hanging greenery dominate the dining room. It is obvious that the management has concentrated on creating a setting that appeals. The same cannot be said for its food. Tortellonis with spinach and cheese appear in a heavy, floury sauce, a fillet of sole (flounder?) is sautéed in a nondescript batter, and the veal, in a red wine sauce, is tougher than it should be. The fruit tarts are more dough than fruit; avoid them. Redeeming features include beautiful, buttery string beans al dente and a better-than-usual list of Italian wines in the $12 to $15 range.

At dinner, there is a medaillon of veal with white truffles. Given the price of these truffles on the retail market, this is good value—and stands out as a good dish to order. It will cost you $35 or more per person to enjoy the surroundings and the music from the piano bar up front. At that price, though, you deserve a good meal, as well.

## 14 ♡
## The Captain's Table
**860 Second Ave. (46th St.)**
**697-9538**
*Lunch and dinner daily until*
*11:00 P.M.; Sat. until midnight;*
*closed Sun.*
*AE, V, MC*
Seafood

Sole from the English Channel and rouget (like red snapper) and loup (bass) from the Mediterranean are flown in regularly to supply this small Midtown fish restaurant and its parent establishment in the Village at 410 Avenue of the Americas (between 8th and 9th Streets). The fish taste remarkably fresh, fresher than what is routinely offered from waters this side of the Atlantic at the more ostentatious fish houses. The owners are Gino Musso, from the Piedmont region of Italy, and his wife, Sabine, from Lyon. They have combined to give New York an outstanding restaurant, where diners can order fish cooked the way it is cooked along the Mediterranean coast or the New England coast. Either way, it is excellent.

As is the custom at many restaurants along the Mediterranean, the maitre d' hôtel shows the fish on a basketlike tray, so the diner can see what is available. Whole fish are a specialty, simply grilled with fennel and herbs, or briefly poached with a light cream sauce. Appetizers reflecting the owners' European background include mussels marinière, scungilli or calamari salad, and a seafood coquille. But if you want the real flavor of New England, try the clam chowder. It puts most versions around town to shame.

Fish that fly the Atlantic don't come cheaply. You pay (a la carte) $22.50 for loup with a mousse stuffing, or $20 for a grilled rouget. Counterparts from waters closer to home are four to five dollars cheaper. The nonfish eater can choose veal piccata ($12.95) or steaks up to $16.95.

There are dry white wines from California, Italy, France, and a couple of German whites and a handful of reds, mostly from Italy and France. Most are reasonably priced: the Orvieto Secco, for example, is only $9.50. But your meal is apt to be relatively expensive, even with a reasonable bottle of wine, $35 to $40 per person.

## 13 ♧
## La Cascade
**645 Fifth Ave.**
**(entrance between**
**Madison and Fifth**
**Ave. from either 51st**
**or 52nd St.)**
**935-2220**
*Mon. to Fri., Noon to 3:00 P.M.,*
*6:00 P.M. to 10:30 P.M.*
French (nouvelle)

You are one floor below the street-level lobby–atrium of the Olympic Tower in a small, formal dining room with beige banquettes and handsome flower arrangements, looking through windows onto a remarkable indoor scene: water dropping fifty feet down a flat wall into a receiving pool right beside your table. The rippling, splashing flood is caught by giant mirrors on each side.

Guy Pascal, proprietor here and of several Délices la Côte Basque pastry shops around town (one is upstairs in the lobby–atrium), makes it possible to admire this setting and to enjoy an exceptional meal at the same time.

The menu is classic French with some nouvelle overtones. The artistry in the kitchen is evident from the start. Excellent appetizers include an interesting salad of duck, lobster, and watercress; scallops in a butter sauce and puff pastry, and the traditional Burgundian fish dumplings in a lobster sauce, known as "La Quenelle de Brochet Nantua." Among the entrees, the medaillons of veal are extraordinary, the lobster (out of the shell) is succulent, and the whole baby salmon in a red wine sauce is exquisitely poached and seasoned. Desserts are less exciting, but there are the faultless pastries of Délices la Côte Basque, including an unforgettable chocolate, mocha, and almond cake.

The wine list is short and not as exceptional (nor relatively as expensive) as the food. You can have perfectly good bottles from $12 to $20, or a Château Duhart-Milon Rothschild (1976), if you want to match the quality of what you are eating and are willing to pay $38. You will pay close to $100 for two for this experience, but then you can spend more and get less at quite a good many places around town. The waterwall can also be enjoyed in the lobby–atrium at Le Café, where sandwiches, quiches, pastries and drinks can be had at more moderate prices.

## 14 ♧
## Le Chantilly
**106 E. 57th St.**
**751-2931**
*Lunch and dinner daily until*
*10:00 P.M.; closed Sun.;*

Not as famous as La Grenouille or La Caravelle, this classic restaurant attracts more or less the same clientele. It's a comfortable place, rather than luxurious, and everything, including the welcome, the service (supervised by Paul Dessibourg), and the cooking (under chef Roland

*reservations necessary*
French (classical)

Chenus) indicates that the staff is composed of professionals who are scrupulous and attentive to detail. Don't expect any inspirations from this soberly classical cuisine—certain dishes are even rather disappointing, such as the bland salmon in an average pastry crust, or the tender but not overly tasty quail (obviously commercially raised game) accompanied by wild rice that is much too salty. Nevertheless, the general level of cooking is very satisfactory: a delicate terrine of sweetbreads and watercress; a good mousse of two different fish; a delicious combination of saddle and rack of lamb; one of the best calf's liver with green grapes, very tasty and tender, we've had in a long time; and an excellent strawberry soufflé convinced us of that. The wine list, quite limited, is badly thought out, and leaves out too much necessary information. $30–$60.

## 13 ☕
## Le Cherche Midi
**936 First Ave.
(51st-52nd Sts.)
355-4499**
*Lunch and dinner Mon. to Fri. until 11:00 P.M.; Sat. dinner only; closed Sun.
MC, V*
French (provincial)

Last fall Sally Scoville, an attractive New Yorker, brought a little piece of France to New York. What with the white stucco walls, the pink terracotta floors, you sense that somewhere outside blazes the Provençal sun. The restaurant consists of two narrow dining areas and a minuscule garden in the back. The tables are on top of each other. No matter, this is a convivial setting, and you will find it easy to exchange pleasantries with diners at adjacent tables.

Ms. Scoville worked in kitchens in Provence, operated her own restaurant in Cambridge, Massachusetts, and participated in a catering venture on New York's West Side. Now she has brought the time-honored bourgeois cooking she learned in the South of France to a kitchen of her own. Her sauces are light. Appetizers include an excellent soup of the day, a pâté, and some salads. But Sally is at her best in the entrees. Try the roast chicken, with its sauce well laced with cognac and garlic; the ragoût of seafood (the mussels are in their shells) with the perfume of Pernod in the sauce; or the lamb, with its interesting game marinade. The bread on the table, imported from a brick-oven bakery west of the Hudson, suggests the crust and tartness of a San Francisco sourdough.

Desserts include Sally's own dacquoise (too dry on one occasion), an acceptable fruit tart, and a tasty crème brulée. The espresso is as strong and lusty as the main dishes. Wines are modestly priced, a good Côtes du Rhône recommended as the house wine, $11. Top priced is a Puligny Montrachet at $22.

Sally has settled somewhere between bourgeois and nouvelle. She is comfortable there. Judging by the immediate success that she has experienced, so are a great many New Yorkers. You'll need a reservation and $60 or more for two to find out what the raves are all about.

## 12/20
# Christ Cella
**160 E. 46th St.**
**697-2479**
*Lunch and dinner Mon. to Fri.*
*until 10:30 P.M.; dinner only Sat.;*
*closed Sun.*
*All major credit cards*
Steaks

Oblivious to changing mores, Christ Cella basically remains a man's steakhouse. Women are not made unwelcome, of course, and there will always be a few around, but this is a stomping ground for males; mostly males with big appetites and big wallets. The small dining rooms downstairs and the larger one upstairs resemble the barrooms that you might find at some suburban golf club: plain wood floors, plain walls with an unexciting print here and there, and waiters in white shirts and butcher aprons. At the rear, near the kitchen, there is an oval community table seating eight where men without a lunch date can take their noon meal in the company of others in a similar predicament.

Christ Cella, once among the best steak houses in the city, is still good if you stick to the staples: steaks, chopped steak, roast beef, double lamb chops (still tops), or plain steamed or broiled lobster. But then at the prices charged you should expect something above the usual. However, if you stray too far you can be disappointed. The grilled fish, usually bass or red snapper, is fresh but probably will be served overcooked. Hashed brown potatoes with a crust routinely accompany most dishes. They used to be cooked to order, but they are now prepared in quantity and they are apt to be better at the corner diner. Ask that they be cooked to order. On one occasion the superb spinach salad was so drowned in the dressing that the fresh leaves became soggy and hardly edible.

A simple lunch of salad, fish, a glass of wine, and coffee will cost you $32. A dinner with steak or chops could easily run to $40. But at Christ Cella there is no menu, blackboard or otherwise. And it seems like bad form to ask the waiter for the price of a dish after he has rattled off the day's offerings.

Are you man enough for Christ Cella? If the answer is yes, one or two shortcomings should not discourage you.

## 16 🍷
# La Côte Basque
**5 E. 55th St.**
**688-6525**
*Lunch and dinner daily*
*until 10:30 P.M.; closed Sun.*
*AE*
French
(classical/nouvelle)

The illustrious Henri Soulé, who during World War II launched French haute cuisine in New York, also founded this restaurant, which enjoyed considerable success for some thirty years. Perhaps this was as much for the colorful trompe l'oeil frescoes on the walls as for his form of cooking, which was all the rage on both sides of the Atlantic for such a long time. Soulé passed away, and La Côte Basque gradually sank into a mediocre stupor. But since it was simply copying itself, our New York colleagues believed that it still was an exceptional restaurant. Then suddenly two years ago, a chef named Mr. Rachou bought La Côte Basque, had the pretty colors of the frescoes brightened up to turn them into one of the most ravishing decors in town and spent a small fortune modernizing the kitchen, installing a wine cellar, and reorganizing the service. He also, and most importantly, modified the menu, rejuvenating and enriching it. He invented new dishes and new ways of presenting them. An international set was tempted back, while perplexed critics eyed it skeptically. Its success having been assured in the meantime, it's now finally beginning to be acknowledged in gastronomic coteries that Mr. Rachou is a masterful professional. It's true that the new Côte Basque still offers a cooking style that is, for our taste, a tinge pompous: too many sauces with truffles and foie gras, too many wine and cream sauces. But the ingredients are admirable (for example, the simple roast chicken), the vegetables exquisite, and several of the preparations (all are superbly presented) deserve our highest praise. Delicious pâtés and terrines, a salad of scallops, lobster ragoût with morilles, noisettes de veau with cucumber, duck aux deux sauces, three-color bombe. Our last meal, as simple as we could keep it, overjoyed us, with a salad of lightly chilled crab and lobster with sauce verte, a marvelous pinkish roast veal with chanterelles and a vegetable purée, and a fruit sherbet to finish. Now, quite understandably, this isn't dirt cheap, but the perfect service and the attentive suggestions of the chef will make you forget the coming horror of the check.

## 13 ♧
## Le Cygne
**53 E. 54th St.**
**759-5941**
*Lunch and dinner daily until 9:30 P.M., Sat. 11:30 P.M.; closed Sat. afternoon, Sun., and during August; jacket and tie required AE, CB, DC*
French (classical)

Neither lame duck nor strutting cock, this swan, revered by so many New Yorkers, is nothing but one of the many classic French restaurants that dot the French countryside. But it's fashionable, and everyone who's anyone in New York gathers in a new and terribly elegant room, decorated in a harmony of blues. Actually a cuisine that is unimaginative (pike quenelles, frogs legs Provençale, artichoke bottoms with Périgueux sauce, chicken in Champagne sauce, veal kidney Beaugé), it does perhaps deserve a single toque for its salmon soufflé (although the sauce isn't particularly delicate), coquilles St. Jacques with saffron, chicken casserole, lamb chops (slightly overcooked), and no compliments whatsoever for its ultra-dry veal farci, lifeless potatoes and insipid green beans, or too-heavy chocolate soufflé. Evenings, prix fixe at $38.75; lunch about $25 without wine.

## 14 ♧
## Felidia
**243 E. 58th St.**
**758-1479**
*Lunch and dinner Mon. to Fri. until 11:00 P.M.; Sat. for dinner; closed Sun.*
*All major credit cards*
Italian

This is one of the most intimate of the small, new restaurants serving what is being described as northern Italian. Actually, the emphasis here is on dishes of the Italian northeast—the area between Trieste and Venice. After a somewhat shaky start, the kitchen and staff now have their act well together, and a meal here can be an experience to be remembered—and not because the bill will run $40 or more per person.

The prosciutto and figs (marvelously fresh and sweet) are an interesting change from the conventional prosciutto and melon. The Venetian cold fish salad under a refreshing, light olive oil of good quality is another appetizer worth trying. A poached bass or red snapper, in a seasoned broth, with onions and a garnish of clams and mussels in their shells, is well executed and a veal chop stuffed with broccoli and imported fontina cheese is better than most of the competition around town. One complaint: the portions are too large. Ingredients of other dishes are fresh and of top quality. Even in preparation of the vegetable accompaniment—a purée of Swiss chard and bits of potato—there is ample evidence that the management cares. A word about the pastas. You can order the fresh pasta prepared on the premises as an entree for $10, or an imported dry pasta for $9. Pay the dollar. The gnocchi al pesto, among others, is outstanding. For dessert you find the berries in season selected for their freshness and ripeness. Ask for a zabaglione sauce, here prepared from whole eggs instead of yolks alone, a delightful addition to your serving of fruit. The wine list is short, but there are good bottles starting at $12. You won't regret the extra dollars if you order a zesty San Gimignano white for $18.

You could walk right by Felidia without seeing the small sign: only the handsome woodwork framing two mythological figures etched in the window. Inside, the main dining area is small and sometimes cramped. Ask for a table in the gallery a flight up under the skylights and greenery hanging against the stark, white stucco walls.

The proprietors are Felice and Lydia. One toque is hardly enough for the two of them; they are working strenuously for a second. They could have it before too long.

## 11/20
## La Fenice
**242 E. 58th St.**
**759-4660**
*Lunch and dinner daily until midnight*
*All major credit cards*
Italian

If the use of alcohol burners were a criterion of quality for New York's Italian restaurants, La Fenice would be without any doubt Manhattan's top spot. As in an old movie, the two maitres d'hôtel in this pleasant trattoria with rough white walls and red fake-leather seats stubbornly insist on warming each dish right before your eyes, while the waiters perform a complicated ballet, bustling about so much they seem to be rushing to catch a train.

As for the rest, La Fenice's cuisine (supposedly northern Italian) is not exactly thrilling: honest fettuccini, an "opiedolini romana" (otherwise known as cheese and ham brioche) which Caesar might have used on the Christians, vitello Fenice in far too much cream, "pollo valdostana" in an unidentifiable sauce, a fearsome zabaglione prepared right at your table (on the alcohol burner, need we add?) and garnished with strawberries that seem to have just been defrosted. Cheerful atmosphere, noisy, an elegant clientele that doesn't dive into what is served, but is quick to kiss the maîtres d'hôtel on both cheeks. About $25–$35.

**12/20**

## Fonda la Paloma
**256 E. 49th St.**
**421-5495**
*Lunch and dinner daily until*
*1:00 A.M.; Sun. until 10:30 P.M.;*
*reservation suggested*
*All major credit cards*
Mexican

Ladies galore at lunchtime fill the two small, extremely picturesque dining rooms where, in the evening, guitarists serenade the diners. Service is particularly attentive, and the cooking has an aura of authenticity that takes the place of delicacy. A good introduction is the dish that combines enchiladas, tacos, tostadas, tamales, and arroz con frijoles, in itself a pleasant meal for less than $8, which you can wash down with an excellent Mexican beer and finish off with an honest flan.

**17**

## Four Seasons
**99 E. 52nd St.**
**754-9494**
*Pool Room: Lunch and dinner*
*daily until 11:00 P.M.; no lunch*
*Sat.; closed Sun.; formal;*
*reservation necessary*
*Bar Room: Lunch and dinner daily*
*until midnight; closed Sun.*
*All major credit cards*
French
(classical/nouvelle)

Should we have eaten here four times, once each season, just to be sure? We were here three times recently, and to be honest, our last meal was not the best. It was a rather frustrating combination of some delicious dishes, and others that were disappointing, such as the ragoût of Bay scallops and tough, dry shrimp, in a tomato sauce almost indistinguishable from ordinary ketchup. Another mistake was the cannelloni, too thick and insufficiently cooked, but stuffed it's true, with an absolutely exquisite purée of fresh, exquisite American cèpes, and served with a quite fabulous sauce, also made of cèpes. On the other hand, the small baked potatoes, cut in half, then fried and stuffed with Swedish whitefish roe, striped bass baked in sea salt and black pepper, very crisp duck served with peaches, sherbets and apricot soufflé, are not subject to any criticism whatsoever, and in each are recognizable the sure hand and the finesse of Chef Renggli (a Swiss), who has succeeded in giving a modern touch to the Four Seasons cuisine without ever succumbing to the temptations of useless complication or invention for its own sake. After tasting dishes as refined and as well prepared as his sole sautéed with grapefruit and orange, artichoke soufflé, calf's liver with avocado, or the pheasant with cabbage, you will agree that his talent is indisputable. Yet one can't help noticing a certain unevenness in the cooking, perhaps attributable to the size of this always crowded restaurant (which would, of course, stand to gain from reducing the number of place settings).

Be that as it may, a meal in the Pool Room next to the large square pool, as fresh as a murmuring spring, is a veritable feast for the eyes, with the wonderful sight of the setting sun reflected in the glass-walled skyscrapers beyond the dining room's high windows and curtains of shimmering steel beads. The immense three-story dining room may disconcert those who think that a good restaurant has to look like a Louis XV salon. In our opinion, this already classic modern style, the dark woodwork, fine leather, and marble corridor, where an immense stage curtain by Picasso hangs in all its glory, all belong to New York's finest cultural heritage—and are absolutely unique. We can't say the same for the Bar Room where, at lunchtime, big names from the world of business and journalism jostle each other while eating mediocre smoked salmon and worthy grilled meats:

despite the lively and scintillating ultra-chic crowd, the setting's somber austerity has something funereal about it. We shouldn't forget to mention the wine cellar, run by Tom Margittai and Paul Kovi—one of the most perfect in New York, and especially interesting for its choice of California wines (superb Chardonnay Ventana 1979 and Jordan Cabernet Sauvignon 1976), its great French vintages, Champagnes, and German, Italian (Nardi Brunello di Montalcino 1973), Spanish, and Hungarian wines.

## 13 ⌂ Gaylord's

**50 E. 58th St.**
**759-1710**
*Lunch Mon. to Fri.; dinner daily until 11:15 P.M.*
*All major credit cards*
Indian

From the Maharani of Jaipur to Dustin Hoffman, from Jackie Onassis to Zubin Mehta, this Indian restaurant welcomes an uninterrupted stream of celebrities during their stopovers in New York. Proof positive that it's possible to be fashionable and at the same time uphold the best traditions. Of all Manhattan's Indian restaurants, Gaylord's is indeed one of the most authentic, and most concerned with quality. Unlike most elegant exotic restaurants, this one does not content itself with keeping up its decor. With its dark red tones, deliciously soft armchairs, walls of mirrors, Rajasthan dolls, and Mogul motifs, its setting is as warm as it is comfortable.

But that's only secondary. The main thing is the delicious and subtle cuisine. Whether you choose mild dishes, like the Delhi Badshahi Korna (chicken with almonds and coriander, invented for the great eighteenth-century Mogul) or spicier preparations like the sag meat (lamb cooked with fresh, highly spiced spinach) you'll discover, at particularly mild prices, the refinements and harmony of the best Delhi and Bombay cooking. For no more than $10 you can enjoy a small fixed meal offering some of the establishment's classics. But don't hesitate to plunge into the mysteries of the entrees, as it's here that you'll discover the great specialties of Indian culinary art, and at prices that are still very reasonable. And don't neglect the desserts, such as the marvelous pressed cheese floating in cream perfumed with pistachio and vanilla. Then finish off your meal with some very sweet spiced tea.

## 13 ⌂ Gloucester House

**37 E. 50th St.**
**755-7394**
*Lunch and dinner daily until 10:00 P.M.*
*All major credit cards*
Seafood

Neither our American colleagues nor the New York public at large seem to judge this surprising seafood restaurant at its real worth. It's perhaps too Southern for their taste, certainly over-priced, and probably under-sauced to meet the criteria of local gastronomes. We won't deny that certain dishes are blatant failures, such as the (frozen?) shrimp sautéed in garlic butter and with the taste of none-too-fresh whiting—and the swordfish, as dry and compact as tinned tuna. But even if you leave aside the ground floor and mezzanine's charming open beige-and-white setting with their large pumpkins and copper-branched chandeliers or the informative, considerate waiters, how can you fail to appreciate the incredible choice of oysters—Blue Points, Cape Cod, Long Island, Canada—the miraculous small clams, the thirty-odd types of fresh fish, grilled or fried, the fresh crabmeat (something of a rarity in the United States), and above all, the incomparable small Maine lobsters, steamed to perfection, which are as good as any to be found in France? An excellent Chardonnay, and a check that is steep indeed. Note that although there is no compunction about serving you on bare pinewood tables, you are expected to wear a tie. (You can borrow one, if necessary.)

13 🙞
## La Grenouille
**3 E. 52nd St.**
**752-1495**
*Lunch and dinner daily until 10:30 P.M.; closed Sun.; jacket and tie required*
*AE*
French (classical)

"I'll try, but I can't promise anything. It's going to be difficult." Heroically, the waiter departs, imbued with the gravity of his impossible mission. Five tense minutes pass, he returns, and, with a glance of complicity murmurs, "Don't worry, it's been taken care of. The chef was in a good mood." The object of all this intrigue? A simple sole meunière. . . . Yes, we almost caused a revolution in the famous kitchens of La Grenouille by asking for a sole meunière not listed on the menu. Fortunately, the chef was "marvelous." He said yes! Marvelous—the sole, somewhat less so. Overcooked, but in the face of such an exploit, how could we not be indulgent?

Opened in the '60s by Charles Masson, former maitre d'hôtel at Le Pavillon, La Grenouille immediately took its place as one of the best French restaurants in New York, perhaps even the entire United States. In a decor neither ostentatious nor terribly imaginative, but warm and friendly with its almond-green walls, mirrors, and small table lamps, the run-of-the-mill commonplaces of American French cuisine were served, with the difference that here they were prepared with extreme care and real talent. Following the death of her husband in 1975, Gisèle Masson courageously took over the reins, careful not to change a thing. Everything seems to justify her decision, since it's as difficult as ever to obtain a table at La Grenouille, where New York's highest society crowds in twice a day. The cuisine, too, continues to be the subject of flattering reviews, and the chef, André Joanlanne—now fifteen years at the stoves—has nothing to worry about. And, judging by the evidence, he doesn't worry either, continuing imperturbably to serve the same menu, the same Billi-Bi mussel soup, the same frogs legs Provençale, veal Orloff, and pike quenelles in Pernod-scented sauce. Such fidelity is touching, but dangerous, because in cooking as in all else, if you don't go forward, you go backward. In the long run, traditions become habits, and it's the bad habits that tend to gain the upper hand. True enough, you can still dine well at La Grenouille, but not as well as the prices lead you to believe. If you were served in another, less famous and prestigious, restaurant the same bisque (agreeable, but nonetheless not without starch, in which the bits of lobster are abnormally tough), the passable terrine of foie gras, good grain-fed herbed chicken garnished with excellent green beans and carrots, but accompanied by a far too spicy sauce, the excellent chocolate meringue cake, but very mediocre oeufs à la neige that were barely caramelized and served with a custard sauce that probably did not contain the standard eight eggs per quart of milk, or the thick cookies unworthy of any self-respecting pastry chef . . . to sum up, were you served these same no-more-than-honorable dishes anywhere else, you wouldn't waste too many words on them. But at La Grenouille, the prices force you to do so. Even if you avoid the dishes with supplementary charges, it will still cost about $40 for a dinner of soup, a main dish, and dessert—not to mention the wine, where the management doesn't go in for half-measures either. We don't really care that they ask $600 for a Latour 1959, or $575 for a Margaux 1961, because we're not crazy enough to order them. But $36 for a very ordinary Chablis is absolutely unjustifiable. At lunch, about $25 without wine.

## 14 ♤
## Hatsuhana
**17 E. 48th St.**
**355-3345**
*Lunch and dinner daily until 11:00 P.M.; no lunch Sat.; closed Sun.*
*All major credit cards*
Japanese

Here, whatever the weather, you will see lines of eager sushi and sashimi lovers overflowing onto the sidewalk, willing to wait up to thirty minutes and more to experience the taste sensations that await them inside. Hatsuhana is essentially a sushi bar, although there are a few tables. Up front, a tiny liquor bar serves the usual assortment of drinks, some of which find their way to the customers outside.

You seat yourself at the sushi bar. A kimono-clad waitress greets you with a smile and a hot towel, then takes your order. Sushi barmen of remarkable dexterity slice, pack, roll, and garnish a wondrous medley of tuna, eel, squid, sea urchin, smelt, clams, scallops, and shrimp. You are observing artists at work.

The "All Japan" lunch at $8 could be the most delectable in town at the price. The main dish consists of several raw fish, shrimp fried in a light batter, plus an assortment of carefully trimmed vegetables. There is soup, steamed rice, and Japanese tea to boot. The same lunch is available with broiled salmon teriyaki as the main dish. Shrimp tempura is $7.50. The raw fish is perfectly fresh, the vegetables crisp and well seasoned. And the sushi barmen before you deserve cards from Actors Equity.

## 13 ♤
## Hee Seung Fung (H. S. F.)
**578 Second Ave.**
**689-6969**
*Lunch and dinner daily until 11:00 P.M.*
*All major credit cards*
Chinese

Dim sum are those small dishes steam-cooked in bamboo baskets so incredibly popular in the south of China, and this is their temple. The bare dining room, scarcely illuminated by spotlights sunk into the ceiling, is perfectly sinister, but the multitude of small dishes that the waiter unveils (there is no menu at all) make you quickly forget its austerity. Fine, delicate cooking, prepared at lightning speed. A festival of subtle and unusual flavors that will cost barely more than $15 for some ten or so different dishes. There is also another establishment in Chinatown, at 46 Bowery (374-1319), renowned for Chinese Sunday brunches, from 11:00 A.M.

## 11/20
### Helmsley Palace
**455 Madison Ave.
(50th St.)
888-7000**
*Lunch and dinner daily until
11:00 P.M.
AE, DC, V*
French (classical)

Two dining rooms that make up the most pompous restaurant imaginable are quite in place in New York's most pretentious hotel. Keep out of the Trianon, which is about as warm and restful as a train station, and stick to the Lunch Room, whose dark wood paneling and luxurious armchairs summon up images of the hunt, Hollywood-style. A maitre d'hôtel who is a dead ringer for Danny Kaye, although much taller and without the sense of humor, greets you with utter. contempt, doubtless thinking to appear distinguished. And the food? It's a feeble imitation of real French; at its best, it's international in style. You can eat without too much displeasure if you stick to the simpler dishes: the chicken liver mousse en gelée, the smoked trout with horseradish, and some excellent Nova Scotia smoked salmon with cheese. That isn't the case for the seafood salad: the shrimp, scallops, and crab meat seem to have been incompletely thawed, or to have been taken out too late from the fridge, and are absolutely tasteless. Avoid the desserts (vanilla ice cream minus the taste of vanilla, and an absolutely appalling chocolate cake) and, above all, the execrable "espresso" with the unforgettable flavor of burned rubber. Lunch is about $28 with a carafe of white wine served at room temperature. Dinner is about $60, proceeding by trial and error through the hearts of palm in sherry vinegar, the turtle consommé, pheasant Trianon, and veal cutlet à la Holstein.

## 13.
### Hostaria del Bongustaio
**75 E. 55th St.
751-3530**
*Dinner nightly until 10:30 P.M.:
closed Sun.
MC, V, AE*
Italian

It's obviously impossible for us to predict what will become of this establishment. For the time being, this tiny restaurant with room for about sixty diners will titillate you with its fresh decor, immaculate white walls, floral-covered banquettes, well-balanced lighting, and friendly, very efficient waiters—and its cuisine that, although without true genius, is carefully prepared and authentic. The menu is too large to be judged in its entirety, but two visits allowed us to appreciate the tortellini in cream, the white and green pasta with mushrooms, the risotto alla rustica (a mixture of perfectly prepared rice, not sticky, mixed with an assortment of very tasty fresh vegetables), fish stew alla livornese—which would improve with a bit more seasoning—the very good chicken sautéed in white wine sauce garnished with excellent peas, the "saltimbocca alla romana" (a tender veal cutlet with sage and ham), and a remarkable zabaglione with strawberries. $25–$35.

## 13 ♀
# Hunam
**845 Second Ave.
(near 45th St.)
687-7471**
*Lunch and dinner daily until
10:30 P.M.
AE, DC/CB*
Chinese

As the owners of the Hunam were kind enough to reduce the decor to its simplest terms, we can save ourselves the description. Suffice to say that the tablecloths are pink, the rice bowls made of plastic, the lighting superior to that of most aquariums, and the food quite well prepared. This establishment is said to have been the first to introduce New Yorkers to the specialties of the province of Hunam (also known as Hunan), one of whose characteristics is, as you know, that it is very hot, like the cuisine of neighboring Szechuan. Among its specialties you will enjoy in particular a superbly fresh sea bass, cooked to perfection and served with sauce, snow peas, and dried peppers, which we recommend you don't swallow; the lamb tripe in hot sauce, smoked duck, and a delicious dish of lamb marinated in a sweet-and-sour sauce sprinkled with dried orange rinds. They have an unpleasant habit here of serving all the different dishes together on one large plate, so that they tend to get mixed together. Ask that they be served separately; and good luck, because the Hunam's waiters seem less zealous to understand than they are to serve you.

## 12/20
# Hyo Tan Nippon Restaurant
**119 E. 59th St.
751-7690**
*Lunch and dinner Mon. to Fri.
until 10:00 P.M.; Sat. dinner until
10:30 P.M.; closed Sun.
All major credit cards*
Japanese

This is an ideal spot for lunch after a morning's shopping at Bloomingdale's, less than a block away. It is a friendly place with tables and a circular sashimi (no sushi) bar, which is particularly pleasant if you are alone. The friendly barman puts your order on a small, wooden tray at the end of a pole, cautiously extends it to your place, and graciously beckons for your attention. The attractive sashimi (raw fish of several varieties with a colorful garnish of interesting vegetables) are a masterpiece at $10.50. Or he will order from the kitchen a tasty shrimp tempura. After a sake and hot Japanese tea, you will feel ready to get up and go back to Bloomingdale's.

At dinner, the same good food and cheer will greet you. There is an exquisite lobster with sake and soy sauce, or a complete steak (teriyaki or plain) dinner. There is informality here, and the ambience is plain. But when you leave, the barman will suggest that you return soon, and you will want to oblige.

## 13 ♀
# Il Nido
**251 E. 53rd St.
753-8450**
*Lunch and dinner daily until
10:15 P.M.; closed Sun.; jacket and
tie recommended
All major credit cards*
Italian

No, you're not mistaken. The hazards of the restaurant business have seen this lovely English farmhouse transformed into an Italian restaurant. The new owner must have found it easier—or at any rate cheaper—not to change a thing, and now there's the additional exoticism of being able to twirl your spaghetti and sip your Chianti in an atmosphere reminiscent of a Sussex country inn. At the same time, the starched white tablecloths and sparkling crockery, the dark, highly polished wood paneling reflected in the beveled mirrors, and the impeccably polite staff will make you think you're in Oxford. The wine cellar contains a few remarkable bottles, like the Pinot Grigio, and the quality of the Bolognese cuisine is fine, although not as high as its overrated reputation would have it: thin slices of dried beef (bresaola); green lasagna with four cheeses; scampi in a caper and anchovy sauce and very delicate chicken, both "dei Sette Colle," boned and served with artichokes in a wine sauce, or cooked just as well "dei colli lucchesi" with olives and vegetables, a superb steak; and a few delightful desserts, like the chocolate cake and the Saint Honoré. A pleasant idea for smaller appetites: you can order half portions of the pasta dishes.

## 14 ♧
## Inagiku
**111 E. 49th St.**
**355-0440**
*Lunch and dinner daily until*
*10:00 P.M.; closed Sun.;*
*Sat. dinner only*
*All major credit cards*
Japanese

a spray of Sakura
in the beak
of an American
eagle

. . . thus might a poet's haiku describe Inagiku, a very good Japanese restaurant tucked away in the Waldorf Astoria Hotel. It is worth pushing through the grand fussiness of the lobbies to experience the cool elegance of the Japanese interior below. The attractive Kinakaku Room, inspired by a fifteenth-century shrine erected by a spendthrift shogun, is the centerpiece of the restaurant. Guests sit at a large curved bar watching a corps de ballet of tempura cooks under the stern gaze of the chef. They wear maroon happi coats, white aprons, and what appear to be black tea cosies on their heads.

Appetizers are excellent and one can make a meal of them, encouraged by a couple of sake-martinis at the bar. Chicken yakitori on bamboo skewers is delicately sauced and the sashimi of raw tuna and fluke sea-fresh and immaculately served. A small portion of seafood and vegetable tempura netted from the bubbling low-calorie oil was marvelously light and crisp and the negima yaki of broiled beef stuffed with scallions slipped down well between mouthfuls of hot sake. Two soups, a smoky akadashi of spiced miso and a light consommé called smashi, with pretty "objets trouvés" at the bottom of the bowl, cleared the palate nicely for the teriyaki sirloin, perfectly broiled in Inagiku's own teri sauce.

In addition to the Kinakaku Room, you can squat zashiki-style on tatami mats in the Hakone Room or, if your prefer, take a seat Western-style in the smaller Imperial Room. Purists may grumble at Inagiku's success in pleasing Western eyes and palates, but we found the cuisine authentic as well as excellent, relying on the best and freshest ingredients. The spendthrift shogun who built the original shrine wouldn't lose face here. About $25 with sake or Kirin beer.

## 11/20
## Iperbole:
## Enoteca
**137 E. 55th St.**

A pretty setting is not always enough to attract the crowds. The proof: it would be hard to find an Italian restaurant more tastefully decorated than this one, with its light

# THE RESTAURANTS/East 42nd to 59th Streets

**759-9720**
*Lunch and dinner daily until 11:00 P.M.; closed Sun.*
*AE, DC, CB*
Italian

wood walls, green brocade panels, chandeliers, antiquarian books, and stuffed birds. Why does this attractive restaurant remain so desperately empty? Perhaps it's the lack of someone to welcome you with a smile, waiters happy to serve you, and a cook who knows how to juggle his flavors and spices in such a way as to recreate a bit of the Mediterranean sun. It's true that the menu lists dozens of dishes. All the classics are there and, with the exception of the desserts (which aren't at all good), they are honestly prepared and generously served, and their cooking times precisely judged, but they lack the spark that can turn an ordinary Italian meal into a feast. In a word, one tends to get bored very quickly with the cold sumptuousness of a soulless restaurant. Only the wines will help you forget the solemnity of the place: there are hundreds of wines and vintages from different lands—in particular, from Italy, France, Germany, and California—it's a dazzling selection, a true library of wines. And that's the nickname of this fearsome and ruinous "Enoteca," which is one of the most expensive Italian restaurants in New York.

**8/20**
## Joe and Rose
**747 Third Ave.**
**(46th-47th Sts.)**
**980-3985**
*Lunch and dinner daily until 10:00 P.M.*
*AE, DC*
Italian

On our last visit it looked as if George Raft and Edward G. Robinson had been raised from the dead to return in their most famous roles. How gaily they congratulated and hugged each other, blowing kisses from one table to another with cigars clenched between their teeth. The descendants of the "Godfathers" of yore are apparently just like their predecessors, with the same open gaiety, and the same appetite. When they get together at Joe and Rose, under the pretty frescoes, they smilingly swallow enormous dry and tasteless oysters, a minestrone as thick as Mama used to make it in Little Italy (except that here the vegetables are drowned and completely bland), great quantities of pasta, and gargantuan portions of veal parmigiana (you never know: cousins may arrive from Milan unannounced) in a sauce so dense you can barely guess its ingredients. But why disturb the rich clientele of Joe and Rose by hinting that the cuisine in their favorite refectory may not really be on a par with its prices ($40 with a glass of Italian wine), or by whispering that what they take for espresso is quite possibly only filtered coffee with the surprising taste of water and iron? Yes, why disturb all these people who come here to converse in unison, in the same humdrum gaiety, about their daily affairs? Joe and Rose is one of the Italian restaurants in Manhattan we recommend most highly to avid aficionados who dream of meeting face-to-face the protagonists of *Scarface* and *Little Caesar*.

**10/20**
## Kegon
**80 E. 56th St.**
**421-8777**

Kegon serves a typical Japanese (New York) menu with tempura, sukiyaki, teriyaki, sashimi, and sushi. Service by waiters and waitresses in Japanese dress is generally good. At noon, there are boxed meals to take out.

70

*Lunch and dinner Mon. to Fri.*
*until 10:15 P.M.; dinner Sat. and*
*Sun. until 9:45 P.M.*
*All major credit cards*
Japanese

The management seems to be more interested in food presentation than in its preparation. There are bamboo plates for tempura and attractive, individual black marmites for yose-nabe, fish and vegetables in a broth on a bed of cabbage and transparent noodles. Some dishes are prepared at the table. On the whole, however, dishes lack distinction. The blandness of some specialties suggests the chef is catering to a clientele unfamiliar with Japanese food. He would do better to stick to the seasonings he learned to use at home.

Upstairs, there is a nightclub with live Japanese entertainment and drinks, but no longer any food. The large number of Japanese customers at night at the nightclub attests to its authenticity; the same can no longer be said of the dining rooms downstairs.

Lunch of appetizers and a main dish cost $10 to $15, dinner $20 to $25. Beers, wines, and sake drinks are available.

**12/20**
# Kuruma Sushi
**423 Madison Ave.
(48th-49th Sts.)
751-5258**
*Lunch and dinner Mon. to Fri.*
*until 10:00 P.M.*
*AE, DC*
Japanese

You may have trouble finding this tiny sushi restaurant. Here are the directions. From Madison Avenue, use the entrance of the Dosanko Japanese restaurant. Once inside, make a right and climb the stairs. At the first-floor landing, avoid the Dosanko communal dining room at the right and the various doors ahead of you. Instead, take a sharp left and don't hesitate to slide open a somewhat mysterious-looking glass door. Walk in. You have entered Kuruma Sushi. To the left is the liquor bar; to the right the sushi bar, with twelve seats. Straight ahead, along the Madison Avenue windows (one flight up) there are two alcoves, each seating four, where you can eat cross-legged and shoeless, Japanese-style. An interior alcove can seat six or eight in similar fashion.

Is it worth the effort to climb the stairs and penetrate this little piece of Japan? Yes, if you are a sushi lover. The offerings are generally fresh and tasty, and the service is courteous. There is no menu.

At lunch, there are $6 and $10 sushi specials. Try the $10 version with its portions of abalone, bass, salmon, tuna, sea urchin, plus the roe of salmon and smelt. The bean soup is particularly invigorating. Prices jump at dinner, and are on the high side. But a sake or two will permit you to accept the fact that you are paying a few dollars more than you should. Furthermore, there's no entertainment charge for watching the sushi barmen prepare your meal.

**14**
# Lello
**65 E. 54th St.
751-1555**
*Lunch and dinner daily until*
*10:30 P.M.; closed Sun.*
*All major credit cards*
Italian

An Italian restaurant of the sort we like: elegant, but not ostentatious (the ground floor, with its mirrors and filtered light, is far more attractive than either room on the second floor), an attentive welcome, qualified and smiling waiters, and remarkably clean, light cooking with very precise flavors. Primarily inspired by northern Italian cuisine, the menu is classic, but never boring. The fresh pasta is marvelously delicate, and we've rarely eaten, even in Italy, linguine ai frutti di mare and spaghettini primavera as good as those here. Also, the stuffed mushrooms (funghi ripieni con lumache), the filetti di soglio al imperiale (unfortunately, a mite overcooked), the pollo Perugina sauteed in Marsala and truffles (and garnished unnecessarily with green beans), scallopine Boscaiola in Marsala, ham, and wild mushrooms, the crème caramel with ginger, and the zabaglione all bear witness to a mastery of authentic Italian cooking, of which we never tire. About $30–$35 with a good Chianti.

## 18 〰️
## Lutèce
249 E. 50th St.
752-2225
*Lunch Tues to Fri.; dinner Mon. to Sat. until 10:00 P.M.; formal*
*Reservation necessary*
*AE, DC, CB*
French
(classical/nouvelle)

This restaurant has become so popular that three people are now employed just to answer the telephone, and reservations are taken three months in advance. In the '60s, André Surmain, himself no cook but endowed with a good sense of advertising, invented as a slogan to launch his new Lutèce: "The most expensive restaurant in New York." His chef, André Soltner, who is the sole owner today, could (were he not so modest) use a different and far more likable one: "the best restaurant in New York." Perhaps nowadays people are less impressed by stratospheric checks than by fine cooking—and at Lutèce the cooking approaches perfection. This state of grace is relatively new: it's true that one has always eaten well at Lutèce, but it was only quite recently, following the eruption of nouvelle cuisine and its shock waves that rocked France and later the United States, that André Soltner realized that he had to try something new, to demonstrate his creativity and to free himself from a menacing routine. Prudent like all Alsatians, he didn't rush headlong into the new fashion for the simple pleasure of following the crowd. Instead he shook up his menu a bit, dropped the conventional and boring dishes on which the important French restaurants in New York prided themselves ten years ago (remember the steak Diane and the tournedos Rossini?), and gave his cuisine an air of freedom that—even when it remains strictly classical—is absolutely enchanting.

But that's not the reason why one dines so well at Lutèce. This is the only restaurant of its caliber in New York whose owner is also its head chef. Sole master of his team of eighteen cooks and apprentices, and admirably assisted by Christian Bernard, he is able to give a cohesiveness and unity to his establishment that other luxury restaurants—where owners, kitchen staff, and waiters are usually divided and often at odds—cannot achieve. Soltner does not accept walk-on parts: he isn't content with lording it over his tables and shaking hands. He keeps a watchful eye on his stoves and the quality of ingredients used. In that field too, he has developed. Formerly, he swore by French imports only. Today, he defends American products, and putting aside his Gallic chauvinism, is happy to be able to find almost everything he needs in New York, from local scallops (better than the

Breton) to farm-raised pigeons, sweetbreads, and even the sweet butter. "Over the past five years," he says, "the change has been spectacular," which, by the way, is also true of his cuisine. Our next-to-last meal was exquisite: hot saucisson en croûte, as good as the best you could find in Lyon (Soltner makes his own sausage), little vol-au-vent with snails, porgy in tomato sauce with fresh mint, scallops served with their coral (why, in America, is this delicious part usually thrown away?), young pigeon with chanterelle mushrooms and snow peas, a beef aiguillette with carrots, almond tarts, and a divine bitter chocolate mousse.

But it was the last, absolutely spectacular meal that incited us to raise the rating by a point. It was a dinner executed with all the brio of a John McEnroe tennis match. It began with tender pink duck's liver, sautéed in tarragon vinegar and accompanied by a small salad of delicate greens and celery, steeped in that same wonderful liquid; bay scallops in a sauce with a hint of tomato, to which the mollusks had given an agreeable suggestion of the ocean; a delicate fillet of fresh salmon, barely cooked and served with an admirable mustard seed sauce; then a good, hearty homemade dish of veal knuckles with carrots, turnips, and mushrooms from the Catskills, on which the perfection of the cooking and the delicacy of the lightened sauce (not a grain of starch or flour) had conferred a rare distinction. And, in perfect harmony, some splendid wines, such as an all too unfamiliar Château Rayas (a red Châteauneuf-du-Pape), chosen from a fairly short but judicious wine list; well presented too, which is unusual in New York, where the names of vineyard owners and wine merchants are often omitted. But, quite obviously, it is the menus-dégustations composed of six or seven courses and served to groups of at least four or five that best demonstrate the talent of André Soltner and his team, assisted by French waiters and staff devoted to their profession. And, whether you're seated on the ground floor in the fresh and amusing decor of an old-fashioned winter garden, or in the elegant and intimate smaller rooms upstairs, you're sure to see a few famous faces. $90 will allow two to dine well at Lutèce, without wine.

**8/20**

## Madras Woodlands
**310 E. 44th St.**
**986-0620**
*Lunch and dinner daily until*
*10:00 P.M.; closed Tues.*
*All major credit cards*
Indian (vegetarian)

The bizarrely colorful Madras Woodlands, with its red flock wallpaper, folkloric murals, and transport-cafe chairs, is an authentic southern Indian vegetarian restaurant with authentically bad service.

Vegetarians are traditionally nonviolent, but on this occasion quite a good many mild-mannered diners were in the mood to stone their waiters to death with onion bhajis—if, that is, they could have gotten their hands on either the waiters or the food. Service was virtually nonexistent. The orders took hours to arrive, and when they did were usually wrong. To add to the confusion few waiters spoke English, and a simple request for a coffee sent them scurrying for an interpreter. Our neighbors—formerly staunch fans—who had failed even to obtain a glass of water, could be heard telling the distraught manager that they would never come again. He, poor fellow, was offering apologies and tearing up bills all over the room. This is a great pity, because the place has always had a faithful following not just with vegetarians or macrobiotics, but with the impoverished young, who can stuff themselves silly for about six dollars.

The food itself is fine provided you like starch—fritters, dumplings, pilafs, pancakes, and breads, with chutneys of coconut, green chilis, tamarind, and coriander to make things less bland, and a little metal container of vegetable curry to help it go down. If you were a prisoner in some primitive Oriental jail you'd probably think it wonderful. For our taste it didn't add up to a particularly varied or appetizing meal.

However, lots of people rave about it. so here are some ways to avoid the main pitfalls. Don't order the Pu-Pu Platter, which includes the totally tasteless iddli, a large white sphere of steamed lentil flour. Try instead any of the different vegetable curries, nicely spiced with ginger, cinnamon, chili, or coriander, and confine your farinaceous intake to a masala dosai. This is starch too, of course, a huge pancake stuffed with potato and onion, but at least it tastes of something, If you can't be bothered with any of this, ask for the tali, a sort of metal-lidded luncheon box with lots of compartments, and a little taste of everything. We can't recommend the rather messy-looking warm halva, but the sweet iassi—an iced yogurt drink—is delicious.

Incidentally, the kitchens with their little household shrines are enormous—big enough to comfortably cater a luxury liner—so the bad service is inexcusable. $6–$10.

## 13 ⌂
## Le Madrigal
**216 E. 53rd St.**
**355-0322**
*Lunch Mon. to Fri.; dinner Mon. to Sat. until 10:30 P.M.; closed Sun.; formal*
*All credit cards*
French (classical)

This is a high-priced, classical French restaurant, popular at the lunch hour with publishers, agents, and (rich) writers. The ambience is bright and airy (there's an enclosed garden at the back), the service is formal and professional, and the food is predictably good, if not exceptional for the prices charged. Fresh flowers and a display of hors d'oeuvres and desserts will greet you as you enter.

The lunch menu includes the usual house pâtés and an unremarkable saucisson chaud, as well as excellent Blue Points and clams. For a main course you might choose tender veal kidneys in a smooth mustard sauce or a poached sea bass hollandaise. The dessert could be lemon mousse or fresh berries. With a glass or two of the house wine, the lunch bill for you and your companion will be $50 to $60.

The dinner menu is more exotic and more expensive. There are a la carte appetizers of smoked salmon, foie gras, and caviar. The price of the entree, which generally covers the full meal, does not include these specials, of course. Entrees include imported Dover sole, chicken with morilles, or rack of lamb. For dessert you can choose from a trolley of sumptuous cakes, ices, ice creams, fruit tarts, or stewed fruits. There is also a cheese tray. The waiter will be as courteous in providing you with the bill for $100 as he has been in serving you. If you are on an expense account, you could have a pleasant evening.

16 🍽️

## Michel Fitoussi's Palace

**420 E. 59th St.**
**355-5150**
*Lunch Mon. to Fri.; dinner Mon. to Sat. until 10:00 P.M.; formal; reservation necessary*
*AE, MC, V*
French
(classical/nouvelle)

A new adventure has begun for what used to be New York's most pretentious and extravagant restaurant. The young French chef, Michel Fitoussi, acquired 50 percent ownership of the business last autumn, and his discreet associates have left him absolute freedom in its management. Thus we bid a fond adieu to Frank Valenza who, with his fortune built on pizzas, dreamed confidently of a more prestigious career and, encouraged by his psychoanalyst, opened this restaurant with the intention of creating nothing less than the best and most expensive restaurant in the United States and incidentally the world. All of New York talked about it, but Polite Society was not supportive: there was too much of everything for the setting to be truly elegant. Too much gold-trimmed china, solid silver, crystal, lace, cut velvet—too many rare Bordeaux at $1,000 and out-of-this-world checks. True, certain persons in dark suits and crocodile shoes were very much at home here among Midwestern billionaires out to do New York in grand style, and clothing manufacturers quaffing Lafite-Rothschild to celebrate their birthdays. Still, they weren't enough to ward off catastrophe, and after years of walking a tightrope, poor Mr. Valenza, crushed by financial problems had to withdraw to lick his wounds.

Michel Fitoussi didn't have to stretch out on the couch before deciding what he was going to do. He realized that meals at $500 per person were no longer in great demand. He instituted a four-course lunch at a set price of $30, and a five-course dinner at $70—which, all the same, are still among the most expensive in New York—introduced several bottles of wine costing about $20, and asked his young wife Marge, shy, but full of good will, to welcome guests who hadn't necessarily appreciated the past pretensions. He is also considering redoing the decor, whose pseudo-chic always struck us as lugubrious. He should at the same time take advantage of the occasion to suppress the spectacular decorations, which he seems to believe must garnish the least of his preparations. If he does all this, he stands a chance of welcoming a regular crowd of gourmets to appreciate the refinement of his generally excellent cuisine without the showbiz. It's possible to have reservations about some of the dishes, such as the fish liver with leeks, whose excellent vinegar sauce doesn't quite manage to pep up its blandness, or the lobster au blanc with asparagus tips, whose flavor is also somewhat pallid, or the chanterelles with Japanese water chestnuts, which could have done with fresh herbs and spices. By contrast, his lobster pâté with foie gras, truffle soup à la Bocuse, fresh pasta with morilles, scallops in a vermouth sauce (delicately seasoned with green peppercorns), the wonderfully creamy salmon that goes extraordinarily with snow peas, the crisp Long Island duckling, the steamed poularde "Lucien Tendret," pheasant with carrots and small Brussels sprouts, his sumptuous chocolate cake, chilled petit fours, and chocolates all bear the mark of great talent and accomplished professionalism. We should only advise him not to give in to the temptation to do too much. As in painting, a great artist knows when to affix his signature.

## 11/20
# Mitsukoshi
**465 Park Ave.**
**(57th St.)**
**935-6969**
*Lunch and dinner daily until*
*10:00 P.M.; closed Sun.*
*All major credit cards*
Japanese

An exceptionally pretty Japanese restaurant situated beneath an extremely expensive store, which specializes in rare Oriental porcelain and lacquerware. At lunchtime it's crammed with businessmen who seem to be using it as a kind of mini-health farm, taking a punishing break between bouts of self-indulgence. Certainly there are few signs of rapture on their faces as they toy with a seaweed salad. Maybe there's a bit of the Emperor's New Clothes attached to Japanese cuisine; it would take a brave man actually to admit that he finds his pickled fluke's fin revolting.

Be that as it may, Mitsukoshi certainly has the most elegant decor, the prettiest lighting, and the most incomprehensible waitresses of any Japanese restaurant in town. Attempts to explain the menu were a total failure, so we settled for a set sukiyaki lunch, cooked at the table, which we'd heard was superb. Our waitress's face fell. "No good cooked at table, not enough room," she announced with unaccustomed fluency, averting her eyes from the empty table beside us, which positively sprouted with outlets and plugs. Off she tripped in her white and gold kimono, to return, suspiciously soon, with what looked like a brimming caldron of some dark brown, overcooked Transylvanian beef stew. Where were those tender morsels of barely cooked beef and vegetables transferred in a flash from pan to plate, moistened only by soy, saki, and their own juices, with a beaten yolk of egg to cool them off? Apart from this fiasco, the rest of the meal consisted of beautifully presented odds and ends, followed by a red bean ice cream (which tasted like vanilla with a few chopped-up beans in it).

It's only fair to add that somewhere in the Mitsukoshi kitchens presides chef Masahiro Ishido, who specializes in kaiseki, a nine-course meal of small but exquisite dishes. This, according to the blurb, is a gastronomic poem, visual, emotional, and edible—in that order. In other words, the art of making things look better than they taste. It is a meal that has more to do with the soul than the body, the script continues, so have a can of beans handy when you get home. With one day's notice this menu can be served to you—sitting in some discomfort on the floor of the Tatami Room—for a mere $50. Set lunches, $15–$17. A la carte about $25.

**7/20**
## Mr. Chow
**324 E. 57th Street**
**751-9030**
*Lunch and dinner daily until*
*11:45 P.M.; closed Sat. and*
*Sun. afternoon.*
*All major credit cards*
Chinese

Yet another Chinese restaurant—but this one is the current darling of up-to-date beautiful people. Until late at night the fashionable set of every sort crowd into this vast, very noisy dining room, whose two levels recreate with flair the 1930s (in the occident), with the customary panoply of black and beige lacquered walls, concealed lighting, and bannisters in gilded metal. The purpose in coming is, apparently, more to be seen in this superb setting than to eat Chinese food; whereas the London restaurant bearing his name enjoys an honorable (although undeniably over-rated) reputation, the cuisine prepared by Mr. Chow's New York branch is absolutely distressing. It's bad enough that you have to wait ten minutes before your knife and fork are replaced with chopsticks, or that it's impossible to get any sort of seasoning whatsoever (soy or hot pepper sauce, etc.) at your table, or that the primary concern of the Italian waiters is to sell you expensive alcoholic beverages. The worst is that the dishes offered on the (as it happens, short) menu bear little relationship to the spirit of Chinese cuisine. On our visit, the heavy, greasy dough of the dumpling resembled bad Italian ravioli, the steamed meatballs tasted disturbingly gamey, the sweet and sour pork had more dough (and badly cooked, at that) in it than meat, and the peppers accompanying it were served cold. The chili chicken was rubbery, the rice, curiously bathed in oil, was totally insipid. Was this punishment specially meted out because we had the pretentiousness to drink nothing but tea? It would seem not, because alcohol drinkers seemed to fare no better. At a nearby table, the glazed Peking duck (although ordered in advance) comprised only one dish, instead of the traditional three, and was composed of saucer-sized pancakes as thick as a finger. At another table, the egg rolls were no bigger than breakfast sausages, though the dough was as thick as tagliatella.

That hardly mattered, as the wine flows freely. We have no idea where Mr. Chow recruits his cooks, but he would gain by sending them to Chinatown for a training course. There, at least, tradition is still respected. It's true that, when you see how his clients, pretending to be gourmets, go into raptures over the canned lichee nuts, you can predict a long and prosperous life for him uptown. About $25 without wine.

## 13 🍴

# Nippon

**145 E. 52nd St.**

**758-0226**

*Lunch Mon. to Fri.; dinner nightly*
*until 10:00 P.M.*
*All major credit cards*

Japanese

Opened by Nobuyoshi Kuraoko nearly twenty years ago
when Japanese restaurants were still a rarity, the Nippon
has retained all of its original authenticity and charm—an
extraordinary blend of functionalism and elegance that
also manages to be quite cosy. The stream, with its
connoisseur's collection of decorative rocks, still
meanders through the main dining room, decked with
plastic ferns. A rather battered bridge overhung with
imitation almond blossoms leads to the bar, where you
can experiment with a sakimi—the Orient's answer to the
martini made with extra-dry saki. This brand, called
Aramasa, is usually only supplied to the royal family, but
one of the owner's relatives has a hotline to the palace.
There's a long cypress-wood bar curving the whole length
of the room. It's supposed to resemble a "nippon" or
gourd, but you have to strain your imagination a bit.
Behind it, chefs in white hats operate the restaurant's fast-
food outlet, rolling up sushi, and tossing tempura in big
copper bowls of sizzling sesame oil.

If you prefer to sit at a table you will be looked after by
girls in kimonos, colored for the season—at our last visit,
russet and gray for the fall—who rush around with a most
ungeisha-like briskness. The boys wear a rather fetching
combination of bow tie and happi coat. They, or the
delightful manager Mr. Matsunaga (known as Mah-jong to
his friends), will help you plough your way through the
bewildering menu, or you can play safe with a set meal. O-
Teishoku gives you ten traditional dishes for $15, or you
can splash out on the royal dinner at $19.50.

Mr. Kuraoka is a seafood fanatic and scours the world
for such unusual delicacies as sea urchins and baby eels,
delicious with oil and garlic. His current craze—cold-
water abalone from Canada—seems less successful. We
were offered a menu featuring no less than fifteen ways to
deal with this rubbery bivalve, but one mouthful was
enough to send two seasoned gourmets diving for their
napkins—it was slippery and knobbly at the same time.
Everything else we tried, however, was perfection. Tatami
rooms with paper screens are also available for traditional
Japanese-style parties, including a special one with a pit
under the table to accommodate Western legs! About
$20–$25 without drink. From $8.50 at lunch.

## 15 🍴🍴

# Oyster Bar

**Grand Central**
**Station, basement**
**level**

**599-1000**

*Lunch and dinner Mon. to Fri.*
*until 9:30 P.M.*
*All major credit cards*

Seafood

The only thing for which we reproach Mr. Jerome Brody is
closing his restaurant on the weekend, thus depriving us
two days every week of the pleasure of eating the best
fresh fish in New York. The white-china-walled Oyster Bar
is in a basement of Grand Central Station, and serves over
two thousand people daily. With the exception of the
shrimp (it's almost impossible to find fresh ones, but
they're still better here than anywhere else), nothing
frozen is offered on the menu, which changes every day
according to what is available fresh, offering truly
miraculous spectra of seafood, including a dozen types of

11-11 @ 1:15
490-6650

oysters, crab, lobster, sturgeon, red snapper, striped bass, pompano, lake and river trout, turbot, and even the authentic wolf fish netted in the North Atlantic, which used to be thrown overboard out of ignorance. Atlantic salmon (not Pacific, which is of inferior quality) is smoked on the premises over applewood, and you'll find none better anywhere in New York. The quality of the ingredients themselves is more important than their preparation, and no effort is wasted on complicated sauces or stuffings. But isn't it a real test of cookery to serve, every day and to perfection, hundreds (even thousands) of fish, as if on an assembly line, and yet keep the natural flavor? On the back of the menu is one of the prettiest lists of California wines (96 different sorts) to be found in the United States. At lunch—there's one sitting at 12:15 and another an hour later—it's possible to reserve a table, or you can just show up when you like and wait your turn.

**11/20**
## Palm
**837 Second Ave.
(near 45th St.)
687-2935**
*Lunch and dinner weekdays until
10:45 P.M.; dinner Sat. until
11:00 P.M.; closed Sun.;
reservation for lunch
All major credit cards*
Steaks

There are some fifteen tables, sawdust strewn on the floor, and the yellowing, slightly peeling walls are decorated with caricatures of all the celebrities who have come to dine on steak and be seen in this establishment over the past fifty years. The crab cocktail is, like everywhere else, infamous. The clam chowder contains, as in other spots, too much flour. And the Maine lobster, so delicious when not overcooked, here serves only to spice up even more a bill that is already hot enough if you stick to one of the double-sized steaks for which the Palm has always been famous. But, as you will have deduced, it's the inimitable atmosphere of New York in the old days that draws people to the Palm, not the cookery. Same for its exact copy, the Palm Too, opened across the street at number 840 on the same avenue.

**8/20**
## P. J. Clarke's
**915 Third Ave.
(near 55th St.)
759-1650**
*Lunch and dinner daily until
4:00 A.M.
No credit cards*
American

It's best to proceed with exteme caution when reviewing a bad restaurant. You tend to gloat, get carried away; and then the next morning you have to repent: you've found a place even worse. All the same, it seems to us that with P. J. Clarke's, we're dealing with a sure thing. What other New York restaurant could manage to ruin so completely a simple steak, or to serve a hamburger both charred *and* cold, which even a starving mongrel wouldn't touch. (A second meal allowed us to revise our opinion: P. J. Clarke's is also quite capable of serving hamburgers both charred and hot.) But that exploit pales in comparison with the difficulty involved in traversing the narrow corridor along the bar, which leads to the small, smoky, dingy, and madly fashionable dining rooms; after dusk the gauntlet is lined by clients of all ages, five or six deep, eyeing each other keenly. Note that a small corner of the bar is reserved for heterosexuals, as established by a sign to this effect: "Men not accompanied by women are not permitted at the end of the bar." And indeed, a certain number of women, whose courage should not go unremarked, offer themselves as volunteers to occupy this bridgehead. Don't hesitate to take your place alongside them, as P. J. Clarke's is easily one of New York's most amusing spots—as long as you ignore its cooking.

**12/20**

## La Petite Marmite

**6 Mitchell Place (east of First Ave. from 48th St.)**
**826-1084**

*Lunch and dinner Mon. to Fri. until 10:00 P.M.; Sat. dinner only; closed Sun.*
*All major credit cards*
French (classical)

A graceful chandelier, its branches flowing like so many inverted tulips, suggests the elegant formality of this (expensive) restaurant close to the United Nations. Dark crimson banquettes and flowery wall coverings confirm the sense of luxury. Moreover, glass dividers and well-spaced tables give the U.N. clientele who frequent the place insurance against eavesdroppers. In this setting, it is not surprising that the menu is in French, without English translations (is French still the language of diplomacy?) and that the menu presents dishes that are classical, or perhaps haute cuisine. As appetizers, try la bouchée Joinville, tiny shrimps and other seafood in a puff-pastry shell with a lobster sauce, or la cassoulette d'Escargots, an individual casserole of snails in a faintly garlicky, Burgundian sauce. The chef makes his own foie gras. You can also pamper yourself with imported caviar at $40 a serving, or domestic at $20. Entrees range from $16 to $22 or more if you opt for the chef's special of the day. A poached bass in a white vermouth cream sauce is correct, if not inspired; a grilled lobster is properly pungent with the aroma of fennel. The combination of two slices from the saddle and two chops of the rack is an unusual lamb presentation and the garnish of julienne vegetables is fresh and crisp. By contrast, the sweetbreads, with imported mushrooms (some looked and tasted like the home-grown variety), were not as fresh and tender as they should be, especially when you are paying $20 to sample them.

Desserts, for the most part, are standard New York French: chocolate mousse, crème caramel, floating island (with a less-than-sensational dribble of raspberry purée giving color to the egg white). The pastries and cakes, made on the premises, are better than average. The great wines of France are listed in profusion in the wine book, at prices that might startle the uninitiated.

Given the elegance of the setting, the excellence of the service, the extraordinary collection of wines, and a bill that can easily reach $125–$150 for two, you are not being unreasonable to expect superlative food on the table. This is rarely the case, and what's more, there is apt to be marked inconsistency from one dish to the other.

**15**

## Le Périgord

**405 E. 52nd Street**
**755-6244**

*Lunch Mon. to Fri., noon to 3:00 P.M., dinner Mon. to Sat., 5:15 P.M. to 10:30 P.M.*

You may now go there blindly. As a matter of fact, that's what we recommend as long as Georges Briguet does not change the fire engine red fabric of his booths nor his flowered drapes, which make you think you just illicitly entered into a young bride's boudoir. But open your eyes

*All major credit cards*
French

quickly to read the new small menu by Antoine Bouterin and to look at the pretty dishes that follow one another on your table. This young chef, whom we met at Quai d'Orsay in Paris, just awakened the old Périgord by bringing, not the "in" cuisine that you can find most anywhere in New York, but a simple and unerring taste, finely tuned cooking times and exquisitely fresh ingredients. We could fault him for a few details, such these superfluous truffles on the very good vegetable tart, coated with clarified butter; an overcooked turbot; his tarte tatin lacking caramel, and the rather bland strawberry cream.

But everything else was enchanting. The lobster soup, without too much cream, and peppered just right; the lamb terrine with ratatouille; the pasta with truffles and fresh basil; the roast duck with glazed broccoli; and the fresh salmon fillet steamed with thyme, had the particular quality of home cooking (performed by a Cordon Bleu) so rare in the French restaurants of New York. Simple and almost perfect. Too few American wines on the wine list but a sensational Château Lascombes 1976 at $28. Prix fixe for dinner at $36.

## 17 The Quilted Giraffe

**955 Second Ave.**
**(50th-51st Sts.)**
**753-5355**
*Dinner Mon. to Fri. until 10:00*
*P.M.; formal; reservation necessary*
*All major credit cards*
French (nouvelle)

We must have been justified in according The Quilted Giraffe a place of honor in the French version of our New York guide published last year. Even those who then spoke of Barry Wine's cooking with some disdain now suddenly find it "delicious," although they still don't give it the rating that, in our opinion, it deserves. The young chef, who abandoned his law office for the kitchen, might well have started as just a gifted amateur; today he's undeniably a true professional. The pseudo-originalities and preciousness that cluttered up certain of his creations have been cast aside. Returning a few months after our first visit, we were convinced that he had, in the interim, progressed even further.

It's entirely possible that his new kitchen, which is larger and better equipped, is partly responsible for this evolution. It wouldn't be the first time we've observed such a phenomenon: an artist needs the proper tools. At the same time, Barry Wine decided to open for dinner, and that too may have permitted him to take better care of his work. At any rate, you can see he's happy in this new and attractive setting created by his wife Suzy and himself. The sheets of engraved art deco glass, the three spectacular enameled ceramics taken from a stove built in Lyon in the nineteenth century, the large porcelain plates known in France as "American" yet so rare in New York despite their obvious handiness—all attest to a sense of style that will not make you regret the passing of the previous somewhat infantile obsession with giraffe imagery. Not to mention the elegant second-floor dining room, or the stunning washrooms that deserve to be in a museum.

In short, everything has been so arranged as to allow you to best appreciate the finesse of an inventive style of modern cooking reminiscent, although not a copy, of Michel Guérard's cuisine. Which is not surprising if you know that Mark Chayette, a young American formerly a member of Guérard's team, is at Barry Wine's side.

After having hugely enjoyed their wild mushroom and truffle soup, lobster and scallop ragoût with tarragon, their roast veal kidney with black pepper, and the best rack of lamb (Montana lamb is one of the world's tastiest) with Chinese mustard and herbs we've ever tasted, we "discovered" this time the swordfish steak with fresh herbs and snow peas in a divine cream sauce with thyme, in which tiny Japanese mushrooms from California (enokitaki) had been cooked. And also, although less interesting, a salad of partridge fillets with chanterelles, some tender, pink lamb chops garnished with delicious vegetables "cooked in a veil," some Indiana goat cheese that could almost turn a champion French she-goat green with envy, and to finish, coffee ice cream in a chocolate pecan sauce capable of turning an ascetic into a gourmand. Yes! Yes! Yes! Vive La Giraffe! which fully deserves our three toques. Let's only hope its head doesn't swell too much to wear them. Our enthusiasm, however, doesn't make the bill any easier to swallow—it's not nearly as light as the cooking, especially if you let yourself be tempted by the Ventana Chardonnay 1979 and the superb H. M. R. Zinfandel 1976 (San Luis Obispo), recommended by a sommelier who knows his trade admirably. Menu-carte at $45, and full menu at $65.

**9/20**
# Regine's
**502 Park Ave.**
**(59th-60th Sts.)**
**826-0990**
*Lunch Mon. to Fri.; dinner Mon. to Sat. until midnight; jacket and tie required*
*AE, V, DC*
International

An urgent task is at hand: to disabuse anybody of the disastrous notion that it is still possible to enjoy a trace of Michel Guérard's admirable cooking at Regine's. The present chef offers at lunch a menu worthy of a luxury hotel in Eastern Europe (although, in all fairness, we have to admit we've never seen a restaurant offer a strawberry jam omelet as a main course, not even in Bulgaria) and flings at you some wretched hors d'oeuvres, including a distressing fish pâté stuffed with sliced raw carrots, then a pike quenelle Nantua whose principal merit is that it's microscopic, a rubbery suprême de volaille in a Champagne sauce that's not too bad, a tasteless crème caramel, an edible chocolate mousse, and a drinkable espresso.

It's true that $15.75 (the set price for lunch) is not too much to pay for the excellent service, ravishing black and silver art deco setting, and smart looking diners (whom we would not, nonetheless, ask for a list of their favorite restaurants).

## 11/20
### The Rendez-Vous
**Berkshire Place Hotel**
**21 E. 52nd St.**
**753-5800**
*Lunch and dinner daily until 10:30 P.M.; brunch on Sat. and Sun.; reservation suggested*
*All major credit cards*
International

This large, friendly establishment, with its square bar, green plants, two glass ceilings lit from above, and waiters in red-striped jackets, seems to hesitate between the states of luxury restaurant and common cafe-bistro. The guests, who seem to be mostly the beautiful people who stay in this elegant hotel, lunch on fare that leaves you somewhat perplexed. The dishes vary from the very mediocre to the fairly good, in the most haphazard way. Thus, for instance, you can go from a fresh marinated baby salmon, which has undergone some mysterious treatment to remove all its flavor, to a well-cooked and well-spiced sautéed red snapper with shallots—or from an indescribable vegetable soup in which a couple of shipwrecked clams float to an excellent strawberry cheesecake, or from a thin, overcooked Dover sole aux fines herbes to a very acceptable grenadine of veal à l'orange et au citron. Because the Rendez-Vous' menu offers steamed salmon–nouvelle cuisine its cooking passes in town for avant-garde. The only thing modern about it are the prices ($18 for the grenadine of veal).

## 13 ♤
### Restaurant Laurent
**111 E. 56th St.**
**753-2729**
*Lunch and dinner Mon. to Sat.; Sun. dinner only*
*AE, DC, CB*
French (classical)

The passageway is nondescript, but it takes you from the street into old-world grandeur: a somber room of immense proportions, a twenty-foot ceiling with decorative molding, dark paneled walls, subdued blue banquettes, elegant table settings, and dominating the scene, an enormous bar. Another door leads to the somewhat brighter main dining room, with light wood paneling and red banquettes.

French (New York-style) haute cuisine is served in either room, at high prices, particularly at lunch when prices are even higher than you might expect: a grilled sole with a mustard sauce for $21. Dinner entrees include squab in a casserole, rack of lamb, medallions of veal, and the usual steaks. The wine collection is one of the best in the city—over twenty thousand bottles according to the management. There are numerous rare bottles, but also quite a number of good buys: a house wine by Bouchard from France for $9 and a Louis Martini Cabernet Sauvignon from California for $12.50, to name just two. There are no surprises here, unless it is that the kitchen continues to maintain a generally high standard, and that the service continues to be what it should be in these surroundings. This is where the captains of industry eat—can you afford their company?

## 10/20
### Russian Bear
**139 E. 56th St.**
**355-9080**
*Lunch and dinner daily until 11:30 P.M.; dinner only Sat. and Sun.*

Seldom the hardiest of blooms, Russian restaurants suffer from a proverbially high mortality rate. Not the Russian Bear, however, which if legend is to be believed, has been going its grizzly way since 1908. Dimly lit, its wood paneling decorated with dancing bears and carousing

*All major credit cards*
Russian

peasants, this hostelry exudes just the right mix of Slav gloom and nostalgia to make anybody weep happily into their vodka.

There is a long curving bar at which you can imbibe one of the many plain or flavored vodkas, with or without the statutory pickled gherkin. Our own advice is to accompany this dangerous ritual with a hearty portion of zakuska or appetizers, that great Russian institution orginally devised to revive guests delayed by iced roads, blizzards, or wolves. The choice includes Maatjes herrings, garlicky calves'-foot jelly and, notably, blini pancakes with red caviar and sour cream. The food at the Russian Bear had been vacillating from bad to worse, but since the recent arrival of Valia, a professional cook from Riga, things have looked up. Rumor has it that on at least one occasion she has cooked for Big Bear Brezhnev himself.

Stick to the ethnic dishes—flavorful borscht and pirojok, the small savory meat pie traditionally served with soups, or stuffed cabbage rolls in a rich tomato sauce. Nalesniki, chicken-filled blintzes, were good, as were the pelemeni, plump Russian ravioli in consommé or with lashings of sour cream. Caucasian grills are popular and Tatiana, the proprietress, claims that her lamb fillet shashlik is marinated for three days according to an old Georgian recipe. There is also chakhombili, a spicy casserole of chicken said to have been Stalin's favorite dish.

From 7:00 P.M. to 2:00 A.M. there is live music, though not by the wildest stretch of Slav imagination can the resident trio be described as an abandoned gypsy ensemble. Customers will love singer Ludmilla with her repertoire of Russian songs, guaranteed to wring tears from the hardest Madison Avenue aparatchik. $25 with wine or vodka.

## 10/20
# Shun Lee Palace
**155 E. 55th St.**
**371-8844**
*Lunch and dinner daily until 10:30 P.M.; Fri. and Sat. until 11:30 P.M.*
*AE, DC*
Chinese

Lunch at Shun Lee Palace is gregarious and noisy, with only the waiters impassive as they shuffle through a forest of arms waving to attract their attention. The decor is a chop suey of bad taste, with glittering chandeliers and dazzling metallic wallpapers. Seating is elbow-to-elbow and you are likely to overhear the product formula for a new shampoo loudly and clearly from a neighboring table.

Chef Wang's mainly Hunan and Szechuan menu is ambitious, but years of pandering to American palates have made the cooking bland and blurred the distinct regional flavors. A brown and boring unisauce seems to prevail. Yet some dishes pass muster, such as the spicy Yanchow chicken soong, a tasty macédoine of fowl and vegetables in a lettuce cup; cold duck in Hunan sauce; and, on a good day, steamed dumplings. Chef Wang's creations include rabbit in barbecue sauce and tangy pheasant (in season); but we found more comfort in the Hunan section, where whole sea bass glazed in a rich spicy sauce and an unusual dish of peppery calves' liver garnished with spinach both lived up to expectations. The renowned General Ching's chicken, a great standby and China's answer to poulet marengo, was good, but the sauce did not quite tingle as promised. However, side dishes of extra hot sauce are provided for those who prefer more incendiary fare.

Shun Lee Palace is one of those popular restaurants that has paid the price of assimilation. Like other members of the chain, it is unmistakably successful, but Chef Wang must know in his heart that the kitchen gods are frowning. $25 with wine.

**12/20**
## Sichuan Pavilion
**322 E. 44th St.**
**986-3775**
*Lunch and dinner daily until*
*11:00 P.M.*
*All major credit cards*
Chinese

Sichuan Pavilion is widely regarded as the flagship of authentic Chinese cuisine in New York. Small wonder, for what other establishment can boast ten ranking, hand-picked chefs direct from the People's Republic?

Restful and elegant, it is decorated with a plethora of pandas, stuffed, scrolled, and depicted on huge murals. You can feast admirably off the varied hot and cold appetizers: steamed dumplings in a Sichuan sauce, small and delicate spring rolls and pan-smoked fish fillets. Tiny spare ribs rolled in rice flour and served in small metal steamers and "Unusual Taste Chicken" in a multi-flavored dressing both had the real taste of Sichuan. Well-chilled Chinese vodka makes a perfect accompaniment to such a minifeast, surely one of the best ways of getting to know a new restaurant.

Hot and spicy Sichuan dishes are marked with a star, while a red dot indicates specialities "first time served in America," as the menu proudly proclaims. Setting aside such delicacies as home-style sinews and sea cucumber— that ubiquitous and slithery marine echinoderm—it pays to try some of these authentic Sichuan concoctions. Chengdu-style sea bass in its dark, sweet, and mildly incendiary sauce, and the quaintly named "Tinkling Bells," in which sizzling pork shreds and vegetables are poured onto a red-hot skillet, were both good. Rabbit chunks cooked with chili and peanuts were disappointing, coarsely cut, oily, and leaving an unpleasant aftertaste. Buddha duck, curiously named since he was certainly a vegetarian, was better, simmered with vegetables; but the tea and camphor duck could have been crisper.

On the whole we found the cuisine erratic, with more than a hint of cooking by committee: too many chefs, perhaps? One of the best Chinese restaurants in New York? Probably, but there is a disquieting lack of finesse in both cooking and presentation. Maybe authentic Chinese cuisine does not travel. Still, with such a concentration of talent in the kitchen, Sichuan Pavilion merits more than one visit. $30 with wine.

**9/20**
## Sparks Steak House
**210 E. 46th St.**

Sparks is "in." It gets publicity, and crowds. But the question is, "What is all the fuss about?" One visit answers the question. The fuss is about the remarkable

**687-4855**
*Lunch and dinner Mon. to Fri. until
11:00 P.M.; Sat. dinner only;
closed Sun.*
*All major credit cards*
Steaks

wine list—not about the steaks or the handful of other dishes on the menu. There are nearly three hundred wine selections, of which almost one-half are California bottles. Most of the California wines are catalogued under their varietal names, which adds to the joy of browsing through the list. For example, you find 36 under Cabernet Sauvignon and twenty under Chardonnay, as well as bottles listed under Pinot Noir, Zinfandel, Petite Sirah, Merlot, Gamay Beaujolais, Chenin Blanc, Sauvignon Blanc, Fumé Blanc, and so on. The "house" wines are Beaulieu Vineyards (1977) Cabernet Sauvignon and Mirassou (1977) Zinfandel, each good value at $12. But insofar as the wines are concerned, Sparks is a place where you will probably want to experiment. And the wines have been so well selected that you you can't really go wrong. Your decision may come down to price. Among the Cabernet Sauvignons, the Clos du Val (1975) at $18.50 and the Château Montelena (1975) at $19.50 are good choices. Among the Chardonnay, the St. Clément (1979) at $19.50 is particularly worth trying. If you are supremely ambitious, you can have a bottle of the Latour Reserve of Beaulieu Vineyards (1970) for $79. The list of Italian and French wines is of almost equal interest, although the French bottles are generally more expensive.

The ambience, if not the food, is conducive to tasting. Smoked-glass partitions, etched with the letter *S,* separate the wall booths. But you will have to put up with mediocre (and relatively expensive) food as you work your way through the wines. Insist that your steak be cooked to order. Otherwise, you may be served a steak that has been sitting around too long. The same for the potatoes. The fish is apt to be overcooked, dry, and heavily coated with bread crumbs. The only dessert worth ordering is the Italian ice cream in a bittersweet chocolate coating. Everything you order is a la carte. Count on $35 per person, plus wine.

**9/20**
# Tandoor
**40 E. 49th St.**
**752-3334**
*Lunch and dinner daily until
10:30 P.M.; no lunch Sun.*
*All major credit cards*
Indian

The heavy and handsome carved doors of this posh Indian restaurant would not look out of place in the Red Fort in Delhi. Named after the beehive-shaped clay oven in which marinated lamb, chicken, and seafood are roasted to a ruddy hue, it is plush and comfortable with fretted brass lamps casting a soft glow on the red upholstery and ocher tablecloths. The overall effect is muted and clublike. Houris in green saris greet you on arrival, hands folded in ritual welcome just below their caste marks. Tandoor watchers, indulging in a new and diverting spectator sport, can observe the chefs performing inside their glass-encased kitchen, in full view of the main restaurant. Two can share a tandoori dinner ($11.95), which in addition to giving you a taste of lamb and chicken straight from the oven includes a selection of curries, pilaf rice, lentils, chutneys, pickles, and last but not least, naan bread, baked on the inner walls of the tandoor itself. At that price you can afford a well-chilled bottle of Tavel rosé, though many Indian friends recommend lassi, a cold yogurt drink, dubbed Indian penicillin by the irreverent. To follow, try the makhni chicken first tandoored, then finished in a buttery tomato sauce. Or, if you prefer your curries hot, the fiery lamb vindaloo.

The Tandoor is proud of its extensive vegetarian menu and the special thali amounts to a mini-feast. Not to be missed, mildly spiced navrattan curry of nine different vegetables cooked with nuts and cream. Cool off with a mint-flavored yogurt raitha or sample one of the syrupy and satisfying Indian sweets from the trolley. There is also a daily buffet luncheon that offers unlimited opportunities for the greedy at moderate prices.

Tandoor is a worthy and competently run restaurant with food that won't set you afire. Nor will it burn a hole in your pocket. About $20 with a sobering goblet of lassi.

## 10/20
### Toscana
**246 E. 54th St.**
**371-8144**
*Lunch and dinner Mon. to Fri. until 10:30 P.M.; Sat. dinner only until 11:00 P.M.; closed Sun. All major credit cards*
Italian

At first glimpse, this small, bright, frill-free dining room with the staff busy preparing pasta in chafing dishes among the tables, seems a place where serious eaters could find good northern Italian cooking. Looks deceive. The fettucine with clams and the trenette al pesto (actually the same fettucine) are much too salty, and the garlic is too strong in the pesto. The paglia e fieno, green and white pasta, is gooey with too much cheese. The veal in the veal piccata is tough. A poached bass is flaky, the broth well flavored, but the accompanying mussels and clams in their shells are overcooked.

The desserts—except for the excellent zuccotto cake—are pedestrian. Does the cannoli have to be so soggy in what purports to be a fine eating establishment? Italian wines start at $14, and are generally modestly priced. What is the Riserva Ducale Oro, 1949, doing on this list at $235? The quality of northern Italian restaurants has been improving in New York. Do Toscana's habituees know they can do better elsewhere for about the same $35 per person that they pay here?

## 12/20
### Les Tournebroches
**153 E. 53rd St.**
**(Citicorp Center)**
**935-6029**
*Lunch and dinner daily until 10:30 P.M.; closed Sun. All major credit cards*
French (provincial)

In New York's frenetic restaurant world, almost anything is possible. Lower prices at dinner than at lunch? Yes, at Charles Chevillot's small restaurant (seats 65) in the Citicorp Center, which features meat and fish grilled on an open hearth in the dining area.

The credit card crowd at lunch can afford a veal chop ($17), a filet mignon ($18), or a rack of lamb for two ($38); and grilled swordfish ($11). By contrast, at dinner there are a la carte entrees at reasonable prices that don't even appear on the luncheon menu: chopped sirloin ($5.50), chicken Calvados ($8), brochette of fish ($7.75) or of beef ($8.50). Furthermore, there is a fixed-price dinner menu at $8.50 that includes soup, roast chicken or grilled fish or mixed grill, salad, and coffee! "Well," says personable Sophie, who manages the entreprise for M.

Chevillot, "we have a completely different clientele in the evening." And a lot smarter, too. The main courses come hot from the fire at dinner as they do at lunch, the fruit tarts made on the premises are equally good at either meal, the carafe of wine at $9.50 in the evening is better than some estate-bottled imports costing twice as much, and the service is better if anything in the evening, when there is not quite so much of a rush.

**11/20**

## Trumpets
**Grand Hyatt: 42nd St. (between Park and Lexington Aves.)**
**883-1234**
*Lunch Mon. to Fri.; dinner Mon. to Sat. until 11:00 P.M.; reservation recommended; jacket required*
*All major credit cards*
Continental (nouvelle)

No need to trumpet the opening of the so-called "paradise of nouvelle cuisine." It would seem that the interior decorator has more talent than the chef. Without overdoing it, but using very attractive materials (wood paneling, beveled mirrors, brown velvet upholstery, a subtle pink ceiling that goes well with the brick-colored rug), he has given this somewhat sad room an elegant touch of art deco. The quality of the cooking, unfortunately, is no higher than the chairs, which are so low that one is tempted to ask for a telephone book. Wanting to appear à la mode, the kitchen has a fling with nouvelle cuisine: for example, placing a few slices of kiwi fruit onto a tarragon chicken that is of good quality, but whose sauce is too highly seasoned; or thinking it fashionable to serve turnips raw; and forcing a marriage of tough, insipid asparagus with too salty Westphalia ham, all of which is drowned in hollandaise sauce. Nor did we find the fried wild mushroom omelet to be a soaring triumph of nouvelle cuisine. True, the attractive brunette who served us in black pants and bow tie politely warned, "Don't order that, it's not very good!" But, regrettably, she neglected to mention that the oeufs à la neige—strangely resembling cottage cheese—is the world's worst. There remained, to save the meal from being a complete disaster, an honorable fillet of red snapper with watercress, a good bittersweet chocolate mousse, and excellent coffee. The plates, white with a thick burnt-siena border, are exquisite. It's a pity they put food on them. $30–$50.

# West 34th to 59th Streets

**7/20**

## Algonquin Hotel
**59 W. 44th St.**

Rumor has it that the food at the Algonquin is bad. This information is absolutely erroneous. In fact, it is *terrible*. Old, limp salads, sticky spaghetti, rubbery meats—the

**840-6800**
*Lunch and dinner daily until
1:00 A.M.; closed Sun. evening
AE, DC, CB, V*
Continental

desserts are quite a lot better, especially a good coffee cake—these are the gastronomic pleasures that await you at this once famous meeting place for writers and journalists (the *New Yorker's* offices are close by). Since the paneled Oak Room and the Rose Room, in theory open for dinner after the theater, played such an important part in the New York intellectual scene of yesteryear (Dorothy Parker, Robert Benchley, and Alexander Woollcott held their famous literary lunches at the Algonquin), we recommend that it be transformed into a museum, and its waiters, who are quick to get aggressive, into wax statues.

**10/20**

# American Charcuterie

**51 W. 52nd St.**
**751-5152**
*Lunch and dinner daily until
1:00 A.M.; closed Sun.
All major credit cards*
Continental

"A table for twelve-thirty? No, be here at twelve-twenty." At the American Charcuterie, a reservation is no joking matter, and thus, at twelve-twenty on the dot, we punched in like workers at a factory. It's a luxurious factory to be sure, at the foot of the CBS Building, and with its tall granite columns, it looks more like a posh bank than a restaurant. This used to be The Ground Floor, one of New York's most "in" spots fifteen years ago, decorated by the Finnish master Saarinen. It has a glacial grandiosity about it, but the crowds of people manage to warm up this immense freezer. Our preparations notwithstanding, it was of course necessary to wait in line a good quarter of an hour and, after we had identified ourselves at least three times, we were finally admitted into the Holy of Holies.

In New York, charcuterie is an ultrachic word, but it is no more than a word. If you come here hoping to drink in the heady odor of spicy pork sausages, you might as well spare yourself the trouble. Here, like everywhere else, you'll dine on sandwiches—fairly good ones—hamburgers, eggs Benedict, or a poor imitation of a salade Niçoise. Seated at a table no bigger than a handkerchief, elbows tucked in at our sides, we did our best to swallow an indefinable sort of quiche, which could almost have smothered the chef's remorse, and a slice of swordfish that tasted like blotting paper, garnished with ultrahard green beans that made us wish we'd brought a drum. A piece of cheesecake to top it all off, and you're stuffed.

As we got up to leave, we recalled the immortal phrase of that famous critic, James Beard, who boasted of having eaten at the American Charcuterie "the best chicken soup in my life." It must be a sad life. . . .

**8/20**

# Bangkok Cuisine

**885 Eighth Ave.**
**(52nd–53rd Sts.)**
**581-6370**
*Lunch and dinner daily until
11:30 P.M.; Sun. until 10:00 P.M.*

This long-established Thai restaurant has a rather tired and tacky air, its gloomy decor reminiscent of some Oriental flea-market. The food, too, with a few exceptions, seems depressingly lackluster.

Overcooked pork saté sticks, with a sauce like sweetened peanut butter, were followed by mee krob, usually a crisp delight of deep-fried noodles and shrimps

*AE, V, MC*
Thai

in a subtle sauce: the Bangkok's offering resembled a bad breakfast cereal, flabby and overly sweet. On the credit side were the prawn patties (tod mun pla), fresh and not too chewy, with a sharp relish of cucumber, and an absolutely superb chef's special, gai yang, moist but crunchy nuggets of chicken with a garlicky crust. These were garnished with coriander and served with a wonderful sauce—a blend of chili, vinegar, sugar, and garlic that had almost the color and flavor of an apricot purée.

After that, nothing else was quite up to scratch—the frogs' legs with basil (gob pad bai gra prou) had jumped once too often and were like old leather (no taste of basil either). The nam sod, a dish of minced pork, astringent with lime and outrageously over-gingered, was not improved by half a pound of raw onions as a garnish. The chicken with "Port Winee" sauce was not a great success either.

Obviously the thing here is to stick to the chef's specials of the day—he seems to be bored stiff with everything else on the menu, and may well be assigning them to a lesser menial. Considering New York's current love affair with Thai food, and that so many good new places are coming along, the Bangkok Cuisine needs to look to its laurels. About $12 with tea or a Thai beer.

## 12/20
## Le Biarritz
**325 W. 57th St.**
**245-9467**
*Lunch and dinner daily until 10:30 P.M.; Sat. for dinner only; closed Sun.*
*AE, DC, V*
French (classical)

The Lincoln Center area is not famous for good restaurants. Le Biarritz is an exception. Here, you can still enjoy a solid, if not sensational, three-course French meal for $15, plus wine and tip. This might include a seafood crêpe nicely browned under the broiler, frogs legs with the right amount of garlic (for most people), a fruit tart and coffee (espresso is an extra $1.30). There are daily specials in the $15 range, such as soft-shell crabs, grilled bass, and roast lamb. There is a list of wines on the menu and some extraordinary values, a Pommard at $22.50 to name just one, and for only $10.25 you can order a Muscadet or a Beaujolais. If you wish to explore the house's wine cellar further, ask for the separate, more complete wine list.

Copper pans and paraphernalia of the French countryside adorn the walls. These are comfortable surroundings and the service is professional. At these inflation-resistant prices, Le Biarritz has to be one of the best values in town, especially at a five-minute walk from Lincoln Center.

## 15 🍲
## The Bombay Palace
**30 W. 52nd St.**
**541-7777**
*Lunch and dinner daily*

It's hard to believe this place is only one-and-a-half years old, so mellow and well established does it look, what with its spice-brown walls and an impenetrable gloom, unrelieved even by candlelight. The entrance—just opposite "21"—is a heavy, metal-studded door behind

*until 11:00 P.M.*
*All major credit cards*
Indian

which looms a bearded Sikh of intimidating size. Doorman or bouncer? In fact he's just a pussycat, and spends most of his time chatting with the prettier female diners.

The food here is quite exceptional, some of the best Indian cuisine we've encountered, delicate yet sophisticated with a marvelous spectrum of contrasting flavors. After a creamy lamb pasanda with yogurt and almonds we had a vegetarian dish, mattar paneer—little squares of rather chewy homemade cottage cheese braised with peas, onion and tomato. The light, puffy onion kulcha, an Indian bread stuffed with onions and dried mangoes, made a great accompaniment. Best of all was an astonishing butter chicken, marinated in yogurt, ginger, garlic, and cloves, rubbed with cumin and cardamom and semi-roasted in a clay tandoor oven before being finished in cream. It was the perfect blend of sweet, hot, and savory, and not once did we find ourselves reaching for the relish tray.

After all this we had no room for the barbecued tandoori dishes, which looked most impressive, carried aloft by waiters on sizzling platters. We tried instead three superb sweets—a homemade ice cream with nuts and saffron, little spheres of pearly cottage cheese in cool, sweetened milk (rasmalai), and the deep golden gulab jamun, a sort of miniature rum-baba in rose-water syrup.

There's a buffet upstairs at lunchtime—eat all you want of curries, salads, or grills for $7.95—or you can sit at the bar and nibble on Oriental finger-food, samosas, pakoras, and the like. If you drink, say, a Tavel rosé, which suits this type of food very well, a meal will cost you about $30—or $25 with a glass of chilled yogurt and rose-water.

## 11/20
# Brittany du Soir
**800 Ninth Ave.**
**(53rd St.)**
**265-4820**
*Lunch Mon. to Fri.; dinner Mon. to Sat. until 10:00 P.M.*
*AE*
French (provincial)

Shortly after the end of World War II, Marie and Yves Seveneant opened Café Brittany on the west side of Ninth Avenue between 53rd and 54th Streets. Crew members from the French liners, which then berthed regularly at Hudson River piers nearby, and a generation of young New Yorkers seeking hearty French food at fair prices, kept the place jumping from the very start. Eventually, Mr. and Mrs. Seveneant opened an annex across the Avenue to handle the overflow—the present Britanny du Soir.

Today, 36 years later, Mr. Seveneant has died and the original restaurant is closed, but Mrs. Seveneant, her son, and a granddaughter carry on. The menu has hardly changed and some of the original costumed waitresses (smiling grandmothers now) are on hand. The value is as good as ever: coq au vin, boeuf bourguignon, and poulet à l'estragon at $8.25, tournedos and entrecôte at $14. A giant carafe of lusty red wine is $10; a smaller one $5.

At lunch there are the button-down collar males with their slender, chic female colleagues from the TV studios on West 57th Street. At dinner, the crowd is different, perhaps a bit older and more subdued. They have come some distance to eat and drink heartily in this outpost of French Brittany, with its broad-beamed ceiling and prints of regional French costumes.

**11/20**
## Café Un, Deux, Trois
**123 W. 44th St.**
**354-4148**
*Lunch and dinner daily until 2:00 A.M.*
*AE, V, MC*
French (provincial)

An American, Billy Murs, and two Frenchmen, Georges Guenassian and Gérard Blanés, got together around five years ago to open this brasserie, whose decor is vaguely reminiscent of that of Paris' La Coupole. The spot is highly fashionable, and serves some six hundred meals daily in a very fun, absolutely New York atmosphere. The welcome is friendly, the service rapid, and the cooking isn't dishonest if you stick to a bowl of (good) lentil soup—unless you prefer a salad with blue cheese dressing, described as, "au bleu de Brest" (sic)—steak and french fries, or sirloin grilled with herbs, and finish off with a chocolate mousse or a strawberry charlotte. Cooked from beginning to end by a Thai chef.

**14**
## La Caravelle
**33 W. 55th St.**
**586-4252**
*Lunch and dinner daily until 10:30 P.M.; closed Sun.; jacket and tie required*
*All major credit cards*
French (classical)

For over twenty years a saloon for the Kennedys, Marlene Dietrich, and the Duke of Windsor, La Caravelle enjoys the unanimous respect and esteem of its guests as well as New York critics. Therefore we won't be the slightest bit offensive about this monument to Francomania. Its setting is pleasant and well lit, with frescoes in the colors of the French flag; its staff is plentiful, well trained, and efficient; its atmosphere is of old money; its management is a memorial to Henri Soulé who, in the 1940s, founded haute cuisine in New York, of which La Caravelle is one of the last surviving altars. (Roger Fessaguet, the smiling former chef, is now a part of the management.)

You will doubtless have gathered that we are not overly impressed by haute cuisine. We launched the nouvelle, and we have a distinct preference for simpler, lighter fare. It's undeniable, though, that at La Caravelle the haute is prepared with the greatest attention, without excessive pomp (but with too much sauce). Going over the menu, we noted a few dishes whose simplicity enraptured us, especially as they are all prepared with admirable ingredients. Finally lingering doubts whether American oysters really do come from the ocean, or whether Maine lobster (lightly cooked) has any flavor, will be dispelled. The crab with a gribiche sauce, grilled veal steak, baby salmon with vegetables, and the superb roast veal are convincing. And on the whole, despite the slightly precious, artificial aspect of the cooking (a pink seafood terrine), the overwhelming sauces (sweetbreads with snails) and the somewhat aberrant garnishes (green beans mixed with rice to accompany a quite ordinary salmon mousse), modern cooking doesn't suffer too badly at the hands of Chef Moisan: the scallops in puff pastry with tarragon, or bass with cucumber, for example. Not to mention the magnificent desserts, the superb French wines, and the majestic bill (about $70 per person).

**11/20**
## Century Café
**132 W. 43rd St.**
**398-1988**
*Lunch and dinner daily, until*
*2:00 A.M.; bar open until 4:00 A.M.*
*AE, V, MC*
American

Only time will tell if the proprietors were right to settle near Times Square instead of a fashionable district like Columbus Avenue. They have, at any rate, done the decor rather well: consisting of a large staircase, loggia, black ceiling, bare white walls, and an old Loew's marquee over the bar, it's supposed to evoke Hollywood in the thirties. Charming waitresses bring you dishes almost too huge to get through, although they're of very honest quality. We aren't certain that the carpaccio, the salad of smoked duck and ham, tartare smoked salmon, the open-face sliced London broil, the New York shell steak, the grilled lamb with sorrel, and the praline cheesecake are really the legitimate offspring of American nouvelle cuisine, as the owners seem to think, but at any rate they are carefully and fairly well done.

**10/20**
## Charley O's
**33 W. 48th St.**
**(Rockefeller Center)**
**582-7141**
*Lunch and dinner daily*
*until midnight; closed Sun.;*
*reservation required*
*All major credit cards*
American/Irish

The full name of this establishment is "Charley O's Bar and Grill and Bar." The repetition in the name tells all. There are green borders on the straightforward meat-and-potato, corned-beef-and-cabbage menu. Framed photos of the great (W.C. Fields) and the notorious (ex-Mayor Jimmy Walker) hang on the walls. The cramped booths are separated by mahogany and etched-glass partitions, and there is a drinking man's bar where a drinking man can get a huge drinking man's sandwich of roast beef after downing some clams or oysters with his beer chaser.

At lunch, this is a busy and noisy hangout in the heart of Rockefeller Center. Try the prawns in beer batter. Service is good. At night, you can park your car free next door, eat an uncomplicated (and undistinguished) meal, and walk to the theater. In New York, that adds up to quite a plus.

**10/20**
## Copenhagen
**68 W. 58th St.**
**688-3690**
*Lunch and dinner daily until*
*10:30 P.M.; closed Sun.; jacket;*
*reservation suggested*
*All major credit cards*
Scandinavian

The charm of Copenhagen, now in its 36th year in New York, is in the hospitality of the management, the friendliness of the service, and the intimacy of the small bar with its handful of tables. In the dining room to the rear, Danish koldt bord, elsewhere known as smorgasbord, is the main attraction, although what is offered is not by any means exceptional. Selections include various preparations of herrings, combination salads, cold roasts of beef and ham, sections of roast chicken and duck, and fresh fruits in season. Koldt bord, despite what you might suppose, is not confined to cold dishes. This buffet offers hot items such as meatballs, small frankfurters, and baked beans, which do not improve with time spent in their respective chafing dishes. But you can stuff yourself and enjoy a rich dessert and coffee for $11.75 at lunch and $16.75 at dinner, when gravlax is one of the added choices. For dessert the lemon mousse and the Danish apple cake, a sort of brown betty, are tasty enough. Akvavit (the bottle encased in a block of ice) is the accepted drink with the koldt bord, to be followed by Carlsberg Beer. The wine list has acceptable bottles in the $10–$14 range. For those who do not care for the buffet, there is a menu of Scandinavian and other more universal dishes.

The ambience is pleasant, but regrettably the same cannot be said for everything that comes from the kitchen. A broiled halibut, listed as a special at $9.75, was overcooked and dry, the vegetables overcooked and too long in water. But several akvavits and beer chasers will ease your way through the main courses to the desserts. They will leave a good taste in your mouth. You might even want to return.

13 ♡
**Gallagher's**
228 W. 52nd St.
245-5336
*Lunch and dinner daily*
*until midnight*
*DC, CB, MC, V*
Steakhouse

Formerly a speakeasy in the roaring twenties. Jerome Brody has retained the authentic atmosphere of this New York institution with polished wood and yellowing photographs of little remembered actors. People from the worlds of business, sports, and journalism dine on magnificent pieces of beef that are aged right where you can see them, in a large windowed refrigerator near the entrance. Forget about cuisine—Gallagher's is the great steak and roast beef roundup, a paradise for anyone who really loves meat. Start with a few oysters, finish with a slice of cheesecake, and don't get riled if the waiters have eyes only for their regular customers. It's up to you to become one.

11/20
**Keen's Chop House**
72 W. 36th St.
947-3636
*Lunch and dinner daily until*
*12:30 A.M.; closed Sun.;*
*reservation required for lunch*
*All major credit cards*
American

Founded in 1885, this extremely picturesque English country inn located in the theater district has just been resuscitated, following several years of abandonment and its closing in 1976. Good news, as few places have managed to keep alive the good old days atmosphere that reigns here. A visit is a must, if only to see the extraordinary collection of 72,000 clay pipes hanging in clusters from the ceiling, the photographs of actors famous in the '20s, and charming Early American paintings on the walls.

The proprietors have hired a chef about whom we've heard a lot of good things. Unfortunately, the meal we were served did not allow us to verify whether his reputation is justified. The capellini with smoked salmon and rosemary had a strangely Chinese look and an international blandness, the ballotine of duck was fairly good but rather greasy, the grilled lamb chops only acceptable (the house specialty, grilled mutton chops, was not available), and the chocolate mousse undeserving of any particular comment. Be that as it may, Keen's merits inclusion on any true New Yorker's itinerary. The Old Taproom, where a wood fire burns in the winter, specializes in seafood, and there's also a large dining room upstairs.

## 14 ⌂
# Kitcho
**22 W. 46th St.**
**575-8880**
*Lunch Mon. to Fri.; dinner*
*Sun. to Fri. until 10:30 P.M.;*
*reservation required*
*AE, DC, CB*
Japanese

Set in a busy midtown side street, the entrance to Kitcho is so demure you'd hardly notice it. The inside is equally understated, with austere panels of black, white, and orange, but this must be the most uncompromisingly genuine Japanese restaurant in New York.

Expect no giggling geishas here—you will be under the wing of stern but benevolent governess-figures, ladies of a certain age who, like Nanny, will see that you eat what's good for you. When, in a fit of childish petulance, we insisted on yam cakes (expecting something golden and fluffy), we got a dark-brown slithery substance smelling like ten-day-old mushrooms. The red caviar (which we like) came with white horseradish, (which we don't) but there was no escape. "You eat it like *this*" our mentor said firmly, wrenching the chopsticks from our hands and making a mix of it. Again she was right, the contrast was superb.

Our main dish, Kushi Katzu, was unusually filling for this type of ethereal cuisine—morsels of pork, pepper, and mushroom breaded and deep-fried on skewers, a satisfying contrast of firm, soft, and crunchy textures. It came with a saucer of what looked suspiciously like A-1 sauce, but may have been something more exotic. If you keep your eyes peeled you may spot other tables enjoying interesting oddities not on the menu—hot rocks, for instance, sealing up beef or seafood in their own juices, or spidery soft-shell crabs. You devour them, crisped on the griddle, claws and all, the very essence of crabbiness. Watch out for the little white mound on the side—it's not salt but M.S.G. Our meal was crowned by a soothing hot-pot called to-banyaki, a black iron casserole with pieces of chicken—some more desirable than others—in a sublime, seasame-scented broth.

At lunch a set meal is good value at $9—in the evening you can splurge on a feast of the chef's favorite delicacies, about $25–$50 dollars for a seven- to ten-course banquet. Toshio Morimoto is both owner and chef here, and "Kitcho" means good omen—need we say more?

## 14 ⌂
# Lavin's
**23 W. 39th St.**
**921-1288**
*Lunch and dinner Mon. to*
*Fri. until 9:00 P.M.;*
*reservation required*
*All major credit cards*
International (nouvelle)

Mr. Lavin, a former lawyer who has also had experience in ready-to-wear, restored this Midtown club, and its large, severe room with carved panels adorning the walls houses some of the most promising of the new generation of young American chefs. Mr. Lavin looks for promising but only perfunctorily-trained cooks, then shows them his methods. Much of what they know was learned from cookbooks. We'd like to know which books our discreet cooks studied. At any rate, it's certain that Mr. Lavin has succeeded in creating a synthesis of French, Italian, Chinese, and Japanese cuisine, variously drawing inspiration from these traditions but each time creating unique dishes where the flavors are mixed with rare tact and subtlety. Their presentation alone raises them to the realm of art. Try the soup of the day, cooked as in bygone days on the farm; the bamboo steamer of fresh vegetables, served with two dipping sauces; the carpaccio Gold (a stunning salad of onions, slivers of raw prime shell steak, accompanied by mushrooms, Gruyère, rice, and watercress); the fresh mussels in white wine with saffron, served on shreds of red cabbage with a salad of rice and marinated scallops; the warm apple tart, flavored with cinnamon, and the grapefruit creme de cassis with vodka. You'll be charmed by the delicacy and flavor of the cooking, which is sometimes a touch naive, but generally convincing. Lavin's now houses the American branch of Paris' Academie du Vin. Wine-tasting courses are offered, and diners can sample fourteen different wines by the glass.

## 10/20
## Lou G. Siegel
**209 W. 38th St.**
**921-4433**
*Lunch and dinner daily*
*until 8:45 P.M.;*
*reservation suggested*
*All major credit cards*
Kosher

This kosher restaurant serves no dairy products and advertises that it is under the continuous supervision of the Union of Orthodox Jewish Congregations of America. Nonetheless, the menus at lunch and dinner include a broad range of conventional dishes such as roast turkey, veal and lamb chops, calf's liver, roast chicken, omelets, and broiled fish, as well as desserts. Entree prices at dinner are in the $12–$16 range, but there is a four-course set meal with several entree choices which is better value. For example, you can order an appetizer, soup, prime rib, and dessert for $19.95.

Regrettably, the standard of preparation is mediocre at best. Fish and meats are apt to be overcooked and dry. The delicatessen-type meat sandwiches, hot and cold, are generally good, but it is troublesome that the food overall is not better. The restaurant is a garment-district institution, and the main dining room is spacious and comfortable enough for relaxed dining. The founder's goal in 1917 "to establish an institution which would be a pride to Judaism" hasn't been achieved yet. How long must New Yorkers wait?

## Luchow's
**1633 Broadway**
**(50th-51st Sts.)**
German

As we went to press, Luchow's was about to move uptown to the theater district. This huge German restaurant has been a New York institution for a hundred years on East 14th Street, once the hub of the city's commercial and cultural life. But with New York's inexorable push north, the 14th Street area has deteriorated and taken on some of the squalid appearance of the old Bowery. Hence, the move.

Luchow's menu at 14th Street featured the usual German fare (sauerbraten, roast goose, game in season) prepared with a heavy hand in generous portions. As eating habits changed under the influence of Oriental and French nouvelle, Luchow's stubbornly stuck to thick flour sauces and giant portions that were the vogue 100 years ago.

Uptown, Luchow's promises to recreate the atmosphere of 14th Street (dark-wood paneling, mirrors, chandeliers) and to make some concessions to the revolution in eating tastes (but they will also serve the old standbys).

Time will tell whether Luchow's can make it into the 20th century.

## 15 🍽

## Maurice
**119 W. 56th St.**
**(Hotel Parker**
**Meridien)**
**245-7788**
*Lunch Mon. to Fri.; dinner nightly*
*until 11:30 P.M.; formal;*
*reservation required*
*All major credit cards*
French (nouvelle)

You can't accuse the Meridien chain of being short on ambition. In Houston, Boston, Montreal, and New York, it has brought in the greatest French chefs to train the cooks, establish menus, and control quality at regular intervals. In New York, Alain Senderens of the famous Parisian restaurant L'Archestrate was entrusted with the supervision of Maurice, a restaurant set a half-level above the hotel's main floor, in a decor of light wood, mirrors, and rugs, which may lack gaiety but not elegance. Senderens developed one of New York's most imaginative and exciting menus, in which you'll find some of L'Archestrate's most popular dishes, like the hot oysters with curry and spinach, ragoût of scallops in rose butter, admirable lobster with spinach and watercress in a vanilla sauce, pheasant in pastry with pears and spinach, émincés of lamb in curry cream sauce, and exquisite roast pigeon in a confit of leeks. It would obviously be unreasonable to expect that this ultra-refined cooking be a carbon copy of what Senderens himself prepares for the forty fortunates who dine at his Paris restaurant. Also, working conditions in a large hotel are not at all like those in a small, family-run restaurant where no more than eight people work in the kitchen: mistakes and failures are likelier to occur than in the smaller place. In addition, this type of cooking is extraordinarily complex, and every detail counts. Still, Christian Delouvrier, the chef, offers a faithful and often enough a superb version of Senderens' work, even if he does err at times (putting, for example, too many breadcrumbs on the exquisite goujonnettes of lamb napped in a perfect béarnaise sauce, or undercooking a chicken that a few more minutes would have made superb). Be that as it may, the talent is there, and Maurice's success is proof positive that it was high time nouvelle cuisine was given a place in a large hotel. We mustn't forget to mention that the pastries (raspberry millefeuille, caramelized pears with strawberry syrup, coffee charlotte with a chocolate sauce flavored with cinnamon) are among the best in New York, and that the choice of wines—mostly French—is first-rate. $22.50 at lunch. A la carte about $40–$50 with wine.

## 10/20
## Moshe Peking
**40 W. 37th St.**
**594-6501**

When the late Martin Soshtain's mother cooked vegetables, she boiled them to rags—"you don't touch them till they're dead," she told young Martin—which is probably why, after escaping from the Rabbinate, he

*Lunch and dinner Sun. to Thurs.
until 10:00 P.M.; dinner only Sat.
(one hour after sunset); closed Fri.
All major credit cards*
Chinese Kosher

opened a Chinese Kosher restaurant. Set in the middle of Manhattan's garment district, it soon became popular with his orthodox friends. After all, if you've been up to your ears in knishes ever since Momma first slapped a yarmulke on your curls, spicy Chinese food and undercooked vegetables must come as a revelation from Mount Sinai.

Substitution proved easy—veal for pork, seabass for shrimp, pastrami for ham—and they already had the chicken soup with dumplings. There are a few jokes on the menu, such as "pho-nee shrimp with mock lobster sauce," but on the whole it's as authentic as most uptown Chinese restaurants—apart, that is, from a pu-pu platter that lives up to its name.

The chef comes from Nanking via the Catskills, and we enjoyed his hot-and-sour soup, fried dumplings and sea-spiced beef, but, as in all the main dishes, the meat was not cut finely enough—apparently if it is it gets sent back. In a community not exactly renowned for anorexia small delicate portions are seen as a threat to survival—so expect to be overfed.

There's also an American-Jewish menu for parties, and one suspects a certain amount of commuting goes on— the meatball that starts life on a bed of kasha may end up bathed in sweet-and-sour sauce on the flaming pu-pu platter. Super modern decor with an illuminated plastic tree; great comfort; and good service under the eye of John Chang, a most friendly and efficient manager. If you see a burly figure in a dark hat leaving the kitchen with a large briefcase, don't worry—it's only the rabbi, who has just completed his weekly checkup for the Beth Din. From $10 at lunch, about $20 at dinner.

**11/20**
## Orsini's
**41 W. 56th St.**
**757-1698**
*Lunch and dinner daily
until 1:00 A.M.; closed Sun;
jacket and tie required
DC, CB, MC, V*
Italian

"Right this way, Mr. Kennedy," said the maitre d'hôtel to us with a bow, as we turned the stairs. It was intended for someone else, another client famous like so many, who come here to snack on a salad and to nibble at a few noodles. The place is delightful, especially on the second floor, with black brick walls, paintings, delicate antiques, and tiled tables that are the repositories of very uneven food. You won't risk anything with the simply cooked pasta (remarkable with mushrooms), whose last touches are ostentatiously administered at your table, or the risotto, or any of the salads. But despite a delicate garlic butter sauce the scampi are distinctly tough and not overly fresh, and the osso buco is rather like steel dipped in canned tomato sauce. No matter—you'll spend a highly elegant evening over a glass of Soave, two tables away from an up-and-coming politician, or a diva coiffed with a feathered Stetson.

**12/20**
## Patsy's
**236 W. 56th St.**
**247-3491**

John Mazzola, the very discriminating president of Lincoln Center, visits regularly to satisfy his nostalgia for spaghetti marinara, homemade ravioli, and tripe in tomato sauce.

*Lunch and dinner daily
until 10:45 P.M.; Fri. and
Sat. until 11:45 P.M.
AE, DC, CB, V*
Italian

All the garlic-scented odors of southern Italy waft through the warm, noisy rooms of this down-to-earth restaurant, which has managed to hold onto its youthfulness as well as the authenticity of a cuisine that is not particularly light, but very colorful. Every day, seven different specialties are offered in addition to the standard menu, including lentil soup, veal with green peppers, and rigatoni, none of which would leave the divas and tenors of the Metropolitan Opera weak from hunger in the middle of the third act. About $25, with wine.

**8/20**
## Pearl's
**38 W. 48th St.**
**586-1060**
*Lunch and dinner daily until
10:00 P.M.; no lunch Sat. or Sun.
No credit cards*
Chinese

What is it that makes all New York run to this Chinese restaurant, this pale corridor behind a concealed door where television and advertising people are herded together beneath the watchful but aloof eye of Mrs. Pearl, a Chinese lady with a wizened face? It's certainly not in order to see or be seen—the stingy lighting makes women look ugly (and the food wan)—or for the setting, reminiscent of a tennis club locker room, or for the joys of conversation—you'd think you were in a suburb-bound train at rush hour, and anyway, they punctiliously throw you out after an hour. And it's positively not for the food, which used to be good, but has completely lost its way. We had heard about the dim sum: there was only one, and it was heavy, greasy, dense, and tasteless. And the famous won-ton soup is, yes, a meal in itself, but a bad meal, made of different meats boiled in the taste of tallow, thick won-ton, and (good) vegetables in a (good) bouillon. The sautéed shrimp with broccoli tasted of a burnt frying pan. That leaves, among other dishes, the expensive lobster in egg sauce; the inevitable yook soang, a mixture of pork and water chestnuts wrapped in a lettuce leaf; the beef with lotus, rescued by a curious, tough vegetable in the shape of a motorcycle wheel; and the mushrooms and snow peas, which are always exquisite. Perhaps they come for the wine, you suggest? There's nothing but a sad Chablis. Or for the service? It's both apathetic and hectic. Perhaps for the prices; or maybe people are turned on by Sino-masochism.

**12/20**
## Pierre au Tunnel
**250 W. 47th St.**
**582-2166**
*Lunch and dinner daily until
11:45 P.M.; closed Sun.
AE*
French (provincial)

One of New York's least expensive and least known French restaurants, although its owner, Pierre Pujol, has devoted himself over the past 35 years to making good French provincial cooking known in America. No doubt he lacks the flair for publicity or the whiff of inventiveness—or both—that have made so many other chefs famous.

Nonetheless, his basement restaurant near Times Square is always full, and there's a family-like atmosphere among the regulars who meet in this small room decorated like a hunting lodge, with a scene from a deer hunt adorning the fireplace, bare brick walls, artificial beams, and batteries of copper pots.

The menu itself stays well within the limits of French

gastronomy as it's conceived in foreign lands: homemade pâté, mussels ravigote, split pea soup, coq au vin, tripes à la mode de Caeu, calf's head à la vinaigrette, and the like. It's all essentially very honest, but unfortunately Grandma's style of cooking requires attentiveness and long periods at the stove—which a New York restaurant owner, even a well-intentioned one, can hardly permit himself.

That said, the ingredients are of good quality, the portions enormous, and this 100 percent French establishment (including waitresses) is extremely pleasant. Excellent French wines (between $15 and $20 per bottle) and a respectable filter coffee.

## 11/20
### Pongsri Thailand Restaurant
244 W. 46th St.
502-3392
*Lunch and dinner daily until 11:30 P.M.*
*AE, DC, CB*
Thai

Start with a crunchy Thai omelet filled with bean sprouts, peanuts, and fresh coconut, or fried shrimp patties, both served with a tangy cucumber sauce. There is also a mouth-watering dish of crispy rice noodles topped with tender butterfly prawns in a sweet-and-sour sauce. By contrast, beef saté was disappointing, the meat tough and tasteless. A Thai version of tripe and onions appeared on a bed of lettuce, but for sheer excellence don't miss the sliced charcoal-broiled steak, rolled in roasted ground rice and tossed in a lime juice, mint, and chili dressing. It takes a dish like this to explain the growing appeal of Thai cooking.

Curries should certainly be explored, as they differ substantially from their Indian counterparts. More than a dozen spice mixes figure in their preparation, and our medium-hot beef and coconut curry was excellent, fiery and subtle at the same time. It was accompanied by white rice served in an elegant silver tureen. After the curry it seemed a good idea to clear the palate with a chicken broth fragrant with preserved lemons, squash, and mushrooms.

Sweets include coconut sherbet and a rather daunting glazed banana fried whole in batter. Thai beer is excellent and wine is available. As we were leaving, a long-haired Thai pop group was seen moving in their instruments for the following night's dance (tangos and cha-chas are the rage, it appears). So if you are allergic to loud sounds, note that Thursdays, Fridays, and Saturdays are nights to avoid. $15 with Thai beer.

## 12/20
### Raga
57 W. 48th St.
757-3450
*Lunch: Mon. to Fri.; Dinner nightly until 11:15 P.M.; jacket and tie; reservation suggested*
*All major credit cards*
Indian

There's not much to say about the Raga. Its very grand, expensively decorated, quite pricey, and enormously dull. It has everything you would expect to find in such a milieu—carved wooden pillars, soft lighting, dark-suited captains, and ladies in floating saris. Musicians in white tunics sit scraping and twanging away on a raised platform—they're very loud, and it's great when they stop. The food?—Well, it's painstakingly prepared, but it doesn't exactly knock you out, or tickle your palate to tingling ecstasy—in a word, it's mediocre. Our first sampling of the tandoori bits and pieces was not spectacular. The chicken was fine, but the promised "morsels of baby lamb" were simply huge chunks of rather old sheep, with that unmistakable taste you sometimes encounter in Indian bazaars. As for the seafood, it just wasn't there. The two dishes we had particularly wanted to taste were the stuffed chicken, and the fabled lobster Malabar, "smothered in rare condiments from the Malabar Coast." Unfortunately one was no longer on the menu, and the other, though ordered, never arrived.

The nicest dish was a murg Hyderabadi, chicken in a sweetish curry sauce tasting of aniseed. Apart from that, the mutton with spinach was just that, the kofta lajavab was rather like a potato croquette, and the hot bread arrived puffy but soon went limp. The sweets—an Indian ice cream decorated with thin strips of beaten silver, and a confection of white curds in a cool spiced milk—were pleasant enough, if a bit grainy.

This is a great place for impressing visiting delegations or V.I.Ps, but it's not a load of fun, and the food just doesn't match up to the decor. Portions are not particularly large, so you won't satisfy your appetite at much under $28 a head, with wine.

## 12/20
## The Rainbow Room
**RCA Building, Rockefeller Plaza (49th-50th Sts.)**
*Dinner nightly until 1:00 A.M.; brunch on Sun.; formal*
*All major credit cards*
Continental

A place to dine and dance in a Hollywood movie setting perched on the 65th floor of one of Manhattan's most attractive skyscrapers. Hardened New Yorkers may sneer, but out-of-towners will be riveted. The perfect place to celebrate a golden wedding anniversary, especially if you're seated at a table near the bay windows that show the city lights mixed with the starry skies. All that's missing is the voice of Frank Sinatra crooning "Strangers in the Night." Not impossible, by the way—many great singers and jazz musicians have performed in the Rainbow Room. The mostly Italian waiters look after you with consideration, and serve an honest, if banal, cuisine (crab crêpes, lamb chops, duck à l'orange, and above all some very good desserts). A la carte, about $30 to $40.

## 15
## Raphael
**33 W. 54th St.**
**582-8993**
*Dinner Mon. to Fri. until 10:00 P.M.*
*AE, DC*
French (nouvelle)

You'll pay dearly for these pleasures, too dearly ($50 to $70). It's true that the very intimate setting (cozy, eggshell colored, with beams and reproductions of paintings by Raphael, and a small winter garden in the back), the professionalism of both the welcome (by one or the other of the co-owners), and the service, as well as the delicacy of the cuisine, all tend to make you indulgent. The cooking is as French and as nouvelle as possible—not yet perfect, but full of inventiveness and a freedom rare in New York. A superb jowl of salmon (lightly cooked) with marvelous truffles; a pleasant sole (American, with the taste of whiting) very well steamed on a bed of lettuce; a delicious rare magret of duck in honey (an amusing taste of beeswax) and the incomparable wild rice; and very pure grapefruit sherbet, with the superb Château Talbot '71, will make for a fairly memorable evening.

## 13 ♀
# René Pujol
**321 W. 51st St.**
**246-3023**
*Lunch and dinner daily until*
*11:30 P.M.; closed Sun.*
*All major credit cards*
French (provincial)

A sinister district, a decor that could have been taken from the suburbs of Toulouse in the '50s, and a menu that will bore you to death. Nevertheless, this is a good, small, New York French restaurant. Scattered here and there throughout the dining room, under the stuffed deer's head, the copper warming-pan, or the appliqué in sculpted wood, are two or three regulars, born and bred in the southwest of France. And in New York, what more could you ask for to make a place fashionable? Especially as the banality of the menu hides a style of cooking whose simplicity and good taste are absolutely successful. We should add that René Pujol is well connected with the great French chefs, and masters his art with skill. He offers shellfish salad, served with warm lobster claws and a julienne of vegetables; a very pleasant duck terrine containing chunks of duck; truffle dishes and foie gras mousse; superb lamb chops (a little overcooked); exquisite calf's liver of irreproachable quality sautéed with onions and good accompanying vegetables (unfortunately, the same ones with all the dishes); and an authentic beef bourguignon. Good French wines. Service is not overly cheerful, but it's pleasant and efficient.

## 9/20
# Romeo Salta
**30 W. 56th St.**
**246-5772**
*Lunch and dinner daily until*
*11:15 P.M.; closed Sun.*
*All major credit cards*
Italian

It is out of a sense of professional duty and in tribute to our New York colleagues that we carefully read their reviews and guidebooks. And we make a point, whenever they record an exciting "discovery," of visiting the place ourselves. It was thus that we wound up in this restaurant, which with five other establishments was awarded the highest rating in a guide brought up-to-date for 1981. What, we wonder, could have so misled our colleagues (other than the building's charming facade)? This was, it should be added, the same guide that put the Quilted Giraffe in last place. A spacious beige decor, service both remote and obsequious, a suburban clientele, and an immense menu filled with the banal Italian favorites: pasta swimming in floury, insipid sauces, scampi (large seemingly frozen shrimp) that would have been tasteless were it not for the excessive amounts of garlic used. Overwhelmed with disappointment, we fled, but not without leaving behind about $30 per person—which also paid for the butter, billed separately, that they forgot to use in the kitchen.

## 12/20
# The Russian Tea Room
**150 W. 57th St.**
**265-0947**
*Lunch and dinner daily until*
*12:30 A.M.; jacket required*
*All major credit cards*
Russian

It's always crowded, in part by beautiful women, avid readers of *Vogue,* in the large "Muscovite" room on the ground floor, where people are packed like herrings in a barrel. The upstairs has recently been redecorated, and offers more living space, but it's less lively. Don't bother to bring your Russian dictionary, or to mention that you've come because you particularly admire Dostoevsky—neither owners nor staff has the slightest idea what da or nyet might mean.

To what miracle then should we ascribe the fact that the cuisine has lost none of its original accents? Without losing a word of your neighbor's conversation, you will enjoy the best borscht in New York, as well as okroschka (a cold soup with sour cream and diced meat and cucumber), Pojarski veal cutlets, chicken Kiev, golubtze (stuffed cabbage), and Caucasian shashlik, which are none the worse off for having made it over the ocean. $25 to $35 with a carafe of white wine, but you can dine for less on a salad or even a sandwich.

### 10/20
### Sardi's
**234 W. 44th St.**
**221-8440**
*Lunch and dinner daily until midnight; jacket and tie recommended; reservations required on matinée days*
*All major credit cards*
Continental

There's nothing we could possibly say about this famous "star-studded" restaurant that you haven't already heard. All we can add is a small word of warning: if you want to be seated upstairs, on the left, in the Belasco Room, to be able to say hi to Barbra Streisand and Lauren Bacall, the simplest way is to come with them. The famous cannelloni with cheese, seafood crêpes, and veal scallopini in marsala won't be any better for their company, but they will be served with a noticeable increase in enthusiasm by veteran waiters who have experienced all the triumphs and disasters of innumerable Broadway opening celebrations. There's no point in dining here during normal hours, when Sardi's is just another mediocre restaurant.

### 7/20
### Sea Fare of the Aegean
**25 W. 56th St.**
**581-0540**
*Lunch and dinner daily until 11:00 P.M.*
*All major credit cards*
Seafood

The decor of this Greek seafood restaurant is supposedly modeled on the famous palace at Knossos, on Crete. It's too bad that the cooking isn't put safely under lock and key in some museum cabinet. It would have spared us the sorry task of masticating the Santorini shrimp covered with gluey cheese, and a red snapper exhausted by cruelly prolonged cooking. Frank Sinatra, we were told, patronizes this establishment, which for some reason we've not been able to fathom, has enjoyed a flattering reputation for many years. Someone else we won't ask for the names of his favorite restaurants.

### 13
### Seeda Thai
**204 W. 50th St.**
**586-4513**
*Lunch Mon. to Sat.; dinner daily until 11:00 P.M.*
*AE, MC, DC*
Thai

Those nostalgic for the pleasures of Bangkok come to this small restaurant two minutes from the theater district to enjoy all the flavors of Southeast Asia. The lemon grass soup is delicately spiced, the crisp-fried fish with ginger is perfectly cooked and seasoned, the chicken is served with a velvety, very aromatic coconut sauce, the mee krob (grilled noodles) are exquisite, and the beef saté quite successful, although the meat did not seem to be of the best quality. Rapid and smiling service, as is almost always the case in Thai restaurants.

### 9/20
### Shezan
**8 W. 58th St.**
**371-1414**

As the chef descended the few stairs that lead to this elegant and austere basement restaurant two minutes from the Plaza Hotel, a number of recipes and spices must

*Lunch Mon. to Fri.; dinner nightly until 10:45 P.M.; jacket and tie DC, CB, MC, V*
Indian/Pakistani

have accidentally fallen out of his turban. Indeed, there was little here to remind us of the delicacy, subtlety, and very authentic character of the cuisine as prepared at the original Shezan in London. It's not so bad that the menu has been shortened, but what was served really had very little flavor—neither the tandooris and lamb curries, nor the Kyberi chicken with fresh herbs, nor even the naans, an unleavened bread that is always exquisite at the British mother house. Whatever happened to the intoxicating odors of Indian cuisine, one of the most voluptuous in the world? You may be able to answer that for yourself—at least we could. As we went to the washroom, we were entranced and detained by a fabulous perfume of cinnamon, no doubt wafting in from the nearby kitchen where the chef was probably fixing his own lunch. We won't mention the service—it would be cruel to wake up the staff when they're sleeping so soundly.

11/20
# Siam Inn
**916 Eighth Ave.
(54th-55tSts.)**
*Lunch and dinner daily until 11:30 P.M.; no lunch Sun. AE, DC*
Thai

The cuisine of this recently opened, small Thai restaurant enjoys a reputation that is, in our opinion, excessive. Never in Bangkok have we seen pork curry with coconut milk served with lettuce and candied cherries! Anyway, the pork itself is much too tough, and although they prepare an exquisite chicken soup with lime juice and coconut milk, neither the king fish cake with cucumber sauce, nor the Thai pad (shrimp, rice, and broccoli), nor the chicken sautéed with ginger gave evidence of the powerful but subtle flavors that confer on Thai cuisine its very special character. Fresh herbs, lemon juice, and combinations of spices are not lacking, but you still get the impression that the chef is afraid he'll set New York's palates on fire—to the point that his pumpkin custard is perfectly tasteless. This timidity is of course regrettable, and we would have liked to try the dishes he prepares for himself—they certainly couldn't be any less authentic. We should add that the small establishment is impeccably maintained and very friendly, and that for $12 to $15 per person, with a rather bland tea, you won't regret a visit.

# Top of the Sixes
**666 Fifth Ave.
(53rd St.)
757-6662**
*Lunch and dinner daily until midnight*
*All major credit cards*
Continental

Connoisseurs come here on Sunday, when it's closed. To be perfectly honest, we haven't been back to this 39th floor panoramic restaurant for two years. The meal was high above New York, but far below our expectations. This time, at the last minute, our courage failed us. Mr. Stouffer, please forgive us.

12/20
# 21 Club
**21 W. 52nd St.
582-7200**

"Cooking at the 21 is irregular; sometimes it's bad, other times it's worse." A tired joke, recounted by a New Yorker who lunches there at least three times a week. His vision

*Lunch and dinner daily until midnight; closed Sun.; jacket and tie required*
*All major credit cards*
Continental/American

of hell (ours too, as we absolutely adore this institution) is not being able to visit the club. There are thousands of people in politics, finance, or showbiz, from high society and the underworld, whose lives will continue to be worth living as long as 21 remains open. As at Harry's Bar in Venice, and at Maxim's in Paris, people don't come here to eat, but to be seated. So what difference does it make if the crab tastes like cardboard, if the duck is cooked once too often, or if the 21 burger, exalted to the ranks of one of the house specialties, differs in no way from any ordinary hamburger except that it costs three times as much? Or, for that matter, if the gazpacho is honest, the crabs not badly done, or the roast beef juicy?

Anyway, it would be extremely inappropriate to serve excellent food here. Refined cuisine would either steal all the attention, which would have a disastrous effect on conversation, or more likely would go completely unnoticed, which would make the chef extremely unhappy.

The main problem, of course, is not the food, but getting into this former speakeasy, a pseudo-club that is open to everyone, but not just anyone. When the doorman informs you, "There's no room," you understand of course that what he really means is, "There's no room for people like you." But it would be most unusual if you didn't find among your friends or the concierges in the better hotels, someone who can get you into this sanctuary of the New York Good Old Days—even if it means accepting a table in the back room, the "17," nicknamed "Siberia" because that's where unfamiliar faces are deported. The "19" is infinitely more civilized, but the Holy of Holies is the "21," the first room you go through. Always full from morning to night, a setting of brownstone and polished wood where a faint whiff of Prohibition still lingers, despite the beautiful diamond-draped ladies and the very tanned gentlemen in tweed. Miniature planes and trucks are suspended from the ceiling above the solid mahogany bar, reproductions of private vehicles belonging to favored clients. From Kissinger to Nureyev to Sammy Davis, Jr., how many people figure on charming Sheldon Tannen's lists? Twenty thousand, some say, of whom about half have a private account (only those who merely sign the bills can consider themselves as truly belonging). The others will never be anything more than guests . . . Blue Point oysters, roast beef with roast potatoes, and a small crème au chocolat won't set you back more than $30, wine not included—but we should point out that the 21's wine cellar is a treasure trove, and contains most of the best wines and finest liqueurs from France.

13 ⌂
## Wood's
**148 W. 37th St.**
**564-7340**

This stylish (and often hectic) restaurant in the heart of the garment district offers some of New York's most interesting nouvelle cuisine. The setting is a bit stark, but

*Weekdays for lunch and dinner until 9:30 P.M.; reservations required*
*All major credit cards*
American (nouvelle)

attractive in a crisp, clean way. A bar topped with imitation marble greets you in the small vestibule, and you will probably have to push your way through the bar crowd to let the maitre d'hôtel know you have a reservation. Once seated, which can be awhile even though your reservation is confirmed, tables are close and the partitions hanging from the ceiling like so many theater curtains do little to reduce the noise level. The menu changes often; at our visits appetizers included shredded duck salad with ginger and wild rice; a seviche of salmon and sole; and a herbed, fried Brie cheese that, somehow or other, comes off. Main courses included some with an Oriental touch, but the chef is uninspired concerning the way the food should look on the plate, or for that matter the amount of food to put on it. An order of what is described as stir-fried chicken with broccoli and ginger was overwhelmed by the addition of no fewer than five other vegetables. Enough for two. Maybe three. But there is definite talent in the kitchen. The scallops (in season) are well seasoned with oregano and garlic, and the grilled fish is fresh and unusual with a sherry-soy dressing. There is a daily pasta and salad.

The wine list is adequate, with French, Italian, and Californian selections. Luncheon entrees run from $9.75 to $16, and prices are somewhat higher at dinner, which seems a bit much, even for this expense-account crowd. There are seatings at noon and 1:30 P.M. In the evening there is a 6 P.M. pre-theater seating and another at 7:45 P.M.

Wood's at 37th Street is a relatively new outcrop of the less ambitious Wood's on Madison Avenue in the 60s. The management was not ready for their instant success at the new establishment, and brusqueness (rudeness?) seems to be the rule, at least at the busy lunch hour. Service is not yet professional. Given the generally high quality of what goes on the table, the kitchen—and the public—deserve better.

# East 59th Street and Above

10/20
## Adams Rib
**23 E. 74 St.**

This is a comfortable, conservative, English-style dining room off the lobby of the old Volney Hotel, now

**535-2112**
*Lunch and dinner daily*
*until 10:30 P.M.*
*All major credit cards*
Steaks

converted to cooperative apartments. It is a favorite of the art gallery impresarios in the neighborhood.

At lunch there are sandwiches, hamburgers, and omelets, ranging from $4.95 to $6.95. The dinner specialty is Adam's Rib, a generous cut of roast beef (you can order it on or off the bone), with Yorkshire pudding and horseradish sauce ($16.50). Eve's Rib, with unblushing disregard for equal rights, is a smaller cut, available at $13.25. Also featured are steak, duck, and an Alaskan king crab plate. Desserts include a rich bavarian cream and a bittersweet chocolate pie, both quite good. If you long for roast beef, this is probably as good as you'll find in New York. If you are looking for excitement in the food or the surroundings, you'll be happier elsewhere.

14 ♧
# Andrée's Mediterranean Cuisine
**354 E. 74th St.**
**249-6619**
*Dinner nightly until 9:30 P.M.;*
*closed Sun. and Mon.;*
*reservations necessary*
*No credit cards*
Middle Eastern/French

If you want to find the sunshine of the Riviera, Greece, Egypt or Lebanon on your plate, visit this little brownstone house, bringing your own bottle of wine. Andrée, whose apartment is just above the kitchen, has fixed up a dining room for about thirty diners. When she leaves her stove momentarily in order to greet you, this dark, enthusiastic little woman, who gave up a job in publishing several years ago to open this restaurant, is captivating. Of French and Egyptian extraction, she lived first in Cairo, then in the south of France, which enabled her to become familiar with several Mediterranean cuisines, the flavors of which she combines with consummate skill. The eclectic menu is an invitation to a long and delicious culinary voyage. One goes from the stuffed vine leaves or the mushrooms à la grecque (exquisitely spiced) to the Lebanese tabouleh ( a salad of crushed wheat, parsley, and scallions with a delicious dressing of oil and fresh lemon); from the Egyptian falafel to the striped bass Corfu, perfectly cooked in phyllo; from Algerian couscous (lamb, chicken, turnips, carrots, chickpeas, onions, sweet black raisins, and finely-cooked grain), to the rack of lamb Méditerranée, Andrée's star attraction in itself worth the visit. The lamb is perfectly coated in garlic and fresh herbs; the juicy meat melts in your mouth, leaving an irresistible fragrance of the herbs and spices. Andrée lavishes the same love and care on her desserts as on everything else, drawing surprising flavors from all of them, whether the crème caramel, the coffee ice cream (studded with bits of black chocolate) or the fruit compote (composed of stewed apricots, prunes, raisins, pistachios, slivered almonds, and pine nuts in a rosewater syrup).

This is unpretentious family cooking with a hint of Greece. It compensates for many pretentious meals we've had, which were insipid and shamefully expensive. Service is assured by charming young women, to whom Andrée is teaching her culinary secrets. You'll have a really pleasant evening without spending more than $25 to $30, in addition, of course, to the cost of your own wine.

**12/20**
## Le Boeuf
## à la Mode
539 E. 81st St.
249-1473
*Dinner nightly until 11:00 P.M.;*
*closed Mon.*
*AE, V, DC*
French

Charming Cecile, whose husband Étienne is in the kitchen, will greet you warmly at the door of this Upper East Side neighborhood restaurant. Colorful murals of Paris and the French countryside will heighten a serene feeling that you are away from the heart of the city. This is more or less standard New York French cuisine, but with a difference: the value is extremely good. A dinner of appetizer, soup, entree, salad, and dessert will cost you from $16 (for the French pot roast for which the restaurant is named) to $19 (for the sirloin, filet mignon, or chateaubriand). The leeks in a zesty vinaigrette are a refreshing starter. The onion soup is better than most around town. Steaks are carefully grilled to order. Salad is fresh with a good dressing. Desserts are so-so; the chocolate mousse is your best bet. The house wine at $9.75 is a good buy. There are better Bordeauxs in the $14–$17 range.

There are disappointments, too, such as the vegetables accompanying the main dish (overcooked) and the fruit tart (poor crust). But a complete steak dinner at $19 plus wine and tip in these pleasant surroundings is something to moo about.

**5/20**
## Café Geiger
206 E. 86th St.
734-4428
*Lunch and dinner daily*
*until midnight*
*All major credit cards*
German

No, we don't consider this the worst restaurant in the world; however, if a general vote were to be taken this one would certainly be in the running. Whether it's the sausages or the schnitzel, the roulade of beef or the pork cutlets, everything tastes exactly the same. The food is delivered by older waitresses who speak English with a stupefying accent and must have been trained, as the cook seems to have been, in a barracks. If after this combatant's course you're still breathing, order the twelve-layer cake and try calling for help. The Mecca of Yorkville, the Café Geiger, with its beer drinkers, its roars of laughter, and its tumultuous digestion, is really not to be missed.

**12/20**
## Café San
## Martin
1458 First Ave.
(76th St.)
288-0470
*Dinner nightly until midnight;*
*Sun. brunch*
*All major credit cards*
Spanish

Inexpensive Spanish cuisine, which, for once, hasn't forgotten its origins along the way, served in a rather pleasant decor (white walls, green plants). Forget the Alaskan crab in a too-heavy sherry sauce; try instead the excellent little sausages in red wine, the gambas with garlic, a seafood zarzuela, a Valencian paella, or even a lobster (seemingly frozen). You'll have a reasonable meal, washed down with a good Rioja, for between $20 and $30.

**11/20**
## Casa Brazil
406 E. 85th St.
288-5284
*Dinner nightly until 9:30 P.M.;*
*closed Sun.; jacket and tie*

New York's most serious food critics have praised highly this little restaurant in a fancy part of town. Its sign led us to expect hearty Brazilian frenzy; the batida, tall, supple girls, and spicy food with a samba in the background. At first, we thought we had made a mistake. Where is Brazil

*recommended*
*No credit cards*
Brazilian/International

in this family "pension" of the '50s, with its flowered tablecloths and little bouquets of flowers on the tables, its walls covered with autographed photos of stars forgotten for the past thirty years, and a rather stuffy clientele that appeared to have come to attend a Mass? In actual fact, Brazil appears here only on the passport of Donna Helma, the robust owner. This redoutable matron, whose air is only remotely connected with the exuberance of the Rio carnival, must have a better sense of humor than it would seem. For more than fifteen years she hasn't hesitated to label as Brazilian a cuisine that has absolutely nothing to do with that of her native land (except when she offers her version of the traditional feijoada Wednesday evenings). It's as though a restaurant dubbed Casa Romana specialized in Japanese cuisine five days out of six.

As for the menu, it is Donna Helma who has determined its composition from time immemorial. It started as usual with hearts of palm (canned) drowned in béchamel au gratin, in which the presence of bits of ham and hardboiled egg could be surmised. After this curious introduction, a sad young woman served us crab claws in mayonnaise, accompanied, believe it or not, by scarcely warm little croissants. Both, we must admit, were of quite exceptional quality. Let us add that this combination is astonishing. But why not, after all? The main course arrived after a perfectly seasoned lettuce salad (a rarity in the United States). Suddenly open-minded, Madame Helma left the choice of several house specialties (equally immemorial) to her clients. These included beef Wellington, in which the meat was very tasty but the crust that evening was infinitely too salty; roast duck, perfectly fine but served without a drop of sauce; lamb chops served pink the way we like them. Nothing really extraordinary but for an astonishing hot sweet-and-sour preparation, a mixture of candied carrots and exotic braised fruits, that accompanied all these dishes. This little marvel, in which are to be found at last the great Brazilian flavors, was really the only thing that makes the trip worthwhile.

There were several undistinguished desserts, although the lemon mousse was perfectly prepared. It was almost 11:00 P.M. when without a word of explanation, Donna Helma reduced the lighting by half, then by three-quarters. The proprietress was sleepy. Well trained, the regular customers got the message and left to finish their conversations outside.

13
## Chez Pascal
**151 E. 82nd St.**
**249-1334**
*Dinner nightly until 11:00 P.M.;*
*closed Sun.*

This is a long, pleasant little dining room, with white walls in pink brick, woodwork, paintings, almond green banquettes and chairs, antique gold coffered ceiling (plastic?), and bustling, short-bearded mâitres d'hôtel. The waiter offers you a little saucisson en brioche and, in

*All major credit cards*
French (classical)

French, suggests an a la carte menu. Then you are served generous dishes, prepared with care, on huge plates. These range from slightly insipid bouillabaisse to spring chicken with garlic, from green bean, crab, and kiwi-fruit salad to veal with lime; all concessions to fashion. We found the green and white pasta du jour excellent, delicate in a slightly tomatoey sauce. Unfortunately, we came across it again (with a little white wine and orange, and good all the same), this time accompanying a superb red snapper. Good salads, and a delicious chocolate mousse.

15 🍴

## Le Cirque
**58 E. 65th St.
(Mayfair Regent
Hotel)
794-9292**
*Lunch and dinner daily until 10:30 P.M.; closed Sun.; formal; reservations necessary*
*AE, DC, CB*
French (classical)

One meets clowns in a circus. We have too much respect for the New York Establishment to suggest that Sophia Loren, Henry Kissinger, Princess Margaret, and all the beautiful people who frequent this bright, attractive dining room might belong to this profession. In any case, Sirio Maccioni, the proprietor, can flatter himself with having one of the most fashionable waiting lists in the city. This dapper, smiling man, with his slight resemblance to the young John Wayne, runs his restaurant—where he is always present—with the masterliness of a pro. We must admit, however, that we have never been enthusiastic about his menu. Tournedos Rossini, suprême of chicken Gismonda, veal chop à la Milanaise, and cassolette de filets de sole, no matter how well prepared, are not among our favorite dishes. Therefore, for a long time we considered Le Cirque's cuisine to be conventional and, in a word, boring. It seems we should have paid more attention to chef Alain Weill's daily specials, which show a little more imagination. After exquisite American oysters we tasted a remarkable warm salad of Bay scallops from Long Island on a bed of fresh greens; fresh pasta with Oregon chanterelles, garnished with white Italian truffles; a perfectly baked red snapper with peppers and sliced lemon, unfortunately swimming in oil; a Canadian partridge with a miraculously gamey taste in a good juniper berry sauce, accompanied by undercooked chestnuts and a superfluous slice of bread. We also tried the roast duckling, rosy and tender, but whose green peppercorn sauce must, alas, have been forgotten in the kitchen; an excellent Roquefort; and a superb chocolate cake.

15 🍴

## Claude's
**205 E. 81st St.
472-0487**
*Dinner nightly until 10:45 P.M.; closed Sun.; jacket and tie required*
*All major credit cards*
French (classical/
nouvelle)

Claude Baills (who vaguely resembles Alain Senderens), his smile partly covered by his black beard, is in an awkward position, straddling the ancienne and the nouvelle cuisines. As he has a sense of equilibrium, everything is all right; his is at present one of the best French restaurants in New York. It's also one of the most refined, albeit a little cold, with its lacquered red panels from China, its mirrors and its superb art deco carpets. Miraculously, you don't need a flashlight to read the very short menu, to which are added several dishes to be ordered in advance, such as the truffle soup Paul Bocuse, steamed capon Lucien Tendret, or the Catalonian bouillabaisse. For the past twelve years Claude has worked in the best places in New York, and was chef at the Palace before opening his own restaurant. His sauces are excellent, he uses first-rate produce, and his preparations are rigorous. If there is nothing really astonishing in his cooking, he does know how to lend grace to the most ordinary dishes, such as delicious sweetbreads in tarragon cream sauce, chicken wing with herbs, or a succulent piece of beef grilled with a Brouilly wine reduction. He's not quite as lucky with the fish pâté, whose spicy tomato sauce alone cannot cover up its insipidity. His smoked salmon millefeuille and his exquisite California crayfish salad with kernels of corn prove that he can stray from the beaten track and not get lost. There are five or six desserts, among them very good oeufs à la neige et aux violettes. The French service is well executed and this is one of the rare places where it is possible to prolong dinner without having the staff try to push you toward the exit in order to give your table to new arrivals. Very good choice of French and California wines, whose prices are not too astronomical.

## 12/20
## La Cocotte
**147 E. 60th St.**
**832-8972**
*Lunch and dinner daily until*
*10:30 P.M.; closed Sun.;*
*reservation and jacket required*
*All major credit cards*
French (classical)

Consistency in the kitchen is perhaps the most difficult of culinary virtues to achieve. Over the years, La Cocotte under Ernest Guzmits has achieved it to an unusual degree. For a New York French restaurant the menu is not exceptional (escalope de veau, poulet sauté archiduc, frogs' legs, roast duck, rack of lamb), but there are always seasonal specialties such as whole baby salmon, soft-shell crabs, squabs from the Carolinas, or game.

The wine list covers most of the best-known regions of France, and the service is genial and professional.

At the entrance, there is a cash register, small bar, and a few tables for regulars who enjoy this informal bistro environment. There is a more formal dining area to the rear, and a few steps down a glass-enclosed garden, which is a rare find in the city.

A complete dinner runs from $15.50 to $22, plus wine and tip, which doesn't seem too much in this high-priced neighborhood. Given the more than acceptable standards of the kitchen and the professionalism of the service, it is hard to go wrong at La Cocotte.

## 9/20
## David K's
**1115 Third Ave.**
**(65th-66th Sts.)**
**371-9090**
*Lunch and dinner daily*
*until midnight; weekends*
*until 1:00 A.M.*
*AE, DC, CB*
Chinese

When we pointed out pleasantly to the maitre d'hôtel that the plates were dirty, he gave us the same withering glance as a warlord about to shoot. No doubt in order to punish us, he keenly recommended the fresh blue crabs with Hunan sauce, forgetting to add that they had been fresh during the Ming dynasty.

This was our second visit to "the most beautiful Chinese restaurant in New York." It's worthy of the title if one limits oneself to the quite spectacular decor, with its giant stone dragons standing on guard at the door; its aquariums containing disturbing exotic fish; its big, round, well-dispersed tables; and its veranda full of flowers and plants. Unfortunately, there's the rest: remarkably inefficient, contemptuous service, and the cooking. The latter is highly spoken of when chef Teng has a special reason to prove his talent (for instance, when you order a banquet in advance, or Danny Kaye wants to dine at his friend David's). For the ordinary customer, it fluctuates between the mediocre and the satisfactory, with several happy exceptions, including excellent firm, spicy shrimps, or the sliced lamb Hunan style. There is nothing to justify a bill that easily comes to $30, including a glass of wine. It's true that the restaurant is always full, at least for dinner, as we did have lunch in a sort of Gobi Desert. David Kay, a charming man in other respects, has no reason to worry.

## 11/20
### Demarchelier
**608 Lexington Ave. (62nd St.)**
**223-0047**
*Lunch and dinner daily until 11:30 P.M.; closed Sun.*
*All major credit cards*
French (provincial)

Saturday lunch is when the fashion models of New York, their escorts, and other chic types visit the bistro opened by fashion photographer Patrick Demarchelier. Here, the melon prosciutto, the grilled fillet of sole, the veal scallopini with lemon, and the crème à l'orange have the good taste not to stand out too much, as the public is the real star.

## 8/20
### Elaine's
**1703 Second Ave. (88th St.)**
**534-8114**
*Lunch and dinner daily until 2:00 A.M.; no lunch Sat. or Sun.*
*AE*
Continental

One has the impression of being in a dingy aviary. The once-fat Elaine (who has lost forty kilos) rarely smiles, and does so with the charm of a slammed door. In fact, this impossibly unpleasant former waitress has a flair for public relations. The public will stoop to anything in order to get an table and have the right to eat second-rate spaghetti next to the mournful sight of Woody Allen hunched over an osso buco. Elaine knows her customers; she sends some to hell and the others to the semiobscurity of her paradise, thus competing with God the Father. When the earth's population reaches eight billion we'll need lots of places like this one in order to give certain people the impression they exist. Around $15 to $20, unless you are careless ordering wine.

## 11/20
### Elio's
**1621 Second Ave. (84th St.)**
**772-2242**
*Dinner nightly until 11:00 P.M.*
*AE*
Italian

The smart set, the jet set, the fashion set—you name it, they crowd into Elio's late into the night. Is this simply an outcropping of Elaine's? No, Elio—once an employee of Elaine—now controls what has become Upper East side's latest modish eatery. Outside, old-fashioned globe lights glimmer like full moons. Inside there is understated chic: heavy mahogany bar, dark-paneled walls, and ceiling spotlights illuminating potted plants and wine racks.

People-watching and conversation are the two real specials here, but the waiters are patient (and intelligent) in explaining the short menu and the daily specials. Pastas are good. Fettuccine with four cheeses is worth ordering, when it is available. Some appetizers, such as the cold seafood salad, lack distinction. The main dishes are acceptable, but are apt to be underseasoned. Chicken dishes are preferable to the veal, although the breaded, stuffed veal chop can be very good. Desserts are pedestrian.

Wines are reasonably priced and there are good selections in the $12–$14 range. A Pinot Grigio at $12.50, followed by a Barbera Vignarey at the same price, will give your meal and your conversation a lift. Four persons can enjoy the scene with two bottles of wine, tip included, for $120.

## 10/20
## La Folie
**21 E. 61st St.**
**765-1400**
*Lunch and dinner daily until*
*midnight; closed Sun.;*
*jacket required*
*All major credit cards*
French (classical)

There are restaurants in which you feel right at home. La Folie is unlikely to figure among them, unless you are the sort to entrust the late Frederick P. Victoria and David Barett with decorating your apartment. If such is the case, nothing could make you happier than this delirious hodgepodge in which blue and red marble clash with pillars ostensibly in Russian malachite but obviously plastic; parrot-green banquettes; a bar standing on shod and stockinged dummys' legs, a bronze Charlie Chaplin; and paintings that resemble those of Van Dongen, but aren't. It's breathtaking and quite amusing, like a party game. The trouble is, chef Bernard Norget seems to have lost his recipes in this heterogeneous decor. We can't swear that it was he who prepared the meal we had (perhaps there's a replacement at lunch). In any case, despite the kindness of the maitre d'hôtel, it was difficult for us to finish our meal, except for the marvelous oysters and exquisite apple tart. The mushroom feuilleté was even worse than the one an innocent young bride might botch with frozen pastry; the scallops à la nage were perfectly fresh but served without a drop of sauce, and garnished with mediocre rice and almost raw green beans, as was the blanquette de veau à l'ancienne, a totally insipid concoction, engulfed in pure glue. We concluded the meal with twenty-one little raspberries on a plate, which made us regret not having brought a microscope. It is entirely possible that the "gourmet dinners" at $28 are outstanding, but you may want to wait a little longer before finding out. Lunch: $17.50; Dinner: $28.

## 11/20
## Fortune Garden
**1160 Third Ave.**
**(67th-68th Sts.)**
**744-1212**
*Lunch and dinner daily*
*until 11:00 P.M.*

This pleasant restaurant, very comfortable and always full, is wrongly considered one of the best Chinese restaurants in the city. Let's say that whether it's a question of the coquilles Saint Jacques in velvet sauce (made of soybeans and vegetables), the chicken smoked with tea, the very spicy sautéed chicken Hunan, or the beef with ginger, orange, or garlic (among the house specialties), the

All major credit cards
Chinese

## 13 🍴
## The Gibbon
**24 E. 80th St.**
**861-4001**
*Lunch and dinner daily until
10:30 P.M.; closed Sun.; jacket and
tie required*
*All major credit cards*
French/Japanese
(nouvelle)

cuisine is honorable, but only just. It is true, however, that we didn't try the Peking duck, of which some speak very highly. Around $20 to $25.

If Hanae Mori or Kenzo were to open a restaurant in Manhattan, they couldn't do any better. One is received (if not welcomed) at The Gibbon by a terribly chic and moderately amiable Japanese Rudolf Valentino with a delicate moustache and plastered-down hair. It's the latest thing: Japanese chic. The decor is as ascetic as a tea house from which the furniture has been removed; one fears a smile would seem terribly incongruous and even wonders whether it is actually acceptable to open one's mouth to eat. The cuisine is also perplexing: is it Japanese or Western? We seem to discern an attempt at a new-style, hybrid cuisine—prepared, furthermore, by a veritable artist. Astonishingly enough, he doesn't sign each of his plates. We think we recognized a sashimi (quite exquisite) and, after a long moment of reflection over the jumbo shrimp with lotus seeds and strawberry vinaigrette (yes!), we must admit that even if the shrimp were not fresh, the sauce is so extraordinary that one would eat it anyway. After, we had a red snapper stuffed with crab and veal in watercress sauce, whose insipidity made them unmemorable. Let's admit it: even though there were six of us at the table, from that moment on we did not pay much attention to what we were eating. We were as hesitant as the cuisine seemed to be, as though we were confronted with a new type of mutant. There's no doubt that we must return, but next time with the proper material: microscopes, stethoscopes, and X-rays.

## 11/20
## Gino's
**780 Lexington Ave.**
**(60th-61st Sts.)**
**223-9658**
*Lunch and dinner daily until
10:30 P.M.; no reservations;
Sun. brunch*
*No credit cards*
Italian

Why do fashionable New Yorkers from the worlds of entertainment, fashion, advertising and business rush to this noisy, uncomfortable little restaurant, with its idiotic decor, every Saturday at noon? It's not because of the Italian (and primarily Neapolitan) cuisine, which is nice and no more (top marks, however, for the tagliatelle with clams). It's not because of the wines, which are nothing special, nor the kind owner who takes only superficial care of his customers. What, then, makes New Yorkers crowd into Gino's, aside from the pleasure of standing in turbulent line in order to get a table? Well, we'll tell you: it's the certainty, for the past several decades, of finding fashionable New Yorkers from the worlds of entertainment, fashion, and so forth, there. Around $20 to $25. Much sought-after Sunday brunch with Champagne.

## 9/20
## La Goulue
**28 E. 70th St.**
**988-8169**
*Lunch and dinner daily until*

Very charming decor, that of an old bistro in Paris or Lyon. You'd think you were there, what with the somber woodwork, the etched windows, the heavy lace curtains, the tulip bracket-lamps, the bar, the real cashier behind

*11:00 P.M.; jacket and tie recommended*
*All major credit cards*
French (classical)

the real till, the waiters in long aprons, all French. On reading the menu, you're less convinced. It's banal, poor: egg in aspic, artichoke vinaigrette, crudités, snails, onion soup, duck à l'orange, veal chops with morilles, Brie, chocolate mousse. Once the meal is served, the illusion vanishes. The duck terrine was dreadfully insipid, the spinach salad (with spinach as hard as cardboard) was redeemed by good mushrooms; the "grilled" chicken (reheated how many times?) and the greasy french fries were abject. There remains an American dish, always good in New York: little coquilles Saint Jacques meunière, unfortunately swimming in too much butter. Several great, relatively inexpensive Bordeaux wines ($60 for the best vintages) and an exquisite Cabernet Sauvignon '77 from Mondavi. That's hardly what France is all about.

## 11/20
## Greener Pastures
**117 E. 60th St.**
**832-3212**
*Lunch and dinner daily until 9:30 P.M.*
*No credit cards*
Natural Food

This is a natural-food restaurant, entered through a small natural-food retail shop. Keep going through dining room one, at the back, and dining room two, on the right, and you will find yourself in a cheery greenhouse, the greener pastures you have been looking for.

You can order from an extensive menu of appetizers, salads, sandwiches (on excellent coarse-grained bread), and vegetarian, chicken, and fish dishes. The "beef" stroganoff and steaks are prepared from protein and shaped to look like the real thing. A couple of chicken dishes and sole, scrod, bluefish, snapper, halibut, bass, and salmon *are* the real thing. Oriental sauces are a favorite; vegetables are quick-cooked and usually crisp. Entrèe prices range from $5 to $10.95 at lunch, and not much more than a dollar is added at night. There is a $2 service charge (portions are generous) for shared dishes. Box lunches to take out are available.

If you are a vegetarian, the wide selection and the low prices will appeal to you. If you are not a vegetarian yet, you may appreciate the character of the meat substitutes, and you will surely like the prices of the vegetarian dishes. You may never go back to T-bone, sirloin or shell.

## 12/20
## Hoexter's Market
**1442 Third Ave.**
**(81st-82nd Sts.)**
**472-9322**
*Dinner nightly until midnight; Sun. brunch*
*AE, CB, V, DC*
International/American

Plunge into the stylish throng where there's a nightly crush to get to the bar. White wine or cocktail in hand, cross the red cordon, after proving that you have a reservation. There you are, a place utterly characteristic of New York: a former meat market metamorphosed into a fashionable restaurant. Nothing is missing: neither the brick walls covered with tapestries and lithographs retracing the history of Manhattan, nor the soft lights, nor the ravishing girls, nor the denizens of the world of advertising, film, and European society. Let it be said that slender young people can find only happiness here in the form of healthy foods, simply prepared with obviously first-class produce. In addition to these dishes, there are more substantial ones, but always superbly honest.

Choose among gazpacho, breast of smoked chicken, carpaccio with capers, tortellini al dente (with lumpfish eggs), grilled chicken, paillard de boeuf, steak tartare, and the immense, superb Hoexter's salad. Then finish with the chocolate cake. For between $30 and $35 (which includes a good Californian wine) you'll have a perfectly straightforward dinner or supper, while trying to place two or three well-known faces. Slip away at midnight when the disco begins. This subdued civilized restaurant suddenly becomes infernal.

13 ♧
# Hunan Manor
**1464 Second Ave.
(76th-77th Sts.)
570-6700**
*Lunch and dinner daily
until 11:00 P.M.
All major credit cards*
Chinese

As soon as you enter this plain but comfortable Hunanese restaurant you know you are in good hands. A contented purr seems to rise from the assembled congregation, whose heads are lowered, chopsticks flickering purposefully over their rice bowls. It is an atmosphere you only get when a good chef is in charge, and this one's name is Ho. Formerly with Uncle Tai's and David K's, he is now culinary Lord of his own Manor.

Both the hot-and-sour and the snow-white fish soups, (the latter a sort of chowder), were outstanding. Assorted hot appetizers (for two) proved to be a mini-cornucopia of honey-glazed spareribs, sesame shrimp toast, scallop puffs, chicken in foil, and skewered spicy beef. Alternatively, try the Hunan dumplings in red-hot oil or the brutishly named hacked chicken in a smooth, delicious sesame dressing. Vegetable package turned out to be a delicate fry-up of tiny tofu cubes with crisp mixed vegetables to be eaten from shells of iceberg lettuce. There is a hotter version of this dish with diced chicken. A side order of sweet-and-sour cabbage salad goes well with both.

Moo shu pork with scrambled eggs, lichens, and straw mushrooms, was let down by the tough and leathery wrap-around pancakes. Whole sea bass, crisp beneath its unctuous and multi-flavored Hunan sauce, was enjoyable, as were the two-flavor prawns, hot and bland and separated by a dark green wall of kale. Both dishes belied the claim that chefs from inland provinces like Hunan don't do justice to seafood. All dishes in a garlic or "sea spice" sauce were classically cooked and we liked Ho's orange beef, juicy with a crunchy crust flavored with tiny chips of dried orange peel. Lovers of lamb will enjoy Ho's hot, sour, and spicy version; eggplant with garlic sauce, and sautéed green beans with a ground pork and shrimp topping.

Two dishes disappointed: the shredded dry-sautéed beef with carrots and celery was chewy and rubbery; and the glazed sesame banana was unaccountably encased in an armor of heavy pastry. So stick to fresh pineapple or orange sorbet for afters.

Chef Ho does not immure himself in his kitchens but wanders in and out of the restaurant dispensing good cheer. He has also found time to open another restaurant. Hunan Manor is one of the best of a growing band of Hunanese restaurants in New York. Beware of imitations. $20 with wine.

13 ☖
## Il Valetto
**133 E. 61st St.**
**838-3939**
*Lunch and dinner daily*
*until 11:30 P.M.*
*All major credit cards*
Italian

It's extremely smart to arrive at precisely one o'clock at this chic, crowded, noisy bistro, where women of fashion stand in line (with a smile, if you please) while waiting for a table. But what compels smartly turned-out high society to come here and fight among themselves in order to spend $11 for the most insignificant pasta dish, and to pay a bill of $45 without batting an eyelash? The decor undoubtedly has nothing to do with it, consisting as it does of travel-agency posters singing the praises of Italy and tables with little space between them. It's true that there is some atmosphere. The other day Gina Lolabrigida chattered gaily under the eyes of the waiters, who seemed to have seen worse. What is particularly striking is the quality of cuisine, which, without rising to great heights, is perfectly honest, restoring all their authenticity to the dishes of the Abbruzes. The capelletti is tasty, the saltimboca alla Romana rather delicate, and the sauces light even if the portions are copious (which perhaps accounts for their price). The daily specials vary between the osso buco with fetuccine and the pollo valdostana. By contrast, the desserts are less exciting (cassata with a strong taste of food coloring). However, if you have lots of money and the urge to see society, don't hesitate. The welcome is amiable, despite the crowd.

11/20
## Jim McMullen
**1341 Third Ave.**
**(76th St.)**
**861-4700**
*Lunch and dinner daily until*
*4:00 A.M.; no reservations*
*No credit cards*
International/American

Brick walls, etched glass, interior garden, lots of models, actors, and journalists. In short, a made-to-order spot for trendy New Yorkers. Jim McMullen, the handsome young man who greets you (when his numerous friends leave him the time to do so), runs his ship with great ease, even though his friend Kathy (with whom he established this restaurant) took off to try her luck in California. The cooking reflects the owner: relaxed, unpretentious, and very neat. The cold mussels vinaigrette or a salmon steak, followed by calf's liver with onions and bacon ( a little overcooked), a dessert, and a Californian wine will cost you about $20. You may have to wait a long time for your table while sipping a drink among the very busy singles at the bar, but they'll be polite about it.

12/20
## Le Lavandou
**134 E. 61st St.**
**838-7987**
*Lunch and dinner daily until*
*10:00 P.M.; closed Sun.*
*AE*
French
(classical/nouvelle)

This was the sort of vision of "Paris" that delighted New Yorkers during the '60s: gaudy frescoes of dubious French landscapes, Louis XVI imitation chandeliers, tables very close together, lots of noise, ultra-French service (more recently Chinese). Let's add to this snails in pastis, quenelles in Pernod, cassoulet Toulousain, tournedos with leanings toward the conventional Rossini variety, lobster bisque, and duck au poivre vert. Nothing very reprehensible, but it's really overestimated: too many cream sauces, too much overcooked food, and too little invention. In short, a good kitchen whose cassoulet de coquilles Saint Jacques with seafood and shellfish we liked (although we couldn't find any lobster). We detested the enormous serving of inordinately overcooked, insipid sweetbreads in Madeira sauce, but served with excellent vegetables. Lovely, fresh asparagus and a nice nouvelle salad with green beans and foie gras. A familiar refrain, not to mention the soupe aux truffes de Bocuse! Dinner menu at $28 plus extras and wines, with a good selection from the Bordeaux region (a Pichon-Lalande '72 for $15 is quite reasonable).

## 12/20
## Manhattan Market
**1016 Second Ave.**
**752-1400**
*Lunch and dinner daily until midnight; Sun. brunch (but no dinner)*
*AE, MC, V*
American

David Liederman has won his case. This former gourmet lawyer, who gave up law for catering, has in fact opened one of the nicest, smartest little restaurants in Manhattan (customers include models, publishers, lawyers, and journalists—if you consider journalists part of the smart set). Although Liederman himself underwent a period of training in France with the Troisgros brothers, he does not aspire to the gastronomic summits. It is limited to simple but perfectly prepared dishes, using first-class fresh produce. Take for example the terrine de canard aux poivrons verts et aux pistaches; the pasta au pistou (unfortunately too salty); the green bean salad with goat's milk cheese and pecans; the excellent "Market Burger" covered with minced onions and served in a delicious homemade roll garnished with light, crisp homemade french fries; the chicken with sour cream mustard sauce; or the veal cutlet with herb butter. Just the sort of cuisine one needs after a tour of the "grands restaurants." The desserts deserve special mention. The crème brûlée with lemon is a marvel, and nowhere will you eat such delicious cookies. This is hardly surprising, really, as they come from the shop next door, David's Cookie Kitchen, where the best cookies and the best French baguette in New York are made. $20 to $30.

## 10/20
## Maxwell's Plum
**1181 First Ave.**
**(64th St.)**
**628-2100**
*Lunch and dinner daily until 1:00 A.M.; Sun. brunch (reservation recommended)*
*All major credit cards*
American/Continental

Warner Leroy, son of Mervin and nephew of Jack Warner, created this, his first decorating masterpiece, about fifteen years ago, and it seems a tribute to his folks in moviedom. He was subsequently definitively honored by art historians as the leader of the P.T. Barnum school (which, as we know, went through several periods), for his major work, the Tavern on the Green. Maxwell's Plum belongs, in our view, to the "lost property period." It's impossible to draw up an inventory, but let's mention a few at random: several hundred hippopotami, rhinoceroses, giraffes, lions, zebras, Tiffany lamps, mirrors, pots of flowers, imitation bronzes, imitation virgins, genuine rich people, fake poor people, old young people, young old people, loners in groups, loners alone. . . . Even if the cuisine were unspeakable, it would be absolutely essential to visit Maxwell's Plum, just as in Paris one visits Sacré Coeur, or the Tussaud museum in London, or Lenin's tomb in Moscow. But there's a difference. One has infinitely more fun in this immense, always crowded cafe where, from seven in the evening on, a rain-forest-honed machete would help to clear a path to the giant horseshoe bar or the tables on the veranda where hamburgers and cheesecake are served. Mink and tuxedos later invade the far end of the dining room (the Back Room). There's no mistaking the effects; it's the reproduction of an imitation of an inaccurate copy of a fake twin of Maxim's. One journalist, either drunk or a practical joker, wrote one day that a fabulous cuisine is served here. It is no longer possible to count the number of people who have resorted to contemptible actions in order to secure a table in this sanctuary and partake of the exquisite pleasures of a very comical chicken salad Troisgros, reheated moules marinière, chateaubriand with béarnaise sauce and tarte Tatin with schlag, that is, "mit whipped cream." Following that, the management could decree a hunger strike without causing any damage. In fact, the cuisine is irrelevant to Maxwell's Plum's immense success; it is, above all, an extravagant, exciting, marvelous lounge where people chat, look at each other, and pick each other up.

## 12/20
## Meat Brokers
**1153 York Ave.**
**(62nd St.)**
**752-0108**
*Dinner nightly until midnight;*
*Fri. and Sat. until 1:00 A.M.*
*All major credit cards*
Steaks

In a Stock Exchange-like atmosphere near the East River, excellent steaks and, in the winter, some fresh fish, are served. There are few wines, but there is a large selection of beers, which are gulped down by a dense crowd of businessmen who make Meat Brokers their canteen at noon. This typical New York restaurant was opened in 1979 by a very representative quartet: an Englishman, a Jew, an Italian, and an Irishman. In the meantime, there have been several changes, but the clients pretend to believe in the durability of this holy alliance.

## 10/20
## Mme. Romaine de Lyon
**32 E. 61st St.**
**758-2422**
*Lunch daily; closed Sun.*
*No credit cards*
French

We had to go to New York to learn that the omelet is a specialty of Lyon. What's certain is that Mme. Romaine was born in Lyon and that she hit pay dirt twenty years ago by serving only omelets and a few pastries in her restaurant. There are 520 varieties of omelets, with everything and anything else you can think of. The customers, mainly women, come at noon, between errands, and celebrate this cult of the egg, about which a food critic can say little, but a psychoanalyst certainly a great deal. The prices are not particularly moderate nor is the welcome particularly cordial.

12/20
## Il Monello
**1460 Second Ave.
(76th-77th Sts.)
535-9310**
*Lunch and dinner daily until
midnight; closed Sun.
All major credit cards*
Italian

It is a well-known fact that the faces of certain women are not the same at night as they are in the morning. The same goes for certain restaurants. Our first visit to Il Monello, under the same management as the excellent Il Nido, was a catastrophe. This dark dining room, slightly vulgar and over the hill, was three-quarters empty at lunchtime; the minds of the maitre d'hôtel and the waiters were clearly elsewhere, and they seemed totally uninterested in service. As for the meal itself, it was completely worthless. Everything was either tasteless or too salty, and one could have used the white sauce from the tortellini with four cheeses to glue the chef to his stove, which would have been a just revenge. Therefore, it was reluctantly that we returned to Il Monello by chance several days later, this time for dinner.

The decor (pure comic opera) was no more refined than before, obviously, but in the now-full dining room there reigned a convivial atmosphere. The waiters were taking care of their customers; by some miracle, the cuisine improved. Certain dishes were even well executed, as for example the crostini di Polenta (triangles of crisp cornmeal topped with a ragout of procini mushrooms), a splendidly earthy dish with Parmesan freshly grated, as it should be, at the table. The white truffles of Alba arrived in a jar of raw rice along with a risotto Milanese, which was yellow and fragrant with saffron, moist, yet with each grain separate. The zuppa di pesce of sea bass, red snapper, and octopus was perfectly cooked in a pale orange broth, and the vitello juliano, which consists of a tender veal cutlet coated with egg and freshly grated Parmesan, fried in butter and finished in white wine and lemon at the table, was delicious.

For those who wish to round off their meal in true Italian fashion, try a plate of Grano (prime Parmesan with sliced pears and walnuts). Wash this down with a noble 1850 Madeira from the owner's reserve.

Listings of great Italian vintages and "riservas" are formidable, some wines spanning close to half a century. About $30, with Chianti.

10/20
## Mortimer's
**1057 Lexington Ave.
(75th St.)
861-2481**
*Lunch and dinner daily until
midnight; supper: 11:00 P.M. to
2:30 A.M.; reservations for parties
of 5 or more
All major credit cards*
Continental

If one were to ask Oona Chaplin, Gloria Vanderbilt, Diana Vreeland, William Paley, and the scores of other beautiful people who regularly haunt Mortimer's why they chose this cafe over another, they would undoubtedly reply, "Because we feel good here." And why do they feel good there? First of all, because they are there, and it is always more pleasant to look at famous people, or those who are going to become famous, than to look at anonymous alcoholics. Also, because the place has charm, with its very solid bar, several lovely old paintings, and its trompe l'oeil windows. Glenn Bernbaum, the owner, sensibly reserves the good tables for his good customers, but the staff seems happy to see one and all. The cuisine is obviously only a pretext, but thanks to its complete lack of originality, it can be eaten without comment, whether you're having the smoked chicken, the gray sole, the twinburgers, the roast leg of lamb, the crème brûlée (particularly well made), or, quite simply, sandwiches for lunch. Sunday brunch is an important, fashionable event not to be missed.

At two in the morning, you're sure of being able to have one more for the road at the bar. Around $15 to $20.

13

## Pamir
**1423 Second Ave.
(74th St.)
734-3791**
*Dinner nightly until 11:00 P.M.
V, MC*
Afghan

The Bayat brothers have taken over an old bar on Second Avenue, installed a samovar, covered the walls with exotic rugs, and put little embroidered waistcoats on the staff. The Tiffany lamps and swiveling bar stools in well-worn leatherette are obviously part of a previous incarnation. We say "staff," but family would be a better word—all five brothers are involved here, political refugees from Afghanistan. In Kabul they would have been doctors, teachers, or pharmacists—here they have opened a restaurant, and as they have excellent taste, and one of them at least is a born cook, Kabul's loss is New York's gain.

The food is exactly what they would serve at home, with no compromises, and in case the word "Afghan" conjures up an uncouth image—rough food for mountain tribes—be reassured. It is less fiery than the Indian cuisine, not as coarse as the Russian—something of a Persian refinement about the flavors, with fragrant notes of orange, rose-water, coriander, and cardamom.

The menu falls naturally into two sections: the starters that would normally be served on feast days, and the everyday dishes based on delicious combinations of meat and rice—food originally designed to be eaten with the hands. Of the appetizers, on no account miss the bulanee gandana. Thin, crisp triangles of pastry, rather like the Greek phylla, are filled with green scallions and eaten with a tantalizing dip of walnuts, mint, green pepper, and coriander. Aushak is also delectable, velvety-smooth dumplings with a meat, yogurt, and mint topping.

For your main course, combine a pilaf with the Pamir kebab, a sampler of all their excellent grills—meat balls, lamb chops, cubed lamb, and chicken, all marinated, skewered, and grilled to perfection. The nicest pilaf to our taste is the norange palaw, a quite extraordinary blend of rice with thinly sliced orange peel, pistachios, cardamom seeds, and rose-water, with tender well-flavored chunks of lamb lurking within. Try a side dish of sabsi, spinach cooked with lime-juice, which tastes almost like sorrel.

Of the three desserts baklava is the heaviest. Goshefeel is preferable, a crackling disc of the finest pastry, fried in butter and strewn with sugar and pistachios, or firnee, a lovely, bland, nursery custard, with nuts and spices. You won't be tempted by any fiery local liqueurs, as the

Moslems are teetotalers, so finish with a most digestive hot cardamom-scented tea—the definitive "chai." About $15 for an absolute feast.

15

## Parioli Romanissimo
**1446 First Ave.**
**(76th-77th Sts.)**
**288-2391**
*Dinner nightly until 11:00 P.M.;*
*closed Sun. and Mon.*
*AE, DC*
Italian

You may have to wait two weeks for a reservation and you'll have to reconfirm your reservation 24 hours in advance. Such is the popularity of this expensive and exclusive Upper East Side bastion of New York's power elite. They may eat lunch at 21 where they can see and be seen, but at dinner they want to relax. Laurence A. Tisch, chairman of Loews' Corporation, has said that Parioli is the best restaurant in New York. Not true, but it is considerably better than the average Italian restaurant around town. It's not that the menu is more imaginative, but there is a light hand in the kitchen, lending elegance to more or less standard pasta, chicken, and veal dishes. The hot antipasto, with perfectly poached shellfish, comes in a beautifully scented tomato sauce. The capellini alla arrabiata is full of zest with its garnish of capers, olives, and peppers. For entrees try the breast of chicken in a delicate Calvados-flavored cream sauce, or the tender veal with artichokes and mushrooms. The breaded veal cutlet is excellent, although it would be more satisfying with a vegetable garnish. The cheese tray and the desserts are worth ordering, something that cannot be said for most Italian restaurants in New York. The fruit tart, for example, consists of an exquisite, flaky pastry, and the zabaglione, made at the table, is exceptionally frothy and flavorful.

The wine list is unusual in that there are only Italian and French white wines and only Italian reds, except for the 1971 Château Latour at $165. Whites start with a refreshing San Gimignano at $15.50, and Pinot Grigio and Orvieto at $18.50. Then there are outstanding 1979 Burgundy whites, including a Drouhin Puligny Montrachet at $56 and Le Montrachet Marquis Laguiche at $105. There are solid Chiantis at $18.50, and more substantial reds priced all the way up to the $165 Latour. But the clientele at Parioli need not stop there. They can go for collector items: Brunello di Montalcino, Biondi Santi, the 1955 at $1,450, the 1945 at $1,850, and the 1925 at $4,350. Are these bottles only to be talked about? No, the crowd at Parioli can afford to drink them. If you cannot, you still may dine among those who can for $65, with a perfectly acceptable wine. And chances are your meal will be exquisite.

11/20

## Parma
**1404 Third Ave.**
**(79th-80th Sts.)**
**535-3520**
*Dinner nightly until 12:30 A.M.*
*AE*
Italian

A relatively new darling of the Upper East Side, the Parma is a good-looking 1900s-style bistro with a mahogany bar, retro globes, posters under glass, and very unimaginative but correctly prepared Italian cuisine. The prosciutto melone (exquisite) shares the menu with a tomato and mozzarella salad straight from the refrigerator and flavorless. The tortellini, rather delicate in a cream sauce, rub shoulders with an overcooked sirloin steak. The raspberries with zabaglione are an honest finish. But beware of the wines kept at room temperature, meaning much too warm. We tried a harsh, acidic Bardolino that would have been perfect for seasoning the salad. It is important to note that in order to get a table at the Parma, it is almost mandatory to wait in line at the bar, even if you have a reservation. Also, it will cost you $35 for the right to sit down among the tables full of models and executives.

## 14 ⌂
## Périgord Park
**575 Park Ave.**
**(63rd St.)**
**752-0050**
*Lunch and dinner daily until*
*10:30 P.M.; no lunch Sat.; Sun.*
*brunch; jacket and tie required*
*All major credit cards*
French (nouvelle)

When the great chefs of France go on an outing to New York, they always dine with the eloquent, impassioned, bearded owner of Périgord Park. Do the same—without, however, expecting to dine at the Troisgros brothers. The big, elegant dining room, decorated with colonnades and medallions of trompe-l'oeil on a green background, is pleasant and overcrowded. The Franco-Mediterranean service is bustling; the menu is rich, with a nouvelle cuisine aspect; prices are almost reasonable; and the American wines are remarkable. Aside from the littleneck clams, which are always exquisite, the shellfish were rather disappointing. The fish tartare, poorly deboned and scaled, was pleasant and very fresh. The lacquered duck with truffles and endives was good, but not very well lacquered; other good dishes were the justly famous roast lamb on Sunday and the delicate sole mousse. Lovely desserts and good strawberries year-round.

## 9/20
## La Petite Ferme
**973 Lexington Ave.**
**(70th-71st Sts.)**
**249-3272**
*Lunch and dinner daily until*
*10:00 P.M.; closed Sun.*
*All major credit cards*
French (provincial)

New Yorkers in search of the authentically French speak highly of this modest basement. Its tables in pale wood, straw-bottomed chairs, checked tablecloths, slate menu, and the owner's name, Charles Chevillot, seem a guarantee of the virtues of the native soil. Poor soil! That the entire menu can practically be enumerated on the fingers of one hand (mussels vinaigrette, tarragon chicken, poached trout, sole meunière, steak Maître d'Hôtel, and strawberry tart) is one thing. What is more serious is that the mussels have the cottony consistency of products left too long in the refrigerator, and that the chicken succumbs under an abundantly creamy and totally insipid sauce. Only the wine slate offers any consolation, although courtesy dictates that American vintages also be suitably represented. It will be pointed out, no doubt, that we "came at the wrong time." Even so, we find it serious that such simple dishes were botched.

## 10/20
## La Place
**21 E. 62nd St.**
**838-4248**
*Lunch and dinner daily until*
*midnight*

This small, typically "Madison Avenue" restaurant with a terrace has been uninterruptedly crowded ever since it was opened last fall by a Frenchman who used to work promoting French tourism in New York. The cuisine here plays a supporting role—there's little to say about it,

All major credit cards
French (classical)

except that the artichoke à la barigoule (stuffed with mushrooms) bears no resemblance to the original, that the grilled striped bass with hollandaise sauce is good, and that the raspberry tart is undistinguished. But we could go on at length about the attractive young women and men who fill this dining room.

13 ♡

## Le Plaisir

**969 Lexington Ave.
(70th-71st Sts.)
734-9430**
*Dinner nightly until 10:30 P.M.;
closed Sun.*
All major credit cards
French (nouvelle)

For three years, Le Plaisir was among a handful of New York restaurants serving nouvelle cuisine comparable in style and delicacy to the best available in France. While the restaurant was closed for alterations during the summer of 1981, the talented Japanese chef, Masataba Koboyahi (known as Masa) dropped by and announced to the owners that he was leaving to open his own restaurant in Napa Valley, California. In January 1982, Le Plaisir reopened under the new management of Pierre Jourdan, twenty-four, of the Jourdan shoe-store clan, with Guy Reuge (formerly of La Tulipe) as chef.

Masa's dramatic renditions of nouvelle are a hard act to follow. But the ambitious menu developed by Guy and Pierre suggests that they are determined to try. The results are mixed, but perhaps it is too early to make a conclusive judgment. The oysters in Champagne sauce are perfect, and the salad of scallops and artichokes is fresh and invigorating; but the mousse of trout and salmon is not light and fluffy enough. The tender slices of squab with wild mushrooms is extraordinary, as is the fillet of veal with fresh pasta. The lobster with julienne vegetables totally misses the mark.

The cheese tray offers only three varieties, a triple crème, a chèvre, and a French blue; but each has reached the point of ripeness for total enjoyment. The French bread is of exceptional quality, crisp and tasty, rare on this side of the Atlantic. A pear cake and a raspberry chocolate cake are rich and exotic, but the chocolate soufflé with crème Anglaise is pedestrian.

The wine list is even more ambitious than the menu. The great wines of France are represented, and some of the most notable years. Prices reflect the reputations of the labels, with dozens of selections in the $50 to $200 range. A good, moderately priced choice is the Canon de Brem (St. Émilion '78) at $24.

Le Plaisir is still one of the few intimate and elegant establishments remaining in New York (seats 46). Shadow box frames against the textured coral-tinted walls hold interesting works of contemporary artists. These works change every several months, as you would expect in a gallery on 57th Street.

The prix-fixe dinner was $35 when Masa held forth in the kitchen: it is now $46. The question is whether Pierre, with Guy at the stove, can build the following that Le Plaisir knew when Masa was there. The dinner with a modest wine can easily run to $70, when you include wine, tax, and tip. That kind of bill won't help Le Plaisir attain the popular acclaim it once enjoyed, even if Guy should make it to the summit where Masa already stands.

**12/20**
## The Post House
**28 E. 63rd St.**
**935-2888**
*Lunch and dinner daily until 11:00 P.M.; no lunch Sat. or Sun.*
*All major credit cards*
Steaks/Continental

Sort of a big brasserie on the main floor of the Lowell Hotel. Its pleasant but rather cold decor of pale woodwork and pottery tiles is warmed by the presence of a life-size oil painting in a period frame of a woman who, apparently a victim of the 1929 crash, covered her nudity with one of the living room curtains. Evenings are less lively, but at lunch, the clientele is served excellent steaks that spill over the edge of the plate (ask for the smaller lunch steak, which is sufficient for two), spareribs, red snapper, very good spinach, an honest pine-nut cake, and an espresso that would have been perfect had it been better filtered. Around $25, including a glass of white wine.

**8/20**
## Praha Czechoslovak Restaurant
**1358 First Ave.**
**(73rd St.)**
**988-3505**
*Lunch and dinner daily until 11:00 P.M.*
*All major credit cards*
Continental

If you are starving and need to fill your stomach without spending your last penny, why not go to Praha? The portions are enormous, and heaped bowls of sauerkraut, red cabbage, and dumplings are placed in the middle of the table, family-style, if there are several of you. The menu of Czech specialties is extensive, but the dishes that come from the kitchen seem to have languished too long, and have lost their zest. The boiled beef can be tough, but the accompanying dill sauce makes the dish worth trying. You might also try the duck (or goose when available) or the rabbit in a nicely seasoned white cream sauce. The palacinky (crêpes with apricot or prunes) are so-so, and the apple pie is definitely not the article that G.I.'s fought for.

The main dining room is cheery, if a bit noisy with the banter of hearty diners. A black-and-white wall panorama of Prague reminds you that the Czech capital city is not forgotten. The price of the daily special varies from $10 on Monday (potato soup and duck) to $13.50 on Saturday (liver dumpling soup and fillet of beef), and the price includes the appetizer, entree, and dessert. With steins of imported beer at $1.50, two can gorge themselves for $25–$30, which these days is something to write home about.

**13** ♤
## Primavera
**1570 First Ave.**
**(81st-82nd Sts.)**
**861-8608**
*Dinner nightly until midnight; closed Sun.*
*All major credit cards*
Italian

Don't forget to reserve a long time in advance, as people jostle each other at the entrance to this long, little Italian restaurant, with its somber bricks, attractive paintings, bar-style chairs, tulip-shaped lamps, distinguished customers, serious and pleasant service, and noise. Avoid the dismal, varied hors d'oeuvre (antipasto) and choose a good plate of pasta, a remarkable house specialty, even if the "pasta of the day" in chicken liver sauce was somewhat heavy the other evening (the tortellini with peas and ham are exquisite). The gambaroni (jumbo shrimp) were admirably cooked in a garlicky butter sauce; the grilled fish was very fresh, and the huge veal chop was very satisfying. With a chocolate cake, an honest Italian wine (a delicate Travaglini Gattinara in a rather curious bottle), dinner will come to around $40.

**8/20**
## Quo Vadis
**26 E. 63rd St.**
**838-0590**
*Dinner nightly; closed Sun.; formal*
*All major credit cards*
French (classical)

If you asked a friend, in Latin, "Where are you going for dinner?" and he replies, "XXVI Via LXIII," don't accompany him. We were told that this pompous restaurant was gradually getting back its luster of old. In that case, it must have started again from scratch. Oh, happiness can be found beneath the Pompeian ceilings, in the chef's pâté, a salad, and sautéed vegetables. If you're not too demanding about the quality of the produce, if the efficient but charmless service and the company of dinosaurs appeal to you, you'll be pleased. But in our case a metallic-tasting eel au vert, a dilapidated sole meunière, and little sautéed scallops, of which our teeth still conserve a few fibrous souvenirs, were quite enough. The "quo" may, if the Roman gods are kind, improve under its new management.

**8/20**
## Rao's
**114th St.**
**(455 E. Pleasant Ave.)**
**534-9625**
*Dinner Mon. to Fri. until*
*10:00 P.M.*
*No credit cards*
Italian

It's probably because he cooks in a cowboy hat that the owner of this little Italian bistro is so well liked by New York columnists. Indeed, we see no gastronomical reason at all to visit a dismal neighborhood on the borders of Harlem, little frequented by taxis. The cuisine is disconcertingly insipid, the Parmesan is mediocre, the vegetables are not drained, the desserts are nonexistent. Only the white Corvo from Palermo added a little sunshine to this bleak menu.

**12/20**
## Le Refuge Restaurant
**116 E. 82nd St.**
**861-4505**
*Lunch and dinner daily until*
*11:00 P.M.; closed Sun.*
*No credit cards*
French (classical)

The tile sign over the curtained window reads: "Plats Chauds—Le Refuge Restaurant—Boisson." Inside, you are in the dining room of a provincial French inn. An ancient tapestry interrupts the plainness of the white wall to your right. Your eye picks up the warmth of the table settings; blue ironstone plates and tall, etched stemware on the handful of bare wood tables. There is evidence all around that the moving spirit here, a young Frenchman named Pierre Saint Denis, has taste. He also has a light-handed way in the kitchen, that combines to make this an extremely popular neighborhood restaurant. Among his best dishes are an appetizer of chicken livers with the slightest taste of blueberries, entrees of calf's brains with capers, tiny soft shell crabs in season, and a chicken of the day in a light cream reduction with a hint of orange. Unfortunately, some of his sauces don't come off so well. The snails (an appetizer) were submerged in a sweet-tasting concoction with raisins, and a chicken of the day "au Calvados" had a surprising sweetness that overwhelmed the tartness of the apple brandy. The apricot soufflé was too sweet.

This French chef would be well advised to resist the temptation to appeal to the American sweet tooth. When he resists that temptation, the result is quite good.

Young, second generation Franco-Americans, fluent in both languages, provide friendly and efficient service. Three-course a la carte dinner for two with a pleasant enough Château Simard will run to $60.

## 12/20
## Le Relais
**712 Madison Ave.**
**(63rd St.)**
**751-5108**
*Lunch and dinner daily until*
*11:00 P.M.; reservations necessary;*
*AE*
French (classical)

A relatively recent creation popular in the world of fashion models, couturiers, affluent foreigners, and the like. It has one of the rare terraces in New York, a crowded bar, and a main dining room decorated with mirrors, old engravings, and knickknacks. Saturday lunch is particularly sought-after, but one must fight for a table any day of the week. It is understood that the cuisine is unremarkable, and that people go there essentially to see and be seen. All things considered, one eats decently there (at decent prices): céleri rémoulade, endives with Roquefort, grilled steak béarnaise, and several fussier dishes, such as chicken with raspberry vinegar (quite adequate, but on which the chef, just to be smart, tossed a handful of fresh raspberries).

## 12/20
## The Restaurant
**35 E. 76th St.**
**(Carlyle Hotel)**
**744-1600**
*Lunch and dinner daily until*
*10:00 P.M.; reservations necessary;*
*formal*
*All major credit cards*
Continental

This dining room is one of the most civilized in New York, with its large mirrors, chocolate-brown suede walls, sumptuous bouquets of flowers, white linen-covered tables, and chandeliers glimmering through the semi-obscurity. In such a decor, it is only right to speak in a lowered voice, to wear real jewels, to have a Cézanne hanging in one's living room, and to pick at distinguished dishes, which, like the grilled fillets of sole, the cold poached salmon, or the tournedos béarnaise, are too elegant to draw attention to themselves. If they're not wildly exciting, these dishes are at least of impeccable quality and are perfectly served by the best personnel in the city.

## 9/20
## Serendipity
**255 E. 60th St.**
**838-3531**
*Lunch and dinner daily until*
*midnight; reservations necessary;*
*wine and beer only*
*All major credit cards*
American

The T-shirts, Texan boots, dolls, and cakes of soap sold in this amusing boutique are likely to be more easily consumed than the sautéed chicken livers, the feeble curried chicken or the red caviar, served under attractive Tiffany-style lamps. The place is typical of New York, and it's possible to be undamaged by an openface roast beef sandwich, lemon pie, and an espresso or a hot chocolate with cinnamon, while admiring the attractive customers out of the corner of your eye.

## 7/20
## Sign of the Dove
**1110 Third Ave.**
**(65th St.)**
**861-8080**
*Lunch and dinner daily until*
*midnight; no lunch Mon.; jacket*
*and tie recommended*
*All major credit cards*
Continental

Dine with your eyes only in this exquisite 1900s-style winter garden with its plants and beautiful people. You'll enjoy yourself and avoid one of the most disastrous meals possible in Manhattan (for around $35), served promptly by young men in yachting blazers who tack this way and that, as though they had too much wind in their sails. Yes, you'll say, but how can one avoid the gratin de fruits de mer Neptune and the duck with brandy? It's easy. Just stay at the bar.

## 13 ♔
## Szechuan East
**1540 Second Ave.
(near 80th St.)
535-4921**
*Lunch and dinner daily until
11:30 P.M. (weekends until
12:30 A.M.)
AE, DC*
Chinese

This is one of the most commendable and popular among the restaurants of every sort of origin, notably Chinese, that line Second Avenue near 80th Street. A good-natured clientele comprising both young people and families is always crowded into the big, simple dining rooms, in which the only ethnic indications are several imitation antique engravings. The cuisine, by contrast, sacrifices nothing of the hearty traditions of Szechuan province. Choose dishes marked with one—or better still, two—red asterisks. These include hot and sour soup, Szechuan East special beef, ta-chien chicken, or the sauteed shrimp in hot pepper sauce (the crisp assorted vegetables will alleviate the burning). You will thus partake of a marvelously spicy meal that will not merely set fire to your mouth, but also delight you with its vigor, precision, and authenticity. Don't get carried away when you're ordering, though, as the portions are gargantuan.

## 12/20
## Trastevere
**309 E. 83rd St.
734-6343**
*Lunch and dinner daily until
11:00 P.M.; reservations necessary
AE*
Italian

You might as well be in the Trastevere. Ten or so tables are crowded together, several engravings of Rome hang on a crudely painted white wall, recorded bel canto is belted out at full volume, there's a mama at the stove (who can be seen through the open door), and her sons Paul and Maurizio take care of the rest with Roman liveliness and good spirits. The opening of this tiny restaurant last year was welcomed by certain food critics with somewhat excessive enthusiasm. Did not one of them go so far as to speak of 'Italian nouvelle cuisine?' It exists, but certainly not at the Trastevere, where the owners are content (in itself a very good thing) to serve classic, robust dishes in which fresh herbs and garlic are used liberally. Unfortunately, the use of garlic is a bit heavy-handed; its overpowering presence crushes the finesse of the delicious capellini with peas, of the huge, tasty, breaded veal cutlet Trastevere, and of the chicken alla Gaetano in its delicate wine and mushroom sauce. The gâteau St. Honoré, the zuppa inglese, and the chocolate pie alla Rebecca, all delicious, were happy exceptions. The espresso coffee was mediocre. We're very tempted to give a toque to the Trastevere, but the deadly recollection of the garlic keeps coming back; perhaps another time. $20 to $30 with house wine.

## 13 ♔
## Uncle Tai's
**1049 Third Ave.
(62nd-63rd Sts.)
752-9065**
*Lunch and dinner daily until
11:00 P.M.
AE, DC, CB*
Chinese

At last, a Chinese restaurant that doesn't kowtow to the American dislike of hot peppers. Take advantage of it in order to discover some of the specialties of Hunan, a province in central China; its heavily spiced cuisine helps the people resist the rigors of its interminable winters. As is often the case in the United States, the decor of this restaurant rigorously avoids Chinese curios. You'll discover dishes that are among the heartiest in Asia, such as sliced duck with young ginger root, beef à l'Uncle Tai, or the superbly seasoned vegetable plate, in an austere dining room decorated in rather chilling blue tones.

Everything here displays refinement. As for the prices, they're remarkably reasonable considering the quality. Count on around $17 for a veritable banquet, as tasty as it is surprising.

**12/20**
## Uzie's
**1442 Third Ave.**
**744-8020**
*Dinner nightly until 12:30 A.M.;*
*brunch on Sat. and Sun.*
*No credit cards*
Italian

We've lost it, but if you're really interested, we can find the name of the owner of this little restaurant-bar where for some time ultrasmart New Yorkers have jostled each other nightly. If memory serves us, he is the former husband of an American millionairess. In any case, you have only to ask him: he's there every evening, very urbane, surrounded by a galaxy of pretty women and men in good tweeds. It's difficult to find a seat, but despite appearances Uzie's is not a club. Ask in advance and you'll get a poor table. The good ones—that is, those in the bar—are given to the faithful and to celebrities passing through. In any case, the place is cheerful, pleasant, the service is amiable, and the Italian cuisine is not bad at all. In addition to the menu, the waiters announce six or seven daily specials, and we did well to order good tortellini with spinach and ham followed by a slice of perfectly cooked swordfish garnished with saffron rice. Finish up with a remarkable ricotta cheesecake, try some white Toscany Nozzola; and for around $30 you'll have a pleasant evening.

**13** ♟
## Le Veau d'Or
**129 E. 60th St.**
**838-8133**
*Lunch and dinner daily until*
*10:30 P.M.; closed Sun.*
*AE*
French (provincial)

*11-12*
*7:30*

An imperturbable old French bistro with an idiotic but friendly decor (photos, a painting of a sleeping calf), a smiling welcome, bustling service; it's also noisy, good-natured, and crowded. In Paris this sort of place is gradually disappearing, and it's not what is served here (artichokes vinaigrette, tomato salad, onion soup, pâté de campagne, spring chicken "grand-mère," leg of lamb, or loin of pork) that will bring them back into fashion. In New York, people are delighted to find this simple, generous cuisine, carefully prepared with excellent produce. Our most recent lunch: fresh mussels rémoulade, fresh seafood platter, tender pork roast with mashed potatoes, well-chosen cheeses, and a rum parfait. Nothing surprising in any of it, except for a refreshing honesty. A la carte, count on spending $30 to $45, including a house Beaujolais.

**14** ♟
## Vienna Park
**33 E. 60th St.**
**758-1051**
*Lunch and dinner daily until*
*10:00 P.M.; Sat. dinner only;*
*closed Sun.*
*All major credit cards*
Continental (nouvelle)

There is a bit of old-world elegance here: the subdued colors of the plain walls and banquettes; prints of Vienna's famed "lippizzaner"—white horses—on the walls of the club-like room to the rear; the tiny frosted-glass vases holding fresh flowers on each table. At lunch, Madison Avenue types achieve sanity; at dinner one senses that the clientele neither needs to see who is at the next table nor cares very much. The kitchens of Vienna have felt the impact of French nouvelle; sauces are lighter and seafood is more commonplace than it once was.

Vienna Park has brought this cuisine to New York. This is not by any means a carbon copy of Vienna 79, under the same management, which continues to serve the traditional cooking of old Vienna. You can order more than acceptable old standbys, such as excellent boiled rib of beef with horseradish sauce, chicken with apples and apple brandy, or a whole baby chicken with a creamed paprika sauce. But more interesting are the dishes where the chef has borrowed more heavily from the French nouvelle cuisine. At night, you can feast on a whole baby salmon with two sauces or at lunch on sole with a mousse of scallops and lobster sauce.

You would expect first-rate desserts and you would be correct. Try the moist almond cake with bittersweet chocolate coating, the sachertorte, or the apple strudel with cream whipped the way the chef learned at home. Or an excellent raspberry soufflé.

Service is professional and there are wines to fit every pocketbook. Lunch for two, with a couple of glasses of wine, will run $50 or more, and the dinner for two $75, or a lot more if you go for a big bottle from the comprehensive wine list.

## 12/20
# Vienna 79
**320 E. 79th St.**
**734-4700**
*Dinner nightly until 11:00 P.M.;*
*closed Sun.*
*All the major credit cards*
Austrian

Four or five years ago, this was a favorite Mafia restaurant under a different name, so much so that one evening three gentlemen in dark glasses armed with submachine guns burst in and sprayed the seemingly placid customers with bullets. Alas! They got the wrong target and hit some harmless Jewish butchers from Brooklyn who were celebrating a birthday. The killers disappeared, three innocent butchers died, and the police closed the place. It opened later under the name "House of Vienna," without achieving the success expected. But now, directed by a team of real Austrians, this elegant but rather stiff restaurant has become a success. Unfortunately, Viennese cuisine is one of the most trying in the world except for Hungarian dishes, which are full of fire and character. Of course, customers are no longer assassinated at Vienna 79; one is content to smother them a little with overcooked trout à la Mozart, schnitzel, fillet of beef Metternich, and several other typical dishes that don't exactly have the lightness of a Viennese waltz. Nonetheless, we know the restaurants of the Austrian capital well, and we can confirm that this one would figure among the top few traditional ones. The cuisine is deadly dull, but at least it uses good produce scrupulously prepared. The best dish is apparently the very classic tafelspitz (boiled beef and vegetables with horseradish sauce), a treat of the Emperor Franz Josef. Good marks for the desserts as well, which are enormous and plumed with whipped cream; less extraordinary to eat than to look at, but charming all the same. Around $35 to $45.

## 11/20
# Vivolo
**140 E. 74th St.**
**628-4671**

This is a busy (and noisy) establishment that draws crowds deep into the evenings as if there was no other place to eat in the neighborhood. At street level, there is

*Dinner nightly until 11:15 P.M.*
*All major credit cards*
Italian

dark wood paneling on the walls and tables cluttered around the bar. Upstairs you are in the brighter, calmer atmosphere of what once was the drawing room of a private house.

Among the more interesting appetizers are mozzarella cheese dipped in batter and bread crumbs, then deep-fried, with an anchovy butter on the side. Also an Adriatic-style cold seafood salad, flavored with a light olive oil dressing. Both are tasty. Regular entrees include fettuccine with tomatoes, prosciutto, and onions and a veal chop, stuffed with mozzarella and prosciutto. There are daily specials of pasta, veal, chicken, and fish. Unfortunately, the kitchen cannot always keep up with the crowds, and what appears on your plate may not be as carefully prepared as it should be. Sometimes the ingredients (the veal for example) are not the best.

But Vivolo is full of life, and the crowds keep coming. And on the whole, the food is better than the neighborhood competition. About $30.

## 10/20
## Wood's
**718 Madison Ave.**
**(63rd-64th Sts.)**
**688-1126**
*Lunch and dinner daily until*
*11:00 P.M.; closed Sun.;*
*reservations necessary*
*AE, MC, V*
French
(classical/nouvelle)

Spotlessly clean and pleasantly arranged (although the tables are small and too close together), Wood's is the typical Madison Avenue restaurant where young women lunch after the hairdresser or a morning of shopping. The menu is not without interest, but the dishes don't live up to expectations. The steamed bass is overcooked, the sauce for the pepper steak is mediocre. One can choose among generally well done hors d'oeuvre from a trolley, excellent steamed vegetables in lemon butter, and to conclude, a cheesecake. Fairly crowded, with higher prices in the evening, when despite everything the atmosphere is duller.

# West 59th Street and Above

## 13
## Café des Artistes
**1 W. 67th St.**
**877-3500**
*Lunch and dinner daily until*
*11:30 P.M.; no lunch Sat.;*
*Sun. brunch*

Journalists, Columbia University professors, Lincoln Center types, and much of the West Side intelligentsia eat here among the plant life and splendid paintings of young nudes of the late '20s. The cuisine is solid, different every day, honestly prepared, and served promptly, at very moderate prices. Dishes include, for example, a good pâté "du chef," a delicious salmon

131

All major credit cards
French (provincial)

marinated in dill with mustard sauce, a hearty Provençal fish soup with garlic, well-made pot-au-feu (boiled beef with vegetables), lovely lamb rather curiously accompanied by béarnaise sauce, and admirable chocolate cake. Around $30 with a carafe of good California wine, and an excellent espresso.

**11/20**

## Hunan Balcony

**2596 Broadway
(98th St.)
865-9200**
*Lunch and dinner daily until
11:00 P.M.
All major credit cards*
Chinese

The Hunan Balcony is situated on a large, light corner site, far pleasanter than most of the rather sleazy restaurants on upper Broadway "Strip," with comfortable chairs and a bar that can make a good martini.

The food is largely Hunanese from the late Chairman's home province, and its hot, spicy character is said to have contributed to his aquatic prowess and longevity. Excellent griddle-fried dumplings and cold duck in bean sauce. Cold noodles with a sauce of sesame, soy garlic, and scallions were compulsively edible, sprinkled with tiny shreds of Sichuan pickle for crispness.

Alas, the sea bass was heralded by a whiff, suggesting less than perfect freshness, that preceded it to the table, and was confirmed once the crunchy skin was cut into. The sauce was agreeably thickened with chopped vegetables rather than the usual cornstarch, and laced with lots of ginger that almost masked the shortcomings. "Never on Sunday," must be our advice to sea bass fanciers in Chinese restaurants.

General Ching scores again with his chicken, crispy morsels that are moist inside with a hot, pungent sauce, garnished with steamed broccoli. Asked for the recipe, the manager brusquely disclaimed any knowledge of kitchen secrets: "I am not a cook," he barked. Indeed service was conspicuously lacking in charm and our waiter appeared to be blind and deaf on one side—ours. Knowing the intimidating size of New York's Chinese helpings, we enquired about half portions. "Chef too busy to make half portions," came the elliptical reply.

Yet in spite of surly service, this is a very good restaurant indeed. Hunan pork, four-flavored beef, Hunan lamb, and scallops in garlic sauce were all good, and we particularly enjoyed the tofu in a black bean sauce that really penetrated and flavored this intractable curd. Light banana fritters stuffed with sweet bean paste were perfect, washed down with sustaining cups of an unusual dark, aromatic tea. We would have liked to know its name but didn't dare ask.

No wine list, but the dry white house wine is admirable. $15 with wine.

**12/20**

## Indian Oven

**285 Columbus Ave.**

The powerful odor of the spices in this tiny, tidy white Indian restaurant immediately reassures you, as does the honest cuisine which is served to apparently enthusiastic

132

**(73rd St.)**
**362-7567**
*Lunch and dinner daily until*
*11:00 P.M.; closed Mon.*
*All major credit cards*
Indian

regulars. We won't class Indian Oven among the best Indian restaurants in the city; for the price (less than $10), it is certainly a good place to know. The bread is delicious, the mulligatawny soup well made; we particularly liked the shajahani curry (chicken with saffron rice) recommended by the waiter. Try the finely malted Indian Eagle beer.

**8/20**
## Museum Cafe
**366 Columbus Ave.**
**(77th St.)**
**799-0150**
*Lunch and dinner daily until*
*2:00 A.M.; no reservations*
*No credit cards*
American

After a visit to the Museum of Natural History, whose cafeteria should be avoided, one can sit down on the terrace of this amusing cafe on the Upper West Side, which is currently being revived. You'll do so more to look at the crowd than to eat overcooked bluefish and undercooked vegetables. In the evening, the bar is very lively, and the pleasant encounters there help you forget the cuisine.

**8/20**
## O'Neals' Baloon
**269 Columbus Ave.**
**(opposite Lincoln Center)**
**399-2353**
*Lunch and dinner daily until*
*11:30 P.M.*
*All major credit cards*
Continental

O'Neals' advertises itself as a "drinking and eating establishment" and "New York City's first saloon." Whatever the claims, certainly the liquid refreshments and surrounding activities are more important than what is offered on the menu.

Consider the bar. It is fifty feet long, and two rows of seventy stem-up glasses hang overhead. Bar patrons from their stool perches can gaze out through the windows separating the bar from the sidewalk cafe, and see Lincoln Center across Columbus Avenue. The inside dining area is 1900s vintage Bowery—dark wood, imitation gas lamps, brass railings separating tables and nooks and crannies on several levels. The Baloon seats 265. The menu offers chili con carne, chicken pot pie, spare ribs, and ravioli with salad, as well as a few burgers, salads, and desserts. There are half a dozen wines, reasonably priced.

O'Neals' is a place to have a drink, a snack, or a bit more, before (or after) a Lincoln Center performance. The crowd itself puts on a pretty good show. After a couple of drinks, you may not want to cross the street for a professional performance at prices three or four times what you'll find on your bill at O'Neals'.

**10/20**
## Ruelles
**321 Columbus Ave.**
**(75th St.)**
**799-5100**
*Lunch and dinner daily until*
*2:00 A.M.; reservations suggested*
*in the evening; Sun. brunch*
*All major credit cards*
Continental

The cuisine is rather banal, but you can savor the atmosphere of Columbus Avenue, which is becoming a new Village, while eating an unremarkable salad and steak on the terrace in summer. Ruelles is certainly one of this area's most representative and best known bistros.

**13** 🍴
## Shun Lee West
**43 W. 65th St.**

When a restaurant starts having financial difficulties, it's Orientalized, and the problems are over. That's what happened at Le Poulailler (originally opened by the

**595-8896**

*Lunch and dinner daily until 10:30 P.M.; dim sum until midnight; dim sum brunch Sat. and Sun.; reservation suggested AE*

Chinese

owners of La Caravelle) which was sold recently to Michael Tung, who runs several of New York's most famous Chinese restaurants (Shun Lee Palace, Shun Lee Dynasty, and the Hunam). The new decor is not exactly inspiring, and the tea room next to the street that features dim sum is a failure. But the staff is efficient, the menu extremely original and varied, with Hunan, Szechuan, and Pekinese specialties and most importantly, the cooking is perfectly executed and rigorously authentic. We were in China not too long ago, and we would have been quite content had we been served more often such delicious, delicate, and well-seasoned dishes as the shrimp with garlic and scallions, herbed spareribs, crispy fried Hunan-style sea bass, sesame chicken, and an exquisite crispy orange-flavored beef. The hot and spicy dishes are marked with an asterisk on the menu, and are, in our opinion, the most interesting ones. Even the tea, undeservedly neglected by so many Chinese restaurants, has a delicious aroma. Chef Wang and his team offer as well a selection of some fifteen dim sum for a quick bite before or after an evening at nearby Lincoln Center; these are prepared with the same attention as the more elaborate dishes.

**9/20**

## Simon's

**75 W. 68th St.**
**496-7477**

*Lunch and dinner daily until 11:00 P.M.; late supper until 2:00 A.M.; no liquor AE*

American
(nouvelle)

It's unfortunate that Jon Simon did not partake of our meal, as he could have written a very interesting article about it. Jon Simon was a food critic before opening this uncomfortable little restaurant, whose decor veers from "trapper's cabin" to art deco, in an unpleasant basement near Lincoln Center. It is always embarrassing to say disagreeable things about a former colleague, but he has gone over to the other side, so too bad for him. Anyway, he'll get over it. His restaurant is always full, his fashionable clientele seems delighted, and ever since Walter Cronkite gave his farewell dinner there he has had no cause for concern, since it is now terribly "in." There are two kinds of nouvelle cuisine: the real and the fake. Jon Simon seems to have opted for the second, which is his right. But it's also our right to gripe vigorously, after eating carpaccio curiously cut in thick slices, without the slightest drop of olive oil or lemon juice; green noodles with basil that would have been good if they had been salted; a chicken and mango salad of very vague flavor, containing string beans cut up and practically raw (the curse of American cooking), and to top it all off, an iron-clad and barely cuttable profiterole (filled, on the other hand, with an excellent coffee ice cream). As you read the rest of the menu—presented by honest but totally inexperienced waiters who place dishes destined for the next table under your nose—you think you're dreaming: lobster bisque, ham omelet, Chinese vegetable salad, tournedos with eggs. . . . Where is the nouvelle cuisine in all that? Jon Simon will no doubt reply that we have only to come in the evening, when the dishes are decidedly more elaborate. Perhaps, but when one doesn't know how to prepare green noodles, is one better able to prepare lobster beurre blanc, beef tournedos, veal with a poached pear, or red shrimps and medallions of lotte with mousse of red peppers? Lunch: around $15: dinner: $25 to $30 (not including wine).

## 8/20
## Tavern on the Green
**Central Park West (67th St.)**
**873-3200**
*Lunch and dinner daily until 1:00 A.M.; Sun. brunch; reservations suggested*
*All major credit cards*
American/Continental

This immense greenhouse, transformed at a cost of millions of dollars into an extravagant restaurant, makes you think of some set from a '50s musical. Ceilings in Viennese-style whipped cream, Venetian chandeliers, Moorish columns, life-size plaster deer: it would be difficult to dream up anything more staggering and at the same time more entertaining than this junk shop in the middle of the park, where the ill-assorted crowd is celebrating ten birthdays at different tables, and where a battalion of waiters bustle hither and thither clearing out customers to make way for those waiting to get in. Some time ago the menu announced, in large letters, the presence of "the extraordinary Daniel Dunas, head chef of the Connaught in London for 12 years." The menu was incredibly uninteresting and, after careful consideration, the presence of this artist must have seemed less necessary to Warner Leroy, the Tavern's owner; he had the good sense to replace him with nobody. It is indeed likely that the food served in the Tavern is created by spontaneous generation. Under no circumstances can one reproach the chef for serving an omelet with onions and a foreign object vaguely resembling a dog's ear, which finally turned out to be a fossilized croissant; reheated bacon, first-class meats drowned in grease, giant french fries still in their skins, and a banana cheesecake that would have smothered Desdemona more quickly than her pillow. One of the great moments in the life of Tavern on the Green is Sunday brunch. By reserving three days in advance, you can hope to secure a table for around 3 o'clock in the afternoon. It's one of the most celebrated attractions in New York, and if you want to see a middle-class dream come true—strawberry omelet and American Champagne—it's not to be missed. But don't take it upon yourself to ask the maître d'hôtel to prepare a steak tartare for you. He'll reply, as he did to us, while rolling his eyes filled with alarm: "A steak tartare? But it takes too much time!"

## 12/20
## Teacher's
**2249 Broadway (80th-81st Sts.)**
**787-3500**
*Lunch and dinner daily until 1:00 A.M.*
*All major credit cards*
American/Continental

Teacher's is a neighborhood pub that serves surprisingly good and interesting food—and at reasonable prices. It has become so popular that the management opened a twin, Teacher's Too, a block north at 2271 Broadway. The Thai chef (he supervises the kitchen at both establishments) is adept at preparing the spicy dishes of his homeland as well as many classical French, Italian, American, and even Mexican dishes. So appetizers include Thai pork with a tangy peanut sauce, French snails and country pâté, Italian avocado with pimiento and clams casino, American chopped chicken liver, and Mexican guacamole with toasted tortillas, perhaps the freshest and tastiest around town.

Chicken, beef, and shrimp dishes with Thai seasonings stand out among the entrees. But less adventurous pub crawlers can order a bucket of steamed littleneck clams with broth and drawn butter, spare ribs, hamburger with potatoes, or various pastas. Specials on the blackboard can range from a perfectly poached scrod with a delicate white wine reduction (the chef knows nouvelle, too) or chicken Kiev.

Two desserts stand out: a moist orange cake and a raspberry yogurt pie. The wine list appears on a single blackboard that travels from table to table. Bottles have been carefully selected for quality and price. Try the Soave or Bardolino, at $6.25. Or celebrate your anniversary with a California Korbel brut for $11.95. Prices are not much more than you'll find at the corner retail liquor shop.

You won't be enchanted with your surroundings, which include lots of mirrors, some art deco prints, exposed ducts and vents overhead—and diners attired in almost anything but tie and jacket, or skirt. Concentrate on the food (and the pretty waitresses) and you'll probably want to return to see what new things the chef has up his sleeve. But reserve ahead. Even with Teacher's Too, the management is having difficulty taking care of the Upper West Siders who have been careful not to tell their friends across town about their neighborhood pub. Dinner $10 to $15, not including wines.

## 12/20
## Tovarisch
**38 W. 62nd St.**
**757-0168**
*Lunch and dinner daily until*
*11:00 P.M.; closed Sun.*
*V, MC, AE*
Russian

Less than a "verst" from Lincoln Center lies Tovarisch, the latest addition to the rather meager Russian eating scene in New York. Patently misnamed, Tovarisch aspires to a touch of prerevolutionary grandeur; its future is unlikely to lie with meatballs and kasha.

Owner Marvin Safir has been lucky to secure the services of Boris Blekh, a talented young chef who recently defected from Arbat, one of Moscow's most fashionable restaurants. Safir, who drives to work on a motorbike and whose trademark is a raffish black eyepatch, stakes his claim to being a Russian restaurateur on having a Russian great aunt and having been the first postwar U.S. tourist in Moscow. In any event, he and Boris have created a restaurant that with proper care may yet put Russian cooking back on the map.

The two-room restaurant is friendly and attractive with a bar where you can drown your sorrows in a choice of plain or flavored vodkas served at permafrost temperatures. Service is getting better and mine host frequently vaults over the bar, Polovtsian style, to replenish your glass. As befits a Russian restaurant, there is a good zakuska table with appetizers ranging from maatjes herring fillets and sturgeon to eggplant "caviar" and basturma, the wind-dried beef from the Caucasus.

But no true believer could resist "blini imperial" ($15.75 per person), the complete and perfect starter. Hot, yeasty pancakes arrive as the center-piece of a lazy Susan, encircled with different kinds of caviar, smoked fish, and other vodka-compatible tidbits. You set to work with melted butter and sour cream, pausing only to down your glass. The staff will ensure that it is never empty. A word of warning—go easy on the blini: this starter could finish you off!

Lamb and pork shashlyks are served with tart plum sauce and pomegranate juice respectively, and we liked chicken tabaka. You eat with your hands, dipping the pieces in Tkemali sauce, the hot and spicy plum ketchup of Georgia, USSR. Siberian pelemeni poached in consommé were outstanding and connoisseurs of cheese blintzes will warm to the alternative blinchiki, filled with kasha and mushrooms. Lunch can be a jolly affair, but if you have to clock in afterwards, stick to Russian mineral water.

Prices are moderate, although caviar cravers may be in for a rude shock. Here's hoping that Safir lives up to his house slogan, "Let them eat caviar—at proletarian prices." $30 with wine or a couple of vodkas.

# Brooklyn and the Bronx

13 🏠
## Amerigos
**3587 E. Tremont Ave.**
**The Bronx**
**792-3600**
*Lunch and dinner daily except*
*Tues. 11:00 until midnight*
*(2:00 A.M. Fri. and Sat.)*
*All major credit cards*
Italian

When Amerigo and Millie Coppola opened their little pizzeria in the Bronx over forty years ago, the neighbors little suspected they were harboring the Ludwig of Bavaria of the pasta belt. To Amerigo (named for the man after whom America was named), small was never beautiful, and now he has achieved his dream palace, a huge two-room restaurant of quite amazing vulgarity where he serves some of the best Italian food in the city. Everything is crimson, the carpet, the walls, the waiters—there is even a twenty-foot-wide crimson waterfall, fronted by a broken pillar and a statue of an athlete scratching his foot—no doubt Signor Coppola's gesture toward classic grace.

Millie is still in the kitchen, which on inspection proves to be of quite staggering cleanliness and efficiency.

137

Amerigo and his maître d'hôtel, Toni, rule the front of the house. Even the waiters carry beepers in their pockets like surgeons, to insure speedy service. The homemade pastas are delicious—you should try the gnocchi, which recently won a competition against all comers, or the capelle d'angeli provinciale, fine noodles in a great sauce of olives, prosciutto, peas, pimentos, and capers. The chicken cacciatore was treated classically, cooked al bianco in the frying pan, with white wine, garlic, and mushrooms—not a trace of the ubiquitous tomato sauce that can ruin this dish. Hot vegetables proved too oily, but a dark, slightly bitter salad of arugula and radishes was crisply refreshing. There is a lot of good, fresh seafood here, but make sure its simply prepared—the over-spicy sauce diavolo is a real killer.

A word of warning—lay off the scrumptious Abruzzese bread, or crunchy sesame-coated grissini. Portions are enormous; in fact one helping of pasta could well serve four people as an appetizer. Sweets are mostly brought in from Ferrara's bakery, but there's a good ricotta-based cheesecake. If you are rash enough to follow this with a cappucino you'll surely regret it—it's a dessert in its own right, a goblet of coffee topped with a pyramid of sweet whipped cream. The wine list ranges from sound Italian vinos to top Burgundies and clarets.

Amerigos is situated five miles south of the Westchester border, and a good thirty minutes by cab from the center of town—it's a long trek, but worth it. About $25 with an Italian wine. Booking essential at weekends.

---

**12/20**

# Gage and Tollner
**372 Fulton St. (between Smith and Pearl Sts.) Brooklyn
875-5181**
*Lunch and dinner daily until 9:00 P.M.; closed Sun.
All major credit cards*
American

This, one of the oldest restaurants in New York, opened in 1879, and it's one of the few whose reputation has crossed the East River. The panels of old cherry wood, flocked garnet-red wallpaper, etched mirrors, gas-burning copper chandeliers, and big marble bar haven't changed for more than a century—and, one is tempted to add, neither have the waiters. An emblem indicates their seniority (a golden eagle for twenty-five years of service, a gold star for five years, etc.), and if all of them are not yet centenarians, they'll still be working when they are. Go to Gage and Tollner for lunch, when lawyers take over the place, choosing from among seventy-six different preparations of oysters and clams (very good New England-style clam chowder), ten preparations of coquilles Saint Jacques, eleven of lobster, and so on. Also very fresh fish, which you should ask to have prepared in the simplest way possible. The meats, grilled over charcoal, are first-class. If you're hungry, order a sirloin steak; otherwise, the minute steak will do. Few interesting desserts, aside from a good rice pudding. A good choice of American wines. $25 to $40.

## 12/20
## Peter Luger
**178 Broadway
(Driggs Ave.)
Brooklyn
387-7400**
*Lunch and dinner daily until
9:30 P.M.; closed Sun. afternoon
No credit cards*
Steaks

Peter Luger, at the foot of the Williamsburg Bridge, is within a year or so of rivaling Gage and Tollner which claims the title of oldest restaurant in the city. The ambience is rather banal, vaguely German, and the Wall Street customers are served grilled steaks (porterhouse, T-bone, or filet mignon) of irreproachable quality, washed down with good German beers (Beck's) or American wines. Less atmosphere than at Gage and Tollner, but a serious restaurant in the fine tradition of New York steakhouses.

## 17
## The River Café
**1 Water St., Brooklyn
(Cadman Plaza W.)
Brooklyn
522-5200**
*Lunch and dinner daily until
11:00 P.M.; Sat. and Sun. brunch;
reservation necessary
AE, DC*
American/French
(nouvelle)

A good number of our New York friends used to be surprised when we maintained that the River Café was a good spot. "Oh yeah," they said mistrustfully, "you mean there's a nice view." The place still called to mind the distant memory of a rundown shack by the waterfront, where the only consolation for the food served was one of the world's most exalting panoramas.

Today, everyone in New York knows that The River Café is a good spot, and masses of fashionable people crowd in for lunch and dinner; but what everyone may not know is that the cuisine is better than "good." Young Larry Forgione, who worked at Connaught's in London and under Guérard at Regine's, has really taken off on his own, and the last meal we were served, in front of the magical spectacle of the Brooklyn Bridge with its forest of illuminated towers, unquestionably deserved three toques.

Larry Forgione is convinced, as we are, that the future belongs to the young up-and-coming generation of American cooks, and that a revolution in taste is in full swing on this side of the Atlantic. This American nouvelle cuisine—similar to the French nouvelle cuisine without being merely a pale copy of it—has, in him, its most enthusiastic and convincing apologist. It isn't out of chauvinism that he endeavors to use only 100 percent American ingredients (Bellingham Bay smoked salmon from Washington, California crayfish and snails, fresh forest mushrooms, fresh Key West shrimp, Illinois Brie, Calistoga goat's cheese), but because he believes that they can rival the best in the world (a belief with which we have always concurred), and because the American public isn't always aware of this.

But what's most important here is the way he uses these ingredients. "Manhattan's best restaurant is in Brooklyn," said one of our New York guests at the end of our last meal. You would undoubtedly have agreed, after tasting the hot sea urchins in tomato sauce with cucumber and shallots, garnished with an exquisite spinach sauce; the fabulously tender and perfectly cooked sweetbreads in a light pastry shell; a mixture of lamb chops in tarragon sauce (an absolute marvel) with veal (a bit too firm) in vegetables cooked to perfection; a dream salad of savory lettuces, unusual greens, and goat's cheese, in a dressing of California olive oil seasoned with fresh basil; and to finish off (this was the meal's weak point) hot apple tart or chocolate cake. After this superb, airy light meal, we almost wanted to sit right down again and start over, this time to taste the salmon trout in ginger and the Eastern lobster in watercress.

We should point out that the wines are perfectly chosen (a remarkable Lambert Bridge Cabernet Sauvignon '78), the maître d'hôtel friendly and efficient, and the clientele prodigiously "New York," with all that this entails in terms of beautiful women, lovely clothing, and controlled eccentricities.

Of course, with these crowds (the wait, even when you have a reservation, is sometimes almost intolerable) and with room for three hundred guests, one may doubt whether the miracle will endure. There will inevitably be failures, like everywhere else, and meals that are less successful than others, but so what . . . it's a chance we'll gladly take.

# Toque Tally

## 18/20

**Lutèce**  p. 72

## 17/20

**Cellar in the Sky**  p. 23
**Four Seasons**  p. 63

**Quilted Giraffe (The)**  p. 81
**River Café (The)**  p. 139

## 16/20

**Côte Basque (La)**  p. 60
**Michel Fitoussi's Palace**  p. 75

**Tulipe (La)**  p. 42

## 15/20

**Bombay Palace (The)**  p. 90
**Cirque (Le)**  p. 110

**Oyster Bar**  p. 78
**Parioli Romanissimo**  p. 122

Claude's  p. 110
Maurice  p. 97

Périgord (Le)  p. 80
Raphael  p. 101

=== 14/20 ===

American Harvest Restaurant (The)
    p. 16
Andrée's Mediterranean Cuisine  p. 107
Caravelle (La)  p. 92
Captain's Table (The)  p. 57
Chantilly (Le)  p. 58
Felidia  p. 61
Gauloise (La)  p. 37
Hatsuhana  p. 66

Inagiku  p. 69
Kitcho  p. 95
Lavin's  p. 95
Lello  p. 71
Périgord Park  p. 123
Restaurant (The—World Trade Center)
    p. 24
Vienna Park  p. 129

=== 13/20 ===

Acute Café  p. 15
Amerigos  p. 137
Ararat  p. 45
Café des Artistes  p. 131
Cascade (La)  p. 58
Chanterelle (La)  p. 30
Cherche Midi (Le)  p. 59
Chez Pascal  p. 109
Coach House (The)  p. 36
Cygne (Le)  p. 61
Da Silvano  p. 36
Gallagher's  p. 94
Gaylord's  p. 64
Gibbon (The)  p. 114
Gloucester House  p. 64
Greene Street Restaurant  p. 30
Grenouille (La)  p. 65
Hee Seung Fung (H.S.F.)  p. 66
Hors d'Oeuvrerie (L')  p. 24
Hostaria del Bongustaio  p. 67
Hunam  p. 68
Hunan Manor  p. 116

Il Nido  p. 68
Il Valetto  p. 117
Madrigal (Le)  p. 74
Market Dining Room (The)  p. 24
Mon Paris  p. 51
Nippon  p. 78
Pamir  p. 121
Plaisir (Le)  p. 124
Primavera  p. 125
René Pujol  p. 102
Restaurant Laurent  p. 83
Sabor  p. 41
Say Eng Look  p. 28
Seeda Thai  p. 103
Shun Lee West  p. 133
Szechuan East  p. 128
Texarkana  p. 41
Uncle Tai's  p. 128
Veau d'Or (Le)  p. 129
Wise Maria  p. 33
Wood's (West)  p. 105

=== 12/20 ===

Ambassador Grill  p. 53
Balkan-Armenian  p. 46
Biarritz (Le)  p. 90
Bistro (Le)  p. 55
Black Sheep  p. 34
Boeuf à la Mode (Le)  p. 108
Café 58  p. 57
Café San Martin  p. 108
Christ Cella  p. 60
Cocotte (La)  p. 111
Colombe d'Or (La)  p. 46

Dragon Garden  p. 25
Fish Place  p. 37
Fonda La Paloma  p. 63
Gage and Tollner  p. 138
Hoexter's Market  p. 115
Home Village  p. 26
Hwa Yuan  p. 27
Hyo Tan Nippon Restaurant  p. 68
Indian Oven  p. 132
Kuruma Sushi  p. 71
Lavandou (Le)  p. 117

Little Szechuan  p. 27
Manhattan Market  p. 118
Meat Brokers  p. 119
Métairie (La)  p. 39
Il Monello  p. 120
Mr. Lee's  p. 50
Patrissy's  p. 40
Patsy's  p. 98
Peking Duck House  p. 27
Peter Luger  p. 139
Petit Robert (Le)  p. 40
Petite Marmite (La)  p. 80
Pierre au Tunnel  p. 99
Post House (The)  p. 125
Raga  p. 100
Rainbow Room (The)  p. 101
Raoul's  p. 31

Refuge Restaurant (Le)  p. 126
Relais (Le)  p. 127
Restaurant (The—Carlyle)  p. 127
Russian Tea Room (The)  p. 102
Sichuan Pavilion  p. 85
Silver Palace  p. 28
Teacher's  p. 135
Tenbrooks  p. 21
Tournebroches (Les)  p. 87
Trastevere  p. 128
Tovarisch  p. 136
21 Club  p. 104
Uzie's  p. 129
Vienna 79  p. 130
Wings  p. 32
Z  p. 52

# 11/20

Ballato's  p. 29
Benihana  p. 55
Benito's I and II  p. 25
Box Tree  p. 56
Brasserie (La)  p. 56
Bread Shop Cafe (The)  p. 17
Brittany du Soir  p. 91
Cafe Espanol  p. 34
Café Loup  p. 35
Café New Amsterdam  p. 35
Café Un, Deux, Trois  p. 92
Caliban  p. 46
Capsouto Frères  p. 18
Casa Brazil  p. 108
Century Café  p. 93
Delphi  p. 19
Demarchelier  p. 112
Elio's  p. 112
Fenice (La)  p. 62
Fortune Garden  p. 113
Gino's  p. 114
Greener Pastures  p. 115
Helmsley Palace  p. 67
Hunan Balcony  p. 132

Il Cortile  p. 25
Iperbole: Enoteca  p. 69
Jim McMullen  p. 117
John Clancy's Restaurant  p. 38
Keen's Chop House  p. 94
Louisiana  p. 50
Marylou's  p. 39
Mitsukoshi  p. 76
Odeon  p. 19
One Fifth Avenue  p. 39
Orsini's  p. 98
Palm  p. 79
Parma  p. 122
Pongsri Thailand Restaurant  p. 100
Rendez-Vous (The)  p. 83
Sammy's Roumanian Jewish Restaurant  p. 20
Siam Inn  p. 104
SoHo Charcuterie  p. 32
Sweets  p. 20
Trumpets  p. 88
Vincent Petrosino  p. 21
Vivolo  p. 130
Ye Waverly Inn  p. 45

# 10/20

Adam's Rib  p. 106
American Charcuterie  p. 89
Bernstein-on-Essex Street  p. 34
Bourse (La)  p. 17
Caffé da'Alfredo  p. 35
Camelia (La)  p. 57

Charley O's  p. 93
Copenhagen  p. 93
Elephant and Castle (The)  p. 30
Folie (La)  p. 113
Fraunces Tavern  p. 19
Garvin's  p. 37

## 9/20

## 8/20

## 7/20

## 6/20

# 5/20

**Café Geiger**  p. 108

**Oh-Ho-So**  p. 31

# NO RATING

**Luchow's**  p. 96

**Top of the Sixes**  p. 104

# THE DIVERSIONS

# Bistros • Tea Rooms

## La Brasserie
**100 E. 53rd St.**
**751-4840**
*Daily 24 hours*

Listed as a restaurant (you can enjoy a good, hot meal here), La Brasserie can also be recommended outside dinner hours for its snacks, and for late-night dinners, when the crush has receded somewhat.

## Cafe Madeleine
**405 W. 43rd St.**
**246-2993**
*Daily until 10:30 P.M.,*
*(midnight on Sat.)*

An adorable little French cafe in the theater district, with brick walls, lace curtains, and on the menu a platter of assorted fish pâtés, cheese, and delicatessen items, and good salads. The dishes are fresh, delicate and don't cost over $5. No liquor license, yet, so there's no wine to wash down the goat's cheese.

## Caffe Reggio
**119 MacDougal St.**
**(W. 3rd and**
**Menetta Ln.)**
**475-9557**
*Daily 11:00 to 2:00 A.M.*
*(Sat. and Sun. to 4:00 A.M.)*

Two blocks from Washington Square, try the best espresso (hot or iced) in New York, in an Italian renaissance setting, plus cappucino and hot chocolate as creamy as can be, perfumed teas, and, for the starving, toasted prosciutto and cheese sandwiches, and Italian pastries. This is not so much a spot for gourmets as for æsthetes, with a trendy crowd in a very romantic setting. Absolutely the place to go for an after-dinner coffee and to be encircled by the intellectual fringe of fashionable New York.

## Cupping Room Cafe
**359 W. Broadway**
**(Broome and**
**Grand Sts.)**
**925-2898**
*Daily 9:00 to 1:00 A.M.*
*Sun. 8:00 A.M. to*
*8:00 P.M.*

SoHo's best selection of coffees, teas, and hot chocolate, served with homemade croissants and a good choice of snacks. Friendly atmosphere.

## Délices La Côte Basque
**1032 Lexington Ave.**
**(73rd-74th Sts.)**
**535-3311**
*Daily until 9:00 P.M.*

As exquisite as its name suggests. Everything is good: the pâté, the croissant with ham, the quiche. Try the assorted cheese plate with a glass of wine, leaving a bit of room for the succulent desserts: lemon cake, chocolate cake, and Saint Honoré.

## Fay and Allen's Foodhall
**1241 Third Ave.**
**(71st St.)**
**794-1101**
*Mon. to Thurs. 9:00 A.M. to 11:00 P.M., Fri. and Sat. 9:00 A.M. to 12:30 A.M., Sun. 9:00 A.M. to 10:00 P.M.*

You'll be surrounded by cakes and different dishes as you munch a croissant stuffed with all sorts of good things. In particular try the foodstuffs from abroad: salmon roe, herring, Westphalian ham (sold in the grocery department), or one of the large and acceptable specials of the day. As for dessert, just use your eyes. . . .

## J. S. Vandam
**150 Varick St.**
**929-7466**
*Daily until midnight*

A brasserie transported from Montparnasse in the 1930s right next to the SoHo lofts, J. S. Vandam has a certain distinguished, artsy air about it. People collapse at night on the red leather seats and discuss nothing in particular over an avocado with crab or roast duck, unless they opt for the long wooden bar, an excellent observation post looking out over the large, cozy room with subdued lighting. Like the lounge on a liner, you can almost hear the ocean.

## Kleine Konditorei
**234 E. 86th St.**
**737-7130**
*Daily until midnight*

You could be in Germany: right next to the Bremen House sits a cafe-restaurant-delicatessen for those with distinctly hearty appetites: beef croquettes, chicken-liver kebabs, a house herring salad, beets, onions, black bread. The food is quite good (goulash, meatballs) but desperately slow service is provided by robust waitresses who are not exactly ingratiating, and the setting is a touch sinister, to say nothing of the insistent music. Huge Bavarian pastries you could smother yourself in, if you're feeling suicidal, aren't at all bad.

## McFeely's
**565 W. 23rd St.**
**929-4432**
*Daily until 2:00 A.M.*

It's not a very wholesome neighborhood (beautiful young men loiter about the streets where scenes from *Cruising* were shot), but this Victorian saloon is elegant and seductive, with its stained-glass ceiling, art nouveau frescoes, large bar, and well-spaced tables. The restaurant, which offers, for example, salads and sole "grenobloise," is ideal for an inexpensive look at nocturnal decadence. It is near the wholesale meat market, and not far from the Hudson Street transvestites.

## Nyborg Nelson
**937 Second Ave.**
**(50th St.) 2nd floor**
**753-1495**
*Daily 10:00 A.M. to 7:00 P.M.*
**153 E. 53rd St.**
**(Citicorp Center)**
**223-0700**
*Daily until 9:00 P.M.,*
*Sun. 11:30 A.M. to 6:00 P.M.*

A cornucopia of smoked fish (herring, trout, salmon) and Scandinavian cheeses served assorted on platters or in sandwiches. Also several hot daily specials. A rustic setting to enjoy these simple and excellent products, as good as those in a real restaurant but at coffee-shop prices. Cold, dry white wine.

## Promenade Cafe
**Lower Plaza,**
**Rockefeller Center**
**757-5730**
*Daily until 11:30 P.M.*

One of Manhattan's "musts." A large, rather dark, distinguished terrace (although the restrooms show signs of wear), where you can eat a slice of apple pie tasting vaguely of vanilla, and drink a coffee seemingly perfumed with Javelle water. We didn't dare to dine here, but in winter the view of the ice skaters and the crowd in front of the RCA building is worth three stars.

## The Rainbow Grill
**30 Rockefeller Plaza**
**757-9090**
*Daily until 1:00 A.M.*

The ideal place for an after-the-show drink, and to admire the lights of Manhattan and the Verrazano Narrows Bridge in the distance. With an authentic art deco interior and subdued lighting, it thumbs its nose at the Rainbow Room bar, from which, at night, you can

147

perceive only the darkened moors of Central Park. Cocktails, fruit juices, and atmosphere—at reasonable prices.

## Richoux of London
153 E. 53rd St.
(Citicorp Center)
753-7721
*Daily 24 hours*

English comfort: leather, wood, and a cozy atmosphere. A very varied menu for breakfast, lunch, tea, or dinner, served with a smile. The chocolates are renowned.

## Rumpelmayer's
50 Central Park South
755-5800
*Daily 7:30 A.M. to 12:30 P.M.*

An old-fashioned tea room offering Viennese and French pastries, ice cream, and winsome waitresses in a kitschy and comfortable fake marble atmosphere. This is an annex of the St. Moritz hotel, whose clients prefer Rumpelmayer's reasonable prices for lunch and dinner to the more pompous Harry's New York bar next door. No sweeping gustatory impressions, but good for a tranquil moment after shopping on the Avenue of the Americas.

# Delis

## Carnegie Delicatessen
854 Seventh Ave.
(55th St.)
757-2245
*Daily 6:00 A.M. to 4:00 A.M.*

The most famous, and one of the oldest, of the Midtown delis. Not far from Times Square and the big Broadway shows, it attracts both audience and actors. (All delis boast of their starry clientele.) Leo Steiner, the owner, is a celebrity in his own right, as is the head waiter, Milton Parker. The sandwiches are standard fare, but you can also enjoy homemade soups, such as the matzoh ball or meatball soups. The pastrami is fresh, and not too salty. A big bottle or jar of pickles sits on every table, a tradition in New York delis. Waiters are attentive and emotional. Long lines Sunday morning.

## Katz's
205 E. Houston St.
(Essex St.)
254-2246
*Daily until 11:30 P.M.*

If Ratner's is the number one Lower East Side dairy, Katz's is unquestionably the area's most famous deli. A large, popular self-service restaurant where you'll bask in the turn-of-the-century atmosphere—the decor seems to belong to those distant times, as do the rare waiters. And you would swear that the other diners are immigrants just off the last steamer. Incredible! At very low prices (not much over $2 per dish) you can choose between knubelwurst (sausages flavored with garlic), pastrami, liver, kasha balls, potato pancakes. No wine. It's the atmosphere that counts.

## Ratner's
**138 Delancey St.**
**(Norfolk and Suffolk)**
**677-5588**
*Daily 24 hours*

Opened in 1905, Ratner's is the most famous dairy on the Lower East Side, probably in all of New York. Vast (it resembles the waiting room in a Central European train station), it can serve close to two hundred people at any one time—Jascha Heifetz, Elia Kazan, and the mayor, Ed Koch, have all been spotted there. It was also used as one of the shooting locations for *The French Connection.*

The waiters are grouchy; their motto appears to be: The customer is rarely right. At Ratner's, everything (or almost everything) is bad, from the tasteless borscht to the spongy gefilte fish. The Israeli army could use the blintzes in their cannons. The specialty, kasha varnishka (kasha with onions and small noodles) is dense to the point of being, in our opinion, barely edible. It's true that the prices are low, except for the Ratner special, a gigantic combination of smoked carp and salmon with cream cheese, lettuce, and tomato—a sort of dairy nightmare! Cakes, especially Ratner's famous cheesecake, are enormous, too sweet, but otherwise tasteless. A well-stocked wine list, but the house white wine is practically undrinkable.

In conclusion: a spot typical of the Lower East Side, to be visited (for delicatessen, pastries) but absolutely avoided at mealtimes unless you insist on reliving the gustatory experiences of Stetl cuisine a century ago. There are huge reception rooms for marriages and bar mitzvahs.

## Second Avenue Deli
**156 Second Ave.**
**(10th St.)**
**677-0606**
*Daily until midnight*

On the boundary of the Lower East Side, this is one of New York's most famous kosher delis, and also its best. The Lebenwohl family (father, mother, and two daughters) have taken great pains to recreate a 1900s Lower East Side atmosphere, when immigration was at its height. In a nostalgic setting, big, motherly waitresses unload chicken soup (excellent) with matzoh balls, boiled beef, goulash, Romanian-style steak with chili peppers. New York humorist Sam Levenson claimed that the reason the Second Avenue Deli's cooking is so salty is that the Jewish mothers sob while cooking at the stove. All the dishes are accompanied by kasha, kugel (noodle pudding) knaidlach (dumplings), kishka stuffed beef intestine. The gefilte fish deserves special attention: it's made of whitefish or carp seasoned with onions and eaten with horseradish. Considering the psychological pressure exerted by the waitresses, it's difficult not to order the chopped liver ($5.15) as an appetizer. It's a tradition, and Abe Lebenwohl claims he serves the best chopped liver in the world—the only one made according to the rules: liver (fresh daily), vegetable oil, chicken fat, eggs, and onions. He's so proud of it that if you ask, he'll let you taste it for free.

## Stage Delicatessen
**834 Seventh Ave.**

Closer to Times Square, the Stage rivals the Carnegie for supremacy in matters of pastrami and matzoh ball and meatball soups. Bigger and fancier (the waiters wear

**(53rd St.)**
**245-7850**
*Daily 6:30 A.M. to 2:30 A.M.*

scarlet jackets), this is one of the rare delis that makes an effort in its decor. The Stage also offers regular American cooking (hamburgers, cheeseburgers). It has its regulars, its fanatics, and its enemies.

## Wolf's Sixth Avenue
**101 W. 57th St.**
**586-1110**
*Daily 6:30 A.M. to 1:30 A.M.*

Lucky New Yorkers. For less than $10 right in the middle of Manhattan, they can enjoy varied, good-quality, and pleasantly served full-course meals in an attractive setting that is at once practical and cheerful. Of all the delis in the Central Park area, Wolf's, on the corner of Avenue of the Americas, enjoys the greatest turnover. From salads and omelets to the Reuben sandwich and boiled beef in a pot (a single portion is more than enough to fill two people), there's an immense choice of the Central European dishes New Yorkers are so crazy about.

# Diners

## Empire Diner
**210 Tenth Ave.**
**(at 22nd St.)**
**243-2736**
*Daily 24 hours*

The Empire is an art-deco railway car that welcomes a mixed bag of superb cover girls, leather-jacketed bikers, and establishment types from the area willing to swallow anything as long as there's ketchup on it. The elderly "Queen of the Piano," Miss Bea, resurrects pre-war hits. Highly recommended for breakfast around 4:00 or 5:00 A.M.

## Market Diner
**572 11th Ave.**
**(43rd St.)**
**244-6033**
*Daily 24 hours*

Less atmosphere than at the Empire Diner, but a decor that is outstanding, immortalized by the painter John Baeder. No artist's hand was at work, unfortunately, on our inedible "veal and peppers."

# Fast Food

## The Automat
**200 E. 42nd St.**
*Daily from 6:30 A.M. to 10:00 P.M.*

This huge, square dining room is the last bastion of a historic chain of fast food restaurants. Innumerable glittering vending machines spew forth (fairly bad) dishes for 50¢ or $1. A self-service section offers quiches, hamburgers, and pizzas at more than reasonable prices. There is very friendly service in this amusing artifact of bygone days.

## The Big Kitchen
**World Trade Center (Concourse)**
**938-1153**
*Daily from 7:00 A.M. to 7:00 P.M., closed Sun.*

If the words "fast food" evoke for you the smell of burning grease, a prison atmosphere, and gastric punishment, you owe yourself a visit to the complex of restaurants that takes up most of the concourse in the World Trade Center. You'll see that it's entirely possible to feed the multitudes good, healthy food simply prepared, and offered in a relaxing atmosphere at ridiculously low prices. What strikes you at first is that, although thousands of meals are served here daily, you never get the impression that there's a crowd. The space is divided into a number of warm and intimately lit zones in attractive colors with comfortable seats, each zone arranged around a particular stand. From hamburgers to roast chicken, from seafood (including oysters that Europeans will find staggeringly inexpensive) to pastries (167 different sorts), from international delicatessen fare to the 42 different types of bread available at the bakery, you're offered hundreds of hot and cold dishes prepared the same day, which you can take out or eat at the attractive tables. In short, for about $4 to $5 (provided your willpower is strong enough to resist temptations) you can lunch at the Big Kitchen—lightly, it's true, but in a remarkably appetizing manner. Owners of assembly-line-type restaurants would do well to spend some time studying under Toni Aigner, the manager of this extraordinary restaurant giant.

## Dosanko
**135 E. 45th St.**
**697-2967**
*Daily until 10:00 P.M., 8:00 P.M. weekends*

Japanese cuisine calls to mind delicate, perfumed soups, noodles fried with soy, spicy dumplings . . . and that's exactly what you'll find here, served with the politeness and efficiency characteristic of the Far East. Japanese wines and beer. Tea and coffee. Copious, but light and tasty dishes, which leave no unpleasant memories. The only thing "fast foodish" are the prices (under $5 per dish). Take-out service. Various locations.

## Nathan's Famous
**1482 Broadway (Times Square at 43rd St.)**
**594-7455**
*Daily until 2:00 A.M.*

When Eddie Cantor and Jimmy Durante, singing waiters at nearby night spots, used to drop in after work at Ida and Nathan Handwerker's pint-sized snack bar in Coney Island, the all-beef hot dog was five cents. Sixty-five years later, Nathan's is big business (a dozen locations in the Metropolitan area and franchises in Florida and California), and the original hot dog is 89 cents.

At the cavernous Times Square location, cafeteria-style counters offer hamburgers, pizzas, chili con carne, fresh little neck and cherry stone clams, deep-fried chicken and seafood, deli meats, ice cream (Good Humor), domestic beers and soft drinks. The meats are available to take out either in sandwiches or by weight, a quarter pound and up. Everything is self-service, but there is table seating on street level and, by escalator, a floor below. Prices are right even if the environment is a bit tawdry and some of the fried items are not as crisp as they might be. Stick to Nathan's original and a cold glass of beer.

# Ice Cream

## Agora
**1550 Third Ave.
(87th St.)
860-3425**
*Mon. to Thurs. 11:30 A.M. to
11:30 P.M.; Fri. and Sat. to
1:00 A.M.; Sun. to 10:00 P.M.*

"Agora" means "marketplace" in ancient Greek, a place where people buy and sell just about everything. Here the word refers especially to clothes and ice cream, because this extraordinary shop is divided into two entirely distinct sections: a men's and women's clothing store on one side, and an ice cream parlor and restaurant on the other. You can enjoy the best ice cream sodas in town (twenty-five varieties, from the most classical to the most unlikely, and twenty-one very good ice cream flavors) in an authentic late nineteenth-century setting: stained-glass windows, frosted mirrors, beaded chandeliers, beautiful hand-carved mahogany cabinets, and an onyx soda fountain at the entrance. All of which makes for an unusual spot to eat ice cream and more (the window terrace restaurant offers a complete menu). Certainly worth a visit.

## Le Glacier
**1022 Madison Ave.
(78th-79th Sts.)
249-2975**
*Daily to 10:00 P.M.*

Frozen yogurt (vanilla, chocolate, raspberry, lemon, peach) made on the premises is exceptional. But the owner is Austrian so you might want to try his hot fudge sundae (Sedutto ice cream), topped with whipped cream that will bring memories of your last visit to Vienna.

## Häagen-Dazs
**2323 Broadway
(85th St.)
877-4556**
*Daily until 11:00 P.M.,
Fri. and Sat. to 12:00 P.M.*

Häagen-Dazs convinced New Yorkers 21 years ago that there is more to ice cream than sugar and artificial flavors and colors. The product is rich and creamy and contains only natural flavors and ingredients. With ice cream parlors springing up all over town, Häagen-Dazs remains among the best. Try the coffee or strawberry—honest-to-goodness flavors—that will captivate you, if you cherish the real thing. Various locations.

## Peppermint Park
**666 Fifth Ave.
581-5938**
*Daily to midnight, Sat. to 1:00 A.M.*

A classic ice cream parlor, modern, light, and appropriately decorated in peppermint green. For pies, ice creams, and homemade chocolates of only average quality. A pretty spot nonetheless.

# Pizzerias

## Goldberg's Pizzeria
**996 Second Avenue**

Larry Goldberg tried 44 jobs (salesman, radio/tv announcer, standup comic, etc.) before he discovered that for him, pizza was the total experience. Today, Goldberg is

**(52nd-53rd Sts.)**
**593-2172**
*Daily until 11:00 P.M.*

described as the Pizza King of New York, and his distinctive neon sign was selected to be a part of the Smithsonian permanent collection in Washington D.C. What distinguishes the Goldberg Pizza: fresh, tasty ingredients baked in a deep pie tin to be eaten with knife and fork. Try the SMOG pizza: sausage, mushroom, onion, and green pepper at this or two other East Side locations—1443 York Avenue (76th St.) or 253 Third Ave. (20th-21st Sts.) also open daily until 11:00 p.m.

## Pizza Pino
**981 Third Ave.**
**(58th-59th St.)**
**688-3817**
*Daily until 11:00 P.M.*

Acceptable pizzas cooked in a wood oven before your eyes, and a good choice of Italian dishes in a very New York setting: brick walls, mirrors, and green plants. Recommended: the pastas. You can choose from six types of sauces, including a very tasty seafood sauce. Try to be seated at the back on the ground floor, as it's much more pleasant than in front or on the second floor. Take-out service.

## Ray's Pizza
**465 Avenue of the**
**Americas**
**(11th St.)**
**243-2253**
*11:00 A.M. to 9:00 P.M., closed Sun.*

In the Village, this is one of the best pizzerias among the hundreds in New York. Over two thousand people eat pizza whole or by the slice every day.

# Sandwiches

## Between the Bread
**141 E. 56th St.**
**888-0449**
*Until 5:00 P.M., closed Sun.*

The most delicious sandwiches and salads imaginable in this small, self-service bistro: from pâté, to duck (from the 3 Petits Cochons), from cream cheese to vegetables, from mushrooms to shrimp. You choose two slices of French bread, German pumpernickel, raisin bread, or pita. And a choice of homemade desserts; in particular the chocolate brownies and pecan pie, much better here than anywhere else. Twenty different types of muffins with fruit, and a few fancy groceries to take out: olive oils and vinegars, English fig and rhubarb jams, jars of exotic fruits and natural sea salt (hard to find in New York). Delivery available.

## Jackson Hole Burgers
**232 E. 64th St.**
**371-7187**
*10:30 to 1:30 A.M., closed Sun.*

Our thanks to Gerry Frank ( *Where to Find It, Buy It, Eat It, in New York*) for having singled out these burgers. We won't go so far as to proclaim, as he does, that they are the best in New York. Still, they are very thick, very juicy, and very well prepared—in a word, excellent. Good sandwiches too. Various locations.

## Manganero's Hero Boy Restaurant

**492 Ninth Ave.**
**(38th St.)**
**947-7325**
*Daily 7:30 A.M. to 7:30 P.M.,*
*closed Sun.*

Lovingly prepared by Italian hands, these sandwiches are among the most famous and the biggest in New York. (The Champion can feed twenty-five people, and must, of course, be ordered in advance.) Several hot Italian dishes, rather nondescript, although the place boasts of having served Frank Sinatra a meal.

# Vegetarian

he first time I ate in a vegetarian restaurant (this is Christian Millau speaking), I was deathly ill the entire night that followed. I suffer from an unfortunate allergy to any food even remotely considered "healthy." My stomach, accustomed to wretched excess of foie gras, red meat, butter and cream sauces, rebelled at the contact with these ersatz foods. A second attempt, this time in London, proved just as disastrous. But little by little I've gotten used to it. Still, I don't pretend to be an expert, and I hope I will be forgiven for not having visited more of New York's vegetarian restaurants. The fact that I'm still alive and writing indicates at least that those I did visit aren't so bad.

## Brownies

**21 E. 16th St.**
**255-2838**
*Mon. to Fri. 11:00 A.M. to 8:00 P.M.,*
*Sat. noon to 4:00 P.M.*

Long before the current health-food fads took hold, Edith and Sam Brown were preaching the virtues of carrot juice and ribs of celery. Today, they run a boutique (91 Fifth Ave.), have published a recipe book, and run one of the most immaculate and appetizing restaurants in town. The soups and salads are delicious, and the homemade desserts very likeable. The check is somewhat less so as, in the end, vegetarian restaurants are as expensive as anywhere else.

## Greener Pastures

**117 E. 60th St.**
**832-3212**
*Daily until 9:30 P.M.*

A fruit juice bar, with three dining rooms (an attractive indoor garden) where charming but quite incompetent young waiters serve dishes abundant in quantity, but not always in flavor. You would be wise to steer clear of the vegetarian beef stroganoff, although the salads, broiled fresh fish, and vegetable sandwiches are excellent.

## Health Works

**153 E. 53rd St.**
**(Citicorp Center)**
**586-1980**
*Daily to 7:30 P.M., 6:00 P.M. Sat.*
*and 4:00 P.M. Sun.*

A sort of fast-food nouvelle cuisine: raw or cooked finely diced vegetables in an assortment of salads (both vegetarian and other) with the dressing of your choice (all using as a base fresh tomatoes, yogurt, and mixed herbs). The menu offers as well a very light quiche, a soup of the day, and a few pastries and cookies. The setting is always agreeable, and sometimes even more than that (as on Madison Ave.). No alcoholic beverages (it goes without saying), but no sodas either—they're fattening. Coffee and fruit juices. Various locations.

# THE NIGHTLIFE

# On The Town

New York at night is like a wild game preserve, an immense, fenced-off expanse guarded by selective Cerberuses. Most of the trendier establishments are about as impenetrable, if not as the Underworld, then at least as Castel's in Paris. Unless you have the right introductions, the right friends, a face the doorman likes, and clothes he approves of, you run every chance of being locked out like an untouchable. There are always ways of getting around this, like calling your hotel concierge to the rescue or renting a limousine with a knowledgeable chauffeur—but isn't that too much trouble just for the right to admire celebrities who haven't the slightest interest in you? In short, you might as well face the fact that most of the truly dazzling nightspots you've heard so much about are not nearly as interested in you as you are in them. But not to despair—first-rate (and accessible) nightspots abound in New York.

There's nothing like New York nightlife anywhere else on earth. First of all, it can last all night—for many, dawn is a normal hour to end an evening. Secondly, it has something for everyone, from the simplest of pleasures to the most exotic of whims.

Nightlife here is like a mercurial woman—blink your eyes and she changes. Last month's trendiest club might be empty now, and the place no one frequented last week is suddenly "in."

All this is enough to give any conscientious guidebook writer a headache. Still, we've tried to provide you with a few addresses beyond the trusty classics (the accessible ones), treading delicately all the while—no guaranteeing you'll be able to get in, if the place still exists, or that it will deserve your attention if it does. And if you have an overwhelming desire to be up-to-the-moment, check the gossip columns of the daily papers—if the name of a bar or supper club appears more than twice in three days, it's the new place to go.

Going out at night ought not to be a hit-or-miss exercise; the locals don't approach it that way and neither should you. Decide what you want out of a particular evening, then find the place that stands the best chance of giving it to you. A little research and planning can save a lot of regrets at four in the morning.

Just as individual nightlife action moves and shifts, neighborhoods and certain areas of the city change from "out" to "in." Columbus Avenue (on the West Side of Manhattan from Lincoln Center to 86th Street) has suddenly become *the* place for bar-hopping and people-watching. The hottest spot in town is on this street (Ruelles, Columbus Avenue and 75th Street) as are a few dozen other cafes, bars, and restaurants. A summer-night stroll along this paseo (just you and three thousand other folks) is a *must*—you'll either love it or hate it.

Many other areas are equally appealing and equally safe. Greenwich Village is still interesting with street musicians, dope dealers, artists, and religious zealots jockeying for space with intelligentsia, hustlers, uptown sophisticates, and wide-eyed tourists. The Village jumps all night (especially Christopher Street, world-renowned as the gay ghetto) and warm weather brings people out to see, be seen, and enjoy the spectacle. Or stroll along Second Avenue between 55th and 62nd Streets; this is the district of singles bars, cafes, and a youthful group on the make. An evening without danger and reasonably exciting.

Ah, there's that word—*danger*. Contrary to popular belief, New York nightlife is not completely overrun with muggers, thieves, and the like. Most streets in Midtown Manhattan are pretty safe, but be realistic—being out at 4:00 A.M. can be dangerous no matter *where* you are. Some areas are more dangerous than others, and one should be careful (unless one's thirst for adventure cannot be quenched through normal channels). Areas like Hell's Kitchen (34th Street to 59th Street, Tenth Avenue to the Hudson River), the Lower East Side (any place east of First Avenue and below 14th Street), Chinatown (lots of young Oriental street gangs are having a "turf" war down there), and Harlem (any place above 100th Street on the East and West Sides) should be approached with extreme caution. Many taxi drivers refuse to travel in certain areas of New York, so even if you get from your hotel to a danger zone in a taxi, there's no guarantee you'll be able to find one to get out.

New York's exotic blend of glamor, excitement, danger, and fun appeals to the widest possible range of people. It's the pulse of the city and its rhythm will make you enjoy!

Please note that we have given you a ballpark price quote and indicated whether or not a cover charge is required, whenever appropriate.

# Cabarets

Cabarets come in all shapes and sizes, from big and brassy to small and elegant, with everything in between. A visit to at least one of the places listed below should be high on your "things to do" list—for sheer pleasure and value, these are among the best forms of nighttime entertainment that New York has to offer.

## Broadway at O'Neal's Times Square
**147 W. 43rd St.**
**869-4200**
*Nightly until 1:00 A.M.*
*Moderate: cover charge*
*All major credit cards*

Brand new restaurant/cabaret/bar in the heart of Times Square. Red and black art deco decor, lots of room and lots of action. Curt Davis' "New York Nightlife" originates from here, and it's fast becoming the hottest cable television show in town. Recommended.

## Dangerfield's
**1118 First Ave.**
**(61st St.)**
**593-1650**
*Nightly until 4:00 A.M.*
*Moderate: cover charge*
*All major credit cards*

The owner is comedian Rodney Dangerfield and he appears regularly. When he's absent, other talented performers (especially newcomer Dennis Blair) take over. Large space with a Las Vegas atmosphere . . . everyone seems determined to have a good time. Very good if an evening of comedy is desired.

## Duplex
**55 Grove St.**
**(near Christopher St.)**
**255-5438**
*Daily until 4:00 A.M.*
*A bargain: cover charge*
*No credit cards*

It's the oldest continuous cabaret room in New York and has spawned the likes of Woody Allen, Joan Rivers, and Rodney Dangerfield. Most of the unknown performers appearing in the tiny upstairs cabaret room are good, and some are better than that. A visit to the downstairs piano bar late on Saturday night is a must. Broadway chorus boys and girls, plus assorted singers, performers, and Greenwich Village residents pack themselves around the piano and sing every show tune ever written . . . and you're invited to participate. A New York institution and highly recommended.

## Freddy's
**308 E. 49th St.**
**888-1633**
*Nightly until 4:00 A.M.*
*Expensive: cover charge*
*AE, MC, V*

Up-and-coming jazz singers, former Broadway show-stoppers, and famous female impersonator Charles Pierce strut their stuff on this club's tiny stage. Recommended.

## Marty's
**1265 Third Ave.**
**(73rd St.)**
**249-4100**
*Nightly until 1:30 A.M.,*
*midnight Sun.*
*Expensive: cover charge*
*AE, MC, V*

The perfect cabaret/jazz club for the expense account crowd. Good food, plushy surroundings, and the likes of Sarah Vaughan, Mel Tormé, and Sylvia Syms singing for their supper (note: Sinatra drops in sometimes, just to see and hear Sylvia).

## Les Mouches
**260 Eleventh Ave.**
**(26th St.)**
**695-5190**
*Daily until 4:00 A.M.*
*Expensive: cover charge*
*All major credit cards*

Housed in an office building one block from the Hudson River, this restaurant/cabaret/disco/art gallery would be the best cabaret in New York if it were more accessible. Even so, it has everything you could want—a mirrored cabaret room featuring fine entertainment, a decent restaurant, and an excellent gay/straight disco with plenty of room to dance, and a very bouncy, good-humored atmosphere. Highly recommended.

## The New Ballroom
**253 W. 28th St.**
**244-3005**

Formerly in SoHo and noted for its art-world clientele, this new cabaret/bar/restaurant/theater is very appealing and very comfortable. Two-level bar and restaurant in the front with piano music; spacious cabaret in back with top

*Daily until 4:00 A.M.*
*All major credit cards*

entertainment; theater downstairs featuring new plays and musicals. At the moment, it's the hottest cabaret in town. Highly recommended.

## Panache
### (at The Magic Pan)
**1409 Sixth Ave.**
**(57th St.)**
**765-5080**
*Showtimes: 8:00 P.M. weeknights,*
*8:30 and 11:30 P.M. weekends.*
*Moderate: cover charge*
*AE, MC, V*

A new place with a little atmosphere and a lot of space. Mini-revues are the norm for entertainment, and the performers are usually unknown and usually talented.

## s.n.a.f.u.
**676 Sixth Ave.**
**(21st St.)**
**691-3535**
*Nightly until 2:00 A.M.*
*Moderate: cover charge*
*All major credit cards*

Bar/cabaret with eclectic entertainment including rock groups, Quentin Crisp ("The Naked Civil Servant"), and a transvestite opera company. The crowd is as varied as the performers (sometimes the show at the tables is better than the one onstage) and the ambience borders on bizarre. You'll love it! Recommended.

## Sweetwater's
**170 Amsterdam Ave.**
**(near 68th St.)**
**873-4100**
*Daily until 3:00 A.M.*
*Expensive: cover charge at tables*
*All major credit cards*

A pretty, mirrored, multilevel cabaret/bar/restaurant with the forced trendiness New York seems prone to. Good food and top-notch performers are sometimes overshadowed by the pseudo-sophisticated ambience. Worth a visit; the headliners on stage are usually great.

## Ted Hook's Onstage
**349 W. 46th St.**
**581-8447**
*Daily until 2:00 A.M., closed Sun.*
*Expensive: cover charge*
*All major credit cards*

Former chorus boy saves money and creates his idea of a 1940s New York nightclub—and succeeds! It's all white and silver and polished and lacquered (with a little glitter thrown in) and lots of people love it. Performers range from unknowns to former greats (Rosemary Clooney, Margaret Whiting), the food is awful; but somebody famous (or nearly so) is always in the audience.

# Cafes • Bars

There are hundreds of bars and cafes in New York, and each has its supporters and detractors. Listed here are some of the more interesting places . . . at least one of them should suit your needs. Be adventurous and try something new: it might make an interesting evening.

## Adam's Apple
**1117 First Ave.**
**(61st St.)**
**371-8650**
*Daily until 4:00 A.M.*
*Inexpensive: admission charge with*
*free drinks*
*All major credit cards*

A three-level bar/restaurant with disco dancing on two tiny floors and lots of room everywhere else (this is a singles bar, and dancing plays second fiddle). The decor is ersatz Garden of Eden and the clientele is young and randy.

## Boodles
**1478 First Ave.**
**(77th St.)**
**628-0900**
*Daily until 2:00 A.M.*
*Inexpensive: no cover or admission*
*All major credit cards*

Another pleasant meeting spot for singles: a lively bar-restaurant with an acceptable menu (daily fresh fish) and speedy service. Sunday brunch. Set meal ($6.95) or a la carte ($10 to $15).

## Cafe Central
**320 Amsterdam Ave.**
**(75th St.)**
**724-9187**
*Daily until 4:00 A.M.*
*Moderate: no cover charge*
*All major credit cards*

Friendly neighborhood bar with some of the most ornamental faces to be seen anywhere. Good food, lots of conversation, and impossible to get into on weekend nights . . . the entire West Side of New York drops in to see and be seen. Recommended.

## Charley O's Bar and Grill
**33 W. 48th St.**
**582-7141**
*Daily until midnight*
*Moderate: no cover or admission*
*All major credit cards*

Your basic bar/restaurant, if crowded, warm, and lively surroundings are desired. Lots of television and advertising agency people, pretty women, and minor celebs hang out here.

## City Lights Bar
**World Trade Center**
**938-1111**
*Daily until 1:00 A.M.*
*Sun. until 10:00 P.M.*
*Moderate: no cover or admission*
*All major credit cards*

Off the mainstream of Midtown Manhattan, this beautiful, comfortable bar rests atop one of the tallest buildings in the city—outstanding view and ambience. Recommended.

## Daly's Dandelion
**1029 Third Ave.**
**(63rd St.)**
**838-0780**
*Daily until 2:00 A.M.*
*Moderate: no cover or admission*
*All major credit cards*

Busy, pub-like à la mode atmosphere, and young, à la mode crowd. Hamburgers, salads, and quick-witted waitresses.

## Demarchelier
**808 Lexington Ave.**
**(62nd St.)**
**223-0047**
*Daily until 12:30 P.M., closed Sun.*
*Moderate: no cover charge*
*All major credit cards*

Tiny bar in a chic East Side restaurant. Wood paneling, fresh flowers, and coveys of fashionable fellows and girl models make this a perfect place for an after-dinner drink.

## Friday's
**1152 First Ave.**
**(63rd St.)**
**832-8512**
*Daily until 1:00 A.M.,*
*4:00 A.M. weekends.*
*Inexpensive: cover charge on*
*weekends*
*AE, MC, V*

A lively young crowd provides the ambience in this famous First Avenue singles bar. First Avenue is "singles country" par excellence, with such establishments all along it. The menu is typically American: hamburgers, steaks, barbecued spareribs, fried chicken in a basket . . . all in copious servings. The Champagne brunch on Sundays is also known for its abundance.

## Garvin's
**19 Waverly Place**
**(near Broadway)**
**473-5261**
*Daily until 2:00 A.M.*
*Inexpensive; no cover charge*
*All major credit cards*

Attractive decor, young and well-dressed crowd, good place to meet all kinds of people.

## Harvey's Chelsea Restaurant
**108 W. 18th St.**
**243-5644**
*Daily until 2:00 A.M.*
*Inexpensive; no cover charge*
*AE, MC, V*

Dick Harvey has brought this red mahogany saloon back to its former splendor, and serious drinkers (preferably intellectuals) come from everywhere. Definitely worth a visit.

## Jim McMullen
**1341 Third Ave.**
**(76th St.)**
**861-4700**
*Daily until 4:00 A.M.*
*Moderate; no cover charge*
*All major credit cards*

One of New York's friendliest bars, and a hangout for top sports players. Baseball, football, soccer, tennis, and hockey stars practically *live* here . . . as do some of the prettiest models. Crowded and popular.

## Joe Allen's
**326 W. 46th St.**
**581-6464**
*Daily until 2:00 A.M.*
*Inexpensive; no cover charge*
*All major credit cards*

Before and after the theater, the bar is packed with actors and others who enjoy the atmosphere and the hamburgers. Highly recommended.

## J.S. Vandam
**150 Varick St.**
**(near Broadway)**
**929-7466**
*Daily until 2:00 A.M.*
*Moderate; no cover charge*
*All major credit cards*

Started by two former employees of Raoul, this fairly mediocre restaurant attracts the "fashion crowd" around the bar in a pleasant art nouveau decor.

## Landmark Tavern
**626 Eleventh Ave.**
**(W. 46th St.)**
**757-8595**
*Daily until 4:00 A.M.*
*Inexpensive; no cover charge*

Dick Harvey, owner of Harvey's Chelsea Restaurant, has saved this old Irish bar from disaster. In the evening, and above all on weekends, this 1880s establishment attracts a crowd of merry, thirsty souls.

## Maxwell's Plum
**1181 First Ave.**
**(near 64th St.)**
**628-2100**
*Daily until 4:00 A.M.*
*Moderate; no cover charge*
*All major credit cards*

One of the best singles bars in town. It's like a Hollywood musical—huge, popular, colorful. The bar area is maddening, the restaurant area is frantic . . . and it's a "must see" for everyone. The Tiffany glass is a dream. Highly recommended.

## McFeeley's
**565 W. 23rd St.**
**929-4432**
*Daily from 5:00 P.M. to 2:00 A.M.*
*Inexpensive; no cover charge*
*AE, MC, V*

Pub-like atmosphere at the bar and, above the mahogany woodwork, a handsome painted ceiling (apparently the only one of its kind in New York). A place to drink but definitely not to eat . . . they obviously forgot to restore the kitchen.

## McSorley's
**15 E. 7th St.**
**473-8800**
*Daily until midnight*
*Inexpensive: no cover charge*
*No credit cards*

Irish pub with Lower East Side atmosphere and assorted writers, artists, and neighborhood folk heroes hanging about. Perfect place for singing along with the records on the jukebox.

## Nicola's
**146 E. 84th St.**
**249-9850**
*Daily until midnight*
*Moderate: no cover charge*
*No credit cards*

This comfortable and very elegant bar just drips with style: dress Wall Street or preppy on a spree and you'll fit right in.

## Old Town Tavern
**45 E. 18th St.**
**473-8874**
*Daily until 11:00 P.M.*
*Inexpensive; no cover charge*
*No credit cards*

Three blocks west of Gramercy Park lies one of the most authentic vestiges of the nineteenth-century saloon in New York. Superb mahogany decor and an interesting clientele.

## One Fifth Avenue
**1 Fifth Ave.**
**(8th St.)**
**260-3434**
*Daily until 3:00 A.M.*
*Inexpensive; no cover charge*
*All major credit cards*

Lots of young people, piano played in the evening (good jazz trio) . . . typically New York.

## Pete's Tavern
**129 E. 18th St.**
**(Irving Place)**
**473-7676**
*Daily until 3:00 A.M.*
*Inexpensive; no cover charge*
*All major credit cards*

About a hundred years old, this place credits itself with being the "oldest original bar in New York." Customers drink to the health of O. Henry, who lived just across the street.

## P. J. Clarke's
**915 Third Ave.**
**(at 55th St.)**
**355-8857**

Lots of places around town have tried, but this is the original and the best. An authentic "saloon," immortalized in Ray Milland's *The Lost Weekend*. Advertising executives, secretaries, literary types, fashion models, and Jackie Onassis all love the informal atmosphere. Last report had

*Daily until 4:00 A.M.*
*Inexpensive; no cover charge*
*No credit cards accepted*

## Rascal's
**1300 First Ave.**
**(71st. St.)**
**734-2862**
*Daily until 3:00 A.M.*
*Inexpensive: no cover charge*
*No credit cards*

## Redbar
**116 First Ave.**
**(7th St.)**
*Daily until 4:00 A.M.*
*No credit cards*

## Ruelle's
**321 Columbus Ave.**
**(75th St.)**
**799-5100**
*Daily until 4:00 A.M.*
*Moderate; no cover charge*
*All major credit cards*

## Le Saloon
**1920 Broadway**
**(64th St.)**
**874-1500**
*Daily 11:30 A.M. to 4:00 A.M.*
*Moderate: no cover charge*
*All major credit cards*

## September's
**1442 First Ave.**
**(75th-76th Sts.)**
**861-4670**
*Daily until 4:00 A.M.,*
*2:00 A.M. Sun.*

## Spring St. Bar
**162 Spring St.**
**(near Broadway)**
**431-7637**
*Daily until 4:00 A.M.*
*Inexpensive: no cover charge*
*MC, AE, V*

## Tuesday's
**190 Third Ave.**
**(18th St.)**
**533-7900**

the owner refusing an offer of $3 million to sell the place. Highly recommended.

The same sort of American style pub as Friday's, with sawdust-strewn floors, brick walls, and the menu handwritten on large blackboards. The same dishes, and more or less the same crowd as Friday's, but as Rascal's is less well known, this is the place to come when Friday's is full. Gorgeous staff.

The counterculture hangout of the 1980s. The whole place serves as a backdrop for the crowd . . . New Wave girls with pink hair, fashion designers with hip boots, punk rock groupies with mohawks (guys) and leather (girls). Not at all cozy but, well, interesting. Worth a visit.

This is it, folks; as of this writing, this bar/restaurant is the hottest place around . . . a transplanted East Side singles bar with a "gotta score" atmosphere. The bar is huge, there's a crowded sidewalk cafe in the summer (it seems as if the entire city walks by on a warm night), and the clientele like to think they're the trendiest folks in town. Go, if only to experience an honest-to-God singles bar in New York. Recommended.

Just across from Lincoln Center. Actors from Broadway shows and the after-the-theater set frequent this very crowded saloon, which can hold some three hundred people. The Italo-Sino-Franco-International-American menu is as big as a small-town telephone directory, and offers a gratinée à l'oignon and a boeuf stroganoff (so much for the Franco element). "The chef is wild," confided a waiter as he glided past the bar on roller skates. Have a Manhattan as your ears are pummeled by rock blasting from the speakers, and forget the hours slipping by and Broadway's dimming lights.

A welcoming, warm, cheerful, down-to-earth spot, diligent waiters, and in the evening, a band to add to the charm. Very typical. A friendly New York meal.

Downtown bar, SoHo neighborhood, arty/literary crowd, attractive decor, lively atmosphere.

Charming American bar decorated with old photos and etchings, lit by Tiffany lamps. Rustic menu: steaks, salads, and hamburgers, served on red-and-white checked tablecloths. Young atmosphere, and extremely pleasant

*Daily until midnight*
*Moderate: cover charge*
*AE, MC, V*

## Top of the Sixes
**666 Fifth Ave.**
**(near 53rd St.)**
**757-6662**
*Daily (except Sunday)*
*until midnight*
*Moderate: no cover charge*
*All major credit cards*

## Uzie's
**1442 Third Ave.**
**(near 81st St.)**
**744-8020**
*Daily until 2:00 A.M.*
*Moderate: no cover charge*
*All major credit cards*

## Wine Bar
**422 West Broadway**
**(near Prince Street)**
**431-4790**
*Daily until 2:00 A.M. weekdays,*
*4:00 A.M. weekends*
*Inexpensive: no cover charge*
*AE*

Sunday brunch. Other places in the same style: Wednesday's, 210 E. 86th St. (535-8500), until 4:00 A.M., closed Monday; and Thursday's, 57 W. 58th St. (371-7777), daily until 2:00 A.M.

A superb view of New York from the 39th floor. Terrible food, but good drinks—the whole place has a "we're celebrating our wedding anniversary with a night on the town" atmosphere.

Pretty women and good-looking men, all fashionably attired and all having a good time in this discreetly good-looking spot.

One of the many SoHo bistros installed in a loft with big Vogue magazine posters adorning the painted brick walls. Small tables, lit by candles in the evening, where people eat pâté, cheese, desserts, or the hot daily special, accompanied by a glass of red or white wine chosen from a spectacularly long list. The idea is originally from London, but is currently all the rage in New York. Very informal clientele and atmosphere. This is unquestionably one of the best spots for getting a sense of New York.

# Discos

## Bond's
**1526 Broadway**
**(45th St.)**
**944-5880**
*Nightly until 4:00 A.M.*
*Moderate: admission charge*
*No credit cards*

## Cachaca
**403 E. 62nd St.**
**688-8501**
*Nightly until 4:00 A.M., closed Mon.*
*Moderate: cover charge*
*All major credit cards*

A former clothing store enjoying new life as the largest disco in New York. It tries very hard to be hot and pulsating but falls short most of the time . . . it's just too big! A huge dance floor with a laser light show, a two-story indoor water fountain, lots of places to sit, and live entertainment are the advantages: a Times Square location, surly employees, and its rejected-from-the-best-crowd are disadvantages. Usually easy entry except weekends when mostly gay people claim pseudo-membership.

A Brazilian disco with the proper music and a carioca atmosphere. Attractive locale and an international crowd who appreciate the less-than-frantic demeanor. Live bands perform bosanova. A slice of carnival. Recommended.

## Empire Rollerdisco
**200 Empire Blvd. (Brooklyn)**
**462-1570**
*Daily, 8:00 P.M. to 1:00 A.M., closed Mon.*
*A bargain: admission charge*
*No credit cards*

The original roller disco. Largely black clientele and the best skaters in town. The pace is fast and furious and *very serious*—recommended for roller wizards only. Neighborhood and distance should discourage all but the true aficionado.

## High Roller Disco
**617 W. 57th St.**
*Nightly until 1:00 A.M., closed Mon.*
*A bargain: admission charge*
*No credit cards*

In Midtown, but far on the West Side. All types of music all night long. Hordes of people, a stage show on Wednesday nights, and lots of action.

## Magique Disco
**1110 First Ave. (61st St.)**
**935-6060**
*Nightly until 4:00 A.M.*
*Expensive: admission charge*
*AE*

A good-sized disco with a circular floor, lots of glitter on black walls and floor, and a decent sound and light show. Pretty girls abound, and there's a party atmosphere from floor to ceiling. Very crowded on weekends: entry is usually not difficult if you arrive before 11:00 P.M.

## Paradise Garage
**84 King St. (near Varick)**
**255-4517**
*Fridays and Saturdays 1:00 A.M. to 10:00 A.M.*
*Moderate: admission charge*
*No credit cards*

Reconverted parking garage housing the best, the hottest, the most incredible gay disco in New York. The latest and best music played on a mind-boggling sound system by a renowned disc jockey. Clientele is mainly young blacks and Latinos and the huge dance floor throbs. Out-of-the-way location but very safe. No alcohol served. Extremely difficult entry (members and guests only) but try calling ahead . . . the owner is understanding. Highly recommended.

## Regine's
**502 Park Ave. (59th St.)**
**826-0990**
*Daily until 4:00 A.M., closed Sun.*
*Expensive: cover charge*
*All major credit cards*

New York version of the international disco franchise. Pretty decor, pretty people, tiny dance floor, and sophisticated ambience. Those who *should* be here already know what to expect.

## Ritz
**119 E. 11th St.**
**254-2800**
*Nightly until 4:00 A.M.*
*Moderate: admission charge*
*No credit cards*

Hot, crowded, and a "must" visit for rock music fans. Disco plus live stage shows, and a huge movie screen showing cartoons and films. All the top rock stars appear here (The Talking Heads, Tina Turner, etc.) and the atmosphere is sweaty, pulsating, and a bit frenzied. Young clientele, lots of beer drinking, casual/sleazy dress code. Recommended.

## Roxy Roller Disco
**515 W. 18th St.**
**675-8300**
*Daily until 2:00 A.M.*
*Inexpensive: admission includes skate rental*
*No credit cards*

The "Studio 54" of roller discos, although entry is relatively easy. Huge rink, lots of action, lots of good-looking skaters, celebs who like to skate (Diana Ross, Cher, Alan Alda) drop by often. Frequently closed for private parties so phone ahead. Recommended.

## The Saint
**105 Second Ave.**
**674-8369**
*Saturday and Sunday all night*
*Expensive: admission charge*
*No credit cards*

The current "in" gay disco. Good music, spectacular surroundings, throbbing atmosphere (both the place and the patrons) and an experience that shouldn't be missed if you like disco. Extremely difficult entry (members and guests) but try calling ahead. Recommended.

## Studio 54
**254 West 54th Street**
**(near 7th Avenue)**
**489-7667**
*Nightly until 4:00 A.M.*
*Expensive: admission charge*
*No credit cards*

Reopened after the scandal that rocked New York's nightlife, the granddaddy of discos has been picking up steam although it has lost some of its celebrity crowd and status to rival Xenon's. Revamped with new lights, new sound system, and new decor, it's still difficult to enter . . . but that's only an attempt at recapturing the old mystique. Worth a try and a visit: it's still a first-class experience. Recommended.

## Underground
**860 Broadway**
**(near 18th St.)**
**254-4005**
*Nightly until 4:00 A.M.*
*Moderate: admission charge*
*No credit cards*

A phenomenon in Lower Manhattan. Gay disco invites a lady and her television camera to interview its patrons— soon all of New York's nocturnal in-crowd beat down doors to see and be seen. Every celebrity, from Halston to Baryshnikov, and Valentino to Ryan O'Neal, smiles and preens before Nikki Haskell's camera . . . and the loud music and steamy dancers only add to the fun. Another *must* if trendiness is important . . . but phone ahead, as it's often closed for private parties. Recommended.

## Wednesday's
**210 E. 86th St.**
**535-8500**
*Daily until 1:30 P.M., closed Mon.*
*Inexpensive: admission charge*
*All major credit cards*

An underground disco/bar/restaurant that continues on and on for an entire city block. The long, narrow dance floor is usually crowded with dancers, with plentiful diversions to merit a visit. It doesn't attract the trendiest crowd in town, but you'll have a good time anyway.

## Xenon's
**124 W. 43rd St.**
**221-2690**
*Daily until 4:00 A.M.*
*Expensive: admission charge*
*No credit cards*

Studio 54's replacement as *the* place to dance. Nighttime headquarters for movie stars, media stars, sports stars, Broadway stars . . . and social climbers with stars in their eyes. Big, brawny doormen block the entry of anyone but the "right" crowd, but try if your ego can stand the probable rejection . . . you might be lucky and pass inspection. The place has no real ambience and employs the surliest waiters in town; but no one cares because it's *the* place! For the moment, anyway . . .

# Entertainment

New York: "If I can make it there, I'll make it anywhere."
The world's greatest entertainers have a love/hate relationship with New York. It's a jaded, hypercritical town but the rewards can be stupendous . . . if New York loves you, she *loves* you. Opportunities to see

and hear an entertainer at his best are frequent. On the following list are the nightclubs, discos, and country/western bars where live entertainment is a mainstay.

Now would seem to be the time to mention another fact of New York nightlife: the use and availability of stimulants (other than alcoholic beverages). Marijuana, cocaine, uppers, downers, and so on *do* exist and are used rather openly in some clubs and discos. We neither support nor condemn the practice thereof; we just mention that you'll probably encounter it at some point during your nighttime excursions.

## The Bottom Line
**15 W. 4th St. (Mercer St.)**
**228-6300**
*Nightly until 1:30 P.M.*
*Moderate: admission and minimum charge*
*No credit cards*

Eclectic entertainment roster highlights one of the city's most popular theater/clubs. The best jazz, new wave, country/western, and pop musicians play here—check the newspapers to find out who's in town and showtime. Not a gorgeous facility, but the entertainment makes up for it.

## CBGB and OMFUG
**315 Bowery (at Bleeker St.)**
**982-4052**
*Nightly from 9:00 P.M. to 2:30 P.M.*
*Inexpensive: cover charge*
*No credit cards*

New York's unofficial rock and new wave music headquarters. Many of the best groups perform here along with some excellent newcomers making a bid for the big time. Scruffy jeans and multicolored hair are everywhere, and it's a required pilgrimage for true rock 'n roll lovers.

## City Limits
**125 Seventh Ave. (10th St.)**
**243-2242**
*Daily until 4:00 A.M.*
*Moderate: cover charge*
*No credit cards*

The music in this country and western bar is so good that even the sound system is famous. *The* place to wear cowboy boots and Stetson hats while dancin' the two-step. Entertainment nightly. Good place to visit when the rodeo is in town—the cowboys hang out here and at the Lone Star Cafe.

## Lone Star Cafe
**Fifth Ave. at 13th St.**
**242-1664**
*Daily until 3:00 A.M.*
*Moderate: cover charge*
*All major credit cards*

Top-notch country and western music, and hot chili have made this place the best "Texas-style bar in town. The crowd is lively, friendly, and they are real down-home folks (even the ones from Trenton, New Jersey). If the names Jerry Lee Lewis, Kinky Friedman, and Aztec Two-Step are familiar, this is the place to see and hear them.

## Mineshaft
**12th St. and Washington Ave.**
*Nightly (all night)*
*Inexpensive: admission charge*
*No credit cards*

Women are discouraged and leather attire is encouraged at this leather bar. Dress up or you might not get in; nor might you want to—this is a serious place, with S & M (sadomasochism) on the menu for those so inclined. Several scenes from *Cruising* were filmed here, and many consider it a "must" when surveying the gay scene.

## Mudd Club
**77 White St.**
**(near Broadway)**
**732-3560**
*Nightly until 4:00 A.M.*
*Inexpensive: admission charge*
*No credit cards*

This wonderfully grungy-looking club has succeeded CBGB as *the* new wave club, and seems reasonably long-lived. Raucous, bizarre, quite enjoyable.

## O'Lunney's
**915 Second Ave.**
**(near 49th St.)**
**751-5470**
*Nightly until 2:00 A.M.*
*Inexpensive: cover charge*
*All major credit cards*

Country/western music in an appropriate decor. Restaurant features spareribs and chili, beer is guzzled by the gallon, and everybody has a good time drinkin' and eatin' and foot stompin'.

## Sundown
**227 E. 56th St.**
**755-1725**
*Daily until 3:00 A.M.*
*Inexpensive: cover charge*
*No credit cards*

Country and western purists might find this large, raucous bar a bit disappointing but everyone else will have a good time. Live music, lots of dancing, cheerful patrons, and two bars (one upstairs overlooking the dance floor) are the main attractions . . . they even give free dance lessons (learn the two-step and become a star) on Sunday afternoons. Recommended.

## Tramps
**125 E. 15th St.**
**(Irving Place)**
**777-5077**
*Daily until 4:00 A.M.*
*Moderate: admission charge and minimum*
*No credit cards*

Stucco walls, small tables, and the best rhythm and blues or reggae music in town. Old-timers like Big Joe Turner and Luther Allison sing while the clientele shake their hips (no dancing, but people come real close to cuttin' a rug). Noise level is high, conversation is impossible, but the music is great. Recommended.

## Trax
**100 W. 72nd St.**
**799-1554**
*Daily until 4:00 A.M., closed Mon.*
*Moderate: Admission charge*
*All major credit cards*

Difficult to find (no sign, no lights, small door) but make the effort if rock music and rock musicians are your thing. Everyone hangs out here—Mick and the Stones, Rod Stewart, assorted groupies, society types. Live bands and jam sessions abound (the later it gets, the better it gets) and often the celebs will jam right along with the band. The atmosphere is frantic, a bit bizarre, and highly recommended.

# Harlem

During its heyday, a visit to Harlem was a required item on every trendy traveler's agenda. The heyday has passed, and unless you are local, we suggest you content yourself with the Harlem of your memory. It is no longer the safe, friendly neighborhood that travelers knew and loved—street crime and drug addiction have made it one of the least safe areas in New York.

There are still some very good clubs and bars in Harlem—The Cotton Club (West Side Highway at 125th Street) has reopened and it features excellent singers and bands, and the Lickity Split (138 Adam Clayton Powell Boulevard) is a good, small, classical jazz club. However, barhopping along 125th Street is not the same as barhopping along First Avenue, and the venturesome are warned that caution should be exercised.

# Jazz

Mellow—that's the word for jazz buffs. Their clubs, too. For the most part, relaxation reigns. Conversation spreads from table to table, friendships develop, and you don't need to be a hard-core fan. People of all ages come to have a good time, not to pray to the memory of Charlie Parker.

Forget splendors of cuisine or decor, of course. Jazzmen are famous for their anti-style and are oblivious to the surroundings in which the music is played. Next to them, rock 'n' rollers seem like so many peacocks. So, luxury addicts, seek elsewhere.

Jazz lovers in New York have a novel problem. Choice. One is, after all, confronted with more than a hundred spots. The very well informed can call Jazz Line (423-0488), a five-minute recording that will tell you everything that's happening in the jazz world this week. But for those with less expertise, magazines such as the *New Yorker, New York,* and the *Village Voice* publish up-to-date listings. The most reliable clubs are the following.

**The Cookery**
**University Place 8**
**(8th St.)**
**674-4450**
*Daily until 2:00 A.M.*
*Moderate: cover charge*
*MC, V*

This contemporary-styled club and restaurant in Greenwich Village presents the very best jazz artists (with a penchant for female singers). The legendary Alberta Hunter makes her home here, and should be seen at least once. Recommended.

**Eddie**
**Condon's**
**144 W. 54th St.**
**265-8277**
*Daily until 2:00 A.M.*
*Moderate: cover charge*
*All major credit cards*

One of the traditional New York jazz clubs and still going fortissimo. Small bands and enthusiasm. Next-door neighbor (Jimmy Ryan's) is also noted for swing and bebop music . . . spend an evening between the two and hear jazz at its best.

## Fat Tuesday's
**190 Third Ave.**
**(17th St.)**
*Daily until 2:00 A.M.*
*Expensive: cover charge*
*AE, MC, V*

Elegant music in elegant surroundings. Mainstream jazz (as opposed to traditional) with the best musicians in the business playing and singing. Highly recommended for the jazz buff—others might feel a bit intimidated.

## Greene Street
**101 Greene St.**
**925-2415**
*Daily until 2:00 A.M.*
*Expensive: cover charge*
*All major credit cards*

*The* SoHo jazz club/cabaret/bar/restaurant/hangout. It's big, beautiful, and infuriatingly noisy for music lovers—performers (from singers Cissy Houston and Judy Kreston to musicians James Moody and David Lahm) fight a losing battle with table chatter and clanging dishes. Still, it's worth a visit . . . the food is good, the ceiling is lofty, and the experience is rewarding. Highly recommended.

## Gregory's
**1149 First Ave.**
**(63rd St.)**
**371-2220**
*Daily until 4:00 A.M.*
*Moderate: cover charge*
*All major credit cards*

Modern jazz in a small, intimate club. Great for a nightcap.

## Jazzmania Society
**40 W. 27th St.**
**532-7666**
*Daily until 3:00 A.M.,*
*closed Mon. and Tues.*
*Sun. 2:00 to 5:00 P.M.*
*Moderate: cover charge*
*No credit cards*

New spot with masses of space and atmosphere. Very, very good musicians (Chet Baker, Mike Morgenstern) perform here, and the clientele is varied and full of bonhomie. Dancing.

## Jimmy Ryan's
**154 W. 54th St.**
**664-9700**
*Nightly until 2:00 A.M.*
*Moderate: cover charge*
*AE\ V*

Next door to Eddie Condon's, which it very much resembles. Dixieland and swing music in an easy setting.

## Michael's Pub
**211 E. 55th St.**
**758-2272**
*Nightly until 1:00 A.M., closed Sun.*
*Moderate: cover charge*
*All major credit cards*

East Side jazz club featuring singers and musicians from old-timers like Blossom Dearie and Dizzy Gillespie to newcomers like Jonathan Schwartz and Woody Allen (playing clarinet on Monday nights with a ragtime band). Woody's presence sometimes attracts those simpleminded fans that British jazzmen call "Hooray Henries."

## Mikell's
**760 Columbus Ave.**
**(97th St.)**
**864-8832**
*Daily until 4:00 A.M.*
*Moderate: cover charge*
*AE, MC, V*

The top jazz musicians in New York appear here (Art Blakey, Noel Pointer, Mongo Santamaria are regulars) and the performance roster changes often, so phone ahead. The clientele is a mix of jazz fanatics, neighborhood singles, and mellow executives. Recommended.

## Red Blazer Too
**1576 Third Ave.
(near 88th St.)
876-0440**
*Daily until 4:00 A.M.
Moderate: cover charge at tables
AE*

One of the friendliest bar/restaurants in town with Big Band music and New Orleans jazz as the main attractions. Old movie posters adorn the walls, there is a buzz of conversation in the air, and the music comes from good live bands. A bit crowded on weekends. Recommended.

## Seventh Avenue South
**160 Bleecker St.
(near Thompson)
475-5120**
*Nightly until 2:00 A.M.,
closed Sun. and Mon.
Moderate: cover charge
No credit cards*

A small bar downstairs and a roomy, two-level jazz club upstairs. Good, solid jazz musicians and a very interesting crowd lend splendid atmosphere. Recommended.

## Sweet Basil
**88 Seventh Ave.
South at Bleecker St.
242-1785**
*Nightly until 2:00 A.M.
Moderate: cover charge
AE, MC, V*

One of the most popular club/restaurants in Greenwich Village. Pleasant ambience and lots of good music. Recommended.

## Village Gate
**160 Bleecker St.
(near Thompson)
475-5120**
*Nightly until 2:00 A.M.,
closed Sun. and Mon.
Moderate: cover charge
No credit cards*

A New York institution. Larger than most clubs, the Gate is catnip to jazz enthusiasts. Even the discomfort and awkward seats prove no deterrent. Programs vary from jazz to salsa to whatever, and are almost always terrific. One visit is essential.

## Village Vanguard
**178 Seventh Ave.
(11th St.)
255-4037**
*Nightly until 2:00 A.M.
Moderate: cover charge
No credit cards*

This gloomy basement opened in 1935, and jazz greats from Charlie Parker to Miles Davis have created wonder there ever since. Like its sister club, the Village Gate, it's a required visit for those seeking the true New York jazz scene. It, too, lacks comfort—but who cares?

## West Boondock
**114 Tenth Ave.
(17th St.)
929-9645**
*Nightly until 1:30 A.M.
Moderate: cover charge
All major credit cards*

A plate of spareribs, a jug of wine, and good modern jazz music make the trip (it's way, way on the West Side) worthwhile. Recommended.

## West End Cafe

**2911 Broadway
(115th St.)
666-9160**

*Daily until 4:00 A.M.
A great bargain: $3 minimum
AE, MC, V*

Way uptown, close to Harlem and in the heart of Columbia University's campus, there lives a student cafe that is fun, entertaining, lively. Excellent jazz and 1940s music featured nightly. Like the West Boondock, it's worth the trip. Recommended.

# Late Night Sports

## Plato's Retreat

**509 W. 34th Street
627-1959**

*Nightly until 4:00 A.M., closed Mon.
Admission to couples and single
women only.
Admission $50*

So many lies, distortions, and pure creations of the imagination have been written and perpetuated concerning this venerable New York institution, that it's about time someone finally re-established the naked truth. Plato's Retreat is, in fact, an athletic club where people, either in groups or in couples, engage in all sorts of extremely healthful corporal activities, such as Swedish gymnastics, French boxing, Roman wrestling, swimming, horseback riding, rugby, karate, jogging, and archery—to name only the principal pursuits. In an age when communication between individuals is fraught with such difficulties, we can only applaud this vast collective spirit which enables members of the most diverse ethnic origins, social classes, age categories, and sexes to meet and get to know each other better—in spite of the semi-obscurity that can only be explained by the management's civic-minded attempt to reduce energy consumption.

One might wonder why so many men and women willingly pay to enjoy sports they might otherwise practice at home for free. But that would be to overlook the inestimable virtues of emulation, which is one of the foundations of democracy.

On a mattress or by the pool, individuals attempt to surpass themselves, sometimes even to establish new records—in any case to show their neighbors what stuff they're made of, and no one can deny that this healthy confrontation awakens passions that had gone to sleep, and tightens conjugal binds that threaten to come undone. But no one is obliged to do anything against his or her will, and if, perchance, you're not in a romantic mood, there's no penalty reserved for those who don't get into the swing of things. At Plato's Retreat, everything is permitted—even nothing. You can perfectly well enjoy a quiet evening seated, reading the complete works of Woody Allen or Shakespeare. Or simply take your weekly bath—the management obligingly provides a towel upon request—or widen your knowledge of the cinema by watching a few neglected masterpieces full of delicacy and tact, whose authors, alas, will never be discovered. The sighs and other sub-verbal exclamations which serve as dialogue in these film shorts have the advantage, among others, of transcending linguistic boundaries, and will be comprehensible to all—including foreign visitors and the feeble-minded.

The gastronomic activities, on the other hand, are sadly less well developed than the cultural ones. Chance had it that we visited Plato's Retreat during celebration of a birthday party, and we were looking forward to treating you to an enthusiastic description of the giant cake artistically sculptured in the form of a phallus. The idea, at least, was charming. Unfortunately—and we regret to have to point this out—the mocha cream was not up to the task.

# Piano Bars

Piano bars usually offer subdued lighting, music to have civilized conversations by, and an urbane atmosphere. A perfect place to meet before or after the theater, dinner, or a night on the town.

## Backstage
**318 W. 45th St.**
**581-8447**
*Daily until 4:00 A.M., closed Sun.*
*Moderate: no cover charge*
*All major credit cards*

Restful and good-looking, this piano bar/restaurant is close to most Broadway theaters and is the brainchild of Ted Hook, former B'way dancer. Lots of theater people swapping war stories. Couldn't be more New York. Recommended.

## Cafe Carlyle
**35 E. 76th St.**
**744-1600**
*Nightly from 10:00 P.M. to*
*2:00 A.M., closed Sun. and Mon.*
*Expensive: cover charge*
*All major credit cards*

This intimate piano bar housed in a distinguished hotel is the home of pianist Bobby Short. His drop-in-for-a-drink buddies include Jackie O., Frank S., and Princess Grace. Bobby sings a specialized gamut from Lorenz Hart to Cole Porter in a style that is at once witty and poignant, suave and sentimental. Highly recommended, despite the sometimes plodding service.

## Hanratty's
**1754 Second Ave.**
**(91st St.)**
**289-3200**
*Nightly until 2:00 A.M.*
*Moderate: cover charge*
*AE*

Several excellent pianists take turns playing in this attractive, comfortable bar. Very pleasant atmosphere.

## L'Hors d'Oeuvrerie
**1 World Trade Center**
**938-1111**
*Nightly until 12:45 A.M.,*
*closed Sun. and Mon.*
*Moderate: cover charge*
*All major credit cards*

There's a pianist, alternating with a small jazz group, and there's a gee-whiz view, since we are, after all, on the 107th floor. Nice music in a nice spot.

## Peacock Alley
**49th St. and Park Ave.**
**(Waldorf Astoria Hotel)**
**355-3000**
*Daily until 2:00 A.M.,*
*closed Sun. and Mon.*
*Moderate: no cover charge*
*All major credit cards*

Force yourself. Have a drink at the lobby bar in the city's largest hotel, if only to hear pianists Jimmy Lyon and Ronny Whyte show verve and style playing (apparently) every song ever written. The atmosphere may be stuffy, conversation inhibited, but, what the hell, it's music, music, music.

## Regency Room
**61st St. and Park Ave.**
**(Hotel Regency)**
**759-4100**
*Nightly until 1:45 A.M., closed Sun.*
*Moderate*
*All major credit cards*

Piano bar in the beautiful setting of this proud hotel. The atmosphere reeks of sophistication, the clientele often seem to have walked out of advertisements in *Town and Country*, and the music plays second fiddle to the experience. Recommended.

## The River Cafe
**1 Water St. (Brooklyn)**
**522-5200**
*Nightly until 1:30 A.M.*
*Moderate: no cover charge*
*AE, CB/DC*

Yes, it's quite a trip from Midtown Manhattan to a piano bar/restaurant beneath the Brooklyn Bridge, but the extraordinary view of Downtown Wall Street and the East River make it thoroughly worth doing. Crowded, but full of life and always a good place to impress a companion.

## Rupperts
**1662 Third Ave.**
**(93rd St.)**
**831-1900**
*Daily until 4:00 A.M.*
*Moderate: no cover charge*
*All major credit cards*

Two-level piano bar/restaurant with lots of polished wood and lots of polished ambience and lots of polished people. Upstairs a tinkling of piano and soft lights make for an easy atmosphere. Recommended.

# THE HOTELS

# Renaissance and Revival

By the end of 1982 at least five large new hotels will have opened, adding some five thousand rooms to the hundred thousand already available, but even this will probably not be enough to satisfy the constantly rising demand. Finding a hotel room in New York is never easy, even during the summer months when visitors keep pouring in despite the stifling heat.

For a long time New York hotels were—a few elegant exceptions notwithstanding—among the most mediocre in the entire United States. Even today one is shocked in certain hotels (even some with certain pretensions) by their conditions; it's as if the owners were waiting for everything to collapse before starting again from scratch. Happily, attempts have been made in the past few years to change the situation. Still, it's a good idea to choose a hotel that has recently been renovated and redecorated: if it doesn't guarantee perfection, at least you will be sure of comfort and relative cleanliness. There are, of course, also the few luxury hotels, as well as numerous sleeping factories, which, although completely impersonal, have the merit of being well equipped and functional. On the other hand, one is as likely to find the equivalent of the smaller, "quaint" European hotel as of striking oil under the World Trade Center. What is known as a "small" hotel in New York rarely has less than 150 rooms, and the price of land per square foot is such that only a philanthropist could dream of opening a forty-room hotel both attractive and affordable.

A word about service: it's best not to demand the impossible. Service is deteriorating so rapidly that one wonders, if it continues to decline at the same rate, whether the clients won't soon be serving breakfast to the staff. The status of hotel staff domestics now tends to be viewed as demeaning in the United States, and only a few elderly men and women still carry out their duties with any semblance of pride and grace. The newcomers grumble as they work, and seem indifferent to the feelings of their charges. Although it's often irritating, a little understanding is in order. Since many of them are recent immigrants who do not speak English well, they *are* badly paid. It's better to vent your frustration on a grouchy janitor, or a porter who fills his pockets just for raising his hand to beckon a taxi, without a word of gratitude.

**P**lease remember that prices listed are subject to change, and may already have been raised. In all cases, it's necessary to add state and municipal taxes (8.25 percent). Be sure to ask your travel guide or agent, airline reservations agent, or hotel reservations agent about special rates for weekends, groups, and conventions/ meetings (i.e. if you're a jeweler and the jewelry convention is in town, you might get a special rate at some hotels . . . even if you're not attending the convention). Many times a room charge can be reduced by 35–50 percent because you checked in on Friday and took a weekend package (meals are often included)—it's the same room, the same facilities, the same service, but a lot less expensive.

Hotel burglaries are on the rise and most hotels have a list of precautions that guests receive upon registration. New safety locks (some opened with a computer card instead of a door key) have been installed in luxury hotels like The Harley: it's an insurance against lost keys and random access to hotels by strangers.

**T**here exists no official classification of hotels in New York. We have grouped them into categories according to price based on single occupancy. Within each category we have listed the hotels alphabetically, and given each zero, one, two, or three or four symbols, according to our personal preferences.

# From $120

●●●●
## Carlyle
**35 E. 76th St.**
**744-1600**
*All major credit cards*

The poor wretches you see riding around in their Rolls Royces, who buy their emeralds at Cartier and their slippers at Gucci, are all of one mind: the Carlyle is one of the few places in New York where it is "possible" to stay. Some of these unfortunates keep an apartment here, and you won't necessarily get a room just because you want one in this small palace, where room service is unfortunately not always on a par with the sumptuous surroundings. You can give no better address to your couturier or art dealer, nor can you meet more distinguished chihuahuas than those that stroll through the neo-Louis XVI lounges. On the ground floor, The Restaurant, one of the most elegant in New York, and the charming Cafe Carlyle, are congenial and discreetly lively.

Single: $150–$175; double: $160–$185; suite: $300–$600.

## The Inter-Continental New York
**111 E. 48th St.**
**755-5900**
*All major credit cards*

For more than fifty years, the quiet, conservative Barclay Hotel has watched presidents, kings, and movie stars pass her by and sleep with her next-door neighbor, the Waldorf-Astoria. A few savvy travelers knew about it, and they kept the information to themselves—but that has changed since the Inter-Continental chain began pouring $30 million worth of renovations into the Barclay's lap. All of a sudden, she's the new lady in town—beautiful, gracious, and charming. For our money, there is no finer hotel in New York.

Everything has been changed and improved, yet the ambience and graciousness remain (and have, if anything, increased). Each room has been redecorated from floor to ceiling, and is comfortable, quiet, and elegantly furnished. The 350-member staff seem eager to please, from the doorman who ushers you into the beautiful lobby to the 24-hour room service waiter who delivers breakfast on time. A gourmet restaurant is on the premise, as are Caswell-Massey (the oldest pharmacy in New York and worth a visit all by itself) and Leonard's of London (the hairstylist who supervised "Murder on the Orient Express" and trimmed the locks of the Princess of Wales' bridesmaids). The entire enterprise is a world apart from most New York hotels . . . it seems that a guest's comfort and well-being are of paramount importance to everyone here.

Single: $150 ($84 weekend rate); double: $170 ($89 weekend rate); suite: $190–$750.

## Pierre
**Fifth Ave. and 61st St.**
**838-8000**
*All major credit cards*

This posh hotel, located in the heart of Manhattan a few steps from Central Park, is almost as famous for having been the scene of one of the most brilliant holdups in hotel history as it is for having played host to Henry Kissinger, Pierre Cardin, Yves Saint-Laurent, and the gilded vagrants of the international set. Although not always perfect, service is clearly above average, and if one has the means to take one of the luxurious and exorbitant 39th-floor apartments overlooking Central Park, it's difficult to feel hardly used.

The calm that reigns at the Pierre, where thick green carpets muffle footfalls, contrasts with the din characteristic of most New York hotels. We will only add that the vast, well-lit, and variously decorated rooms are perfectly comfortable, and that the bathrooms offer everything one might possibly expect from a bathroom.

Single: $150–$190; double: $165–$205; suite: $465–$575.

## Regency
**Park Ave. and 61st St.**
**759-4100**
*All major credit cards*

Still one of New York's most elegant spots. Although with five hundred rooms it's far from being a family-run boarding house, thanks to its antique furniture, marblework, and attentive service the Regency has kept up the manner of a luxury hotel. The rooms are particularly spacious, although it must be admitted that their "French Classical" decoration is a trifle dull. An extremely pleasant bar where, in the evening, solitary travelers will find all sorts of reasons not to remain so.

Single: $120–$185; double: $135–$200; suite: $230–$600.

### •••
### United
### Nations
### Plaza Hotel
**44th St. at the**
**U. N. Plaza**
**355-3400**
*All major credit cards*

Because in New York hotels small is chic, the U. N. Plaza, administered by the Hyatt chain, has to be one of the most exclusive addresses in Manhattan—it has just over 250 rooms, and starts at the 28th floor. In short, a family-run boarding house—where your fellow elevator passengers may be the American Secretary of State or the Egyptian Minister for Foreign Affairs, and where one sleeps soundly alongside the world's heads of state, knowing they are in the nanny-like care of strapping soldiers packing concealed firepower.

The hotel offers other distractions: tennis 24 hours a day; a magnificent swimming pool; and a bird's-eye view of the U. N. offices. With a pair of binoculars you can play at being a spy.

Single: $125–$160; double: $137–$175; suite: $200–$595.

### •••
### Waldorf-
### Towers
**100 E. 50th St.**
**355-3100**
*All major credit cards*

There are two Waldorfs: one, the Waldorf-Astoria (see *From $70*), which ends on the 20th floor. This lower part is a teeming caravanserai, a Tower of Babel for wheat merchants from the Midwest, German salesmen, Japanese industrialists, and Austrian farmers. Above that is The Towers, a hotel within a hotel, with its own private, French-style reception and management, which offers special treatment to those lucky mortals who manage to secure a place between the 21st and 40th floors. Even here there are distinctions, though. The Towers suites from the 21st to the 27th floors, are not really the be-all and end-all housing as they are mere rooms, albeit pleasantly decorated and extremely comfortable. The true sanctuary begins on the 28th floor. Here there are apartments, many of them leased by the year (to notables who have included General MacArthur and the Duchess of Windsor), the others temporarily occupied by the greats of the world (King Faisal of Saudi Arabia and his modest entourage had to make do with eleven apartments and twenty rooms).

But the ultimate glory, of course, consists in making it to the 40th-floor Presidential Suite. Furnishings of all epochs and styles are mixed here, for better—and especially—for worse. (Perhaps the U.S. should elect an antique dealer after its first actor.)

Waldorf Towers: double: $230; suite: $310–$430.

## •••
## Westbury
**Madison Ave. at
69th St.
535-2000**
*All major credit cards*

Conveniently located on Madison Avenue in the heart of the museum and boutique district. Trusthouse Forte, the British group, now owns this venerable hotel, and it has returned to its youthful glamor under the supervision of Henri Manassero, the former director of the Pierre. Its relatively modest dimensions, the comfort of its nicely redecorated rooms, and its almost family-style atmosphere have made it a preferred address for (among others) those who come to do their shopping at Sotheby's and the Madison Avenue art galleries. The restaurant—the Polo Lounge—is soon to be entirely redecorated.
Single: $135–$170; double: $150–$185; suite: $300–$500.

# From $95

## ••
## American Stanhope
**Fifth Ave. at 81st St.
288-5800**
*All major credit cards*

This relatively small hotel situated just across from the Metropolitan Museum doesn't have the fame of the Carlyle, but it is frequented by many fashionable folk. They appreciate its calm and discretion, and the extreme good taste of the Rembrandt Room, whose subdued lighting shows off its paintings, engravings, and furniture at their best. (The Stanhope, uniquely, is furnished with authentic antiques.) There's nothing more chic than to hold one's wedding reception in one of the Stanhope's small lounges. The rooms, by contrast, are distinctly more modest.
Single: $100–$140; double: $120–$160; suite: $200–$500.

## •••
## Berkshire Place
**21 E. 52nd St.
753-5800**
*All major credit cards*

Numbering only 416 rooms and 20 suites, this relatively small hotel was thoroughly renovated after its takeover by Aer Lingus, and it is now a particularly "choice" address. The reception area has been done in the colonial style, with bamboo furniture and plants. The rooms are elegant and the service is quite human—something rather unusual for New York.
Single: $110–$130; double: $145–$165; suite: $185–$385.

## ••
## Doral Park Avenue Hotel
**70 Park Avenue at
38th Street
867-7050**
*All major credit cards*

Just a stone's throw from Grand Central Station, yet away from the hustle and bustle of Midtown sits the Doral Park Avenue . . . close enough to theaters and nightlife, but quiet and elegant enough to be a relaxed and gracious home-away-from-home. Beautifully furnished rooms, a very popular bar and lounge, an outdoor cafe that's perfect for people-watching during warm weather—it's all here. A definite bargain for the savvy traveler.

Single: $80–$90; double: $95–$105; suite: $170–$350.

## Dorset
**30 W. 54th St.**
**247-7300**
*AE, CB, DC*

Located near the Museum of Modern Art and the boutiques on Fifth Avenue, this reasonably sized hotel will appeal to people who appreciate discreet luxury. Two hundred well-maintained rooms are painted in pleasant spring colors but are, unfortunately, not very well lit. Excellent service.

Single: $95–$125; double: $107–$140; suite: $240.

## Drake
**440 Park Ave.**
**(56th St.**
**421-0900**
*All major credit cards*

One of New York's most elegant hotels, and most popular too, since Swisshotel purchased it from the Loew's chain and entrusted its management to the expert Fred Laubi, previously the director of the Ritz in Montreal, and Monte Carlo's Hôtel de Paris. The five hundred rooms have been entirely redecorated. Very spacious (the bathrooms somewhat less so) and decorated with very cheerful fabrics and flowered wallpaper, they are delightful. The staff is friendly and efficient. The reception lounges are very elegant, and the Wellington Grill will shortly be enlarged and luxuriously redecorated. The Drake is the perferred address of such movie folk as Gina Lollobrigida.

Single: $110–$155; double: $125–$170; suite: $240–$360.

## Elysée
**60 E. 54th St.**
**753-1066**
*All major credit cards*

This small, kitschy establishment run by a Spaniard, in the heart of the elegant East Side, is highly regarded in the world of arts and letters. A friendly atmosphere of relaxed good taste reigns in the hotel, whose rooms are all decorated in different styles.

Single: $85–$95; double: $95–$105; suite: $125–$245.

## Essex House
**160 Central Park South**
**247-0300**
*All major credit cards*

Facing Central Park, this large hotel (part of the Marriott Chain) is in the "luxury-commercial" category. Somewhat impersonal, it nonetheless is perfectly comfortable and has all the facilities of a modern luxury hotel.

Single: $95–$150; double: $110–$165; suite: $275–$610.

## Grand Hyatt
**42nd St. and Grand Central Station**
**883-1234**
*All major credit cards*

Built on the remains of the old Commodore, this hotel is alongside Grand Central Station, from which it can be entered, and vice versa. One of the latest of the Hyatt chain of hotels (whose passion for original and spectacular architecture is well known) this is no rival to its stunning older brother in San Francisco. Floor space here is much more limited, and with the atrium several stories high it seems slightly cluttered, with mirrors, mobiles, and gurgling fountains. This doesn't keep this 34-story tower-mirror, which reflects the facades of surrounding buildings and the vagaries of the heavens, from being attractive. With 1,407 eminently comfortable though sometimes cramped rooms, including 87 suites, the Grand Hyatt caters to the business community. A sort of Waldorf-Astoria of the 1980s, minus the eccentricity.

Single: $95–$140; double: $120–$165; suite: $300–$2,100.

## •• Halloran House
**525 Lexington Ave.**
**755-4000**
*All major credit cards*

If ever an example is needed of the value of hotel renovation, this former residential hotel for men could serve as the perfect role model. Everything is fresh and sparkling and new: the British club-type chairs of the richly appointed lobby; the redesigned and redecorated rooms with a telephone in every bathroom (a convenience that every hotel manager in New York points out nowadays); a wall safe in every closet; an Olympic-sized pool and full health spa right downstairs. It's all peppy and young . . . seekers of the subdued won't find it here.

Single: $93–$108; double: $108–$123; suite: $275–$425.

## ••• The Harley of New York
**212 E. 42nd St.**
**490-8900**
*All major credit cards*

Every morning from 6:00 to 10:00 A.M., a man rides a special elevator equipped with fresh, hot coffee, warm croissants, and cold juices. When you ask room service for a continental breakfast, this man prides himself on being able to deliver your order minutes after you hang up the phone. New York's newest luxury hotel is full of wonderful little touches like that: Irish linen on the towel racks, the ubiquitous phone-in-the-bathroom, and eight hundred attractively decorated rooms. The staff is courteous and pleasant; the ambience is European and elegant; the attention to detail seems never-ending. Harry Helmsley's latest hotel venture appears to be quite remarkable . . . he has succeeded in combining Old World comfort with New World know-how.

Single: $99–$108; double: $114–$129; suite: $280–$430.

## ••• The Helmsley Palace
**455 Madison Ave.**
**888-7000**
*All major credit cards*

Where are we? Rome? No, but, a few minor details notwithstanding, this ponderous building (apparently chocolate-covered) is an exact replica of la Cancelleria in Rome and was built for Henry Villard, a leading financier of the 1880's. The palace later became the headquarters of Cardinal Spellman's entourage, and then of the important publisher, Random House, before Harry Helmsley got his hands on it and decided recently to transform it into New York's premier hotel.

Of course, he made a point of preserving the woodwork, marble, crystal, plasterwork, frescoes, colossal fireplaces, and the rest of the superabundant detail from this monument of the "Gilded Age." He had the means to do so: Harry Helmsley is one of America's richest developers.

Unfortunately, the result is excessively tedious. The decor might have turned out ugly but amusing: it is merely somewhat pretty and deadly dull. It's marked by all the trinkets of Old Europe, some of which are disastrous mistakes, like one rug of appalling hue. Even the bar is a flop, and so cramped at one end there's hardly any room for two people to pass. Without wishing to insult Mr. Helmsley, who, it seems, prides himself on his ability as a decorator, the Palace is now nothing more than a copy of a copy.

In fact, it's less; just a gimmick, because the 975 rooms and apartments are obviously not located in this three-story palace. They're in a 55-story tower that has sprung up behind it like a huge crystalline mushroom, as though something out of science fiction. That said, it's true that the rooms had to go somewhere, and that their great comfort must be commended.

Single: $95–$180; double: $115–$200; suite: $350–$800.

## ••
## Loews Warwick Hotel
**65 West 54 Street near Sixth Avenue**
**247-2700**
*All major credit cards*

Lots of savvy travelers keep their information about this hotel to themselves. It's just a stone's throw from the Hilton Hotel, but in a class by itself. Nicely appointed rooms, a huge and comfortable lobby, and a very efficient staff combine to make this hotel one of the nicer ones on the west side. Lots of celebrities seem to favor the Warwick, probably because of its good service.

Single: $85–$105; double: $100–$120; suite: $150–$350.

## ••
## Lombardy
**111 E. 56th St.**
**753-8600**
*AE*

A small hotel made up primarily of apartments. Studio couches in the rooms, which can serve as very livable studio apartments during the day. Several very luxurious suites decorated in modern Italian baroque style, with fully equipped kitchens.

Single: $90–$105; double: $105–$120; suite: $195–$245.

## •
## Lowell
**28 E. 63rd St.**
**838-1400**
*No credit cards*

Nicely placed between Park and Madison. A banal facade and a feeble attempt at imitation Louis XV within. But the hotel is tranquil, well run; its rooms are comfortable, and some even have fireplaces in which wood fires can be lit—the last word in chic in New York.

Single: $95; double: $100; suite: $250–$350.

## •••
## Mayfair Regent
**610 Park Ave.**
**(65th St.)**
**288-0800**
*All major credit cards*

Popular with the beautiful people, from Marisa Berenson to Rex Harrison. This small, very exclusive and elegantly furnished hotel has attentive service and a European atmosphere. Many of the rooms are occupied by year-round residents, and although there are theoretically 150-odd rooms and apartments available, many seem to be reserved for "friends of friends."

Single: $105–$150; double: $115–$135; suite: $185–$250.

## •••
## Parker-Meridien
**118 W. 57th St.**

A French hotel on New York soil—that was the challenge set, and met, by the Meridien Chain. In opening its second hotel in the United States (the first, in Houston, has been in operation since June 1980), this Air France subsidiary

**245-5000**
*All major credit cards*

did things right: a location in the very heart of Manhattan, two minutes from Central Park, between Sixth and Seventh Avenues; the 100 apartments and 703 small rooms are air-conditioned and soundproof; health club with squash courts, jogging track, sauna, swimming pool, and so on; convention facilities for six hundred people; and several bars and restaurants. Among the latter, Chez Maurice (Maurice Chevalier remains popular in the United States) keeps the flag of French nouvelle cuisine flying in New York City skies. Not satisfied with merely increasing the number of comfortable rooms available, Meridien sets out to promote the "art of living," French-style. And it does it well.

Single: $95–$160; double: $115–$180; suite: $215–$435.

•••
**Park Lane**
**36 Central Park South**
**371-4000**
*All major credit cards*

This ultramodern 46-story tower, whose bay windows overlook Central Park, has a fashionable clientele. The rooms—only sixteen per floor—are decorated in different styles (from contemporary to traditional), but always with elegance. The service is attentive, and the staff at the reception desk speak ten languages or so, including Estonian (reassuring for our Baltic readers). Superb suites, each with two bathrooms, bar–refrigerator, two color TVs, and of course a fantastic view, as they are located at the summit of this tower.

Single: $95–$160; double: $115–$180; suite: $280–$490.

•
**Plaza Hotel**
**Fifth Ave. and 59th St.**
**759-3000**
*All major credit cards*

It is wise not to venture into the reception areas, lounges, restaurants, or halls of the Plaza unless armed with maps, a pair of sturdy hiking boots, and emergency flares, as you run the risk of being caught by nightfall in the middle of your journey. The story is told of a gray-haired old lady who, as a young girl early in the century, went to the Palm Court for a cup of tea and who, unable to find her way out, has remained there ever since. Others may not have been so fortunate. Their bleached bones probably rest between the different floors—one shudders at the thought of what the thousands of cupboards in this New York Marienbad may conceal. But how, you may well ask, is it possible to get lost in the dense crowds that flow imperturbably through this temple to the 1900s? The explanation is simple: so many different and unexpected tongues are spoken here that one is never sure of being able to make oneself understood. Be that as it may, and regardless of the dangers, the Plaza unquestionably merits a visit, if only to be able to experience the sense of pride that comes from having gotten out.

You should know as well that, contrary to (not very prevalent) rumors, the Oak Room is not New York's finest restaurant. Indeed, at lunch and dinnertime it's one of the worst. The Victorian woodwork, muffled conversations, elegant monotony and smoked salmon tasting of papier mâché are extremely fashionable, though. The Sunday brunch is likewise an event in the life of the city.

Single: $110–$255; double: $135–$275; suite: $300–$700.

## St. Regis Sheraton

**2 E. 55th St.**
**753-4500**
*All major credit cards*

With its period furniture, European atmosphere, and chic guest list, this used to be one of New York's most prestigious establishments. It's popularity waned awhile back, and it still has not regained its former prestige. That shouldn't be long in coming, however, thanks to the vast renovations undertaken by the Sheraton's new management. Service has markedly improved, and the St. Regis is beginning to welcome back the distinguished European and South American guests who were its splendor in the great days of John Jacob Astor.

Single: $98–$150; double: $118–$170; suite: $225–$450.

## Sheraton City Squire

**790 Seventh Ave.**
**(53rd St.)**
**581-3300**
*All major credit cards*

Right in the heart of Manhattan, New York's biggest motel (720 rooms), recently renovated.

Single: $82-$100; double: $95-$115; suite: $150-$200.

## Sheraton-Russell

**46 Park Avenue near**
**36th Street**
**685-7676**
*All major credit cards*

Another one of those out-of-the-way, quiet, comfortable hotels on the lower end of Park Avenue. This one has a very nice bar for quiet meetings, nicely appointed rooms, and a very friendly staff.

Single: $98–$130; double: $118–$150; suite: $175–$225.

## The Tuscany Hotel

**Park Avenue at 39th**
**Street**
**686-1600**
*All major credit cards*

The owners of this hotel call it the "biggest little hotel in New York" and they are almost correct. The aim of the management, staff, and everyone else is to offer service and comfort. Located in the heart of the Murray Hill district and surrounded by stately mansions and famous clubs, the Tuscany blends into the residential mood of the neighborhood perfectly. The rooms are tastefully decorated and furnished; most rooms have a butlers pantry, all bathrooms have a telephone—and the whole enterprise is just wonderful. It's worth a visit.

Single: $95–$100; double: $110–$115; suite: $150–$275.

# From $75

## Algonquin Hotel

**59 West 44th Street**

Home of the famous Roundtable and for many years a bastion of artists and writers, this sturdy hotel has seen better days. Yet it remains a good place to escape the

**near Sixth Avenue**
**840-6100**
*All major credit cards*

hustle and bustle of New York life. The subdued atmosphere and comfortable surroundings (not luxurious, just comfortable) mask the hint of old age, and the staff is pleasant and accomodating. The sleeping quarters have comfortable beds and huge bathtubs . . . and you never know if Dorothy Parker and Alex Woollcott shared your particular room.
Single: $84–$88; double: $89–$94; suite: $162.

## Barbizon-Plaza Hotel
**106 Central Park South**
**247-7000**
*All major credit cards*

Of all the hotels that border Central Park this one is probably the worst. It is still a cut above a lot of other places in the city, but it's not in the same league as its neighbors (Plaza, Park Lane, Pierre). The rooms and facilities are adequate but no more; the service is functional but no better; the food is mediocre but digestible. Stay here if you must have a Central Park South address but are operating on a budget.
Single: $75–$95; double: $75–$95; suite: $190–$325.

## Loew's Summit Hotel
**Lexington Avenue at 51st Street**
**752-7000**
*All major credit cards*

Another Midtown hotel that's been completely redone. It's a bit tacky with bright orange couches in the lobby and plastic decor in the rooms, but it's comfortable, centrally located, and very friendly. The restaurant (Maude's) has an all-you-can-eat buffet lunch that is one of New York's better bargains . . . the food's not gourmet, but it's edible.
Single: $75–$90; double: $88–$103; suite: $125–$250.

## •Mayflower Hotel
**15 Central Park West at 61st Street**
**265-0060**
*All major credit cards*

Central Park is across the street, Lincoln Center is around the corner, and the trendiest street in town (Columbus Avenue) is a block away. A good restaurant and singles bar (The Conservatory) is on the ground floor, the rooms are nicely furnished (some offer great views of the Park), the staff is friendly and helpful; it's a good place to stay and a good place to keep as your own little secret.
Single: $75–$105; double: $90–$120; suite: $145–$200.

## ••New York Hilton
**1335 Avenue of the Americas (53rd-54th Sts.)**
**586-7000**
*All major credit cards*

A block from Fifth Avenue, the Hilton boasts 2,153 rooms. Staff and guests speak a good thirty languages, and the walls are so thin that you can brush up on your Japanese or Hebrew from your neighbors (at least you could in the room which one of us occupied). The half-dozen restaurants, the coffee shops and bars, boutiques, and nightclub seem overrun by the sort of people one meets in airport duty-free shops. In addition, of course, all the services one can expect from a Hilton, meaning minimal. Unless you can afford one of the two luxury penthouses costing over $800 per day, which offer one of the most fabulous views over New York.
Single: $73–$113; double: $95–$135; suite: $235–$395.

## New York Sheraton Hotel
**Seventh Avenue at**

What's to say? If you've seen one Sheraton, you've seen them all. This one is huge, very popular, very busy, and very ordinary. It's well located for theater-goers and sightseers, and close to Central Park and the Coliseum. A

**56th Street**
**247-8000**
*All major credit cards*

convention group or two will probably be in residence while you're there . . . so you'll take your chances.
Single: $82–$105; double: $95–$125; suite: $175–$330.

## St. Moritz Hotel
**50 Central Park South**
**755-5800**
*All major credit cards*

A large and lovely hotel across the street from Central Park; very European atmosphere and very charming ambience. The rooms are large, comfortable, and nicely appointed; try to get a room with a view of the Park and you'll fall in love with New York all over again.
Single: $80–$120; double: $90–$135; suite: $165–$400.

## Salisbury
**123 W. 57th St.**
**246-1300**
*All major credit cards*

Near Carnegie Hall, this moderately priced hotel has been entirely renovated. Its rooms are on the small side, and not always the brightest, but they're clean and well outfitted, including sizable dressing rooms.
Single: $69; double: $78; suite: $130–$179.

## Sheraton Center
**Seventh Ave.**
**at 52nd St.**
**581-1000; toll-free**
**U.S. reservations:**
**800-325-3535**
*All major credit cards*

The former Americana redone in a style that's short on personality but very comfortable. There are 1,800 rooms. The five upper floors, bearing the name Sheraton Towers, have been specially converted for business people and have a separate reception desk and elevator.
Single: $64–$110; double: $64–$125; suite: $225–$425.

## Vista International New York
**3 World Trade Center**
**938-9100**
*All major credit cards*

Business people can now stay practically on top of Wall Street. The first hotel built on the southern tip of Manhattan since 1836, the Vista International has set its 22 stories of glass and concrete right between the twin towers of the World Trade Center. Though low on nightlife, the Vista's neighborhood abounds with New York history. The 825 rooms in light colors and modern style are all equipped with large offices. Business people, whose domain this is, have at their disposal everything necessary for their well-being: bookstore, research service, secretaries, offices that may be rented by the day, swimming pool, health club, squash courts, and even a jogging track.
Two restaurants: the Orangerie (devoted especially to seafood) and the American Harvest, offering classic American dishes prepared with local produce.
Single: $75–$135; double: $100–$160; suite: $205–$390.

## Waldorf-Astoria
**301 Park Ave.**
**50th St.**
**355-3000**
*All major credit cards*

If Tutankhamen had lived in Manhattan, he could simply have arranged to be buried in the Waldorf-Astoria. All exits would have been sealed, which might not have been such a bad idea. It's hard to believe, when visiting this 42-story, 1,900-room monument, that it's possible to sleep here as well. But we must submit to the evidence: some people stay at the Waldorf. In fact, there are so many that the employees pay them absolutely no attention, and one can traverse miles of corridors laden with burdensome luggage without arousing any response from them. Only Buddhist monks attain such extraordinary detachment. Also, you have to get used to certain small details, such as being obliged to wait in line fifteen minutes to get your room key, and having to cross the lobby four times before finding the right elevator, and having to wait three quarters of an hour for your breakfast. It's true that the Waldorf doesn't have exclusive rights on these rigors and, in any case, it may be better to endure a little suffering in the midst of all the gold, velvet, and bronze gone wild, than to die of boredom in some large, cold, and impersonal hotel.

Single: $70–$150; double: $105–$185; suite: $235–$360.

# From $45

### Blackstone
50 E. 58th St.
355-4200
*All major credit cards*

Much more comfortable than one would guess from the somber exterior and cramped reception area. All rooms have air-conditioning and color TV, the staff is devoted, and this modestly priced hotel is well known to only a select few.

Single: $50–$55; double: $60–$75; suite: $75–$150.

### Century-Paramount
235 W. 46th St.
246-5500
*All major credit cards*

Clusters of haggard tourists linger in the lobby of this bunker on Broadway which, considering the masses of luggage, looks more like a checkroom than a hotel. The decoration of its 650 rooms seems to have been left to the staff plumber; still, every room has a bed, bath or shower, air-conditioning, and TV. Prices, as might be expected, are reasonable. It would be unreasonable if they weren't.

Single: $45–$60; double: $50–$70.

### Doral Inn
541 Lexington
Avenue at 50th Street
755-1200
*All major credit cards*

Across the street from the Waldorf-Astoria and in the heart of midtown Manhattan, the newly-refurbished Doral is an attractive, comfortable inn with lots of "extras" that will delight most guests: four squash courts, 24-hour coffee shop, multi-lingual staff, his-and-her terry cloth robes in each room. Nicely furnished rooms and a courteous staff make this hospitable hotel well worth a visit.

Single: $68–$88; double: $80–$99; suite: $150–$350.

### Gorham
136 W. 55th St.
243-3700
*MC, V*

Located near Fifth Avenue, this is a commercial hotel whose decor is not uplifting, but which has earned a faithful following thanks to its good location, modest prices, and the honest comfort of its rooms.

Single: $48–$58; double: $55–$70; suite: $70–$95.

## Milford Plaza
**270 W. 45th St.**
**869-3600**
*All major credit cards*

The lobby has all the charm and refinement of an Albanian airport, and a pushing and shoving crowd resembling those encountered in Woolworth's at rush hour. But this large, commercial hotel is not without its good points: completely redone on the premises of the old Royal Manhattan, it offers acceptable comfort; it's located in the heart of Broadway near the theaters and Times Square; and, above all, its prices are very reasonable.
    Single: $52–$77; double: $66–$87; suite: $160–$260.

## Shoreham
**33 W. 55th St.**
**247-6700**
*All major credit cards*

Small brick building well located a stone's throw from Sixth Avenue. Hospitable. Rooms done in a bare modern style. Quite comfortable. Unfortunately, individual (and thus noisy) air-conditioning.
    Single: $50–$60; double: $64–$74; suite: $80–$100.

## Statler Hilton Hotel
**401 Seventh Avenue at 33rd Street**
**736-7000**
*All major credit cards*

If you have business to conduct at Madison Square Garden, or on Seventh Avenue, you might want to stay at the Statler . . . otherwise, think twice. It's big and old, with small rooms, a hustle/bustle atmosphere, and a rather inconvenient location. In her heyday, the Statler was a grand old lady; today, she's just an old lady.
    Single: $59–$98; double: $75–$114; suite: $165–$250.

## Tudor
**304 E. 42nd St.**
**986-8800**
*All major credit cards*

Near the United Nations, a peaceful and quite pleasant hotel with an international clientele. Indifferently decorated but well-maintained rooms, all with bathroom and television.
    Single: $50–$60; double: $66–$75; suite: $88–$250.

## Wentworth
**59 W. 46th St.**
**719-2300**
*All major credit cards*

A small hotel whose 207 rooms are also small, albeit comfortable. Charming wallpaper and flowered curtains. Modest, but obviously well kept.
    Single: $45; double: $55.

# From $35

## Chelsea
**222 W. 23rd St.**
**243-3700**
*MC, V*

The Chelsea presides with a sort of seedy splendor over the brownstone district of Lower Midtown known as Chelsea. Since its opening in 1884, this red-brick, black-balconied edifice has been home to such literary folk as William Dean Howells, O. Henry, Arthur Miller, William Burroughs, Vladimir Nabokov, Dylan Thomas and Brendan Behan. In 1938 Thomas Wolfe assembled *You Can't Go Home Again* from thousands of manuscript pages he kept in packing crates. Around the corner, in 1951, Jack Kerouac typed his first complete draft of *On*

*The Road* nonstop onto a 120-foot roll of teletype printer, to begin the "beat" generation. The lobby is frequented by today's beats, the new wave crowd.

Single: $35–$65; double: $45–$85; suite: $100.

### Earle
**103 Waverly Place**
**777-9515**
*MC, V*

On the corner of Washington Square, on the limits of Greenwich Village, a very modest, small hotel. Refurnished, but not very clean—we saw cockroaches in some rooms.

Single: $25; double: $29–$40.

### Murray Hill Hotel
**42 West 35th Street**
**near Fifth Avenue**
**947-0200**
*AE, MC, V*

A small, out-of-the-way hotel that's functional and not much else. It's inexpensive, clean, friendly, and a good place to check if everyplace else in town is booked.

Single: $35; double: $45.

### Wales
**1295 Madison Ave.**
**(92nd St.)**
**876-6000**
*AE, MC, V*

On the upper limits of East Side chic, but nevertheless in close proximity to the museums, this hotel ( 150 rooms with baths) was recently redone, thus making it worthy of recommendation—especially because its location obliges it to offer more reasonable prices than elsewhere.

Single: $35; double: $60.

# For The Young

### International House
**500 Riverside Dr.**
**(123rd St.)**
**678-5000**

This large building overlooking the Hudson River, donated by the Rockefeller family, lodges young travelers on a daily, weekly, or even monthly basis from mid May to late August. Showers, cafeteria, TV rooms, and gymnasium.

### International Student Center
**38 W. 88th St.**
**787-7706**

A sort of "emergency bed" center, in a turn-of-the-century building facing Central Park. Dormitories for men and women, more or less private rooms, showers, and help in hunting down other lodging in the city.

### International Student Residence
**Broadway and**
**116th St.**
**280-2775**

Columbia University's John Jay Hall has accommodation for students of both sexes from mid May to late August. Private rooms and showers.

### YMCA— Vanderbilt Branch
**224 E. 47th St.**
**735-2410**

A well-equipped center with 438 rooms, each with one, two, or three beds, some with baths. Swimming pool and gymnasium. Open to families and single people of both sexes.

# THE SHOPS

# Open Season

New York is a shopper's paradise. You can find just about anything here in this international marketplace. And traditional seasons often don't exist; with all the magazines' and advertising agencies' off-season photography shooting schedules, the city is a goldmine of unusual merchandise year-round. As much as we'd love to list all the fantastic shops, boutiques and out-of-the way places in New York, we have had to limit ourselves to those we especially like. All the information was confirmed pre-publication, but we apologize if prices, times and even locations have changed. New York is always in its state of flux, and what's here today may be gone tomorrow. We suggest that you do as the New Yorkers do, and walk throughout the city to discover its special treasures and unexpected finds. If you have enough self-discipline, you may be able to resist the temptations that run rampant. We know it's hard. But window shopping can be the better part of shopping valor.

# Antiques

We haven't attempted the impossible: a comprehensive list of the innumerable antique dealers and secondhand shops in New York, and their specialties. We offer you, simply, an overview of the field. We think they are the most interesting and the most promising.

## AMERICAN ANTIQUES

**American Folk Art Gallery**
19 E. 76th St.
794-9169
*Tues. to Fri. noon to 6:00 P.M.; Sat. to 5:00 P.M.*

The most beautiful examples of American folk art can be admired here. Almost everything is a museum piece. Look for unusually shaped weather vanes with their original paint, early handmade quilts featuring vivid geometric designs, charming, naive paintings (in many cases the work of children), folk toys, cigar-store figures and hitching posts. Everything is quite delightful and, alas, quite exorbitant.

## America Hurrah
**316 E. 70th St.**
**535-1930**
*Mon. to Sat. noon to 7:00 P.M.*

A treasury of very attractive and amusing American antiques: weather vanes, signs painted on tin, folk art, a few old paintings and photographs, and especially a magnificent collection of very reasonable priced quilts. A captivating shop.

## Benjamin Ginsburg Antiquary
**815 Madison Ave.**
**744-1352**
*Mon. to Fri. 9:00 A.M. to 5:00 P.M.;*
*Sat. by appointment*

Very pretty English and American furniture and decorative objects, including needlework, pottery, glass, Chinese export porcelain, and textiles.

## Bernard and S. Dean Levy
**961 Madison Ave.**
**(76th St.)**
**second floor**
**628-7088**
*Tues. to Sat. 10:00 A.M. to 5:00 P.M.*

The highest-quality American antiques at a store that has been in business for three generations: furniture, silverware, and paintings alongside a superb collection of English china and pottery.

## The Gazebo
**660 Madison Ave.**
**(61st St.)**
**832-7077**
*Mon. to Sat. 9:00 A.M. to 6:30 P.M.;*
*Sun. 1:00 P.M. to 6:30 P.M.*
*AE, MC, V*

Two equally stunning collections of quilts: antique quilts from around the turn of the century, and new quilts made according to traditional methods and based on old designs (from $200 to $1,200 and from $225 to $525, respectively). As well, a section for wickerwork, silk flowers, embroidered cushions, and other delicious accessories.

## George Schoellkopf
**1065 Madison Ave.**
**879-3672**
*Tues. to Sat. 10:00 A.M. to 5:00 P.M.*

An extremely attractive gallery for fine American folk art. Charming painted furniture, weather vanes, and quilts. Well-seasoned prices.

## Israel Sacks
**15 E. 57th St.**
**753-6562**
*Mon. to Fri. 10:00 A.M. to*
*5:00 P.M.; Sat. to 3:00 P.M. (July*
*and August, Sat. by appointment)*

Israel Sacks has two floors on which you will find a wide choice of American furniture dating from 1650 to 1825: William and Mary, Queen Anne, Chippendale, Hepplewhite, and Pilgrim items, even a few rare John Seymour pieces are to found here. There is something a bit melancholy in the array. You feel twinges of nostalgia for the Newport "cottages"—but these are prices only collectors can afford.

## Kelter Mace Antiques
**361 Bleecker St.**
**989-6760**
*Mon. to Sat. noon to 8:00 P.M.*
*AE, MC, V*

A big, attractive selection of quilts (from $200) and other highly unusual early American art objects and painted furniture. Antique toys and folk art, not to mention an interesting collection of Pennsylvanian rugs.

## Laura Fisher Country Things

Laura speaks several languages, and will be only too happy to tell you in any one of them anything you want to know about her quilts ($200 to $400) and collection of

**1050 Second Ave. (56th St.)**
**838-2596**
*Daily 1:00 to 6:00 P.M.*
*Gallery 73*
*44 W. 96th St. 866-6033*
*(by appointment only)*

folksy arts and crafts. Her gallery, right at the back of the third floor in the big Second Avenue antiques center, may be difficult to find, but it's well worth the effort.

## Made in America
**1234 Madison Ave. (89th St.), second floor**
**289-1113**
*Mon. to Fri. 10:30 A.M. to 6:30 P.M.; Sat. 11:00 A.M. to 5:30 P.M.*

Three collectors, all young women, run this inviting boutique, recently installed in an attractively paneled shop. It offers a good selection of admirably preserved quilts from the '20s and '30s, with light and bright colors and very graphic designs: flowers, rosettes, and geometric constructions, all charming. A standout among the quilt shops that have invaded the city. Also look over the antique toys and utensils, and a few contemporary articles made in the old-fashioned manner. And, if you'd like to know more about quilting and quilts, Made in America organizes night courses for beginners and intermediates (6:30 to 8:30 P.M.; $65 for six evenings).

## The Secret Garden
**252 E. 62nd St.**
**753-3077**
*Mon. to Sat. 11:00 A.M. to 7:00 P.M.*

If you have a weakness for things antique, delicate fabrics and subtle colors, don't miss this minuscule and marvelous shop full of delicate delights. An enchanting array of American bibelots and furniture from 1840 to 1930 (Victorian to art deco).

## Thos. K. Woodward American Antiques and Quilts
**835 Madison Ave. (69th-70th Sts.)**
**988-2006**
*Mon. to Sat. 11:00 A.M. to 6:00 P.M.*

The crème de la crème of quilts can be scrutinized in this pretty shop. There are antique quilts in excellent condition dating from 1800 to 1925, with highly original patterns (from $60 for an unlined top quilt to $600 for an entire quilt and, of course, quite a lot more for the rarest pieces, of which there are a couple of extraordinary examples. Also dolls' quilts, antique country furniture; and—a touch of modernity in this traditionalist museum—a large selection of new all-cotton American prints.

# AUCTION HOUSES

New York has now joined London in importance as an art market. A tour of these auction houses' showrooms will often show you the treasures destined for sale. These are the largest establishments, with their specialties: note that during the winter (between Labor Day and Memorial Day) both Sotheby and Christie's are open Sundays and have lectures.

## Christie's
**502 Park Ave. (59th St.)**
**546-1000**

With branches in New York for some five years now, this is the second biggest name in the business. Numerous top-quality auctions in all domains. Christie's East (219 E. 67th St. 570-4141), a subsidiary, features sales of lesser importance, young collectors' items.

## Phillips, Madison Avenue
**867 Madison Ave.**
**(72nd St.)**
**570-4830**

Another well-thought-of firm for fine arts auctions. The Madison Avenue branch features paintings and valuable items. The 72nd Street store (Phillips East, 525 E. 72nd St., 570-4842) is for furniture and larger pieces. The third-ranked in London . . . and in New York.

## Sotheby Parke Bernet
**980 Madison Ave.**
**472-3400**

In business for over twenty years in New York, this prestigious establishment now does business from three addresses. The original location (Madison Avenue) is where the action is in fine arts and jewels. The other two branches offer decorative arts, stamps, coins and books.

Additional stores at 1334 York Ave., 472-3512 and 171 84th St., 472-4825.

## Swann Galleries
**104 E. 25th St.**
**254-4710**

A small establishment where auctions organized around a central theme are held every Thursday. The items are on show the two preceding days.

## William Doyle Galleries
**175 E. 87th St.**
**427-2730**

Finally, an American-styled, American-owned, American auction house! Fourth on the hit parade, it is increasingly fashionable, and increasingly well esteemed. Thus, increasingly few bargains.

# BOOKS

## Antiquarian Booksellers Center
**50 Rockefeller Plaza**
**246-2564**
*Mon. to Fri. 9:30 A.M. to 5:30 P.M.*

A few shelves with rare tomes in all languages and on all subjects. You may also obtain here a list of the best rare book dealers affiliated with the Antiquarian Booksellers Association.

## Appelfeld Gallery
**1372 York Ave.**
**(73rd St.)**
**988-7835**
*Mon. to Fri. 10:00 A.M. to 5:00 P.M.*

A European-style place. Antiquarian books are Mr. Appelfeld's long-time passion—he was smitten over forty years ago, in France. His collection of rare books, first editions, some in sets, some illustrated, line the walls of his pleasant little shop, where they can be browsed through at ease. For more information, send for a copy of his catalogue.

## Argosy Bookstore
**116 E. 59th St.**
**753-4455**
*Mon. to Sat. 10:00 A.M. to 5:30 P.M.*

An entire townhouse given over to old books, bindings, maps, and engravings. More than just a bookstore, this is a real library, where researchers come to consult all sorts of documents from the elderly to the ancient, classified alphabetically and by subject, in a number of fields. Their collection of maps on the second floor in particular is the most complete in New York. An excellent choice of old engravings and posters, some at very reasonable prices. Also some luxurious bindings. A reference library has a nicely old-fashioned air about it.

## J. N. Bartfield
45 W. 57th Street
Suite 201
753-1830
*Mon. to Sat. 10:00 A.M. to 5:00 P.M.*

Known to collectors as the specialist in bindings. One would be tempted to say he offers them by the yard, just like any other way to decorate your living room walls—more expensive, it's true, than wallpaper, but not as dear as old master paintings. Anyway, the books themselves, sold mostly in sets, are not totally devoid of interest. There's a bit of everything: art, philosophy, history, natural history, but especially Anglo-American literature. The bindings are varied, in good condition, and certainly decorative. A place for everybody but bibliophiles.

## Hacker Art Books
54 W. 57th St.
757-1450
*Mon. to Sat. 9:00 A.M. to 6:00 P.M.*

One of the largest selections in the world of books on art and architecture, both old and rare, as well as a few engravings.

## H. P. Kraus
16 E. 46th St.
687-4808
*Mon. to Sat. 9:30 A.M. to 5:00 P.M.*

One of the best antiquarian book dealers, both eclectic and specialized, Kraus stocks an admirable collection of books from around the world dating for the most part from before the seventeenth century: medieval manuscripts, incunabula, cartography, and Americana. There are items here in many fields, in a profusion of languages, and in every size. The only exception to the rule about age here is magnificent series of nineteenth-century French illustrated books. For serious bibliophiles only.

## Lucien Goldsmith
1117 Madison Ave.
(83rd-84th Sts.)
879-0070
*Mon. to Fri. 10:00 A.M. to 6:00 P.M.*
*Sat. to 5:00 P.M.*

A true French art bookstore, established in New York forty years ago and the first on the continent to be interested in books by painters (Picasso, Matisse, Rouault, Bonnard), and to represent French illustrated books. He was the co-editor of the correspondence of Toulouse-Lautrec, and organizes once or twice a year excellent exhibitions around a particular theme. His collection comprises continental books exclusively: French, Dutch, and Italian, from fifteenth-century incunabula to modern books from the 1950s. Mr. Goldsmith also has a large selection of engravings and drawings by European artists from 1800 to 1950, superior in quality to his books. In short, there's no one else like him in New York. But he is the first to recognize this superiority, and appears ever so slightly condescending at times to the ordinary customer.

## Leonard S. Granby
1168 Lexington Ave.
(80th-81st Sts.)
249-2651
*Mon. to Sat., noon to 6:30 P.M.*

A delicious little shop with a superb stock of rare books and limited editions on all sorts of subjects, including, among others, the Surrealists and French Impressionists. Lots of everything in this honest jumble where you're invited to take your time and browse, and where you won't be treated stuffily if you don't buy anything. Mr. Granby's shop is rivaled in its charm and pleasantness only by Mr. Appelfeld's.

## Philip C. Duschenes
**699 Madison Ave.
(62nd-63rd Sts.)
838-2635**
*Daily 9:45 A.M. to 4:30 P.M.
Closed Sat. and Sun.*

A surprising spot if there ever was one. The setting is gloomy, but the quality of what it offers is beyond reproach: almost exclusively illuminated manuscripts, fine press books, fine printings and bindings, and first editions of American literature.

# CLOCKS AND WATCHES

## Clock Hutt Ltd.
**1050 Second Ave.
(55th St.)
759-2395**
*Daily 10:00 A.M. to 6:00 P.M.,
Sun. 1:00 P.M. to 6:00 P.M.*

Visit the basement of the large Second Avenue center for antiques to see this dealer in European clocks (French, British, German) of all sizes and periods and in every sort of material: bronze, porcelain, copper, and wood. Complete repair service.

## William Skolnick and Joseph Fanelli
**1001 Second Ave.
(53rd St.)
755-8766, 355-1160**
*Mon. to Fri. 11:00 A.M. to 5:30 P.M.*

Marvelous English and French clocks, carriage clocks, and above all fobs, at this specialist who carries only the best. For connoisseurs only. Excellent catalogue. Ships all over the world. Repair service with free estimates. The best spot in New York.

# CURIOSITIES

Here are a few likely spots for charming miscellanea, a mass of small antique items, both useful and quite useless, plus a few specialized shops for collectors.

## Ann Philipps Antiques
**899 Madison Ave.
(72nd St.)
535-0415**
*Tues to Sat. 10:00 A.M. to 6:00 P.M.*

The specialty of this seductive Madison Avenue boutique is what you might call the pop art of yesteryear: pamphlets, posters, paperweights, and diverse objects from before the First World War. Fascinating, but rather costly.

## Bottles Unlimited
**245 E. 78th St.
628-8769**
*Open daily noon to 7:00 P.M.*

A collection of antique American bottles, for the most part handmade, dating from 1770 to 1904, in all shapes and sizes: big blue, brown, or clear pharmaceutical flasks, as well as bottles with very attractive labels. The only display of its kind in New York.

## Maya Schaper
**1022 Lexington Ave.**

Two lovely boutiques: the one on the East Side mostly stocks French and English knick-knacks and accessories and a few pieces of oak and pine furniture. The West Side

**(73rd St.)**
**288-9522**
*Mon. to Sat. 11:00 A.M. to*
*6:00 P.M.*

has two kinds of merchandise—an unusual combination, but appropriate—appetizing cheeses and hams, on the one hand, and ravishing nineteenth-century English earthenware cheese and butter dishes, on the other. A feast for eye, nose, and mouth.

## Oldies, Goldies, and Moldies
**1609 Second Ave.**
**(83rd-84th Sts.)**
**737-3935**
*Mon. to Fri. noon to 7:30 P.M.;*
*Sat. 10:00 A.M. to 8:00 P.M.;*
*Sun. noon to 8:00 P.M.*

A minuscule shop with a big name, crammed with good art deco pieces and furniture. Don't miss the second floor, which is larger than the first.

## Patina Antiques
**334 Bleecker St.**
**(near Christopher St.)**
**929-3170**
*Mon. to Sat., noon to 7:00 P.M.;*
*Sun. 1:00 to 5 P.M.*

A pretty, and very varied, display of curiosities (boxes, vases, jewelry), many European in origin, in this charming Village boutique.

## Philip W. Pfeifer
**900 Madison Ave.**
**(72nd St.)**
**249-4889**
*Mon. to Fri. 10:30 A.M. to*
*5:30 P.M.; Sat. and in August by*
*appointment*

For collectors of scientific, medical, astronomical, and mathematical instruments, a superb display of items from the eighteenth and nineteenth centuries: microscopes, telescopes, all sorts of desk seals, and such other curiosities, as boxes, candlesticks, snuffboxes, walking canes, magnifying glasses, and antique corkscrews.

## Side Show
**184 Ninth Ave.**
**(W. 21st St.)**
**675-2212**
*Tues. to Sat. 11:00 A.M. to*
*6:00 P.M.*

Amusing flea-market type wares such as old kitchen utensils, painted tin signs, and diverse nineteenth-century mementos; in Chelsea, a very up-and-coming district.

# ENGLISH ANTIQUES

## Arthur Ackerman and Son
**50 E. 57th St.**
**753-5292**
*Mon. to Fri. 9:00 A.M. to 5:00 P.M.;*
*Sat. to 4:00 P.M.*

Exquisite eighteenth-century English furniture, handsome English prints and paintings of the hunt and other sporting scenes. Quality china (mostly English); ask to see the Battersea boxes.

## Florian Papp
**962 Madison Ave.**
**(76th St.)**
**288-6770**

It should be stated at the outset that this antique store was the first in New York, being set up in the first year of this century, and for three generations it has been offering a marvelous collection of seventeenth- and eighteenth-

*Mon. to Fri. 9:30 A.M. to 5:30 P.M.;*
*Sat. 10:00 A.M. to 5:00 P.M.*

century English furniture of the highest of quality. There are also a few American and Continental pieces, as well as some decorative objects and accessories that turn over quickly, such as china, mirrors, chandeliers, and grandfather clocks. Excellent investments.

## Hyde Park Antiques
**836 Broadway**
**(12th-13th Sts.)**
**477-0033**
*Mon. to Fri. 9:00 A.M. to 5:15 P.M.;*
*Sat. 10:00 A.M. to 3:00 P.M.*

This shop located in the antique dealers district in Greenwich Village stocks a large number of pieces of eighteenth- and nineteenth-century English furniture. The accent here is more on quantity than quality, and the only problem is to decide among the abundant pieces. Moderate prices.

## The Incurable Collector
**42 E. 57th St.**
**755-0140**
*Mon. to Fri. 9:30 A.M. to 5:30 P.M.*
*(5:00 P.M. in summer); Sat.*
*10:30 A.M. to 4:30 P.M.; closed*
*Sat. in July and August*

A subsidiary of Stair and Company specializing in eighteenth- and nineteenth-century paintings and fine furniture, both English and Oriental. Good selection of Chinese lacquer, and a few very attractive oil paintings; landscapes, marine scenes, and still lifes.

## Phillip Colleck of London
**122 E. 57th St.**
**753-1544**
*Mon. to Fri. 9:00 A.M. to 5:00 P.M.*

Established in New York since 1938, this very fine London establishment has no fewer than five floors of fine eighteenth-century English furniture (Queen Anne and Chippendale, especially) as well as all sorts of accessories: mirrors, lamps, and chandeliers of the same period.

## Vernay and Jussel
**825 Madison Ave.**
**(69th St.)**
**879-3344**
*Mon. to Fri. 9:00 A.M. to 5:30 P.M.;*
*Sat. 11:00 A.M. to 4:00 P.M. (closed*
*Sat. in summer)*

The oldest and most respected antique dealer in New York for seventeenth- and eighteenth-century English antiques: furniture, clocks, globes, mirrors, china—produced in the days of Queen Anne and the four Georges. Not long ago he broke all records for the highest price ever obtained for a Queen Anne cabinet: $500,000. The store is managed by Christian Jussel who, at 31, is New York's youngest antique dealer.

# FRENCH/EUROPEAN ANTIQUES

## À La Vieille Russie
**781 Fifth Ave.**
**(59th St.)**
**752-1727**
*Mon. to Fri. 10:00 A.M. to 5:00 P.M.*

In our opinion, the most attractive antique store in New York. In a superb shop on two floors are shown magnificent Russian icons and objets d'art, marvelous eighteenth-century French furniture, an admirable display of paintings, antique jewelry, and a ravishing collection of gold snuff boxes, many of which were made by Fabergé, the famous jeweler to the court of the czars. No superlative is out of place when speaking of this dealer.

## L'Antiquaire, Inc. and Connoisseur, Inc.
**717 Madison Ave. (near 63rd St.)**
**751-1570**
*Mon. to Sat. 9:00 A.M. to 5:30 P.M.*

Two small antique dealers, associated with each other, who specialize in French and Italian furniture from the fifteenth to eighteenth centuries with a few pieces from Spain. Jewelry, ceramics, and objets d'art, too.

## Le Cadet de Gascogne
**1021 Lexington Ave. (73rd-74th Sts.)**
**744-5925**
*Mon. to Sat. 10:00 A.M. to 6:00 P.M.; closed Sat. in the summer*

The only French antique dealer in New York. Born in the southwest of France, he returns to his native land every year to acquire antiques. Everything in his store is authentic, and in its original state. His specialties: Louis XIII, XIV, XV, XVI, and Directoire, as well as a few pieces from the Second Empire. Prices are reasonable for the quality offered, as you aren't charged for restorations. You can treat yourself to some lovely smaller pieces from $1,000 to $7,500—rarer items are, of course, much higher. A former stockbroker, he is one of the most agreeable and interesting dealers around.

## Dalva Brothers
**44 E. 57th St.**
**758-2297**
*Mon. to Sat. 10:00 A.M. to 5:00 P.M.; closed Sat. in summer*

Five floors of the handsomest French classical eighteenth-century furniture in New York. The best of Louis XIV, Louis XV, and Louis XVI, as well as a few well-made Italian and Chinese pieces. Louis XVI clocks and vases from the Sèvres factory, magnificent inlaid work, a few desks, as well as paintings and screens: all in perfect condition, at prices which, although high, are not as excessive as in France. We shouldn't forget to mention the marvelous library on the top floor, with books on furniture and art dating from as far back as the eighteenth century. Nor the friendly welcome.

## Didier Aaron
**32 E. 67th St.**
**988-5248**
*Mon. to Fri. 10:00 A.M. to 6:00 P.M.*

A famous Parisian dealer. The quality of the furniture, objets d'art, and paintings on display here is equaled only by the setting in which they are presented: a superb townhouse decorated in eighteenth- and nineteenth-century European styles. In addition, don't miss the collection of art deco pieces, Oriental furniture and objects, and Victorian English furniture. A very eclectic shop run by Hervé Aaron, the son of Didier.

## Garrick C. Stephenson
**50 E. 57th St., 7th floor**
**753-2570**
*Mon. to Fri. 10:00 A.M. to 5:00 P.M.; appointment advisable*

This is the place to see the most exclusive pieces available on the New York market. Each one, whether a Ming buffet, Japanese table, Louis XIV wardrobe, art deco commode, or Portugese chest, is the work of master craftsmen. The choice, as imposed by the quality, is limited, and the prices limit purchasers to a select group, but if you're lucky enough to belong, you shouldn't forget that this shop exists.

## Malmaison Antiques
**29 E. 10th St.**

New York's greatest specialist in Empire and Directoire styles. His collection of furniture—mostly French, but with some American and Russian pieces from the same period—is extremely impressive: there are over a

**473-0373**
*Mon. to Fri. 10:00 A.M. to 6:00 P.M.*

thousand, of which necessarily only a few are exhibited; the rest can be studied in photographs. Prices very from $500 for a chair to $75,000 or $100,000 for the best pieces, with most of the smaller items around $1,000. Quality of wares and of welcome go hand in hand: a visit here is a real pleasure.

## Matthew Schutz
**1025 Park Ave.**
**876-4195**
*Mon. to Fri. 9:00 A.M. to 5:00 P.M.; by appointment only*

High-quality French furniture from the late seventeenth to the early nineteenth century. The choice of pieces is abundant and, considering their quality, prices are fair: in the middle to high range. Lots of Chinese lacquer furniture. An excellent spot.

## Paul Martini Antiques
**833 Broadway**
**(12th-13th Sts.)**
**982-5050**
*Mon. to Fri. 9:00 A.M. to 5:00 P.M.*

An excellent selection of French eighteenth-century and some nineteenth-century furniture. This dealer used to be on Madison, and his store is well worth a trip downtown. His quality is recognized, and his prices are not as high as those uptown.

## Provence Antiques
**857 Madison Ave.**
**(near 71st St.)**
**288-5179**
*Mon. to Sat. 10:00 A.M. to 6:00 P.M.*

There are quality pieces, especially Louis XVI, at this small dealer, where the only thing Provençal is the name. Rare lacquer pieces from Europe and the Orient, an excellent selection of Chinese and Japanese art objects, and magnificent eighteenth-century paneled rooms. For Provençal furniture, you have to visit his rival, across the street: Pierre Deux Antiques.

## Rosenberg and Stiebel Inc.
**32 E. 57th St.,**
**5th floor**
**743-4368, 888-5007**
*Mon. to Fri. 10:00 A.M. to 5:00 P.M.; appointment preferable*

An exclusive art dealer if there ever was one. For over a hundred years they have been an uninterrupted source of outstanding works of art, for both museums and private collectors. No specialty per se, but a limited, magnificent choice of works in a number of domains: medieval and Renaissance art, bronzes and objets d'art, European and Chinese porcelain from the eighteenth century, French and Italian furniture from the same period, and Old Master paintings and drawings by such artists as Jordaens, Tiepolo, Drouais, and Hubert Robert. Museum quality throughout.

## York House Antiques
**1150 Second Ave.**
**(60th-61st Sts.)**
**755-9543**
*Mon. to Fri. 10:00 A.M. to 5:00 P.M.*

A very pretty and tranquil spot, off the beaten path, stocking all sorts of furniture and bibelots, principally from the Empire and Restoration periods. A few Chinese and English items as well. A small choice of excellent craftsmanship.

# JEWELRY

## À La Vieille Russie

Sumptuous antique European jewelry dating from the fifteenth century to 1920 sumptuously presented at this,

**781 Fifth Ave.**
**(59th St.)**
**752-1727**
*Mon. to Fri. 10:00 A.M. to 5:00 P.M.*

the most admirable antique store in the city. And a collection of indisputably authentic Fabergé creations.

## Antique Buff
**321 Bleecker St.**
**(near Christopher St.)**
**243-7144**
*Mon. to Sat. 2:00 to 8:00 P.M.*

A small Village store run by a slightly grumpy but nonetheless very likable older gentleman holds enough jewelry to fill many treasure chests. Trinkets from 1800 to 1900, including a good collection of Victorian rings, as well as silverware and other miscellaneous items from the same era.

## Ares Antiques
**961 Madison Ave.**
**988-0190**
*Mon. to Sat. 11:00 A.M. to 5:30 P.M.*

A wide range of enamels, cameos, mosaics, and jewelry dating from antiquity to the late twentieth century—at Madison Avenue prices.

## Fred Leighton
**763 Madison Ave.**
**(66th St.)**
**288-1872**
*Mon. to Sat. 10:00 A.M. to 6:00 P.M.*

The rarest, the most beautiful, and the most extravagant jewelry from 1800 to 1950 available in New York. The collection of art deco jewelry from the '20s is far better in quality than anything you can see elsewhere. The Cartier pieces are pure marvels. High quality at high prices.

## Ilene Chazenor
**46 E. 73rd St.**
**737-9668**
*By appointment*

Her art deco and art nouveau jewelry is every bit as good as that found at her more famous rivals and, what's more, is offered at better prices.

## Jan Skala
**1 W. 47th St.**
**246-2942, 246-2814**
*Mon. to Sat. 8:30 A.M. to 5:30 P.M.*

This jeweller on the outskirts of the "diamond center" has stunning nineteenth-century watches and jewelry as well as Russian enamels and, as you might expect, diamonds—at accessible prices.

## Macklowe Gallery, Ltd.
**982 Madison Ave.**
**(near 76th St.)**
**288-1124**
*Mon. to Fri. 10:45 A.M. to 6:00 P.M.; Sat. 10:45 A.M. to 5:00 P.M.; closed Sat. in July and August*

A spacious place adjoining Sotheby Parke Bernet, with an impressive selection of George V, Victorian, art nouveau, and art deco jewelry signed by Kohn, Tiffany, Cartier, Lalique, and more. Tiffany lamps, Gallé vases, clocks, and mirrors of exceptional quality.

## Primavera Gallery
**808 Madison Ave.**
**(68th St.)**
**288-1569**
*Mon. to Sat. 11:00 A.M. to 6:00 P.M.; closed Sat. in summer*

An art deco atmosphere holds sway in this small, fetching store filled with vases, furniture, standard lamps, silver, paintings, but above all jewelry from this era, signed by Cartier, Tiffany, Boucheron, and Lalique.

# MUSIC BOXES

### Nathaniel's Music Boxes
**290 Columbus Ave.**
**787-3388**
*Daily from 11:00 A.M. to 9:00 P.M.*

"A house without music is like a heart without a song"— that's not Confucius, but rather Nathaniel, whose charming shop is full of objects from yesterday, today, and even tomorrow: inflatable and electronic robots that respond to your voice, tin boxes, cuckoo clocks, and, of course, a fine choice of antique and modern music boxes from all over. Wind yourself up and go.

### Rita Ford Music Boxes
**19 E. 65th St.**
**535-6717**
*Mon. to Sat. 9:00 A.M. to 5:00 P.M.*

You'll find nothing better or prettier in the way of antique music boxes than in this store where Rita Ford has amassed rows of American and European treasures dating from 1830 to 1910. All are in working condition. If you're a true lover of music boxes, it will take lots of time to try them all. Modern music boxes, too, are at very accessible prices (from $15), and there are charming musical carousels that light up (from $350). You can sometimes choose the music you want to go in the box of your choice.

# ART NOUVEAU/ART DECO

### Lilian Nassau
**220 E. 57th St.**
**759-6062**
*Mon. to Sat. 10:00 A.M. to 5:00 P.M.*

This is the place to go and the person to see for anything to do with art nouveau and art deco. She has the biggest collection of Tiffany glass and lamps in the world, all authentic, as well as all sorts of furniture and decorative objects. She is a famous figure in the antiques world.

### Minna Rosenblatt
**816 Madison Ave.**
**(69th St.)**
**288-0250**
*Mon. to Sat. 11:00 A.M. to 6:00 P.M.*

Lots of glass here: Tiffany, French cameo glass—Gallé, Daum—molten glass, statuettes; all add up to a very attractive whole, despite the sad brown walls.

### Muriel Karasik
**1094 Madison Ave.**
**(82nd St.)**
**535-7581**
*Mon. to Fri. 10:00 A.M. to 6:00 P.M.*

An attractive gallery that pays attention to presentation. Everything of the highest quality, whether furniture, sculpture, objets d'art, lamps, silver, posters, art nouveau and art deco jewelry—to say nothing of a large collection of Oriental nineteenth-century lacquer boxes. Ask to see the back room, where other delights are crowded. It is not, in theory, open to the public, but Mrs. Karasik will gladly show it to you.

### Simon Lieberman
**989 Madison Ave.**
**(near 77th St.)**
**Mon. to Sat. 12:30 to 5:00 P.M.*

Art nouveau and art deco furniture, painting, and glass, all of good quality. The combination of objets d'art (Tiffany, Daum, Gallé, Marinet), furniture (Gallé, Majorelle), and original framed posters (Toulouse-Lautrec, Jules Cheret, Emile Grasset) creates a happy ambience.

# ORIENTAL ANTIQUES

## E. J. Frankel, Ltd.
**25 E. 77th St.**
**879-5733**
*Mon. to Sat. 10:00 A.M. to 5:30 P.M.*

One of the most attractive galleries for Chinese and Japanese art in the world. Jade ornaments, ceramics, bronzes, jewelry, furniture, paintings, rugs, textiles, and robes, dating from the Shang Dynasty in China (1700 B.C.) and the Jomon Period in Japan (5000 B.C.) to the present time. Absolutely stunning. There is a reason why Mr. Frankel is Chairman of the Far Eastern Department at the New School.

## Felice Fedder Oriental Art
**348-7497**
*By appointment only*

Mrs. Fedder will be of interest primarily to the advanced collector; every one of her pieces of Chinese, Korean, and Japanese art is a small treasure. Ceramics, painting, furniture, screens, lacquerware, jade ornaments, and sculptures are magnificently represented here, and each item is carefully selected and displayed.

## Frank Caro
**41 E. 57th St.,**
**2nd floor**
**753-2155**
*Tues. to Sat. 9:30 A.M. to 4:30 P.M.*

A very attractive collection of Indian, Asian, and Chinese art dating from the Shang Dynasty to the eighteenth century, including furniture and objets d'art.

## G. Malina
**680 Madison Ave.**
**(61st-62nd Sts.)**
**593-0323**
*Mon. to Fri. 11:15 A.M. to 5:00 P.M.; Sat. 11:30 A.M. to 4:00 P.M.; closed Sun.*

A small shop offering Chinese porcelain and jades, dating from 220 B.C. to the mid nineteenth century. Each piece is handmade and has been authenticated.

## Hartman Rare Art
**978 Madison Ave.**
**(76th-77th Sts.)**
**794-2800**
*Mon. to Fri. 9:30 A.M. to 5:30 P.M.*

The most attractive and biggest collection of Oriental art in the United States, with works from the Shang to the Ching Dynasties. The Tang Dynasty pottery, the Shang and Chou Dynasty bronzes are outstanding, and there are Japanese metal works and ivory (netsuke, cloisonné, and Satsuma). Everything is beautifully displayed in this newly designed space on Madison. The Hartmans own a second

## Joseph Rondina
**27 E. 62nd St.**
**758-2182**
*Mon. to Fri. 10:00 A.M. to 5:00 P.M.; Sat. afternoon*

This famous dealer's selection of furniture and objets d'art has the air of a private collection. There isn't really any one specialty, although the accent is clearly on high-quality Oriental art. But there are also French and Italian antiques, chosen with immense care, and extremely seductive. A dealer in true luxury.

## Korean Art and Antiques
**963 Madison Ave.**
**(75th St.)**
**249-0400**
*Mon. to Sat. 10:00 A.M. to 5:00 P.M.*

The skill and imagination of Korea are perfectly represented by this shop's ginkgo and elmwood cabinets with brass fixtures, its reproductions of well-known ceramics, and folk paintings. Nothing is truly ancient (about 150–200 years old) but nothing is wanting in charm on that account.

gallery located in the Manhattan Art and Antiques Center, 1050 Second Avenue (between 55th and 56th Streets, 794-2812, same hours). This shop features an enormous and magnificent collection of English, American, and Continental silver, enamels, porcelain, Oriental accessories and a few pieces of French furniture.

## Madison Galleries
**1023 Second Ave.**
**688-1994**
*Mon. to Sat. 9:00 A.M. to 5:30 P.M.; closed Sat. in summer*

This is an excellent source of Oriental and Continental art, well known to collectors, interior designers, and people in the trade, with its stock of porcelain, screens, bronzes, ivory, hardstones, Chinese lacquer and furniture. Everything isn't the rarest of the rare, so the price range is broader.

## Mitsukoshi
**465 Park Ave.**
**(57th St.)**
**935-6969**
*Mon. to Sat. 10:00 A.M. to 6:00 P.M.*

The largest department store in Japan, Mitsukoshi's New York branch is a haven of Oriental beauty and tranquility in the midst of Manhattan. It offers attractive hand-painted Satsuma porcelain, both antique and modern, in a wide range of prices, as well as screens, lacquered boxes, kimonos, fans, tea sets, each item more bewitching than the last. In the basement is a restaurant where you can lunch or dine, Japanese style, to the accompaniment of that country's haunting music.

## Ralph M. Chait Galleries
**12 E. 56th St.**
**758-0937**
*Mon. to Sat. 10:00 A.M. to 5:30 P.M.; closed Sat. in summer*

The oldest shop of its kind in the United States established in 1910 carries magnificent pieces of Chinese art: bronzes, hardstones, pottery, jade work, and enamel, from the Neolithic period to 1800, as well as porcelain from the seventeenth and eighteenth centuries, and a few highly original pieces of fine silver from the late nineteenth century. The only gallery in New York equipped with a private laboratory for authentification and thermoluminescence dating.

## Vajra Arts
**975 Madison Ave.**
**(near 76th St.)**
**249-1677**
*Mon. to Sat. 11:00 A.M. to 6:30 P.M.*

An opulent choice of Indian, Nepalese, and Tibetan objets d'art of all kinds: bronzes, terra-cotta, stone, sculpture, wood carving, and jewelry—and at reasonable prices, meaning you don't have to be a wealthy collector. But if you should happen to be, ask to see their admirable selection of pieces dating from the second century A.D. to the eighteenth century, all of which are of museum quality.

## Weisbrod and Dy, Ltd.
**906 Madison Ave.**
**(near 73th St.)**
**934-6350**
*Mon. to Sat. 10:00 A.M. to 5:00 P.M.*

A small quantity of Chinese treasures, dating from the Neolithic era to the eighteenth century: archaic bronzes from the twelfth and thirteenth centuries B.C., porcelain, pottery, and stoneware. This small gallery's selection is constantly getting better. Wide range of prices.

# PORCELAIN

## Antique Porcelain Company
**48 E. 57th St.**
**758-2363**
*Mon. to Fri. 9:30 A.M. to 6:00 P.M.*

Very attractive eighteenth-century European porcelain and earthenware in an eclectic shop that also stocks French furniture, Renaissance jewelry, and objets de vertu.

## Armin B. Allen
**4 E. 95th St.**
**289-0345**
*By appointment only*

A small private dealer specializing in European ceramics and works of art from the eighteenth century and earlier. Pottery, porcelain, and glass.

## La Ganke and Co.
**1093 Second Ave.**
**(57th-58th Sts.)**
**688-9312**
*Mon. to Sat. 10:00 A.M. to 6:00 P.M.*

A true "bull" in a china shop! After twenty years of honorable service in a brokerage firm, the owner gave up his job and went into porcelain, to the great joy of the most demanding collectors. The pieces he deals in are superb and rare, and include the greatest names in eighteenth- and early nineteenth-century porcelain and pottery, such as Meissen and Sèvres, English Staffordshire, Chinese export. Also a good choice of nineteenth-century American ceramics (from before 1840) and Georgian glass. He offers an appraisal service for private collectors, and is an important source for the big museums.

## Philip Suval
**17 E. 64th St.**
**794-9600**
*Mon. to Fri. 9:00 A.M. to 5:00 P.M.;*
*by appointment only*

Breathtakingly beautiful porcelain and pottery await at one of New York's oldest antique dealers. Lots of China-trade goods, but also enchanting pieces from the best English factories—Worcester, Chelsea, Liverpool, and Wedgwood—dating from the eighteenth and nineteenth centuries. Both single objects and dinner services. A small collection of English and American furniture from the same period.

# RELIGIOUS ARTS

## Morjan Antique Judaica
**699 Madison Ave.**
**(62nd-63rd Sts.)**
**751-7090**
*Mon. to Fri. 9:00 A.M. to 5:00 P.M.;*
*Sat. 9:00 A.M. to 4:00 P.M.*

There is an admirable display of Jewish ritual and ceremonial art in this gallery devoted to antique Judaica from the sixteenth to twentieth centuries: Chanukah lamps, Torah ornaments, antique textiles, manuscripts and books, wedding rings, and illuminated marriage contracts. The quality and quantity of this collection are unequaled anywhere.

# SILVER

**James Robinson**
**15 E. 57th St.**
**752-6166**
*Mon. to Sat. 10:00 A.M.
to 5:30 P.M.; closed Sat. in July and
August*

The biggest and best collection of eighteenth- and nineteenth-century (from Georgian to Victorian) English silver and jewelry. Also, a small selection of modern handmade sterling silver flatware. On the 6th floor are sets of hand-painted crockery (mostly earthenware), a few of which are absolutely extraordinary (yet seem reasonably priced), as well as a collection of Regency brass and papier mâché boxes, lots of Victorian and Edwardian jewelry and silver, and, in back to the left, a section of inviting copperware, including dolls' furniture from the same era.

# TOYS

**Fun Antiques**
**1174 Second Ave.**
**(61st-62nd Sts.)**
**838-0730**
*Mon. to Fri. 11:00 A.M. to
5:00 P.M.; to 4:00 P.M. Sat.*

A stupendous collection of nearly fifty thousand antique toys, the oldest dating back to 1880, and the newest from the last World War. This very small shop is run by a former actor passionately interested in his treasures, and we should point out in particular the large store window full of animated merry-go-rounds, a miniature ferris wheel, and other marvelous automata. Very expensive—of course—with a few exceptions.

**Second Childhood**
**283 Bleecker St.**
**989-6140**
*Mon. to Sat. 11:30 A.M. to 5:30 P.M.*

Old and antique toys from 1850 to 1950 in painted tin, wood, and porcelain. A lovely collection of figurines and lots of other items too, including an impressive series of brand new Japanese robots—an admittedly surprising intrusion from the future.

**S. J. Shrubsole**
**104 E. 57th St.**
**753-8920**
*Mon. to Fri. 9:30 A.M. to 5:30 P.M.*

English jewelry and silver, mostly Victorian. Also a few reproductions of American silver. Not as rare, so not as expensive, but interesting all the same.

**S. Wyler, Inc.**
**713 Madison Ave.**
**(63rd-64th Sts.)**
**838-1910**
*Mon. to Sat. 9:00 A.M. to 5:30 P.M.*

Authors of an accepted reference book, *The Book of Old Silver,* Seymour B. Wyler and son Richard are acknowledged to be true experts in the field. Nor is their competence limited to that subject: as their collection of fine antique silver, porcelain, Sheffield plate, and Victorian objects proves. A store where there's a lot to learn—and spend.

# Beauty • Health

## BODY SHOPS

### Makeovers

**Ann Keane**
16 W. 57th St.
3rd floor
586-2803

This slightly old-fashioned looking but reputable beauty shop offers a pleasant welcome and good treatment. The specialty: aroma therapy, a massage using essential natural flower oils; more relaxing than stimulating, followed by a mask, for $35.

**Christine Valmy**
767 Fifth Ave.
(58th St.)
752-0303
153 W. 57th St.
581-9488

Almost a medical institute, this shop works in close collaboration with dermatologists, using a proved Swiss method of treatment. You will be well treated, and can take advantage of the low-priced facials done by their students (call 581-1520 for an appointment: only $10). In the salon, a facial by the regular staff costs $30 and up, depending on method. Pedicure, manicure, cellulite treatment, and makeup lessons are also available.

**Elizabeth Arden Salon**
691 Fifth Ave.
(near 54th St.)
407-7900

A day spent in this superb salon ($125 for five hours of steam bath, exercise, facial, makeup, manicure, pedicure, and a light lunch will make you feel ten years younger. If you don't have the time, opt for the half-day miracle morning ($90), or just a massage followed by a shower at alternating temperatures ($40), or a paraffin bath to stimulate and clean your skin ($30). Another way to keep fit: a series of ten gymnastics lessons given by Marjorie Craig. A full-service salon on seven floors!

**Georgette Klinger**
501 Madison Ave.
(52nd St.)
838-3200

A huge, luxurious salon for men as well as women, where you can have a massage (by hand only) for $30, or undergo one of the superb facials using herbal steaming, nourishment masks, and carefully studied individualized makeup for a contemporary look. Before you leave, you'll be given a home-care program outlining the necessary steps you should take and the products you should use (from among the 350 unscented, minimum-preservative items made in their own laboratory).

**Lancôme**
at Bloomingdale's
Beauty Center:
1000 Third Ave.

Its reputation in Paris is high, and for its New York institute, Lancôme has imported a team of Paris-trained estheticians. The treatment rooms are very comfortable, the skin-care program is adapted to each type of skin, and

(59th-60th Sts.)
8th floor
223-6772

the results are entirely satisfactory. Specialized service available for face, neck, hands, hair removal, makeup; and—of course—you can also purchase their excellent products.

## Make-up

### Citi Cosmetics
643 Lexington Ave.
(54th-55th Sts.)
752-3505

As modern and sparkling as its neighbor, the Citicorp Center, this attractive mirrored shop offers every beauty aid imaginable. All the best names are represented, such as Dior, Borghese, Orlane; such perfumes as Opium by Yves Saint Laurent and the new scent from Van Cleef and Arpels; also attractive ornaments for your hair, accessories for manicures, and vitamins. A beauty-care service is also available to give you advice about makeup and grooming. Every week experts from different cosmetic companies give free lessons and beauty analyses. A highly professional spot.

### Lydia O'Leary
575 Madison Ave.
753-4600

An expert in makeup to mask scars, broken veins, and other marks. A good spot for problem skin, and for special delicate attention.

### Make-Up Center
150 W. 55th St.
977-9494

A large, modern, and friendly shop–salon crowded with everyone from fashionable and trendy New York: models, actors, and dancers come here to stock up on theatrical makeup, which is the Center's specialty—including their own famous, moderately priced On Stage line. In addition to their own products, they offer one-hour consultations (by appointment for only $25, all-inclusive). They teach the use of makeup for daytime, evening, or on stage, as well as how to conceal scars resulting from accidents or birthmarks ($50). They give all sorts of facials, too ($25 and up). Private rooms and their own extraordinary products. Waxing and nail care also available.

### Il Makiage
Salon: 107 E. 60th St.
371-3992, 593-2880
Store: 50 E. 58th St.
750-8858, 750-8859

The Fiorucci of makeup: a small, very fashionable, and slightly eccentric shop that does makeup of all kinds, but excels in the unorthodox. You can receive all the usual kinds of treatment, as it's a full-service salon—but if you want to have your eyelashes dyed, your fingernails lengthened, your hair treated with henna, or have yourself done over with a new punk look and get covered with sparkles, this is the place. Their own line of very expensive products features all sorts of extraordinary colors. Makeup lessons at $45 an hour. Eye makeup $25, and full-face application $35. A special program for teenagers is planned, to teach young women thirteen and older proper grooming and the use of makeup.

### Merle Norman Cosmetics

A team of beauticians is available in this spacious and modern shop to make you up. They will advise you (at no charge) on which products and which colors suit you

**5 W. 57th St.**
**980-6970**

best, how to minimize all your little flaws (if flaws there be), and how to transform yourself for a special occasion. You'll be given a small personalized instructional guide. All these services are free: you're only charged for the products (exclusively from their own line) you buy. This is the largest chain of stores for cosmetics in the United States, with nearly thirty thousand shops across the country.

## Treatments

# Anushka
**11 E. 67th St.**
**3rd floor**
**249-3615**

Anushka is located in a small townhouse entirely devoted to body care: it's well known for its complete treatments, the head-to-toe and the neck-to-toe ($70 and $55 respectively) treatments, consisting of massage, paraffin and cream applications that make you so relaxed that it's hard to stay awake. Another of its programs is the cellulite treatment and diet program conducted on another floor. In these charming surroundings you can be completely made over, practically from inside out.

# Nicole Ronsard
**1010 Third Ave.**
**(60th St.)**
**833-6408**

Here you're in the hands of a great cellulite specialist, known the world over for her services in this domain. Each case is studied and treated individually. If cellulite isn't a major source of worry, drop by for her hour-and-a-half Body Facial ($85).

# FRAGRANCE

# Dans un Jardin
**143 E. 57th St.**
**980-1177**
*Mon. to Fri. 10:00 A.M. to 6:00 P.M.; Saturday 11:00 A.M. to 5:00 P.M.*

Soft green and white, with occasional touches of pink: that's the setting conceived by Lucile de Baudry d'Asson, a young Frenchwoman who gave up her job as a vice-president at the Chase Manhattan Bank for the world of perfumes. She has just opened this dream shop in New York, after similar ventures in Paris, Milan, Brussels, and Buenos Aires. Perfumes aren't sold here, but you'll find a line of fifty exclusive and enchanting flower, fruit, and wood fragrances that you can mix to create an entirely personal perfume to match your taste and mood.

The essences are marvelously fresh and striking, all different, and all wonderful. Your own combination can be made into eau de toilette, beauty milk, soap, and shampoo. There are also readymade lines of jasmine, lotus, apple, rose, verbena, and sandalwood. Scented vinegars to rinse your hair and skin, and as the perfect treatment for sunburn, are also offered. The prettiest lacquer boxes, kits, bathrobes, embroidered evening bags, china, and matching linen—all in pink, green, and white, are located at the back of the store. You'll also discover a selection of green jade, pink coral, and other Chinese jewelry.

## Crabtree and Evelyn

30 E. 67th St.
734-1100
1310 Madison Ave.
289-3923
*Mon. to Sat. 10:00 A.M. to*
*6:00 P.M.*

There's a very Olde London atmosphere in these two shops lined with painted shelves imported from England. Their products are no less English: assorted soaps, shampoos, and bath oils scented with almond, corn, or oatmeal; seashell soaps and kids' soaps in the shape of Babar and Alice in Wonderland; and marvelous rosewood hair brushes and shaving brushes, one of their specialties. All sorts of goodies, such as cookies, jams, and unusually flavored and packaged teas, are available in very attractive gift baskets ($10 to $150, depending on the contents).

## Scentsitivity

39 E. 65th St.
988-2822
*Mon. to Fri. 10:00 A.M. to*
*6:00 P.M.; Sat. noon to 6:00 P.M.*

Below street level in this fashionably located townhouse you'll find soaps, potpourris, oils, bath foams, and other treats for delicate epidermi. Here, too, you can create your own perfume using any of their hundred varieties of aromatic oils (the latest of which is Lady Diana—as you might have expected!) elegantly presented in one-of-a-kind bottles. Attractive bath accessories, candles, scented books, and ravishing made-to-order gift baskets.

## Soap 'N Accents

243 E. 59th St.
421-6347
*Mon. to Fri. noon to 7:00 P.M.;*
*Thurs. to 9:00 P.M.*
*V, MC*

The center for the entire line of Roger et Gallet soaps and lots of other perfumes, unsinkable duck-shaped bars of soap for children, a few superb peignoirs, towels, cushions, and stylish Italian porcelain and glass, all of which will be gift-wrapped in attractive black-and-white striped boxes for $1 extra.

## Soap Opera

31 Grove St.
(Bleecker-
Christopher Sts.)
929-7756
*Mon. to Sat. noon to 9:00 P.M.;*
*Sun. 1:00 to 6:00 P.M.; closed Sun.*
*in July and August*

Soap, soap, and . . . well, tea. This small Village store specializes in the English Crabtree and Evelyn products. Delicious fruit-scented soaps, body creams, shaving soaps, jams, cookies, and teas are sold in an attractive shop, where the staff's manners wouldn't have delighted nanny.

## Soap Scents

245 E. 77th St.
861-3735
*Mon. to Fri. noon to 7:00 P.M.;*
*Sat. noon to 6:30 P.M.*

There are soaps of all shapes, colors, scents; bath oils, shampoos, and eaux de toilette; and lots of fragrant gift ideas in this tiny shop located just below street level. We were charmed by the painted boxes filled with soaps shaped like birds and butterflies ($9), Beatrix Potter and Charlie Brown characters (for $3 or $4), and even pasta shapes!

# PHARMACIES

## Boyd Chemists

655 Madison Ave.
(60th St.)
838-6558
*Mon. to Sat. 9:30 A.M. to 7:00 P.M.*

You'll find most lines of European beauty products in this universally known shop. You'll also find their own line of Fabriella products, plus current items in the way of soaps, shampoos, hairbrushes, and barrettes. Several estheticians are available for makeup consultations (eye $25, face $50) and demonstrations. In short, a mecca for beauty products frequented by the beautiful people—and those who would like to be. Drug and prescription service as well.

## Cambridge Chemists
702 Madison Ave.
(62nd-63rd Sts.)
838-1884
*Mon. to Fri. 10:00 A.M. to 6:00 P.M.*

A very good classic pharmacy that, despite its small size, is well stocked with domestic and imported cosmetics, beauty products, and toiletries, including the Cyclax line from London, used by Her Majesty Queen Elizabeth, only stocked by Cambridge in the United States. That should give you an idea of this shop's style.

## Caswell Massey Co., Ltd.
518 Lexington Ave.
(48th St.)
755-2254
*Mon. to Sat. 10:00 A.M. to 6:00 P.M.*

This spot in the Inter-Continental Hotel deserves at least one visit. Established in 1725, it's the oldest apothecary shop in the United States. If you'd like to try the eau de cologne used by George Washington and his friend the Marquis de Lafayette (Washington sent it to Lafayette as a gift), or the special cream prepared for Sarah Bernhardt, or one of their extraordinary soaps (they have the largest selection of imported soaps in the world), or if you simply want to contemplate the marvelous apothecary jars, some of which date from the eighteenth century, don't hesitate—there's nowhere else like it in the country.

## Clayton and Edwards Chemists
1004 Lexington Ave.
(72nd St.)
737-1147
*Mon. to Sat. 9:00 A.M. to 7:00 P.M.*

Two excellent corner pharmacists of a type that scarcely exists anymore, these shops' traditionalism is matched by their professionalism. The one on Lexington specializes in beauty products and perfumes, while the York Avenue store (1327 York Avenue, 737-6240) deals more in pharmaceutical items. Both stores carry unmarked brands of products, excellent in quality and lower in price.

## Kiehl's Pharmacy
109 Third Ave.
(near 13th St.)
475-3400
*Mon. to Fri. 10:00 A.M. to 6:00 P.M.;Sat. to 5:00 P.M.*

Kiehl's is certainly the most seductive of the New York pharmacies: it's a long, narrow, fragrant apothecary shop where you're sure to be made welcome. On the shelves are rows of jars full of the marvelous ointments, potions, and drugs they've been making since 1851, using herbs and natural products exclusively. Natural henna, musk oil, herbal facials, botanical drugs, and everything for men's and women's body care, are available in jars, bottles, or sachets,—everything of irreproachable quality. A full line of homeopathic remedies. Kiehl's counts among its staunchest clients a good number of people who frequent health stores and clubs, and who have an ecological frame of mind.

# SALONS

## For Children

## Michael's
1263 Madison Ave.
(near 90th St.)
289-9612

After Paul Molé's, the next most popular children's haircutting salon is Michael's. The salon is nothing much and is badly kept up, but is nonetheless very friendly and pleasant—and there are lollipops for the kids to suck on while being shorn. Ask for Dino. Cut costs $6. No reservations.

# THE SHOPS/Beauty • Health

## Paul Molé Barbershop
**1021 Lexington Ave.**
**(73rd-74th Sts.)**
**535-0461**

This is a real turn-of-the-century barbershop, clean and old-fashioned, with comfortable old leather chairs. It deals with an impressive number of children every hour, and always seems to be full. Certainly it is fast and efficient, and the barbers are very friendly. What more could you ask?

## For Men and Women

### Cinandre Beauty Space
**11 E. 57th St.**
**2nd floor**
**758-4770**

An institution in New York for several decades. A small, somewhat dumpy salon where the service is personal and talkative: you tell your life story and bare your secret desires while they give you a therapeutic cut. Not for when you're in a hurry.

### La Coupe
**694 Madison Ave.**
**(62nd St.)**
**371-9230**

The best cut in town. This is a truly dynamic salon, rapidly on the way up, which boasts some of New York's most gifted hairstylists. Whether you want your hair styled into a sophisticated chignon or intricate braids, or simply want a cut that's easy to live with and care for, you're sure to find what you're looking for. But you have to reserve long in advance as the spot is well known, to men as well as women. La Coupe also sells some pretty finery for your hair, available individually or in sets, and will do your makeup.

### Davir
**789 Madison Ave.**
**(67th St.)**
**2nd floor**
**249-3580**

This large, bright, and elegant European-style salon overlooking Madison Avenue, is the ideal spot to have your hair done rapidly (there's never any waiting) and perfectly by friendly, discreet stylists. A cut costs $25, and a blow-dry $20, and you are given a relaxing neck and back massage before the shampoo. Special prices for young clients.

### Hair Power
**27 St. Marks Place**
**982-6300**

For followers of fashion. New Wave styles (bizarre) and colors (extreme). Not for everybody! Men and women.

### Jean Louis David
**at Henri Bendel**
**10 W. 57th St.**
**6th floor**
**247-1100**

A very prestigious name, yet we do not recommend him very warmly. The team of stylists, although trained on the job in Paris, do not always share the master's talent. Instead, try the Jean Louis David special arrangement: the salon takes walk-ins (no reservations, so you may have to wait) at only half-price. Considering the results, this is not as much of a risk. Full service salon for men and women.

### Kenneth
**19 E. 54th St.**
**752-1800**

Kenneth is to New York what Alexandre is to Paris: a famous hairstylist specializing in very elaborate hair constructions and scaffolding—anything but simple cuts. Reserve several weeks ahead—especially if you want to put your head in Kenneth's own hands. The salon is located in a superb five-story townhouse.

## Linterman's
**21 E. 62nd St.**
**2nd floor**
**421-4560**

Roger Resca, a lively native of Nice, presides over everything in this small, intimate salon that, although internationally known and respected, retains an almost family-style atmosphere. He is the great, unrivaled specialist of the dry cut, which lets him adapt the cut to the individual's hair and gives clients advance warning of the final results. He is adept at natural hairstyles that need little care beyond a morning shampoo. A good cut doesn't need a blow-dryer—and his don't.

## Monsieur Marc
**22 E. 65th St.**
**2nd floor**
**861-0700**

Marc de Coster is the coiffeur par excellence of the fashionable set. You can sip a hot cup of his special-mixture tea and gossip among the flowered wall hangings, rococo chairs, and indistinct paintings. As for the methods, the blow-dryer plays a negligible role, with curlers and crimping firmly ensconced in this bastion of tradition. The results? You'll walk out looking fifteen years younger—with a lovely 1965 creation to adorn your head. But that's obviously what many right-thinking ladies are looking for. Likable staff.

## Pierre Michel
**6 W. 57th St.**
**3rd floor**
**757-5175, 593-1460**

Another furiously fashionable spot for having your hair done in whatever sexy, original, or romantic fashion you wish in a plush atmosphere. This is the place where "everybody" goes; that is, the sort of people who do their shopping at Henri Bendel, which is just a minute away. Also serves men.

## Raymond and Nasser
**747 Madison Ave.**
**737-7330**

An immense salon with a very modern atmosphere, as much because of the mirrors and brightly colored walls as for its style of cuts and clients. It's a very efficient place, and in less than an hour (by appointment, of course) you'll leave shampooed and set, without looking as if you were on your way to a wedding. It's a full service salon too, offering manicure and makeup. Your greeting may be fairly frenetic, but the results are entirely satisfactory, and it's especially recommended for henna. Prices that, considering the neighborhood, should not come as a surprise. Men and women.

## Le Salon
**16 W. 57th St.**
**2nd floor**
**581-2760**

Simplicity and efficiency are the order of the day in this salon, run by an Italian and his polyglot team who cut women's hair as well as men's. Specialists in tinting. The cuts themselves are like the decor: clean and simple. Excellent products, facials, manicures, and pedicures.

## Suga
**115 E. 57th St.**
**421-4400**

The owner of this dazzling white and mirrored salon is considered to be the best hair stylist presently working in New York: he can do everything, from the most natural to the most sophisticated, from the simplest to the most extravagant hairdos. What's more, this talented Japanese has surrounded himself with a diligent and highly competent staff that caters to a clientele of very up-to-date men and women. $35 for a cut, $65 to $85 for a permanent, $50 and up for coloring. Manicure and pedicure too.

# Books • Stationery

## BOOKS

### Barra Books
**819 Madison Ave.**
**(68th St.)**
**988-1770**
*Mon. to Sat. 10:00 A.M. to
5:30 P.M.*

This basement bookshop is by far the best in New York for reference books on art and antiques. You've hardly entered before an erudite young man steps up, offering to help you locate out-of-print books that interest you. A clientele comprising academics, collectors, and employees of institutions and museums. A singular shop.

### Book Branch East
**63 E. 8th St.**
**260-3999**
*Mon. to Thur. 10:00 A.M. to
11:00 P.M.; Fri. and Sat. to
midnight; Sun. noon to 9:00 P.M.*

A fetching little bookstore filled with books and magazines on theater and dance, as well as foreign periodicals and classical records.

### Books and Company
**939 Madison Ave.**
**(74th St.)**
**737-1450**
*Daily 10:00 A.M. to 7:00 P.M.*

A very special mention for this splendid store, both for its style and for the quality. You won't find just current best-sellers, but, carefully presented, the complete works of most good authors, as well as American and foreign poetry magazines, beautiful books on photography, art, architecture, philosophy, and a very pretty selection of children's books. Also a fine and complete paperback collection. Not quantity, but quality.

### Brentano's
**586 Fifth Ave.**
**(47th St.)**
**757-8600**
**20 University Place**
**(8th St.)**
**674-3480**
*Mon. to Fri. 9:45 A.M. to 6:30 P.M.;
Sat. 10:00 A.M. to 6:00 P.M.;
Sun. noon to 5:00 P.M.*

An entire world of books and other articles on three floors: this is a perfect store for finding presents. The good classical music department in the basement stocks records, instruments, and scores. A gift gallery of objets d'art—Italian vases, jewelry, music boxes—is on the ground floor, along with everything imaginable to amuse children: dolls from the world over, stuffed animals, educational and electronic toys, amusing and charming puzzles, and picture books. The second floor is filled with used books and collectors' items. There's more than enough to occupy you for a few hours.

### Eeyore's
**1066 Madison Ave.**
**(near 81st St.)**
**988-3404**

A bookstore exclusively for children, the only one in New York. It's charming, friendly, and will delight children of all ages. Children, from infancy to adolescence, will find a book or record to enchant them, and every Sunday

**2252 Broadway
(81st St.)
362-0634**
*Mon. to Sat. 10:30 A.M. to
6:00 P.M.; Sun. 10:30 A.M. to
5:00 P.M.*

morning there's a captivating storyteller. Go once at least.

## Forbidden Planet
**821 Broadway
(12th St.)
473-1576**
*Mon. to Sat. 10:00 A.M. to 7:00 P.M.*

This temple of science fiction offers an astronomical selection of science-fiction books, magazines, drawings, models, gadgets, and toys. Also similar items about rock stars. Fan heaven and cultist's delight.

## Four Continents
**149 Fifth Ave.
(21st St.)
533-0250**
*Mon. to Sat. 9:30 A.M. to 5:30 P.M.*

Impropaganda? Books, magazines, and newspapers from Russia, Poland, Czechoslovakia, and other Eastern European countries of which some, but not many, are translated into English and Spanish. Records, comic books, posters, and small souvenirs, too.

## Gotham Book Mart
**41 W. 47th St.
757-0367**
*Mon. to Sat. 9:30 A.M. to 6:30 P.M.*

A hub of literary activity, past, present, and future: the biggest selection of American poetry (mostly twentieth-century) and some 250 literary and underground magazines clutter this narrow bookstore. This is the place for information about poetry events all over the city. "Wise men fish here" says the wooden sign over the door, and we won't contest that.

## Librairie de France and Libreiria Hispanica
**610 Fifth Ave.
(Rockefeller Center)
581-8810**
*Mon. to Sat. 9:30 A.M. to 6:15 P.M.*

We can't say that the atmosphere, display, or prices are particularly attractive, but still, you'll find a good selection of magazines (not always the current issues), new novels and, on the French side, such Gallic glories as the Astérix books. Other location at 115 Fifth Avenue, 673-7400.

## Metropolitan Museum of Art Bookstore
**Fifth Ave. and
82nd St.**
*Tues. 10:00 A.M. to 8:45 P.M.; Wed.
to Sat. 10:00 A.M. to 4:45 P.M.;
Sun. 11:00 A.M. to 4:45 P.M.;
closed Mon.*

If you're not tempted by the major reproductions in the Metropolitan Museum of Art's gift store on the ground floor, keep walking. You'll surely be interested in the superb collection of art books in the Met's bookstore—without a doubt, the best in New York. Not only is the selection exhaustive (everything from prehistoric to contemporary), but the store is handsome and very well-organized.

## New Morning
**169 Spring St.
(W. Broadway)
966-2993**
*Daily 10:00 A.M. to midnight*

A wide choice of underground American and foreign publications and a good selection of underground comic books.

## Oscar Wilde Memorial Bookshop
**15 Christopher St.**
**255-8097**
*Daily from 10:00 A.M. to 6:00 P.M.*

A famous gay thoroughfare is home to a shop specializing in books of interest to homosexuals: novels, essays, magazines, as well as T-shirts proclaiming one's affiliation.

## Rizzoli
**712 Fifth Ave.**
**(near 56th St.)**
**397-3750**
*Mon. to Sat. 9:30 A.M. to 6:00 P.M.*

The wood-paneled walls covered with their freight of multilingual books make you think you're in a library rather than a bookstore. There is a perfect art section, as well as European newspapers in a section at the back to the right, a small art gallery, and a department for classical and jazz records on the mezzanine. You'll browse to the accompaniment of opera or refreshing chamber music for a change, instead of the almost inescapable disco tunes.

## South Street Seaport Book and Chart Store
**25 Fulton St.**
**(near Water St.)**
**766-9030**
*Daily 11:00 A.M. to 6:00 P.M.*

A life-preserver's throw from the Fulton Fish market, a bookstore quite appropriately given over to the sea. The complete works of Herman Melville take their place among sailing magazines, guides to navigation, travel books, how-tos for building your own boat, and—since the shop is also a government supplier—very attractive maps. Everything is neatly organized—no storms or heavy seas on the horizon here.

## The Strand
**828 Broadway**
**(12th St.)**
**473-1452**
*Mon. to Sat. 9:30 A.M. to 6:15 P.M.*

"The biggest used bookstore in the world." Over seven miles of new and used books. Everything you're looking for in history and art departments. A few copies of the latest titles sold at half-price. An institution.

## Supersnipe Comic Book Euphorium
**1617 Second Ave.**
**(84th St.)**
**879-9628**
*Mon. to Fri. 12:30 P.M. to 5:30 P.M.; Thur. to 7:00 P.M.*

As far as we know there's nowhere else like it outside of Hollywood. A true paradise for comic book aficionados, it features over 300,000 old and new comic books, including 1934-vintage collector's items. Plus complete sets of books and magazines, as well as first, rare, and current editions—enough to satisfy occasional fans and the most demanding collectors. A small, messy, and wonderful shop.

## Wittenborn Art Books Inc.
**1018 Madison Ave.**
**(78th St.)**
**2nd floor**
**288-1558**

This bookstore devoted to the visual arts (painting, sculpture, architecture, tapestry, furniture, and so on) looks like an over-crowded archive, but the disorder is only superficial, classification is rigorous, and the choice a wonder.

## Woman Books
**201 W. 92nd St.**
**873-4121**
*Tues. to Sat. 10:00 A.M. to*
*7:00 P.M.; Sun. noon to 6:00 P.M.*

This shop will be of great interest to women engaged in the struggle for women's rights. Books written by and for women, plus non-sexist children's books.

## Zen Oriental Bookstore
**142 W. 57th St.**
**582-4622**
**521 Fifth Ave.**
**697-0840**
*Mon. to Fri. 10:00 A.M. to*
*11:00 P.M.; Sat. to 8:00 P.M.;*
*Sun. noon to 8:00 P.M.*

Everything in the way of books about Japan: philosophy, culture, and cuisine. There are also records, sumi artistic supplies, toys, prints, and crafts in these shops whose clients are almost exclusively Japanese. A small cafeteria on the mezzanine is perfect for relaxation at one spiritual level or another, over a cup of tea.

# STATIONERY

## Ffolio 72
**888 Madison Ave.**
**(72nd St.)**
**879-0675**
*Mon. to Sat. 10:00 A.M. to 6:00 P.M.*

You'll find everything you need in the way of formal and classic visiting cards at Tiffany's or at Cartier, but for more original and creative ideas, this shop will print your own letterheads to order. Also invitations, visiting cards—formal or eccentric, depending on your mood. If you're a model, for instance, and would like a card with your portrait on the back, just ask them—nothing's simpler, and they'll be ready within a few weeks ($145 for 300, $175 for 700).

## Greetings
**740 Madison Ave.**
**734-1865**
*Mon. to Fri. noon to 9:00 P.M.;*
*Sat and Sun. 11:00 A.M. to*
*7:00 P.M.*

Among the long rows of well-displayed cards, you'll find a series of lovely card-collages ($3.50), as well as posters, clips, and colorful stickers to affix to your letters and gift wrapping. Stationery in all the colors of the rainbow is sold by weight. An amusing spot. Another location at 35 Christopher Street, 242-0424.

## Hallmark Gallery
**720 Fifth Ave.**
**(56th-57th Sts.)**
**489-8320**
*Mon. to Sat. 9:30 A.M. to 6:00 P.M.*

A large, spacious, and well-lit shop for party decorations, cards, candles, trinkets, various puzzles, children's books and jewelry. You can choose at your leisure from among five hundred types of card covering almost any occasion. Only divorces seemed to be missing. Many other branches throughout the city.

## Under Attack
**187 Columbus Ave.**
**724-6865**
*Mon. to Fri. 11:00 A.M. to midnight*

Attractive and extravagant cards from 40¢ and up, and very New Yorkish posters in this West Side shop.

## Untitled Art Postcards
**159 Prince St.**
**982-2088**
*Mon. to Sun. 1:00 to 5:00 P.M.*

A minuscule shop that nonetheless houses the biggest international collection in the world of art postcards in all areas: science, photography, painting, literature, classed by author or subject. A very interesting spot.

# Children

## CLOTHES

### Au Chat Botté
0 to 4 years:
**888 Madison Ave.**
**(72nd St.)**
**772-7402**
5 to 15 years:
**1065 Lexington Ave.**
**(75th St.)**
**938-3482**
*Mon. to Sat. 10:00 A.M. to 6:00 P.M.*

The most elegant and attractive children's clothing (mostly from France and England) imaginable. Everything is admirable in both taste and quality, whether it's sportswear or dress outfits (for boys and girls), babies' clothes or plaid skirts, finely embroidered baptismal robes or top-quality shoes (which account for 40 percent of their business). The best European brand names, some of which are to be found only here. If you're not afraid to spend a lot of money on clothes that are absolutely worth it, don't pass by these two shops.

### Broadway Baby
**2244 Broadway**
**(80th-81st Sts.)**
**580-0493**
*Mon. to Sat. 10:00 A.M. to 6:00 P.M.*

A discount shop offering clothes by all the good designers at unbeatable prices. Sasson jeans, for example, and hooded sweaters for less than $10.

### Cerutti
**807 Madison Ave.**
**(68th St.)**
**737-7540**
*Mon. to Sat. 9:00 A.M. to 5:45 P.M.*

A reliable classic for children up to sixteen. The window may not be particularly well kept up or arranged, but the clothes inside are beyond reproach, and the many Madison Avenue mothers who come here regularly can't all be wrong. In addition to a good selection of ready-to-wear (not always made in Europe), you can also have smocks and outfits made to measure for twenty or thirty dollars more. Good accessories and underwear (Dior panties and Doré tights) and a very elegant choice of shoes and flats. Madison Avenue prices.

### Chocolate Soup
**946 Madison Ave.**
**(74th-75th Sts.)**
**861-2210**
*Mon. to Sat. 10:00 A.M. to 6:00 P.M.*

The specialty here is imaginative clothing in colors ranging from the reserved to the frankly audacious, and smocked Liberty dresses designed for the store at reasonable prices. Corduroy overalls with patterns sewn on the front, Oshkosh overalls dyed specially for the shop in solid colors or stripes, and a wonderful choice of toys and knickknacks: old-fashioned metal mechanical toys, and others in wood painted with nontoxic paints; wood, plastic, and cardboard dinosaurs, dolls and doll houses, and the Danish schoolbags that are all the rage in New York. A fascinating, minuscule shop, only a few square yards in size, colorful and crammed with goods, not to mention the bustle of clients.

### Little Bit of the Sixties
**1036 Third Ave.**

Specializing in their own line of handmade clothing, including embroidered overalls and jeans with children's patterns, using rivets and heavy thread, and western outfits

(61st-62nd Sts.)
838-5961
*Mon. to Sat. 10:00 A.M. to 7:00 P.M.*

with fringes. Mini-western boots for the mini-cowgirl or boy, patchwork, and charming accessories. A small store full of delightful surprises.

## Pamper
322 First Ave.
(19th St.)
677-0604
*Mon. to Sat. 10:00 A.M. to 6:00 P.M.*

A good and very friendly store run by two Hawaiian-born ladies who don't push you to buy, but try to help you, as far as possible, to find what you're looking for, even to the point of suggesting other likely stores if they can't deliver the goods themselves. The quality and variety of the clothes (mostly American, with some European) and the relaxed atmosphere make this large-size small store the one we recommend most heartily to people in the neighborhood.

## Pinch Penny Pick-a-Pocket
1242 Madison Ave.
(89th St.)
831-3819
*Mon. to Sat. 10:00 A.M. to 6:00 P.M.*

The specialty here is clothing made according to traditional methods: hand-sewn overalls in all the colors of the rainbow, and charming dresses made by American and French designers. A tiny store with a very Village atmosphere right in the middle of Madison—for kids up to sixteen years old.

## Second Act
1046 Madison Ave.
(89th St.), 2nd floor
988-2440
*Mon. to Fri. 10:00 A.M. to 5:00 P.M.*

The best-known shop in New York for secondhand children's clothes. Very well organized and crowded with hand-me-downs in good condition and clean, if not new. Most of them excellent brands (Absorba, Cardin) at excellent prices. A more than useful spot.

## Small Business
101 Wooster St.
966-1425
*Mon. to Sat. 10:30 A.M. to 6:00 P.M.*

Attractive handmade quilts, jackets, and sweaters in dazzling colors. Lots of classics (Oshkosh, T-shirts) and sophisticated items (nightgowns, negligées) at affordable prices. A spacious and airy SoHo store, and well-organized (which can't be said about all its competitors). We also liked their fur-lined shoes and Indian moccasins, at very good prices.

## Stone Free Junior
1086 Madison Ave.
(81st-82nd Sts.)
744-7152

## Stone Free Kids
124 W. 72nd St.
362-8903
*Daily 10:00 A.M. to 6:00 P.M.*

Lovely handmade patchwork vests ($25 to $40), a line of Oshkosh overalls in every color imaginable ($14 to $17.50) and sweaters, as well as hand-decorated sweatshirts and T-shirts. Jackets in Chinese silk, smocked Liberty dresses, most of them exclusive items, with the accent placed increasingly on eccentricity—which is sometimes unfortunate, given the quality of the all-natural-fiber clothing (cotton, wool, silk, and animal hide). The West Side shop is more fun and better stocked with a particularly marvelous collection from the Appalachians, but the one on Madison Avenue is more spacious and better arranged—as you'd expect from the district.

## Tru-Tred
1241 Lexington Ave.
(84th St.)
249-0551
*Mon. to Sat. 9:30 A.M. to 5:00 P.M.*

A store that always seems to be jammed with people, and it wouldn't be surprising if you had to register before being served—at any rate patience, and plenty of it, is de rigueur. But that will give you time to look over all the models and styles offered and, if you can't decide yourself, one of the efficient salespeople will eventually help you make a wise choice of shoes for your child. You can't go wrong, as all are of excellent quality and well made by American manufacturers such as Sebago, Capezio, Stride-rite, Nike, and Timberland, and their European competitors such as Kickers, Mob 8, Adidas, and so on. They also sell some sports shoes for adults—not very stylish, but sensible, the sort that won't go out of style. Shipment available throughout the U.S.

## Wendy's Store
**1046 Madison Ave.**
**(80th St.)**
**861-9230**
*Mon. to Sat. 10:00 A.M. to 6:00 P.M.*

A wonderful jumble where you can find absolutely everything. Wendy's specialties include clothing hand-knitted specially for her, with delightful animal designs, in a wide range of colors (sweaters, vests, bonnets, socks), quilts for cribs, hand-painted T-shirts, embroidered sneakers, jeans for the newborn, elegant imported clothing from France, miniature toys, and more. Also a terrific choice of children's books with old-fashioned illustrations. As you would expect, Wendy herself used to illustrate children's books before opening the store. Reasonable prices, on the whole.

# TOYS

## Childcraft Center
**150 E. 58th St.**
**753-3196**
**155 E. 23rd St.**
**674-4754**
*Mon. to Sat. 10:00 A.M. to 6:00 P.M.*

Educational toys, mostly wood, plus puzzles, construction sets (from the already conventional Leggo sets to the latest American creations). Laboratory equipment for budding scientists, musical instruments, artistic supplies, and books. Education and amusement for children up to fifteen. Not to mention some furniture, such as rustic-style children's tables and chairs (from $35).

## Dolls and Dreams
**454 Third Ave.**
**(31st St.)**
**684-4277**
*Mon. to Sat. 10:00 A.M. to 6:00 P.M.*

There's not a single mass-produced toy in this charming shop devoted to quality imported or handmade toys. Stuffed animals, wood toys, the famous British Sascha dolls with lovely painted faces and enviable wardrobes, very well-made children's outfits, and excellent quality art supplies (such as all the Caran d'Ache supplies from Switzerland). Nothing is cheap, of course, but the least of these items is sure to surprise and please. Off the beaten path.

## F.A.O. Schwarz
**745 Fifth Ave.**
**(58th St.)**
**644-9400**
**5 World Trade Center**
**(concourse level)**
**775-1850**
*Mon. to Fri. 9:30 A.M. to 8:00 P.M.;*
*Sat. to 7:00 P.M.*

Is there any grownup who can't remember his first visit to the biggest and most prestigious toy store in the United States—and the most expensive? Three world-famous floors of toys, many exclusive items, including the famous life-size stuffed animals, miniature radio-controlled vehicles, and the electric trains (2nd floor). Dolls, electronic games (all the rage among the younger set), kites, and above all that Ambassador of Charm, the famous Snoopy doll, which won't fail to delight in any of its sizes. Not to mention the section of turn-of-the-century toys on the 2nd floor. Prices are higher than elsewhere, but a visit

221

is a must. At Christmastime, the animated windows provide one of Fifth Avenue's most popular attractions. Note the puppet shows given Monday and Friday at 2:30 P.M.

## Flosso-Hormann Magic Company
**304 W. 34th St.**
**2nd floor**
**279-6079**
*Mon. to Sat. 10:30 A.M. to 5:00 P.M.*

The oldest magic shop in the United States, which has been run by a series of celebrated prestidigitators since its founding in 1865. Free demonstrations for children and tours of the Museum of Magic on Saturday. Said to be Orson Welles' favorite store.

## Go Fly a Kite
**1434 Third Ave.**
**(81st St.)**
**472-2623**
*Mon. to Sat. 10:00 A.M. to 6:00 P.M.*

Kites from around the world in all shapes (birds, animals, planes), sizes, materials (plastic, paper, cloth) and in a wide range of prices ($5 to $80). The Chinese kites—especially the dragon—are stupendous, and inexpensive. And most can be folded up, so they're easy to transport. A sort of gallery of flying sculptures, well known to New Yorkers, as it has been around for over fourteen years.

## The Laughing Giraffe
**147 E. 72nd St.**
**570-9528**
*Mon. to Sat. 10:00 A.M. to 5:30 P.M.*

The few steps leading down into this minuscule shop will introduce you to a world of original and creative toys, carefully selected (space demands it) by the owner, a former elementary school teacher. Everything is amusing and intelligent, encouraging children to stretch their capabilities while having a good time. A particularly irresistible selection of stuffed-animal puppets ($15 and $25, depending on size). An excellent choice of children's books.

## Mary Arnold Toys
**962 Lexington Ave.**
**(70th St.)**
**744-8510**
*Mon. to Sat. 9:00 A.M. to 5:45 P.M.*

Stuffed animals, dolls and doll houses, all sorts of toys, stationery, art supplies, helium-filled balloons, books for readers of all ages, and a good selection of party favors. A shop particularly dear to the hearts of younger mid- and uptowners, as they can leave a "wish-list" here for their birthday or other special occasions. What's more, owner Pamela is also a charming party planner, and will organize the big event to suit your wallet and the number of guests you've invited. She can arrange clowns, cartoons, balloons, prettily wrapped gift packages . . . everything will be taken care of.

## Muppet Stuff
**833 Lexington Ave.**
**(64th St.)**
**980-8340**
*Mon. to Sat. 10:00 A.M. to 6:00 P.M.*

The Sesame Street bunch has recently opened this store where, in addition to the much-in-demand figures of Miss Piggy and her cohorts, you can also find clothing, linen, puzzles, and games, all bearing the portrait of these favorite TV characters.

## Play It Again
**129 E. 90th St.**
**876-5888**
*Tues. to Sat. 11:00 A.M. to 5:00 P.M.*

Lots and lots of secondhand toys in working condition, some of them practically (if not actually) new: dolls, stuffed animals, books, puzzles, bicycles, party games—an enormous variety at very good prices. Keep this place in mind.

## Polk's
**314 Fifth Ave.**
**(32nd St.)**
**279-9034**
*Mon. to Sat. 10:30 A.M. to*
*6:00 P.M.; Thur. to 9:00 P.M.;*
*Sun. 11:00 A.M. to 5:00 P.M.*

The only, the unique, the incomparable shop for models, radio-controlled toys, racing sets, personal computers, science equipment, and the like. This is where all serious model-makers and hobbyists come to acquire the latest kits, the boats, airplanes, cars, and trains, which enchant children of all ages, including our own. Five floors.

## Toyworks
**114 E. 86th St.**
**427-6611**
*Mon. to Sat. 10:00 A.M. to*
*7:00 P.M.; Sun. noon to 5:00 P.M.*

The Big Apple finally has a supermarket for toys, something common in the suburbs, but only about a year old here. The store is, as you'd expect, absolutely immense and very well stocked, especially with educational toys and games. A superb doll section and much, much more, at reasonable prices. Lots of happy family Sundays in store.

## Youth at Play
**1120 Madison Ave.**
**(84th St.)**
**737-5036, 737-5037**
*Mon. to Sat. 10:00 A.M. to 7:00 P.M.*

A veritable bazaar of toys, offering a chaotic but enormous selection for children of all ages. Every available bit of space is filled with electronic games, party games, games of skill, and educational games—for adults as well as children—as well as sports equipment such as roller skates and skateboards. Plus, more traditional toys (doll carriages and tricycles), puzzles, an armory of toy weapons, and costumes (which you can also order specially if they're not otherwise available) plus a party goods department, school supplies, on and on. We can't list everything, but trust us, it's all here; and if you should happen not to find what you're looking for amidst the disorder, call on one of the helpful sales staff. Prices are slightly higher than in department stores but, unquestionably, there is a better selection.

## Dolls

## Doll House Antics, Inc.
**1308 Madison Ave.**
**(93rd St.)**
**876-2288**
*Mon. to Sat.*

A treat for young eyes: an enchanting presentation of doll houses with stupendously exact reproductions. From the familiar ketchup bottle to the attractive bedspreads, everything is miniaturized with exquisite taste, and looks more real than the originals. The frequently changed window, too, is a marvelous accomplishment in itself.

## Iris Brohm Antique Store
**253 E. 57th St.**
**593-2882**
*Mon. to Sat. 11:00 A.M. to 6:00 P.M.*

Mrs. Brohm isn't the sort of person who will force you to buy something: she's much too attached to her wonders to part from them willingly, and you'll understand her feelings. She posesses what is undoubtedly the most tempting collection of antique dolls in New York. Porcelain and biscuit dolls from Victorian times, each one prettier than the last, fill a glass case on one side of this shop. The case on the opposite wall is devoted to doll's furniture from the same era—pure marvels. A few attractive pieces of period clothing as well. Nothing here dates from after the nineteenth century (except Mrs. Brohm, who, however, cares so much for her dolls that she has come to resemble them). They're expensive, but justifiably so: the smallest (about eight inches high) cost about $400, and the biggest (about twenty inches) are, well . . . She also buys dolls and repairs them.

## Manhattan Doll Hospital/ The Doll House
**176 Ninth Ave. (21st. St.) 928-4000**
*Mon. to Sat. 10:00 A.M. to 6:30 P.M.*

The German owners of this shop have been in the doll business for over forty years, which is to say that they are specialized connoisseurs of dolls and doll houses and that they offer a very attractive range of wares in a wide range of prices ($25 to $2,000). There are preassembled houses, houses you put together yourself, and in particular a wonderful assortment of separate rooms that you can arrange to create the doll house of your dreams—and kits to make reproductions of old homes. And, the store claims, there's no piece of furniture that goes into a real house which you won't find here: typewriters, bathroom accessories, tea sets—nothing's missing for the comfort of your dolls.

They also offer a very good collection of antique dolls, including the first Madame Alexander ever made. And, what's more, Jenny and Herman repair antique porcelain, rag, and rubber dolls. Experts offering expert services.

## New York Doll Hospital
**787 Lexington Ave. (62nd St.) 838-7527**
*Mon. to Sat. 10:00 A.M. to 6:00 P.M.; closed in July*

You don't often visit a more charming and authentic shop or meet a store owner as friendly as Irving Chass who, in his doll-filled attic, performs delicate operations on dreadfully sick porcelain bodies and unstuffed animals. Mr. Chass has spent 35 years reviving, repairing, and reconstituting dolls of all sorts (wood, porcelain, plastic, rag) and animals of irreplaceable value to their young owners, and is probably one of the only remaining craftsmen of his type in the world. It's more than a livelihood for him—dolls are a passion he shares with his parents and grandparents, who opened the Doll Hospital in 1900. He also possesses an extraordinary collection of antique European and American dolls, some of which date back to 1875. He has a few of the first doll-automatons as well as an exact replica of Queen Elizabeth II as a young girl (with very blue eyes, and fitted with a flowered candy-pink hat); a number of Shirley Temple dolls complete with blonde ringlets; adorable French and German dolls from the turn of the century; and W. C. Fields and Charlie McCarthy dolls (ahh, fame and immortality!). Plus new old-fashioned accessories like socks and shoes, wigs, and more. Heaps of little wonders waiting to be discovered among big boxes full of sick dolls.

Prices, you will have guessed, vary considerably. Accessories are inexpensive, but the older dolls cost, on the average, between $250 and $2,000. Repairs will run from $10 to $20. A unique store undisturbed by tourists.

## Tiny Doll House
**231 E. 53rd St. 752-3082**
*Mon. to Sat. 11:00 A.M. to 5:30 P.M.; Sat. to 5:00 P.M.*

An appealing spot that specializes in furnishings and accessories in every style: rustic, modern, art deco, and so on, and of every sort: paintings, newspapers, dishes, mirrors. . . . Absolutely bewitching and incredibly small—a triumph of technology.

# Clothes

## ACCESSORIES

### Broomes of Broome Street
**351 West Broadway
(Spring St.)
431-7885**
*Tues. to Sun. noon to 7:00 P.M.*

This isn't "art wear" here, and the offerings displayed have nothing to do with the artistic creations exposed a little farther up the street. Instead, these are amusing and whimsical accessories made from very varied and colorful materials—leather, paint, plastic, macramé, papier mâché, and diverse weavings. Jewelry, hats, scarves, belts, and purses—everything sufficiently unusual and original that you don't risk showing up at a party and finding a competitor wearing the same thing, unless her taste is as eccentric as your own.

### Cachet
**1159 Second Ave.
(61st St.)
753-1650**
*Mon. to Sat. 11:00 A.M. to 7:00 P.M.*

A good spot for inexpensive fashionable handbags in the latest styles, from the smallest to the biggest, made from quite unexceptional hides and materials. Acceptable belts, and a very attractive and up-to-date collection of evening bags, including some in mother-of-pearl, natural or dyed (about $120) and some very good plastic imitations ($40) for those who don't want to invest too much in any one item. Some scarves and hats as well. It's nothing extraordinary, but well informed about fashions.

### Furla
**705 Madison Ave.
(62nd-63rd Sts.)
755-8986**
*Mon. to Sat. 10:00 A.M. to 6:00 P.M.*

Italian accessories at honest prices in this small, pleasant shop. The jewelry is inexpensive and very elegant ($20 to $50), the braided leather purses ($140 to $175) bearing a little golden F are absolutely representative of discreet Italian chic, and the belts in hammered metal and soft leather embroidered with delicate designs are very appealing.

### Gindi
**153 E. 57th St.
753-5630
816 Madison Ave.
(69th St.)
628-4003**
*Mon. to Sat. 10:00 A.M. to 7:00 P.M.*

Superb and stunning: Gindi is the sort of boutique where, even when your mind is on something else, you suddenly stop in your tracks because something has caught your eye—a small decorative object, a piece of jewelry, or an unusual and attractive accessory—deserving a few seconds' contemplation. And you won't be disappointed: the jewelry, belts, hairpins, and combs are extraordinary. Particularly beautiful imported ivory jewelry, mother-of-pearl, ivory, and golden metal evening purses, brilliant butterfly-shaped hairpins, silvery handbags. . . . Very, very beautiful trinkets, which don't look cheap and aren't. But you get a very neutral (not to say cold) welcome.

## Medusa
**1207 First Ave.**
**(65th St.)**
472-1166
*Mon. to Sat. 10:00 A.M. to 6:00 P.M.*

Very art deco accessories in this minuscule boutique brimming with brooches, necklaces, barrettes, pins, copies of period pieces, mostly plastic but very well done. A pretty, large pearl necklace will only set you back $48, and the barrettes they design themselves about $6 to $10. All sorts of bibelots as well, plus music boxes and embroidered, gold, and serpentine evening purses. Prices are reasonable.

## Uncle Sam's Umbrella Shop
**161 W. 57th St.**
247-7163, 582-1976
**7 E. 46th St.**
687-4780
*Mon. to Fri. 9:00 A.M. to 5:00 P.M.;*
*Sat. to 5:45 P.M.*

The pioneer in parasols and umbrellas, established in 1866, they've had more than enough time to develop a few models, and now have some fifty thousand umbrellas and a thousand walking sticks and canes in stock. Not all of them are on display, of course; their small shops couldn't manage it. Still, you're more or less certain that, if you ask for a particular size of a particular model in a particular color, they'll eventually find it. Not that polite service is their strong point—rather, their umbrellas are, and they're excellent, whether classical or amusing, old-fashioned or up-to-date, and they aren't the sort that will collapse with the first gust of wind. Attractive beach and garden parasols, plus a good repair service for all items, at reasonable prices.

# ═ANTIQUE/RECYCLED CLOTHES═

## Born Yesterday
**1193 Lexington Ave.**
**(81st St.)**
650-0683
*Mon. to Sat. 11:00 A.M. to 6:00 P.M.*

Three antique dealers share the same shop: to your left, old clothing; secondhand goods (lots of silver bibelots) to the right; and in the middle a magnificent collection of deco jewelry and antique beaded purses ($18 to $100), mostly French.

## Brascomb & Schwab
**148 Second Ave.**
**(9th St.)**
777-5363
*Mon. to Sat. noon to 8:00 P.M.*

Its collection of clothing from the '20s, '30s, and '40s is considered to be the best in New York, and the best priced too. At any rate, its window, decorated weekly, is certainly the prettiest and most tempting. Good prices for period furniture as well.

## Canal SoHo Flea Market
**369 Canal St.**
**(West Broadway)**
226-8724
*Thur. to Sun. only 11:00 A.M.*
*to 7:00 P.M.*

A real flea market with shops offering clothing and other wares. Several dealers share the three floors. On the ground floor toward the back, Harriet and Michael offer 1900s clothing made of pretty fabrics in more or less good condition, at prices that are negotiable; on the top floor, booth 42, Yesterday's Dreams has a selection of antique clothing of the highest quality. Art deco items, as well—everything covered with dust, but there are good finds.

## Cherchez
**864 Lexington Ave.**
**(65th St.)**
**737-8215**
*Mon. to Sat. 11:00 A.M. to 6:00 P.M.*

A personal attic shop full of treasures: antique shawls, an assortment of late nineteenth- and early twentieth-century clothing, period linen in perfect condition, a good collection of purses, and their specialty, subtly fragrant herb potpourris.

## Early Halloween
**180 Ninth Ave.**
**(21st St.)**
**691-2933**
*Tues. to Sat. 1:00 P.M. to 7:00 P.M.*

The '20s, '30s, '40s, '50s, and even the '60s in this shop dear to the hearts of Jane Fonda, Geraldine Page, Julie Christie, and many others. Superb things here include a handsome collection of early twentieth-century shoes: over a thousand pairs in fine leather, from $15 to $50 for those never worn. A somewhat unlikely location, but unquestionably worth the effort.

## The Good Old Days
**351 Bleecker St.**
**242-0554**
*Tues. to Sun. noon to 8:00 P.M.*

"The old, the unusual, the interesting" is how they define their stock—which translates into a collection of clothing and accessories from the '40s and '50s at reasonable prices. You'll even find authentic Miller's cowboy shirts in cotton gabardine, labels still intact, with mother-of-pearl buttons ($18). A pretty shop with a good reputation.

## Harriet Love
**412 West Broadway**
**966-2280**
*Tues. to Sat. noon to 7:00 P.M.;*
*closed in August*

A ravishing peach-colored boutique, one of New York's finest for antique clothing. Everything shines: the wooden floor, the mirrors, and the clothes are immaculate. A few Victorian skirts, as well as Chinese embroidered dresses, Hawaiian shirts, a superb collection of '20s and '30s scarves, and beaded change purses, everything at very high prices. A store for celebrities.

## Jezebel
**265 Columbus Ave.**
**(72nd St.)**
**787-5486**
*Mon. to Sat. noon to 7:00 P.M.*

Named for a 1938 William Wyler film starring Bette Davis and Henry Fonda, the shop caters to all people nostalgic for the splendors of the past, in an authentic theater set—including a fifty-year-old cash register. Lots of Victorian petticoats and camisoles, gabardine shirts and a pretty selection of lingerie. Very wide range of prices. The best of its kind on the West Side, if not of all New York.

## Joia
**1151 Second Ave.**
**(61st St.)**
**754-9017**
**149 E. 60th St.**
**759-1224**
*Mon. to Sat. 10:00 A.M. to 7:00 P.M.*

An art deco atmosphere in this pleasant shop filled with dresses, kimonos, embroidered sweaters, camisoles, and scarves from the '20s, '30s, and '40s. Furniture is sold in the long store on 60th Street, where the sumptuous decor and the choice of furniture alone are worth the visit.

## Lydia Antiques
**21 E. 65th St.**
**861-8177**
*Mon. to Sat. 9:00 A.M. to 6:00 P.M.*

For this quality of merchandise, the word "antique" is much more appropriate than "secondhand." The items sold here are true museum pieces, some of which date back as far as the eighteenth century. Jewelry, shoes, and accessories too, all at (rich) collectors' prices.

## Victoria Falls
**147 Spring St.**
**226-5099**

The prettiest store of them all, extreme refinement in a typically New York setting: a large wooden floor surrounded by brick walls. You'll find an assortment of Victorian blouses, camisoles, and dresses with starched

Mon. to Sat. noon to 7:00 P.M.;
Sun. 2:00 P.M. to 6:00 P.M.

white lace, absolutely divine, and contemporary embroidered sweaters and vests, for the most part unique items, original to the point of being extravagant, but so pretty and well displayed that a visit is a must. Extremely romantic. High but not excessive prices.

# THE CLASSICS

## Antartex
**903 Madison Ave.
(72nd St.)
535-9079**
*Mon. to Sat. 10:00 A.M. to 6:00 P.M.*

The odor of leather and sheepskin wafts through this store, a true Scottish family-run business that raises its own sheep and makes most of its clothing near Loch Lomond. Displayed on the natural-wood shelves are quality articles made to last decades and to age handsomely: leather shirts and coats as well as attractive Irish and Nordic hand-knit sweaters ($120 to $180), English Shetlands, mohair shawls ($50), Scottish kilts ($100), and Harris tweed blazers for men and women. Sensible clothing at sensible prices.

## Brooks Brothers
**346 Madison Ave.
(44th St.)
682-8600**
*Mon. to Sat. 9:15 A.M. to 6:00 P.M.*

Situated in the heart of New York's British enclave—Madison Avenue in the '40s, the paradise of genteel shopping—this is *the* department store, a monument to Anglo classicism. Four floors devoted to the latest styles in kilts, solid tweeds, and button-down collar shirts for gentlemen, ladies, and little preppies. The specialty here is undoubtedly the striped and solid shirts ($23 for women, $30 for men, and $14 in children's wear). The children's sizes are large, so try this department first for styles absolutely identical to those sold in the men's and women's sections. We recommend caution in the men's suits: the fabrics are superb, but the cuts, alas, often leave something to be desired. They'll do adjustments, but you're better off sticking to the plaid or striped long-johns, which are very stylish and cost only $7.50. A basic spot, neither expensive nor inexpensive, where the salespeople have a ruddy open-air look.

## Burton
**475 Fifth Ave.
(41st St.)
2nd floor
685-3760**
*Mon. to Sat. 9:00 A.M. to 6:00 P.M.;
Thur. to 7:00 P.M.*

It's a little Paul Stuart, a tiny Brooks Brothers, slightly less stylish and far less expensive, but more casual and entirely acceptable. The choice of shirts is at least as wide as at the other two places, and the cost 30 percent less—less the famous label too, of course. The Shetland knits, Madras jackets, suits, and shoes are all very elegant, and the womenswear perfect for the preppy look. Only the display sometimes leaves something to be desired, but this placid store lets you take your time.

## Harbour Knits
**22 E. 65th St.
472-0695**
*Mon. to Sat. 10:00 A.M. to 6:00 P.M.*

This isn't genteel England here, it's genteel Boston, knit or woven on Nantucket Island. Heavy sweaters and scarves in mohair or thick wool, handwoven ascots and shawls and Bermuda bags. A bit of local craftwork and, the only decoration in the shop, a light wood loom. Yes, yes, we believe you: everything is handmade here.

## Paul Stuart
**Madison Ave.**
**at 45th St.**
**682-0320**
*Mon. to Sat. 9:00 A.M. to 6:00 P.M.*

The basic British look is on display here, featuring superb and expensive Shetlands, flannels, and velvets; shirts with every type of collar imaginable and, if you desire, made to measure (minimum of four); and the famous Buck shoes, comfortable and solid. On the mezzanine, a line of womenswear offers cashmeres, tweeds, silks, leather, and suede, everything of the highest quality. An elite store for those who have the means.

## San Francisco
**975 Lexington Ave.**
**(71st St.)**
**472-8740**
*Mon. to Fri. 10:00 A.M. to 7:00 P.M.; Sat. 11:00 A.M. to 6:00 P.M.*

Impeccably tailored tweeds with careful attention to detail, soft cashmere skirts and blouses in crepe de chine, for women; for men, the famous Jefferson shirts with small buttons on the collar points, extremely elegant nightwear. Everything presented in a store resplendent with gleaming wood and shining copper. Unforgettable prices.

## Sils Mara
**999 Lexington Ave.**
**(72nd St.)**
**988-3900**
*Mon. to Fri. 11:00 A.M. to 7:00 P.M.; Sat. to 6:00 P.M.*

A small, warm selection of the prettiest clothing that England, Ireland, and Scotland have to offer, in a very charming shop whose prices are much more affordable than at their illustrious neighbor, San Francisco. Tweed, wool, sweaters, shawls, and preppy blouses ($40 for some fine examples) are agreeably displayed in wood compartments: good taste, excellent quality, and superb prices.

## Stewart Ross/ Stone Free
**754 Madison Ave.**
**(65th St.)**
**744-3870**
*Daily 11:00 A.M. to 6:00 P.M.*

The sort of things English countrywomen knit by the fire—there's nothing better. The proof is that Woody Allen, Shelley Duval, and Paul Simon are among this shop's faithful customers. And the sweaters, all hand-knitted with pompoms here and there, have a warm, genteel, Olde England character to them. The blazers in cashmere or mixtures of wool and silk also have the same sort of simple elegance that is never boring—strict without being straitlaced and subtle without being mawkish—which accounts for their success. In summer, cotton, silk, and linen.

# ETHNIC

## Chinese Emporium
**154 W. 57th St.**
**757-8555**
*Mon. to Sat. 10:00 A.M. to 6:30 P.M.*

A pretty store for Chinese fashions hardly reminiscent of Mao. A large choice of reversible embroidered jackets ($60), blouses, silk and cotton tunics, caps, sandals, and bibelots—all very Chinese—plus some sportswear and canvas pants with many gussets, at modest prices. Pretty, inexpensive fashion.

## Chor Bazaar
**801 Lexington Ave.**
**(62nd St.)**
**838-2581**
*Mon. to Sat. 10:00 A.M. to 6:30 P.M.*

Three blocks down from Putumayo, another quality bazaar, though slightly more commercial and gaudy. Romania, Afghanistan, India, Mexico, Japan, and China are all represented here in an assortment of pretty things: skirts, tunics, kimonos, superb Afghan shawls, and boots ($100 to $150). Everything is made of natural fibers, such as cotton, wool, and silk. The children's department is particularly exquisite and the department for antique Afghan clothing on the second floor is worth a visit. You can also order a dress in the color, fabric, and size you want, and have it made within a week by the store's tailor. Very pleasant service.

## Five Eggs
**436 West Broadway**
**226-1606**
*Tues. to Sun. 12:30 to 7:00 P.M.*

An exquisite little shop where everything is Japanese, and either useful or beautiful or both. Superb-quality pure cotton and flannelette (for winter) kimonos ($29 long, $19 short). You can also stock up on rice paper, mattress cushions for a cup of tea on the floor (futons), and various fine, delicate objects. Nothing flashy or gaudy.

## Greco-philia
**132 W. 72nd St.**
**877-2566**
**1143 First Ave.**
**(63rd St.)**
**688-0190**
*Mon. to Sat. 10:30 A.M. to 7:30 P.M.; Sun. noon to 6:00 P.M.*

It's true that the shop is run by a Greek, and that there is some Greek cotton clothing, handmade sweaters in winter and charming gauze shirts, skirts and pants in summer. But, in fact, most of the articles come from California and New York, for fashion that is young, well-designed, and affordable. An excellent shop for small pocketbooks.

## Greek Island Shop
**217 E. 60th St.**
**355-7547**
*Mon. to Sat. 11:00 A.M. to 7:00 P.M.*

All the flavor of the Greek Islands in the heart of Midtown: cushions, wool bags, shawls, and bonnets woven in bright colors. A very handsome collection of art books and travel books on Greece.

## Kembali
**425 West Broadway**
**(near Spring St.)**
**431-7616**
*Tues. to Sun. 1:00 P.M. to 7:00 P.M.; Sat. from noon*

Across the street from Paracelso, a very pretty shop with a very good selection of exotic clothing, particularly from China and Indonesia. The Chinese wedding gowns are museum pieces—they're exhibited here on the wall—and the Indonesian garments are of exquisite refinement. A few batiks in original colors and designs are heaped together in a basket, and other carefully selected articles are sure to catch your eye.

## Paracelso
**432 West Broadway**
**966-4232**
*Tues. to Sat. 12:30 P.M. to 6:30 P.M.; Sun. 2:00 P.M. to 6:00 P.M.*

Run by a gentle and mysterious Italian woman with dark, heavily made-up features, who goes by the surprising pseudonym Luxor Tavella, this is certainly New York's most exotic clothing shop. You feel you might have stumbled into a scene from the *Thousand and One Nights,* as the brilliant silks mix with embroidered muslins and multicolor velvets—from Turkey, Afghanistan Ethiopia, Japan, and China. It's absolutely sumptuous, particularly the spangled scarves, harem pants, and the antique Afghan jackets and wedding gowns. The prices are quite affordable for such incomparable quality. And Luxor's smile is brilliant.

## Putumayo
**857 Lexington Ave.**
**(64th-65th Sts.)**
**734-3111**

This marvelous store features both clothes imported from Bolivia, Ecuador, Guatemala, India, and Afghanistan, many in hand-woven cotton, and their own line of clothing—Afghan robes personalized with an original detail (pattern,

**339 Columbus Ave.**
**(76th St.)**
**595-3441**
*Mon. to Sat. 11:00 A.M. to 6:30 P.M.*

fabric). There is a collection of priceless antique jewelry from Nepal, China, and India, plus some primitive painting on wood and canvas from Mexico and Ecuador. Lots of handmade accessories. The welcome is charming.

## Sermoneta
**740 Madison Ave.**
**(64th St.)**
**744-6555**
*Mon. to Fri. 10:00 A.M. to 6:00 P.M.; Sat. 11:00 A.M. to 6:00 P.M.*

Pretty cottons from Peru, Ecuador, India, and Italy, in very sober colors and stylized shapes. Superb sweaters in the winter. Little variety, but everything is very elegant: the style of this boutique is more Madison Avenue than bazaar, but the prices are moderate all the same.

## Swing Low
**1181 Second Ave.**
**(63rd St.)**
**838-3314**
*Mon. to Fri. 11:00 A.M. to 9:00 P.M.; Sat. to 7:00 P.M.; Sun. 1:00 to 7:00 P.M.*

Very attractive hand-knit wool articles in this small shop run by two young women who import jackets and sweaters from South America (Uruguay, Bolivia, and Ecuador) as well as from Canada (warm jackets), India, and Italy. They will, also hand-knit to order whatever it is you're looking for. Very varied models, and superb-quality wool, for reasonable ($20 to $90) and negotiable prices. A few shirts are rather banal. A good shop for people with cold feet and warm hearts.

# FURS

## Emilio Gucci Furs
**333 Seventh Ave.**
**(28th St.)**
**2nd floor**
**244-5875**
*Mon. to Thur. 9:00 A.M. to 6:30 P.M.; Fri. and Sun. to 6:00 P.M.; closed Sat.*

The biggest factory and the largest salon in New York, offering very beatable prices. A store that relies on its gaudy and excessive advertising—still, they're handsome ads.

## Fur and Sport
**333 Seventh Ave.**
**(28th St.)**
**6th floor**
**594-8873**
*Mon. to Fri. 9:30 A.M. to 6:00 P.M.; Sat. 10:00 A.M. to 2:00 P.M.*

Excellent quality and good advice at this small furrier who chooses the pelts and designs and makes the coats himself. Very good cleaning service, plus repair and storage. Just as good as some in more fashionable districts, and less expensive.

## Hy Fisherman's Fur Fantastic
**305 Seventh Ave.**
**(27th St.)**
**6th floor**
**244-4948**
*Mon. to Sat. 9:00 A.M. to 5:00 P.M.; Sun. 11:00 A.M. to 5:00 P.M.; closed Sun.*

This manufacturer–designer has thousands of coats in stock in all sizes and styles, at good prices. Friendly service.

231

## Maximilian Fur Company
20 W. 57th St.
3rd floor
247-1388
*Mon. to Fri. 10:00 A.M. to
5:00 P.M.; Sat. 11:00 A.M.
to 4:00 P.M.*

Superb, expensive, ultra-chic. Everything from sporty playclothes to the most elegant coats.

## New Yorker Thrift Shop
822 Third Ave.
(50th–51st Sts.)
355-5090
*Mon. to Fri. 9:00 A.M. to
6:00 P.M.; Sat. to 5:00 P.M.*

Their marked-down and almost-new furs sell from $50 to $3,000. Most of them originally belonged to celebrities.

## Peter Duffy Furs
305 Seventh Ave.
(28th St.)
18th floor
255-5144
*Mon. to Fri. 9:00 A.M. to 6:00 P.M.;
Sat. to 2:00 P.M.*

Higher up in the same building as Hy Fisherman, Peter Duffy is well liked by New Yorkers. According to many of our friends, he offers "unbeatable choice and prices"— which means wholesale prices and fashionable furs.

## Revillon Fur Salon
at Saks Fifth Avenue
611 Fifth Ave.
(50th St.), 3rd floor
753-4000
*Mon. to Sat. 10:00 A.M. to
6:00 P.M., Thur. to 8:00 P.M.*

This store offers the most chic and expensive furs: mink blouses and parkas, skunk trench coats, and other sports furs for active people who can afford them. Excellent sales in February.

## The Ritz Thrift Shop
107 W. 57th St.
265-4559
*Mon. to Sat. 9:00 A.M. to 5:00 P.M.*

Internationally known, renowned, and respected, a high-class "thrift shop" that offers perfectly clean, glossy, and adjusted (free) almost-new furs. For men as well. Good deals.

## Vison Creations
333 Seventh Ave.
564-8047
*Mon. to Sat. 9:00 A.M. to 5:00 P.M.*

The specialist in mink: all shades, dark and light. Some classic styles, and others more fashionable. Readymade and custom-made furs at very good prices (around $4,000).

# JEWELRY

### Quality

## Bulgari
Pierre Hotel,
795 Fifth Ave.

Decidedly bad manners have been mistaken for a sign of quality by many illustrious merchants. Unless you are a billionaire or a celebrity, you are paid little attention in

**(61st St.)**
**486-0086**
*Mon. to Sat. 10:30 A.M. to*
*5:30 P.M.; closed Sat. in summer*

## Carimati Jewelers
**773 Madison Ave.**
**(66th St.)**
**734-5727**
*Mon. to Sat. 10:00 A.M. to 6:00 P.M.*

## Cartier
**653 Fifth Ave.**
**(52nd St.)**
**753-0111**
*Mon. to Fri. 10:00 A.M. to*
*5:30 P.M.; Sat. to 5:00 P.M.*

## David Webb
**7 E. 57th St.**
**421-3030**
*Mon. to Sat. 10:00 A.M. to 5:30 P.M.*

## Fortunoff
**681 Fifth Ave.**
**(54th St.)**
**758-6660**
*Mon. to Sat. 10:00 A.M. to*
*6:00 P.M.; Thur. to 8:00 P.M.;*
*Sun. noon to 5:00 P.M.*

## F. Staal
**743 Fifth Ave.**
**(58th St.)**
**758-1821**
*Mon. to Sat. 9:30 A.M. to 5:30 P.M.*

this shop. The place, incidentally, is so small and common that you wonder for a moment if you've gone in the wrong door, what with the rattan armchairs. But the jewelry is both stylish and beautiful—a very Italian combination that's difficult to resist. A specialist in colored stones juxtaposed in the same ornament, or mounted in gold, and brilliant. But the stones, alas, are not first-rate—that's public knowledge.

Enrico Carimati seems to be surrounded by more art in his store than most galleries. The atmosphere is as Italian as the superb and, on the whole, very wearable jewelry. Carimati is also distinguished by a weakness for stones of unusual color—yellow sapphires, for example. All pieces are unique, and start at $4,000.

An entirely different atmosphere than in the Paris shop. The greeting here is anonymous, and you can wander freely without attracting the slightest attention or seeming to disturb anyone at all. So even if the prices are out of reach don't deprive yourself of the pleasure, as the variety of the jewelry is immense, to say nothing of the objects and accessories. Although you may already be familiar with their famous "Musts," you may not have seen their even prettier "S," or their boutique collection, or their sterling silver department—which is one of the most affordable and original sections in the shop. There's tableware, as well: Limoges porcelain, silver table settings, a few very beautiful crystal glasses, some objets d'art and antiques, and more. We haven't forgotten the jewelry; it speaks for itself. It has to, sometimes: this great store too often treats its customers with icy aloofness.

David Webb believes in originality at any price, and pulls it off. He makes jewelry of every kind and for every age, pieces that are, on the whole, very easy to wear—the sort of jewelry you can use, and not abandon to the safety deposit box. His boutique is decorated in earth tones, which are elegant if a touch gloomy, and the welcome is perfect.

A sort of department store—four floors of jewelry, silver, table settings, watches, clocks, and alarm clocks. A luxury shop, if not of the highest sort, but the choice is good, the service helpful, and the atmosphere somewhat bazaar-like but agreeable. Not in the least pretentious—and absolutely unbeatable prices. A name to remember.

A small jeweler among the big names, and yet a store which has enjoyed a reputation for exquisite quality of stones and gold, conscientious work, and perfect service for over a hundred years. The jewelry here is aimed at connoisseurs, and its understated elegance will satisfy the most demanding. In addition to the modern pieces, F. Staal has a very fine collection of secondhand jewelry. He is one of those rare dealers who proves that jewelry is a fine art.

## François Hérail
**31 E. 64th St.**
**593-0124**
*Mon. to Sat. 10:30 A.M. to 6:00 P.M.*
*By appointment*

If you're looking to invest in precious stones, François Hérail is not the man to consult. But if, on the other hand, you want to treat yourself to the most appealing jewelry imaginable, either absolutely simple or madly baroque, which you can wear just as easily with jeans as with an evening gown, this is the place to go. The most gifted young French jeweler of his generation (Poiray, rue de la Paix in Paris) opened in May 1982. The boutique carrying his name, decorated in trompe l'oeil, is furnished along old-fashioned lines, where he offers stylized jewelry, combining with brio cabochons and colored stones with gold or blued steel, wood or mother of pearl. Superb, but expensive: $1,500 to $30,000.

## Gérard
**21 E. 57th St.**
**832-6640**
*Mon. to Sat. 10:00 A.M. to 5:30 P.M.*

Gérard is something of a legend: he started out at Van Cleef as a salesman, and it was there that he discovered his passion for jewelry. After 25 years with Van Cleef, he decided to go into business for himself. In the ensuing twelve years, he opened eight boutiques, of which the one in New York is the latest, following Paris, London, Monte Carlo, Cannes, Lausanne, Geneva, and Gstaad, and he is now the premier French jeweler. Sumptuously situated in a five-story townhouse decorated in navy blue and gray, Gérard's is the "haute couture" of jewelry. He himself designs unique and exceptional pieces. It is obvious that all work is done by hand, and it may take four to seven years to collect stones of a compatible quality to complete a necklace. He is the only jeweler who brings out two collections annually, one in winter and another in summer, and he manages to follow fashion and still maintain his high standard. He also offers a boutique collection in gold and slate gray that includes watches, cufflinks, and other objects, as well as a few crystal necklaces that are not as costly, but extremely well made nonetheless. The shop is run by Gérard's charming and competent daughter, Dominique.

## Harry Winston
**718 Fifth Ave.**
**(56th St.)**
**245-2000**
*Mon. to Sat. 10:00 A.M. to 5:30 P.M.*

The premier American jeweler, Winston is internationally known for his fine and costly work. The collections are superclassic, made with superb stones unfortunately mounted in a slightly boring and conventional manner. Their lack of warmth and originality is reflected in this huge shop itself, but the pieces are nonetheless good investments. A luxury jeweler where you're treated very well.

## House of Jerry Grant
**137 E. 57th St.**
**371-9769**
*Mon. to Sat. 12:30 to 6:00 P.M.*

This charming little jewelry shop creates original pieces in impressive quantities, and bearable prices. You can pick out one of the unusually shaped and stylish rings or bracelets without being a petrodollar princess. You can also order other models, or have your own stones mounted: Jerry Grant designs and makes elegant eighteen-carat gold settings in the workshop next door, which accounts for his speed and reasonable prices. And, if you suffer a cruel blow of fate, you can take him your own jewels: he'll either offer to sell them on commission or buy them outright. A shop that really is a bit different.

## Tiffany
**727 Fifth Ave.**
**(57th St.)**
**755-8000**
*Mon. to Sat. 10:00 A.M. to 5:00 P.M.*

You absolutely must visit this treasure house. Examine the jewelry, clocks, watches, and precious stones; then go to the upper floors, and check out the silver, crystal, and china. Service is very friendly, and most people will find something within their reach. You'll find jewelry designed for daytime and for nighttime wear, as well as the collection designed by Paloma Picasso (from $400 to $60,000). Not to mention the largest yellow diamond in the world (128.5 carats) displayed on the ground floor, a mere bauble at an even million.

## Van Cleef and Arpels
**744 Fifth Ave.**
**(57th St.)**
**644-9500**
*Mon. to Sat. 10:00 A.M. to 5:00 P.M.*

The store bearing the mighty name Van Cleef and Arpels is located in Bergdorf Goodman. The salon has a rather ordinary look, like a duty-free shop. It's rather airport in quality, too. Although the jewels are imported from Paris, they're mostly in quite a different style from the French line. There is, however, a good selection of the famous Piaget watches. And, for the finest jewelry, the welcome is more in keeping with all those zeros.

## Costume

## Artwear
**409 West Broadway**
**431-9405**
*Tues. to Sun. 11:00 A.M. to 6:00 P.M.*

A shop for contemporary art in the form of jewelry made of acrylic, copper, silver, gold, and more or less anything else. It is often adventurous with necklaces, bracelets, earrings, hairpins, belts, and all sort of other creations admirably displayed. Artists and exhibitions change, making this a spot worthy of regular visits. Variable prices, some of which are quite affordable.

## Ciro
**711 Fifth Ave.**
**(55th St.)**
**752-0441**
*Mon. to Sat. 9:30 A.M. to 5:30 P.M.*

Five shops offering a varied choice of fake diamonds, of which the prettiest cost around $800 to $900. But there are also very satisfactory copies of Bulgari for $75 to $150, with a complete set (earrings, bracelet, necklace) coming to about $250 to $300. Perfect for arousing the envy of your friends at low prices.

## Jolie Gabor
**699 Madison Ave.**
**(62nd-63rd Sts.)**
**838-3896**
*Mon. to Sat. 10:00 A.M. to 6:00 P.M.*

A small, beribboned boutique run by Zsa Zsa's mother, in which you'll find the loveliest and most expensive copies of famous jewelers' creations made with cultured pearls, colored stones, and brilliants that have all the flashiness and chic of the '50s. For instance, a superb eight-carat diamond (cubic zirconia), a copy of a Van Cleef ring, for the tidy sum of $700. Luxury costume jewelry for gala evenings.

## Ophélie
**673 Madison Ave.**

A small and charming store for fantasy jewelry of good quality that is not too whimsical. Everything is imported from France, down to the leather showcases, which show

**(60th St.)**
**593-0124**
*Mon. to Sat. 10:00 A.M. to 6:00 P.M.*

off the pretty pieces particularly well. Lots of very delicate eighteen-carat chains, rings, earrings (starting at $60), but also ambrolyth bracelets for $30 and necklaces with large crystals for only $45, all designed exclusively by their own artists. Gallic elegance.

## Richard Gould
**545 Madison Ave.**
**(55th St.)**
**888-6012**
**20 E. 58th St.**
**753-7696**
*Mon. to Sat. 10:00 A.M. to 6:00 P.M.*

This is the lower end of the scale, in price, but not in quality—you can find such costume jewelry as Dior pieces here for a few dollars. The shop may not look like much, and the reception may be mediocre, but you don't risk going broke.

## The West Side Boutique
**239 W. 72nd St.**
**(between Broadway and West End Ave.)**
**787-5472**
*Mon. to Sat. 10:30 A.M. to 7:30 P.M.*

Everything here is one of a kind. Two different collections are displayed side by side: one, for modern silver and gold jewelry beautifully mounted with fine stones, like tiger's eye, onyx, and lapis lazuli, all designed by the owner; and the other of superb ethnic jewelry imported from India, South America, Morocco, Tibet, and Kenya. The ivory jewelry is particularly sumptuous, and plentiful. The rest is also of a rare quality and sometimes at surprisingly low prices.

## Watches

## Bucherer
**730 Fifth Ave.**
**(57th St.)**
**757-8140**
*Mon. to Sat. 9:45 A.M. to 5:30 P.M.;*
*closed Sat. in summer*

A luxury watch store. There's no use dropping by if you have less than $500 on you—unless it's to have a watch repaired, as they have a workshop on the premises with some ten or so craftsmen who provide rapid and competent service. They carry the best watches, and only the best, but not all the best: they have, to begin with, their own, in eighteen-carat gold exclusively, plus Rolex, Baume et Mercier, and Vacheron watches, as well as classical watches in gold with snakeskin straps, all-gold watches, and watches of gold and diamond, plus a few in stainless steel (Rolex and a few Cartier). Need we add that the prices reflect the quality (going as high as $6,200), as does the welcome, which is very friendly.

## Gubelin
**745 Fifth Ave.**
**(57th St.)**
**755-0053**
*Mon. to Sat. 10:00 A.M. to 5:30 P.M.*

This Swiss institution opened in New York some ten years ago and offers only the very best watches, such as their own (one in 21-carat gold and diamonds for $61,000) and examples by Audemars Piguet, Omega, and Patek Philippe, each more splendid and expensive than the last. Some jewelry as well, also of the finest craftsmanship. There's no point in walking through the door unless you have a few thousand to burn. An excellent repair service for all the watches they sell, in New York and in Switzerland—that's the least they could do!

## Hausmann & Cie

Hausmann began making watches and jewelry in 1794, and has upheld the highest standards ever since. They

**635 Madison Ave.
(59th St.)**
**832-9000**
*Mon. to Sat. 10:00 A.M. to 6:00 P.M.*

carry only watches by such names as Rolex, Phillipe Patek, Baume et Mercier, Concorde, and Piaget, as well as their own, which are quite in keeping with the beauty of the collection as a whole. They also sell pieces of jewelry created exclusively for them by the best Italian goldsmiths. But they aren't cheap.

## Tourneau
**500 Madison Ave.
(52nd St.)**
**758-3265**
*Mon. to Sat. 10:00 A.M. to 6:00 P.M.*

Tourneau offers quite simply the loveliest choices of watches in the loveliest jewelry store in New York. All the Swiss watchmakers are represented: Audemars Piguet, Baume et Mercier, Omega, Piaget, Ebel, Jaeger, Lecoutre, Longines, and many others. There are also watches by Rolex and Seiko, the "Must" from Cartier, and by Tourneau themselves, which are far from being the worst of the lot. As you'd expect from a store of this class, all styles are represented—youthful, classic, formal—and prices range from $115 to quite a lot higher. Clocks are another of their specialties: small copper clocks, carriage clocks, and alarm clocks, as well as traveling alarm clocks, the latest of which comes in a small English enamel case decorated with flowers and birds, a small wonder at $265. Also gold quartz fobs ($700 to $3,000), and a few elegant accessories, like Dupont lighters and pens.

# MENSWEAR

## Ready-To-Wear

## Blue and White Men's Shop
**50 E. 58th St.**
**421-8424**
*Mon. to Sat. 10:00 A.M. to 6:30 P.M.*

Sportswear and men's accessories of a quality you seldom see. Of the dozens and dozens of other shops, however prestigious, we visited in New York while preparing this guide, none came close to this elegance. No other crêpe de chine shirts were as soft as these, no other loafers as supple, no other leather raincoat as fine. Antelope-hide parkas, cashmere sweaters, alpaca, mohair—the quality of the clothes here, all handmade and woven and mostly imported from Italy, is equalled only by their discretion, the sobriety of their colors, and the simplicity of their tailoring. And the service is on a level with the rest: Carlo Bonini welcomes you into his tiny shop with all the charm and unostentatious friendliness you'd quite naturally expect in a man with so much taste.

## Denoyer
**219 E. 60th St.**
**838-8680**
*Mon. to Sat. 10:00 A.M. to 6:00 P.M.*

A small selection of quality classic clothing in this small store run by a likable and friendly Frenchman. Everything he offers is superb: impeccable suits, very soft Jacquard weave cashmere sweaters, attractive ties, supple leather shirts, comfortable raincoats, a few pairs of very stylish shoes, and in the back of the shop, a choice of womenswear that is just as judicious, with attractive silks in the winter and charming swimsuits for the summer.

## Gian Pietro
**205 E. 60th St.**
**759-2322**
*Mon. to Sat. 10:00 A.M. to 6:00 P.M.*

A few yards along the same street, this Italian shop stocks sophisticated sportswear and formal wear, as well as one of New York's dandiest collections of silk shirts. The ladies will swoon.

## Rive Gauche Saint Laurent for Men
**543 Madison Ave.**
**(55th St.)**
**371-7912**
*Mon. to Sat. 10:00 A.M. to 6:00 P.M.*

The style and quality are unsurprising—but the prices still stun.

## Discounts

## BFO and BFO Plus
**149 Fifth Ave.**
**(21st St.)**
**2nd and 6th floors**
**254-0059, 254-0060**
*Daily 9:30 A.M. to 5:30 P.M.*

Shirts and sweaters from Yves Saint Laurent, Cerrutti, Ralph Lauren, and more between $15 and $40 on the 2nd floor; suits, coats, and pants by the same designers for $20 to $100, fine ties with labels from Cardin, Lauren, and Liberty of London for $8 (normally priced at $30)—these are the kinds of buys offered at this shop, frequented by the best-informed New Yorkers, famous ones included. But the cut, even when signed Yves Saint Laurent, is not always the most elegant. So take a good look in the mirror before making up your mind—inelegant tailoring is much more noticeable than the label. An excellent spot all the same.

## Dollar Bills
**99 E. 42nd St.**
**867-0212**
*Mon. to Fri. 8:00 A.M. to 6:30 P.M.;*
*Thurs., Fri. to 7:00 P.M.; Sat*
*10:00 A.M. to 6:00 P.M.*

Situated a few minutes from Grand Central Station, this is among the best discount menswear stores in New York. The choice of clothing is selective, but covers a wide range of articles: all the best designers are represented at very good prices. And owner Marcel always has a friendly word. One of the most accessible and affordable shops.

## Merns Mart
**525 Madison Ave.**
**(54th St.)**
**371-9175**
**75 Church St.**
**(near World Trade Center)**
**227-5471**
*Mon. to Sat. 9:30 A.M. to 6:30 P.M.;*
*Thurs. to 8:00 P.M.*

Up to 50 percent off well-made French, British, and American suits. Shoes, jeans, and sportswear as well on the street level. The store on Madison Avenue is eight times bigger than the other, and is discreet and sober, relaxed and friendly—all rare qualities in discount stores. What's more, the buys are excellent, even outrageously good, depending on your taste and luck. A quick glance on the way to Brooks Brothers or Paul Stuart might save you the extra walk and quite a bit of money. A womenswear section too.

## Oxford Handkerchief Co.
**51 Orchard St.**
**226-0878**
*Sun. to Thur. 9:00 A.M. to 5:00 P.M., Fri. to 3:00 P.M.*

Christian Dior, Yves Saint Laurent, Oscar de la Renta at 30 to 50 percent off—this shop may be of interest.

## Syms
**45 Park Place
(Church St.)
791-1199**
*Mon. to Sat. 9:00 A.M. to 7:00 P.M.;
Thurs. to 5:00 P.M.; Sat.
to 6:00 P.M.*

Three-piece velvet suits for $70, designer's shoes for $20, flannel pants for $20 . . . maybe you don't believe us? Well, head down to Syms, the discount department store: it'll clothe you from head to foot without taking you to the cleaners. The collection of shirts (from $7 to $20) on the 2nd floor is breathtaking. Nor are women left out. An entire floor is given over to clothes for them by big-name designers at 50 percent off. It's easy to verify the discounts, as all articles bear their original price tags. Sales staff is friendly, and the merchandise well organized. The store doesn't carry the latest fashions, but you can't have everything. Note: minors under the age of eighteen are not admitted.

## Victory Shirt Company
**96 Orchard St.
677-2020**
*Sun. to Fri. 9:00 A.M. to 5:00 P.M.*

A plethora of pure-cotton shirts in the purest of English styles: oxford, basketweave, and broadcloth, sold under Victory's own Lord Carlton label, or under that of the department stores, at 25 percent less than uptown in a shop run by a Brit who knows his shirts like the back of his hand. Or neck.

## Large/Small Sizes

## Cadet General Store
**523 Hudson St.
989-6428**
*Tues. to Sun. noon to 8:00 P.M.;
Sun. to 6:00 P.M.*

Opened about a year ago, this store is run by Joe de Filippis, who measures 5 feet 5 inches, and knows what he's talking about. It's the perfect shop for small men who've had enough of dressing in the boy's department or paying a fortune for alterations or made-to-measure clothing: suits from 34 short up ($135 to $180), leather shoes ($35), sport shirts, belts, socks, even sunglasses smaller than normal size. The shop's ceiling has been lowered, the shelves placed at reachable levels, and none of the sales staff measures over 5 feet 6 inches. Free alterations and special orders.

## Imperial Wear Men's Clothing
**48 W. 48th St.
541-8220**
*Mon. to Sat. 9:30 A.M. to 6:00 P.M.;
Thurs. evening*

Too big or too tall to get your clothes at Barney's? In that case, go straightaway to Imperial, the specialists in dressing large sizes, both height and width, with some chic. Here, you can obtain everything (except hats), American-made and very good quality. Prices are honest ($20 to $30 for the shirts) and their choice excellent. Their brands include Pierre Cardin, Givenchy, Christian Dior, Ralph Lauren, Lanvin, and London Fog.

## London Majesty
**1211 Avenue of the Americas
(near 48th St.)
221-1860**
*Mon. to Sat. 9:00 A.M. to 6:00 P.M.;
Thur. to 8:00 P.M.*

English and European fashions within everyone's reach— the smallest and the biggest—in this, the first New York outlet of a well-known European chain: cashmeres and wool knits are the specialty; very English fabrics for their suits, jackets, and sportswear; silk for the pajamas and shorts. English chic to the smallest detail.

## Shirts

### A. Sulka
**711 Fifth Ave.**
**(55th St.)**
**980-5200**
*Mon. to Fri. 9:30 A.M. to 6:30 P.M.;*
*Sat. 10:00 A.M. to 5:00 P.M.*

You'll have to wait about four to six weeks for delivery of your made-to-measure shirt, available in a wide choice of silks and cottons (from $40). For sensitive skins there are silk pajamas (about $200) and even silk briefs ($50) custom-made.

### Bancroft Haberdashers
**363 Madison Ave.**
**(45th St.)**
**687-8650**
*Mon. to Fri. 9:00 A.M. to 6:00 P.M.;*
*Sat. to 5:00 P.M.*

The largest selection of ties and men's shirts in New York, mostly in a no-iron cotton-synthetic mixture. The many branches of this store are rather dreary, but the shirts are not, and the prices are less so ($10 to $20).

### Custom Shop, Shirtmakers
**618 Fifth Ave.**
*Mon. to Sat. 9:00 A.M. to 5:45 P.M.,*
*Thur. to 7:45 P.M.*

This chain of stores carries an enormous choice of styles and fabrics. The made-to-measure shirts have the same affordable price as their ready-to-wear ones ($20 to $40), but you have to order at least four—which, at these prices, is not a problem (four weeks preparation).

### Duhamell
**944 Madison Ave.**
**(74th St.)**
**737-1525**
*Mon. to Sat. 10:00 A.M. to 6:00 P.M.*

These are not just any old fabrics: Swiss net, broadcloth Egyptian cotton, silk, sea island, and more in over seven hundred models, each more elegant than the last (minimum order of six, three weeks delivery). In addition to their shirts, Duhamell makes custom suits and very handsome leather articles, and sells accessories, casual wear, and even jewelry.

## Shoes

### Bally of Switzerland
**347 Madison Ave.**
**(45th St.)**
**986-0872**
*Mon. to Fri. 9:00 A.M. to 5:45 P.M.,*
*Sat. 9:30 A.M. to 5:00 P.M.*

A brief mention of this company whose quality and reputation continue to grow, to the detriment of the service they offer: shoes (about $175) and briefcases are fine and classic. Several locations.

### Billy Martin's Western Wear
**812 Madison Ave.**
**(near 68th St.)**
**988-3622**
*Mon. to Sat. 10:00 A.M. to 6:00 P.M.*

The wherewithal to turn you into a cowboy from head to foot in this store, which was opened two years ago by an authentic Yankee. It offers cowboy boots from the simplest to the most exotic ($60 to $450), handmade leather jackets ($950), shirts with original Indian designs ($100 and up), and more. Plus a line of children's wear, with superb belts, fringed jackets, and moccasins. Dude ranch stuff.

### Church's English Shoes
**428 Madison Ave.**
**(49th St.)**
**755-4313**
*Mon. to Sat. 9:30 A.M. to 5:30 P.M.*

Classic English shoes of good reputation and quality. $80 during sales.

## McCreedy and Schrieber
**213 E. 59th St.**
**759-9221**
**47 and 55 W. 46th St.**
**719-1552**
*Daily 9:00 A.M. to 7:00 P.M.;*
*Mon. and Thur. to 9:00 P.M.;*
*Sun. noon to 6:00 P.M.*

New York's most eclectic shoe store for every kind of shoe imaginable. You can be shod like a cowboy (this is the only store in New York to carry Look Easy, the best brand of cowboy boots), Italian playboy, or in sturdy walking shoes (Bass Weejuns) and sports shoes (Topsiders). Everyone should find the shoe that fits amongst this unbelievable (and moderately priced) selection. Several models of women's boots.

## Nino Gabriele
**1022 Third Ave.**
**(60th St.)**
**935-9280**
*Mon. to Sat. 10:00 A.M. to 7:00 P.M.;*
*Mon. and Thur. to 9:00 P.M.*

The avant-garde of the latest fashion—for both sexes. But a few classic models as well, and marvelous quality leather.

## Serendipity
**225 E. 60th St.**
**838-3681**
*Mon. to Sat. 11:30 A.M. to 7:00 P.M.*

You have to walk down a few steps to enter this minuscule and charming general store-restaurant, and then climb a few more to see the superb selection of very original Texan boots, from simple suedes and leathers to patent leather or lizard-skin dyed in slightly sour colors like apple green or tender pink. The designs are very intricate, and the price range on the high side ($190 to $250). Not for everyday wear, but certain to dazzle your friends.

## To Boot
**100 W. 72nd St.**
**724-8249**
*Mon. to Sat. 11:00 A.M. to*
*7:00 P.M.; Sat. to 6:00 P.M.*

The biggest collection of Texan boots in New York, florid or sober, high or low, leather or other, light or dark, displayed by the hundreds against the wall of this superb shop.

## Tailors

## Chipp
**14 E. 44th St.**
**687-0850**
*Mon. to Sat. 9:30 A.M. to 6:00 P.M.*

Classically styled made-to-measure suiting including riding clothes, in fine shetlands and flannels. On the 2nd floor is a collection of more contemporary clothing, in some of the gaudiest colors you can imagine. Suitable for surprising friends and acquaintances—but it will cost you dearly. Ready-to-wear as well.

## Dunhill Tailors
**65 E. 57th St.**
**355-0050**
*Mon. to Sat. 9:30 A.M. to 6:00 P.M.*

The most beautiful made-to-measure suits in all New York. Their celebrated clients happily pay $1,000, with four-week delivery. For the less well-heeled, there's excellent ready-to-wear of a comparable quality.

## F. R. Tripler
**300 Madison Ave.**
**(46th St.)**
**682-1760**
*Mon. to Sat. 9:00 A.M. to 5:30 P.M.*

Here you can choose from all sorts of fabrics and styles and then, six weeks later, take delivery of the exact suit you wanted, for a price that won't be higher than for off-the-rack merchandise. Custom-made shirts too (two months). Also an excellent selection of shoes (Bally, Church, and the like) and cashmere sweaters. A women's department featuring the same quality and tradition in New York for almost a century.

# TRENDY/DISCO

## Betsey Johnson
**105 Thompson St.**
**925-0129**
*Tues. to Sun. noon to 7:00 P.M.*

A minuscule candy-pink matchbox boutique where the "enfant terrible" of New York offers disco-style outfits in appropriately electric colors. Her "thing": multicolor red, green, pink, white, black, and yellow stripes on miniskirts, maxidresses, maxisweaters, jumpsuits, and knickers. Everything in synthetic—it's gaudier.

## Camouflage
**141 Eighth Ave.**
**(near 17th St.)**
**741-9118, 929-7237**
*Mon. to Fri. noon to 7:00 P.M.;*
*Sat. 11:00 A.M. to 6:00 P.M.*

A boutique in the Chelsea district offers "American clothing made in America," a rarity of which the owners are justifiably proud, as their clothes are pleasing, easy to wear, made of classic fabrics, and always have an imaginative detail to distinguish them from more ordinary creations. The shop clothes both sexes.

## Ciciobello
**462 West Broadway**
**(Prince St.)**
**475-1345**
*Daily noon to 8:00 P.M.*

Fashion craziness! This is one of the latest of SoHo creations, and its avant-garde inventors want everyone to (we quote) "sing, dance, and feel light, to appreciate the magic energy of colors." In other words, you'll need a serious sense of humor to wear the least of the (expensive) clothes and accessories sold here. A must on any tourist's itinerary.

## Fiorucci
**125 E. 59th St.**
**751-1404**
*Mon. to Sat. 10:00 A.M. to*
*6:00 P.M.; Mon. and Thur. to*
*8:00 P.M.*

Fiorucci's reputation is firmly ensconced as the most capricious, whimsical, and sophisticated of stores, and even if it's not your style, you owe yourself a visit, if only to have a look at the salescreatures (most of whom are purebred new wavers) and the shop itself. This is superbly decorated, spreads over two vast floors, and features numerous happenings throughout the year. Anyway, not all its clothing is exaggerated, the shoes are made of good Italian leather, and some of the accessories are delicious. And there's a good section for beauty products on the ground floor where you can have yourself made up— trendy or otherwise.

## Flash
**221 E. 59th St.**
**593-0493**
*Mon. to Sat. 11:30 A.M. to 7:00 P.M.*

More daring even than Fiorucci, Flash is staffed by tattooed salesmen who look at you mistrustfully if you're not attired as they are. This is really the most outrageous store imaginable, with its lamé T-shirts, outfits in shiny vinyl and panther, eccentric boots, and jazz shoes. Not for all tastes!

## Fonda's
**168 Lexington Ave.**
**(30th St.)**
**685-4035**
*Mon. to Fri. 10:30 A.M. to 7:30 P.M.;*
*Sat. to 6:30 P.M.*

This marvelously eclectic store has a most unusual stock, including women's loose jackets of Victorian lace as well as blouses and dresses made of antique fabrics, plus unique sweaters and outfits from good American designers at discount prices, old and new accessories, their own line of patchwork quilts, silk kimonos, and so on. It's a world of beautiful things in limited quantities, rigorously selected, at very reasonable prices. The only place like it is perhaps Reminiscence, in the Village, slightly more commercial and less exquisite. A very personal boutique, for women who don't want to dress like everyone else.

## Le Grand Hotel and Tales of Hoffman
**471 West Broadway
(Houston St.)
475-7625**
*Tues. to Fri. noon to 7:00 P.M.;
Sat. to 6:30 P.M.*

The Grand Hotel sells clothing, Hoffman sells shoes. Both are semi-haute couture and displayed on brick walls for ease of choice. The prices are sometimes quite uneasy—still, there are affordable items, especially in summer, and a line of inexpensive shoes called Shoe String, which are pretty and of poor quality. A large selection of pointed-, round-, and square-toed cowboy boots.

## Ian's
**1151 Second Ave.
(60th-61st Sts.)
838-3969
49 Grove St.
(near 7th Ave. South)
675-1062**
*Mon. to Sat. 11:30 A.M. to 6:30 P.M.*

It aims to be gaudy and succeeds: intended for theater people, night club performers, and the like. Tight-fitting dresses with seersucker flounces, outrageously baggy red skirts, leather and imitation pantherskin miniskirts, rock star-style fringed blouses, colored glasses and eccentric shoes which, of course, arrive for the most part from England, the homeland of glitter rock. Mercifully inexpensive fashion for limited occasions.

## Macondo
**150 Spring St.
431-3224**
*Mon. to Sat. 11:00 A.M. to
6:00 P.M.; Sun. noon to 7:00 P.M.*

This is extravagance of quite another kind: artistic extravagance, where clothing is treated as art, and where its strangeness is the result of authentic invention. Five hundred different craftspeople work for this shop, creating a collection of unusual and marvelous articles, in much greater number and at much lower prices than at Julie Artisans—$15 to $1,600. Combinations of various fabrics and materials, such as leather, wool, and feathers seem to be the order of the day, and sometimes give superb results. The owner, Katrena Wood, is from Kenya and very handsome African masks, statuettes, and jewelry are also for sale.

## Mano A Mano
**421 West Broadway
925-6066**
*Tues. to Sat. noon to 7:00 P.M.;
Sun. 9:00 A.M. to 6:00 P.M.*

Good and bad, casual and formal wear in this large and friendly SoHo boutique specializing in European imports. The leather jackets are very handsome, the ties elegant, the shoes quite good, and the prices average.

## Miso Clothes
**416 West Broadway
(Spring St.)
226-4955**
*Daily noon to 7:00 P.M.*

A trendy boutique featuring wearable fashions, the latest creations of the youngest and newest Seventh Avenue designers. Lots of pretty, delicate silks, dresses and blouses, some in a Southern-belle mode. Old-fashioned lingerie as well. And a very amusing toys and trinkets department, where you can buy candles in the shape of the Empire State and Chrysler Buildings, New York's trademarks, for $6, plus mechanical toys, metal music boxes, and miniature puzzles for only a few dollars.

## Parachute
**121 Wooster St.**
**(Spring-Prince Sts.)**
**925-8630**
*Mon. to Sat. noon to 8:00 P.M.;*
*Sun. 1:00 to 7:00 P.M.*

An immense loft turned into a store for pseudo-uniform outfits, such as overalls and sophisticated blouses, similar in style to Thierry Mugler: catering to a clientele that is ready for anything except, it seems, parachuting. A visit is a must. Very New York.

## Skin Clothes
**25 E. 65th St.**
**2nd floor**
**988-0554**
*Mon. to Sat. 11:00 A.M. to 7:00 P.M.*

For rockers, wealthy punks and fantasizers, to dress in leather from head to toe: T-shirts, leather trousers in twenty colors, and fifteen colors of suede. A bizarre specialty: the leather print in gold or trimmed with metallic snakeskin! And, if Anouchka and Michel's inventions aren't enough, come armed with your own ideas and a thick wad of bills, and have them make a custom design leather outfit. To hell with stinginess and common sense!

## Steve
**97 Wooster St.**
**925-0585**
*Tues. to Sun. noon to 7:00 P.M.;*
*closed Sun. in July and August*

One of the best menswear boutiques in New York for sporty, comfortable, well-tailored, and modish clothing, which attracts a clientele in part female. A wide range of prices and friendly service.

## Susuya
**130 E. 59th St.**
**688-8835**
*Mon. to Sat. 10:00 A.M. to 7:00 P.M.*

This shop, across the street from Fiorucci, is less far-fetched, but still lively, youth-oriented, and up-to-date. Modish, fun clothing is imported from Italy and Japan: shoes, socks, belts, brooches, jumpsuits. Everything is so well presented, colorful, and reasonably priced you'd like to buy the lot. A charming shop where new merchandise comes in every day.

# ═══════ WOMENSWEAR ═══════

## Chic/Contemporary

## Agora Boutique
**1550 Third Ave.**
**(87th St.)**
**860-3425**
*Mon. to Thur. 10:00 to 9:30 P.M.;*
*Fri. to Sat. 10:00 to 12:00 A.M.;*
*Sun. 12:00 to 7:00 P.M.*

An unusual spot, to say the least, where the original art deco setting is beyond words, and the men's and women's fashions are as good as the ice cream. Unquestionably the most original pairing of services in New York.

## Ann Taylor
**3 E. 57th St.**
**832-2010**
*Mon. to Sat. 10:00 A.M. to*
*6:00 P.M.; Thurs. to 8:00 P.M.*

An attractive, spacious, well-organized boutique featuring relatively inexpensive clothing by Norma Kamali, Carol Horn, Diane B., Perry Ellis, Cacharel, and other designers, plus Italian shoes by Joan and David. A good selection, within the reach of most people, brings in a varied clientele. The fashions are reasonable, almost sober, and in very good taste, even when highly original: a fetching department store in miniature. Gourmets should take note that the SoHo Charcuterie is located on its 3rd floor.

## Betsy Bunky Nini
**746 Madison Ave.**
**(64th St.)**
**744-6716**
*Mon. to Fri. 10:30 A.M. to 6:00 P.M.;*
*Sat. 11:30 A.M. to 6:00 P.M.*

This charming little shop done in light wood doesn't carry a huge selection, but has very attractive wardrobe components for day and evening. They like a young and active look, and stock pleated skirts, leather outfits and the latest evening wear—all reasonably priced. Among their strong points are their superb, comfortable sweaters, and the hand-woven dresses, jackets, and scarves. A mixture of BBN's own designs and European imports.

## Diane B.
**729 Madison Ave.**
**(64th St.)**
**759-0988**
*Mon. to Sat. 10:00 A.M. to 6:00 P.M.*

This store is to small boutiques what Henri Bendel is to department stores: synonymous with the best. In a setting of brown and aubergine, you'll find wearables by Castelbajac, Dorothée Bis, often in single copies, and Kansai Yamamoto's eccentric sweaters. A few unusual accessories. Everything rather dear, of course.

## Julie Artisan's Gallery
**687 Madison Ave.**
**(61st-62nd Sts.)**
**688-2345**
*Mon. to Sat. 11:00 A.M. to 6:00 P.M.*

A "gallery" for clothing. The first shop of its kind in New York (several others have since opened, in SoHo and elsewhere), it sells and exhibits incredible sartorial creations made by artists and craftspeople. Each piece is original, made of feathers, pearls, straw, and who knows what else, and sold at prices commensurate with their artistic uniqueness. As in any gallery, the hangings change often; but they're always beautiful, surprising, and full of wit. A spot that shouldn't be missed. A new you? Who knows.

## Madeleine
**237 E. 60th St.**
**688-3115**
*Mon. to Sat. 10:30 A.M. to 6:30 P.M.*

Madeleine, the newest of the innumerable shops to appear on 60th St. between Second and Third Avenues, has two specialties: its sells only evening wear, and it is a showcase for offbeat designers. As a result, you'll find here original outfits for on-the-go young women, and absolutely nothing with the "mother of the bride" look. Their credo is that casual evening wear—lamé knits, baggy breeches, and the like—will triumph over traditional formal gowns. Individualistic, eye-catching styles by Judy Hornby, Stephen Burrows, Ralph Rucci, and more—very reasonably priced.

## Miya and Yoshi
**366 West Broadway**
**(Broome St.)**
**226-1990**
*Tues. to Sun. noon to 7:00 P.M.*

A New York classic: it was the Japanese designer Yoshi who brought out the first of those long down-filled winter jackets that now keep half the city warm in cold spells. He specializes in natural materials, hand-dyed in such subtle colors as parma violet, jade green, gray, and crimson, and his designs have an attractive, almost conservative simplicity.

## Patricia Fields
**10 E. 8th St.**
**254-1699**
*Mon. to Sat. noon to 8:00 P.M.;*
*Sun. noon to 6:00 P.M.*

A young, up-to-the-moment designer, not as well known as Norma Kamali, but striking and innovative. Her boutique contains her own unusual, colorful creations at affordable prices, as well as clothing from other avant-garde designers.

## Pierre D'Alby
**610 Fifth Ave.**
**541-7110, 541-7111**
*Mon. to Fri. 10:30 A.M. to
6:30 P.M.; Sat. 10:00 A.M. to
6:00 P.M.*

Not one of the greatest French designers, but not one of the least either. His shop is crammed with clothing that is mostly attractive and inexpensive, his sportswear being much more successful than his formal wear. His blouses, shirts, divided skirts, pants, sweaters, and dresses are colorful, in pleasant materials, and very easy to wear. Some admirable clothing by Daniel Hechter, too—don't miss it.

## Riding High
**1147 First Ave.**
**(63rd St.)**
**832-7927**
*Mon. to Sat. 10:30 A.M. to
8:00 P.M.; Sun. noon to 6:00 P.M.*

A "high-tech" setting for this mini Bendel. The choice of clothing, lingerie, and accessories seems aimed at *Vogue* sophisticates. Some are American, some imports, and many are unique—which explains their prices.

## Sharon Bovaird
**927 Madison Ave.**
**(73rd St.)**
**288-4749**
**1116 Madison Ave.**
**(83rd St.)**
**794-8865**
*Mon. to Sat. 10:00 A.M. to
6:00 P.M.; Sun. 1:00 to 5:00 P.M.*

A very eclectic boutique. Very pretty cashmere sweaters and dresses, and a breathtaking collection of accessories, such as belts, evening purses, jewelry, hats—there's absolutely everything here (except for shoes). At the store on 73rd Street you can have yourself made up to go with the color of the dress you've just bought. Excellent sales two or three times a year.

## Street and Company
**2030 Broadway**
**(near 69th St.)**
**787-2626**
*Mon. to Sat. 10:30 A.M. to 8:30 P.M.*

Are you a chic female executive? This is the place for Wall Street-style suits, coordinated jackets, skirts, and silk blouses, sober cashmere creations, well-cut high-quality dresses, and even tuxedos for evening wear—with lace bow ties for a feminine touch. Prices will certainly not exceed your budget (from $80 for the blouses to $300 for the suits), and services are available that will be useful to a woman of your station: wardrobe planning, on-the-premises tailoring, and delivery. A small investment of time and money to tame the bulls and bears.

## Yves Saint Tropez
**251 E. 60th St.**
**759-3784**
**4 W. 57th St.**
**765-5790**
*Mon. to Sat. 10:00 A.M. to 7:00 P.M.*

Elegant, inventive, and expensive French and Italian ready-to-wear can be found in these shops, whose prefabricated name corresponds well to their style: a cross between Saint Laurent and St. Tropez. Their clientele can obviously afford to buy more than one outfit, since few of the models are what you'd wear anywhere, anytime. Attractive accessories and shoes, and a men's shop. Some advice: those who balk at the prices can always try their luck at Yves Saint Tropez II, 46 E. 57th Street, 2nd floor, 751-2222, which sells all the leftovers from previous collections at drastic savings. For the more classic models, this can be an invaluable opportunity.

## Designer

**Adolfo**
**36 E. 57th St.,**
**4th floor**
**688-4410, 688-4411**
*By appointment only*

We start alphabetically with Adolfo, which is quite appropriate since he dresses the First Lady. Cuban-born, Adolfo has perfectly understood the mentality of the elegant American woman, who wants to look like her European counterpart, but just a bit later, when she has grown used to new styles. Adolfo specializes in copying the best French couturiers, especially Chanel. His braid-trimmed knit suits with matching blouse strangely recall those of the French Grande Dame ($950 to $1,200). So infatuated is he with her style that one year he dedicated his entire collection to her. He also has classic formal dresses for evening wear, from $1,600. His showroom on 57th St. is reserved for his most faithful clients and department store buyers. Commoner mortals can see his creations at (among other places) Saks Fifth Avenue.

**Boutique Valentino**
**677 Fifth Ave.**
**(53rd St.)**
**421-7550**
*Mon. to Sat. 10:00 A.M. to 6:00 P.M.*

A highly talented and original Italian designer, whose models range from the simplest (daytime outfits) to the most extravagant (formal evening wear). He uses superb natural materials, like cotton, linen, wool, and silk, often in their most exotic forms: tulle, embroidered, spangled, or crocheted organza. A beige boutique, ravishingly done up and perfumed, where you know, the moment you walk in, that prices are extravagant.

**Courrèges**
**19 E. 57th St.**
**755-0300**
*Mon. to Sat. 9:30 A.M. to 6:30 P.M.*

You'll immediately recognize the Courrèges look in this small "design" shop white from ceiling to floor and decorated with mirrors, just as you'll recognize the famous angular shapes in the short dresses with nursery colors, the cotton knits, and other light clothing, all bearing the familiar initials. But you'll have to pay the price: $350 for an ordinary cotton-knit dress—which seems rather dear for what it is.

**Emmanuel Ungaro**
**803 Madison Ave.**
**(68th St.)**
*Mon. to Sat. 10:00 A.M. to 6:00 P.M.*

Delightful fabrics and perfect cuts—exorbitant marvels ($1,200 for a blouse, $2,000 for a skirt) for lovers of very simple, very "haute couture."

**Georges Rech**
**711 Madison Ave.**
**(63rd St.)**
**832-3147**
*Mon. to Sat. 10:00 A.M. to 6:00 P.M.*

This is high Parisian chic. Consider the elegant suits with striped or solid-color flannel pants in elegant autumn colors, and the superb evening gowns in luminous taffeta with ruffles—as becoming as can be—at high but not exorbitant prices. This lovely boutique shows France at its best and, of course, its worst: the staff is perfectly disagreeable.

**Giorgio Armani**
**701 Madison Ave.**

This relatively small boutique on two floors shows Italian fashion at its finest. The styles are audacious, sometimes eccentric, but undeniably chic. When you pay about $250

**(63rd St.)**
**838-4330**
*Mon. to Sat. 10:00 A.M. to 6:00 P.M.*

## Halston Boutique
**813 Madison Ave.**
**(68th St.)**
**744-9033**
*Mon. to Fri. 10:30 A.M. to 5:45 P.M.; Sat. noon to 4:45 P.M.*

## Martha
**475 Park Ave.**
**(58th St.)**
**753-1511**
*Mon. to Sat. 9:30 A.M. to 6:00 P.M.*

## Norma Kamali
**6 W. 56th St.**
**245-6322**
*Mon. to Sat. 10:00 A.M. to 6:00 P.M.; Thurs. 10:00 A.M. to 7:00 P.M.*

## Saint Laurent Rive Gauche
**855 Madison Ave.**
**(71st St.)**
**988-3821**
*Mon. to Sat. 10:00 A.M. to 6:00 P.M.*

for a silk blouse, or $280 for a subtly shaded knit, you're paying for talent, not for the label.

This American designer is known the world over for creations to suit every pocketbook and every taste—especially dressed-up middle-class taste: lots of flourishes and swags, "couture" dresses for $1,000 or more in vivid colors that have won over all of America. Halston has something for everyone: he offers several different collections designated by different numbers, from the very affordable Halston IV label to his very expensive originals. Perfumes, gloves, pants, casual and formal dresses, ponchos—there's a bit of everything, not to mention his five new collections each year, including one that comes out for those privileged to spend the winter months in more balmy climes. Halston has become an industry, a sort of fashion multinational offering.

This isn't a shop devoted to any one couturier, but rather an haute couture salon representing good designers in general: Martha purchases her line all over Europe, and elsewhere. She offers a very classic, dressy look, with a few more whimsical creations, thus allowing elegant New York womenfolk to choose clothing perfectly adapted to different situations: strolling along Park Avenue, having a tea at one's club, playing a few hands of bridge in the afternoon, and appearing at a fund-raising dinner or a cocktail party. Silk, crêpe, lamé, and muslin are scattered throughout the spacious salmon and beige shop, and there are private showrooms available to clients who wish to study the models more closely. An atmosphere of unobtrusive luxury reigns, matching the clientele. Martha is an institution who dresses upper-crust types from New York, Palm Beach, and all over.

A very imaginative and individualistic designer whose style is essentially aimed at the young. Who else would dare to wear black cotton minidresses, which are about as unflattering as possible, or extravagant gold synthetic evening dresses, other than someone in the bloom of youth, whose silhouette will be accentuated by the deliberate imbalance in design? A very fun, loud, and expensive style (short dresses $500, long dresses $1,000 to $2,000). Excellent sweatshirts copied the world over.

It would be more polite to pass this over in silence—the Saint Laurent merchandise in New York is disappointing. There's little that's original or attractive in the velvet, pleated, and plaid skirts, the suits, the exorbitant pleated pants ($890 for the blazer, and $400 for the pants)—or the flawlessly banal evening dresses. These conventional offerings don't correspond in the least to his image as an imaginative designer. The label is simply not enough. Is it just that his New York buyer is deficient? Also a few perfumes, scarves, purses, and shoes.

## Ted Lapidus
**666 Fifth Ave.**
**(53rd St.)**
**582-5911**
**1010 Third Ave.**
**(60th St.)**
**751-7251**
*Mon. to Sat. 10:00 A.M. to 6:45 P.M.*

Another famous name complete with well-known symbol: a simple and elegant Parisian designer whose classic creations allow you to go from office to cocktail party without changing. Delicious accessories, including purses and hand-painted silk scarves, at prices that more than justify the multipurpose usage.

## Discounts

## A. Altman
**204 Fifth Ave.**
**(25th St.)**
**889-0782**
**182 Orchard St.**
**(Houston St.)**
**982-7722**
*Daily 10:00 A.M. to 6:00 P.M.*

Your first stop on the Lower East Side; the most "in" and the best-stocked with European imports, including an excellent choice of fashionable, low-priced silk blouses. The store on Fifth Avenue is the more pleasant, but you should on no account expect friendly help in either.

## Bolton's
**225 E. 57th St.**
**755-2575**
*Mon. to Sat. 10:00 A.M. to 6:45 P.M.*
*(Mon. and Thur. to 8:45 P.M.),*
*Sun. noon to 4:45 P.M.*

A well-known chain of discount stores where you'll find the worst as well as the best, but more of the best, from Halston, Ralph Lauren, Anne Klein, and even Dior, at 20 to 50 percent of the retail prices. A good selection of formal dresses, elegant coats, and fashionable accessories. A store that has shown its mettle over the past 25 years, well organized in its stock, styles, and prices.

## Cacharel
**290 Veterans Blvd.**
**in Rutherford,**
**New Jersey**
**(201) 933-7649**
*Tues. to Sat. 10:00 A.M. to 5:00 P.M.*

You've doubtless heard of this classic French designer. But you may not know is that he opened an excellent warehouse outlet for all his men's, women's, and children's sportswear about a year ago. A spot for the smart!

## Damages
**169 E. 61st St.**
**2nd floor**
**688-6388**
*Mon. to Sat. 10:00 A.M. to 7:00 P.M.*

A huge store, the length of the block, filled with rows of clothes racks on which hang blouses, dresses, and outfits by good and sometimes even very good designers, mostly French and Italian, such as Christian Dior, Yves Saint Laurent, Balmain, Franck Olivier. It takes a lot of time to go through this accumulation of clothes, much of which is without interest, so don't forget that the finest items are displayed right at the entrance and on the platform at the right. Invaluable for silks, marvelous for inexpensive blazers and accessories, like the very elegant Italian leather purses, belts, and shoes. For men and women.

## The Emotional Outlet
**242 E. 51st St.**
**838-0707**
*Mon. to Sat. 11:00 A.M. to*
*8:00 P.M.; Sun. noon to 6:00 P.M.*

The savings aren't enormous—about 20 percent—but the shops are pretty, and you're greeted with a cup of coffee or a glass of fruit juice as if you were a regular client at a select boutique, and you're shown a very attractive selection of elegant and young-looking sportswear, dresses, lingerie, shoes, and accessories, made by good tailors at prices that are moderate, and sometimes even very inexpensive (d'Alby cotton blouses for $15, Anne Klein silk dresses for about $80). A very friendly spot. Other locations throughout the city.

## European Liquidators
**1404 Second Ave.**
**(near 73rd St.)**
**879-9140**
*Mon. to Fri. 11:00 A.M. to*
*8:00 P.M.; Sat. to 7:00 P.M.;*
*Sun. noon to 6:00 P.M.*

This is one of the best stores of its kind; well stocked, quite stylish, and with a very friendly atmosphere. The silk skirts and the jeans are particularly good buys—and you won't have to pay for your savings by putting up with impatient service (or no service whatsoever). On the contrary, the charming salesladies will go out of their way to help you find what you're looking for.

## French Connection
**1211 Madison Ave.**
**(87th St.)**
**348-4990**
*Mon. to Fri. 10:30 A.M. to*
*7:00 P.M.; Sat. to 6:30 P.M.;*
*Sun. noon to 5:00 P.M.*

Wool, silk, and gabardine outfits, mostly European imports; but lots are made in Korea too. Prices are good and the styles are classic, but don't have a fit if your blouse runs when it's washed: at these prices, you can afford to take it to a dyer. A store that has attracted some publicity—good, but only that. Other locations.

## Giselle Sportswear
**143 Orchard St.**
**673-1900**
*Sun. to Thur. 9:00 A.M. to 6:00 P.M.;*
*Fri. 9:00 A.M. to 5:00 P.M.*

The best European and American designers offer their latest creations here, at noteworthy wholesale and retail prices. You'll find the current season's Kenzos, Anne Kleins, Cathy Hardwicks, Cacharels, and Dior USAs, at a third of their value. No commentary is needed—the store speaks for itself.

## Loehman's
**9 W. Fordham Rd.**
**(and Jerome Ave.)**
**The Bronx**
**295-4100**
*Mon. to Sat. 10:00 A.M. to 9:30 P.M.*

Loehman's has been an institution for generations. What is it that lures shoppers from as far away as Manhattan? Quite simply the best discount store in the entire region: 2,500 articles of clothing arrive daily and are snapped up as quickly, because most of them are current fashions by the best designers, like Perry Ellis and Calvin Klein, offered at ridiculously low prices. The choice varies, justifying the frequent visits that some shoppers make; but whatever the frequency of your trips, it would only be by incredibly bad luck that you'd leave empty-handed, because Loehman's is truly miraculous. Take your time, however, when choosing, and try on all purchases in one of their immense dressing rooms, because there are no exchanges or refunds. Other branches in Brooklyn and Queens.

## Peta Lewis
**1120 Lexington Ave.**
**(78th St.)**
**2nd floor**
**744-7660**
*Mon. to Sat. 11:00 A.M. to*
*6:30 P.M.; Thur. to 9:00 P.M.;*
*Sun. 1:00 to 5:00 P.M.*

A good discount (30 to 50 percent) on good designers: Ted Lapidus, Oscar de la Renta, Evan Picone, Diane B., and more. There are dresses, sweaters, and well-cut suits in this second-floor location that proves the New York adage: a few steps more, many dollars less.

## Lingerie

### L'Affaire
**226 Third Ave.**
**(19th St.)**
**254-1922**
*Mon. to Fri. 11:00 A.M. to 7:00 P.M.;*
*Sat. 11:00 A.M. to 6:00 P.M.*

A very imaginative shop that imports alluring and capricious undergarments from Italy, France, Switzerland, and England. Pretty materials in charming styles—what more could you ask?

### Criscone/Ora Feder
**248 E. 60th St.**
**838-2843**
*Mon. to Sat. 10:30 A.M. to 7:00 P.M.*

Very sexy sets of lace panties and bras, soft, flowing negligées and nightgowns in silk and a variety of gauzes— inviting without being vulgar, being both sensuous and tasteful. Their secret is, of course, that they're from France, and thus blend elegance with charm and imagination with quality. Plus, a small deco section, with big embroidered butterflies, and some sizzlers with plunging necklines and rustling muslins. The prices are reasonable: $40 for the bras, $50 for the panties, or $80 for a set, plus nightgowns from $75 to $120 for the most sophisticated ones. A few evening gowns as well, made along the same lines. These are outfits for "total women"!

### Monte Napoleone
**789 Madison Ave.**
**(67th St.)**
**535-2660**
*Mon. to Sat. 10:00 A.M. to 6:00 P.M.*

A store offering exclusively Italian and French lingerie— the last word in refinement. Even the polyester satin used in so many of the articles here takes on a noble character: silky-soft, and decorated with lace from Switzerland, France, and Italy. The lingerie and undergarments are in delicate tones, and the items in silk, linen, crêpe de chine, and cotton have classical elegance and simplicity. This is lingerie as art, sold at collectors' prices (about $200)—but the collectors seem to be rare in New York, as this elegant light-gray shop is usually terribly quiet. Custom-made lingerie (two months waiting) and free alterations.

### Roberta
**1252 Madison Ave.**
**(90th St.)**
**860-8366**
*Mon. to Sat. 10:00 A.M. to 6:00 P.M.*

This shop's window (frequently redecorated) is so tempting, its salesladies so helpful, and its lingerie so dashing, that we could probably be induced to buy anything in it, whether we needed it or not. Negligées, soft satin panties, slips, and for winter, flanelette pajamas— everything has perfect taste and a delicate texture that makes it a delight to wear. The store also carries Dior lingerie and fine choice of one-and two-piece swimsuits, in a wide range of prices that make these silky indulgences even soft on the pocketbook.

## Large/Small Sizes

### Ashanti
**872 Lexington Ave.**
**(65th-66th Sts.)**
**535-0740**
*Mon. to Fri. 10:00 A.M. to 6:00 P.M.*

Have a look at this lovely store for women sizes 12 to 26. The styles are for the most part exclusive, and made of quality fabrics, such as silk, wool, and cotton, in very tasteful patterns and colors. Elegant classicism, carefully conceived, at reasonable prices: formal dresses for $285, wool coats from $200 to $350, silk evening dresses from

$400, and cottons from $65. A limited number of woven articles, as well, including some very attractive scarves. Also very stylish jewelry. The best spot of its kind.

## Helga Howie
**733 Madison Ave.
(64th St.)
861-5155**
*Mon. to Sat. 10:00 A.M. to 6:00 P.M.*

Not a specialty shop per se, but one that caters to large sizes among others, and offers pretty, classic styles, often handmade and one-of-a-kind, agreeably feminine. Its silk outfits, blazers, and crocheted sweaters are perfect, and its ambience is warm.

## Mikko Fur Co.
**121 E. 57th St.
2nd floor
753-1155**
*Tues. to Sat. 11:00 A.M. to 7:00 P.M.*

Here are dresses and blouses, most of them in silk and in small sizes, which aren't all that easy to find in New York. The shades and patterns are of perfect refinement, and the prices are by no means excessive ($150 to $300 for a silk dress hand-painted according to original Japanese drawings, $90 for the blouses and tunics). Plus, as the name indicates, coats in winter and warm suits. The welcome is very Japanese too—reserved but delicious.

## Piaffe
**830 and 841
Madison Ave.
(69th St.)
744-9911**
*Mon. to Sat. 10:00 A.M. to
6:00 P.M.; Sun. noon to 5:00 P.M.*

Piaffe is the perfect spot for women under 5 feet tall who don't want to wear only little-girl fashions. These two elegant Madison Avenue boutiques offer a wide variety of clothing and lingerie in sizes 2 to 8, and even smaller, which are elegant, well cut—some are imported from France and Italy—and reasonably priced: silk dresses, for instance, at $125 to $200, and very pretty three-piece outfits for $135. A store that will make you happy to be small.

## Maternity

## Lady Madonna
**793 Madison Ave.
(67th St.)
988-7173**
*Mon. to Sat. 10:30 A.M. to 6:00 P.M.*

The most famous boutique for pregnant women, and the first to dress them in something other than a potato sack. Pleasant and very varied fashions: dresses and sweaters as well as tennis outfits, bathing suits, pants, lingerie. Prices are moderate, but the quality is rather mediocre: you won't find any silk dresses or cotton tunics. This store offers only synthetics, and although the styles are pretty, they'll still scratch you in winter or stick to your skin in the summer. And if you happen to be a fanatic about no-iron polyester, you'll find the prices at Alexander's even lower.

## Mater's Market
**237 E. 53rd St.
355-7977, 688-4286**
*Mon. to Sat. 10:30 A.M. to 5:30 P.M.*

Future mothers will find everything they need in this charming little shop. Not only a wide selection of Laura Ashley-style dresses ($35), tunics, T-shirts, and pants, but pretty lingerie and various items for your baby-to-be as well. Complete, mostly attractive, and reasonably priced.

## Romantic/Lace

## Anita Pagliaro
**1030 Lexington Ave.**

A very pretty shop run by a very pretty young lady whose hobby is lace. Dresses and blouses are made with new lace appliqués modeled for the most part on antique

**(73rd-74th Sts.)**
**737-2684**
*Mon. to Sat. 11:00 A.M. to 6:00 P.M.*

## Dora Herbst
**611 Madison Ave.**
**(57th-58th Sts.)**
**935-1457**
*Mon. to Sat. 10:00 A.M. to 6:00 P.M.*

## Laura Ashley
**714 Madison Ave.**
**(63rd St.)**
**371-0606**
*Mon. to Sat. 10:00 A.M. to 6:00 P.M.*

## Rubicon Boutique
**849 Madison Ave.**
**(70th St.)**
**861-3000**
*Mon. to Sat. 10:00 A.M. to 6:00 P.M.*

## Sara's
**150 Spring St.**
**2nd floor**
**226-5303**
*Fri. and Sat. noon to 8:00 P.M.;*
*Sun. to 7:00 P.M.*

## Bally of Switzerland

patterns, with Victorian effect. Several articles in original lace, most of which are one-of-a-kind, and priced accordingly: blouses $100 to $200, dresses $200 and up.

Dora is lucky enough to live on Ibiza, a small Spanish island that serves as a refuge for artists, idle epicureans, and sun-worshippers in general. The styles she designs are made for her in local workshops and are radiant with this soft, luminous lifestyle. Her small New York boutique is a haven of romanticism, an oasis of feminine charm in the midst of Madison, with its tiled floor, handhewn wood beams, white stucco walls decorated with fans and tambourines, and, all around you, a gala of lace, gauze, ottoman, embroidery, and patchwork made into dresses, skirts, blazers, and shirts in indescribable and inimitable styles. The lace is new, Swiss-made, and has been prewashed to remove sizing. The applications of different laces in one blouse or skirt give an extraordinarily delicate effect. From $100 to $500, depending on the amount of work involved.

Well-brought-up young ladies didn't wait for Lady Diana to wear these charming white cotton camisoles with small flounces, or these pretty flowing skirts and printed velvet dresses. The princess merely added a royal seal of approval to a feminine style and fashion that has survived all the hazards of capricious taste. The choice of clothing and lingerie in this ravishing shop is no less exquisite for being familiar, and at prices that even young ladies without dowries can afford. A limited selection of children's wear, as well, plus a line of light perfumes, and a collection of fabrics and accessories.

You can create some appealing Victorian-style 1980s dresses by patiently reattaching antique lace to new fabrics, but when can you wear them without looking as if you're on your way to a fancy-dress ball? The answer is simple: at weddings. The clients of this store are either brides-to-be or their proud mothers, bringing the "modesties," gorges, and other original lace-work back to splendid life for a few hours, if at no mean price ($500 to $600).

This small shop deserves mention for two reasons: first of all, for its friendliness and, secondly, for the perfection of its clothing, all handmade in the adjoining workshop, and all in old-fashioned styles, often using antique fabrics. The silk chemisettes are pure marvels ($180). Limited choice, but rare quality. For a larger choice in the same style, try Victoria Falls.

## Shoes

An elegant selection of imported footwear: the Swiss classics, but, above all, the Italians—Bally knows its

253

**681 Madison Ave.**
**(62nd St.)**
**751-2163**
*Mon. to Sat. 9:30 A.M. to 6:00 P.M.*

## Botticelli
**Women's:**
**612 Fifth Ave.**
**(50th St.)**
**582-6313**
**Men's:**
**666 Fifth Ave.**
**(53rd St.)**
**582-2984**
*Mon. to Sat. 10:00 A.M. to*
*6:30 P.M.; Thurs. to 7:00 P.M.*

## Carina Nucci Uomo
**1071 Third Ave.**
**1073 Third Ave.**
**(63rd-64th Sts.)**
**888-1033**
## Riff's Boutique
**1075 Third Ave.**
**688-1754**
*Mon. to Sat. 10:30 A.M. to 6:00 P.M.*

## Carrano
**677 Fifth Ave.**
**(53rd St.)**
**752-6111**
**782 Lexington Ave.**
**(61st St.)**
**832-8182**
*Mon. to Sat. 10:30 A.M. to*
*6:30 P.M.; Thur. to 8:00 P.M.*

## Charles Jourdan
**700 Fifth Ave.**
**(55th St.)**
**541-8440**
**769 Madison Ave.**
**(66th St.)**
**620-0133**
*Mon. to Sat. 10:00 A.M. to 6:00 P.M.*

## Ferragamo
**717 Fifth Ave.**
**(56th St.)**

clientele. Average prices for the neighborhood. ($150 to $250).

Two shops, one for women and one for men, offering, of course, the same style: classic and classy. Lots of beige, camel, brown, and black, but some patches of color, as in the men's cowboy boots ($350). Prices for men's and women's shoes vary from about $120 to $220.

Four very Italian and good-looking boutiques that shoe such famous feet as those of Vitas Gerulaitis and Shirley MacLaine. The leathers are soft, the shapes delicate, and the colors exquisite, and there's usually a touch of eccentricity, which you can get away with because of the quality—Italian extravagance is always in good taste. The stores also carry shoes by Andrea Pfister with matching evening purses. Riff's Boutique also specializes in men's shirts, blazers, and pants that are casual and elegant, if just a wee bit affected; Carina Nucci on 57th Street carries a very pretty collection of dresses, suits, pants, blouses, sweaters, and leather clothing for day and nighttime, aimed at sophisticated as well as somewhat more sober ladies. Wool outfits $95, leather pants $480 to $500, blouses $200.

A weakness for gold, gray, blue, and silvery green is obvious here, which gives a very fashionable look to the otherwise classic shapes of most of the boots and shoes. Lots of lizardskin flats in all colors and in a wider range of prices than its competitors: $85 to $185 for the shoes, and from $150 to $900 for the boots. There's a more conventional men's department, plus a few leather articles of clothing that are in without being too eccentric.

Classic footwear at not very reasonable prices (shoes $98 to $225 and boots $125 to $395) in a wide range of high-quality skins—leather, suede, snakeskin, patent leather—stylish shoes that won't go out of fashion, and of a comfort that's always in style. Very pretty accessories: handbags and belts, some in crocodile skin, and a ready-to-wear section offering a choice of leather garments. You can't go wrong here.

Florentine old-hat: moccasins and flats with wide toes and low heels—at least you won't risk twisting your ankle. The colors (brown, black, navy blue) are strong rather than

# THE SHOPS/Clothes

**759-3822**
*Mon. to Sat. 10:00 A.M. to 6:00 P.M.*

## Gucci
**689 Fifth Ave.
(54th St.)
826-2600**
*Mon. to Sat. 9:30 A.M. to 6:00 P.M.*

## Helène Arpels
**665 Madison Ave.
(61st St.)
755-1623**
*Mon. to Sat. 10:00 A.M. to 6:00 P.M.*

## I. Miller Shoes
**11 E. 54th St.
753-2577**
*Mon. to Sat. 9:15 A.M. to 6:00 P.M.*

## Jerri's Shoe Outlet
**538 Second Ave.
(30th St.)
889-6491
2611 Broadway
(99th St.)
866-2820**
*Mon. to Sat. 10:30 A.M. to 6:30 P.M.*

## Mario Valentino
**5 E. 57th St.
486-0322**
*Mon. to Sat. 10:00 A.M. to 6:00 P.M.*

## Maud Frizon
**210 E. 60th St.
753-8978
49 E. 57th St.**

stylish. Their leatherwear department, however, is younger and of very good quality. For women and men.

No surprises in store here—either good or bad—for Gucci fans. Lots of moccasins and flats for women ($110 to $120) and, for men, a bigger choice, including some very handsome moccasins for summer ($160). Buckle World.

Paloma Picasso, Nancy Reagan, and lots of other glittering ones frequent this antiquated and inhumanly dull store. Shoes, dresses, and hats made in very few copies, if not one-of-a-kind, at prices that remain an absolute secret, known only to store and client. It's better that way, too, because you can enjoy the impression, when paying three or four times the normal price, that you're not like everybody else—which is the whole purpose. The styles themselves are as "old maidish" as the shop: paragons of platitude and conformism, perfect, say, for an official receiving line. Still, we shouldn't be too nasty—Helène Arpels is the First Shoemaker.

This shop offers the broadest choice of French and Italian imports in the district: without ruining yourself, you can pick out a pretty pair in any style and at all prices from $26 for espadrilles with heels, to $180 for elegant lizardskin flats. Winter boots, evening sandals, classic moccasins— there's everything here, plus luggage and clothing designed by Étienne Aiguet. You don't always have to pay the highest prices for quality accessories.

These two stores are popular for their discounts of 20 to 50 percent on pretty, well-tailored shoes, boots, and sandals by Yves S. Laurent, Ungaro, Anne Klein, and their ilk, in magnificent leather ($10 to $40 during the sales) and also for a few good-quality purses. The shop on Second Avenue with its shiny chrome is the prettier of the two, but the one on Broadway is bigger.

An attractive shop featuring shoes from Naples for men and women. Classic and elegant models, some more successful than others. But, more important, an absolutely magnificent section of leather goods, including clothing. Their latest collection of skirts, cardigans, and jackets in leather and suede and in solid-colored and printed Italian cotton, is breathtaking. But they're not for all tastes, for every budget. Men and women.

Maud Frizon means imagination and quality, unusual designs and colors, and the sort of striking detail that sets her work apart. It means superb and sophisticated sandals and boots for cover girls and smart young women, at

980-1460
*Mon. to Sat. 10:00 A.M. to 6:00 P.M.*

prices that will send chills down your spine. The recent opening of a shop on 57th Street coincided with their unveiling of a line of hide luggage as supple and elegant as their shoes, at prices just as record-setting. Shoes for both sexes.

## Santini E Dominici
697 Madison Ave. (62nd-63rd Sts.) 838-1835
*Mon. to Fri. 10:30 A.M. to 6:30 P.M.; Sat. to 6:00 P.M.*

New York's most charming Italian shoe store, with the friendliest prices. A very modern and good-looking shop, done entirely in white marble and black carpeting and decorated with only a few bouquets of red tropical flowers—a treat! And, it's the only one of its kind to provide reasonable prices for handsome Italian shoes and boots designed with a native Roman's sure taste. The collections are limited, but more than sufficient to seduce you: pretty Italian leather, simple and fashionable styles embellished with a few discreet details that make them the height of chic—this is exactly the sort of store New York lacked until now. Nothing costs more than $200, and, for only $25, you can pick out a pair of very appealing plastic boots in rainbow colors. An elegant choice of men's shoes, too ($95), and a children's department is slated to open—impatiently awaited by hard-to-please mothers. This is the only Italian shoe store that advertises its prices—the others don't dare to!

## Susan Bennis/ Warren Edwards
440 Park Ave. (56th St.) 755-4197
*Mon. to Sat. 10:15 A.M. to 6:30 P.M.*

The most extravagant "design" leather-goods store in New York. Created by two highly inventive young designers, this very large shop, neither quite round nor quite octagonal, offers an extraordinary collection of shoes and boots at absolutely alarming prices. The mixture of materials used—snakeskin and leather; colors—golden and matte; and styles—heels of every height, various inlays—is unusual and successful. Reptiles reign: python, lizard, and crocodile are abundant and, if you don't balk at spending $6,000, you can walk away with the prettiest pair of boots in the entire United States. Average prices are from $250 to $950 for women's shoes, and from $225 to $1,250 for men's shoes in slightly more classical styles. An appealing line of luggage and clothes. For well-padded wallets.

## Vigevano
969 Third Ave. (58th St.) 755-9090
*Mon. to Fri. 10:00 A.M. to 7:00 P.M.; Mon. and Thurs. to 9:00 P.M.; Sat. to 6:00 P.M.*

An immense shop offering a vast, superbly Italian selection, including Bally shoes, plus a custom-made service. A true bootmaker, who won't make you look like a bumpkin.

## Vittorio Ricci
1019 Third Ave. (60th-61st Sts.) 355-3377
*Mon. to Sat. 10:00 A.M. to 7:00 P.M.*

Very elegant and very exclusive—this shop wins all the awards hands down for the most eye-catching, inventive, and often changed store-window displays.

256

# Department Stores

In many respects, department stores are the best way to take on life in New York and its shopping-oriented natives. Consider, for example, the role the shopping bag plays in the metropolis. It is for the '80s what the hat was at the turn of the century: a symbol of social status and prosperity—so much so that some people would rather walk the streets barefoot than be caught without a shopping bag emblazoned with the initials of the store or designer they frequent. It reassures its possessor and gives its bearer a sense of belonging to a larger group.

There are ten or so department stores that count in New York, offering more or less the same type of wares, but whose personal character and tone is defined by the style of service they offer and, still more, by the clientele that frequents them. On the following pages you'll find a general guide to the front-runners, their specialties, their styles, the tastes they cater to.

## B. Altman
**Fifth Ave. and 34th St.**
**679-7800**
*Mon. to Sun. 10:00 A.M. to 6:00 P.M.; Thurs. to 8:00 P.M.*

Less exclusive than Bergdorf, less fashionable than Bloomingdale's, less dowdy than Lord and Taylor, and better maintained than Macy's, Altman is a good New York classic where the accent is on quality and service. The merchandise is completely acceptable, and the prices average; particularly noteworthy are the linen department (4th floor) and the children's department, offering all the best American easy-to-care-for brands. Its lower Midtown location means that it's not really in the fashionable shopping district, but it's still a very complete and tasteful store, a bit old-fashioned (in the best sense of the word).

Restaurant: the Charleston Gardens, on the 8th floor. A popular spot serving well-prepared traditional Southern cooking.

## Barney's
**Seventh Ave. and 17th St.**
**929-9000**
*Mon. to Sat. 9:00 A.M. to 9:30 P.M. Sat. to 7:00 P.M. in summer*

The resident genius for men's fashion: since 1923 five floors completely given over to men, with a recent and ravishing women's duplex of shops (6th floor and penthouse) linked by a stunning art deco stairway and capped with a huge greenhouse, where ladies can stroll in the sun (you'll get enough fluorescent lighting elsewhere) from one boutique (the best decorated and most personalized in New York) to another, featuring such designers as Giorgio Armani, Missoni, Gianni Versace, Agnès B, Kenzo, Perry Ellis, Norma Kamali, and some sportswear by SoHo designers.

257

Men, whether tiny, tremendous, or in-between, whether their taste runs to classic English tweeds, American-styled shoulders, or Italian chic, will find articles of interest at Barney's. All the best-known American designers are represented, in every size, style, and price range. An entire floor is devoted to Giorgio Armani creations, Basile and Cerutti; a Tokyo boutique represents the latest Japanese designers; and hostesses on every floor will direct you to the section you're looking for. The biggest (if not the only one) of its type in the world. A true must!

## Bergdorf Goodman
**754 Fifth Ave.
(58th St.)
753-7300**
*Mon. to Sat. 10:00 A.M. to 6:00 P.M.;
Thur. to 8:00 P.M.*

The most elegant of all the department stores, where you can outfit yourself for $50 or $4,000 (more often the latter). Sophisticated New York ladies come here for creations by their favorite designers, like Yves Saint Laurent, Chanel, Givenchy, Christian Dior, and the best Italian names (Armani, Montana, and the like), and, of course, domestic designs, plus the famous Italian furs made by the Fendi sisters. The 2nd floor lingerie department presents a stupefying gradation of glittering and shimmering colors. The men's section is just as elegant, offering magnificent fabrics like silk, linen, Shetland wool and gabardine. Everything bathes in an atmosphere of calm and luxury, among a clientele composed of self-consciously "Bergdorf" ladies.

## Bloomingdale's
**1000 Third Ave.
(59th-60th Sts.)
355-5900**
*Mon. to Sat. 9:45 A.M. to 6:00 P.M.;
Mon. and Thur. to 9:00 P.M.*

Of all the department stores, Bloomingdale's is unquestionably the most appealing, the most agreeable, the pleasantest, the most brilliant, and the best known. Bloomingdale's sets fashion trends for the young and in crowd (Saturday's Generation in the basement), plays host to Kenzo, Cacharel, Anne Klein, and more, and gives new designers their big break. Only at Bloomingdale's are the decor and presentation at least as well conceived and carried out as the merchandise itself. The Beauty section (ground floor, on the Lexington Avenue side) in black marble and gleaming metal merits a visit if only to see it; so does the Men's Furnishings department (also on the ground floor), a storehouse that recalls Ali Baba's cave filled with cashmere socks, swimsuits, Lacoste polo shirts in all the colors of the rainbow, ties, and shirts. The basement houses the collection of suits and jackets by famous designers, of which a good number, even of the latest fashions, are always on sale at very attractive prices. The Activewear and Lingerie departments (subway level) present the greatest and most elegant choice available in New York of these goods. As for the accessories, they have nothing short of the best department in town (2nd floor). Nor should you overlook the Delicatessen (59th Street entrance) with its Petrossian and Lenôtre stands. By all means have a look at the Dior, Calvin Klein, Givenchy, Ungaro, Nina Ricci, Valentino, Fendi, Halston, Ralph Lauren, and Jourdan boutiques (Yes department and Place Élégante on the 3rd, 4th, and 5th floors), which are ravishingly laid out and displayed, and whatever else you do, don't miss The Main Course on the 7th floor, the prettiest housewares department in the city. You'll find a profusion of sheets and towels on the 6th floor, including the famous Vogue designs, and an excellent beauty salon (featuring Orlane, Lancôme, and more) on the 8th. Furniture is on the 6th floor, offering showrooms designed by top decorators, along with a good choice of light fixtures. In fact, all the floors merit a visit: you feel at home here in the midst—alas—of an enormous crowd, among which you're sure to see a few friends on an autumn or winter Saturday afternoon. It goes without saying that you'll have to do a little song-and-dance routine to catch a salesperson's eye, and that the cash registers are always brimming over with customers. But it's all good fun, and more than worth the effort. Note as well that the store regularly organizes its famous special shows highlighting clothes, food, and art from near and faraway countries and all of Bloomingdale's adopts a sort of folkloric flavor.

There are four eating spots: L'Espresso Bar on the subway level, a chic spot to nibble on a quiche, a platter of pâté, or a fruit cup, washed down by a glass of Champagne, Perrier, or beer; 40 Carrots (basement), with a restaurant-counter popular for such health-food fare as yogurt with fruit; The Green House (8th floor) for its sandwiches, salads, quiches, and crêpes; and, above all, Le Train Bleu (6th floor), looking out over the 59th Street entrance, a European-style restaurant serving full-course meals (liquor license) in an Orient Express atmosphere.

## Bonwit Teller
**4-10 E. 57th St.**
**593-3333**
*Mon. to Sat. 10:00 A.M. to 6:00 P.M.; Sun. noon to 5:00 P.M.*

Very classic and conservative, Bonwit recently reopened in the Trump Tower and is operating at full capacity. The best department is for accessories (main floor), offering a limited but high-quality selection of items both trendy and basic. A complete collection of sportswear, dresses, coats and suits, evening collections, lingerie, designer clothes, and furs on various floors. Another of New York's symbols of sophistication, represented by the romantic bouquet of violets that adorns their shopping bags, walls, and credit cards.

## Gimbel's
**1275 Broadway**
**(33rd St.)**
**564-3300**

## Gimbel's East
**125 E. 86th St.**
**348-2300**
*Mon. to Sat. 10:00 A.M. to 6:00 P.M.; Mon. and Thur. to 8:30 P.M.*

New York opinion is divided about these two stores: some shoppers will not enter them under any circumstances because their setting is so depressing, while others swear by these stores that sell many of the same items as Macy's and Bloomingdale's at much better prices. The store on Broadway, right next to Macy's, is larger but also darker and dustier than the other. Everything is of acceptable quality, and the lingerie department stocks a more varied and original selection than what is usually displayed. There are also charming new fashions, designers' clothes, and some very good bargains scattered among the heaps of mediocre, low-priced items. The upper floors, given over to housewares and furnishings, are very good.

## Henri Bendel
**10 W. 57th St.**
247-1100
*Mon. to Sat. 10:00 A.M. to 5:30 P.M.*

A special mention for this department store aimed at sophisticated and fashion-minded women, unlike any other retail outlet in New York. It consists exclusively of a collection of boutiques, each more luxurious than the last, and each representing the highest point of fashion. New York's most famous doorman greets you at these superbly decorated, ultra-chic, and extremely expensive premises. You'll find the best (and only the best) in each department: Jean Louis David will do your hair, Eli Zabar will cook for you, Shoe Biz (main floor) will adorn your feet, and Castelbajac, Mary Macfadden, Sonia Rykiel, Emmanuelle Khanh, Carol Horn, Perry Ellis, Jean Muir, and some of their most distinguished colleagues will attire you in the finest silks, brocades, cottons, and gauzes, a pure enchantment of colors and materials. Ravishing accessories and sundries, charming stationery, and more make this a paragon of refinement.

## Lord and Taylor
**424 Fifth Ave.**
**(38th St.)**
391-3344
*Mon. to Sat. 10:00 A.M. to 6:00 P.M.; Thur. to 8:00 P.M.*

This is Brooks Brothers for women: very conservative, a traditional and pleasant store where the salespeople don't pounce on you and force you to buy: on the contrary, you can linger and reflect on your purchases without ever being hurried. A good choice of sportswear by such excellent designers (mostly American) as Bill Blass, Ralph Lauren, and Calvin Klein. There are some attractive household furnishings, like the antique Chinese porcelain lamps (9th floor) and an attractive collection of Kilim rugs (8th floor). There is no sign of frivolity in this store, only of reassuring good taste and the most pleasant service. Excellent sales in January and July.

## Macy's
**W. 34th St. and Broadway**
685-4409
*Mon. to Sat. 9:45 A.M. to 6:15 P.M.; Mon., Thur., and Fri. to 8:30 P.M.; Sun. noon to 5:00 P.M.*

Unquestionably the biggest of all (an incredible 2.2 million square feet) with an overwhelming choice of relatively inexpensive moderate to better fashions, but no designer labels. Macy's has recently revamped its image, and attracts a very mixed bag of customers. It is, among other things, a haven for teenagers, with a striking selection of sweatshirts, jeans, outfits, and accessories (2nd and 3rd floor). An entire floor (the 4th) is given over to sheets, quilts, and towels of a variety and quality clearly above average, including linen by Pratesi and Descamps. The 5th floor is recommended for its magnificent toy department as well as its children's clothes, while the Cellar (basement) is noteworthy for its antiques, contemporary art gallery ($25 posters and $4,000 art nouveau lithographs), and above all for its food and housewares departments where everything is in perfect taste.

## Saks Fifth Avenue
**611 Fifth Ave.**
**(50th St.)**
753-4000
*Mon. to Sat. 10:00 A.M. to 6:00 P.M.; Thur. to 8:30 P.M.*

A store offering quality in a classic setting, recently and very appealingly redecorated, where you're neither rushed nor subjected to the weight of crowds, and are very well served. You'll find a very fine choice of sports and elegant wear; a lovely infants' and children's wear department (7th floor); a good selection of teenagers' wear and tasteful shoes in a wide range of prices (6th floor); and very refined lingerie (4th floor). One floor down are the Revillon fur salon and one of the best maternity boutiques in the city. On the ground floor, the collection of men's shirts is reputed for its quality. The luggage department includes a Vuitton boutique featuring articles manufactured in California—thus reasonably priced, but not as solid as otherwise. Don't overlook their very luxurious household linen department, reminiscent of Porthault in style, but not in price—or their stand for cats and dogs, or their sumptuous art gallery (entrance at 15 E. 49th St.) worthy of comparison with the best Madison Avenue galleries. The entire store, including its clientele, bathes in an atmosphere of luxury and wealth.

# Flowers

## FLORISTS

### Bouquets à la Carte
**222 E. 83rd St.**
**535-3720**
*Mon. to Fri. 9:00 A.M. to 5:00 P.M.;*
*Sat. 10:00 A.M. to 1:00 P.M.*

And a very special menu it is, too: floral arrangements using fresh or paper flowers adorned with ribbon, candy, stuffed animals, and various other gifts in all sorts of distinctive containers: vases, baskets, teapots, bottles of Champagne, or cedar crates. Their specialty: a giant bouquet of multicolored flowers, streaming with ribbons, in a wicker basket. Very original and fun. Don't forget to ask them about their latest creations. More traditional offerings as well.

### Ed. Stiffler
**1190 Third Ave.**
**(69th-70th Sts.)**
**628-4404**
*Mon. to Fri. 9:30 A.M. to 5:00 P.M.*

A superb selection of original cut and silk flowers. Their creations are as stylized as they are superb. Very pretty potted flowers and exquisite wreaths of fresh and dried flowers. A charming welcome in an attractive shop and very reasonable prices, considering the quality.

### Flowers on the Square
**399 Bleecker St.**
**(near 11th St.)**
**243-0218**
*Mon. to Thur. noon to 6:30 P.M.,*
*Fri to 7:00 P.M., Sat. 11:00 A.M. to*
*6:00 P.M.*

Flowers are treated as works of art and arranged in highly stylized displays. It's sumptuous—the antithesis of the corner florist. The orchids are particularly stunning. A second store at 1886 Broadway, 397-5882.

### Irene Hayes Wadley Smythe

If any New York florist enjoys particular fame, it is Irene Hayes, the first lady of flowers. Her delivery trucks are visible throughout the city, making their rounds among

**1 Rockefeller Plaza**
247-0051
*Mon. to Fri. 8:00 A.M. to 6:00 P.M.;
Sat. 8:00 A.M. to 2:00 P.M.*

the initiated. You can rely on her for blooms that are high quality and expensive. Various locations.

## Japan Bonsai Nursery
**782 Avenue of the Americas
(30th St.)**
255-2187
*Mon. to Sun. 10:00 A.M. to
6:00 P.M.*

For lovers of Japanese gardens, this florist specializes in the famous bonsai trees. The trees may be miniature—the prices are not. But you are buying the living proof that a little perfection is worth more than a whole jungle.

## The Jungle Riding High
**1170 First Ave.**
737-0289
*Mon. to Sat. 10:00 A.M. to
8:30 P.M.*

This shop—it is allied with the "Riding High" shop across street—didn't come by its whimsical name by chance. "In the jungle," the owner explains, "you never know what to expect next. By merely pushing aside a few branches, you can discover at any moment the most bizarre and extraordinary things—just as you can here. We go after the original, the unusual." The results are often amazing. For his arrangements he uses exotic flowers such as orchids, sprigs of greenery, and lots of large leaves that he paints gold or silver, giving them a fabulous metallic look and transforming simple flowers and plants into works of artistry. Prices are accordingly high: from $20 or $25 to $500.

## Renny
**27 E. 62nd St.**
371-5354
*Mon. to Sat. 9:30 A.M. to 6:00 P.M.*

A veritable architect of bouquets, a young man who brims with talent and taste and who creates unusual, "designed" arrangements, using imported flowers that are so beautiful that one bloom is sometimes enough.
Another Renny location (1018 Lexington Avenue, between 72nd and 73rd Streets: 371-5354) offers plants and flowers in a spare but striking setting. Floral arrangements from $35 to $80.

## Ronaldo Maia Flowers
**27 E. 67th St.**
288-1049
*Mon. to Sat. 9:00 A.M. to 6:00 P.M.*

The first shop that comes to mind when you try to think of an elegant florist. Everything is delectable: the store itself, located in a charming townhouse, as well as the supremely distinctive flowers and the different sorts of potpourri—one of the house specialties—($12 for four ounces). The arrangements themselves (from $35 to $50) are usually presented in baskets or decorative cachepots. The bouquets cost about $20 to $30. Customers are treated with polish.

## South Flower Market
**Columbus Ave. and 68th St.**
496-7100
*Mon. to Sat. 10:00 A.M. to
10:00 P.M.; Sun. noon to 8:00 P.M.*

A self-service for cut flowers: you arrange your own bouquets, choosing from an immense variety of common and uncommon flowers that arrive daily from all around the world. Fixed, discount prices, with extra savings if you buy any one species in quantity. Lovely long-stemmed roses cost $1.35 each or $13.77 for a dozen.
For same-day delivery of lovely bouquets at reasonable prices call 392-8085. Copious bouquets of assorted

wildflowers in glass jars cost $10, and $61.50 will buy the best in exotic and unusual flowers. Eighteen long-stemmed roses come to $27.36, a real bargain, and regulars get home deliveries.

# ARTIFICIAL FLOWERS

### Diane Love
**851 Madison Ave.**
**(70th-71st Sts.)**
**879-6967**
*Mon. to Sat. 10:00 A.M. to 5:30 P.M.*

Straight out of the *Thousand and One Nights:* a narrow, gray-silk-draped boutique through which wafts an intoxicating odor of a potpourri mixed from rose and jasmine—Diane Love's special concoction. Her magnificent exotic silk flowers have made her name, but they aren't the only attractions. She also sells all sorts of objects brought back from her voyages, or which she herself has designed: lacquer boxes, bowls, and trays, embroidered Chinese handbags and kimonos in old silk from '20s and '30s are among her treasures. But they are not, alas, within everyone's reach. Which accounts for the ever so slightly snobbish atmosphere and clientele.

### La Fleuressence
**1240 Madison Ave.**
**(89th St.)**
**931-4796**
*Mon. to Fri. 10:00 A.M. to 6:00 P.M.*

Say it with flowers—flowers made of silk or dried, hand-painted on sumptuous scarves, woven on antique handbags and silky cushions, necklaces, frames, and diverse knicknacks. Flowers reign here in all their delicacy and subtlety, and make this into a truly enchanting shop. A few Victorian antiques, including some silverware.

### Pamela Duval
**680 Madison Ave.**
**(61st-62nd Sts.)**
**752-2126**
*Mon. to Sat. 9:15 A.M. to 5:00 P.M.*

The window is decorated with old-fashioned cushions embroidered with newfangled mottos such as "Old lovers are better lovers." The shop itself is minuscule, and so crammed with really very ordinary lamps, vases, knickknacks, and so on that it's difficult to clear a path through it. But the silk flowers are magnificent, though much less unusual than at Diane Love, and they are made into very pleasing arrangements. Nothing extraordinary or particularly original, but the perfect sort of thing to adorn a chest of drawers or an elegant store window.

# Food

# BAKERIES

### Baked Expectations
**1312 Madison Ave.**

Appetizing and unpretentious cakes of the type home bakers dream of making, "If only I had the time!" So, if you want to trick your friends into believing that you are

**(93rd St.)**
**427-5382**
*Daily until 6:00 P.M.*

an accomplished cook who effortlessly whips up crunchy and mouth-watering hazelnut cheesecakes or chocolate layer cakes, this is your spot. You can also enjoy these upstairs at the Carnegie Hall cafe.

## Bonté
**1316 Third Ave.**
**(75th St.)**
**535-2360**
*Mon. to Sat. 9:00 A.M. to 7:00 P.M.*

This is New York's best French pastry shop. Selective, with a limited choice—but oh! of what wonders! Year-round specialties (cakes with butterscotch or Grand Marnier, strawberry mousse, mille feuilles, tarte tatin) and seasonal creations (the strawberry pie is perfection) have earned Maurice Bonté the Best Pastrycook award in France and the United States. His croissants, palm leaves, and miniature madeleines would win any prize for excellence hands down. If you want to order in quantity for a party, you'd best call up in advance, as the meticulous craftsmanship that permits such results is incompatible with mass production. But Bonté resembles any other small neighborhood shop, and doesn't seem likely to change its unpretentious style. We hope it doesn't.

## Colette
**1136 Third Ave.**
**(66th-67th Sts.)**
**998-2605**
*Tues. to Sat., 8:00 A.M. to 5:45 P.M. on the dot*

Colette is the progenitor of French pastry shops in New York: her antiquated shop and ageless, unsmiling salesladies testify to that. But Colette has merits: her wide variety of quiches are still the best, and her cakes are of high quality. We should call attention to her delicious brioches, and her very thin butter cookies topped with lemon, apricot, and raspberry, rightfully called "merveilleuses." Colette also offers a few traditional, simply prepared French dishes.

## Creative Cakes
**400 E. 74th St.**
**794-9811**
*Tues. to Fri. 9:00 A.M. to 5:30 P.M.; Sat. 9:00 A.M. to 11:30 A.M.*

Perhaps you're feeling imaginative, and would like a cake in the form of an animal, a car, or a portrait of a friend. Well, look up Stephanie Crookston: with the help of her top-secret family recipes she'll make a chocolate cake to match your fantasy. A good way to cut a despised enemy into little tiny pieces—and not go to jail for it.

## Délices la Côte Basque
**1032 Lexington Ave.**
**(73rd-74th Sts.)**
**535-3311**
**Olympic Tower**
**Arcade, 635 Fifth Ave.**
**(51st St.)**
**935-2220**

The merits of this pastry shop (with Bonté, the best in town) are unquestionable and its growing reputation is admirably earned. As for its sweets, the almond biscuits and petits fours are particularly tasty. The chestnut pastry boats are an unforgettable experience in their own right, and the chocolate cakes are true "délices." The savories? Côte Basque prepares its own pâtés and makes a jambon persillé and sausage en croûte which are both remarkable. These treats can be enjoyed on the spot in their French-style tea rooms. The one at the Olympic Tower is spanking new and includes a cafe, restaurant, and bar—but it's totally devoid of the other's rustic charm, and the service is much too slow.

## Dumas
**116 E. 60th St.**
**688-0905**
**1330 Lexington Ave.**

Everything is good, but the Saint Honorés, meringues, nut and almond rings, and cookies coated with caramel are particularly praiseworthy. Excellent fruit pies with flaky crusts. A reasonable choice of cheeses, quiches, pâtés,

**(88th-89th Sts.)**
**369-3900**
**1042 Madison Ave.**
**(79th-80th Sts.)**
**744-4804**
*Mon. to Sat. 8:30 A.M. to 6:30 P.M.*

## Elysée Pastries
**939 First Ave.**
**(52nd St.)**
**755-5858**
**1397 Second Ave.**
**737-8529**
**1039 Third Ave.**
**(61st-62nd Sts.)**
**838-5248**
*Mon. to Sat. 9:00 A.M. to 6:30 P.M.;*
*closed Sun. (Second Ave. store*
*closed Mon., open Sun.)*

## Erotic Bakery
**73 W. 83rd St.**
**362-7557**
*Tues. to Sat. 11:00 A.M. to*
*8:00 P.M., Sun. noon to 6:00 P.M.*

## Just Desserts
**443 E. 75th St.**
**535-4964**
*Mon., Thurs., and Sat. 10:00 A.M.*
*to 6:00 P.M.; Tues. and Wed.*
*1:00 P.M. to 6:00 P.M.*

## Kramer's Pastries
**1643 Second Ave.**
**(86th St.)**
**535-5955**
*Mon. to Sat. 8:00 A.M. to 7:00 P.M.;*
*Sun. 10:00 A.M. to 6:00 P.M.*

## Lanciani
**275 W. 4th St.**
**(Perry St.)**
**929-0739**
*Tues to Sat. 8:00 A.M. to 9:00 P.M.,*
*Sun. 8:00 A.M. to 7:00 P.M.*

pickles, homemade jams (including wild strawberry), and French bread—everything you need for a simple feast, as long as your palate is not too picky: Dumas is facing stiff competition from talented newcomers. No delivery. Sometimes frosty service.

Started by Jean Claude Szurdak, these pastry shops, although somewhat less prestigious than the two preceding, can nonetheless be recommended. The relative poverty of atmosphere and setting is more than made up for by the appreciable quality of the products. The cakes and pies are comparable to those of Dumas, while the specialty, a fresh orange pie, lightly glazed, is reminiscent of Bonté. A few acceptable cheeses and pâtés, and a freezer full of dishes you can heat up and serve without embarassment. A lobster or mushroom roulé to begin with, followed by duck with turnips or beef à la mode: this isn't haute cuisine, but is nonetheless very proper and reasonably priced. No deliveries.

A part of the movement that burst the straitlaces of WASP America, this shop offers chocolate, sweets, and almond paste in the shapes of sexual organs, naked women, and similar objects. There are also similar pot-holders, brooches, and toothbrushes. Strangely enough, it's not really in bad taste, and the raw materials used are first-rate. Which explains its large clientele from all walks of life. Have a look, even if you don't taste. Cakes for special occasions by order. Various locations.

A minuscule blue and white shop filled with various cakes and pies, most of which have just come out of the oven: layer cakes, raspberry fudge cakes, praline cheesecakes, and almond mousse cakes, as well as all sorts of pies. A veritable roll call of baking. Cakes sold only whole, not by the slice—at very reasonable prices: $7 for a cake that will serve about six.

A newcomer to the scene who deserves special attention because of the quality of his moderately priced desserts. The petits fours, palm leaves, butter and chocolate cookies, and "cigarette russes" are true delicacies, and the fruit pies beg to be eaten. Keep your eyes on this place.

The Italian owner, formerly head pastry chef at the Plaza, now makes quality Viennese and French pastries. His chocolate eclairs, lemon tarts, and cookies are delicious. The Christmas logs and Easter eggs are as good as those at Dumas, and the croque-en-bouches are made according to the best French traditions. Wedding cakes superbly decorated with lace motifs are his specialty. This is our only listing of this class for the downtown area. His products are now available at Pasta and Cheese on Third Avenue and 65th St.

## Miss Grimble
**305 Columbus Ave.
(74th St.)
362-5531
416 W. 13th St.
675-2865**
*Mon. to Sat. 10:00 A.M. to 7:00 P.M.*

The Cheesecake Queen, as she's known here. Miss Grimble's creamy, filling specialty, topped off with various fruits, is well worth the calories. Known too for her pecan and pumpkin pies. New England cooking for hearty appetites.

## Mrs. Herbst
**1437 Third Ave.
(81st-82nd Sts.)
535-8484**
*Mon., Wed. to Sat. 8:00 A.M. to 6:00 P.M.*

A true provincial pastry shop/tea room, whose regulars enjoy the best strudels, poppy-seed cakes, nut crescents, other unpronounceable but unforgettable Hungarian specialties in town, seated at the back of the shop at tiny tables, over a bad cup of coffee or a better hot chocolate. Good homemade jams, and reasonably appetizing petits fours, but at exorbitant prices. A curious spot—one quite obviously not tourist oriented.

## Sarabeth's Kitchen
**412 Amsterdam Ave.
(79th St.)
496-6280**
*Wed. to Mon. 10:00 A.M. to 7:00 P.M.*

The charm of Sarabeth's smile is matched by that of her attractive boutique filled with tasty goodies fresh from the oven: fresh-fruit pies, individual or family size, small golden, crusty palm leaves, brownies, "health-food" cookies, shortbread, white or whole-wheat breads and rolls, and mouth-watering mixed fruit jams. Beware! This seemingly harmless shop, full of rustic pleasures, is a hotbed of temptations. We should point out that everything here is made with natural products, without artificial coloring, preservatives, or anything of that sort.

## William Greenberg Jr. Desserts
**1377 Third Ave.
(79th St.)
861-1340
57 Seventh Ave.
674-6657**
*Closed Sunday*

## Butter Cake Squares
**1100 Madison Ave.
(82nd St.)
744-0304**
*Mon. to Fri. 8:30 A.M. to 6:00 P.M.
(Seventh Ave. store open on weekends)*

Excellent, typically American pastry shops, they have such specialties as Danish rings, almond coffee rings, cinnamon coffee loaves, pies, cheesecakes, and chocolate layer cakes, not to mention the spectacular cakes available by special order at the Third Avenue store. The brownies, butter cookies, and honey buns are reputed to be the best in the metropolis, and are perfect for an American-style tea. As its name suggests, the Madison Avenue shop specializes in variously flavored butter cakes. No layer cakes, but everything else, which is saying a lot. Mr. Greenberg is a true New York pastry chef who knows his clientele well, but who is not particularly willing to make the effort necessary to attract new customers.

# BREADS

Both bakeries and croissanteries are numerous today, as the croissant craze has taken over New York; and growing interest in high-quality cheeses has called up a demand for bread to go with them. The quality varies; here are a few specialized places we can recommend, in addition to the pastry shops already listed.

## Au Bon Pain
**Citicorp Center,
53rd St. and
Third Ave.
838-6996**
*Mon. to Fri. 7:00 A.M. to 8:30 P.M.,
Sat. and Sun. 10:00 A.M. to
8:30 P.M.*

Bread made with authentic French flour—it's supposed to make a big difference in the taste of their rolls and loaves of French bread. The croissants and brioches are better than in many other places, but are nonetheless quite unexceptional.

## Betsy's Place
**144 E. 74th St.
2nd floor
734-1855**
*Mon. to Fri. 8:30 A.M. to 5:00 P.M.;
Sat. 10:00 A.M. to 5:00 P.M.*

If you like bread with fruits, dates, ginger, spices of all kinds, or if you are tempted by the idea of tasting among the best chocolate-bar cookies and butterscotch brownies in town, climb up the few stairs that separate this shop from the street level. An attic-like setting swimming with colors, odors, and shapes. Very attractive gift boxes to offer your gourmet friends.

## Bonjour Croissants
**701 Lexington Ave.
(57th St.)
980-5066**
*Mon. to Sat. 7:00 A.M. to 8:30 P.M.*

A tiny shop where the croissants are delicious, fresh, piping hot, and available in a striking variety. The ham and spinach are popular, as are the chocolate and apricot croissants, but they come in lots of other flavors too, and all are hefty. A true success story in a high-competition field—the owner, a Moroccan, is going to open a larger outlet on the corner of 57th and Avenue of the Americas. Delivery and catering.

## Le Croissant Shop
**459 Lexington Ave.
(45th St.)
697-5580**
*Mon. to Sat. 7:00 A.M. to 8:00 P.M.*

Two to three thousand croissants freshly baked and sold each day—that's the difficult goal set and reached by a couple of young Frenchmen, who have managed to recreate in this blue boutique the atmosphere of a Parisian corner bakery. Sit at the typical French "counter-tables" to try these famous croissants served with fresh butter, or cinnamon, ham, or cheese croissants, sausage pies, quiches, apple turnovers, almond macaroons, chocolate mousse, and Alpen Zauber ice cream, washed down with a good cup of coffee or a glass of milk or fruit juice. A tasty and inexpensive treat in the French style. A counter for crusty breads as well. Delivery and catering service.

## Croissant Show
**148 E. 57th St.
759-9603**
*Daily 8:00 A.M. to 8:00 P.M.*

There is an agreeable little room where you can sit over a bowl of soup and a croissant but, apart from that, there's nothing to say about this shop, an exact replica of the one on the Boulevard St. Germain in Paris, except that here the croissants are very bad. Owner Michel Axel, a well-known Parisian designer, would do well to stick to his shirt collections, which are surely more his line.

## David's Cookie Kitchen

This cookie king is quite new to the scene, but has handily beaten other pretenders to the throne. His cookies made with tender, creamy Linot chocolate, and his French

**1018 Second Ave.
(54th St.)
888-1610**
*Mon. to Thur. 10:00 A.M. to
11:00 P.M., Fri. and Sat. to
midnight, Sun. noon to 11:00 P.M.*

## J. P.'s French Bakery
**54 W. 55th St.
765-7575**
*Mon. to Fri. 7:00 A.M. to
8:00 P.M.; Sat. 8:00 A.M.
to 7:00 P.M.; Sun. 9:00 A.M. to
5:00 P.M.*

## Pain de Paris
**792 Lexington Ave.
(61st St.)
753-4774**
*Daily 7:00 A.M. to 11:00 P.M.*

bread, the best in New York, are both absolute musts. The smells are Proustian. The shop is often crowded, but the wait is never disagreeable. Modest prices.

Opened last June, this is another exquisite small French bakery where you can stock up on bread, croissants of all sorts, palm leaves, and turnovers. At lunchtime, grab a good pâté, ham, rillette, or cheese sandwich (products from Les 3 Petits Cochons). Takeout and delivery.

A relative newcomer whose name is quite appropriate, even if almost everything about the bakery, from owner to the flour used, not to mention clients and staff, is American. But the bread itself is baked daily on the spot according to French methods and in French-style ovens, and is authentically golden and crusty. Also rolls and Vienna rolls. The pastry section is still modest, but there are attractive croissants (regular, or with ham or cheese), brioches, pains au chocolat, palm leaves, turnovers, and fruit pies—all cooked with good American butter, every bit as worthy as Normandy butter, to judge by the appetizing and tasty results and the long lines of clients.

# CAVIAR

Some readers will complain that the accidents of alphabetical order do not do justice to caviar, which, they maintain, deserves first place.
Since the interruption of Iranian caviar exports, American production has picked up, and North Atlantic sturgeon roe is available just about everywhere. It's far less expensive than Russian or Iranian caviar, but is often not up to par. At best, it's suitable for stuffing soft-boiled eggs. The catch is anarchic, the roe is not very rigorously graded, and salt is added in haphazard fashion. But, when production becomes better controlled and more standard, there's no reason why American caviar shouldn't compete favorably with the best.

## Caviarteria
**29 E. 60th St.
759-7410**
*Mon. to Sat. 9:00 A.M. to 6:00 P.M.*

## Petrossian
**(Bloomingdale's)
1000 Third Ave.
(59th St.)
233-6441**

Eight varieties of fresh caviar, and six in jars: Russian, Iranian, and American too, as well as Kamtchatka, a very good mixture of broken and whole eggs at about $5 for a one-ounce jar. It would be a crime to deprive yourself. Real Swiss chocolate as well.

The specialist from Paris has just opened an extremely attractive outlet on Bloomingdale's ground floor—a replica of his store on the Boulevard Latour-Maubourg. Christian Petrossian swore that he would introduce New Yorkers to the real taste of good caviar. The types he

Mon. to Sat. 9:45 A.M. to 6:00 P.M.,
Mon. and Thur. to 9:00 P.M.

imports are the unfortunate victims of various regulations (such as pasteurization) and restrictions (no borax permitted), and are never quite as good as the caviar he sells in France. He had to submit to the law but, thanks to certain methods (about which he maintains a discreet silence) he has nonetheless been able to offer a fairly remarkable quality of caviar (Beluga, oscietra, pressed)—all from Russia. He also sells a quite extraordinary "extra-royal" Norwegian smoked salmon, salmon roe, Périgordian truffles, and goose and duck foie gras.

## Poliroff
**542 La Guardia Pl.**
**3rd floor**
**254-7171**
*Closed Saturday and Sunday*

This isn't a store where you can browse, touch, and smell. You can only call them up and leave your order for the highest-quality smoked salmon and caviar at the lowest prices. A three-pound Nova Scotia smoked salmon for $80. All varieties of caviar. Prices on request.

# CHEESE

There's no need to list more than a few spots, as good European cheeses can be found just about everywhere these days, such as at the fine grocers listed below (Zabar's probably has the best selection) and in a multitude of other specialty shops with such names as Cheese Board, Cheese Please, and Cheese Unlimited.

Nonetheless, a few shops stand out quite clearly. At some of these you can find (God knows how!) unpasteurized, imported French cheese: Camemberts that taste like Camembert and not like bars of soap, and goat's cheese for which a gourmet would sell his soul.

## Cheese of All Nations
**153 Chambers St.**
**(at West Broadway)**
**732-0752**
*Mon. to Sat. 8:00 A.M. to 5:30 P.M.*

An immense variety of cheese from all over, where you can buy small quantities at normal prices, or wholesale by the case. Bread and hors d'oeuvres as well. The right spot to stock up for a cheese party.

## The Cheese Shop
**161 E. 22nd St.**
**673-7920**
*Mon. to Fri. 10:00 A.M. to 6:45 P.M.; Sat. 9:30 A.M. to 6:15 P.M.*

There are 150 varieties of cheese, of which about a quarter are Italian, in this shop run by an Italian who used to be with Dean & Deluca. His specialty is fresh cheese with various fruits, and a cheese pie made of alternating layers of gorgonzola and mascarponi. All the cheeses are aged on the spot by this connoisseur.

## La Fromagerie
**189 E. 79th St.**
**772-1819**
**1374 Madison Ave.**
**(95th-96th Sts.)**
**534-8923**
*Mon. to Fri. 10:00 A.M. to 9:30 P.M.; Sat. 9:30 A.M. to 7:30 P.M.*

Superb French cheeses sold by a Frenchman—this has been a reality ever since Gérard du Passage, a refuge from the garment trade, opened these deliciously attractive shops not long ago. Mr. du Passage knows what's good and what's not, and at what point a cheese has sufficiently matured for consumption, or for selling to a wholesaler. A warm, friendly sort, he lets his clients taste, advises them, or chooses for them if they wish. It's a wonderful sight: creamy goat's cheeses, soft Saint Nectaires, Marvilles,

Chaources (whole or by the slice), the majority of which are unpasteurized, thus keeping their natural flavor. There are also crusty French breads and rolls, and excellent pastries—in particular, homemade coconut macaroons, fruit pies, and chocolate and Grand Marnier mousses—as well as croissants and brioches from Délices la Côte Basque, salads with tortellini, crab, or tabouleh ($2 to $3 a quarter-pound); pâté—two house specialties, salmon and spinach pâté and pâté panache made with chicken, veal, and ginger, wrapped in bacon, for $6.50 a half-pound; and delicious delicatessen. The prices, alas, are comparable to the quality. And if this description has made you hungry, ask the owner for a Parisian sandwich: buttered roll with ham and pickle. The shop also offers Petrossian products: salmon, foie gras, caviar. Finally, there's a catering service with free delivery for all their delicacies, plus their own specially prepared dishes (such as lobster à la nage). Nothing frozen; it's not their style.

## Ideal Cheese Shop
**1205 Second Ave.**
**(63rd-64th Sts.)**
**688-7579**
*Mon. to Sat. 10:00 A.M. to 6:00 P.M.*

In our opinion, and in that of almost all connoisseurs, this is the best cheese shop in the city: between 250 and 300 domestic and, above all, imported varieties—in particular, velvety goat's cheeses, triple crèmes, Pont l'Évêque, Livarots, Epoisses, Stiltons, and innumerable other superb sorts. Also petits suisses, real French crème fraiche (imported daily), excellent pâté, and a good selection of crackers. Prices are very reasonable, taking into account the superlative quality of the products. A plus: the knowledgeable owner can help guide your purchases, which is not to be underestimated, as this is a field that requires expertise.

## Mad for Cheese
**1064 First Ave.**
**(58th St.)**
**759-8615**
*Daily 10:00 A.M. to 7:00 P.M.;*
*Sat. to 6:30 P.M.; closed Sun.*

This shop, one among several similar, deserves notice for its charm and that of the owner, a young Italian woman. Her wares are honest: a large variety of cheeses, pâté from Les 3 Petits Cochons, fresh salads, quiches, prosciutto, fine groceries, coffee, a good bread section—in short, a friendly corner store. They'll also prepare cold trays for you with an assortment of meats and cheeses for about $10 per person.

# CONFECTIONS

## The Chocolate Garden
**1390 Third Ave.**
**(79th St.)**

A fetching shop that offers temptations to which people succumb not only in the neighborhood, but also from all over New York. Try at least once the "stuffed ice cream," vanilla ice cream coated in a layer of chocolate, and covered with one of twenty different toppings, from

**988-3756**
*Daily 10:30 A.M. to 9:00 P.M.*

cashews to dried apricots, not to mention chocolate chips and M&Ms. The Chocolate Garden is also well known for its jelly beans (six liqueur and twenty fruit flavors), and its white and dark hand-dipped chocolate. We counted over forty varieties, including many made with preserved fruits. A friendly spot.

## Le Chocolatier, Ltd.
**843 Lexington Ave. (64th St.), upstairs**
**249-3289**
*Mon. to Fri. 10:00 A.M. to 5:00 P.M.; Sat. to 3:00 P.M.*

It's quite a surprise to discover the best, the freshest, and the tastiest truffles we've ever eaten in New York in this small shop adjoining an alterations boutique. The owner, a Frenchman who divides his time between his alterations and his chocolates, makes his truffles daily, the way his father did—hence their incomparable freshness. We only hope that his progeny will not alter this routine. In the meantime, we rejoice over his specialties, and wish him an expanded clientele of lovers of truffles, pralines, and marzipan.

## Elk Candy Company
**240 E. 86th St.**
**650-1177**
*Daily 9:00 A.M. to 6:30 P.M.; Sun. 10:00 A.M. to 6:30 P.M.*

Marzipan country: a delicious homemade product that attracts a lot of hard-bitten marzipan munchers to this attractive shop whose pretty window stands out in this neighborhood.

## Godiva Chocolatier
**701 Fifth Ave. (54th St.)**
**593-2845**
*Mon. to Sat. 10:00 A.M. to 6:00 P.M.*

A Belgian firm whose creamy (and for the most part heavy) chocolates have earned a solid reputation. Their velvety taste is well liked by many, and their golden gift boxes make perfect offerings. Godiva chocolates are also sold in many specialty shops, gift shops, and department stores. The prewrapped boxes contain a standard selection, which isn't always the best.

## Krön Chocolatier
**764 Madison Ave. (64th-65th Sts.) upstairs**
**288-9529**
**506 Madison Ave. (52nd St.)**
**486-0265**
*Mon. to Sat. 10:00 A.M. to 6:00 P.M.*

Another highly ranked shop, to judge by its reputation (but not necessarily by quality). Fresh and dried fruit dipped in semisweet chocolate and fresh, attractive truffles (not the tastiest), all made according to Hungarian recipes ($25 per pound). If it's originality in presentation you're looking for, you'll appreciate the unusual sculptures and forms in bittersweet and milk chocolate: life-size female busts and legs ($60 to $75), greeting cards inscribed with a short message, telephones, records, slide rules, tennis racquets, golf balls, monograms, and more at varying prices ($5 to $30). We should mention that their homemade chocolate ice cream is among the best in New York. We won't be too harsh on them, even if the appearance of their products is better than their quality (although at these prices, that's the least they can do).

## Li-lac Candies
**120 Christopher St.**
**242-7374**

All the chocolates (over fifty varieties) are hand-dipped and homemade in this shop, which has been in business since 1923. It has become an institution much appreciated by . . . well, not the most demanding of gourmets. Its best-

271

**987 Lexington Ave.
(71st St.)
734-5219**

## Perugina Chocolates
**636 Lexington Ave.
(54th St.)
688-2490**
*Mon. to Sat. 10:00 A.M. to 6:00 P.M.*

## Plumbridge Confections and Gifts
**33 E. 61st St., upstairs
371-0608**
*Mon. to Fri. 9:30 A.M. to 5:30 P.M.;
Saturday 10:00 A.M. to 5:00 P.M.*

## Sweet Temptation
**436 Avenue of
the Americas
(10th St.)
982-8665**
*Sun. to Thurs. 11:00 A.M. to
10:00 P.M.; Fri and Sat. 11:00 A.M.
to 11:15 P.M.*

## Teuscher Chocolates of Switzerland
**25 E. 61st St.
751-8482
620 Fifth Ave.
(in the promenade
of Rockefeller
Center)
246-4416**
*Mon. to Sat. 10:00 A.M. to 6:00 P.M.*

sellers: fudge and filled chocolates that taste and smell quite ordinary.

The classic Italian imported chocolates, including the famous "Baci" (kisses) stuffed with pralines, so delighted in by the chefs at Le Cygne and The Four Seasons. A very reasonable treat at $12.50 a pound. Admirable gift boxes as well.

A very exclusive shop run by the same family since 1883, which caters to a distinguished American clientele who, for their part, have been stocking their larders here for generations. Candies are typically American (nuts coated with brown sugar and cinnamon, mint chocolates, glazed apricots, jelly beans) from $7.50 to $15 a pound, and a very wide choice of gifts: paper boxes, antique Chinese porcelain plates, toys, and slightly kitschy gift boxes filled with candy—but the kitsch is popular. Plumbridge does most of its business by mail, across the United States and abroad too. For New Yorkers, the 61st Street shop is very friendly, well kept up, and you won't have to wait in line.

These small, old-fashioned shops overflow with candies in all shapes and wrappers: chocolate roller skates, spiders, hats, and cowboy boots; famous Godiva chocolates, and Sedutto ice creams with elaborate and exquisite flavors, which you can order by the cone. Will bring a smile to the most blasé child's face. Various locations.

Packaging and display are also dominant in these small, typically Swiss shops. Not that the chocolates are bad; they're imported weekly from Zürich, thus guaranteeing relative freshness, and are made entirely from natural ingredients. The place smells good when you enter, although your eye and nose will probably be more satisfied than your taste buds, which may be disappointed by a certain native Swiss dullness. But, if you're not too demanding, you'll like the great variety of truffles with nougat, nuts, vanilla, orange, dark or white chocolate, or even Champagne (their specialty), and if you go for crêpe-paper decorations, you'll be delighted by their charming animal figurines, dolls, and bouquets of flowers, handmade in Zürich, that hold some of these sweets. Not to mention the tiny bed inscribed "Good night" for your nighttime chocolate stash. Delightful Christmas gift boxes.

# GOURMET MARKETS

Where can you find high-quality sausage, cheese, pâté, a crusty loaf of bread, fresh salmon, and fine baked goods in New York?

As recently as three years ago, it would have taken some effort to come up with the names of even five acceptable addresses, and these would have been considered strictly luxury boutiques. Since then, New Yorkers have become more demanding, and you can now find high-quality domestic and imported foodstuffs just about everywhere, even in some supermarkets.

Here is a list of the best spots with their specialties, to make your shopping both pleasant and tasty.

## Abbondanza
**1647 Second Ave.
(85th St.)
879-6060**
*Daily 8:00 A.M. to 10:00 P.M., weekends to midnight*

Abbondanza is a success story. It's the latest on the scene, and the most inviting of the lot, being an oasis of taste and refinement in this hearty, once-German district. It's divided into several sections, including a cafe with attractive round white tables and a takeout section in the back of the shop that offers, behind sparkling-clean glass counters, a more than abundant choice of dishes and salads (banal Italian salads, unfortunately). If the dishes are not always perfect, their quality is, on the whole, excellent, and their freshness beyond reproach. A selection of good Italian products (prosciutto, salamis, bread, cheese (limited choice), and pastry (appetizing petit fours and pies), an espresso bar for lovers of Italian coffee, and a small homemade ice cream stand complete the picture. As for the service, it's as warm and friendly as you could wish.

## Artichoke
**968 Second Ave.
(51st-52nd Sts.)
753-2030**
*Mon. to Fri. 10:00 A.M. to 7:00 P.M.; Sat. to 6:00 P.M.; closed Sun.*

A plethora of appetizing items in this attractive little store run by two charming Americans: various salads, but also ten sorts of pâtés from Les 3 Petits Cochons, sausage en croûte, cheese, olive oil, some very fine grocery goods, very fresh French bread, and croissants: a menu that has become a classic, but is still very engaging and served with a smile.

## Balducci's
**422 Avenue of
the Americas
(9th St.)
673-2600**
*Daily 7:00 A.M. to 8:30 P.M.; Sun. 7:00 A.M. to 6:30 P.M.*

Another of the important and large Italian grocers. It takes a bit of effort to find what you're looking for in this jumble, but you always end up finding it, because they have everything—from fine cider in bottles to dry sausage, not to mention the fresh fruit and vegetables, the particularly well-stocked out-of-season produce, fine fresh meat, dried fruit, cheese (some 550 varieties), and unusual beverages. Everything in huge quantities and variety, in a very Village atmosphere.

## B. Altman: The Market
**Fifth Ave. and
34th St., 5th floor
679-7800**
*Mon. to Sat. 10:00 A.M. to 6:00 P.M.; Thurs. to 8:00 P.M.*

The entire range of products from the famous British firm Fortnum and Mason, and a large assortment of Crabtree and Evelyn jams, jellies, and marmalades, as well as items from Chez Faucher in Paris, chutney made by Corcellet, fine oils, coffee, cheese, and more.

## Bloomingdale's Delicacies

On the ground floor (you can also enter at 59th St. between Third Avenue and Lexington), the delicacies shop offers

**1000 Third Ave.**
**(59th St.)**
**355-5900**
*Mon. to Sat. 9:45 A.M. to 6:00 P.M.;*
*Thur. to 9:00 P.M.*

lots of delicious items, in particular, very good and reasonably priced Nova Scotia smoked salmon, an assortment of fresh pasta with accompanying sauces, cheese and charcuterie, superb cakes from Délices la Côte Basque, Godiva chocolates, not to mention counters for items from Petrossian, Gaston Lenôtre, and Michel Guérard (luxury takeout and frozen dishes).

# Dean & Deluca
**121 Prince St.**
**(Wooster)**
**254-7774**
*Daily 10:00 A.M. to 7:00 P.M.;*
*Sun. 10:00 A.M. to 6:00 P.M.*

The most attractive, best-known, and certainly one of the best. Patience is de rigueur while waiting to be served, but it pays off: these are the best fresh pastas in New York, the best olives and olive oils. Also crusty breads, pâtés, cheeses (French and Swiss)—although the selection of cheese is rather banal—delicious-smelling coffees in big burlap bags, and exquisite pastry. Admirably displayed in a pleasing, rustic manner, by an Italian with taste and talent. At the back of the store is a small department of well-chosen kitchen utensils. Service with a smile, but huge crowds on the weekend: the lines sometimes extend to the street.

# Demarchelier Charcuterie
**1460 Lexington Ave.**
**(94th St.)**
**722-6600**
*Daily 10:30 A.M. to 7:30 P.M.;*
*closed Sun.*

We found pâté, dry sausages, country ham, and sausage en croûte in this attractive uptown shop launched by the restaurant of the same name at Lexington and 62nd St. Good bread, coffee, old-fashioned homemade jams; a bit of everything attractively and very appealingly displayed. Prepared dishes as well.

# Donald Sacks SoHo
**120 Prince St.**
**226-0165**
*Mon. to Fri. 8:00 A.M. to 7:00 P.M.;*
*Sat. and Sun. 11:00 A.M. to*
*6:00 P.M.*

Just across from Dean and Deluca, where Mr. Deluca himself first opened shop, a minuscule boutique consisting of an awning, a refrigerated counter, and a work table, which offers a small range of soups, attractive salads, meat and spinach pies, cookies, and the like, all made on the spot. There are small tables for snacking on the street—the only place where you can do so in SoHo.

# E.A.T.
**1064 Madison Ave.**
**(80th St.)**
**753-5171**
**867 Madison Ave.**
**(72nd St.)**
**879-4017**
*Daily 7:00 A.M. to 7:00 P.M.*
*(1064 Madison Ave. closed Mon.)*

This store, started by the sons of Zabar, is everything nearby Fay and Allen's is not, being on the small side, with a very limited and judicious choice of goods. We should call attention to their excellent caviar, fresh foie gras, a large selection of goat's cheese, a few excellent cakes, and their famous brownies in individual packages. Horribly expensive for no apparent reason: their products are good, but not always better than those found elsewhere at lesser prices; but you'll never be unpleasantly surprised. Home delivery and catering service, for a refined and affluent clientele: probably the only spot in New York for true gourmets.

# Elysée Pastries
**939 First Ave.**
**(52nd St.)**
**755-5858**
*Mon. to Sat. 9:00 A.M. to 6:00 P.M.*

There is a very respectable charcuterie department in this store better known for its pastry: their blood pudding, dry sausage, and garlic sausage are highly recommended, and their homemade pâté is quite acceptable.

## Fay and Allen's Foodhall
**1241 Third Ave. (71st St.) 794-1001**
*Daily to 9:00 P.M.; Sun. 11:00 A.M. to 9:00 P.M.*

Masses of good European products in a block-long store: a world of food from France, Italy, Germany, the USSR . . . foie gras, salmon, prepared dishes, cheese, delicatessen items. The bakery-pastry section is particularly attractive, with ten varieties of chocolate cake (to be expected in a store this size), to say nothing of babkas and breads furnished by thirty different New York bakers. A feast for your eyes—and for your stomach, as there's also an espresso bar with a varied menu. Specializes in jams and gift baskets. If you plan on exploring the store in detail, put on a pair of sturdy shoes.

## Food Emporium
**1331 First Ave. (71st-72nd Sts.) 794-8866**
*Open daily to 9:00 P.M.; Sun. to 6:00 P.M.*

At last a supermarket, recently opened, where it's pleasant to shop and wander. The wares are even better displayed than in some of the finest delicatessens, and their quality is higher than in other supermarkets. European-style counters for meat, fish, and delicatessen goods, where products are cut individually for you, and are not prepackaged. The fresh produce, too, is extremely appetizing, and a salad bar offers tempting takeout items. Is this really a supermarket? It's hard to tell these days, when large grocery stores look more and more like supermarkets, and new-style supermarkets like large grocery stores. Various locations.

## Lorenzo and Maria's Kitchen
**1418 Third Avenue (80th-81st Sts.) 794-1080**
*Open daily to 8:00 P.M.*

To judge by the odors that emanate from the back of the shop where they are made, the attractive and varied dishes created here are undoubtedly the work of another talented Italian. Unfortunately we can't be more specific, because chef Maria, submerged with work for her well-to-do clients, didn't want to let us try any. But our gourmet eye didn't miss the seafood salad next to the lobster bisque, or the ratatouille and salads made of pasta and homemade pâtés, which are surely very good. Shelves crammed with fine products from all over.

## Macy's: The Cellar
**West 34th St. and Broadway 695-4400**
*Mon. to Sat. 9:45 A.M. to 8:30 P.M.; Tues. and Wed. to 6:45 P.M.; Sat. to 6:00 P.M.; Sun. noon to 5:00 P.M.*

A series of boutiques off an arcade. The oversized charcuterie is stocked with everything from cheese and pasta to fresh produce and pastries. The selection of pâtés is excellent, the fragrance of chocolate appealing, and the temptations are endless.

## Pasta and Cheese
**756 Madison Ave. (65th St.) 570-0884**
*Mon. to Fri. 10:00 A.M. to 7:00 P.M., Sun. noon to 6:00 P.M.*

Pasta and Cheese isn't one of the biggies; but then, it's not exactly small either. The number of shops and products offered is constantly increasing, and at a rate that threatens to have an adverse effect on quality. But the general level of the store is quite high. Pasta, fresh daily, and accompanying sauces, are the specialties, but there's also an acceptable (no more) choice of cheese, which varies from store to store, a wide choice of salads, which are good but expensive, and a good range of spices and fine foods. Coffee, bread, and prosciutto as well, all nicely arranged in attractive, modern shops, of which the latest—Third Avenue at 65th St.—has a Lanciani pastry department, and a very pleasing cafe with white marble-topped bistro tables. Unfortunately it's only open until 8:30 P.M. There's another little espresso bar at Bergdorf Goodman's, and you can buy their products at Macy's and Zabar's. Supermarkets will probably not be long in following suit. Other locations throughout the city.

## Salumeria Italiana
**348 E. 62nd St.**
**838-4118**
*Mon. to Sat. 6:00 A.M. to 7:00 P.M.*

A sort of Midtown Little Italy: a small, old-fashioned Italian delicatessen run by a couple of austere Italians who brighten up for their regular customers. At any rate, with a smile or without, they sell a superb prosciutto for $7.95 a pound (it's at least $10.95 everywhere else), lots of different coppa and salamis (mild or spicy), good Italian cheese, and other products from the Peninsula: Perugina chocolates, Marsala, green pasta (prepackaged). We like this modest, unpretentious spot for what it is: the antithesis of Pasta and Cheese.

## Self Chef
**1224 Lexington Ave.**
**(82nd St.)**
**288-8824**
*Mon. to Sat. 10:00 A.M. to 7:00 P.M.*

Philippe Bernard, a Frenchman, long-time resident of New York, has been in this little shop for three years. His prepared dishes are excellent: the boeuf bourguignon, chicken "basquaise," veal marengo and paupiettes of veal are quite obviously the work of no amateur. He stocks as well all kinds of salads, a delicious ham brought in specially from Tennessee, quiche lorraine you bake at home, pâtés from Les 3 Petits Cochons, a good selection of cheese, bread, delicatessen items, and chocolates for dessert, or a deliciously light pumpkin mousse, or "New York ice," sherbets low in calories but high in flavor for the diet-conscious. If you're out for something more substantial, ask for his mealbag: it contains an appetizer, a main course, a dessert, and some French bread for $5 to $10. Free delivery.

## Silver Palate
**274 Columbus Ave.**
**(73rd St.)**
**799-6340**
*Daily 10:30 A.M. to 9:30 P.M.;*
*Sat. and Sun. 10:30 A.M. to*
*7:30 P.M.*

The most attractive and the friendliest spot on the entire West Side, and the best place for lovely salads, pastry, and cookies, as well as a great variety of homemade breads (all sorts, from the more customary to bread made with zucchini, carrots, and cranberries). Also excellent sauces and spices and freshly prepared hot dishes, different ones every day. There was chicken fricasseed in white wine when we visited, as well as roast veal in Marsala, pasta with caviar, and chicken breasts for about $5 per person.

## SoHo Charcuterie
**195 Spring Street**
**226-3545**
*Tues. to Sun. noon to 9:00 P.M.*

Opened three years ago by two Frenchwomen, this was one of the first places to combine a grocery department and a restaurant where you can taste the foods, an arrangement that has since become very popular. Pâtés are their specialties, but also try the salads (shrimp, noodles, and tarragon chicken) at reasonable prices. A spot of greater historical than gastronomical note. There's a branch at Ann Taylor, 3 E. 57th Street.

## Les 3 Petits Cochons
**17 E. 13th St.**
**255-3844**
*Mon. to Fri. 11:00 A.M. to 7:00 P.M.; Sat. 11:00 A.M. to 5:00 P.M.*

Installed by three young Frenchmen in what used to be a hotel, and recently renovated and enlarged, this is the first French charcuterie in New York, and it's excellent. Twelve delicious types of pâté, very reasonably priced ($6.50 to $9.50 per pound)—judged by a New York *Times* critic to be delicious, and then rated terrible when the same critic ate them at a nearby restaurant, not realizing of course where they came from. The favorites are the pâté de campagne, the pâté of duck à l'orange, the pâté forestier (Champagne and cognac), and the mousse of scallops—all made with the best ingredients, without additives and coloring. Nor should we neglect the excellent sausage, the brandade, quiches, salads, and cheeses. And for $3.50 (the price of a mediocre hamburger) you can also pick up an assorted lunch-time platter. The choice is yours. Les 3 Petits Cochons also offers an excellent catering service with hot and cold dishes, cooked on the spot. All are superb.

## Washington Market
**162 Duane St.**
**(between Hudson and West Broadway)**
**233-0250**
*Mon. to Sat. 9:00 A.M. to 9:00 P.M.; Sun. to 7:00 P.M.*

A spacious, very old-fashioned store with very up-to-date merchandise. The young women who opened it in the spring of 1981 haven't forgotten any of the things one looks for in this kind of shop: bread, meat, cheese, coffee, condiments; they have added homemade salads (one of the tastiest ratatouilles), pâtés de campagne, and very agreeable pastry.

## William Poll
**1050 Lexington Ave.**
**(75th St.)**
**288-0501**
*Mon. to Sat. 9:00 A.M. to 6:00 P.M.*

William Poll is really a caterer who offers a takeout service in his store, but we list him in this section because, in our opinion, he doesn't merit any better. Still, he is on a different level from Dover and similar places. Prepared dishes range from vichyssoise in jars to more elaborate items, like moussaka and coq au vin. Let's just say, you have to like them. . . . There are rather good accompanying sauces made with lobster or avocado, but the best things here are the appetizers—miniature quiches and cheese feuilletés, both delicious, and commendable biscuits. There's also a banal choice of cheese, a charcuterie section that seems more interesting (an excellent prosciutto), and well-stocked shelves with the usual imported items. Finally, an exquisite smoked salmon.

## Word of Mouth
**1012 Lexington Ave.**
**(72nd St.)**
**734-9483**
*Mon. to Fri. 10:30 A.M. to 7:00 P.M.; Sat. 10:30 A.M. to 6:00 P.M.; Sun. 11:30 A.M. to 5:30 P.M.*

The dishes are more unusual in tone here—one could say, a reflection of the very varied metropolis: ham with apricots, chicken with lemon, goulash, and lasagna. In addition to a few permanent specialties, there's a rotating menu with certain dishes on specific days, as in any diner, except that they're better here—much better. On the shelves you'll find the usual items, such as Scandinavian bread, French mustard and vinegar (in particular, some made by Corcellet), soups and fresh salads, a small cheese and charcuterie section, and a few desserts, among which we recommend the lemon and chocolate mousses. The spot has been around for a while, but it's none the worse for wear.

## Zabar's
**2245 Broadway (80th St.)**
**787-2000**
*Daily 9:00 A.M. to 7:30 P.M.;*
*Sat. to 10:00 P.M.*

The unbeaten champion amongst the bigger stores in all domains: cheese, herbs, meat, smoked fish, coffee, and tea. Plus a large choice of kitchen utensils, gadgets, and mixers. Relaxed West Side atmosphere, with a clientele from all over. You have to take a number and wait your turn (which gives you time to look over the offerings) and then wait in line to pay (which gives you time to regret what you haven't bought). Unfortunately, Zabar's is losing its intimate neighborhood smallness; it is becoming an industry: too much variety, too many people, too much success, too much everything! But Zabar's is an institution and a landmark for New Yorkers who appreciate good food, quality, and the nicer things in life.

# GOURMET CATERERS

## Délices la Côte Basque
**1032 Lexington Ave.**
**523-3311**
**Olympic Tower**
**635 Fifth Ave.**
**935-2220**

Délices has put together one of the most complete catering services in New York, whether for a buffet or a sit-down dinner. You can select your dishes from the many listed on his menu. His buffet à la française is composed of tasty delicatessen, canapés, vol au vents, quiches, and miniature homemade cakes. (As his kitchens are located at the Olympic Tower, it's wiser to go there when you're giving a full-course meal. For buffets made up of appetizers and pastries, the shop on Lexington Avenue will more than meet your expectations.) $15 per person minimum, which is quite a lot, plus full-service catering.

## Demarchelier Charcuterie
**1460 Lexington Ave. (94th-95th Sts.)**
**722-6600**

In the same style as Les 3 Petits Cochons, but not done quite as well, and at prices short on rustic simplicity. Presentation, service, and quality aren't at all stuffy: your guests will think that you alone are responsible for the meal—and you can take credit without any shame, as the level of cooking is honest (without giving you pretensions to being a Cordon Bleu cook). Cassoulet, spring veal, turbot in tarragon, duck in pepper, mustard chicken, and lamb curry are agreeable. The salads and charcuterie are acceptable, and the desserts (crème caramel, white and dark chocolate mousses, different fruit pies) are all quite good and simple. For special orders (dinners, parties) order 24 hours in advance. Demarchelier will look after everything: service, rental of accessories, whatever you need. A complete caterer.

## Donald Bruce White
**159 E. 64th St.**
**988-8410**

The other name in American catering, and for a long time the only one. He's also a specialist in large private and official receptions. Donald and his young American chef (who studied in France) hold office in two superb old-fashioned brownstones. The cuisine, neither American nor French, is a sort of nouvelle cuisine composed of specialties from around the world. If, for example, you long for couscous, he'll make it for you. Like Glorious Foods, he is known and renowned for his imaginative appetizers and perfect service, whether your party is for thirty or three thousand. His meals are served in magnificent copper dishes, which are as heavy as their contents are light. What more can we say?

## Dover Caterers
142-144 E. 57th St.
759-2570

In terms of the numbers it feeds, Dover is the biggest caterer of them all. In terms of what it serves these hordes, it's no better than a run-of-the-mill delicatessen. But you can eat your fill of relatively inexpensive and banal meat and poultry dishes, simple appetizers, mediocre cheeses, potato salads, and coleslaw. Nothing is particularly good or extraordinarily bad—it's filling, and that's all. Dover will look after everything, from floral arrangements to after-the-feast cleanup. As is to be expected, prices are moderate. If you insist on a modicum of refinement, go elsewhere.

## Glorious Foods
172 E. 75th St.
628-2320

In frenzied competition with its colleague and rival, Donald Bruce White, Glorious Foods presents the best in American cuisine. But although the presentation is extravagantly superb, there's not much to put on your plate, and you won't risk enlarging your waistline with these sophisticated dishes. That doesn't make the menu any less mouth-watering: it's an American version of French cooking (the chef is French), and includes an original breakfast with stuffed crêpes, miniature pies, and scrambled eggs. There's a sit-down dinner for twenty or more ($40 to $60 per person) and cocktails for up to four thousand ($15 to $30 per person). Nothing daunts these professionals: their service staff is impeccable and their kitchens, visible at the back of their duplex, are as white as a laboratory. Glorious Foods will look after everything for you: linen tablecloths and napkins, dishes, and even reception rooms. Truly a top caterer, whose doorway alone (a handsome object in massive sculpted wood) indicates its class. Very much in demand, so reserve in advance.

## Jean Claude Caterers
309 E. 75th St.
726-5300

Another Frenchman who shares his kitchens with Jean Pierre Briand, the major difference being that Jean Claude cooks pastry and desserts in addition to other dishes (he's the owner of Elysée Pastries). It shows in the dishes he makes with doughs and feuilletés: bass en croûte, seafood feuilleté, and Brie en croûte, his true specialty and a supreme success. His cuisine is French in orientation, and fancy: paupiettes of sole, rack of lamb aux fines herbes, filet mignon, and saddle of veal are all done very well; and, for dessert, an assortment of hot and cold soufflés, or sliced crêpes with plums. Like Jean Pierre Briand, he refuses to cook for large numbers: his limit for a cocktail party is three hundred people, and he serves dinner for a minimum of four people (about $30 per person). Neither waiters nor accessories, though: Jean Claude simply cooks.

## Jean Pierre Briand
440 E. 56th St.
753-2872

Quality is the first and sole concern of this Frenchman, a self-made cook, both in the cooking, which he himself prepares aided by a single assistant, and in the service (whether for a buffet or a sit-down dinner)—the table decoration, the quality of accessories, silver serving trays, and luxurious linen. Everything is excellent. He does beef fillets or ham en croûte, preceded by small lobsters or seafood vol au vents for a sit-down dinner (minimum of twelve and maximum of fifty) and for cocktails, he will shrink the best in French cuisine to bite-size: salmon mousse canapés, small bits of seafood, foie gras finger rolls, and mini vol au vents. (For cocktails, Jean Pierre limits his production to three hundred people, with a minimum of forty.) This is no food assembly line, and he's quite right to believe that quantity is rarely compatible with quality. Prices per person for a cocktail reception vary from $5 to $20, for buffets from $12 to $20, and for full meals from $35 to $45. Full service is available, including all accessories, waiters, and wine, at extra cost. His desserts are prepared by his friend and colleague, Jean Claude (see above).

## Madame Germaine
38-09 33rd St.
Long Island City
322-7284

Madame Germaine and her husband Marcel are the best French caterers in New York, along with Jean Pierre Briand. Highly praised by the owner of Lutèce, at whose instigation they settled in the United States twenty years ago, they are caterers of great renown, using styles and methods of cooking that represent classical cuisine at its best. Everything is perfectly prepared, without unnecessary frills. Madame Germaine will serve sixteen to one thousand people: prices available on request. Don't be put off by what can be a slightly off-putting welcome on the part of the "maison"—Mme. Germaine doesn't run after business. She doesn't have to; but she will never scorn a true gourmet.

## La Table du Roi, Inc.
675 Water St.
267-6966

Launched by Cécile Arnett some ten years ago, this small catering enterprise has become one of New York's best. It offers made-to-measure catering—that is to say, Cécile will prepare the dishes you want, assisted by a team of cooks from Brittany, for the number of people you've invited, and in the price range you're looking for. She learned the classic French recipes from her mother and grandmother, and her inventiveness knows no bounds. The beef roulade with green peppercorns and chicken in vinegar "façon Troisgros" are succulent. Her Génoise with fruit, torte with nuts, and soufflé glazed with pralines are but a few of her successful desserts. And if you order a buffet, you'll find all sorts of original canapés and bite-sized delights, tasty and perfectly light. Everything at very reasonable prices: $20 per person (for full service, with accessories and waiter) for a buffet, and $50 for a small get-together. Cécile will also choose and provide wines for you.

## Les 3 Petits Cochons
**17 E. 3rd St.**
**255-3844**

For a more relaxed gathering among friends, try this establishment, the only one of its kind despite innumerable imitations. Its charcuterie and salads are far superior to those of its competitors and make for a fine buffet. The cold-cut and pâté platters are the best New York can offer. As for the cooked dishes, they are classics of French rustic cooking, easy to warm up—in fact, the sort that get better the longer they're reheated: civet of pork, potée savoyarde, blanquette of veal, chicken in vinegar, beef bourguignon, bouillabaisse, cassoulet, and the like. French cooking has no secrets for these chefs, who are also initiates into the fine art of leaving things to simmer on the stove for lengthy periods. The desserts, chocolate mousses and cakes, are of the same style, and everything is moderately priced: about $6 for the daily special, and $12 per person for a full-course meal (appetizer, salad, main course, and dessert). Full service (accessories and waiters) available. There are more sophisticated specialties as well: bass en croûte, stuffed piglet—to be ordered in advance.

# Home

## CHINA AND CRYSTAL

## Baccarat
**55 E. 57th St.**
**826-4100**
*Mon. to Sat. 9:30 A.M. to 5:30 P.M.*

Baccarat has been the crystal of kings for over two centuries—Louis XV of France sponsored the company's foundation in 1764. Its fame has since spread to the four corners of the globe, and Baccarat's premier position in table crystal is undisputed. There is a wide choice of glasses, with stems and without, modern and classic; and the prices, though high, are not impossible ($40 and up). It's a crystal with a particularly high lead content, which makes it unusually sparkling and pure. In addition to its own wares, Baccarat New York also carries the extremely attractive Ercuis silverware, the superb Ceralène porcelain by Limoges, and a complete collection of Les Étains du Manoir pewter services and other objects. A very attractive shop on two floors offering a stunning collection of beautiful French accessories for the table.

## Cardel
**615 Madison Ave.**
**(59th St.)**
**753-8880**
*Mon. to Sat. 10:00 A.M. to 6:00 P.M.*

The perfect shop to leave a marriage list, with silverware by Christofle, porcelain by Limoges and Rosenthal, and crystal by Daum, Lalique, and Saint Louis, as well as vases, fruit bowls, dishes, platters, and glasses. This small, crowded shop could set up a newlywed couple for life—in style.

## Carole Stupel, Ltd.

The quintessence of a certain careful sort of taste: everything in this shop is of very good quality, but nothing

281

**61 E. 57th St.**
**260-3100**
*Mon. to Sat. 9:30 A.M. to 6:00 P.M.*

is inventive. And unfortunately, the taste is sometimes questionable. The mannerist ornamentation on this brand-new porcelain, crystal, and silver is sometimes stuffy, dull. The most famous names are represented here, as well as Carole Stupel's own original creations and sculptures in porcelain, sterling silver, and bronze. Prices are exactly what you'd imagine in a store on 57th St. near Madison! A luxury boutique for cautious souls.

## Finkelstein's
**95 Delancey St.**
**(Orchard St.)**
**475-1420**
*Sun. to Fri. 9:30 A.M. to 5:00 P.M.*

Finkelstein's has been selling imported crystal at reductions of up to 50 percent for over sixty years. Unfortunately, things aren't the way they used to be, and the big names in French crystal are now unavailable in good condition. Very pretty German and Polish crystal, and some Chinese porcelain.

## Richard Ginori
**711 Fifth Ave.**
**(55th-56th Sts.)**
**752-8790**
*Mon. to Sat. 10:00 A.M. to 6:00 P.M.*

An Italian boutique, but totally devoid of Italian charm. The layout of this immense store and the display of the merchandise, are conventional to the point of being boring. There are, it's true, some pretty things—the Murano vases and some good French crystal (St. Louis, Daum, Lalique, Baccarat). And there are also the friendly salesladies who help brighten up the place a bit.

## Robin Importers
**510 Madison Ave.**
**(52nd-53rd Sts.)**
**735-6475**
*Mon. to Fri. 9:00 A.M. to 6:00 P.M.;*
*Sat. 10:00 A.M. to 5:00 P.M.*

Good buys in the heart of Madison. This shop doesn't look promising from the outside, but it's the nicest surprise in the district. Everything by way of tableware can be had at discounts that vary from 20 to 60 percent: tablecloths and napkins, porcelain from France (Limoges), Japan, and elsewhere, modern stainless steel cutlery, ovenproof dishes, all in excellent taste, and some really out of the ordinary. They also carry Melior coffee-makers, and can replace broken glasses. They are full of attractive, practical, and advantageously priced items. A best bet in New York.

## Royal Copenhagen Porcelain/ Georg Jensen Silversmiths
**683 Madison Ave.**
**(61st St.)**
**759-6457**
*Mon. to Sat. 9:00 A.M. to 5:00 P.M.*

Danish luxury and refinement reign in a large and tranquil shop. The crystal and porcelain are beautiful, simple, and in the modern mode, and everything, of course, is exclusive. Georg Jensen silverware is another expression of Danish taste—very stylish too, and, very expensive.

## Steuben Glass
**715 Fifth Ave.**
**(56th St.)**
**752-1441**
*Mon. to Sat. 9:30 A.M. to 5:30 P.M.*

Steuben crystal is highest ranked in the United States, perhaps in the world. Its Fifth Avenue showroom is beautiful, and the objects displayed there are admirably simple and of extraordinary quality. Don't miss the red room at the back, where glass sculptures are displayed; pieces whose prices we daren't list. But everything is skillful and inventive. Go elsewhere for wine glasses—here you'll find crystal animals, vases, chandeliers, fruit bowls, or superb bowls like the official wedding present from the United States to Prince Charles and Lady Diana.

# FABRICS

## B & J Fabrics
**263 W. 40th St.**
**221-9287**
*Mon. to Fri. 8:00 A.M. to 5:45 P.M.;*
*Sat. 9:00 A.M. to 4:45 P.M.*

The best spot in New York for fabrics: everything is of the finest quality, and designed by the big names: Anne Klein, Calvin Klein, Perry Ellis, Valentino, Dior. (It should be pointed out that, unlike some other "designers'" fabric stores, the designs here are the latest styles, and not last season's.) Prices are neither particularly high nor particularly low, and the service is uncommonly cordial.

## Fabrications
**145 E. 56th St.**
**371-3370**
*Mon. to Sat. 10:00 A.M. to 6:00 P.M.*

This is the finest fabric store imaginable, a carnival of colors that is a pleasure for the eye, and a danger to the pocketbook. All fabrics are pure imported cotton, and their nursery collection is particularly delightful, with designs of hearts, animals, balloons, and rainbows. The same designs are used on pillows and toys, and you can also buy framed fabric panels, ready-made or in do-it-yourself kits, with charming patterns and at very reasonable prices. Another attraction is the superb collection of Indonesian, Malaysian, and Dutch batiks at the back of the store ($10 to $16 a yard) and the very popular country French printed patterns at equally modest prices, which are wide enough to allow you to make tablecloths and curtains at low cost. The headquarters for up-to-date handypeople.

## Laura Ashley
**715 Madison Ave.**
**(63rd St.)**
**371-0606**
*Mon. to Fri. 10:00 A.M. to 6:00 P.M.*

Laura Ashley's popular prints have conquered the globe, and this is her new outpost. A recent addition: the home furnishings department on the top floor of this small townhouse offers all delicate floral and geometric cottons, as well as matching wallpaper, lampshades, and floor and wall tiles, for the discreetly romantic Laura Ashley look. Moderate prices.

## Liberty of London
**229 E. 60th St.**
**888-1057**
*Mon. to Sat. 10:00 A.M. to 6:00 P.M.*

What could we possibly say that you don't already know about these prints with which the best brought-up little girls are so prettily clothed? We will only add that the shop itself is charming, full of small Liberty accessories, upholstery, dress fabrics, and a superb collection of glazed chintz, whose decorative effect is especially lovely (about $18 a yard). Also a few smocked dresses ($80 to $120) that seem to come straight out of nursery rhymes.

## Marimekko
**7 W. 56th St.**
**581-9616**
*Mon. to Fri. 10:00 A.M. to*
*6:30 P.M.; Sat. to 6:00 P.M.*

You can feel the Nordic influence in this very quiet and stylized shop that displays carved wooden objects, rustic clothing, and attractive accessories—all rather expensive—by this well-known Finnish designer. There is also a very cheerful children's department and the famous line of linen, fabrics, and wallpaper in modern, simple, and colorful patterns, which so quickly captured a large part of the market. Printed cotton: $17 a yard. Sheets with floral or children's patterns: $15 (double size). A very attractive spot, if a bit melancholy and cold.

## Pierre Deux
**870 Madison Ave.**
**(71st St.)**
**570-9343**
**369 Bleecker St.**
**675-4054**
*Mon. to Sat. 10:00 A.M. to 6:00 P.M.*

New York's own bit of sunny Provence, superbly located in a ravishing, country French-styled shop that stocks traditional Provençal printed fabrics by Souleiado, with colorful interlocking patterns, mostly in cotton but also in silk and challis ($15 to $21 a yard) sold with coordinated border prints ($3 to $4.50 a yard). Also a striking collection of accessories made from their fabrics, such as cosmetic bags, address books, and frames, and a children's section filled with expensive but very pretty clothing and toy animals. The clothing section includes a fine selection of shawls, perhaps the best way to wear the vivid Provençal colors.

# ═══ FURNITURE ═══

## Ambienti
**792 Madison Ave.**
**(near 67th St.)**
**249-2811**
*Mon. to Sat. 10:00 A.M. to 5:30 P.M.; Thur. to 7:00 P.M.*

The best dealer in Italian design since its famous rival, Abitare, went out of business. It offers exclusive, simple, and beautiful pieces in superb materials, and while the choice is quite limited (consisting mostly of tables and chairs), there is a varied selection of lamps and home furnishings of handsome quality: crystal salad bowls by Carlo Moretti, marvelously light, handmade alderwood platters, and various steel objects with a matte finish—purity at a price.

## Art et Industrie
**464 W. Broadway**
**(Prince St.)**
**777-3660**
*Tues. to Sat. noon to 7:00 P.M.*

It's difficult to define this unusual spot. Is it, one wonders, a furniture store or a gallery? In fact, it's a bit of both: "high-tech chic" you might say, furniture of the future, inventive, sometimes even creative and colorful. So we'll leave it to you to make up your mind. But at any rate, don't miss it.

## Bien Amié
**231 E. 51st St.**
**688-4643**
*Mon. to Sat. 10:00 A.M. to 7:00 P.M.; Sun. noon to 5:00 P.M.*

Drafting tables ($150 to $300), retractable and extendable tables, folding wooden chairs ($20), classic oak, walnut, and teak shelving. No unusually pleasant surprises—until you get to the cash register. While you're in the neighborhood, look around: the block on 51st Street between Second and Third Avenues is, on the whole, very good for furniture.

## Bon Marché
**55 W. 13th St.**
**620-5550**
**1060 Third Ave.**
**(62nd-63rd Sts.)**
**620-5592**
*Mon. to Sat. 10:00 A.M. to 6:30 P.M.; Mon. and Thur. evenings*

They specialize in wall units, such as bookshelves and desks, mostly in formica. It's all very simple design, nothing extraordinary; but it is sturdy. Attractive glass items, vases, bibelots, and a very good choice of lamps make this our favorite inexpensive shop.

## Brancusi
**1001 Fifth Ave.**
**(55th St.)**

Acceptable, but no more, with an immense selection of tables in every material: glass, stainless steel, chrome, brass, and wrought iron. Chrome mirrors, lamps, and shelves too. Nothing is that bad, but the store itself is so

**688-7980**
*Mon. to Sat. 9:30 A.M. to 6:00 P.M.*

## Conran's
**160 E. 53rd St.**
**(Citicorp Center)**
**371-2225**
*Mon. to Fri. 10:00 A.M. to
9:00 P.M.; Sat. 9:00 A.M. to
6:00 P.M.; Sun. noon to 6:00 P.M.*

## Maurice Villency/ Roche Bobois
**200 Madison Ave.**
**(35th St.)**
**725-4840**
*Mon. to Sat. 10:00 A.M. to
6:00 P.M.; Sun. noon to 5:00 P.M.*

## Mondrian
**1021 Second Ave.**
**(55th St.)**
**355-7373**
*Mon. to Fri. 10:00 A.M. to
7:00 P.M.; Sat. to 6:00 P.M.*

## Wicker Garden
**1318 Madison Ave.**
**(93rd St.)**
**348-1166**
*Mon. to Sat. 10:00 A.M. to 6:00 P.M.*

## Workbench
**470 Park Ave.**
**(32nd St.)**
**481-5454**
*Mon. to Sat. 10:00 A.M. to
6:00 P.M.; Sun. noon to 5:00 P.M.*

dreary it's hard to imagine what the stuff will look like at home.

After London, Paris, and Brussels, New York finally got its own Conran's some four years ago; that is to say, its own inexhaustible supply of furniture, accessories, fabrics, linen, and kitchen equipment, simple in design, easy to live with, and moderately priced. Everything is appealing here, from their collection of sofas, tables, bookshelves, and beds to their children's desks, bunk beds, and folding chairs. The home furnishings department, with its glasses, cutlery, dishes, vases, spices and soaps, lamps, handmade rugs, diaries, and potpourris, is no less fetching. It's hard to walk out empty handed and at these prices, you won't want to.

Good quality furniture whose discreet style has been earning plaudits for many years now. The ground floor has stylized furniture in beautiful materials: leather sofas ($3,300 for three-seated models), Italian marble tables and attractive modern lacquer beds, all clashing somewhat with the American and Scandinavian furniture. The merchandise, however, is obviously extremely well made· Villency is doubtless the most pleasant furniture store in New York, as its relatively high prices attest.

Formerly Furniture in the Raw, Mondrian has been transformed into a superb shop, the most serious spot in New York for built-to-order natural wood or lacquer furniture. They carry few models, and those they have are simple in style and fit in easily with most decors. The colors of their lacquer, too, are superb, very *House and Garden*. As for the wood—oak and maple—it's constructed to your dimensions and colored according to your wishes. They will also put on an outer layer of formica, but this is more expensive and less elegant. Good-quality shelving, wall units, beds, and children's furniture, and magnificent color coordinates at very moderate prices.

A very Victorian atmosphere reigns in this realm of beautifully displayed, beribboned white wickerwork, in which your eye doesn't know where to alight next among the irresistable pastel colors. There are beds, cradles, rocking chairs, and other antique or new objects plus, on the 2nd floor, a children's section, the Wicker Garden's Baby. A paradise for wicker wackies.

Modern, all-purpose furniture in maple, oak, and teak, simplified to the point of the rudimentary, without the slightest ornamentation, at prices that are also very spare. Less quality than Conran's, but better than at many others. Nothing is in bad taste, because it's functional, well conceived, and colorful (which makes up a bit for its coldness). A few sofas upholstered with attractive fabrics. Various locations.

# GIFTS

## Accents et Images
1020 Second Ave.
(54th St.)
838-3431
*Mon. to Fri. 11:00 A.M. to
7:00 P.M.; Sat. to 6:00 P.M.*

Chic, expensive, classic, or bizarre luxury items in a shop that imports its entire stock from Europe. A mixture of unusual articles, many without the slightest interest: decorated dishes, perfumes, fussy trifles, silver frames, address books, ties, and a section of crystal including vases and cups at prices much higher than Tiffany's. The sort of shop you see in hotels and airports for last-minute obligations—at a price.

## Air Import and Export Corp.
17 E. 45th St.
*Mon. to Fri. 8:30 A.M. to 7:00 P.M.;
Sat. to 6:00 P.M.*

This store, which caters to tourists, has an assortment at prices better than at airports and in most specialized shops: Cross and Parker pens; Rayban sunglasses; Samsonite luggage; Wilson, Head, and Spalding metal tennis racquets; roller skates; extra-thin and cordless telephones; a large selection of 220-volt electrical appliances; watches; calculators. A very useful and, above all, a very central shop.

## Any Occasion
209 Columbus Ave.
(69th St.)
580-1049
*Mon. to Sat. 11:00 A.M. to
8:00 P.M.; Sun. 1:00 P.M. to
5:00 P.M.*

Every kind of small gift for the house, the most attractive being the vases in molten glass and silver. In the basement, amusing cards and writing paper. The spot to pick up some pretty presents without ruining yourself ($10 to $40 on the average).

## Barbi International
655 Madison Ave.
(60th St.)
421-4580
*Mon. to Sat. 10:00 A.M. to 6:00 P.M.*

Luxury reigns as undisputed master in this richly carpeted shop, where things are at times a bit heavy, but always elegant, and everything is Italian from A to Z. We particularly admired their Murano vases and glass chandeliers, the simple, heavy porcelain eggs, the gold- and silver-plated frames, and above all the superb glass tables with twisted porcelain supports ringed with metal. A line of sofas, made to measure in rich fabrics, at prices we daren't mention.

## Carrington
854 Madison Ave.
(70th St.)
737-9700
*Mon. to Sat. 10:00 A.M. to
6:00 P.M.*

"Decorative art for the home" is how the young owner defines Carrington. Everything here is handmade, from the dishes and pottery to the low lacquered glass-top tables, which are original and expensive ($2,250 for the medium size), not to mention an attractive collection of glassware, silk and hide pillows, upholstered chairs, strange umbrella holders made of stag's antlers, and the most beautiful object in the entire shop, a round mirror framed in parchment skin—for only $3,250! A very interesting place all the same.

## Cherchez
864 Lexington Ave.
(65th St.)
737-0215
*Mon. to Sat. 11:00 A.M. to 6:00 P.M.*

Cherchez has recently expanded: from an oversized cupboard it has grown into an attic, and the quality hasn't suffered from the diversification. In addition to its classic potpourris, Victorian clothing, and paisley shawls, it now offers such attractive gift items as English soaps, French ribbons, knitted baby toys, stationery designed for the store, some food delicacies, and above all a line of handmade Shetland and mohair sweaters made for them in subtle colors, whose style transcends the whims of fashion, and whose prices are entirely fair ($150 to $300 for a real jacket). Cherchez will not disappoint: it's an exquisite boutique that evades classification.

## Ellen O'Neill's Supply Store
**251 E. 77th St.**
**879-7330**
*Mon. to Sat. 11:00 A.M. to 7:00 P.M.*

A mini-boutique for mini-gifts: baskets, dolls' clothing and tea sets, pencils, pearls, objets d'art—everything is miniature, and displayed on tiny shelves or in minuscule drawers. There are also a few antique quilts and dresses—normal-sized. Nice.

## The Glass Store
**1242 Madison Ave. (89th St.)**
**289-1970**
*Mon. to Sat. 10:00 A.M. to 6:00 P.M.*

A stunning store for glass and crystal. Each article is made in a limited number of copies by craftsmen, some of whom work exclusively for this gallery. There are vases, dishes, paperweights, animals, marbles, buttons, eggs, glass in every shape and in every color. There are also modern works by Baccarat, Daum, and Lalique, as well as attractive jewelry made by Maggie Lane using art deco pearls.

## Gonon
**643 W. 57th St.**
**586-6477**
*Mon. to Fri. 9:00 A.M. to 6:00 P.M.;*
*Sat. to 4:00 P.M.*

A jumble of a bazaar beside the Hudson, where the well-informed buy briefcases, linen (a wide assortment), socks (much more solid than those from Brooks Brothers, which immediately slip down around your ankles), Rayban sunglasses, Samsonite luggage; in short, a variety of objects at prices that make the journey worthwhile. Another Gonon has just opened in the Lexington Hotel at the corner of Lexington Avenue and 48th Street, in the heart of Manhattan, but to get to it you have go through gloomy halls with dirty linoleum, and your destination is not much more inviting. But it's handy for business people in a *very* great rush (Gonon East, 755-4400, ext. 321).

## The Mad Monk
**500 Sixth Ave. (12th St.)**
**242-6678**
*Daily from 11:00 A.M. to 7:00 P.M.; Sun. from noon*

A superb celebration of the potter's art: over a hundred craftsmen work for this gallery, which actually buys their products and doesn't simply sell them. The store is full of inventiveness and variety, and you're invited to touch the works—in itself a rarity. The prices are as varied as the pottery, ranging from $10 to $20 for vases, teapots, and goblets, to more than $1,000 for Georges Hausen's mirrors decorated with bizarre animals.

## Mixed Company
**133 E. 57th St.**
**751-0569**
*Mon. to Sat. 10:30 A.M. to 7:00 P.M.; Christopher Street: Mon. to Fri. 10:30 A.M. to 10:00 P.M.; Weekends to midnight*

Wonderful gadgetery: a realm of multicolor, multiform, multipurpose inventions whose taste ranges from the vulgar (decorative underwear, breast-shaped bells) to the rococo (bird-and cloud-shaped lamps, music boxes) to the inventive (luminous neon panels). Posters, stickers, brooches, cards, decals, pillows, and so on to infinity. Their newest shop, on Christopher Street, carries higher-class materials, such as the attractive ceramic objects created by the painter John Baeder, including boxes in the shapes of theaters, cafes, and the like ($17 to $60). Various locations.

## The Museum Shop
**11 W. 53rd St.**
**956-7544, 956-7545**
*Daily 11:00 A.M. to 5:45 P.M.*

Don't miss this spot close to the Museum of Modern Art if you like simple, modern, and exclusive items, and are willing to pay for them. In addition to art books and posters, they sell the design collection founded by MOMA thirty years ago, which now numbers over two thousand items (some of which are no longer available), most of them copies of Bauhaus designs or creations by contemporary artists. There's a wealth of ideas, whether you're looking for a pretty china bowl, door handles in black rubber, a stylized aluminum platter, unusual gadgets, or simply a tote bag. Very variable prices, but on the whole rather high.

## My Rich Uncle Harry
**1452 Second Ave. (76th St.)**
**734-6666**
*Mon. to Sat. 10:30 A.M. to 7:00 P.M.*

An inexpensive and bizarre assortment of sundries is displayed on iron shelves in this friendly high-tech shop. There's a bit of everything: golden socks, cards, floating crap games, and diverse gadgets, few in number and very low in price.

## Mythology
**370 Columbus Ave.**
**874-0774**
*Mon. to Fri. 11:00 A.M. to 7:00 P.M.; weekends to 6:00 P.M.*

Take the time to inspect the multitude of objects gathered in this small shop: the most interesting are unquestionably the old and new metal toys, and the rubber stamps shaped like letters of the alphabet, animals, and other designs—this is probably the biggest collection in the world. But that's not all: there are also extremely beautiful masks from South America, India, and Ceylon, posters by well-known Japanese and American artists, T-shirts designed especially for the shop, kites, books, and a plethora of attractive objects classified by theme (space, food, magic, education). A high-quality shop that organizes such events as book autographing sessions and, several times a year, exhibitions dealing with a certain theme.

## Only Hearts
**281 Columbus Ave. (73rd St.)**
**724-5608**
*Mon. to Sat. 11:00 A.M. to 7:00 P.M.*

Say it with hearts. Everything in the shop is under the sign of the heart: glasses, pencils, small boxes, brushes, stationery, sweatshirts, lollipops, plates, rattan chairs and waffle irons, and some, with a daring disregard for anatomical realities, situated on garters and undergarments.

## Petit Loup
**107 Columbus Ave. (66th-67th Sts.)**
**873-5358**
*Mon. to Sat. 11:00 A.M. to 8:00 P.M.; Sun. 10:00 A.M. to 6:00 P.M.*

This minuscule, all-white boutique on the West Side is brimming with excellent inexpensive gifts and gadgets you won't find anywhere else, as they're exclusive to this shop and come directly from Japan. How could anyone resist the cushions wrapped in plastic that you would swear were candy wrappers? Or, for that matter, the animal-shaped bags (the Lacoste crocodile is particularly cute)? In short, how could anyone walk out without something sure to provoke pleasure? A charming spot.

## Pottery Plus
**1455 Third Ave.**
**(82nd St.)**
**650-9846**
*Daily 11:00 A.M. to 9:00 P.M.*

You're likely to be slightly overwhelmed by the extraordinary array of bizarre and sundry articles when you walk into this shop—how can you not feel lost? You've come to look at beautiful pottery, and everywhere there are only the ugliest items. . . . Well, look again, because there are pretty things as well: oven dishes, vases, large flower pots, mugs and teapots, all made in California; hand-painted clothing, mirrors, lamps, jewelry, crammed into a little showcase. All in all, a muddle of objects ranging from the ugliest to the okay, and the whimsical staff make this shop quite fun—even with its questionable taste.

## Ribbons and Rolls
**190 Columbus Ave.**
**(69th St.)**
**362-2482**
*Mon. to Sat. noon to 7:00 P.M.*

Miles of ribbons and forests of silky, shiny, and multicolor wrapping-paper rolls. That's all they sell in this narrow shop devoted to the fine art of gift wrapping. For $2 and up, materials not included, you can have your gifts made up into the most inventive objects. Or, if you prefer, just buy the paper and ribbon and do it yourself.

## Romano Paris-Rome Outlet Shop
**628 W. 45th St.**
**581-4248**
*Mon. to Fri. 8:00 A.M. to 5:30 P.M.;*
*Sat. to 4:30 P.M.*

On the waterfront, Romano sometimes offers absolute treasures at unbeatable prices—if you're lucky. Saint-Laurent, Dior, and Cardin bags, luggage, and umbrellas at great discounts. Real buys on Seiko and Rolex watches and Japanese electric lighters. One small problem: when cargo-laden ships have docked and the warehouse is full, it's difficult to move around all the merchandise.

## Sherman and Mixon
**404 Columbus Ave.**
**(79th St.)**
**724-6904**
*Mon. to Sat. noon to 6:30 P.M.*

A bazaar-like shop crowded with all kinds of treasures old and new, where the late nineteenth-and early twentieth-century glasses particularly caught our eye. There are also some charming music boxes, lots of glassware, a few signed, framed lithographs, and an attractive array of items in a wide range of prices.

## S and M Mariners Supply
**651 W. 42nd St.**
**594-0276**
*Mon. to Fri. 9:00 A.M. to 4:30 P.M.;*
*Sat. to 2:30 P.M.*

Located almost on the waterfront, across from the Greyhound Bus Terminal. Ask for Sam, the owner, who'll point out the special of the day: Parker pens, luggage, cameras, Polaroid sunglasses, pocket calculators, cosmetics, Head tennis racquets. The more valuable items are kept in the basement, but Sam or another employee will show them to you. Prices, already rather good, are negotiable.

## Sointu
**20 E. 69th St.**
**579-9449**
*Mon. to Sat. 10:00 A.M. to*
*10:00 P.M.*

Modern, highly stylized objects of Scandinavian inspiration, made from simple materials (metal, wood, glass) in resolutely modern and audacious forms at unflinchingly high prices.

## U.N. Gift Center
**United Nations**
**First Ave. at 45th St.**
**basement level**
**754-7700**
*Daily 9:45 A.M. to 5:30 P.M.*

You must take the time to browse here when you visit the United Nations: gifts, jewelry, and crafts from the four corners of the world are sold and—a nice detail—sold without the 8.25 percent local tax.

# HOUSEWARES/KITCHEN

## Bazaars de la Cuisine
**1003 Second Ave.**
**(53rd St.)**
**421-8028**
*Mon. to Sat. 10:00 A.M. to*
*6:00 P.M.*

Everything for the house and garden: an absolutely remarkable and economical array of imported (Chinese, Japanese, Italian) and domestic articles displayed in every nook and cranny of this large store. Their house and garden furniture, frames, lamps, china, and tableware are all modern and very pleasing. Look here first.

## Bridge Kitchenware
**214 E. 52nd St.**
**688-4220**
*Mon. to Fri. 9:00 A.M. to 5:30 P.M.;*
*Sat. 10:00 A.M. to 5:00 P.M.*

Professionals and amateurs alike are absolutely unanimous that this is the best-stocked store for top-quality kitchen equipment this side of the Atlantic. It's a huge showroom offering the finest in kitchenware: copper and earthenware dishes, French oven-proof porcelain, baking supplies, bowls, pots, graters, coffee-makers, appliances, pastry brushes, all presented in the most functional, and at the same time attractive, manner possible. An entire wall is covered with the world's best knives and there's also a fine display of copper casseroles—it's a magnificent selection of useful items at more than reasonable prices. Browsers are barely tolerated here: this isn't Bloomingdale's and the salespeople, though fairly pleasant, don't waste time on people who can't make up their minds.

## La Cuisinière
**867 Madison Ave.**
**(72nd St.)**
**861-4475**
*Mon. to Sat. 10:00 A.M. to 6:00*
*P.M.*

Alas, the window promises more than the shop itself delivers. It's true that there's a pretty assortment of French earthenware from Gien et Lunéville, a little Wedgwood and Minton, some classic ceramic and iron cookware, and a variety of other kitchen appurtenances—and even some antique English dishes and plates. The welcome is friendly but, in our opinion, this is no more than a chic neighborhood store, not worthy of the fuss people make over it.

## Hammacher Schlemmer/ Plummer McCutcheon
**145 E. 57th St.**
**421-9000**
*Mon. to Sat. 10:00 A.M. to*
*6:00 P.M.*

Gadget heaven: from the smallest to the biggest, the most useful to the most superfluous, the most dear to the cheapest, the most charming to the most egregious. The entire building is devoted to inventions and finds: remote-control car starters, barbecues, vacuum cleaners, jukeboxes, very unusual dishes, Dresden porcelain figures, and oversized hangers for fur coats (unavailable elsewhere).

An entire floor (the 5th) is given over to patent models, all sorts of prototypes are presented in their original packages, even some that date back to the nineteenth century—a true curiosity, like the rest of the store and its catalogue. A rather mediocre welcome, unfortunately, but the store doesn't have to try harder; its reputation is unassailable. Recommended for wedding registry for couples who appreciate original ideas.

## Hoffritz
**331 Madison Ave.
(43rd St.)
697-7344**
*Mon. to Sat. 9:00 A.M. to 5:45 P.M.*

Scissors to cut fabric, paper, nails, hair—these are familiar enough, and you'll find them here, amidst an inventory of the most exotic and ingenious varieties imaginable: scissors for cutting double-knit polyester fabrics, super-speedy scissors, silhouette scissors, or scissors for cutting ribbons. You've probably never seen many of these before, nor ever have any use for them, but they are delightfully inventive. Various locations.

## Johnny Jupiter
**385 and 392
Bleecker St.
(11th St.)
741-1507**
*Tues. to Sun. noon to 7:00 P.M.*

A charming shop for utensils, pots, and other objects—antique (1920–1950) and modern—and jokes, gadgets, and tricks. Everything is unusual, astonishing, and particularly well priced. Enamel plates are only about $3.50, painted clay water pitchers about $11, teapots that play "Tea for Two" are $23, vegetable-shaped notepads $1.10, and art deco lamps $20. There's a section for painted tin toys, jokes and tricks, and very amusing 1930s antiques in the shop at 385 Bleecker Street. But make sure you visit both shops, each as delightful as the other, and both ideal if you're trying to avoid stereotyped industrial design or expensive antiques.

## Pampered Kitchens
**21 E. 10th St.
982-0340**
*Mon. to Fri. 1:00 to 7:00 P.M.;
Sat. 10:00 A.M. to 6:00 P.M.*

A store of long standing that offers items both beautiful and functional—a rare combination. Plus a collection of antique copper instruments, pottery and baskets handmade by craftsmen internationally. A charming and distinctive shop.

## Pottery Barn
**117 E. 59th St.
741-9132**
*Mon. to Sat. 10:00 A.M. to
6:30 P.M. (Mon. and Thur. to
8:30 P.M.), Sun. noon to 5:00 P.M.*

These stores are the most popular for rustic and semicrystal glasses, stoneware, china, and earthenware dishes, various accessories and the latest gadgets, because it's one of the most modern and best stocked with a wide range of inexpensive items. Excellent remainders, seconds, plus four drastic sales per year (especially at the warehouse, 231 Tenth Avenue).

## Spice Market
**265 Canal St.
(Broadway)
966-1310**
*Mon. to Fri. 8:00 A.M. to 5:30 P.M.;
Sat. to 4:45 P.M.; Sun. from
10:00 A.M.*

Everything to enable you to cook well: herbs and spices as well as a large selection of kitchen appliances and espresso machines—at discount prices (it goes without saying in this neighborhood). Particularly good selection of copper and aluminum utensils.

## Turpon and Sanders
**386 West Broadway
925-4040**
*Tues. to Sun. 11:00 A.M. to
7:00 P.M.*

Aesthetics takes precedence over all else here: quite simply, this is a superb shop, one of the immense SoHo lofts where it's so pleasant to stroll, to take your time making a selection far from the madding cries of the department stores and uptown shops. Every item here, be it the simplest (like an earthenware bowl) or the humblest (a broom) is admirably and elegantly (and sometimes amusingly) displayed. There's an attractive housewares section, with such items as simple white china (the sort used in restaurants), giant glass fruit bowls, magnificent simple vases, classic appliances and espresso machines as well as superb diabolical inventions for uncorking bottles and doing all sorts of other things. A section of household goods looks like a super-realist painting, with giant brushes, pure Marseille soap, and various gadgets. Everything is beautiful and tempting— and rather expensive, as you'd expect for this quality and design.

# LIGHTING

Among the department stores, Bloomingdale's lighting department ranks first. It offers a wide variety of models, from modern to traditional, domestic and imported, standard lamps, table lamps and hanging lamps—although none are particularly outstanding. It is, alas, on the whole pretty difficult to find attractive lamps in New York, as, here too, interior decorators jealously maintain control of the best. We offer a few stores that are above average.

## Bon Marché Lamps and Accessories
**74 Fifth Ave.**
**(13th St.)**
**620-5559**
*Mon. to Sat. 10:30 A.M. to 6:30 P.M.*

Aside from the avenue bazaars you won't find any less expensive outlet for modern lamps in New York. Lamps for the office, living room, children's rooms, lamps that stand on desk tops, hang from the wall, stand up, and clamp down—there are lamps here for every use, in every color and every style. Another location at 1060 Third Avenue, 620-5592.

## George Kovacs Lighting
**831 Madison Ave.**
**(near 69th St.)**
**861-9500**
*Mon. to Sat. 10:00 A.M. to 6:00 P.M.*

Well-designed contemporary models in a wide range of prices, but are never very high because nothing is of the highest quality. George Kovacs has an obvious affection for Japanese paper lamps, flexible mountings, and Oriental styles of the sort you see copied in all the department stores and neighborhood bazaars and shops. His models are simple and pleasant, devoid of anything particularly winning or attention-grabbing, except for an occasional nice detail or an unusual shape which, we hope, will stand up to use.

## Light Inc.
**1162 Second Ave.**
**(61st St.)**
**838-1130**
*Mon. to Fri. 10:00 A.M. to 6:00 P.M.; Sat. noon to 5:00 P.M.*

Anyone wishing to let there be light would do well to start at this shop, which is by far the most splendid modern lamp store in New York. If you like styles that are both inventive and aesthetically pleasing, unusual models, stylized forms, contemporary in design, you'll find what you're looking for here. Some of their lamps (most of which are imported from France and Italy) are decorative, others more traditional; but none are banal. A full line of track lighting as well, everything at designers' prices.

## Murano Glass
**217 E. 60th St.**
**838-2770**
*Mon. to Sat. 11:00 A.M. to 7:00 P.M.*

If you prefer romanticism to high tech, and prize craft-work above mass production, you owe it to yourself to pay at least one visit to this delicious boutique, which offers imported Italian lighting still made in Murano according to the famous seventeenth-century methods. The store is a pure enchantment of forms and colors, and even if you don't particularly like their ornate style, you'll admire the amount of work they represent. The hanging lamps look like spring bouquets of incomparable freshness and delicacy—everything here is an homage to glass, to its delicacy and transparency. It is nothing short of stunning. As for the prices, though high, they are far from being excessive.

# LINEN

In addition to the better department stores, we offer these good addresses.

## Beron
**745 Fifth Ave.**
**(57th-58th Sts.)**
**753-6700**
*Mon. to Sat. 9:30 A.M. to 5:30 P.M.*

This boutique sells bed, bath, and table linen of perfect quality. Virtually all of their patterns are exclusive, handmade for them in their own workshops—superb workmanship. The linen is not any the less seductive for its classicism, and the large flowers and wild birds embroidered on napkins, sheets, and tablecloths are decorative. Count on a minimum of $450 for a set of king-size bed linen, and $500 and up for twelve place settings. But there are also less extraordinary sets of bed linen at competitive prices. Also: a very old-fashioned lingerie department.

## Brookhill
**695 Madison Ave.**
**(62nd-63rd Sts.)**
**2nd floor**
**688-1113**
*Mon. to Sat. 10:00 A.M. to 6:00 P.M.*

Although the decor is a bit too modern for our taste this is still an attractive beige shop for fine Victorian-style linen made with both old and new lace. Pillowcases and bedspreads are the specialty, and you can choose from a large selection of lace and ribbons to have your dream pillow ($15 to $150) or coverlet ($275 to $335) made to order, if you don't find it in their ready-made collection. You can even bring in your own family lace. Waiting time three to eight weeks.

## Descamp's
**723 Madison Ave.**
**(near 64th St.)**
**355-2522**
*Mon. to Sat. 10:00 A.M. to 6:00 P.M.*

Easy French chic, unpretentious, good quality, and honestly priced: that is, the Primrose Bordier style, personal but discreet, simple but varied, elegant but reserved. The style is obviously popular because by the end of '82 Descamp's will have almost twenty shops across the United States, offering goods suitable for modern living that aren't too standardized. The fine floral patterns are charming, the new somewhat more masculine line is particularly well conceived, and the accessories for babies and young children are absolutely delicious. Everything is very agreeably displayed in shops that are in the process of becoming a sort of trademark in the U.S. All-purpose linen, not yet for everyone.

## E. Braun & Company
**717 Madison Ave.**

Just a bit up Madison from Maison Henri, another traditional and honorable linen shop that also specializes in made-to-measure orders. The atmosphere is not

**(63rd-64th Sts.)**
**838-0650**
*Mon. to Fri. 10:00 A.M. to 6:00 P.M.*

marked by unbridled gaiety—nor is the linen—but it's of irreproachable quality. This is not the place to go for floral-pattern percales, or for extremely sophisticated embroidery—but rather, for good-quality machine-embroidered cotton or flannelette winter sheets ($45 king-size), for made-to-measure sheets for beds of unusual shapes and sizes, or for lace and macramé tablecloths. The style of service and quality swim against the present current of fashion.

**Frette**
**787 Madison Ave.**
**(67th St.)**
**988-5221**
*Mon. to Sat. 10:00 A.M. to 6:00 P.M.*

Frette means Italian quality and luxury, the beauty and refinement of Venice, high style and class. There's no trace whatsoever here of synthetic fibers: piqués, silks, and cottons have the place of honor, in a quality unavailable elsewhere and at prices that defy all competition: $460 for a set of cotton damask satin queen-size sheets, and $490 for king-size, or $400 for a very attractive terrycloth bathrobe. Comforters range from $315 (cotton cover with polyester-dacron fill) to $900 (embroidered satin cover with down fill). The store can also turn one of their sheets into a comforter cover, or adjust any of their flat sheets to the size of your bed in just two days, with home delivery. A charming Italian welcome, which never hurts.

**Grande Maison du Blanc**
**68 E. 56th St.**
**355-2030**
*Mon. to Fri. 9:30 A.M. to 5:30 P.M.;*
*Sat. by appointment*

The oldest linen shop in the United States, going back four generations, whose style does not seem to have changed much over the last century. But then neither has their quality, which remains irreproachable: sheets, bath towels, table linen are all perfectly made in traditional designs and colors without the least spark of originality. Their cashmere sweaters and blankets are magnificent—the peak of classicism, a trifle mawkish, a trifle boring, but timeless. Custom orders for special sizes or special designs. As for the service, that too is perfect. A venerable store. Prices high, but not extravagant.

**Maison Henri**
**617 Madison Ave.**
**(58th-59th Sts.)**
**355-5463**
*Mon. to Sat. 10:00 A.M. to 6:00 P.M.*

A narrow boutique specializing in expensive and exclusive linens, custom work, but also some delightful and relatively inexpensive infant wear. Indeed, Maison Henri is a store unlike any other in New York. Run by a dynamic, competent, and very welcoming Frenchwoman named Ginette, its service is among the most agreeable and friendly in the metropolis. As for its merchandise, it too is of perfect charm and quality. The price range is immense, of course, but you don't pay here for ephemeral fashions: you pay for quality.

**Porthault**
**57 E. 57th St.**
**688-1660**
*Mon. to Sat. 9:30 A.M. to 5:30 P.M.*

The realm of prints, offering all the charm and French gaiety of flowers and ribbons, bedeck a store whose atmosphere, alas, is much too formal, and whose service is a bit too cold. A large choice of Egyptian cotton towels and silk or cotton voile, the latter costing the modest sum of $1,200 for a queen-size bed set. Porthault recently succumbed to the vogue for wallpapers and upholstery fabrics ($45 the roll or the yard) offered in their classic floral print patterns. It's all very pretty, but high priced: yet though the prices may continue to rise, the quality itself can't go much higher.

## Pratesi
**829 Madison Ave.
(69th St.)
288-2315**
*Mon. to Sat. 10:00 A.M. to 6:00 P.M.*

Like Frette, this is a pretty Italian shop offering taste and luxury, though less refined than its competitor. But the sheets have the advantage of being machine-washable, even the silks. The cashmere blankets and silk sheets are particularly fine—and the prices too are quite striking: $980 for a 92-by-108 inch blanket, $800 for a single twin-size silk sheet, and $124 for a printed cotton-polyester one. All types of custom work possible: oversized tablecloths, quilts made in any thickness, a copy of your tile design embroidered onto towels.

## Upstairs Shop
**238 E. 60th St.
751-5714**
*Mon. to Fri. 10:00 A.M. to 5:00 P.M.*

A shop that sells English-style linen, designed by Elinor Dee, a young British woman with a weakness for fresh colors and flowers. You can coordinate a bedroom–bathroom ensemble from A to Z: curtains, blinds, sheets, towels, lampshades, tablecloths, pillowcases, birdcage covers, dressing gowns, slippers, and gloves—everything matches here, and it gives the place an ingenue atmosphere. Matching wallpapers and fabrics ($20 the roll or yard), paints, and appliquéd pillows to order in the pattern of your choice. Allow eight weeks for delivery.

# PLASTIC

## Lucidity
**775 Madison Ave.
(66th St.)
861-7009**
*Mon. to Sat. 10:00 A.M. to 6:00 P.M.*

One of Madison Avenue's more chic shops—although the store is not extraordinary. It sells good lucite wares, well designed, from France and Italy at reasonable prices. We noticed a particularly elegant table-bar made of a sheet placed on a rack ($37.50 for the sheet and $70 for the rack), large salad bowls ($14.50), and an ice bucket ($28.50). Tables, chairs, desks, and bath accessories.

## Perplexity
**237 E. 58th St.
688-3571**
*Mon. to Sat. 10:30 A.M. to 6:30 P.M.*

All sorts of ultramodern objects at prices much better than in the department stores. Among the frames, furniture, cutlery, and various accessories, you'll find something to your liking at prices you can afford. What's more, the stock is always changing, and the latest creations are always on hand. But the stock is uneven as well: the store obviously has its good and bad days. Custom-made furniture.

# SILVER

## Bucellati
**703 Fifth Ave.
(near 56th St.)
755-4975**
*Mon. to Sat. 10:00 A.M. to 6:00 P.M.*

Italian silver at its best: everything in this elegant store is designed in Milan by Mario Bucellati. He specializes in reproductions of antique Florentine silver—as expensive as they are beautiful and ornate—a very special style that will not appeal to those who prefer pure lines. A few pieces of chic and original jewelry, too, on the ground floor. Everything in an atmosphere of perfect courtesy, helpfulness, and discretion.

## Jean Silversmiths
**16 W. 45th St.**
**475-0723**
*Mon. to Fri. 9:30 A.M. to 5:00 P.M.*

A heavenly hodgepodge: a narrow boutique crammed helter-skelter with piles of silver. You can buy (and sell) everything here: platters, candlesticks, tea services, coffee services, table settings—a striking choice at unbeatable prices based on the weight and quality of silver contained in the pieces (between $20 and $25 an ounce, cleaning and polishing included). There is ridiculously priced silver plate but, above all, there's silver: sterling (98 percent pure) and pure silver (99.9 percent). There's new silver, but Jean Silversmiths specialty is the largest collection of discontinued and obsolete patterns of silver flatware in the country hidden in his cupboards and displayed on his shelves.

## Michael C. Fina
**580 Fifth Ave.**
**(47th St.)**
**2nd floor**
**757-2530**
*Mon. to Fri. 9:00 A.M. to 6:00 P.M.;*
*Sat. 10:00 A.M. to 5:00 P.M.*

On the edge of the diamond district, Michael C. Fina is not a shop like all the others, although it's well known and popular. It offers crystal, china, and jewelry, but above all, an enormous stock of sterling at 20 to 30 percent less than in other stores. Clocks, tea services, various gift items, small jewelry in gold or silver—and, in order to see this fabulous selection, you have to stand patiently in line, give your name to the receptionist, and wait until a salesperson is free to help you. This isn't Tiffany.

## Tiffany
**727 Fifth Ave.**
**(57th St.)**
**755-8000**
*Mon. to Sat. 10:00 A.M. to 5:00 P.M.*

Tiffany merits yet another entry for its silver: the selection, though very classic in style and not all that original, is the best in New York for modern silver, and no more expensive than in other stores. In addition to the tableware, there is also a good choice of accessories in silver plate and sterling (from $15 to $20) which make very attractive gifts in their pretty blue boxes. The best American.

# Image • Sound

Stereo equipment is probably New York's best buy, and prices are about as low as you'll find anywhere except on the black market. But it also calls for shrewdness, as prices vary tremendously from shop to shop and sometimes even from week to week in the same shop. A first rule is to stay away from the bargain stores on Broadway, Lexington, and Fifth Avenue in the 30s and 50s. For listings of sales and best prices read the

*New York Times* on Sunday, particularly the "Arts and Leisure" section, where the biggest and best-known shops advertise their weekly specials. The following reliable stores are worth comparison-shopping.

# PHOTOGRAPHY

## Alkit Camera Shop
866 Third Ave.
(53rd St.)
832-2101
*Mon. to Fri. 8:00 A.M. to 6:30 P.M.;*
*Sat. 9:00 A.M. to 5:00 P.M.*

A shop that stocks the best brands with a friendly atmosphere and excellent service. It rents equipment, does quick repairs, and has a film developing service.

## 47th Street Photo
67 W. 47th St.
2nd floor
260-4410
*Mon. to Thur. 9:00 A.M. to*
*6:00 P.M., Fri. 9:00 A.M. to*
*2:00 P.M., Sun. 10:00 A.M. to*
*4:00 P.M.; closed Sat.*

You'll find everything in this unusual store, but equipment is only sold by catalogue and there are no demonstrator models, so you have to know what you are looking for. The salesmen are all Hasidim and knowledgeable, if hardly jolly, and there are usually interminable lines. That said, the quality and the diversity of the merchandise (exchangeable within fifteen days of purchase) is excellent. Good video department, plus electronic equipment, games, watches, calculators, and film that is much less expensive than elsewhere.

## Hirsch Photo
699 Third Ave.
(44th St.)
557-1150
*Mon. to Fri. 8:30 A.M. to 6:00 P.M.*

Another very good shop in a convenient district, offering all the best brands and a competent and obliging staff. You don't have to elbow your way through crowds here, which is one advantage. Another is that film brought in for development before 9:30 A.M. is ready at 4:30 P.M. No discounts on the merchandise.

## Jems Sound
795 Lexington Ave.
(61st St.)
838-4716
*Mon. to Sat. 9:30 A.M. to 7:00 P.M.*

Two blocks from Bloomingdale's. A good store for photographic, stereo, and electronic equipment featuring all the best brands, many specials, and a diligent staff. A very attractive shop with two floors, which has been developing its stock and lowering its prices for months. Prices are negotiable. A central and practical location.

## Olden Cameras and Lenses
1265 Broadway
(32nd St.), 3rd floor
685-1234
*Mon. to Fri. 9:00 A.M. to 6:00 P.M.;*
*Sat. from 9:30 A.M.*

A marvelous shop teeming with activity where you'll find everything in the way of photographic equipment for amateur and professional: an infinity of lenses, cameras and projectors. That, and the pleasant, competent staff make this a mecca of photography. On Saturday mornings from 9:30 to 10:30 the store holds a special sale of discontinued merchandise and used equipment at incredible prices. Rental department too. Terrific buys in a friendly atmosphere.

## Willoughby's
110 W. 32nd St.
564-1600

A huge shop in the heart of New York's camera corner (31st and 32nd St.) that offers a complete selection of cameras, camera equipment, lighting, and darkroom

Mon. to Fri. 9:00 A.M. to 7:00 P.M.;
Sat. to 6:30 P.M.; Sun. 10:30 A.M.
to 5:30 P.M.

equipment and accessories, with a large used equipment section. Electronic games and gadgets at average prices. A very pleasant and relaxing shop, despite its vastness, well laid out to help you make your choice in peace and quiet—which, with this sophisticated merchandise, is a boon.

# RECORDS AND TAPES

## Bleecker Bob's
**179 MacDougal St.
(8th St.)
475-9677**
*Daily to 3:00 A.M.*

New wave music and punk rock on independent labels and direct imports (tapes and records) from England. If you want to know what's happening in the field—to say nothing of rubbing shoulders with some bizarre rock people—this should be your first stop. New wave is alive and well.

## Disc-o-mat
**716 Lexington Ave.
(57th-58th Sts.)
759-3777**
*Daily 9:00 A.M. to 9:00 P.M.*

New York's best-priced records and tapes (average price: $5.99) in lively pop surroundings. Every week they prepare a list of the top 100 songs on the charts. The singles are only $1. And, every six months, they bring out a "special disco mixer," an L.P. with the season's biggest hits. Various locations.

## Discophile Inc.
**26 W. 8th St.
473-1902**
*Mon. to Thurs. 11:00 A.M. to 9:00
P.M.; Fri. noon to 10:00 P.M.*

New York's biggest outlet for classical music: the best choice of domestic and imported records on all the best and lesser labels—what's more, at prices to match Disc-o-mat's.

## J and R Music World
**For pop and rock:
23 Park Row
732-8600**
*Mon. to Fri. 9:00 A.M. to 6:30 P.M.;
Sat. 10:00 A.M. to 6:00 P.M.*

Unquestionably the best choice of records at the best prices (averaging $3.99 to $5.99). An audio-visual sales department (33 Park Row, 349-0062) stocks the best brands of stereo equipment as well as all sorts of electronic equipment (watches, games) at *truly* discount prices. The rule of thumb in New York is, the further downtown, the lower the prices; but, as a taxi will cost $6 to get here, it's not really worth it for only one or two records. A good choice when you're off to visit the World Trade Center, however. Jazz can be found at 111 Nassau Street, 349-8400.

## Music Masters
**25 W. 43rd St.
840-1950**
*Mon. to Fri. 10:00 A.M. to
6:00 P.M.; Sat. to 3:30 P.M.*

The store for opera lovers. Private recordings of operas, shows, and rare pieces. One of the only stores in New York where you can listen to a record before buying it.

## Record Factory
**17 W. 8th St.
228-4800**
*Daily 10:30 A.M. to 9:00 P.M.*

A complete and inexpensive record shop specializing in American rock and heavy metal, with a well-stocked and (for once) well-displayed selection of cassettes (both prerecorded and not, the latter at $2.90 for the top quality). A wide range of T-shirts, patches, and other items bearing the image or name of your favorite group.

## The Record Hunter
507 Fifth Ave.
(42nd-43rd Sts.)
697-8970
*Mon. to Fri. 9:00 A.M. to 6:30 P.M.*

The best choice of classical music in town, including a multitude of opera recordings. Also jazz and folk and, in back, a small electronics department, with games, watches, and calculators at discount prices. The store is a shambles, but connoisseurs will know how to find their way around. Below-average prices.

## Rock's in Your Head
157 Prince St.
(West Broadway)
228-4557
*Daily 1:00 to 8:00 P.M.*

Another specialist with the same selection, clientele, and atmosphere as at nearby Bleecker Bob's. Plus a few punk accessories.

## Sam Goody
666 Third Ave.
(43rd St.)
986-8480
*Mon. to Fri. 9:30 A.M. to 8:00 P.M.;*
*Sat. to 6:30 P.M.*

The best known of all and the biggest, with a comparable stereo department. Excellent choice of records of every kind at discount specials, not to mention the special weekly sales listed in the Sunday *New York Times*. Don't go anywhere else unless Goody doesn't have what you're looking for. Another location at 1290 Sixth Avenue, 246-8730.

## Rare Records

## Dayton's
824 Broadway
(12th St.)
254-5984
*Mon. to Fri. 10:00 A.M. to*
*6:00 P.M.; Sat. to 5:00 P.M.*

The specialist in nonmusical records, original recordings, film soundtracks, and out-of-print records: used jazz, rock, and classical records, and a few new albums at half price.

## Golden Disc
239 Bleecker St.
(Sixth Ave.)
255-7899
*Mon. to Sat. 11:00 A.M. to*
*9:00 P.M.; Sun. to 7:00 P.M.*

The biggest store in the world for old records: rock, film soundtracks, and old jazz singles.

## Ludus-Tonalis-Gryphon Records
24 Eighth Ave.
(12th St.)
874-1588
*Daily 11:00 A.M. to 7:00 P.M.*

An extraordinary shop for collectors of classical music: every type of recording possible, dating as far back as 1920. An immense stock that includes a number of high-quality imports (at correspondingly high prices). The manager is friendly and competent, and will gladly help you in your search.

## Record Exchange
842 Seventh Ave.
(54th St.)
247-3818
*Mon. to Sat. noon to 6:00 P.M.*

The shop for collectors of rare records and for people nostalgic for such items as old radio recordings. Expensive, but rare—both old and new.

# STEREO/HI-FI

A striking, sometimes discouraging proliferation of equipment of all sorts makes New York seem like an electronic jungle. You'll find everything: telephone answering machines, stereo headphones, games, calculators, and above all, stereos (most of them made in Japan) at unbeatable prices. But there's also a lot of equipment made by second-rate manufacturers, and not all stores sell only the best. You can find these items everywhere (record stores, camera shops, department stores) and, for this reason, we recommend you buy known brands.

And for stereos, we particularly recommend one of the following respected stores. Try to bargain—it's standard practice, and often gives good results.

**Atlantis Sound**
16 W. 45th St.
575-1640
*Mon. to Fri. 11:00 A.M. to 8:00 P.M.; Sat. 10:00 A.M. to 6:00 P.M.*

Models at discount prices from those manufacturers who allow their wares to be sold cutrate: Fisher, Pioneer, Kenwood, Phillips, Onkyo, and more. Less choice but better buys than at Tech Hi-Fi—and prices are negotiable. Excellent after-sales service.

**Canal Hi-Fi**
319 Canal St.
(Broadway)
925-6575
*Daily Mon. to Sat. 9:30 A.M. to 6:00 P.M.; closed Sun.*

A large choice of cassettes at unbeatable prices, videotapes at prices that are competitive, and electronic equipment, including fairly good and very inexpensive speakers.

**Central Electronics**
39 Essex St.
(Grand St.)
673-3220
*Sun. to Fri. 9:30 A.M. to 5:30 P.M.*

Substantial savings offered on Sony, Panasonic, KLH, and Fisher: but only come here to buy what you've seen and tested elsewhere, for the service is very mediocre in this disorderly shop.

**Crazy Eddie**
212 E. 57th St.
980-5130
405 Avenue of the Americas
(8th St.)
645-1196
*Mon. to Sat. 10:00 A.M. to 10:00 P.M.; Sun. noon to 5:00 P.M.*

If you watch television or listen to the radio, you can hardly have missed this place's maddeningly frenetic publicity. But don't be put off: Crazy Eddie is an excellent store for all stereo and video equipment, carrying the best brands and the latest equipment, all at competitive prices. Also, their stores are absolutely gigantic, and sumptuous listening rooms are available. Color TVs, video games, and telephone answering machines, too. In short, everything.

**Grand Central Radio**
155 E. 45th St.

Another store offering an excellent price–quality ratio for a large choice of compact stereos and video games made by respected companies, and offering fast and helpful

**682-3869**
*Mon. to Sat. 9:00 A.M. to 6:00 P.M.*

service. Good location, acceptable merchandise, and advantageous prices. The annex is located at 124 E. 44th Street, 559-2630.

## Harvey Sound
**2 W. 45th St.**
**575-5000**
*Mon. to Fri. 9:30 A.M. to 6:00 P.M.;*
*Sat. from 10:00 A.M.*

A store for professionals, offering a variety of top-quality equipment. But they're no bargains, and this isn't the style of store to encourage haggling. Another branch at 23 W. 45th Street, 921-5920.

## Leonard Radio Inc.
**1163 Avenue of the**
**Americas**
**582-7520**
**18 Warren St.**
**267-0315**
*Mon. to Fri. 9:30 A.M. to 5:00 P.M.*

Unbeatable for receivers: they sell the best brands (Technics, Revere) at prices that are both competitive and negotiable. And if you're looking for something they can't provide, they'll happily tell you where to find it.

## Liberty Music
**450 Madison Ave.**
**(50th St.)**
**753-0180**
*Mon. to Sat. 9:00 A.M. to 6:00 P.M.*

An excellent source of music and video equipment, highly appreciated by music lovers, both performers and listeners. Magnificent listening rooms available for the public to try out equipment manufactured by Sony, Fisher, Naka Michi, McIntosh, and many others. In the video department, you'll find color TVs with giant screens, top-quality equipment, and excellent service.

## Lyric Hi-Fi
**1221 Lexington Ave.**
**(83rd St.)**
**535-5710**
*Mon. to Sat. 10:00 A.M. to 6:00 P.M.*

Great luxury in high fidelity. Here you'll find extremely sophisticated equipment made by Japanese companies unknown to the man in the street. The atmosphere is cocoon-like with its thick wall-to-wall carpeting, and the salespeople are friendly—we'd be friendly too at these prices!

## Rabsons Stereo Warehouse
**119 W. 57th St.**
**247-0069**
*Mon. to Fri. 10:00 A.M. to*
*6:00 P.M.; Sat. to 5:00 P.M.*

New York's best shop for sound and video equipment, carrying the best brands (Sony, Sansui, Marantz) of radios, cassettes, stereos, videotapes, and the like. A superb store offering listening and demonstration rooms, staffed by a team of competent and very obliging salespeople, with *very* discount prices.

## Radio Shack
**385 Fifth Ave.**
**(36th St.)**
**889-0481**
*Mon. to Fri. 9:00 A.M. to 7:00 P.M.*

A sound supermarket: a chain of very cheap, if often melancholy-looking, stores offering an assortment of their own brand equipment at very good prices. For limited budgets. Many Manhattan locations.

## Tech Hi-Fi
**12 W. 45th St.**
**869-3950**
*Mon. to Sat. 10:30 A.M. to*
*6:30 P.M., Sun. noon to 5:00 P.M.*

A large chain of stores offering a good selection of excellent brands (JVC, Kenwood, Pioneer, Thorens, Dual) at discount prices. You can try the equipment in their sound rooms without obligation and at your leisure. Less choice, but better prices, than at Harvey Sound.

# Leathers

The finest hides, magnificently worked, are available in New York, at prices that vary depending on whether you do your shopping on Park, Madison, and Fifth Avenue, or downtown. But on the whole, the very reasonable prices make luggage one of your best buys when visiting the city. In addition to Alexander's (Lexington Avenue at 58th Street, 5th floor), which has a particularly well-stocked and reasonably priced leather department, we suggest the following stores.

## A to Z Luggage
**425 Fifth Ave.**
**(39th-40th Sts.)**
**686-6905**
*Mon. to Thur. 9:30 A.M. to 6:15 P.M.; Fri. 9:15 A.M. to 3:00 P.M. Sun. 10:00 A.M. to 5:00 P.M.*

Every sort and size of luggage and bags here, in leather, canvas, vinyl, and aluminum—all extremely light, strong, and practical—models with wheels, with several grips, with compartments that withdraw into pockets, in complete sets or individually. Plus a line of accessories that every traveler will find useful: traveling irons, pocket radio–alarm clocks, and a hundred other recent gadgets: calendar–clocks, telephone speakers, and other multiple-use items that will no doubt amuse and surprise you. It's hard to believe that such a selection of sophisticated appliances, some of which are quite useful, exists outside of Japan. Various locations.

## La Bagagerie
**727 Madison Ave.**
**(64th St.)**
**758-6570**
*Mon. to Sat. 10:00 A.M. to 7:00 P.M.*

Handbags, handbags, and still more handbags! The emphasis here is on variety, charm, and comfort: easy, up-to-date styles from the classic shoulder purses that made La Bagageries immensely popular in Paris to genteel and luxurious crocodile-skin models. Hundreds of different styles, a new collection every six months, all the product of one man's fertile imagination, and made in their factory in France. Also a pretty collection of accessories, including a particularly modish and original selection of belts, plus more classic and longer-lasting attaché cases and luggage. Truly a charming and friendly shop, which manages to obey both the imperatives of the latest fashions and those of quality, at very moderate prices.

## Bottega Veneta
**655 Madison Ave.**
**(60th St.)**
**371-9218**
*Mon. to Sat. 10:00 A.M. to 6:00 P.M.*

The handsomest Italian leather luggage and accessories, where luxury means refinement and when "your own initials are enough." High-quality leather in subtle and tasteful shades (particularly the lighter ones). Ravishing shoes and boots as well.

## The Coach Store

A store that has nothing in common with its neighbors, distinguishing itself by its simplicity and rusticity. It sells

**754 Madison Ave.
(near 65th St.)
594-1581**
*Mon. to Sat. 11:00 A.M. to 6:00 P.M.*

only Coach bags and Coach belts, all made in New York City by a small private company dedicated to leather. No superfluous sophistication here: there are about fifteen styles, all very classic, made with very soft, natural leather, each of which comes in three different sizes and ten basic colors. Each bag is one of a kind, and has its own registration number stamped into the leather. Prices go from $46 to $160. The belts are neat, elegant, and strong, made either entirely of leather, or of leather and natural fibers, and sell for $15 to $30. The shop itself is simple, like its merchandise, and impervious to the winds and caprices of fashion.

## Crouch and Fitzgerald

**401 Madison Ave.
(48th St.)
755-5888**
*Mon. to Sat. 9:00 A.M. to 6:00 P.M.*

In business for close to 150 years, this store is not the attention-seeking variety. Its clientele is not the sort attracted by flashiness and the latest fashions, but rather by classicism and quality. The luggage, handbags, and leather accessories—sober, solid, the type that are always in fashion—are sold in this old-fashioned, sad-looking store by a staff that is competent, friendly, and unpretentious. New York's most honorable (and honored) store for luggage. It carries, among others, the Vuitton line.

## Desiderio Leather

**698 Lexington Ave.
(57th St.)
751-1797**
*Mon. to Sat. 10:00 A.M. to
6:00 P.M.*

Not as well known, thus not as expensive, as many of the others, the Desiderio stores nonetheless offer very well-made merchandise, with an assortment of very soft bags made in Italian and South American leather, and other charming leather accessories. Exclusively domestic manufacture. Sales in January and July. Various locations.

## Gucci

**689, 697, 699
Fifth Ave.
(54th St.)
826-2600**
*Mon. to Sat. 9:30 A.M. to 6:00 P.M.;
closed 12:30 to 1:30 P.M.*

Luggage, handbags, jewelry, scarves, various gifts, all bearing the famous G Americans are so crazy about. The top floor is given over to fantastic sales, with items at 50 percent or less of their original value. A must.

## Lancel

**690 Madison Ave.
(62nd St.)
753-6918**
*Mon. to Sat. 10:00 A.M. to 6:00 P.M.*

This fine French store, long established on the Place de l'Opéra, recently opened a very attractive New York outlet, its walls hung with leather. There are three floors of its wide range of luggage and accessories, whose style and quality are Continental. This is the haute couture of leather. Not to mention the charming welcome, on a par with everything else.

## Lederer

**613 Madison Ave.
(58th St.)
355-5515**
*Mon. to Sat. 9:30 A.M. to
6:00 P.M.*

A reliable source that imports its handbags, luggage, and accessories from France and Italy, not the least of which are its perfect copies of the famous Hermès handbags, which sell for $75.

## Louis Vuitton
**51 E. 57th St.**
**371-6111**
*Mon. to Fri. 10:00 A.M. to*
*5:30 P.M.; Sat. to 5:00 P.M.*

What is there to be said about this leather maker, whose popularity has borne him across continents and oceans, and whose famous initials LV are rivaled only by Gucci's G? What is there to be said, except perhaps that his new shop on 57th street is superbly pretentious, that the staff there is imbecilic—and that, fortunately, the merchandise speaks for itself. Vuitton is incontestably the best in its genre, a position that is hardly easy to attain. Handbags also carried at Saks Fifth Avenue and Crouch and Fitzgerald.

## Madler Park Avenue
**450 Park Ave.**
**(57th St.)**
**688-5045**
*Mon. to Sat. 9:00 A.M. to 5:30 P.M.*

A wide selection of very fine and expensive Italian and German luggage. A luxurious shop that offers only the finest in imported leather goods.

## Mark Cross
**645 Fifth Ave.**
**(51st St.)**
**421-3000**
*Mon. to Sat. 10:00 A.M. to 6:00 P.M.*

An entire line of elegant and expensive luggage bearing the proprietor's initials MC. Also office accessories, gloves, shoes, belts, and other luxury and high quality items, most made in Italy. A very nineteenth-century "Olde England" saddle shop atmosphere.

## T. Anthony
**480 Park Ave.**
**(58th St.)**
**737-2573**
*Mon. to Sat. 9:00 A.M. to 6:00 P.M.*

Made-to-measure luggage and very exclusive models in this elegant store, where you'll have to pay the price of its fine reputation. One of their specialties is leather book bindings. Another useful service: they'll repair any of their own merchandise free of charge.

# Sports

## The Athlete's Foot
**16 W. 57th St.**
**586-1936**
*Mon. to Sat. 10:00 A.M. to*
*7:00 P.M., Thur. 9:00 P.M., Sat. to*
*6:00 P.M.*

For fanatical runners: all models and brands of shoes for men and women, plus a selection of accessories. And if you can't make up your mind, the sales staff will advise you.

## Conrad's Bike Shop
**232 E. 47th St.**
**753-0092**
*Wed. to Sat. 11:00 A.M. to*
*5:30 P.M.*

According to its clients, this is the best used-bicycle dealership in New York. He has an impressive number in stock, comprising every brand, and at half the normal prices or lower. Renowned for its repair and rental service, too.

## Dream Wheels
**295 Mercer St.**

One of the rare survivors among a plethora of stores that came and went with the winds of fashion. There are preassembled skates, and all the accessories in a wide

**(8th St.)**
**677-0005**
*Tues. to Sun. noon to 8:00 P.M.*

## Feron's Racquet and Tennis Shop
**55 E. 44th St.**
**867-6350**
*Mon. to Fri. 8:30 A.M. to 6:00 P.M.; Sat. 10:00 A.M. to 4:00 P.M.*

## Herman's
**135 W. 42nd St.**
**730-7400**
*Mon. to Sat. 9:00 A.M. to 7:30 P.M.*

## Hunting World
**16 E. 53rd St.**
**755-3400**
*Mon. to Sat. 10:00 A.M. to 6:00 P.M.*

## Kaufman and Sons Saddlery
**139 E. 24th St.**
**684-6060**
*Mon. to Sat. 9:30 A.M. to 5:45 P.M.*

## Miller Harness Company
**123 E. 24th St.**
**678-1400**
*Mon. to Fri. 9:00 A.M. to 5:45 P.M.; Sat. to 4:45 P.M.*

## Paragon
**867 Broadway**
**(18th St.)**
**255-8036**
*Mon. to Sat. 9:30 A.M. to 6:25 P.M.*

## Peck and Goodie
**919 Eighth Ave.**
**(W. 54th St.)**
*Mon. to Sat. 10:30 A.M. to 6:00 P.M.*

## Racquet Shop
**289 Madison Ave.**
**(near 40th St.)**
**685-1954**
*Mon. to Fri. 8:45 A.M. to 6:00 P.M.; Sat. 10:30 A.M. to 4:30 P.M.*

range of quality to make up a custom model to your taste, plus accessories. Organizes evening outings in spring and summer.

A shop offering lower prices than Madison Avenue for a good choice of outfits and racquets for men and women. Also at the Flushing Meadow stadium.

The best brands of equipment for nearly every sport, from the traditional to the exotic. Prices are honest, especially on the tennis and squash racquets, one of the best items to buy here. The shop on 42nd Street is bigger and better stocked than the others. Various locations.

Everything in the way of clothing and equipment (except the guns) for a very comfortable safari. An elegant and expensive shop.

Especially for western saddles, but some genteel English models as well.

For men, women, and children: all the equipment and accessories necessary to ride a horse in the purest of Western traditions: hats, clothing, boots, and accessories all of a very high quality. This store clothes the U.S. Olympic equestrian team.

Very good prices in this surplus-style store, a favorite haunt of New Yorkers. Specializes in outdoor sports: skiing, tennis, hiking, baseball, football, and rollerskating—for adults and children. A staff of young, competent sportspeople quick to serve you.

Skates for ice and asphalt, in every size, for men, women, and children, all in leather, which doesn't make them particularly cheap. But a place to rely on.

The store for professionals: Jimmy Connors, Ilie Nastase, John McEnroe, and Harold Solomon all get strung up here. Professionals and amateurs alike find whatever it is they need: racquets in every material, every weight and size. The tennis-wear department is well stocked and not too expensive.

## Runner's World Sports Warehouse

**275 Seventh Ave.
(26th St.)
691-2565, 243-3947**
*Mon. to Fri. 10:00 A.M. to
6:00 P.M.; Sat. to 5:00 P.M.*

Hiking and running shoes and clothing. Among their staff are several expert marathoners, and all can counsel you wisely.

## Scandinavian Ski Shop

**40 W. 57th St.
757-8524**
*Mon. to Fri. 9:00 A.M. to 6:30 P.M.;
Sat. to 5:30 P.M.; Sun. 11:00 A.M.
to 5:00 P.M.*

An excellent shop for most of the popular sports: skiing, tennis, swimming, and so on. Prices aren't low, as there are neither special bargains nor discounts, but the quality of the merchandise is excellent, and the shop itself superb. A wide range of skis and outfits in season, as well as equipment rental (by the day or the week) and extremely well-organized excursions that leave the shop early in the morning and come back the same or the following evening.

## Sporting Woman

**235 E. 57th St.
688-8228**
*Mon. to Sat. 10:00 A.M. to
7:00 P.M.; Sun. noon to 5:00 P.M.*

For women only: a big store recently opened by the owners of Athlete's Foot, carrying reliable brands of equipment at honest prices for women who run, swim, sail, cycle, dance, play tennis, and lift weights. In short, New York's best selection, neither too functional nor too stylish: a very good compromise between the two that will be perfect for today's sportswomen.

## Stuyvesant Bicycle and Toy, Inc.

**349 W. 14th St.
254-5200**
*Mon. to Fri. 9:30 A.M. to 7:00 P.M.,
Sat. and Sun. to 5:00 P.M.*

An excellent place to stop for all the best brands of American bicycles at good prices. A wide choice of sizes for adults and children, sold by friendly salespeople. Rental service also.

# Tobacconists

## Alfred Dunhill of London

**620 Fifth Ave.
(50th St.)
481-6900**
*Mon. to Sat. 9:30 A.M. to 5:30
P.M.
also at Bloomingdale's*

Dunhill's is, along with Nat Sherman, the premier New York tobacconist. It has been in business since the early years of the century, and does not have to go begging for publicity. Everyone—from the most rabid nonsmoking jogger to the sort of person who puts down his cigar only to go to sleep—knows this name, and the New York branch lives up to its image: it is simply the ultra in quality and price. The most demanding and sophisticated smokers will be completely satisfied: in addition to the famous line of cigars, custom-blended tobaccos, and briar pipes, they will find the sort of handsome and luxurious accessories smokers dream about, such as the superb lighters, carrying cases, tobacco pouches, and cigar humidors. And, should they already be unconditional followers, they will find up a few stairs the part of the shop selling gifts, jewelry, and clothing as exclusive and refined as everything else.

## Don Lou Pipe Shop

**2058 Bath Ave.
(21st Ave.
in Brooklyn)
372-9032**
*Mon. to Sat. 8:00 A.M. to 5:00 P.M.*

For over 45 years Don Lou has been making pipes, by hand. He also carries his own blends of tobacco, and his shop is as friendly and fragrant as a candy store. But his specialty is his custom-made pipes. He can make anything, from a simple briar ($10) to pipes sculpted into different shapes ($100 and up), and uses only such fragrant and spicy woods as Greek briar, Corsican plane, Brazilian oak and rosewood. The lack of varnish or dye preserves all their flavor. A true craftsman of the variety so rare in our time—well worth a trip to Brooklyn.

## J. R. Tobacco Corporation

**11 E. 45th St.
869-8777**
*Mon. to Fri. 8:00 A.M. to 5:00 P.M.;
Sat. to 4:00 P.M.*

A discount cigar supermarket: J. R. carries over three thousand sorts, ranging from the cheapest five-cent variety to the rarest and dearest. Cigars in every size, shape, and color in these two large stores whose display and fluorescent lighting makes them resemble large grocers. A huge stock to please every taste, and at prices well below average. Another location at 219 Broadway, 233-6620.

## Nat Sherman Tobacconist

**711 Fifth Ave.
(55th St.)
751-9100**
*Mon. to Sat. 9:30 A.M. to 6:15 P.M.*

The fragrances of the finest tobaccos mix here with the aromas of comfort and luxury. Nat Sherman has made a name for himself in New York and in the world thanks at first to his Cuban cigars, and then, after the breaking of Cuban–American trade relations, for his delicious and elegant cigarettes made with different blends of tobacco and wrapped in brightly colored papers. You can pick your favorite color and, the height of refinement, have your name printed on them. The selection of cigars (all meticulously maintained at proper temperature in their walk-in humidor), tobacco, and domestic and imported pipes (including the French Dupont pipes, for which he is the exclusive vendor in New York) is extremely attractive. Everything is of high quality, in our opinion—and, if you agree, you can subscribe to his Diary System: Nat Sherman will send you weekly, bimonthly, or monthly shipments (depending on your rate of consumption) of the tobacco of your choice.

## Peterson's Ltd.

**505 Park Ave.
(59th St.)
682-4473**
*Mon. to Fri. 8:30 A.M. to 6:15 P.M.;
Sat. 10:00 A.M. to 6:00 P.M.*

Pipes, tobacco, and cigars are stocked here in an impressive variety, to satisfy every taste and meet every budget. Many imported Danish, Italian, and British pipes ($10 to $270), lots of imported or custom-blended tobaccos (including twelve house blends), cigars from all over (except Cuba), all the accessories to make smoking more pleasant and easier, as well as a repair department. Everything is reasonably priced. If you're not bewitched by big names and fancy decors (the store lacks both), this is the place for you. Peterson's has been in business for three generations.

## Tobacco Center
**130 St. Marks Place (Avenue A)**
**674-2208**
*Mon. to Fri. 9:00 A.M. to 7:00 P.M.*

Tobacco flavored with vanilla, strawberry, chocolate mint, apple, grape . . . it's unlikely you knew they existed, unlikelier still you've ever tried them. (Never underestimate American inventiveness and willingness to try something new!) Well, if the idea appeals to you, visit the Tobacco Center, New York's oldest tobacconist, which sells all this and lots more, by weight (about 55¢ an ounce). All the leaves are cut on the spot to ensure freshness.

## Wally Franck, Ltd., Pipes
**344 Madison Ave. (44th St.)**
**349-3366**
*Mon. to Sat. 8:30 A.M. to 6:00 P.M.*

A good shop offering a wide variety of cigars imported from just about everywhere, in a large selection of sizes, leaves, and prices, with very good bargain prices on certain articles. Also their own line of pipes, accessories, and tobacco blends, on the whole very good. You can also order by catalogue—you won't be disappointed by what the mailman brings.

## Wilke Pipe Shop
**400 Madison Ave. (47th St.)**
**755-1118**
*Mon. to Fri. 9:00 A.M. to 5:00 P.M.;*
*Sat. 11:00 A.M. to 5:00 P.M.*

Well-known to collectors around the world, this is probably the best-informed pipemaker in New York, and his blends of cigar and pipe tobacco are among the best you can find here. Repair service; mail orders accepted.

# Where to Find

## ══════ AN ANTIQUE RESTORER ══════

## Charles Sundquist
**312 E. 23rd St.**
**674-6960**
*Mon. to Fri. 7:30 A.M. to 4:00 P.M.*

A reliable repairman for all kinds of antique furniture from every period. He does conscientious work entirely by hand, offers free estimates in New York City, and charges fair prices. A craftsman recommended and used by the best antique dealers in the city.

## Joseph Biunno
**403 E. 62nd St.**
**744-0907**
*Mon. to Fri. 8:00 A.M. to 4:00 P.M.*

Mr. Biunno and his sons specialize in restoring valuable furniture, both antique and modern. As friendly and charming as he is, don't bother him for an old bargain sofa—he works mostly with decorators, on pieces of the highest quality. That being the case, he'll be pleased to help you, whether you need a piece glued back on, or a complete restoration of some furniture. He won't offer estimates—unless you ask.

## Oxford Antique Restorers
**59 E. 57th St.**
**355-7620**
*By appointment only, Mon. to Fri. 9:30 A.M. to 5:00 P.M.; ask for Mrs. Moran*

Another excellent spot for all repair of antique furniture from the seventeenth, eighteenth, and nineteenth centuries. All sorts of skills and works are available: repairing, rebuilding, gilding, lacquer work, and more. Estimates in New York City: $35.

## Sotheby's Restoration
**440 E. 91st St.**
**472-3463**
*Call Mr. Paul Ranklin for an appointment, Mon. to Fri. 9:00 A.M. to 5:00 P.M.*

This new division of Sotheby Parke Bernet is surely one of the most reliable and competent places for repairs and restoration of antique furniture. Under the management of Mr. John Stair, the son of the founder of Stair and Company, Sotheby's restorers will do any kind of work: cutting, carving, repair, and finishing (gilding, polishing, and lacquer work) on pieces in every style and from every period, whether they were bought at Sotheby's or not. They also offer a service to potential clients of a piece, informing them how about much its restoration will cost, prior to the auction. For your own pieces, they will come to your house to make an estimate for $50, deductible from the cost. Sotheby plans to expand its services to cover metal, glass, and porcelain repairs.

# ═══ A BOOK RESTORER ═══

## Carolyn Price Horton
**430 W. 22nd St.**
**989-1471**
*Mon. to Fri. 9:00 A.M. to 5:00 P.M.; by appointment only*

An expert in the art of restoring antique paper: books, manuscripts, and works of art have been passing through her hands for 25 years, including countless delicate repairs for museums. Count on about two months for repairs. Estimates are free. Carolyn Horton is a skilled artisan in a very difficult field, but is not pretentious about it.

## Deborah Evetts
**532-1538**
*Call Mon. to Fri. evening for an appointment*

Conservator at the Pierpont Morgan Library, Mrs. Evetts also looks after restoration for private individuals—but only if the works are museum-class books printed on flat paper, and the client is willing to wait twelve to eighteen months before delivery and pay top prices for top work. She doesn't simply restore your work, she gives it new life. Don't bring in the old family Bible—she won't even look at it.

## Denis Gouay
**41 Union Square**
**8th floor**
**929-2132**
*Mon. to Sat. 10:00 A.M. to 5:30 P.M.*

A young and extremely likable binder from Lisieux in Normandy who has more than one string to his bow. His competence and talent allow him to do everything concerning books: modern binding, slipcases, art bindings, and restoration of old books and manuscripts. You can give him your rare books and your old with total confidence—he imports the finest leathers from Europe, and best handmade acid-free paper (which won't yellow or otherwise deteriorate for about four hundred years) and copies the original binding and end-papers exactly. What's more, he doesn't charge excessive prices, given the high quality of his work. You'll find in his pretty day-lit studio photographs of his earlier work, as well as samples of the materials he uses and a list of prices.

He also organizes four-week courses in bookbinding (2½ hours a week), for $230, materials included.

## Ffolio 72
**888 Madison Ave.**
**(71st–72nd Sts.)**
**879-0675**
*Mon. to Sat. 10:00 A.M. to 5:30 P.M.; by appointment only*

A very fashionable spot to buy attractive letter paper and to have business cards made, Ffolio 72 also looks after binding of books, family albums, and Bibles, movie scripts, plays, or whatever you like in goatskin—for which it charges chic prices ($250 minimum for a simple rebinding). The service, too, suffers from the store's popularity.

## Froehlich
**18 W. 18th St.**
**4th floor**
**243-1585**
*Mon. to Fri. 9:00 A.M. to 4:30 P.M.*

A specialist in mass-produced leather office accessories and novelties, Froelich will also do leather binding (about six weeks, $60 minimum) and decorating: he can cover your desk top, for example. He also specializes in fake bookshelves—why not camouflage your door with fake but attractive bindings? Something to think about.

# A CLEANER

Broken buttons, burned collars, indelible stains, tears, and creases are all common occurrences, and it's never without some regret that you hand over your clothes to a cleaner. New York has over two thousand, of which we have selected a few very different ones where your entire wardrobe and fine linens will be properly treated.

## Ernest Winzer
**1828 Cedar Ave.**
**The Bronx**
**294-2400**
*Mon. to Fri. 6:00 A.M. to 5:00 P.M.; Pick-up and delivery*

A specialist in cleaning antique clothing and theater costumes, who will look after anyone's dry cleaning with pleasure. His work usually takes two days and, as with the easiest ones, the most difficult cleaning tasks will be delivered immaculate, admirably ironed, and packaged—at incredibly low prices considering the irreproachable and reliable quality of his work.

## Jeeves of Belgravia
**770 Madison Ave.**
**(66th St.)**
**570-9120 (services and account number: 674-7704)**
*Mon. to Fri. 8:30 A.M. to 5:30 P.M.; Sat. to 1:00 P.M. Pickup and delivery around New York*

Jeeves represents a standard of service and quality that unfortunately no longer exists anywhere else. It is the best, both in London and New York, as well as the most sophisticated, with a slight English touch. Its employees are extremely competent and use the finest equipment available. Your clothing will first be thoroughly inspected, and all stains will be marked. Buttons will be resewn and, if necessary, zippers replaced. The quality of the cleaning itself is beyond criticism. Jeeves, like Ernest Winzer, is a specialist in cleaning theater costumes. In addition, he offers a multitude of related services like storage of clothing and furs, wrapping, and anything else you may require. After normal business hours, an automatic answering machine will note your instructions, which will be followed to the letter. A luxury institution—much more, and much better, than your run-of-the-mill dry cleaner.

## Hallak
**1239 Second Ave.**
**(65th St.)**
**832-9015**
*Local deliveries Mon. to Fri.*
*7:00 A.M. to 6:30 P.M.; Sat.*
*8:00 A.M. to 3:00 P.M.*

Joseph Hallak, a native of Marseilles who has been living in New York for over fifteen years, is a cleaner of the highest order: his work is perfect, even on the most delicate of fabrics, and his prices very reasonable. His sturdy wrappings will allow you to keep your clothes in the same condition they were in when he delivered them.

## Perry Process Cleaners
**1315 Third Ave.**
**(76th St.)**
**628-8300**
*Mon. to Fri. 8:00 A.M. to 6:30 P.M.;*
*Sat. to 2:00 P.M.*

Another careful and conscientious cleaner who will take the time necessary to return your clothing to perfect condition. Whereas, for example, most cleaners take two or three days to clean a down coat, and return it to you supposedly dry but with the feathers still damp, Perry takes a few days longer, to make sure that the coat is truly dry and won't go moldy in your closet. Competitive prices.

# AN ESTIMATE

## Sylvia Leonard Wolf
**617 West End Ave.**
**(90th-91st Sts.)**
**595-0264**

Sylvia Wolf, a senior member of the American Society of Appraisers and the Appraisers Association of America, will estimate the value of your furniture, paintings, rugs, china, crystal, silver, and so on at a fee of $225 per hour. The cost may seem high, but includes a visit to your home, inspection and inventory of all the items, and a complete photographic portfolio, as well as of course, the estimates themselves. Sylvia Leonard Wolf is officially recognized by the government, the tax authorities, and insurance companies—her estimates have not been questioned.

# A JEWELRY/WATCH REPAIR

## Fossner Time Pieces Clockshop Inc.
**826 Lexington Ave.**
**(63rd St.)**
**249-2600**
*Mon. to Fri. 10:00 A.M. to*
*6:00 P.M.; Sat. 11:00 A.M.*
*to 6:00 P.M.*

At Fossner's watch repair has been a tradition handed down from father to son for four generations. There is nobody more competent in the field than this Czechoslovakian father, mother, and son. Old and new, clocks and watches, they can repair anything in about a week, and will give a six-month guarantee. They also buy and sell antique watches and clocks, and their collection of fobs, carriage clocks, wrist watches, and big antique pendulum clocks is fascinating. This is more than a neighborhood shop—it caters to connoisseurs. Note: do not confound this shop with the one next door, which also looks after watch repairs, and whose competence we have not tested.

## J. Schwartz
**1372 Broadway**
**(36th-37th Sts.)**
**354-5722**
*Mon. to Fri. 8:00 A.M. to 6:00 P.M.*

A Romanian couple who repair clocks, watches, and jewelry, no matter how delicate. Mr. Schwartz was thirty years with Omega, and you can entrust him with your fobs, watches, and clocks with the greatest confidence. He also sells a selection of watches made by good manufacturers: Swiss (Longines, Morado, Zenith), American (Bulova), and Japanese (Seiko) at prices from $30 to $300. Also some attractive gold jewelry.

## William E. Berger Antique Clocks
**29 E. 12th St.**
**929-1830**
*Mon. to Sat. noon to 6:00 P.M. by appointment only*

An excellent shop for all repairs on antique or modern clocks, mechanical or electric. Free estimates in store or $50 at your home. Mr. Berger comes with recommendations from most of the museums, and works for the best antique dealers.

# A KNIFE SHARPENER

## Fred De Carlo
**(201) 945-7609**

One of the few wandering knife-and-scissors-grinders left, he strolls through the streets with a big bell in hand, his equipment on his back. His territory is the East Side from 52nd St. to 96th St. between Fifth Ave. and the East River, which he covers Monday to Friday, 9:00 A.M. to 5:00 P.M. If you miss him on his rounds, and your knives and scissors are despairingly dull, give him a ring in the evening and he'll arrange an appointment.

# A LAUNDRY

Your splendid linens must, of course, be properly cleaned. The following addresses were all given us by stores that sell fine linen.

## Danielle
**1334 Lexington Ave.**
**(88th-89th Sts.)**
**534-1483**
*Mon. to Fri. 7:00 A.M. to 7:00 P.M.; Sat. 8:00 A.M. to 5:00 P.M.*

Hand cleaning and dry cleaning are both done on the spot at relatively high prices: a silk-covered down comforter will cost about $40. But pickup and delivery are free.

## Jeeves of Belgravia
**770 Madison Ave.**
**(66th St.)**
**570-9130 (services and accounts: 674-7704)**
*Mon. to Fri. 8:30 A.M. to 5:30 P.M.; Sat. to 1:00 P.M. Pickup and delivery in and around New York.*

In addition to their dry cleaning service, Jeeves also looks after fine linen, and does hand laundry at reasonable prices: $1.25 for a bath towel, $1.50 for a pillowcase, and $3.25 for a cotton shirt. In other words, much better prices for much better work than elsewhere. Cleaning takes a week, and pick up and delivery are free for orders over $20.

## Mme. Blanchevoye
**75 E. 130th St.**
**368-7272**
*Mon. to Fri. 7:30 A.M. to 4:30 P.M.*

Sheets cost between $7 and $8.50, pillowcases $1.25 to $1.75, and pickup and deliveries cost a high percentage of the cleaning bill. Unless you have the courage to go up to 130th Street, you'll really be taken to the cleaner's.

## Park Avenue French Hand Laundry
**1305 Madison Ave.**
**(92nd–93rd Sts.)**
**289-4950**
*Mon. to Sat. 8:00 A.M. to 6:00 P.M.*

Your linen and clothing will be washed with care and attention. Delicate sheets and table linen will come back looking like new. A sheet will cost between $6 and $10, depending on size, and table cloths start at $10. Free pickup and delivery for customers with charge accounts.

# A MARBLE RESTORER

## New York Marble Works
**1399 Park Ave.**
**(103rd St.)**
**534-2242**
*Mon. to Sat. 9:00 A.M. to 4:00 P.M.*
*by appointment only*

This restorer's clients include Sotheby Parke Bernet, William Doyle, and the Metropolitan Museum, so he knows what he's doing. He repairs and restores all kinds of marbles: fireplaces, coffee tables, desk tops, and so on, and offers a free estimate if you bring him the object or a photo. Competitive prices.

# PERSONAL SERVICES

Bills to pay, dogs to walk, freezers to fill, parties to organize. . . . Do you never seem to have time to get around to all these tasks, or are you just bored by them? If that's the case, the following organizations will look after you, and put order into the most complicated of lives.

## Let Millie Do It
**Millie Emory**
**Leave messages at**
**532-8775**

If your house is in such a mess that, when you look for your toothbrush, you can only come up with a hairbrush, have no fear: Millie can reestablish order throughout. She can pay your bills, help you do your shopping, take your pets to the vet, and organize your filing cabinet. In other words, she'll help you clear cupboards and conscience for $25 an hour. She works both for companies and for individuals.

## Professional Organizers
**Andrea Adler**
**850 Seventh Ave.**
**suite 705**
**581-6470**

Andrea Adler opened her business only a few years ago, but is already doing so well that she's planning to set up affiliates all over the country. She specializes in moving, and will look after everything—redirect mail to your new address, ship and receive your goods (whether in the United States, or anywhere else), will be there to help you install your new residence according to your instructions— all that will be left for you is to unpack your toiletries bag.

Also, she offers such services as window washing, selling art and furniture at auctions, and taking inventory of your apartment. Further information available by consultation ($35).

## Rent a Mrs.
**Jeanne Ashley and
Carole London
Station Plaza East,
suite 302 in
Great Neck,
Long Island
(516) 621-7750**

Rent a Mrs. offers 32 different services, like paying bills, organizing a party, telephone wake-up, personal shopping, moves, taking clothes to the cleaner, waiting for deliveries, and lots more. The only things it doesn't do are cooking and cleaning—for the rest, your affairs will be looked after and your problems taken care of. Rates vary from $12.50 an hour to $2,500 for arranging a mammoth party—for example, something which takes several months.

## Resources
**Nancy Seifer and
Barbara Peters
33 Riverside Dr.
883-9119 (East Side)
580-8001 (West Side)**

Nancy Seifer and Barbara Peters are professional organizers, and can put order into your apartment or your office. They will water plants, feed and walk pets, do your errands, pay your bills, and, if you authorize them, look after your bank account—in short, take care of all the boring demands of everyday life. They have employees who speak German, French, Italian, and Greek, so they can also work as city guides. Their rates vary, depending on the service required, from $10 upward; and whatever the service, Nancy and Barbara will devote their energies to making your life easy.

## Woman for Rent
**Lisa Dorfman
14 First Ave.
475-0883**

Lisa Dorfman is a young woman who loves her work—which is to look after you. She'll do all the errands you haven't gotten around to—simple laundry, food shopping, looking for an apartment, putting order into your cupboards, organizing a party—and everything for a very reasonable rate of $15 per hour. She has acquired a serious reputation, and her clients don't hesitate to give her their credit cards for shopping, for example. The people who work for her must all meet very strict requirements, and are often university graduates.

# A PERSONAL SHOPPER

## Amelia Fatt
**757-6300 for an
appointment**

Being well dressed doesn't necessarily mean being expensively dressed. That's what Amelia Fatt has been explaining to women for over seven years. She is a counselor in clothing who will come to your home for a two-hour consultation in order to observe and get to know you. You'll talk together about your life, your pursuits and tastes, you'll go through your wardrobe, and she will point out the items that are particularly becoming, those that are flattering and those that don't work for you at all. You'll learn to combine different items in new ways and, keeping your budget in mind, she will choose clothes for you and recommend accessories for your wardrobe. She does this in Manhattan and elsewhere. A two-hour consultation in Manhattan costs just under $100—traveling time is taken into account for places farther away, and if you live out of town you will eventually have to come to New York to try on the clothes she has selected for you.

# ══A PORCELAIN REPAIRER══

## Center Art Studio
**149 W. 57th St.**
**247-3550**
*Mon. to Fri. 10:00 A.M. to 7:00 P.M.; Sat. to 5:00 P.M.*

A luxury craftsman: if you have objects of great value in need of repair or restoration, and are willing to pay for it, Fritz Pohl is your man. He is a specialist in antique porcelain and ceramics, and can do any sort of work necessary, even reconstructing missing pieces. But his skills are not limited to porcelain: he can also carry out repairs on bronzes, ivory, wood carving, gold leaf, furniture, and glassware, whenever their value justifies his expensive rate: $45 an hour plus materials.

## Expert China Repair
**231 E. 50th St.**
**355-7467**
*Mon. to Fri. 11:00 A.M. to 5:30 P.M.; call first*

An excellent and less costly place in a small basement workshop, which will carry out meticulous and time-consuming repair work on fine china and porcelain. The matching of colors, for instance, will take a month at least, and work can take longer depending on the state of the object to be repaired. (Minimum charge of $10 to $20).

## Hess Repairs
**200 Park Avenue South (17th St.)**
**260-2255**
*Mon. to Fri. 10:30 A.M. to 4:00 P.M.; by appointment*

A shop that comes recommended by Steuben, Baccarat, Tiffany, and Waterford; in other words, both reliable and expensive. Porcelain, glass, ivory, and silver have no secrets for Mr. Hess, who can repair the irreparable. Restoration of porcelain takes about three weeks, and work on crystal about fifteen days, Excellent work done on silver too. Minimum charge $10. Maximum—several zeros more.

## Mr. Fixit
**1300 Madison Ave. (92nd St.), 2nd floor**
**369-7775**
*Mon. to Fri. 9:00 A.M. to 6:00 P.M.; Sat. to 5:00 P.M.*

A not-too-exclusive craftsman. Don't hesitate to call on him, even if you're not a shipping magnate, and even it the item to be repaired has no more than personal value. Mr. Fixit repairs everything, without false snobbery. His competence is not limited to his main interest, china, but extends to crystal, ivory, jade, onyx, wood, silver, pewter, tin, copper—in short, anything that needs work. His prices are fair, neither excessive nor ridiculously low. Free in-shop estimate.

## Sano Studio
**767 Lexington Ave. (60th St.)**
**759-6131**
*Mon. to Fri. 9:00 A.M. to 5:30 P.M.; by appointment*

Another absolutely reliable (and expensive) shop for all kinds of restoration of china, porcelain, ceramics, and pottery. William Doyle and the finest decorators in the city are all his clients, cheerfully laying out $20 (to have a small chip repaired) and generally much more because they are confident that the work will be perfect. All surfaces are pasted together and reglazed in colors that exactly match the original. Free estimates. Three months for delicate work.

# A REDECORATOR

## Design Gallery
**847 Broadway
(13th-14th Sts.)
777-4033**
*Mon. to Fri. 9:00 A.M. to 6:30 P.M.;
Sat. to 5:00 P.M.*

Plumbing, electrical work, expansion, construction of new floors and furniture—these are a few of the things Design Gallery can look after. They offer a complete service for redoing and reorganizing your home, and will discuss with you the best way to transform your wishes into reality.

# A SILVER RESTORER

## Cliff Silver Company
**159 E. 55th St.
753-8348**
*Mon. to Fri. 9:00 A.M. to 5:00 P.M.*

An atmospheric place filled with an assortment of pewter, copper, brass, and silver, waiting to be repaired or picked up by their owners. Price is based on the time spent, no matter what the piece, at $28 an hour plus material. A reliable address, which serves Tiffany, Sotheby, and William Doyle, among others. Free estimate. Appointment recommended.

## D & D Silversmith
**1575 York Ave.
(83rd St.)
988-4240**
*Mon. to Fri. 8:30 A.M. to 4:30 P.M.*

A very reliable spot for all polishing, replating, regilding, and repairs on all silverware. D & D also works on such less noble metals as copper and bronze. Estimates are free, prices fair, and the work excellent.

## Thome Silversmith
**328 E. 59th St.
758-0655**
*Mon. to Fri. 8:30 A.M. to 5:30 P.M.*

An excellent craftsman recommended by the best dealers for skillful refinishing, replating, polishing, cleaning, and restoration of any missing piece on gold, silver, copper, or brass. It may take up to three months but, according to his clients, patience is more than repaid. Call for an appointment.

# WRAPPED ATTENTIONS

## Jeeves of Belgravia
**770 Madison Ave.
(near 66th St.)
570-9130 (services
and accounts:
674-7704)**
*Mon. to Fri. 8:30 A.M. to 5:30 P.M.;
Sat. to 1:00 P.M. Delivery and
pickup in and around New York*

For travelers tired of arriving at their destinations with packed clothing wrinkled, Jeeves offers a vacation wrapping service. Your valise will be collected, and your things pressed and wrapped in paper. And, if your things are getting a bit cramped, it will also store any temporarily unwanted clothing to free your cupboards.

316

# THE ARTS

# Galleries

Galleries abound in New York, a capital of art wheeler-dealers. Here is our brief listing of some good addresses to encourage you to do your own wheeling and dealing (or just browsing).

## ═══════AMERICAN PAINTING═══════

**Berry Hill Galleries**
**743 Fifth Ave.**
**371-6777**
*Mon. to Fri. 9:00 A.M. to 5:30 P.M.;*
*Sat. 10:00 A.M. to 4:00 P.M.*

Nineteenth- and early twentieth-century American art, plus paintings from Hong Kong and Taiwan.

**Coe Kerr Gallery**
**49 E. 82nd St.**
**628-1340**
*Mon. to Fri. 9:00 A.M. to 5:00 P.M.;*
*Sat. from 10:00 A.M.;*
*closed in summer*

American nineteenth- and twentieth-century paintings, watercolors, and drawings on five floors of an attractive townhouse. Andrew Wyeth and his son James are represented here, as well as numerous artists of the Hudson River School.

**Daniel B. Grossman**
**1100 Madison Ave.**
**861-9285**
*Mon. to Sat. 10:00 A.M. to 6:00 P.M.*

American and European oil paintings from the nineteenth and early twentieth centuries.

**Graham Gallery**
**1014 Madison Ave.**
**535-5767**
*Mon. to Sat. 10:00 A.M. to 5:00 P.M.*

Nineteenth- and twentieth-century American painting and sculpture. Built in 1857, this is the oldest gallery in New York.

**Hirschl and Adler Galleries**
**21 E. 70th St.**
**535-8810**
*Tues. to Sat. 9:30 A.M. to 5:15 P.M.*

A small museum where eighteenth- to twentieth-century American paintings are shown on two floors of a townhouse against brown-velvet covered walls. A few European paintings as well.

**Ira Spanierman**
**50 E. 78th St.**
**879-7085**
*Mon. to Fri. 9:30 A.M. to 5:30 P.M.*

Nineteenth-century paintings, mostly American. This dealer has been in business for over thirty years at the same location.

## Kennedy Galleries
**40 W. 57th St.,**
**5th floor**
**541-9600**
*Mon. to Fri. 9:30 A.M. to 5:30 P.M.*

Eighteenth-, nineteenth-, and twentieth-century American painting, drawing, and sculpture.

## Kraushaar Galleries
**724 Fifth Ave.**
**(56th-57th Sts.)**
**307-5730**
*Tues. to Sat. 9:30 A.M. to 5:30 P.M.; closed Sat. in summer*

American twentieth-century art is represented here, including the estates of John Sloan, William Glackens, and Jerome Myers.

## Salander O'Reilly Galleries
**22 E. 80th St.**
**879-6606**
*Mon. to Sat. 10:00 A.M. to 5:30 P.M.*

Contemporary abstract and colorfield paintings can be seen here, and one floor of this three-story townhouse is devoted to modernist works.

## Susan Caldwell
**303 West Broadway**
**966-6500**
*Tues. to Sat. 10:00 A.M. to 6:00 P.M.*

This large SoHo gallery shows a variety of contemporary sculpture and painting ranging from the figurative to the abstract.

# CONTEMPORARY ART

## Adler Castillo
**58 E. 79th St.**
**831-3824/5**
*Tues. to Sat. 10:00 A.M. to 5:00 P.M.*

Abstract art from the beginning of the century: Russian constructivism and Italian futurism, and the like.

## Allan Stone Gallery
**48 E. 86th St.**
**988-6870**
*Tues. to Fri. 10:00 A.M. to 6:00 P.M.; Sat. 10:00 A.M. to 5:00 P.M.*

Twentieth-century masters, as well as important contemporary and abstract expressionist works. Also African art, and a collection of Bugatti automobiles.

## Andre Emmerich
**41 E. 57th St.**
**263-3421**
*Tues. to Sat. 10:00 A.M. to 5:30 P.M.; summer by appointment only*

Paintings and sculptures by major postwar and contemporary artists, plus a section of pre-Columbian art and antiques.

## Castelli Graphics
**4 E. 77th St.:**

Castelli is, perhaps, the doyen of art dealers. The West Broadway gallery is dedicated to drawings, paintings, and sculpture by some of the best-known names in modern

**288-3202**
## Castelli Gallery
**420 West Broadway**
**431-5160**
## Leo Castelli
**142 Greene St.**
**431-6279**
*Tues. to Sat. 10:00 A.M. to 6:00 P.M.*

American art: Jasper Johns, Robert Rauschenberg, Andy Warhol, James Rosenquist, Roy Lichtenstein, Claes Oldenburg, Richard Serra, and others. Castelli Graphics has prints and photographs by these same artists, and Leo Castelli, a gallery of impressive scale, is used for the biggest works, as well as for projection of tapes and films. Rental and sales of artists' videotapes and films.

## Marisa Del Re Gallery
**41 E. 57th St.**
**688-1843**
*Tues. to Fri. 10:00 A.M. to 5:30 P.M.*

Highly regarded American and European twentieth-century artists: Motherwell, Dubuffet, Picasso, Masson, Braque, Magritte, de Kooning, and more.

## Marlborough Gallery
**40 W. 57th St.**
**541-4900**
*Mon. to Fri. 10:00 A.M. to 5:30 P.M., Sat. to 5:00 P.M.*

A superb contemporary painting and sculpture gallery with a room full of photographs by Bill Brandt, Berenice Abbott, and Irving Penn.

## Newhouse Galleries
**19 E. 60th St.**
**879-2700**
*Mon. to Fri. 9:30 A.M. to 5:00 P.M.*

Major European and American eighteenth- and nineteenth-century artists.

## Sidney Janis
**110 W. 57th St.**
**586-0110**
*Mon. to Sat. 10:00 A.M. to 5:00 P.M.*

Segal, Marisol, Wesselman, and many more, plus photographs by the greatest masters of this century. One of the best.

## Sonnabend Gallery
**420 West Broadway**
**966-6160**
*Tues. to Sat. 10:00 A.M. to 6:00 P.M.*

Another famous gallery. Contemporary artists, both famous and less well known, with a future ahead of them.

## Paul Rosenberg and Company
**20 E. 79th St.**
**472-1134/5**
*Mon. to Fri. 10:00 A.M. to 5:00 P.M.*

A gallery–museum in a small townhouse dedicated to fifteenth- and sixteenth-century old masters. Superb sixteenth-century drawings, paintings, sculptures, and selected art objects.

## Pierre Matisse
**41 E. 57th St.,**
**4th floor**
**355-6269**
*Tues. to Sat. 10:00 A.M. to 5:00 P.M.; closed July and August*

Paintings and sculptures by Dubuffet, Chagall, and many other artists.

## Schweizer Gallery
**958 Madison Ave.**
**535-5430**
*Mon. to Fri. 10:00 A.M. to 5:30 P.M.*

An older gallery (in business since 1930) specializing in British, Continental, and American painting from the eighteenth century, and earlier, onwards.

## Shepherd Gallery
**21 E. 84th St.**
**861-4050**
*Tues. to Sat. 11:00 A.M. to 6:00 P.M.*

Nineteenth-century European art: sculpture, drawing, and painting. The gallery also has a good service department for framing, restoration, and photography (call 744-3392).

## Wildenstein and Company
**19 E. 64th St.**
**879-0500**
*Mon. to Fri. 10:00 A.M. to 5:00 P.M.*

A fine gallery–museum for Impressionist and contemporary painting. Excellent temporary exhibitions.

# ETHNIC ART

## J. Camp Associates
**380 West Broadway (near Broome St.)**
**966-3372**
*By appointment from noon to 6:00 P.M., except Sat. No credit cards*

Tribal art, with magnificent objects from Africa, New Zealand, and other areas, sumptuously presented.

## Signs Gallery
**37 W. 57th St.**
*Tues. to Sat. 10:30 A.M. to 5:30 P.M.*

This relatively recent gallery is the only one devoted to contemporary Central and South American art in New York. Contemporary artists, mostly from Latin America. You'll discover a world of talent that remains, for the moment, relatively unfamiliar.

# PHOTOGRAPHY

## Daniel Wolf Gallery
**30 W. 57th St.**
**586-8432**
*Mon. to Sat. 10:00 A.M. to 6:00 P.M.*

More vintage ninteenth- and twentieth-century photographs, including works by major contemporary artists.

## Light Gallery
**724 Fifth Ave. (55th-56th Sts.)**
**582-6552**
*Tues. to Fri. 10:00 A.M. to 6:00 P.M.; Sat. 11:00 A.M. to 5:00 P.M.*

Only modern photographers are represented in this large black-ceilinged gallery.

## Marcuse Pfeiffer Gallery
**825 Madison Ave.**
**737-2055**
*Tues. to Sat. 10:00 A.M. to 5:30 P.M.*

An art gallery specializing in photographs, mostly contemporary, but with samplings from all periods.

## Neikrug Galleries
**224 E. 68th St.**
**288-7741**
*Wed. to Sat. 1:00 P.M. to 6:00 P.M.*

Shows nineteenth- and twentieth-century photographs and daguerrotypes, plus rare books, stereographs, and various contemporary photographers. Another museum of photography.

## Photograph
**724 Fifth Ave.,**
**10th floor**
**935-0700**
*Tues. to Sat. 10:00 A.M. to 6:00 P.M.*
*All major credit cards*

This spacious gallery is the latest arrival, and concentrates on art photographs and photojournalism. A small room at the back, the Daguerrean Room, presents nineteenth-century works. A very attractive spot.

## Prakapas
**19 E. 71st St.**
**737-6066**
*Tues. 11:00 A.M. to 8:00 P.M.;*
*Wed. to Sat. 11:00 A.M. to 6:00 P.M.*

An art gallery specializing in modern twentieth-century art, with a special emphasis on photography (Eugene Atget, Man Ray, and more).

## Robert Miller Gallery
**724 Fifth Ave.,**
**11th floor**
**246-1625**
*Tues. to Sat. 10:00 A.M. to 5:30 P.M.*

A beautiful all-white layout and a splendid collection of such twentieth-century photographers as Man Ray, Hans Bellmer, and Robert Mapplethorpe.

## The Witkin Gallery
**41 E. 57th St.**
**355-1461**
*Tues. to Sat. 11:00 A.M. to 6:00 P.M.*

Witkin's is venerable, and looks more like a library or museum devoted to photography than a gallery: there are old books, Tiffany lamps, and a camera on a tripod that dates from the turn of the century. It specializes in vintage nineteenth- and twentieth-century black-and-white photographs and literature on the subject. A few paintings as well. A spot with atmosphere.

# POSTERS

## A and R Studios
**1567 York Ave.**
**650-9498, 744-1627**
*Mon. to Sat. 10:30 A.M. to*
*7:00 P.M.; Sun. 1:00 P.M. to*
*4:00 P.M.*

A few posters and a certain number of original lithographs by artists from America, France, and Switzerland, from Folon to Sonia Delaunay. Prices range from $25 to $5,600. The pleasant owner seems to be willing to bargain about the prices, which are already 15 to 20 percent lower than those on Madison Avenue.

## L'Affiche Gallerie
**145 Spring St.**
**966-4620**
*Tues. to Sat. 11:00 A.M. to 6:00 P.M.; Sun. from noon to 6:00 P.M.*

A good-looking gallery in SoHo for posters and contemporary art reproductions. A pleasant visit to look over a selection of posters accessible to all wallet sizes.

## Cinemabilia
**10 W. 13th St.**
**989-9519**
*Tues. to Fri. 11:30 A.M. to 7:00 P.M.; Sat. 11:00 A.M. to 6:00 P.M.*

The place for cinema buffs: movie posters, magazines, programs, photographs, archives . . . Hollywood in Manhattan.

## Oestreicher's Prints
**43 W. 46th St.**
**757-1190**
*Mon. to Fri. 10:00 A.M. to 6:00 P.M.; Sat. to 5:00 P.M.*

Recommended by all the museums, Oestreicher's is the biggest distributor of American and European reproductions, and has the largest collection of posters in New York. Prices are moderate (most between $10 and $18). The staff is competent and obliging, and the framing service offers an enormous choice of frames in all sorts of materials—from aluminum to hand-sculpted frames with gold leaf.

## Poster America
**174 Ninth Ave.**
**(20th St.)**
**691-1615**
*Mon. to Sat. 10:00 A.M. to 4:00 P.M.; by appointment only*

American and European posters dating from the late nineteenth century, on every subject imaginable. There is also a particularly good movie selection, military and advertising posters of the most extravagant sort. Usually between $100 and $200, but prices can climb as high as $5,000 for rarities.

## Postermat
**16 W. 8th St.**
**982-2946**
*Mon. to Sat. 10:00 A.M. to 10:00 P.M.; Sun. noon to 8:00 P.M.*

Just west of Fifth Avenue, right before Washington Square, this store has an enormous selection of art, cinema, and celebrity posters, and T-shirts.

## Poster Original Ltd.
**924 Madison Ave.**
**(73rd St.)**
**861-0422**
*Mon. to Sat. 10:00 A.M. to 6:00 P.M.; at Spring St., Sun. noon to 5:00 P.M.*

A large selection of American and European art posters from over the past ten years, including the famous Steinberg cover for the *New Yorker* representing the North American continent as seen by egocentric natives. Lots of posters for exhibitions by well-known artists. Prices range from $59 to $250 and up. Plastic coating available for $40, framing for $75. Another location at 158 Spring Street, 226-7720.

## Poster Place
**32 W. 53rd St.**
**586-3740**
*Mon. to Sat. 11:00 A.M. to 6:00 P.M.; Sun. 2:00 to 6:00 P.M.*

Opposite the Museum of Modern Art, this store has lots of contemporary American, European, and Oriental art posters—over two thousand in all, from $10 to $2,000 for some of the limited editions. There are also lively posters from Broadway shows.

## Welcome to New York City
**26 Carmine St.
(near Bleecker St.)
242-6714**
*Tues. to Sat. noon to 9:00 P.M.;
Sun. 1:00 to 6:00 P.M.*

Are you crazy about New York, and nostalgic about how it used to be in the '30s, '40s, and '50s? If so, visit Joe Coppa, who collects and displays all sorts of memorabilia about the city. You'll find Broadway posters from twenty years ago, fifty-year-old *New Yorker* covers, prints made in 1890, and lots more . . . all at very reasonable prices (about $10 to $15).

# PRINTS

## Fitch-Febvrel Gallery
**5 E. 57th St.,
12th floor
688-8522**
*Tues. to Sat. 11:00 A.M. to 5:30 P.M.*

This small gallery, opened about five years ago by Andrew Fitch and his wife, Dominique Febvrel, wasn't long in making its mark. It specializes in black-and-white prints by nineteenth- and twentieth-century artists (mainly European, but also American and Japanese). Their prices are fair, sometimes even below current auction levels. A gallery to be watched.

## Martin Suners Graphics
**50 W. 57th St.
541-8334 and
581-2268**
*Tues. to Sat. 10:00 A.M. to 5:00 P.M.*

Another good gallery for prints by European and American artists from the late nineteenth and early twentieth centuries.

## The Old Print Shop
**150 Lexington Ave.
(30th St.)
683-3950**
*Mon. to Fri. 9:00 A.M. to 5:15 P.M.;
Sat. 9:00 A.M. to 4:45 P.M.*

Founded in 1898, The Old Print Shop, located on the slopes of Murray Hill, has been the best in New York for old American and nineteenth-century French and English engravings ever since. You'll find a particularly good selection of marine scenes, landscapes, cityscapes, and Currier and Ives prints. Old American maps too. A top-rated establishment with a top-rated catalogue (available by subscription).

## Old Print Center of Phyllis Lucas
**981 Second Ave.
(52nd St.)
755-1516**
*Tues. to Sat. 9:00 A.M. to 5:30 P.M.*

Phyllis Lucas is both a dealer and a publisher of engravings and lithographs of all sorts. She can claim credit for the distribution of the very first Dali lithographs and many small illustrated books, and sells a large collection of maps and engravings classified by subject— an excellent source of documentation. Interesting exhibitions are held several times annually in the store's back room.

## Theodore B. Donson
**38 E. 57th St.,
11th floor
355-6970**
*Tues. to Sat. 10:00 A.M. to 6:00 P.M.*

This gallery shows and sells the finest prints from the fifteenth to twentieth centuries. In the fall of '81, for example, an exhibition of fifty Rembrandt engravings was followed by a show of the work of Marc Chagall. The most beautiful prints available on the market regularly appear on their walls. Mr. Donson is also the author of an excellent book on prints.

# Museums

America has gone art crazy. A few years ago, there was a new gold rush, this time for "The Gold of Tutankhamen." Then, in 1980, a million people—seven thousand a day—jostled for place in line to see the nine hundred Picassos at the incredible retrospective organized by the Museum of Modern Art.

These events no longer attract only aesthetes and connoisseurs. Nowadays, almost every new exhibition draws the same teeming, anonymous crowds that fill a ballpark or wait three hours to see a film. New York, like Paris, is now a city of "exhibitionists." There's something disquieting about this frenzy, whipped up by advertising, a hunger for the "not-to-be-missed" exhibition or event. But New York's appetite for art seems insatiable, and you must be ready to stand in line, and elbow (and be elbowed) to attend any exhibition of the slightest importance. You should keep this in mind when planning your museum visits: don't be stingy with your time when devising your schedule.

There are over fifty museums in New York, obviously of unequal interest. We will introduce you to the most famous ones first, and then to a few others, which are not indispensable, but are by no means without interest.

## Guggenheim Museum
**Fifth Ave. and 89th St.**
*11:00 A.M. to 5:00 P.M.*
*(8:00 P.M. Tues.); closed Mon.*

It looks like a French brioche stuffed with a 400-yard spiral ramp. It has provoked myriad jokes (the museum should supply sea-sickness pills with each entrance ticket; it's the architect's revenge on the artist; etc.).

The arguments between Solomon Guggenheim and his architect, Frank Lloyd Wright, aggravated by accounts in the press and the opinions of the Urban Planning Commission, were widely discussed for a long time, and the multibillionaire patron of the arts had been dead for two years before the snail-shaped museum that bears his name finally opened its doors in 1951. After an elevator ride to the top, you begin the descent of this long reinforced concrete spiral—a brilliant creation allowing you to test your cardiovascular conditioning and the endurance of your calves, while feasting your eyes on the treasures displayed.

The museum owns, and exhibits in rotation, some five thousand modern paintings, sculptures, and drawings. The collection, which is both high in quality and intelligently planned, is dominated by the collections of Kandinsky (close to 180 canvases); Mondrian's abstract works, cubist work by Juan Gris, Georges Braque, and

Picasso; works by Paul Klee, Marc Chagall, Picabia, Michaux, Max Ernst, and more, as well as pieces by such important contemporary American artists as Jackson Pollock and Robert Rauschenberg.

The Tannhauser collection, which became a part of the museum in 1965, is of an earlier period and includes 75 pieces (masterpieces, many of them) by Renoir, Cézanne, Van Gogh, Degas, Pissarro, and Picasso (from his "Blue" period).

Temporary exhibits include shows such as "Scandinavia Today," featuring the works of young Scandinavian artists, and an Yves Klein retrospective.

It would unfair not to single out the museum's cafeteria, situated on the ground floor. The food is not only attractively presented, it is actually edible, thus affording the establishment a unique position in the otherwise lugubrious landscape of New York museum restaurants. We particularly recommend the chef's salad and the chocolate cake.

## Metropolitan Museum of Art

**Fifth Ave. and 82nd St.**

*Tues. 10:00 A.M. to 8:45 P.M.; Wed. to Sat. 10:00 A.M. to 4:45 P.M.; Sun. 11:00 A.M. to 4:45 P.M.; closed Mon.*

The biggest art museum in the United States is one of the most dangerous in the world. Visitors risk artistic apoplexy, cultural embolism—or at least of leaving with severe indigestion. Everything you might ever want to see is here—and then there's more. The visitor floats with ecstasy, but gradually dizziness sets in and soon he or she is swaying on his feet, and ends up waving the white flag, wishing dire misfortune on the authors of those guides that enjoin, "The Metropolitan—a full day or nothing."

Three hours, twelve minutes, twenty-eight seconds—that is our absolute record. Of course, one does what one can, but if you want our opinion, anything over two and a half hours borders on the foolhardy. Above all, never enter with the intention (unless you're feeling suicidal) of roaming at random through these endless floors, halls, and galleries.

A wiser course consists of first finding out what is to be seen. There's usually a temporary exhibition, and as they are generally of great beauty (in 1981, for example, we saw a fantastic collection of Benin bronzes, and a slightly boring but nonetheless spectacular display of Viking art), they are a splendid reason for one's first trip to the museum. Coming in 1983 is a four-month exhibit, "Treasures of the Vatican," but be warned—it will be massively oversold, so start looking for a scalper now if you wish to attend. More accessible will be the new annual (and always spectacular) costume exhibition, for years run by fashion's grand dame, Diana Vreeland.

Then, as one exhibition will probably not have brought you to your knees, treat yourself to a stroll through the new American Wing's twenty rooms, which are, with the Astor Court (an exquisite recreation of a sixteenth-century Chinese garden courtyard), the Met's latest grand achievements. There are more stunning masterpieces to be seen in other sections, but when you're in the lap of modern America, why not discover its past as well? Displayed in a gigantic greenhouse are innumerable pieces of furniture from the eighteenth and nineteenth centuries; paintings by both naive and professional artists; stained glass from the Belle Époque; western bronzes; and Tiffany glass, shown in a natural setting. The message is a sound one. Until recently, America had stuffed its museums with the past of other cultures; but America, too, is a civilization with a past. So much for a first visit: and afterwards?

We must leave that up to you. A large descriptive board at the museum entrance indicates which sections are open at what times. But remember that among the events in the museum's own recent past was the opening of a permanent gallery (the Sackler Gallery) of Assyrian art, with a spectacular display (in a different part of the museum) of the remains of the Egyptian temple at Dendur. (The Egyptian section is, after the Cairo Museum, the Louvre, and the Berlin Museum, the biggest in the world.)

You should also trot off to the galleries where many Impressionist masterpieces are displayed—you've seen them in reproduction, but here they shimmer before your eyes. Then lose yourself in the Lehman Collection, a series of rooms crammed with eighteenth-century paneling, important pieces of French furniture, Italian, Flemish, and French painting, tapestries, and magnificent classical drawings.

Just completed is the latest giant addition to the Met, the Rockefeller Wing for Primitive Art. Like everything else here, it is done on a grand scale and is packed with ancient treasures.

Try to make time another day to visit the galleries of Asian and Islamic art, the fifteen or so rooms with reconstructions of interiors of European chateaus and mansions (the exquisite Cabris mansion at Grasse, and a marvelous Louis XVI storefront from Île Saint-Louis in Paris, among others), or the overwhelming section of medieval art. Don't overlook the ground-floor boutique, either, where in addition to numerous art books there are many excellent reproductions and all sorts of attractive objects that make reasonably priced gifts.

## Museum of Modern Art
**11 W. 53rd St.**
*11:00 A.M. to 6:00 P.M. (9:00 P.M. Thurs.); closed Wed.*

Here too, the Rockfeller Foundation distributed its magical manna to make the "MOMA" into one of the most exciting museums in the world. Created in 1929 to introduce the public to the Paris School, it later broadened its scope considerably, aiming to present not only all the most important currents in modern art from French Impressionism to American Abstract Expressionism (via German Expressionism, Dadaism, and Surrealism) but also to follow as well all facets of contemporary art, including architecture, photography, cinema, and furniture. In addition to its permanent collection it displays a variety of temporary exhibitions, such as its incredibly successful Picasso retrospective, which proved the museum to be too small and resulted in the undertaking of a three-year expansion program. The temporary exhibitions are generally held on the main floor, including, more recently, a superb series of exhibitions of early photographs by Eugène Atget. The charming sculpture garden is closed, but movies are shown regularly in the afternoon, free to visitors (an immense retrospective of French cinema was recently sponsored), and art lovers can catch their breath in the cafeteria on the first floor in the new building.

In Fall 1982 look for an exhibit of sculpture of Louise Bourgeois, and Eugène Atget returns in a new exhibit, "Atget—Old Paris."

## Whitney Museum of American Art
**945 Madison Ave. (70th St.)**
*Tues. to Sat. 11:00 A.M. to 6:00 P.M.; Sun. noon to 6:00 P.M.*

This granite and concrete blockhouse, the work of Marcel Breuer, looks like a truncated pyramid. It was opened in 1966 to house the excellent collection of contemporary American painting and sculpture amassed since 1930 at the instigation of Gertrude Vanderbilt Whitney, herself a sculptress. It now contains over six thousand works, most from the twentieth century, and there are fine temporary exhibits. Its Bienniel Exhibition, set to begin in Spring 1983, is a major survey of contemporary American art shown throughout the museum. Just opened is the Whitney's Midtown branch in the Phillip Morris headquarters on 42nd St. across from Grand Central Station.

# OUTSIDE OF MANHATTAN

## Brooklyn Museum
**Eastern Parkway, near Washington Ave., in Brooklyn**
*10:00 A.M. to 5:00 P.M. (noon to 5:00 P.M. Sun.); closed Mon. and Tues.*

This massive fin-de-siècle building (since enlarged) stands at the northeast entrance of a vast botanical garden, remarkable in particular for its reconstruction of a sixteenth-century Japanese garden. It is not a cheery place, and low on signs of life since African, Oceanic, and Native American cultural artifacts are seldom the stuff that works up the crowds. But if you're interested in Egyptian art, pay the place a visit. The Brooklyn Museum houses an excellent collection of sculptures, bas-reliefs, small bronzes, ceramics, and jewelry, dating from the predynastic period until Ptolemaic and Coptic times.

There are also usually interesting temporary exhibits such as "The Dinner Party" by Judy Chicago, a curious work dedicated to important women in history: it was presented in the form of a huge banquet table, laid out in a triangle set with large plates abundantly decorated with sexual symbols. The "Architect of Fashion" show from October 1982 to January 1983 will exhibit the costumes of Charles James.

## The Cloisters
**Fort Tryon Park**
*10:00 A.M. to 4:45 P.M. ( noon to 4:45 P.M. Sun. ); closed Mon.*

Overlooking the Hudson, beyond the Washington Bridge, lies the admirable collection of medieval art presented by the Metropolitan Museum with the financial assistance of the Rockefeller family. Whole buildings are exhibited and rooms from such monasteries as Saint-Guilhem-le-Désert have found sanctuary in the New World. These marvels, to which are added stained glass, tapestries, and sculptures, are presented with great style. Even the gardens are a work of both beauty and scholarship.

# ═══OTHER MUSEUMS═══

## American Craft Museum
**44 W. 53rd St.**
*10:00 A.M. to 5:00 P.M.; closed Mon.*

Right across from the MOMA, this small, brand-new museum presents often interesting exhibitions devoted to costume and contemporary applied arts.

## American Museum of Natural History
**Central Park West at 79th St.**
*Daily 10:00 A.M. to 4:45 P.M.; Sun. and hol. 11:00 A.M. to 5:00 P.M.; Wed. and Fri. to 9:00 P.M.*

This immense and pompous hodgepodge is populous on Sundays with large families and boy scout troops. The miles of cabinets display global fauna and flora, from prehistory on, including a ninety-foot-long (fiberglass) blue whale. The just opened Gardner D. Stout rooms show off a vast enthographical collection from Asia and the Middle East, but the museum might have been more rigorous in its organization.

The museum also offers free hour-long "Highlight Tours" (873-1300, ext. 538), and two films, *To Fly* and *Living Planet. To Fly,* an excellent 30-minute film, is shown daily at the Naturemax Theatre ($2 for adults and $1 for children), and the two films are shown together for $3.50 on weekend nights at 6:00 and 7:40 p.m.

You might also visit the Hayden Planetarium, where presentations on astronomy are given in the Guggenheim Space Theater. On the whole, though, these are less successful than those at the Reuben H. Fleet Space Theater in San Diego.

## The American Numismatic Society
**Broadway and 155th St.**
*Tues. to Sat. 1:00 to 5:00 P.M. Note: ring bell to enter*

What do Herodotus, George Washington, and Caesar have in common? Their faces are all artfully engraved on various bronze, silver, and gold discs, expertly displayed in the American Numismatic Society. Ring the doorbell and you will be ushered into vaulted rooms where currency spanning the period from its invention to the inflationary present can be seen. Two special exhibits trace the evolution of American currency and international medals and decorations.

## Cooper-Hewitt Museum
**Fifth Ave. and 91st St.**

The Carnegie Mansion provides a sumptuous setting for the permanent collection of European furniture, wallpapers, porcelain, glassware, antique textiles of every possible origin, bronzes, wrought iron, and silverware

329

*10:00 A.M. to 5:00 P.M.;*
*Tues. to 9:00 P.M.; Sun. noon to*
*5:00 P.M.; closed Mon.*

(along with a rich selection of drawings and architectural and decorative prints). This fascinating museum also presents temporary exhibits of the highest quality. Alseep for years, the museum is presently experiencing a renaissance.

## Frick Collection
### 1 East 70th St.
*10:00 A.M. to 4:00 P.M. Wed. to*
*Sat. in the summer, and Tues.*
*to Sat. in winter; 1:00 to 5:00 P.M.*
*on Sun.*

On the ground floor of this Louis XV- Louis XVI-style mansion, built in 1913 for the industrialist Henry Clay Frick, awaits a very exceptional collection of European painting—Bellini, Rembrandt, Holbein, Velasquez, Vermeer, Fragonard, Boucher, Claude Lorrain—shown as they were intended to be, in the living rooms and boudoirs of a (very grand) private house. A characteristic example of the (good) taste of an American tycoon in the robber baron years who grew passionate about "art," and took good advice in acquiring it.

## The Hispanic Society of America
### Broadway and 155th St.
*Tues. to Sat. 1:00 to 4:30 P.M.;*
*Sun. 1:00 to 4:00 P.M.*

This exhibit of Iberian (Spanish and Portugese) painting, sculpture and decorative arts is located in the center of the Audubon Terrace. The interior courtyards and galleries contain items of art and archaeology from the earliest Spanish civilizations to the present (including colonial America), but the most interesting art pieces are paintings by such masters as El Greco, Goya and Velasquez.

## International Center for Photography
### Fifth Ave. and 94th St.
*11:00 A.M. to 5:00 P.M. Wed. to Sat.;*
*Tues. to 8:00 P.M.; closed Sun.*

This center possesses a rich collection of works by the greatest photographers of the twentieth century. Its exhibitions are always of interest.

## Jewish Museum
### Fifth Ave. and 92nd St.
*Noon to 5:00 P.M. Mon. to Thurs.;*
*Sun. 11:00 A.M. to 6:00 P.M.;*
*closed Fri. and Sat.*

This small, very active museum devoted to Jewish art and culture (manuscripts, coins, textiles, paintings, pottery, and so on) often presents provocative exhibitions. A little while ago Andy Warhol's "Portrait Gallery" (the likes of Einstein, Freud, Kafka, the Marx Brothers) caused much controversy in the press.

## Museum of the American Indian
### Broadway and 155th St.
*Tues. to Sat. 10:00 A.M. to*
*5:00 P.M.; Sun. 1:00 to 5:00 P.M.;*
*closed Mon. and holidays*

Probably the most complete collection of Indian culture anywhere in North, South, or Central America. A very clear presentation provides enormous amounts of information concerning the native peoples, whose self-evident artistic talents are highly valued by collectors. Located in the beautiful Audubon Terrace complex, you'll find an astonishing number of Indian treasures, from jewelry to weapons to costumes.

## Museum of the City of New York
### 1220 Fifth Ave. (104th St.)
*10:00 A.M. to 5:00 P.M.; Sun. and*
*hol. 1:00 to 5:00 P.M.; closed Mon.*

This absolutely fascinating museum is located in a handsome neo-Georgian building, and contains remarkable models of New York's early development, and of interiors throughout the centuries. There's a delightful collection of toys and doll's houses, John D. Rockefeller's bedroom from the 1880s, puppets, and an audio-visual presentation on the history of New York.

### New York Historical Society
**Central Park West and 77th St.**
*Tues. to Fri. 11:00 A.M. to 5:00 P.M.; Sat. from 10:00 A.M.; Sun. from 1:00 P.M.; closed Mon.*

A visit to this museum agreeably rounds out a tour of the previous one. Here are superb collections of antique toys, New York silverware from the eighteenth and nineteenth centuries, and nineteenth-century furniture, as well as portraits, carriages, and nearly all of John James Audubon's marvelous watercolor originals (433 of 435) for his *Birds of America.*

# Music

Who brought Mozart out into the streets? The Salzburgers in Austria? No, the New Yorkers!

"Mostly Mozart" has become *the* event of the summer. The open-air festival presented free by the best musicians attracts enormous crowds to the esplanade at Lincoln Center between 62nd and 66th Streets west of Broadway. A popular triumph—not surprisingly, a popular line of T-shirts bears the effigy of Wolfgang Amadeus—it includes drama, ballet performances featuring the New York City Ballet and the American Ballet Theater, and of course, concerts.

The importance that Lincoln Center—founded twenty years ago by John D. Rockefeller III and entirely subsidized by private grants—has assumed in New York's cultural life is extraordinary. It's a melting pot where students, the public, and major artists meet to make art more accessible, less stuffy, to take it out of the ivory tower. Meetings with performers, including the most famous, are easier for the general public than anywhere else in the world. Every day from 10:00 A.M. to 5:00 P.M. there are organized tours of Lincoln Center, and if you take the trouble to call up beforehand (877-1800), you can participate in the "Meeting the Artists" program, which will take you backstage, allow you to sit in on a rehearsal, or even gain you entrée into the artists' dressing rooms, where you can ask questions and talk quite informally. Tour tickets are $3.75.

The tour lasts about an hour and is conducted by very competent guides. It will give you a good overview of Lincoln Center, a super shopping center of the arts, and all its buildings (their architectural and decorative qualities vary quite a lot). On the left, the elegant New York State Theater (2,700 seats), conceived by Philip Johnson, an important figure in American architecture, houses both the New York City Ballet, directed by George Balanchine, and the New York City Opera. The Metropolitan Opera House—the "Met"—can hold 3,800: it has a glass facade, two murals by Chagall, and a movable stage, the only one of its kind in the world. A fascinating behind-the-scenes tour of the world of

331

opera and ballet. Tours held Monday to Friday at 3:30 P.M. and Saturday at 10:30 A.M. Phone 582-3512. The Avery Fisher Hall (2,700 seats) is the home of the New York Philharmonic Orchestra; after solving various problems, its concert hall now offers exceptional acoustics. Behind this building rises the Vivian Beaumont Theater, brainchild of the great Finnish architect Saarinen. It includes an extremely elegant theater-in-the-round and the smaller Mitzi Newhouse Theater. And finally, by way of a footbridge spanning 65th Street, you arrive at the Juilliard School, which has become the best conservatory in America for music, opera, and the dramatic arts. It recently instituted an ambitious educational program, and now trains four hundred public school arts teachers annually.

If visiting Lincoln Center is so easy, then how does one actually get to see the New York City Ballet doing "Nutcracker," Luciano Pavarotti in "La Boheme," or Leonard Bernstein directing the Philharmonic, when tickets for all major shows are sold out months in advance?

As soon as you arrive in New York, head for Lincoln Center and look over their program. There are always so many concerts, operas, and plays being presented that you're bound to find a seat for something interesting. Even for those shows listed as sold out, it's always worth your while to try your luck at one of the ticket agencies.

Note as well that Lincoln Center organizes very good film festivals.

Finally, if you get the chance, attend a concert at Carnegie Hall, at the corner of 57th Street and Seventh Avenue. The hall, built in 1891, is acoustically speaking one of the best in the world.

# Theater

*Broadway!* The word has a magical resonance in every country around the world, though the reality is less dazzling. True, "Broadway," which means that part of that boulevard around Times Square, has the highest concentration of theaters in the world, and the stage-struck may be tempted to remove their shoes as they approach this holy place. But they are often disappointed when first setting eyes on their mecca, which is surrounded by porno movie houses, live sex shows, and sordid street life. Yet if you look for it, the glamour and the glitter are still lurking behind the somewhat dreary theater façades, for Broadway is full of treasure, with as great an amount of talent and professionalism, especially in musicals, as anywhere in the world—not to mention the talents responsible for the increased popularity of off and off-off Broadway shows.

Now it's true that there aren't only winners on Broadway. And when a show crashes, no one bothers to tally the wounded and the dead, because the sums of money at stake are usually astronomical.

But when the reviews are encouraging and the public verdicts favorable, it means superpacked houses for months, even years on end, simultaneous road shows all over the country, and tickets scalped in enormous quantities. And the successes are numerous. Broadway now sells nearly ten million tickets a year—an increase of 78 percent in seven years—but the problem for anyone arriving in New York is still: how can I get tickets?

No need for panic: there are several possibilities. The first, if you're traveling on your own and staying in one of the bigger hotels, is to include with your reservation a request that the tickets you want be obtained for you—it's best to list a number of possible dates. If you wait until you arrive—there's always an agency in the better hotels or at least a concierge who, for a few dollars, can arrange things. There are also commercial agencies in town, among which Golden and LeBlang (207 W. 45th Street, 944-8910) is one of the best. You'll pay a bit more, it's true, but the commission is reasonable, since the cost of theater tickets for Broadway is so high ($25 to $40 on the average).

If you're not daunted by the prospect of waiting in line, a big ticket kiosk has sprung up at the intersection of Broadway and 47th Street, which has become very successful: TKTS is a nonprofit organization to help theaters, and by means of its computers all the tickets available on any particular day are rounded up and sold at about *half price*. But only tickets for shows the same day are sold. The shows for which tickets are available are listed outside, and tickets go on sale at noon for matinees, at 3:00 P.M. for evening shows—but it's best to show up at least an hour early.

Then there are the people who hover around ticket booths, with the air of conspirators: the scalpers, who sell tickets on the black market, and they're to be found hanging around theaters where something currently hot is playing. Beware! These ticket traffickers have a particular knack for palming off worthless tickets. A final possibility: show up at the theater somewhat early—there are often last minute cancellations. The method is risky, but often successful.

Wednesday the large Broadway theaters have matinees at 2:00 P.M. It's "Housewives' Day"—they flock to the theaters by bus, subway, or car from all over suburban New York.

One last word: Broadway, yes, but not just Broadway. There is very good theater in SoHo, the Village, and neighboring off Broadway areas. Avant-garde plays, theater workshops, and new plays which are

333

being broken in. You risk being bored. You may catch the next hit play. At least, you will see hopeful actors working.

For a detailed list of plays and musicals, with brief critiques, consult the *New Yorker* or *New York* magazines, or the *New York Times.*

# THE SIGHTS

# The Bronx

The Bronx (no one calls it just "Bronx"), the only borough not on an island, is best known for its zoo and its baseball team, the latter sometimes mistaken for the former.

The ever-colorful, headline-making Yankees, who can stir up more passion in New Yorkers than a power failure, make baseball history every summer in Yankee Stadium. Built in 1923 during the heyday of Babe Ruth, the stadium resounded with cheers and (sometimes) jeers for such immortals as Lou Gehrig, Joe DiMaggio, Mickey Mantle, Roger Maris and Reggie Jackson.

Only sociologists will enjoy a visit to the South Bronx, a zone blighted by neglect and crime, and unredeemed by the promises of politicians. But an hour's drive, and a universe away, you will find City Island, which is a wonderful anachronism—a New England fishing village on Long Island Sound, where a summer saunter will take you past antique shops, seafood restaurants, and the nodding masts of fishing boats.

## Bronx Park Zoo
**185th St. and Kazamiroff Blvd.**
**220-5100**
*Daily 10:00 A.M. to 4:30 P.M.*
*Adults, $2, children 75¢*
*(Tues. and Thur. free)*

With the largest collection of animals in America—over three thousand animals of a thousand species—the Bronx Zoo is among the world's most innovative wildlife sanctuaries and is worth the half-hour trip from Manhattan. Unobtrusive moats border the open domains of wild deer, moose and yak in the "African Plains." The "World of Darkness" houses nocturnal birds. The "World of Birds" aviary simulates a South African rain-forest thunderstorm daily at 2:00 P.M. Lions, monkeys, snow leopards, reptiles, great apes, penguins and elephants all roam in reasonable simulations of their natural settings. Not to be missed is the Bengali Express monorail ride through "Wild Asia," a habitat for gazelle, antelope, and zebras.

## Bronx Park Botanical Garden
**Kazamiroff Blvd. and 200th St.**
**220-8700**
*Daily dawn to dusk; 10:00 A.M. to 5:00 P.M. for conservatory*
*Admission free; conservatory $2.50 adults, 75¢ children*

Finally, after a lengthy period in New York's asphalt jungle, we recommend a visit to the real thing. The world-famous Botanical Garden consists of 250 acres of trees and flowers from all over the world. Don't miss the orchids and exotica in the Enid A. Haupt Conservatory (closed Mondays), a national landmark. You can wander through two deserts, two jungles, and a one-acre rose garden—or lose yourself in the 40-acre Hemlock Forest, through which the Bronx River meanders. Also take a look at the fern forest, palm court, and rock garden, featuring plants from the world's temperate zones.

# Brooklyn

When asked where in the U.S. he resides, a New Yorker traveling in Europe would probably answer, "New York City." Not so the Brooklynite. He would answer "Brooklyn"—emphatically. While only slightly larger than Manhattan, Brooklyn boasts almost twice the population and equivalent the devotion. Brooklynites are proud, passionate, and provincial, and although they may work and play in Manhattan, their hearts and souls have never left the neighborhood in which they were raised. To them, the only thing Manhattan has that Brooklyn doesn't is a few tall buildings.

Brooklyn's ethnic neighborhoods are just as varied and traditional as Manhattan's. The Italian community flourishes in Bensonhurst and Bay Ridge. Just south of Brooklyn Heights on Atlantic Avenue are the foodshops and restaurants of a thriving Middle Eastern community. Bedford-Stuyvesant is a Black and Hispanic ghetto neighborhood in the center of Brooklyn. Many Hasidic Jews dwell in Williamsburg at the base of the Williamsburg Bridge. And there are so many Russian Jews in Ocean Park, near Coney Island, that this area is known as "little Odessa by the sea."

## Brooklyn Heights
**Just across the Brooklyn Bridge**

Brooklyn's answer to Greenwich Village is Brooklyn Heights, an attractive enclave of brownstones and townhouses nestled in a fifty-block area on a hill overlooking lower Manhattan. Its wide Promenade above the East River provides a spectacular view of Wall Street skyscrapers, the Brooklyn Bridge and the Statue of Liberty. At sunset, it can be the most romantic spot in the city. These tree-lined streets around Montague Street have attracted some of America's greatest writers, including Walt Whitman, Herman Melville, Thomas Wolfe, W.H. Auden, Carson McCullers, Arthur Miller and Norman Mailer.

## Botanical Garden
**Eastern Parkway**
**622-4433**
*10:00 A.M. to 6:00 P.M.*
*Tue. to Sun.*
*Admission Free*

Just east of Prospect Park, the Botanical Garden is a serene, tranquil breath of fresh air. In April and May the flowers and lanes of cherry trees are magnificent. The rose garden flourishes in June, and you'll find pathways and small gardens filled with botanical jewels. The greenhouse, an exercise in elegant Victorian design (admission 25¢ on weekends) overlooks a series of lotus pools. The garden also has such unusual features as a Japanese Garden (closed in the winter) with authentic Shinto gardens (open weekends 11:00 A.M. to 1:00 P.M. and 2:00 P.M. to 4:00 P.M. admission 25¢), America's largest bonsai tree collection, and a fragrant garden designed specifically for blind people, complete with braille markers.

## Coney Island

Coney Island is not what it used to be (housing projects now have taken over from the miles of midways and arcades)—but still, on hot summer weekends, up to a million New Yorkers migrate to the end of the subway lines to wedge themselves onto the crowded beach for a cool dip in the Atlantic. Coney Island still has Nathan's famous hot dogs (the original), the skeleton of a 250-foot parachute jump (from the 1939 World's Fair), several roller coasters (the Cyclone is still thrilling after so many years), and a two-mile boardwalk. But a visit to this once legendary, now downtrodden amusement park is for hard-core nostalgics only.

## The New York Aquarium
**Surf Ave. and W. 8th St.
266-8500**
*9:00 A.M. to 5:00 P.M. Mon. to Fri.
Adults $2, children 75¢*

The New York Aquarium, celebrating its 25th anniversary in Brooklyn, houses hundreds of the world's marine animals, both fresh and salt water. The 35 aquariums have fish of every color and size, including some fierce looking sharks. Also of note are three seal pools and a whale pool.

## Prospect Park
**Grand Army Plaza**

Central Park may be twice as large, but Prospect Park, in the center of Brooklyn, is considered by many (including its landscaper—who also created Central Park) to be the more aesthetically perfect. A large triumphal arch (honoring Civil War soldiers and sailors) stands at the entrance. Within its shaded interior lies a beautiful lake and boathouse, several eighteenth-century homesteads, a few aging, but lovely, pavilions, and a small (rather pathetic) zoo. The park is filled in spring and summer with families, amateur ballplayers, dogs, frisbees, kites, joggers, bicyclists, rollerskaters, and strollers. A few local residents even tempt the fates by fishing in the lake.

# Chinatown

Chinatown is so full of visual and sensual treats, you'll be hungry for more an hour later. Touristy? Maybe. You probably won't escape this enchanting, neon-exotic, Oriental island in downtown Manhattan without buying at least one porcelain Big Apple sake bowl, a pair of I

Love New York chopsticks, or a bag of Jewish fortune cookies for the folks back home, and you'll have a grand time as you wander through this spiderweb of small, shop-filled streets that twist through this district like a human fire dragon on Chinese New Year.

Chinatown is home to over ten thousand people of Chinese descent. The five hundred garment factories scattered in the lofts and tenements above street level employ twenty thousand people, mostly women. The more than 150 restaurants, stand-up lunch counters, and tea parlors employ most of the men.

The underbelly of Chinatown, which you won't see, consists of sweatshops, unhealthy housing conditions, basement gambling dens featuring mahjongg, poker, and fantan (a game played with cups of small stones), and street gangs, extortion and protection units, holdovers from the legendary "tongs" that controlled opium dens and vice in the early twentieth century. But you'll not notice this sweet-and-sour urban condition as you try some Chinese delicacies or see if you can find a bargain in something jade, pearl, silk, or ivory. Meander into the many newsstands (there are seven local Chinese newspapers), bookstores, herb and ginseng shops, and import/export houses for an eyeful of East meets West.

## Chinese Museum
**8 Mott St.**
**964-1542**
*Daily 10:00 A.M. to 6:00 P.M.*
*Admission 75¢*

Don't expect the Prado or Saint Peter's. These are mass tourist exhibits that cater to the quick five-minute look. The very idiosyncratic museum is located inside and above a noisy video arcade, features two well-fed chickens who dance and play tic-tac-toe (you have to see it to believe it!) and is just as fun and kitschy. It's an interesting lark if you want a fifteen-minute self-service learning experience about the more popular areas of Chinese life, including chopsticks, flower arranging, checkers, and calligraphy. There's also an enclosed twelve-foot dragon who, for the small price of a quarter, will light up and shake its head. Ah, the inscrutable Chinese . . .

## Eastern States Buddhist Temple of America
**64 Mott St.**
*Daily 9:00 A.M. to 6:00 P.M.*
*Free admission*

The Buddhist Temple is found in the back room of an adjoining Chinatown souvenir shop. Residents come to kneel before Buddha (who represents compassion and mercy) and to toss joss sticks into urns to pay their respects. Followers of Taoism can also shake Tai Tai (fortune) sticks onto the floor and match the first stick fallen with one of the many fortunes printed on slips of paper that look like bus transfers on the wall.

You'll know you're in Chinatown by the pagoda-shaped phone booths and the neon dragons. All its missing now are "Wok—Don't Wok" signs on the street corners.

# Financial District

When a New Yorker tells you he works "downtown," he means the Financial District, the skyscraper-ridden triangle at the bottom-most tip of Manhattan. Unlike uptown, which follows a logical grid pattern set up in 1811, the Financial District still retains a crooked, spontaneous pattern of streets—unchanged since the seventeenth and eighteenth centuries.

The rhythm of Wall Street fluctuates with the rhythm of the Dow Jones (the pedestrian traffic on Nassau Street is amazing at noontime, when a human flood of thousands of workers converge on it). The best view of Wall Street can be had on the lower section of the street looking up towards Trinity Church on Broadway. Wall Street got its name from a wooden wall the Dutch erected to put off imagined Indians and British invaders . . . it ended up as firewood.

A large statue of George Washington stands before Federal Hall, at the corner of Broad and Wall Streets, commemorating his inauguration on that site. Battery Park lies along the edge of the island (home of an old fort, now called Castle Clinton) just below the ornate Beaux Arts Custom House 1901-1907 with its four monumental allegorical sculptures depicting America, Asia, Europe and Africa by Daniel Chester French. The building houses frequently-changing exhibits on the American Indian. The French Renaissance style City Hall (1811) presides over the three blocks of government buildings to its rear. Inside, if you walk up the twin-curved stairway, beneath the rotunda where Abe Lincoln once lay in state, you can watch New Yorkers in the City Council do their best to "fight City Hall." To the left of City Hall, the sixty-story Woolworth Building explodes in all its Gothic, gargoyle-and-flying-buttress glory. Often referred to as the "Cathedral of Commerce," it was built by F.W. Woolworth from the fortune he made with his 5-and-10 shops. Inset in the lobby's ceiling are such endearing tableaux as Woolworth counting his nickels and dimes and Cass Gilbert, the architect, with a scale model of the building in his arms.

## Ellis Island
**Ferry at Battery Park and Broadway**
**269-5755**
*Daily, May to October, 9:30 A.M., 11:45 A.M., 2:00 P.M., 4:15 P.M. Two-hour tour, including one-hour guided tour of the island Adults $1.50*

Considering Americans spend so much money restoring historical houses of no particular interest, it is a wonder that they have allowed the handsomely turreted Victorian buildings of Ellis Island to crumble like old automobiles along a desert highway; this is a critical part of the American heritage.

It is estimated that 50 percent of the American people have ancestors who passed through Ellis Island on their way to America. The first immigrants were received in 1892, and in the sixty-eight years until its permanent closing in 1954 (immigrants now pass through Kennedy Airport) over twenty-four million immigrants, mostly from Europe, were processed in the halls and examining rooms of its six acres of buildings. When you step off the tour boat in front of the Great Hall, imagine the scene an immigrant faced 75 years before: the anxious crowds of fellow hopefuls, the endless questions and inspections, the fearful waiting, until, if lucky, he could leave the "Island of Hope" to begin his life in America.

It will take 50 million dollars to restore the disintegrating buildings of Ellis Island to their former state, so their future is in doubt. If Ellis Island has significance in your life—go now. This may be your last chance to visit the "gateway to America."

## The Fulton Fish Market

**South St.**
**(Fulton St. and Peck Slip)**
*Weekdays 4:00 A.M. to 7:30 A.M.*

The intrepid tourist (or New Yorker) may decide to visit this early-morning wholesale fish exchange. We did. And it was worth it. Like Billingsgate Market in London, during the early morning hours middlemen sell their suppliers' daily catch (97 percent of which is now brought in by truck from all over the country) to fish purveyors (for large restaurants), supermarket chain buyers, fish store merchants, and Chinese restaurant owners, while the truckers huddle around blazing oil barrels with their coffee.

The two-block market underneath East River Drive (east of the Financial District), shuttered by day, is electric by night—aglow with stark white lights as sellers shovel and hook fish onto their large scales, calling the price and poundage into dangling microphones. Handtrucks loaded with burlap bags of oysters and clams and ice-enclosed fish-laden cardboard boxes wheel about to fill the vans that will take the seafood to consumers throughout the New York area.

The fishmongers get their coffee and breakfast at Carmine's Bar and Grill (corner of Front and Beekman), and at 6:00 A.M. the eggs they served tasted just fine to us.

## New York Stock Exchange

**20 Broad St., 3rd floor**
**visitors' gallery**
*Weekdays 10:00 A.M. to 4:00 P.M., closed hol.*
*Free admission*

A sojourn to the Stock Exchange is as much a lesson in the value of instant electronics and human communications as it is a lesson in security transactions. The old tickertape machines that used to click out a never-ending chatter of market quotations, while providing confetti to shower over national heroes, are gone. In their stead, and essential to the modern workings of the exchange, are the new icons of our age—video screens and electronic scoreboards. Three thousand people work on the paper-littered 90 by 90 foot floor of the stock exchange. To keep them constantly informed about the up-to-the-minute trading activity, the walls of the exchange are lined with pulsating, bannerlike "electronic tickertape" screens. In

341

addition, each of the sixteen trading booths where stocks are actually bought and sold has over sixty monitors. Every sale is immediately recorded and transmitted via satellite to similar screens across the planet. If you've ever bought or sold stocks, you shouldn't miss seeing the human drama that goes into your transaction. If you're a neophyte, why not take in the five-minute description by a stock expert before you enter the viewing area? All of the heiroglyphics, symbols, codes and Wall Street "tribal behavior" will be deciphered for you.

## The South Street Seaport

**Water St.**
**(Peck Slip to John St.)**
**766-9020**
*Daily 11:00 A.M. to 6:00 P.M.*
*Exhibit vessels: adults $3*

The South Street Seaport is one of those areas that is going to change radically, so if you want to see some of Manhattan's oldest landmark brick buildings from the 1800s before graduate-school architects turn them into plate glass, scrubbed-brick "nautical" boutique shopping malls you'd better go soon. That the last vestiges of New York's great nineteenth-century maritime history have lasted so long unchanged in the shadow of the Financial District (with some of the world's highest real estate values) is unbelievable in itself.

The city and state, along with the Rouse Company (who built Boston's Fanueil Hall Marketplace and Baltimore's Harborplace) will soon raise a new marketplace on this site to be finished in 1983 and 1984. They do a good job—lots of people spend money in the refurbished buildings, building up the economy—but the honest ramshackle, sea-weathered look and spirit of the predecessors never remains.

Until the developers "save" this area, you can still visit several shops and exhibits. The entire seven-block area is a museum in itself, with outdoor concerts in summer, children's programs, and tours of the district. The main attraction at present are the tours of the exhibition vessels docked on the piers just east of Fulton Street. Here you can visit the Peking, a 1911 square-rigger, the Ambrose, a 1907 lightship (floating lighthouse), and the Lettie Howard, an 1893 fishing schooner. The Pioneer, an 1885 sloop, sails for passengers in the summer months.

While walking in this historic area, stop under the awning to enjoy the contrast afforded by the whimsical building at 127 John Street (corner Water Street). Step back and read the time on the unusual 60-digit clock. Go through the neon tunnel lobby and ride the bizarre elevators any workday. At night, Christmas lights illumine the engine room on the 15th and 16th floors.

As you approach Peck Slip from Front Street, take time to notice the trompe l'oeil scene painted as a reminder of this seaport in days gone by.

## The Staten Island Ferry

**Battery Park**
*Daily, several times an hour*
*Round trip 25¢*

Ask many Manhattanites what they love most about New York and they'll say, "leaving it." If you want to experience the true meaning of "breathing room" after a week of crowded sidewalks and shoulder-to-shoulder restaurants, take a ten-mile, forty-minute round-trip ride across New

York harbor. For a little less than the price of *The New York Times* you'll get spectacular views of the stalagmite metropolis, the Statue of Liberty and Ellis Island.

## The Statue of Liberty
**The American Museum of Immigration Liberty Island, New York Harbor 269-5755 (ferry), 732-1236 (museum)**
*Daily 9:00 A.M. to 4:00 P.M. Year-round tours every hour on the hour (summer every ½ hour) Adults $1.50*

For almost a century the Statue of Liberty, arm outstretched, torch held high, has been a symbol of freedom and opportunity. What began as an extravagant gift from France to the fledgling American people, the lady cast in bronze has become a romantic symbol for emancipation and hope. Millions of physically fit (we assume, as the climb to the crown is 168 steps and twelve stories up a narrow staircase) people see New York through Liberty's eyes. The vast pedestal houses the American Museum of Immigration, a fascinating place full of authentic photographs, costumes and personal artifacts. Nine slide shows weave the museum's history into a patriotic narration. We particularly love the boat ride; if you're short on time (a visit requires 1½ hours, the round-trip ride is only 45 minutes) just enjoy the fresh air, the view of the harbor, and a new perspective on New York—if you don't mind sharing it with an enthusiastic international passenger list.

## Trinity Church
**Broadway at Wall St. 285-0888**

Historic Trinity Church may be dwarfed by its skyscraper neighbors in the Financial District, but it has an imposing presence nonetheless and is a must for anyone even mildly interested in early America. The Gothic revival building is actually the third Trinity Church to stand on this spot: the first, built in 1696, was destroyed by fire; the second, built in 1777, was torn down for structural weaknesses. The current building, designed by Richard Upjohn, went up in 1846 and is part of the Episcopal Church's extensive property holdings in New York.

For an excellent history lesson or a moment of tranquility amidst the madness of Wall Street, wander through Trinity's colonial cemetary, founded in 1681 (predating the first church). Some of early America's greats and near-greats (Alexander Hamilton, Robert Fulton, William Bradford) are buried here.

## World Trade Center
**Observation Deck, Two World Trade Center, 107th flr. 466-7377**
*Daily 9:30 A.M. to 9:30 P.M., wind and weather permitting Adults $2.50*

First there was the French acrobat Philippe Petit, walking a tightrope between the towers in 1974. Then there was George Willig who scaled the South Tower in 1977 like the "human fly" he claimed to be. Then came the parachutists and hang-gliders who jumped onto and off of the decks. What next? What makes people want to risk their lives to get to the top of a tower they can reach in a scant 58-second elevator ride as eighty thousand people do every day? Presumably it's the quarter-mile-high stage.

The views in all directions from either the 110th-floor open-air viewing platform—the world's highest—or from the enclosed high-tech viewing promenade on the 107th are spectacular. One interesting way to get the feeling of the scale is to look past the two-block park that crosses

Broadway, just east of the tower. At the bottom of the sixty-story Chase Manhattan Building, you'll see a square orange fleck. This is actually Noguchi's nine-hundred-square-foot *Cube*. And around the corner of the Chase, in a plaza, looking like a miniature papier-mâché mushroom, is Dubuffet's fifty-foot *Four Trees*. When you leave the tower, stand next to these "tiny" sculptures as viewed from the clouds, and you'll get a quick lesson in relativity.

# Greenwich Village

A nighttime and weekend playground for non-villagers (anyone who lives above 14th Street) who frequent the many bars, jazz clubs, coffee houses, off-off-Broadway theaters, and movie revival houses, the Village is in daytime a more relaxed, self-sufficient community of New York University students, respectable bourgeois, street hustlers and persons trying to grind out a living in the performing arts; the visual types have all gone to SoHo.

But the Village is still charming and ever-steeped in history. We recommend a leisurely walking tour to get a true sense of life in this well-publicized section of the city. Off of Fifth Avenue, you'll see Washington Mews, a picturesque row of converted stables and carriage houses, now townhouses. West of Fifth, especially on the streets from 9th to 12th, some of New York's most beautiful rowhouses and brownstones from the 1800s can be found. This neighborhood hosted an impressive cognoscenti of the likes of Emily Post, Mark Twain, Marcel Duchamp—all former 10th Street residents. The most intriguing part of the Village can be found in the London-esque jumble of little streets west of Washington Square Park. You're bound to get lost, but then that's part of the fun. You'll find lots of restaurants and bars near Sheridan Square, and a charming district of antique, curio, and specialty stores along Christopher Street. You'll also run into many of the large gay community of New York who reside here. At 75½ Bedford Street, you'll see Manhattan's thinnest townhouse—9½ feet wide (1873). St. Luke's Place, off Seventh Avenue, has beautiful 1860s townhouses and was the setting for *Wait Until Dark*. Don't miss the Jefferson Market Courthouse (1876) at Sixth and 10th Street, one of the best examples of Victorian Gothic architecture in America.

On a more commercial note, McDougal and Bleecker Streets offer the more honky tonk section of the Village, complete with ethnic restaurants, head shops, and beer-and-music establishments. Head east of Broadway for a look at the East Village. Astor Place houses Joe Papp's Public Theater in the converted Astor Library; three large flags herald its location. If punk is your pleasure, check out St. Mark's Place. You'll see new wave fashions a year before they become mainstreamed into American ready-to-wear. But further on Second Avenue the mood shifts; dairy-bars and meat shops retain their Ukranian roots. Cultures cross in the Kiev Restaurant (117 Second Avenue at 7th Street), a 24 hour Russian eatery that sells blintzes and borscht to a rocked-out late-night clientele.

**Washington Square Park**
**Base of Fifth Avenue**

This is the geographic center of the Village. Around the park's central water fountain you'll see four or five groups of street musicians, ventriloquists, comedians, crack frisbee throwers, skateboarding youngsters, magicians, jump roping unicyclists, and disco rollerskaters. The Village elders sit on the benches kibbitzing, or playing speed chess in the corners. The Washington Square Arch (1892) is Stanford White's copy of a wooden arch he made three years earlier to commemorate the centennial of George Washington's inauguration.

# Harlem

**Penny Sightseeing Company**
**303 W. 42nd St.**
**247-2860**
*March to November, Mon. and Thur. 10:00 A.M.; 11:00 A.M. Sat. Price $8*

The days when white people enjoyed nights out at the Cotton Club and Apollo Theater are long gone. Harlem's reputation (in part deserved) feeds on itself, unfortunately. Tourism in Harlem is not something to undertake flippantly.

There are, however, still many interesting pockets of architecture and culture in Harlem, and if you want to see them (like many visitors do), the best and safest way is to take the three-hour bus tour given by the Penny Sightseeing Company. Specialists in Black history, they'll point out sights associated with famous Harlemites, including Marcus Garvey, Malcolm X, Langston Hughes, Ralph Ellison, and James Baldwin. You'll also see the Schomburg Center, with exhibits from its large archive of Black culture; the Abyssinian Baptist Church, where the charismatic Adam Clayton Powell Jr. once preached gospel; the 1765 Morris-Jumel mansion—a Federal style home used by George Washington during the Revolution; and Striver's Row, Harlem's most fashionable block, containing handsome 1800's brownstones.

# Little Italy

Little Italy is not what it was. In the old days, when you walked into the cappucino houses and restaurants, the atmosphere made you feel like the guest of honor at a family meal, presided over by the padrone. These warm, unpretentious havens are being replaced by cold steel and glass, reflected endlessly by floor-length mirrors and strewn with high-tech furniture. Slick and clean, mercilessly modern—you could be anywhere.

True, here and there you find the flavor of the Old Country. But the children of the residents of Mulberry Street, five blocks that are the core of Little Italy, are choosing to raise their families in Staten Island, Brooklyn and the suburbs. In addition, the bordering streets are finding their salami shops turning into dried noodle and fish markets for the burgeoning Oriental population emigrating across Canal Street from Chinatown.

On weekends, however, the children come back to visit. They are joined by the droves of New Yorkers who arrive in search of the perfect veal picata and calamari Siciliana. The result is a throng of humanity, pleased to be sitting under Cinzano umbrellas, sipping wine, watching the traveling circus—the streets literally overflowing with al fresco diners and street vendors. And all under green and red neon signs.

Twice a year Italian street festivals—the Feast of Saint Anthony in June and the Feast of San Gennaro in September—honor local saints. For San Gennaro, Mulberry Street turns into a mile-long arcade, petty gambling zone, and glutton's paradise that shouldn't be missed (unless you're claustrophobic). For Saint Anthony, the festivities move west to Sullivan Street.

# Lower East Side

Why do thousands of women make the pilgrimage every Sunday—by subway, taxi, and limousine, down to this thirty-block dark, shabby semideserted ghetto that so many waves of immigrants—Eastern European Jews, Irish, Italians, and others—sweated so hard in the early 1900s to leave? For bargains. For the incredible buys they find on women's, men's, and children's designer and name-brand clothing—dresses, blouses, pants, shirts, lingerie, shoes, coats, and furs. For discounted home furnishings, linens, blankets, and towels. For handbags, leather goods and luggage, fabrics, appliances, and electronic equipment, all far below retail prices.

Be forewarned , however: this is no Upper East Side street fair. It is in every respect like a large Middle Eastern bazaar, rife with artful pickpockets, confidence men, and "creative" salesmen—you may haggle with someone for an hour, and then go next door and see the item for less.

Visually, this district has remained unchanged in years, and bound by tradition, as you'll see many Hasidic Jews in long, black coats wearing the required scullcap or hat over their ringleted hair, running many of the businesses—especially the older shops selling different forms of Judaica.

### Schapiro's Winery
**126 Rivington (Essex St.)**
*Sundays 10:00 A.M. TO 6:00 P.M.*
*Free admission*

Within the vast Essex Street Market, an enclosed village of small food and vegetable booths reminiscent of a European Sunday market. Drop by Schapiro's for a free kosher wine-making and tasting tour of the "Wine You Can Almost Cut With a Knife."

# Lower Midtown

While in this area, don't limit yourself to the Empire Building and Macy's. This is Manhattan's manufacturing and trading zone, and if you want to experience the "behind the scenes" just walk through the many commercial districts and see real New York at work. There's the garment district, just off Fashion Avenue (Seventh Avenue in the 30s); take care to avoid the clothes racks being pushed through the streets, resplendent with fashions being carted from factory to showroom. The fur district is nestled into a two-block area on 30th Street. The millinery district tops off the area at 38th Street. Within the 14th Street to 34th Street area (from the Hudson to the East River) you'll run across the camera district (32nd and Sixth), the toy center (23rd and Fifth), bookstore row (23rd to 12th on Fifth), the home furnishing center (14th to 30th on Broadway), bed pan alley (23rd to 34th and First) catering to the medical trade, and, of course, the flower district (28th between Sixth and Seventh). It all sounds commercial, and it is, but it's a fascinating area of town!

## The Empire State Building

**Fifth Ave. at 34th St.**
**736-3100**

*Observation deck, daily 9:30 A.M. to midnight, Guinness Records Exhibit Hall, daily 9:30 A.M. to 6:00 P.M.*
*Adults $2.50*

The Empire State Building will always command wonder. Other buildings may be higher, but this is still the big one. The "Eighth Wonder of the World." The personification of the Big City. At nearly a quarter-of-a-mile-high, for years this was the world's tallest building (now it's third), the symbol of New York of no bounds, the beacon of the city of dreams. Its romance was sealed, signed, and delivered in *King Kong* in 1933.

Since 1931, over 50 million people have seen New York from the 86th and 102nd-floor viewing platforms.

A ten-foot promenade surrounds the 86th floor and during the day this is an excellent place to gaze at the splendor below, brushed by the breezes that can sway the building twelve inches in bad weather. We recommend the nighttime view from the 102nd floor—200 feet higher and reached by the third elevator ride of your visit.

Here, in the small dark, circular viewing room, which looks like a combination disco and Flash Gordon set (with twinkling lights on the ceiling, walls of polished silver and mirrors, and exposed steel beams and rivets) you can gaze from twenty-odd circular windows at a glittering, panorama of the world's greatest city. Go very late, or very early, as the lines for this art deco wonder are longest in midafternoon, especially in summer.

The Guinness World Record people have an attraction in the lobby, popular with youngsters: a blow-up photo, scale model, and video exhibit of human achievement and excess. The exhibit contains the world's smallest book and the world's largest Raggedy Ann doll, among other abnormalities.

## Flatiron Building

**23rd St. and Fifth Ave.**

This wedge-shaped building was constructed in 1902 and named the Fuller Building. It gets its nickname from its triangular shape, designed to fit the block. For years, it was the world's tallest building.

## Gramercy Park

**Lexington Ave.**
**(20th-21st. Sts.)**
*Open Monday through Saturday 9:00 A.M. to 4:30 P.M, 50¢*

A lovely private square in the London fashion which will warm any Anglophile's heart. It is surrounded by some of the most elegant brownstones in the city. Theodore Roosevelt spent his first fifteen years at 28 East 20th Street, two blocks west of the park. You can feel his boisterous presence among the extensive memorabilia displayed in this restored Victorian townhouse.

## Pierpont Morgan Library

**29 E. 36th St.**
*Tues. to Sat. 10:30 A.M. to 5:00 P.M.; Sun. 1:00 to 5:00 P.M. Suggested admissions $2*

A sedate and refined literary institution. In the opulent interior of this large Italian Renaissance building, you can see Morgan's private collection of rare books, art and incunabula—including one of the few Gutenberg Bibles in existence.

# Midtown

New Yorkers demand the biggest, the best, the most modern, the most sophisticated, the most up-to-date. If something is not at its peak, New Yorkers will stay away in droves. Million dollar plays close after opening night. Movies will beg for an audience. Manhattanites are obsessive about life passing them by—that's why sometimes (by no means always) they do achieve the remarkable. Midtown is where many of these decisions are made and these goals attained.

A walk through Midtown (34th to 59th, the Hudson to the East River) will show you the stuff that dreams are made of. And money. The areas from the East River to Third Avenue are primarily residential. Sutton Place and Beekman Place (the 50s) are lined with elegant nineteenth-century townhouses and luxury cooperatives, many with stunning river views. In this bastion of old New York wealth are two of the city's most romantic and picturesque mini-parks, located in the cul-de-sacs of 58th and 57th Streets. You'll also find a covey of apartment buildings that evoke privacy, prestige, and affluence.

But Midtown is also the media empire of New York, and some say the world: book publishers, magazine headquarters and the ubiquitous advertising offices that go with them. The *Daily News* building (American home of much of the British press) which should be visited if only for its informative lobby, with flying distances from New York to the world's capitals inlaid in the floor.

Some of the city's most impressive architecture can be found in Midtown. The Seagram Building (Park and 52nd) built by Mies van der Rohe in 1958 in the International style, set a precedent for modern American architecture. Across the street is the "L"-shaped Lever House (1952)—one of New York's first glass-skinned buildings and the first to offer a public plaza on the street. The Byzantine building on Park and 50th is Saint Bartholomew's Church (1919) an exercise in stunning detail and craftsmanship. It is currently the focus of a lively controversy concerning its plans to sell its "air space" for the erection of yet another skyscraper. Over on Fifth Avenue (and 50th) St. Patrick's Cathedral (1858-1906) raises its majestic Gothic spires in defiance of the encroaching (albeit mirrored) high-rises. A visit inside this monument is a must; thirteenth–century France transplanted in the New World. Looking ahead, Philip Johnson's contested A.T. & T. headquarters is underway (Madison and 55th). This skyscraper will bear a striking resemblence to a seventy-story Chippendale cabinet. And there is more construction throughout the city; New York just doesn't stay in place, it is constantly in flux and always changing its face.

Vest pocket parks are urban architects' answer to New Yorkers' need for a touch of tranquility and natural surroundings. The Ford Foundation Building (42nd and Second) was the first to contain an atrium. Citicorp Building (Lexington and 53rd) has the most popular atrium, always filled with New Yorkers sharing this public space and enjoying the free stage concerts (call 559-4259 for schedule). Incidentally, St. Peter's Church is housed in this huge complex—it is a very contemporary structure, complete with its Louise Nevelson chapel. Tiny parks squeezed into small spaces are usually the result of corporate or private donation. They are always an unexpected surprise in a city dominated by gray steel and cold concrete, with no place to sit down. Paley (53rd off Madison), Greenacre (51st near Second), and McGraw Hill Park (48th off Sixth) are just a few of these joys.

## The Chrysler Building
**405 Lexington Ave. (44th St.)**

This celebration of art deco is a must, even if it's just to look at the inlaid wood elevators. Take a moment to examine the African marble and chrome lobby. The famous sunburst spire has recently received new lights that give a City of Oz look to the Manhattan skyline. The details and artisan craftsmanship are remarkable—sadly signifying remembrance of things past.

## Circle Line
**Pier 83 and W. 43rd (at the Hudson) 563-3200**
*Late March to early November, departs from 9:45 A.M. to 5:30 P.M. Adults $8.50*

It's a closely-guarded fact that no New Yorker has ever taken the Circle Line boat cruise around Manhattan, although it's the first thing they tell guests to do when they visit. What New Yorker has three hours to kill seeing the other sides of buildings they see every day? Let the natives fight the crowds on the streets. Experience the trip. When you return from your 35-mile, three-hour voyage, you will have a better idea of the scale of their city than most New Yorkers. Over the loudspeakers, a guide will announce the major points of interest and fill you in on fascinating New York gossip.

And think about this as you recline gracefully in your chair sipping your private stock Campari: Diana Nyad, a young endurance swimmer, swam the same route you follow in seven hours, 57 minutes in 1975. That's one way to get around Manhattan!

## Fifth Avenue

This grand boulevard is flanked by world-famous museums, institutes, elite shops, converted mansions and luxurious apartment buildings, from which emerge the idle rich, the industrious rich, their children, and their dogs. Although Fifth runs from the Villiage to 142nd Street, the Midtown section offers a veritable feast of traditional New York. Many feel that the corner of Fifth and 59th emulates what old New York was all about: dignity, style, grace and beauty. A stroll down Fifth Avenue will tempt your pocketbook, make you dream of fabulous wealth, intoxicate you with the endless possibilities offered by this city, and quite possibly wear you out.

Although most New Yorkers wouldn't be caught dead one of the horsedrawn hansom cabs parked outside the

Plaza, they are amusing and worth the investment, once. The price is listed as $17.50 per half hour, and they will go practically anywhere. We prefer the park, and the total trip will come to about $25 plus tip. Drivers are on duty from 10:00 A.M. to midnight, daily.

### Grand Central Station
**42nd St. and Lexington**

Half a million people pass daily through its 300-foot, ten-story lobby, many of whom take the shortcut through the Pan Am Building. Under the dim but twinkling constellations in the ceiling is the world's largest color slide (it changes monthly), courtesy of Kodak.

### The New York Public Library
**Fifth and 42nd**
**340-0849**
*Mon. to Wed. 10:00 A.M. to 9:00 P.M., Fri. and Sat. 10:00 A.M., closed Thurs. and Sun.*

This is the second largest library in the United States, after the Library of Congress. The Beaux-Arts building is guarded by the famous marble lions, Patience and Fortitude. Which is what you'll need to get through the 5.5 million books housed inside. Don't miss the vast third-floor reading rooms. The variety of colorful characters who loiter out on the front steps are worth volumes in themselves. Library funding is erratic, and therefore the hours can fluctuate, so call first.

### Rockefeller Center
**48th - 52nd between Fifth and Sixth**
**489-2947**
*Observation deck 10:30 A.M. to 7:00 P.M., Oct. to Mar.; 10:00 A.M. to 9:00 P.M.*
*Adults $2.50*
*Center Tour, Mon. to Sat. 10:00 A.M. to 4:45 P.M., every 45 min.*
*Adults $3.35*

Rockefeller Center is rightly praised as a model of urban planning and design. Over 250,000 people pass through its art deco buildings every day and many shop and eat in the 24 acres of underground shops that lie beneath this mini-city. John D. Rockefeller, Jr., who leased the land from Columbia University in 1928 (and the lease is up in 2069), had hoped it would turn out to be an international trade center; thus the Promenade, just off Fifth Avenue, is called Channel Gardens, located between the British Empire Building and La Maison Française.

Below the Promenade, framed by flags of fifty states and presided over by the eighteen-foot bronze and gold-leaf statue of Prometheus (1934) is a space where one can skate in winter or, in summer, dine serenely under the stars.

There's an open observation platform on top of the seventy-story RCA building, which gives splendid and unobstructed views north to Central Park and south to the Empire State Building. You can go up alone, or as part of the Rockefeller Center Tour, which includes a quick trip through Radio City Music Hall and ends on a private garden twenty floors above Fifth Avenue with an eagle's-eye view of St. Patrick's Cathedral.

If you've always wanted to see live TV—here's your chance. NBC, also located inside the RCA building, often tapes shows in front of studio audiences. Ask at the NBC desk near the Sixth Avenue entrance to the lobby if there are any tickets available for shows that day (best to get there early—around 9:00 A.M.—or call at 664-3055).

Also glittering at 50th is Radio City Music Hall (1932) the world's largest theater, with the world's largest chandelier and organ. It seats six thousand and features the world-renowned Rockettes, a chorus line of 36 lithe, long-legged dancers who perform live musical spectaculars for the family twice daily (except Thursdays) on the 144-foot stage. Backstage tours of the complex are run daily (except Thursdays) 10:00 A.M. – 5:00 P.M. (246-4600, adults $3.95.

Down the street, in the lower plaza of the McGraw Hill Building (Sixth and 48th), one can find the "New York Experience" (shows daily 11:00 A.M.–8:00 P.M.: Adults $3.90; 869-0345) slide and sound show that will explain New York's history, peoples, and culture to you in sixty minutes. It might even prepare you for the chaotic, polyphonic, New York "experience" on the street outside.

## The United Nations

**First Ave.
(between 42nd St. and 48th St.
754-7713
(Foreign language tours, 754-7539)**

*Daily guided tours every 15 min. 9:00 A.M. to 4:45 P.M.
Adults $2.50*

It is fitting that the attempt to create a world government is situated in Manhattan, chief borough in an immigrant city. Actually, we should say on Manhattan as the U.N. complex (1947–1953) lies in international territory and the postmark from the U.N. post office downstairs proves it. A visit, in effect, involves "leaving the country."

Le Corbusier, Oscar Niemeyer, and Wallace Harrison (the Met), among others, had a hand in selecting the designs for the familiar riverside buildings. Don't expect much from the tour that parades one million people a year through this symbol of world peace. Most of the time is spent seeing monumental gifts from member nations and walking from building to building. Escalator and air conditioning noises drown out half of the narration. Unless a council is in session, you'll see a lot of empty rooms with colored chairs. The most appropriate thing we saw was the huge neon Pepsi sign through the back window of the Security Council chamber—it has truly become an international symbol of world economic ties. Free tickets for the General Assembly (meets mid September–December) or any other Council's meeting are available on a first-come-first-served basis half an hour before the meeting that day from the main information desk. Sessions are usually held at 10:30 A.M. and 3:30. P.M. To find out in advance what meetings will be held, look on page 2 or 3 of the *New York Times*, or call 754-1234 between 9:30 and 5:00. Earphones allow anyone to follow the debates in English, French, Spanish, Chinese, or Russian—the official languages of the U.N.

The Delegates' Dining Room, overlooking the East River, is open to the public for lunch Monday to Friday 11:30 A.M. to noon and 2:00 to 2:30 P.M.—again on a first-come, first-served (literally!) basis. The delegates eat between sessions, but if they come early or late, eavesdropping can be interesting.

Souvenirs are available in the basement, tax free. And in the Assembly lobby, don't miss the Chagall Windows, Apollo 14 moon rock, the model of Sputnik 1, or the overhead pendulum that shows that no matter what nations may do to each other, the world keeps on turning.

# Queens

In most cases, by the time you get to Manhattan, you've already visited Queens. Twice the size of Manhattan, spacious Queens is host to both Kennedy and LaGuardia airports. Kennedy, which accounts for 75 percent of the air passengers between the United States and Europe, is among the world's busiest airports. If you're there, don't forget to look for Queens' most famous architectural creation—Eero Saarinen's TWA Terminal (1962)—which resembles a huge prehistoric bird in flight. The stainless-steel globe you will see on your way to Manhattan from the airport is the Unisphere, symbol of the 1964 World's Fair.

A home to over two million people, Queens is often referred to as the "Bedroom Borough." The Astoria section of Queens is often referred to as "Greek Astoria" and embraces a miniature Athens of 100,000 Greek Americans. Three quarters of the city's Israeli population lives in Queens, and many Korean immigrants make their home in the Flushing and Kew Gardens districts.

Space also means sports, and enthusiastic New Yorkers come to Queens for baseball and football at Shea Stadium; horse racing at Aqueduct and Belmont racetracks; and tennis at Forest Hills and the USTA National Tennis Center.

# SoHo

The Manhattan artistic community has moved south. Although there is a migration of artists to Tribeca, the Bowery, South Street, and even Brooklyn (for the rents, we presume, not necessarily local inspiration), SoHo (South of Houston) is still one of the most exciting art centers in the world. Every form of the latest in contemporary artistic expression is alive and flourishing in this small, forty-block area, centered on West Broadway. And art not on display in the one hundred-odd galleries is being worn on the streets and can be found in the many intriguing boutiques and craft shops that flank the cobblestoned streets.

But SoHo has another side: many traditional manufacturers of clothing and small metal goods still work out of the expansive loft buildings on Wooster, Greene, and Mercer Streets. And, in 1973, certain sections of SoHo were designated as part of the Cast Iron historic district. The Haughwout Building (1857) at the northeast corner of Broome at Broadway best displays the Venetian palazzo-like cast iron facade for which many of these buildings are noted.

We love to walk throughout this stimulating area, although we agree with residents who are appalled by the hoards of uptown preppies slumming in this new, chic haunt. If you can manage the crowds, wander around to get the feel of the avant-garde shops and the plethora of eateries, and to view the marvelous street scene that never ceases to amaze us.

# Staten Island

The island where the Staten Island ferry deposits its cars and commuters is about 2½ times the size of Manhattan, yet is dwarfed by the mother island in both population and, unsurprisingly, in cultural offerings. The best of the available sights (which you must get to by bus) are: Richmondtown Restoration (351-9414)—an in-process rehabilitation of seventeenth-, eighteenth-, and nineteenth-century buildings which will accurately trace the evolution of a typical American village (when completed); the Snug Harbor Cultural Center (351-9414, only a few miles from the ferry landing), a cluster of nineteenth-century Greek Revival buildings, formerly the home of retired sailors in an eighty-acre setting overlooking the harbor, now being converted by the city into a cultural center; the Jacques Marchias Center of Tibetan Studies (987-3478), which contains the most complete collection of Tibetan art and culture in the United States, set in two buildings resembling Tibetan monastaries surrounded by a peaceful garden; and the Verrazano-Narrows Bridge, a 2½ mile span that arches majestically across Lower New York Bay to Brooklyn, the longest suspension bridge in the world.

# Tribeca

No conversation about art in New York will conclude without mention of Tribeca. In fact, Tribeca is so tragically hip we're almost afraid to include it as a "sight-to-see" for fear of adding to the angst of whatever genuine artisans live in the lofts and spaces of this unspoiled SoHo. But we're going to.

Like SoHo (south of Houston) and NoHo (the loft area north of Houston), Tribeca also has a name made up of location and a street: "the Triangle Below Canal Street." But even the people who live there don't know which triangle (although there seems to be a consensus it's west of Broadway from Canal Street to Chambers Street).

Tribeca was custom-made for a loft colony with its multistoried factory warehouses filled with huge unfinished spaces just begging to be discovered. They have been. The artists had no sooner installed their plumbing before such pioneers as Meryl Streep and Robert DeNiro swooped down and bought lofts, skyrocketing the prices. Now Tribeca is becoming chic so fast that its "bastion-of-the-starving-artists" days may be over before they've begun.

But don't worry. While watering holes (Odeon, Commissary, Laughing Mountain) are popping up throughout the area, there are still some honest bars and restaurants catering to the local butter, egg, and cheese wholesalers (the real "founding fathers" of this area) that are affordable to the authentic working artists of Tribeca.

# Upper East Side

Only the United Nations is more cosmopolitan than the Upper East Side. Here and there among its tree-lined thoroughfares, you will find hundreds of international councils, leagues, centers, consulates, missions, foundations and institutes. This area (from 59th Street to 100th) is teeming with museums, galleries, shops, restaurants, bars, and luxury apartments of the New York elite. This is the land of young executive movers who prowl the watering holes from the 50s to the 90s on weekends. This is the territory of ladies who lunch and shop on sprees. And, this is the neighborhood of traditional New York apartment buildings with their ever-present doormen, cum child, pet, delivery watchers.

Off the East Side in the middle of the East River sit the new middle-income apartments of Roosevelt Island. Once known as "Welfare Island," it was rescued from the decaying hospital buildings and renamed in the mid '70s when the renovation program commenced. A walk around the island can be pleasant (no cars allowed), but the best part of the trip may be the three-minute aerial tramway ride that gets you there. The red tramcar holds 60, costs the same as the subway, and leaves every fifteen minutes from Second Avenue and 60th Street.

The Upper East Side also houses a second homeland for Germans, Hungarians, and Czechs. High-rise towers and high rents are gradually changing the complexion of this neighborhood known as Yorkville (the 70s and 80s between York and Third); but as you explore this district, you'll unearth many small ethnic shops and restaurants that cater to this community.

For thirty years New York's mayors have lived in the large Federal-style building, Gracie Mansion. This is located in Carl Shurz park, at the east end of Yorkville, on 88th, and bounded by East End Avenue. The park has a charming boardwalk/promenade from 81st to 90th that affords splendid views of the East River.

# Central Park

Central Park 59th St. to 110th St.; Fifth Ave. to Central Park West. Free event information: 755-4100 is as manmade as the Empire State Building. Twenty years of loving planning and effort went into creating this natural masterpiece: sculpting the myriad lakes, planting the more than a hundred thousand trees, and shaping the countless sinewy paths that weave their way through this bucolic "countryside." Frederick Law Olmstead and Calvert Vaux, the *wunderkinder* of urban landscape design, planned the park in 1856. The pedestrian paths, bridle paths, and sunken roadways, constantly curving to afford the visitor with new vistas at every turn, are woven into a natural tapestry so that when they cross— they don't cross. One path weaves through a tunnel, while the other arches over one of the 46 bridges (no two alike). This harmonious and seemingly effortless web is so smoothly constructed that none of the roller skaters, horseback riders, bikers, or carriage riders ever have to wait at an intersection—since there are none. And we know how much New Yorkers like that!

The park is a 2½-mile, 26-ring circus, so we'll describe some of our favorite rings.

Just inside the park, off Fifth, a few blocks north of the Plaza Hotel, is the Central Park Zoo (64th Street; open daily 10:00 A.M.–5:00 P.M.). The animals—yes, even lions and polar bears—inhabit indoor/outdoor cages surrounding a seal pond. Above the pond is the delightful Delacorte Clock. Every half-hour several large bronze bears emerge from inside the clock and pirouette to nursery rhymes. Nearby, in a fairyland setting, you can find the Children's Zoo, where farm animals love to be petted.

Farther west, behind the zoo, glistens the Wollman Ice Skating Rink (skate rentals in season: 397-3158) where Ryan O'Neil grieved for Ali McGraw at the conclusion of *Love Story*. A little further north you'll be greeted by the hundred-year-old wooden dairy, built in the Gothic Revival mode. Once a working dairy in the 1800s, it now serves as the Park Information Center (free maps, slide shows, and Ranger tours— 397-3156 for information). Nearby is a rare treat—the Victorian Carousel. Even the most sophisticated parkgoer won't be able to resist a ride on this magical antique merry-go-round. (year round; 10:30 A.M.–6:00 P.M.; weekends only in winter).

Just above the 72nd Street Fifth Avenue entrance is the elliptical Conservatory Pond. Children love to climb on the tree-sized Alice in Wonderland statue and chat to the Mad Hatter while sitting on giant toadstools. Children enjoy story-telling during warm months of Wednesday and Saturday at the statue of Hans Christian Andersen. With "The Ugly Duckling" toddling in front, it looks wistfully out over the pond, which is festooned on Saturday mornings in the summer with motorized regattas of remote-controlled model sailboats piloted from onshore by the citified skippers of the Model Yacht Club. (Saturdays 10:00 A.M.–1:00 P.M.; for race schedules: 397-3156).

If you amble over the hill west of here you will arrive at the bridge-spanned Central Park Lake. At the Loeb Boathouse (74th street) along the shore you can decide to either row or paddle with the ducks, ride a bike around the lake, or, if you're tired of exercise, have a hamburger at the waterside snackbar. (Boat rentals: $2/hour with $10 refundable deposit, June–September, daily 9:00 A.M.–5:00 P.M.; bike rentals $3/hour, small deposit and i.d. required: same season).

Bethesda Fountain looms on the south side of the lake. It is surrounded by a loud, chaotic open-air roller disco mob, which is best viewed from right where you are—far away. The fountain is located at the end of the elongated Central Park Mall, the Park's grand promenade, which serves as a showcase for dozens of aspiring street musicians. During the summer you may be treated to a free concert from the large bandshell at the terminus of the mall.

If you wander north of the lake through the hilly region known as the Ramble, you will notice that most of the couples feature a decided unisex look. If that look isn't to your taste, you might want to avoid this densely wooded area.

If you enter the park from the east '80s, take your picnic basket behind the Metropolitan Museum of Art to the Great Lawn. Here, on summer evenings, you can drink your wine and eat your baguette while listening to the free al fresco concerts given by the New York Philharmonic and the Metropolitan Opera, surrounded by hundreds of thousands of festive New Yorkers. If your taste runs to rock and roll, don't despair. In the hot summer of 1981 Simon and Garfunkel staged a reunion before six hundred thousand children of the '60s. Elton John, the Beach Boys, and other major performers have all passed through here.

Below the lawn is the modern hemispherical Delacorte Theater, home of the free Shakespeare-in-the-Park play series in summer (play info: 598-7100). Behind the theater, perched formidably on the hill arising above the small lake, stands Belvedere Castle (1869), hewn out of stone. It is the former home of the city's weather station, and is about to become an environmental education center.

The upper hinterlands of the park boast Manhattan's water supply. The Reservoir is handsome and occupies much parkland for ten blocks in the 90s. Streaming around its 1.5-mile circumference is a parade of sweatsuits; this is a mecca for uptown joggers.

If rowing, running, or rollerskating sound exhausting, let a dusky appaloosa do the work for you—and why not? If you're an experienced rider and sign a release, you can rent a horse (with an English saddle)from the Claremont Riding Academy, located a block from the park on West 89th Street, and ride off into the sunset down the 4.5 miles of bridle paths. (Claremont: 175 W. 89th Street; $16/hr; open daily from 6:00 A.M.; reservations: 724-5101) Central Park also has tennis, croquet and lawn bowling facilities for permit holders, checkers and chess tables, a bird sanctuary, impromptu folk dancing, and a children's marionette theater.

Except for summer nights when you're surrounded by the concert crowds, remember that when the sun goes down in Central Park, the things that go bump in the night come out of their lairs. Unless you relish free fire zones, enjoy the park at night only from a comfortable window seat at one of the many bars and restaurants that surround it.

# Upper West Side

The Upper West Side is like the Upper East Side, but a la carte—bigger helpings, but not the full dinner. It is said that the only thing that separates the Upper West Sider from an Upper East Sider is Central Park and $500 a month in rent. The Upper West Side does have unique characteristics, though. First of all, it's older—most of the buildings are from the turn of the century and only around Lincoln Center have new apartment towers sprung up. So the feeling on the streets here is a little grimier, a little more "Old New York." Traditionally, the Upper West Sider has been more leftist, more intellectual, and less pretentious than his counterpart on the East Side. Wealthy West Siders don't live in ostentatious high-rises, but rather in sedate, beautiful brownstones that line the streets just west of the park. Status means less here and stores serve a more varied clientele.

Discover for yourself the flavor of this neighborhood as you pass through it on your way to the many cultural centers on its perimeter. Besides the museums and churches, the architecturally interesting apartments have historically been home to many cultural figures. The ornate Astoria Hotel (Broadway at 74th) was once home to Caruso, Toscanni, Stravinsky, and Rachmaninoff, who may or may not be rotating furiously in their graves over the fact that Plato's Retreat is sweating all night below their former home. The Dakota (Central Park West and 72nd), with its dark foreboding exterior, was built in the 1880s to rival the lavish mansions of Fifth Avenue. A small section of Central Park across the street has been officially dedicated as "Strawberry Fields" to the memory of John Lennon. The Hotel des Artistes (1 West 67th) was home of Isadora Duncan, Noel Coward, and Norman Rockwell, a mixed artistic bag at best.

## Cathedral of Saint John the Divine
**Amsterdam Ave. at West 112th St.**
**678-6888**
*Daily 7:00 A.M. to 5:00 P.M.*

Only an optimist would bet on when the final third of this structure will be completed. But when it is, the now ninety-year-old edifice (1892) will be the world's second biggest church, inched out only by St. Peter's in Rome. As it is, you could fit Barnum's entire three-ring big top inside its 250-foot nave and still have room for a hundred elephants in the transepts.

Construction of the cathedral was halted after World War II, and only since 1979 has work resumed—on a less ambitious scale. The initial goal of the present planners is to add two imposing 294-foot Gothic towers, which will frame the majestic front facade.

Completing these will be as difficult as it would have been seven centuries ago. By choice, the planners have elected to employ authentic medieval methods and equipment to erect the towers, each of which will need 12,000 finely cut stones. In the cathedral courtyard one can view apprentice stonecutters preparing the smooth blocks from raw stone. Painstakingly, they design, cut, and hew the limestone blocks with old tools including applewood mallets and hundred-year-old chisels. Since 1979 they've been able to carve about a thousand blocks.

A ten-foot scale model of the finished cathedral is on display in the large cathedral shop. In this nonprofit gift shop one can also "donate" stones to the project: ashlars cost $100, capital stones are $3,000 each, and turrets go for $500,000.

## Grant's Tomb
**Riverside Drive at 122nd St.**

A visit here answers Groucho Marx's question: "Who's buried in Grant's Tomb?" If your answer is Ulysses S. Grant, the great General of the Union Army during the

**666-1640**
*Daily Wed. to Sun. 9:00 A.M. to 5:00 P.M*
*Free admission*

Civil War and later President—you're wrong! Grant and his wife, Julia Dent, lie side by side, not buried, but *entombed* in two twelve-foot, nine-ton black marble sarcophagi, resting 130 feet beneath a beautiful domed rotunda. The open crypt was fashioned after that of Napoleon at the Hôtel des Invalides in Paris. Two rooms flanking the crypt area relate Grant's life and career through a large photographic display.

The times take their toll. With graffiti scrawled all over it, the exterior of the classically designed tomb now looks like a signed high school yearbook. Partly to discourage this, the local community was asked several years back to participate in designing park benches around the building. The result is a somewhat bizarre wavelike, free-form series of molded concrete benches, arches, and who knows what, inlaid with thousands of small colored tile chips forming everyday objects and scenes.

We must admit, under close scrutiny it grows on you. Try to find Mickey Mouse, Donald Duck, and Abraham Lincoln.

## Riverside Church
**Riverside Dr. and 122nd St.**
**Observation Tower and Bell Chamber**
**222-5900**
*Mon. to Sat. 11:00 A.M. to 3:00 P.M.; Sun. 12:30 P.M. to 4:00 P.M.*
*Cost: 25¢*

Imagine gazing out over New York City from four hundred feet up while being buffeted by the sound of 74 pealing bells. In the tower of Riverside Church you will find yourself with bells above you, bells below you, bells all around. The Riverside Church Carillon, the world's largest (and heaviest, with a total weight of 100 tons) is located within the Gothic tower of Riverside Church, a twenty-story elevator ride and 100 twisting steps above Riverside Drive.

Some of the bells ring hourly during the week, but we suggest you go on a weekend, when you'll be able to watch the bells being played through the windows of a small cabin centered among the labyrinthine crosswalks. Three times daily you can see the wooden Carillon clavier (keyboard) being played by expert carillonneurs, who deftly press the 74 wooden levers (attached to the bells by wires) with their hands and feet (the six largest bells chime with the assistance of powerful motors.)

Climbing a few steps further up the tower will bring you to a small, 360-degree balcony, 392 feet above Morningside Heights. Although you must peer through iron gratings and concrete buttresses, you'll get a breath-taking view.

# Sports

Most major sporting events take place outside Manhattan in the boroughs or upstate. The following events are seasonal.

Baseball: The Yankees play in Yankee Stadium, "The House that (Babe) Ruth Built"—uptown in the Bronx. The Mets play in Shea Stadium, Queens. Football: The Jets host opponents in Shea while the crosstown powerhouse Giants dominate Giant Stadium in New Jersey. Basketball: Madison Square Garden houses the Knicks, while the Nets play in the Nassau Coliseum on Long Island. Hockey: The Rangers skate in the Garden, the Islanders in the Nassau Coliseum. Soccer: The Cosmos (with Giorgio Chinaglia and Carlos Alberto) play in New Jersey at the Meadowlands. Boxing and wrestling: Bouts are held at Madison Square Garden. Tennis: In early September the U.S. Open is held at the USTA National Tennis Center in Queens. The Volvo Masters (January) fills the Garden. Other tournaments take place at the West Side Tennis Club, Forest Hills, Queens. Horse racing: Thoroughbreds race at Belmont Park on Long Island, Aqueduct Racetrack in Queens, and the Meadowlands Raceway in New Jersey. Harnessed trotters also run at the Meadowlands, in addition to Roosevelt Raceway in Long Island, and the Yonkers Raceway in Yonkers, north of the city. (Or you can't make it to the track but you've got a sure thing, you can bet at the ubiquitous "Off-Track Betting" parlors throughout the city.)

Although there are no tours of Madison Square Garden (at 33rd Street and Eighth Avenue), the place is worth a visit when the (three-ring) circus is in town, or one of the popular sports teams plays in the 19,500 seat arena. (Information on events, 564-4402.) For bowling afficionados, the Garden has a 48-lane Bowling Center.

But why limit yourself to the role of spectator? New York has facilities for every sport you can imagine, from bocci to fencing, from bicycling to roller derby. A reminder: To play tennis on the public city courts you must have a permit, and often register a week in advance. For permits, call 360-8204. For reservations, at the courts in Central Park call 397-3138.

# Tours

## IN GENERAL

All five major sightseeing companies listed below offer "general overview" tour packages that include the following: downtown (below 59th) and Chinatown (2½ hours, $8.50); uptown (above 59th) and Harlem (2 hours, $8); Combined uptown and downtown (4½ hours,

$11.50); All-day tours (8½ hours, $19). Other tours will add a boat trip to the Statue of Liberty or a visit to the top of the Empire State Building. All companies feature multilingual tours. We've listed the schedule of Gray Line, Manhattan's largest tour company. New York Big Apple Tours specializes in foreign-language tours (French, German, Italian, Spanish) and the staff welcomes any perplexed foreign visitor at their 56th Street offices for free advice in six languages. Big Apple also offers several creative expeditions, including "Harlem Gospel Tours" and "New York Under Starlight."

### Gray Line Sightseeing
900 Eighth Ave. (53rd)          397-2600

### New York Big Apple Tours
162 W. 56th St.          582-6430

### Crossroads Sightseeing
701 Seventh Ave. (47th)          581-2828

### Manhattan Sightseeing Tours
150 W. 49th St.          245-6641

### Shortline American Sightseeing
165 W. 46th St.          246-5500

## THE SPECIALTIES

### Backstage on Broadway
228 W. 47th St.
575-8065
Times vary
Adults $5

Want to hear the roar of the greasepaint? A Broadway veteran will take you backstage at a major Broadway production and explain what goes on behind-the-scenes before the curtain goes up. Early reservations are required.

### Doorway to Design
79 W. 12th St.
339-1542, 924-1919
Daily 10:30 A.M. and 12:30 A.M.
$12 to $14

A professional interior decorator hosts you through exclusive interior design galleries, showrooms, antique dealers, artist studios, and private homes.

### Federal Reserve Bank
33 Liberty St.
791-5000, ext. 6130
Weekdays 10:00 A.M., 11:00 A.M.,
1:00 P.M., 2:00 P.M.

Reserve a week in advance if you want to set eyes on $190 billion in the Fed's gold vault. The one-hour tour also includes the security department and cash counting. This is where the bills marked "B" come from. No free samples.

## Holidays in New York
**152 W. 58th St.**
**765-2515**
*Times vary*
*$20–$25 per hour plus expenses*

Exclusive tours of the most celebrated fashion houses, Jewish landmarks, private artist and dance studios are Holiday's specialty. Multilingual private guides will escort you via limousine or taxi.

## Inside New York
**203 E. 72nd St.**
**861-0709**
*Times vary, $15*

Chat with the famous designers and furriers in their studios. Cruise the Fashion Capital in private tours of Seventh Avenue, SoHo, and the Lower East Side. Multilingual tour leaders.

## New York Times
**229 W. 43rd**
**556-1310**
*Fri., Sept. to June, 12:15 P.M.*
*Free*

Meet at the ninth floor auditorium for a tour of New York's status newspaper. It's an eye-opener.

## Singer's Brooklyn Tours
**Second Ave. and 41st St.**
**875-9084**
*10:00 A.M. to 4:00 P.M.*
*$15*

Call "Mr. Brooklyn," 56-year-old Lou Singer, to find out which of the many novel personalized adventures he's arranging this week: "Historic and Architectural Brooklyn," "Fantastic Flatbush," "Tiffany Fine Arts," "Ethnic Noshing," and many others. Custom tours by car or minibus.

# BY AIR

## Island Heliocopter
**Heliport at 34th St. and East River**
**683-4575**
*Daily 9:00 A.M. to 5:00 P.M.*
*$16–100 (2-person minimum)*

Enjoy superman's view of Gotham City and look the Statue of Liberty straight in the eye from a mere seventy-five yards distance. Five flights range in length from six to forty minutes. We recommend the flight over Wall Street to the Statue of Liberty ($28) or the same route plus a trip up to Central Park ($40).

## Pelham Airways
**Seaplane Deck at 23rd St. and East River**
**828-0420**
*April to October*
*$25 per 25-minute flight*

A seaplane whisks you aloft from the East River for an aerial circumnavigation of Manhattan.

# BY BOAT

## Hudson River Day Line
**W. 41st St. and Hudson River, Pier 81**
**279-5151**
*Daily except Mon. and Fri. in June*
*Adults $7 weekdays, $9 weekends*

A 3,000-passenger boat cruises fifty miles up the Hudson. You can picnic and swim at Bear Mountain State Park or continue on north for a three-hour visit to the military academy at West Point. Sightseeing tour of the U.S.M.A. costs an additional $2.50 for adults, $1.25 for children. This is a peaceful trip, if you don't mind being surrounded by colorful, chattering tourists.

## The Petrel
**Battery Park**
**825-1976**
*Times vary from April to October*
*Lunch sails $5, others $12*

Enjoy a sail (in good weather) on this seventy-foot yawl, which holds 35 passengers. Lunch sails, happy hour trips, and moonlit cruises. Cocktails available. This can be a mini-vacation from your vacation.

## The Pioneer
**South Street Seaport**
**766-9076**
*May to October, weekdays*
*2:00 P.M. and 6:00 P.M.;*
*weekends, 10:00 A.M., 2:00 P.M.,*
*7:00 P.M., $15*

The 102-foot schooner, the Pioneer, cruises New York harbor for three-hour trips, giving passengers their chance for a floating picnic.

# WALKING

## Art Tours of Manhattan
**33 E. 22nd St.**
**772-7888**
*Morning or afternoon*
*$15 per half-day*

A privileged way to discover new art; Ph.D.s provide lectures and tours through private art studios, galleries, museums, and major art districts. For the collector or the curious.

## Friends of Cast-Iron Architecture
**235 E. 87th St.**
**369-6004**
*Sun. afternoons in spring and fall*
*$2.50*

Savants and cast-iron devotees lead you through the world's largest concentration of cast-iron buildings—the factories and lofts of SoHo, Tribeca and Lower Broadway.

## Greenwich Village Walking Tours
**226-1426**
*Daily 11:00 A.M. and 2:00 P.M.*
*$5*

Twice a day you can make a two-hour exploration through this district, so important in the intellectual, artistic, and plain eccentric history of the United States. Phone reservations necessary.

## Municipal Art Society
**457 Madison Ave.**
**935-3960**
*May to October, Weekends*
*2:00 P.M. to 5:00 P.M.*
*$5*

This ninety-year-old civic group offers a different tour each month of New York's most fascinating neighborhoods. Trained guides share their love for, and expertise on architecture, history, and city-planning. Every Wednesday at 12:30 P.M., they offer free one-hour tours of Grand Central Station.

## Museum of the City of New York
**Fifth Ave. and**
**103rd St.**
**534-1672**
*April to October, Sun.*
*$5*

The historic, ethnic, and sociological history of the different neighborhoods of New York—a new one each week—is yours with a tour led by the Museum's urban experts.

# THE BASICS

# Getting Around

## ═══AIRPORT TRANSPORTATION═══

### Buses

Carey buses (632-0500) run every twenty minutes from 6:00 A.M. to midnight between Kennedy (1 hour; $5) and La Guardia (45 minutes; $3.50) and the East Side Airlines Terminal in Manhattan at 38th Street and First Avenue (the La Guardia bus makes one further stop at the sidewalk outside Grand Central Station). A bit of an inconvenience as you must carry your own luggage, and you must take a cab (about $2.50) to your hotel from the terminal.

From Newark Airport: Abbey's Transportation minibuses will drop you off and in most cases pick you up anywhere in Manhattan below 73rd Street from 7:00 A.M. to midnight. Make reservations with your hotel or by calling 586-8280 or 201-961-2535. Buses run every half hour from Newark to Manhattan. The return bus from Manhattan runs hourly. The cost for the half-hour trip is $10 plus tip.

For the economy-conscious traveling from Newark to Manhattan's West Side, Transport of New Jersey has buses to the Port Authority Bus Terminal (41st Street and Eighth Avenue) for $2.70 one way from 5:00 A.M. to 2:30 A.M. When leaving Manhattan, board at Platform 243 and 244 on the Upper Level. For the schedule call 800-526-4514. From 11:00 A.M. to 6:00 P.M. Carey has free mini-bus service between the Port Authority Bus Terminal and the Eastside Airlines Terminal.

Except for the Train to the Plane, public bus and subway service to the airports is arduous travail and we don't recommend it. It will take forever and could spoil the beginning or end of your trip. All buses end up at the Port Authority (Eighth Avenue and 42nd Street) and we wouldn't recommend that you take a trip here unless it's a financial requisite.

### Helicopter

No traffic, this route! New York Helicopter, located where 34th Street meets the East River, has a heliport that serves all airports. Time and cost (excluding tax) between the heliport and airports are as follows: Kennedy (15 minutes; $37.14); La Guardia (6 minutes; $26.67); Newark (10 minutes; $41.90) Connecting limousine service is available by calling 953-1022. Allow for ten-minute check-in. Takes all credit cards. Fares are substantially reduced if you buy your ticket in conjunction with your flight to or from New York on most carriers. Check when you buy your inter-city plane ticket.

## Taxis from the Airport

The New York Taxi Commission says the following rates (including bridge and/or tunnel tolls) are "acceptable" between Midtown and the three airports: Kennedy $17–$23; La Guardia $8–$13; and Newark $24–$35. (You should add a 15–20 percent tip.)

Twenty million people pass through New York's airports each year and horror stories are written about innocents who are overcharged by hundreds of dollars by unscrupulous cabbies. This probably won't happen to you, but prepare yourself—if you aren't familiar with American currency, figure out before you ride what bills will be necessary for the above amounts and keep them ready. (Use a small exchange chart if necessary—it will be helpful for your whole trip.) Cabbies aren't known for their patience, and if you rush to pay at the last minute you may end up spending more than you should. If you think you've been overcharged, find a third party at your destination to mediate. (Or follow the instructions listed in the section on taxis, below.)

If you share a cab from the airport, as single riders often do, you have two options . . . paying by the meter or agreeing in advance on a total dollar price. Take the former. Splitting the meter price will always be cheaper.

Allow an hour to get to Manhattan from either Kennedy or Newark, and forty minutes from La Guardia. Don't let the driver take you on a circuitous route. From Kennedy or La Guardia tell the driver to use the Midtown Tunnel (42nd Street) for Midtown locations (The Queensboro Bridge is a longer ride). For Wall Street, ask him to use the Brooklyn or Williamsburg Bridges downtown. From Newark, insist on the Lincoln Tunnel (39th Street) for Midtown; the Holland Tunnel for Wall Street.

## Subway/Special Bus Combination

The "Train to the Plane" is a combination bus–express subway (with a policeman on board) that connects Kennedy Airport with Midtown. A short bus trip from most terminals will take you to a private subway stop where a waiting express train will whisk you to Manhattan, with stops, along the way in Brooklyn, the Wall Street area, and Midtown on Sixth Avenue. Total cost is $5. The fifty-minute ride runs from 5:00 A.M. to midnight, usually every twenty minutes. For recorded information about where to board: 858-7272. Otherwise call 330-1234. This is recommended only for those who know their way around Manhattan and have light luggage.

## Important Numbers

### Airports
**J.F.K. Kennedy International Airport**
656-4520

**La Guardia Airport**
476-5000

**Manhattan Airlines Terminal**
(tickets) 986-0888

**Newark Airport**
1-201-961-2000

**East Side Airlines Terminal**
(Carey Bus) 697-3374

**East Side Heliport**
895-1695

### Railroads
**Amtrak Penn Station**
736-4545

**Conrail Grand Central commuter lines**
532-4900

**Long Island Railroad Penn Station**
739-4200

**Penn Central**
736-6000

### Subway and Buses (Inter-City)
**New York Transit Authority**
330-1234

**Port Authority Bus Terminal**
564-8484

# AUTO RENTAL

A car is the last thing you'll want in New York. Cabs are easier and less expensive. And parking is almost nonexistent. If you do need a car for any reason, rental companies are all over town, and any hotel desk will refer you to one close by. We've listed the major ones (prices are lower if you rent at the airports). Rates differ with size of car, usage, and so on. Don't be surprised that New York City has higher rates than other parts of the country. Foreign travelers: to avoid having to pay a deposit, you must present a major credit card and an International Driver's License (England excluded). If you have no credit cards, you must show your International Driver's License, passport, and return trip ticket back. You will probably, in this case, be asked for a $50–$75 cash deposit. Avis: 1-800-331-1212; Hertz: 1-800-654-3131; National: 1-800-328-4567.

# BUSES

Just think of it as a sixty-five foot limo that you're sharing with about sixty-five other people. A bus is frequently a pleasant, even scenic way to get where you're going on the island. However, in congested Midtown, buses often crawl, and you might get there faster by walking. Here are the facts: buses run twenty-four hours a day on all avenues and major cross streets. Easy-to-read bus and subway maps are available free at Grand Central Station or the Visitor's Center at Columbus Circle (and also at some subway booths). The cost is 75¢ in any direction. Exact change is required. The driver carries no change (although other riders do!). The driver will also give you free transfers for connecting routes, to be given to the driver of the next bus as you board. Bus transfers can't be used on the subways, but subway tokens can be used on the buses. Signposts with maps along the curbs explain the routes (not all buses at the same stop end up at the same place). Choose your route number (i.e., M1, M5) and get on the bus displaying that number. On weekends, two "Culture Buses" make stops at most of the cultural centers between Wall Street and 162nd Street. The bus driver sells the $2.50 ticket (coins only) good for the whole day. For bus or subway route information call 330-1234 and prepare for a ten-minute wait. New Yorkers call the tinted windowed-buses the "Darth Vader" line, for obvious reasons.

# FINDING STREETS

If you've ever read a corporate graph, you'll figure out how to find your way around the city in a minute. The big avenues are the verticals (north/south), the cross streets are the horizontals (east/west), and Broadway falls across them like the chartline of a company on its way to bankruptcy, going out of business at Battery Park. Below 14th Street, this whole system goes awry, and it's safer not to trust the cabbie's knowledge—find out the cross streets near your destination. Most addresses are like mathematical formulas: Fifth and 54th; 48th and First—and you can figure out walking distances if you remember it's twenty north/south blocks to a mile, and most east/west blocks are twice as long. Fifth Avenue divides street addresses into East and West. For example, 250 West 57th Street is at Eighth Avenue, and 300 East 54th Street is at Second Avenue. To determine the location of an address on an avenue, consult the front of the telephone directory for the bizarre calculations that give you the answer. Better yet, just ask somebody. New Yorkers are really quite friendly and are quick to help. As for Avenue of the Americas, most natives still call it Sixth Avenue, as we have here.

# LIMOUSINES

New York limousines offer everything but cable TV, so whether you just want to be met or dropped off at the airport, or want a personal guide (bilingual on request) to the metropolis, why not have the best and get a limousine from one of the many (competitively priced) services around town?

The average cost is $26-an-hour (plus tolls and 15 percent tip) whether you hire one for an hour, a day, or a week. The hourly charge is "from garage back to garage," so expect to pay for before and after you travel (most are fifteen minutes from Midtown). Excluding tip, these are the approximate prices you will pay to be picked up by a limo at the following airports: Kennedy—$48; La Guardia—$41; and Newark—$53. If you request a sedan, the prices are about $8 less. Prices from Manhattan are usually about $5 less. Most services take all major credit cards. We've listed the largest.

## Carey Limousine
*1-800-336-4646 U.S., 937-3100 local*

## Fugazy Limousines
*247-5800 local*

## Dav-El Limousines
*1-800-223-7664 U.S., 580-6500 local*

## London Towncars
*1-800-221-4009 U.S., 988-9700 local*

# SUBWAYS

Although they are a necessity for the 3.5 million strap-hangers (more than the population of Ireland) who use them daily, here's our advice to the visitor: stay out of the subways. Everything you've heard is true. It is noisy, crowded, frantic, and dangerous down there, and like a sauna in summer. Stay above ground—in taxis and buses. If you want the experience or you've had it with "gridlock" (New Yorkese for tied up intersections), the best, safest, and most modern (and air-conditioned in summer) is the *F* train, which with it's sister *E*, goes halfway across Midtown and all the way down to Wall Street. Its route features all the stops you'll need, including Citicorp, Fifth Avenue, Rockefeller Center, Macy's, Greenwich Village, SoHo, Tribeca, and the World Trade Center (change from the *F* to the *E* at West 4th Street walking up two flights, to continue down to the World Trade Center). All rides cost 75¢ for any distance. Graffiti is free. Subways run 24 hours a day.

# TAXIS

The opinionated New York cabbie of legend is a dying breed. You still occasionally get some politics, a discourse on life, or a short night-club act from the veteran drivers, but now you're just as likely to have to give your own directions to a younger hack, absorbed in his own world, separated from you by a plastic antimugging shield. Some recent immigrant hacks may not even know how to get to your destination, and will willingly listen to directions. Most drivers are honest and won't try to take advantage of you—but just in case, we'll give you the rules of the passenger road.

In New York, there are no taxi "zones." You pay just what's on the meter. The cost is based on the length of the trip only, and not related to the number of passengers. The first 1/9th of a mile costs $1.00 and it's 10¢ for each additional 1/9th mile. Any time the cab stands still, the meter will change an additional 10¢ for every cumulative 45 seconds. There is no charge for luggage, even if it goes into the trunk. The "50¢ charge for trunks" sign refers only to steamer trunks—and who uses them anymore? Whoever uses them probably won't be cabbing it. Tips should be 15 to 20 percent. There is no extra charge for going to any other city borough, but if you go outside the city limits (New Jersey,. Westchester, or Eastern Long Island) you must pay double what the meter reads (because the cab isn't supposed to pick anyone up for the return trip).

A single light on the roof tells when a cab is available. When it's out, the cab is in use. If you see more than one light on top, the cab is either "Off Duty" or "On Radio Call."

Here are some tips: All licensed cabs are yellow, with gold medallions on the hood. Don't ride in "gypsy" cabs or "liveries"—they always cost more. Also, make sure the driver sets the meter to $0.00 when you get in, or you'll end up paying for the previous person's ride. Don't negotiate prices. Pay only by the meter. And if you learn the city, don't be afraid to tell the cabbie what route you want to take. If you think you've been unfairly charged in any way, get the cabbie's name and number and call the Taxi Commission at 747-0930. Even better—get the cabbie to put what he charged you in writing. That should solve any problems fast.

## Radio Taxis

Radio-dispatched taxis will pick you up anywhere in New York City upon telephone request—24 hours a day. You will have to pay whatever is on the meter and usually a premium of about $2–$5 for the service (it's universally accepted—but they aren't supposed to charge it!). They may ask you to share a cab, but you don't have to agree.

# At Your Service

## SAFETY

We wouldn't even include this section, except for the unfortunate fact that crime in New York has been so sensationalized by the media that a visitor might think he'd need an armed escort just to go out at night. Not true. Yes, there are places where the potential for danger is higher than others, but common sense will tell you where not to tread.

Here are some basic rules for travelers anywhere: Keep your money in traveler's checks—they're accepted universally. Put your valuables into the hotel safe when you're not using them. Double-lock your hotel room at night. And when you're strolling along the streets— cover up tempting items like jewelry, gold chains, and cameras.

Most of all—just be yourself. You wouldn't be in New York if you didn't already know how to cope with the big time.

## FOREIGN EXCHANGE

New York may be an international city, but its provincialism shows when it comes to providing money-trading facilities for its foreign guests. Don't expect to exchange money after the sun goes down or on weekends. There are exceptions, but most of the Midtown banks with exchange windows are only open from 9:00 A.M.–3:00 P.M. weekdays, and the private exchanges usually close before 5:30 P.M. If you're caught short on a weekend, and don't want to trek out to Kennedy Airport (where currency exchanges at the International Arrivals building are open from 7:30 A.M. to midnight, daily), you're limited to only three locations: Deak-Perera (41 E. 42nd Street; Saturday: 9:00 A.M.–5:00 P.M.); Thomas Cook (18 E. 48th Street; Saturday: 10:00 A.M.–4:00 P.M.); or the Republic National Bank (1 E. 59th Street; Saturday: 9:00 A.M.–2:00 P.M.). Note that these are closed Sundays. Some major hotels will change money—but only for their guests.

Most currency exchange locations, including banks, are listed in the Yellow Pages phone book under "Foreign Money Brokers." We've listed several exchanges that do not charge the $1 service fee.

## Bank Leumi Trust
*562 Fifth Ave. at 46th; Mon.-Fri.*
*8:00 A.M.-5:30 P.M.*
*579 Fifth Ave. at 47th; Mon.-Fri.*
*8:30 A.M.-3:00 P.M.*

## Barclays Bank
*15 W. 50th at Fifth Ave.; Mon.-Fri.*
*8:30 A.M.-3:00 P.M.*
*9 W. 57th at Fifth; Mon.-Fri. 8:30 A.M.-*
*3:00 P.M.*

## Harold Reuter & Co.
*200 Park Ave. at 45th; Mon.-Fri.*
*8:30 A.M.-4:00 P.M.*

## Swiss Bank Corp.
*608 Fifth Ave. at 50th; Mon.-Fri.*
*9:00 A.M.-4:00 P.M.*

# INFORMATION

## Big Apple Report (events)
*976-2323*

## Police
*911*

## U.S. Customs
*466-5500*

## U.S. Passport Office
*541-7710*

## Weather
*976-1212*

## Listing of Dial-It Numbers (free)
*999-1000*

You'll give yourself more time to enjoy New York if you take a leisurely half-hour at the beginning of your stay to organize your thoughts about what you want to see and do during your visit. Listings for all cultural and special events taking place each week can be found in these weekly magazines: *New York/Cue,* the *New Yorker,* and *The Village Voice.* The city's three major newspapers—the *New York Times,* the *Daily News,* and the *Post*—all carry entertainment listings, with the most comprehensive coverage in the "Weekend" section of Friday's *Times.* The *Gallery Guide,* a small magazine found at most newstands or art galleries, lists all current art gallery exhibits and includes useful maps of gallery districts.

Having a map is always a time-saver, too. Free maps and sightseeing literature are available at the New York Convention and Visitors Bureau at 2 Columbus Circle, just southwest of Central Park (397-8222). A more general publication and probably the easiest-to-use information compendium (and one that fits in your pocket) is a little booklet called *New York in Flashmaps,* which is available at most bookstores. Each page is a map and there's one for buses, subways, museums, theaters, restaurants, hotels—just about everything. Finally, if you want to keep up with events at home, out-of-town and foreign newspapers and magazines are available at Hotaling's Newsstand (142 West 42nd Street; 840-1868) just east of Times Square.

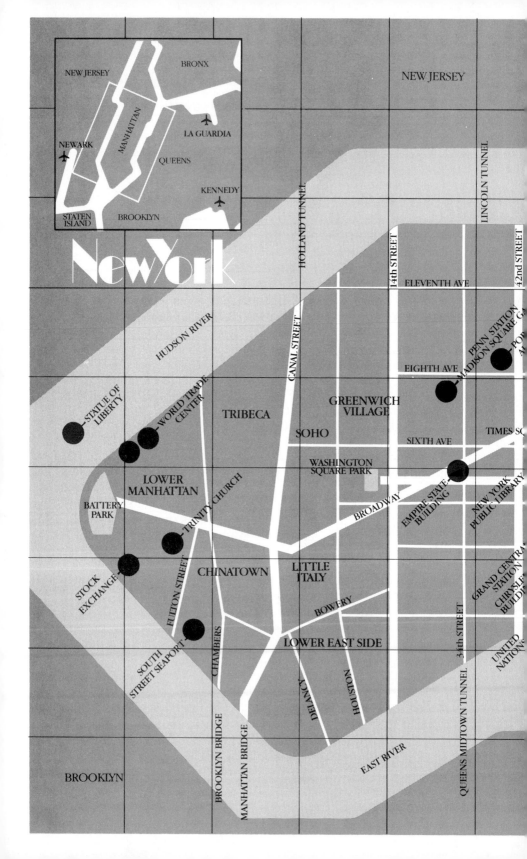

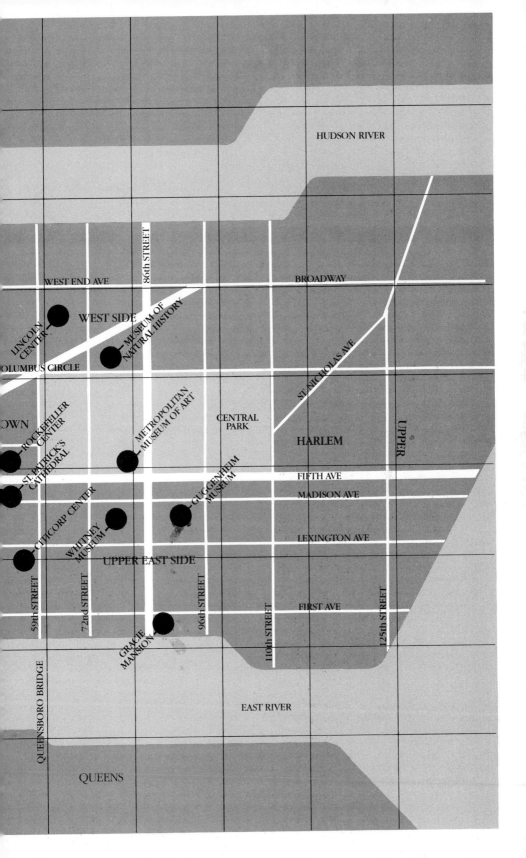

# THE INDEX

## C

# APPENDIX

# The World's Cuisines

The restaurants in this appendix are arranged according to national cuisine.

## A

**Afghan**
Pamir **121**

**American**
American Harvest Restaurant (The) **16**
Bread Shop Café (The) **17**
Caliban **46**
Central Falls **29**
Century Café **93**
Charley O's **93**
'Coach House (The) **36**
Commissary (The) **18**
Fraunces Tavern **19**
Gage and Tollner **137**
Hoexter's Market **115**
Horn of Plenty **38**
Hubert's **49**
Jim McMullen **117**
Keen's Chop House **94**
Louisiana **50**
Manhattan Market **118**
Maxwell's Plum **118**
Museum Café **133**
P. J. Clarke's **79**
River Café (The) **139**
Serendipity **127**
Simon's **134**
Tavern on the Green **135**
Teacher's **135**
Tenbrooks **21**

Texarkana **41**
21 Club **104**
Ye Waverly Inn **45**
Wings **32**
Wood's (West) **105**

**Armenian**
Ararat **45**
Balkan-Armenian **46**

**Austrian**
Vienna 79 **130**

## B

**Brazilian**
Casa Brazil **108**

## C

**Chinese**
Beijing Duckhouse **53**
Bernstein-on-Essex Street **34**
David K's **111**
Dragon Garden **25**
Fortune Garden **113**
Hee Seung Fung (H.S.F.) **66**
Home Village **26**
Hunam **68**

11-11
lunch: Oyster Bar
play:
dinner: Stage Deli

11-12